Integration of Cloud Technologies in Digitally Networked Classrooms and Learning Communities

Binod Gurung
New Mexico State University, USA

Marohang Limbu
Michigan State University, USA

A volume in the Advances in Educational Technologies and Instructional Design (AETID) Book Series

IGI Global
DISSEMINATOR OF KNOWLEDGE

www.igi-global.com

Published in the United States of America by
IGI Global
Information Science Reference (an imprint of IGI Global)
701 E. Chocolate Avenue
Hershey PA, USA 17033
Tel: 717-533-8845
Fax: 717-533-8661
E-mail: cust@igi-global.com
Web site: http://www.igi-global.com

Library of Congress Cataloging-in-Publication Data

Names: Gurung, Binod, 1976- editor. | Limbu, Marohang, 1965- editor.
Title: Integration of cloud technologies in digitally networked classrooms and learning communities / Binod Gurung and Marohang Limbu, editors.
Description: Hershey, PA : Information Science Reference, [2017] | Includes bibliographical references and index.
Identifiers: LCCN 2016037308| ISBN 9781522516507 (hardcover) | ISBN 9781522516514 (ebook)
Subjects: LCSH: Computer-assisted instruction. | Cloud computing.
Classification: LCC LB1028.5 .I5455 2017 | DDC 371.33--dc23 LC record available at https://lccn.loc.gov/2016037308

This book is published in the IGI Global book series Advances in Educational Technologies and Instructional Design (AETID) (ISSN: 2326-8905; eISSN: 2326-8913)

British Cataloguing in Publication Data
A Cataloguing in Publication record for this book is available from the British Library.

For electronic access to this publication, please contact: eresources@igi-global.com.

Advances in Educational Technologies and Instructional Design (AETID) Book Series

Lawrence A. Tomei
Robert Morris University, USA

ISSN:2326-8905
EISSN:2326-8913

Mission

Education has undergone, and continues to undergo, immense changes in the way it is enacted and distributed to both child and adult learners. From distance education, Massive-Open-Online-Courses (MOOCs), and electronic tablets in the classroom, technology is now an integral part of the educational experience and is also affecting the way educators communicate information to students.

The **Advances in Educational Technologies & Instructional Design (AETID) Book Series** is a resource where researchers, students, administrators, and educators alike can find the most updated research and theories regarding technology's integration within education and its effect on teaching as a practice.

Coverage

- Collaboration Tools
- Educational Telecommunications
- Game-Based Learning
- Web 2.0 and Education
- Hybrid Learning
- Social Media Effects on Education
- Instructional Design Models
- Adaptive Learning
- Online Media in Classrooms
- Digital Divide in Education

IGI Global is currently accepting manuscripts for publication within this series. To submit a proposal for a volume in this series, please contact our Acquisition Editors at Acquisitions@igi-global.com or visit: http://www.igi-global.com/publish/.

The Advances in Educational Technologies and Instructional Design (AETID) Book Series (ISSN 2326-8905) is published by IGI Global, 701 E. Chocolate Avenue, Hershey, PA 17033-1240, USA, www.igi-global.com. This series is composed of titles available for purchase individually; each title is edited to be contextually exclusive from any other title within the series. For pricing and ordering information please visit http://www.igi-global.com/book-series/advances-educational-technologies-instructional-design/73678. Postmaster: Send all address changes to above address.

Titles in this Series

For a list of additional titles in this series, please visit: www.igi-global.com

Technological Pedagogical Content Knowledge (TPACK) Framework for K-12 Teacher Preparation Emerging Research and Opportunities
Margaret L. Niess (Oregon State University, USA)
Information Science Reference • copyright 2017 • 122pp • H/C (ISBN: 9781522516217) • US $135.00 (our price)

Handbook of Research on Building, Growing, and Sustaining Quality E-Learning Programs
Kaye Shelton (Lamar University, USA) and Karen Pedersen (Online Learning Consortium, USA)
Information Science Reference • copyright 2017 • 412pp • H/C (ISBN: 9781522508779) • US $225.00 (our price)

Flipped Instruction Methods and Digital Technologies in the Language Learning Classroom
John Paul Loucky (Seinan Jo Gakuin University, Japan) and Jean L. Ware (Tokai University Fukuoka Junior College, Japan)
Information Science Reference • copyright 2017 • 313pp • H/C (ISBN: 9781522508243) • US $165.00 (our price)

Handbook of Research on Foreign Language Education in the Digital Age
Congcong Wang (University of Northern Iowa, USA) and Lisa Winstead (California State University, Fullerton, USA)
Information Science Reference • copyright 2016 • 460pp • H/C (ISBN: 9781522501770) • US $275.00 (our price)

Revolutionizing Modern Education through Meaningful E-Learning Implementation
Badrul H. Khan (McWeadon Education, USA)
Information Science Reference • copyright 2016 • 341pp • H/C (ISBN: 9781522504665) • US $185.00 (our price)

Knowledge Visualization and Visual Literacy in Science Education
Anna Ursyn (University of Northern Colorado, USA)
Information Science Reference • copyright 2016 • 431pp • H/C (ISBN: 9781522504801) • US $205.00 (our price)

Increasing Productivity and Efficiency in Online Teaching
Patricia Dickenson (National University, USA) and James J. Jaurez (National University, USA)
Information Science Reference • copyright 2016 • 327pp • H/C (ISBN: 9781522503477) • US $185.00 (our price)

Wearable Technology and Mobile Innovations for Next-Generation Education
Janet Holland (Emporia State University, USA)
Information Science Reference • copyright 2016 • 364pp • H/C (ISBN: 9781522500698) • US $195.00 (our price)

Editorial Advisory Board

List of Reviewers

Table of Contents

Detailed Table of Contents

Section 2

Cloud technologies offer many pedagogical possibilities for collaboration, ubiquitous learning, and documenting student engagement activities through learning analytics among others. However, effective integration of cloud technologies demands a complex set of teachers' theoretical and conceptual understandings and digital competencies. Furthermore, the teachers also need to re-examine their critical internal barriers such as the lack of digital self-efficacy. A closer look reveals that there is an undergirding notion – the teachers' digital identity – that enables them to develop their conceptual and practical digital competencies and self-efficacy. In this chapter, I critically explore and examine new pedagogical possibilities of integrating cloud technologies into classrooms within the triadic interplay of digital identity, competencies, and self-efficacy (3Ds).

Many students will soon enter high-tech workplace environments that utilize cloud technologies and systems, yet they must be critical of the technologies and infrastructures they use on the cloud. More approaches are needed, however, to facilitate learning environments where students both use cloud technologies and have opportunities to critically reflect on their rhetoricity. The author argues that new vocabularies are needed to describe the use of cloud technologies, especially those used in our pedagogical practices. Utilizing vocabularies and methods informed by actor network theory, instructors can easily identify and diagram the networks that students compose in pursuit of their learning goals. To demonstrate, the author offers network diagrams representing two different writing courses taught in the United States, in turn presenting how instructors can engage in similar diagramming practices and even use the "cloud" and "networks" as crucial points of inquiry for students.

Cloud-based services designed for educational use, like Google Apps for Education (GAFE), afford deeply collaborative activities across multiple applications. Through primary research, the authors discovered that cloud-based technologies such as GAFE and Google Drive afford new opportunities for collaborative cross-platform composing and student engagement. These affordances require new pedagogies to transform these potentialities into practice, as well as a reexamination of contemporary theory of computers and composition. The authors' journey implementing Google Drive as a composing

Although most students regularly interact online for social reasons, many are uncomfortable collaborating for academic work, even work utilizing familiar cloud technology. Because collaborative writing in digital spaces is becoming commonplace in work and academic environments, composition teachers must help students to recognize their individual agency within group work and to develop strategies for a shared writing process. How can we scaffold online writing experiences so that our students' ability to collaborate emerges as a strategic and still-developing part of the learning process? In this chapter we discuss strategies for scaffolding a collaborative writing process using Google Docs in the composition classroom. We describe four sample activities appropriate for undergraduate writing courses: anonymous invention, group annotated bibliographies, group agendas and project plans, and peer review. We suggest best practices for developing individual agency and shared responsibility for group writing in the cloud.

The rapid development of Web-based learning technologies has become a global phenomenon that affects higher education institutions. Both developing and developed countries are eager to take advantage of the multi-modal and asynchronous technical capacities that Web 2.0 can provide to college students. The "E-learning Phenomenon" has also prompted the development of different types of learning tools, ranging from commercially-developed Blackboard, open-source learning platform Moodle, or less popular platform developed by individual universities around the world. This study applied a theoretical concept, Hybrid Interactive Rhetorical Engagement (H.I.R.E.), and a series of quantitative metrics derived from H.I.R.E., to assess the Digital Learning Website developed at Kainan University, Taiwan. Exploratory empirical findings help college instructors to understand whether H.I.R.E. serves a good system design concept explain and predict users' learning behaviors and can be used to assess a variety of web-learning technologies in the market.

In a digitally networked classroom, the learner connects with peers, instructors, and open resources, be they human experts or online resources in non-linear combinations. As a result, the learner must navigate a complex web of associations and pathways. Thus the teacher practitioner who uses the networked medium as the platform for facilitating language learning has the challenge of developing methodologies, task-based activities, and a selection of tools to frame a learning ground that will provide maximum

Preface

With the virtualization of data, communication, and services, cloud computing is opening up many newer horizons in the field of education by offering more efficient technological features and pedagogical affordances. Having emerging interactive features such as creating, saving, sharing, and syncing data and communication in the cloud from anywhere, any device, anybody, and any time bases, cloud-based pedagogies have potential to offer new teaching and learning opportunities. Consequently, there is a growing trend of exploring and using cloud computing in K-12 classrooms and in higher education settings. Cloud technologies such as Google Drive, Dropbox, iCloud, Web 2.0, social media, and other cloud-embedded technologies are rapidly permeating the digitally and/or cloud-based networked classrooms and learning communities. Cloud-based pedagogies are capable of generating new possibilities for improving and transforming existing pedagogical practices and learner engagement. Theoretically, conceptually, and pedagogically, we envision using cloud computing and/or cloud technologies as learning tools, spaces, or systems that can be utilized at the individual, classroom, and institutional levels. Our principal collective research and scholarship interest in this book is to investigate what and how cloud technologies can be used for learning engagement at different levels and diverse contexts. But we also observe that there is a serious lack of theory, research, methodology, and practice on how cloud pedagogies can be conceived, designed, and implemented in the context of emerging digitally networked classrooms and learning communities.

There are several critical elements that remain unexplored within the emerging cloud pedagogies. First, despite the rapid permeation and widespread use of cloud technologies in classrooms (and other learning contexts, e.g., workplaces and networked communities), the theoretical, conceptual, and practical notion of "cloud" still remains cloudy to many educators, researchers, learners, administrators, and policymakers. Second, cloud pedagogies thrive in collaboration and collective intelligence harnessed within the local and global (glocal) learning contexts. This requires cross-cultural, multi-centric, transnational, and global engagement that not only romanticize the presence of the crowd (student population from different continents of the world), but also validate the presence and participation of the "crowd" representing the diverse local and global learners. Finally, cloud pedagogies play important roles to enhance learners' technological knowledge and skills that are highly relevant for preparing themselves as global citizens, professionals, and entrepreneurs in the digitally networked worlds. Thus, this proposed book project will be a timely call to explore the potentials of cloud pedagogies to align with the twenty-first century learners' needs and expectations and to foster meaningful learning engagement.

In this book, our major objective are to critically explore and examine the features and affordances of cloud technologies for pedagogical purposes focusing on the improvement and transformation of existing pedagogical practices (e.g., teaching, learning, training, and collaborative knowledge engagement in general); to capture the uses and impacts of cloud computing in teaching, learning, curriculum, and engendering newer types of student engagement opportunities; to offer new pedagogical strategies for engaging students and/or networked community learners in collaborative knowledge building processes by harnessing collective intelligence in relation to locally and globally networked learning communities. Additionally, our principal objectives are also to investigate and timely address the issues and challenges of integrating cloud technologies for socioeconomically, culturally, and linguistically diverse learners; and to offer conceptual, theoretical, and empirical research insights into using cloud technologies in the context of currently evolving digitally equipped and networked twenty-first century classrooms and learning communities.

Our intended audiences, in this book, include scholars, researchers, college instructors, teachers and teacher educators, professional/business trainers, community members, activists, educational software designers, and undergraduate and graduate students from multiple disciplines such as education, rhetoric and composition, communication, and educationally oriented business education. More specifically, this book will be crucial for those who envision and/or practice of integrating emerging technologies (e.g., cloud technologies, social media, and Web 2.0) in designing curricula, developing learning and training models, and delivering teaching and learning with technology in general.

This book is organized into three major sections. Section 1 highlights the concepts, theories, and practices of cloud technologies and/or cloud- and crowd-based pedagogy. This section primarily deals with conceptual, theoretical, and/or historical aspects of cloud technologies and cloud and crowd pedagogies within the 21st century networked pedagogical landscapes. The chapters in Section 1 discuss what cloud computing is in relation to conceptual, theoretical, and pedagogical contexts, including introductions to the cloud, its history, foundational knowledge about cloud technologies and pedagogies, emerging features, and potentials of the cloud. This section further stresses on what types of cloud literacies are important in cloud pedagogical contexts in a broader horizon (pedagogy inside and outside the classroom practices), why they are important, and how we harness them and/or the cloud affordances for pedagogical purposes. In this section, we also cover epistemological, ontological, and axiological conceptualization of cloud pedagogies such as critical analysis within socio-economic, cultural, political, and psychological terrains on how instructors adopt and/or reject the idea of integrating cloud technologies into pedagogies.

Similarly, Section 2 stresses the dynamics and dimensions of cloud technologies and cloud- and crowd pedagogies. This section mainly explores and examines the dynamics and dimensions of cloud pedagogies including technological, pedagogical, and socio-cultural and linguistic aspects. The chapters of this section mainly cover technological dynamics and dimensions of cloud technologies and cloud pedagogies such as what cloud computing/technology is; how emerging features of cloud computing can be utilized for creating, saving, sharing, and syncing data and communication in the cloud from anywhere, any device, anybody, and any time bases. The chapters, in this section, interpret pedagogical implications for deriving new cloud and crowd-based teaching and learning opportunities based on these cloud features. This section also deals with pedagogical dynamics and dimensions of cloud pedagogy such as what new types of pedagogies can be designed, developed, and delivered by using cloud technologies. In short, the main purpose of this section is to critically discuss what cloud tools and features are; how cloud affordances exist and also could facilitate teaching, learning, curriculum, learning engagement, and learning assessment and evaluation, etc. What cross-sectional potentials can be re-imagined between cloud technologies and pedagogies for devising new and/or improved types of teaching strategies, methods, models, student engagement techniques, and digital learning spaces among others. The chapters also address sociocultural dynamics and dimensions of cloud technology and pedagogy such as how cloud pedagogies intersect with socio-economic, multilingual, translingual, transnational, and multicultural issues/contexts, and how cloud pedagogies address socioculturally and linguistically diverse learners and collaborators in classrooms and learning communities.

Section 3 focuses on research and practice of cloud technologies and pedagogies. We designed and included research-based reports and cases of using cloud technologies in classrooms and learning communities. Section 3 mainly focuses on how specific types of cloud tools, features, and affordances are used for such as creating and sharing; building learning repository and interactivity; facilitating learning processes (e.g., writing, peer review/critique, group project, etc.) and activities; creating remixes, mash-ups, and digital cross-breeding. It also poses questions such as: what new types of cloud learning analytics are emerging that can be used to assess and evaluate student engagement, learning goals, outcomes, assessments, and evaluations?

SECTION 1

Marohang Limbu, in his chapter "Cloud and crowd networked pedagogy: Integrating cloud technologies in networked classrooms and local and global learning communities," argues that our knowledge is constantly shifting from analog literacies to digital literacies, industrial literacies to information societies, paper literacies to screen literacies, and mono-modal literacies to multimodal literacies for which digital technology and/or digital culture has become a dynamic and evolving force. Limbu contends that we are invariably encountering digital technologies' shifts and are explicitly or implicitly embracing such knowledge shift nearly everywhere in the world without any exception, including areas such as business, science, education, and engineering. This knowledge shift demonstrates that digital literacy has become an inescapable component in our daily life in the context of the 21st century's digitally networked communities. In his chapter, Limbu discusses the affordances of cloud technologies and cloud and crowd pedagogies such as what is digital teaching, learning, and writing in the crowd context, how digital pedagogy currently became an inescapable element, and why instructors from any global communities (should) welcome this epistemic shift in the learning and writing processes. Limbu's chapter stresses on how instructors can engage students in the cloud environment, how students can share a complex set of linguistic and cultural narratives, and how students can collaborate and cooperate to create their realities in the context of the 21st century's networked classrooms.

Limbu's chapter succinctly aims to discuss cloud technologies, cloud-based networked spaces, and cloud learning spaces and to critically explore and examine the features and affordances of cloud technologies for pedagogical purposes focusing on the improvement and transformation of existing pedagogical practices (e.g., teaching, learning, training, and collaborative knowledge engagement in general). Limbu's chapter captures the uses and impacts of cloud computing in teaching, learning, and engendering new types of student engagement opportunities; it also demonstrates how newer cloud and crowd based pedagogical strategies function within networked community members and beyond in relation to collaborative knowledge building processes, and it exhibits how cloud and crowd based pedagogy harnesses collective intelligence within networked learning communities and beyond. Additionally, Limbu discusses how cloud-and crowd-based pedagogy promotes cross-cultural, inter-cultural, and inter-epistemic communication/knowledge from the local to global level. In brief, Limbu stresses epistemological, ontological, and axiological conceptualization of cloud pedagogies including critical analysis within socio-economic, cultural, political, and psychological terrains.

Dilli Edingo's "Cloud-Enabled Learning Environment: Optimizing Inclusive Learning Environments and Collaborative Pedagogies and Bridging the Digital Divide" focuses on the emergence and/or advent of cloud computing and how it has changed the ways of thinking, communicating, performing professions, and maintaining socio-cultural and community relations. Edingo argues that capacious cloud storage and its rapidly growing facilities and capabilities in virtualizing human activities and the entire phenomenal entities and in synchronizing them with new digital cloud technologies such as laptops, tablets, smartphones or mobile phones, and personal computers (PCs) have not only increased human capabilities, but also added new creative dimensions to sociocultural, economic, political, epistemological, ontological, and educational fields. And these capacities are profoundly changing the ways of producing, sharing, and acquiring knowledge, teaching, and learning contents. Edingo's chapter critically examines how cloud computing optimizes learning opportunities and transforms teaching and learning pedagogies, and also defines what a cloud-enabled learning environment means.

Edingo's chapter also critically explores how cloud-enabled learning environments and cloud-based pedagogies can address the gaps in education (caused by the digital divide), how cloud-assisted networks of local learning-hubs can contribute to the success of global literacy campaigns, and how cloud computing reaffirms the significance of distance learning or massive open online course (MOOC) and cloud-assisted practices of teaching self. Finally, he states that the rapid shifts in pedagogical grounds from non-virtual paradigms into the virtual world or the cloud clearly indicate that in the future teaching and learning activities and pedagogies become more cloudocratic.

In the chapter "Teaching and Learning in the Cloud: 'Anywhere, Anytime.' Anybody, Too?" Anita August argues that knowledge is no longer produced exclusively in the traditional class-based learning environment because for twenty-first century learners, digitally networked classrooms are the new social spaces where innovative learning perspectives are cultivated. August further stresses that like traditional class-based learning environments, digitally networked classrooms need to be sensitive to the social forces of race, gender, and class that will inescapably invade digital communication and/or global cultures. August contends that even in the cloud, difference as a concept is always already embedded as a contributing element under which knowledge is constructed, disseminated, and maintained. She suggests that a consideration of "difference" and its signifying effect on cloud pedagogy is a useful lens to explore the phrase "anywhere anytime" to the term "anybody" in the digitally networked classroom. Finally, August proposes that the model "anywhere, anytime, anybody" must become part of the basic structure of a democratic and collaborative knowledge building community to democratize teaching and learning in the cloud.

Jason Tham, in his chapter "Genres in the MOOCology of Writing: Understanding Cloud-Based Learning through a Genre-Activity Analysis", contends that with constant emergence of cloud services and platforms for learning at a global scale, the field of education is in the midst of exploring and adapting to new pedagogical features afforded by these environments. Tham further explores that among the most debated cloud and crowd pedagogical environment is the development of MOOCs--short for massive open online courses, which poses questions to the traditional brick-and-mortar teaching model and implore new ways for instruction and learning. Based on Tham's research and writing on MOOCs, he critically argues that although some studies have looked at the effectiveness of MOOCs as a mode of delivery, there still lacks a genre approach to analyzing MOOCs as socio-rhetorical systems that have complex relationships with other social entities in the larger ecology of learning. With an eye toward how writing is taught and learned in the MOOC context, Jason Tham investigates the kinds of course genre invented or reimagined by the cloud technologies and pedagogies afforded by MOOCs, and how those affordances facilitate writing instruction. In this chapter, Tham uses "Activity Theory" to highlight the genre activities specific to two composition MOOCs. By situating these MOOCs as activity systems, he offers an informed observation on the genre components affecting how students learn about writing in MOOC settings. These insights lead to numerous pedagogical implications, including the need to treat MOOCs as an emerging learning ecology that is different from conventional models.

SECTION 2

Binod Gurung, in his chapter "3Ds of Integrating Cloud Technologies into Classrooms: Digital Identity, Competencies, and Self-Efficacy", investigates that cloud technologies offer many pedagogical possibilities for collaborative learning, ubiquitous learning, and documenting learning engagement through learning analytics among others. Gurung further contends that effective integration of cloud technologies demands a complex set of teachers' theoretical and conceptual understandings and digital competencies. Furthermore, the teachers also need to overcome their critical internal barriers such as the lack of digital self-efficacy. A closer look reveals that there is a undergirding notion of teachers' digital identity that enables the teachers' theoretical and conceptual understandings and digital competencies self-efficacy. Gurung critically explores and examines newer pedagogical possibilities of integrating cloud technologies into classrooms within the triadic interplay of digital identity, competencies, and self-efficacy (3Ds).

In his chapter entitled "Critical Cloud Pedagogies: Using Network Diagrams to Name and Visualize Learning Networks," Jack Hennes demonstrates that while many students will soon enter high-tech workplace environments that utilize cloud technologies and systems, they must be critical of the technologies and infrastructures they use on the cloud. Hennes further explores that more pedagogical approaches are needed to facilitate learning environments where students both use cloud technologies and have opportunities to critically reflect on their rhetoricity. Hennes argues that new vocabularies are needed to describe the use of cloud technologies, especially those used in our pedagogical practices. Utilizing vocabularies and methods informed by actor network theory, instructors can easily identify and diagram the networks that students compose in pursuit of their learning goals. To demonstrate, Hennes offers network diagrams representing two different writing courses taught in the United States, in turn presenting how instructors can engage in similar diagramming practices and even use the "cloud" and "networks" as crucial points of inquiry for students.

Brown and Hocutt, in their chapter "Pervasive Pedagogy: Collaborative Cloud-Based Composing Using Google Drive", contend that using personal cloud-based storage has become a way of life for many. Whether it's Dropbox or Google Drive, Microsoft OneDrive or Apple iCloud, free and low-cost personal cloud storage is readily and inexpensively available, enabling users to access their files and content from any networked device. With a networked device, internet connection, and an account, files can be saved and backed up online, shared, and downloaded on demand. This new way of accessing, managing, and sharing information is transforming the tech industry, the workplace, and our personal relationship to technology. Increasingly, cloud-computing plays a role in education, as students use applications located in the cloud, and store and share a variety of media with classmates and faculty. Institutions -- including colleges and universities -- that implement storage and sharing using cloud technology must consider the way that it transforms access, communication, interaction, and relationships between and among the institution and its constituents.

By drawing on Selfe and Hilligos' (1994) theoretical foundation, "Technology changes us, redirects our thinking about the primary tasks of teaching reading and writing" (p. 1), Ramesh Pokharel, in "New Media and Technology: How Do They Change the Notions of the Rhetorical Situations?" contends that new media and technology have an overall impact in our lives including the way we write and read a text, and teach writing. Pokharel argues that by altering our overall literacy practice, new media and technology always creates a new situation, and require the users to use it to explain what cloud technology is. In this chapter, Pokharel creates a narrative that tells stories how new media and technology has created a new situation to redefine, reexamine, remap, or revive the existing notions of the digital rhetorical situation. Pokharel's chapter addresses two major parts: definition of new media and technology and the impact of new media and technology in changing the notions of the rhetorical situation. While in the first part, he delineates the definitions of new media primarily in terms of technology, and discuss overall impact of new media and technology in human life physically and psychologically, in the second part, he discusses how new media and technology has changed the notions of the rhetorical situation.

Jailei Jiang, in "Translingual and Digital Ecologies: A Cloud Pedagogy for Second Language Classrooms", argues that scholarship in cloud pedagogy has provided intriguing lenses through which researchers enhance pedagogical approaches for digital composition classrooms. However, Jiang contends that there is a lack of discussion on how cloud pedagogy could be employed to benefit second language learners of writing. Scholars in both digital and translingual areas of research have touched on conceptualizing their theories through multimodal, collaborative, and ecological perspectives of writing. Based on this conceptual foundation, Jiang looks into the theories and practices of translingualism and explores how translingual writing can be merged and integrated into the multimodal applications of cloud-based learning. Following and expanding the practices of digital composition, chapter aims to argue for an ontological shift to a translingual view of cloud-based writing and examine how it informs second language learning.

Dhruba Neupane, in his "The Digital Third World, Digital Democracy, Cloud Pedagogy: Learning from Multilingual Bloggers," discusses what cloud computing and cloud technology has generated teachers' and scholars' attention as a viable alternative to traditional education. The discourse and rhetoric around cloud—computing, education, pedagogy— seems to romanticize the potential of cloud technology, ignoring, consequently, questions about language, power, and ideology. Neupane, in this chapter, attempts to reintroduce that question and discusses what blog pedagogy offers to multilingual writers and/or how blog pedagogy provides teaching materials free. Similarly, Neupane, in his chapter, demonstrates how language, translation, and transitional exchanges get mediated. Neupane also demonstrate the connection between the digital Third World and issues of equality and access, and how they constitute part of the discussion around cloud pedagogy and practices as a democratic space.

SECTION 3

Katherine Emmons, in her "Doctoral Learning and Cognitive Apprenticeship: Technology Tools for Emerging Scholars," discusses how cloud technologies provide tools to help build the mentoring relationships that are needed for doctoral students to become scholars in their own right. Simmons, in this chapter, draws on observed examples and experiences to discuss a model of cognitive apprenticeship as first described by Collins, Brown, and Newman (1986) and Collins, Brown, and Holum (1991). Emmons argues that this model is helpful for understanding the required relationships and commitments in online doctoral learning, especially between mentors and doctoral students. By referring Kumar, Johnson, and Hardemon (2013), Emmons states when these relationships are formed early in the process of dissertation research, progress in the degree program can be encouraged, and is more likely to culminate in timely completion. Based on her a long term online teaching experience, she contends that technology can foster relationships, particularly for doctoral students who study at a distance, including those enrolled in online programs. In this chapter, Emmons shares her own experiences of using technology in online programs spanning over 15 years, as well as the entry of helpful cloud tools for conferencing, folder and file sharing, scheduling, and community building. In nutshell, she claims that this model is helpful for understanding the required relationships and commitments in online doctoral learning, especially between mentors and doctoral students.

Julia Parra in her "Phases, Scaffolds, and Technology: Cloud-Based Student Collaboration Model for Online and Blended Course Design" argues that with ubiquitous Internet and the related tools, including computational devices and cloud-based technology, has come public access to a world of information literally at one's fingertips. This has to the increased use of use cloud-based student collaboration as a key strategy for engaging students as responsible, creative, and productive participants in the learning process. For the purpose of this qualitative study there are three objectives, 1) update and revise a course design model for cloud-based student collaboration that uses phases and scaffolds, and includes an optimal cloud-based collaboration toolkit identified by graduate students, 2) describe an online course wherein this model has been applied, and 3) share exemplar course materials including guides, learning plans and directions, and content scaffolds in the form of templates, that support this model and can be repurposed by anyone using cloud-based student collaboration in higher education.

Yowei Kang's "Using the Hybrid Interactive Rhetorical Engagement (H.I.R.E.) Metrics to Analyze the Effectiveness of E-Learning Websites" contends that the rapid development of Web-based learning technologies has become a global phenomenon that affects higher education institutions. Kang further argues that both developing and developed countries are eager to take advantage of the multi-modal and asynchronous technical capacities that Web 2.0 can provide to college students. The "E-learning Phenomenon" has also prompted the development of different types of learning tools, ranging from commercially-developed Blackboard, open-source learning platform Moodle, or less popular platform developed by individual universities around the world. This study applied a theoretical concept, Hybrid Interactive Rhetorical Engagement (H.I.R.E.), and a series of quantitative metrics derived from H.I.R.E., to assess the Digital Learning Website developed at Kainan University, Taiwan. Exploratory empirical findings help college instructors to understand whether H.I.R.E. serves a good system design concept explain and predict users' learning behaviors and can be used to assess a variety of web-learning technologies in the market.

Bjyanjana Sharma, in her "Digital literacy: Dilemma for EAL Parents" by bringing the context of the practice of digital literacy in western classrooms, she argues that her chapter shares the views of six English as an additional language (EAL) parents, who just arrived to Australia, and the EAL parents came to Australia from India, Indonesia, Nepal and the Philippines. In this chapter, Sharma shares her studies on five Australian primary government school teachers on digital literacy. The data used here are drawn from a PhD study which explores parents' and teachers' perspectives on the literacy learning of EAL children at a primary school in Victoria. Qualitative data include a questionnaire, focus group interviews, individual interviews, classroom observation and emails. Sharma, in this chapter, shares her research findings that indicate that the teachers are positive towards digital literacy whereas the parents express mixed views, and she affirms that most of the negative comments from the parents have come from their misunderstanding about how digital literacy is included in the school curriculum.

Kate Fedewa and Kathryn Houghton in their "Scaffolding Agency and Responsibility in Cloud-Based Collaborative Writing" argue that although most students regularly interact online for social reasons, many are uncomfortable collaborating for academic work, even work utilizing familiar cloud technology. Because, based on their research believe that, collaborative writing in digital spaces is becoming commonplace in work and academic environments, composition teachers must help students to recognize their individual agency within group work and to develop strategies for a shared writing process. How can we scaffold online writing experiences so that our students' ability to collaborate emerges as a strategic and still-developing part of the learning process? In this chapter, Fedewa and Houghton discuss strategies for scaffolding a collaborative writing process using Google Docs in the composition classroom. They describe four sample activities appropriate for undergraduate writing courses: anonymous invention, group annotated bibliographies, group agendas and project plans, and peer review. Fedewa and Houghton suggest best practices for developing individual agency and shared responsibility for group writing in the cloud.

Jaya Kannan and Pilar Munday, in their "Challenges in Using Cloud Technology for Promoting Learner Autonomy in a Spanish Language Course: Reshaping Pedagogical Design" state that in a digitally networked classroom, the learner connects with peers, instructors, and open resources, be they human experts or online resources in non-linear combinations. As a result, the learner must navigate a complex web of associations and pathways. Thus the teacher practitioner who uses the networked medium as the platform for facilitating language learning has the challenge of developing methodologies, task-based activities, and a selection of tools to frame a learning ground that will provide maximum opportunity for the student to strengthen learning. Kannan and Munday, in this chapter, present a case study of a teacher practitioner's pedagogical design process in an online undergraduate course, "Advanced Grammar and Culture through Social Media." The main focus of this case study is a professional development exercise in which the teacher practitioner went through one cycle of planning, piloting, reflecting on results, and identifying key challenges.

Binod Gurung
New Mexico State University, USA

Marohang Limbu
Michigan State University, USA

REFERENCES

Collins, A., Brown, J. S., & Holum, A. (1991). Cognitive apprenticeship: Making things visible. *American Educator: The Professional Journal of the American Federation of Teachers, 15*(3), 6-11, 38-46. Retrieved from: http://elc.fhda.edu/transform/resources/collins_brown_holum_1991.pdf

Collins, A., Brown, J. S., & Newman, S. E. (1986). *Cognitive Apprenticeship: Teaching the Craft of Reading, Writing, and Mathematics* (No. BBN-6459). BBN Labs Inc. Retrieved from: http://eric.ed.gov/?id=ED284181(ERIC Document Reproduction Service No. ED 284181)

Kumar, S., Johnson, M., & Hardemon, T. (2013). Dissertations at a distance: Students' perceptions of online mentoring in a doctoral program. *International Journal of E-Learning & Distance Education, 27*(1). Retrieved from http://ijede.ca/index.php/jde/article/view/835/1481

Selfe, C. L., & Hilligoss, S. (1994). Introduction. In C. L. Selfe & S. Hilligoss (Eds.), *Literacy and computers: The complications of teaching and learning with technology*. New York, NY: MLA. doi:10.1300/J054v02n01_01

Section 1

Chapter 1
Cloud- and Crowd-Networked Pedagogy:
Integrating Cloud Technologies in Networked Classrooms and Learning Communities

Marohang Limbu
Michigan State University, USA

ABSTRACT

Our knowledge is constantly shifting from analog literacies to digital literacies, industrial literacies to information societies, paper literacies to screen literacies, and mono-modal literacies to multimodal literacies for which digital technology and/or digital culture has become a dynamic and evolving force. Concerning the literacy shifts whether we realize or not, we are invariably encountering digital technologies and are explicitly and/or implicitly embracing such knowledge shift in almost all across the world without any exception. This knowledge shift demonstrates that digital literacy has become an inescapable component of our daily life in the context of the 21st century's digital world. In this chapter, I will discuss affordances of cloud/digital pedagogies such as what teaching, learning, and writing are in digital context, how digital, cloud, or crowd pedagogy currently became an inescapable element, and why instructors from any global communities (should) welcome this pedagogical shift in academic spaces. Additionally, this chapter stresses on how instructors can engage students in the cloud environment, how students can share a complex set of linguistic and cultural narratives, and how students can collaborate and cooperate to create their realities in the context of the 21st century's networked classrooms.

INTRODUCTION

With the virtualization of data, communication, and services, cloud computing is not only opening up many newer horizons in education, business, and politics all alike, but cloud computing is also offering more efficient and effective cloud technologies, networked devices, networked apps, and pedagogical

DOI: 10.4018/978-1-5225-1650-7.ch001

affordances. Having emerging interactive features such as creating, saving, sharing, and syncing data and communication in the cloud from anywhere, any device, anybody, and any time bases, cloud technologies have potential to offer democratic, inclusive, and representational spaces such as networking, crowd-engagement, and writing spaces. Similarly, due to the cloud-based or digital-based writing or collaboration, the so called enormous world has become a tiny global village. Due to the democratic, inclusive, and representational cloud affordances, there is a growing trend of collaborating, communicating, exploring, contesting, and creating in higher education settings. Cloud technologies such as Google-based apps, Google docs, Eli Review (Eli Review is a peer-based review platform that allows writers, reviewers, and students effectively and efficiently review their peer's manuscripts/drafts, in short "Eli"), Wikis, Amazon Web services, Microsoft cloud, institutional cloud (cloud space offered by institutions), Dropbox, myCloud, iCloud, Web 2.0/3.0, social media, and other cloud-embedded technologies are rapidly permeating the 21st century networked classrooms and networked-based learning communities. Networked-based and/or cloud centric-classes are capable of generating pedagogical possibilities for improving and/or transforming existing pedagogical practices and learner engagement. Pedagogically, we (instructors who prefer to embrace cloud pedagogy) envision the use of cloud technologies as learning tools, learning spaces, and networking organisms. Therefore, cloud technologies are preferably utilized at the individual, classroom, and institutional levels as they (cloud technologies) have unimaginable capacities of producing, sharing, disseminating, and maintaining knowledge and/or as they have changed the ways people circulate information across the world (Limbu, 2013, p. 67).

After the advent of the cloud technologies and crowd engagement in the cloud, production of knowledge never remained personal and exclusive because the cloud and/or Web 2.0 offers much more inclusive and representational capacities in the cloud. In such cloud capacity, the binary between writer and reader and/or dichotomy between consumer and producer is blurred. Meaning, in cloud spaces such as blog, vlog, cloud spaces, and YouTube to mention a few, it is hard to affirm who is the reader and who is the writer because even the so called reader is contributing to the production of newer knowledge just like the so called writer; here binary between producer and consumer becomes "prosumer" (producer or consumer). In other words, even (most) readers effectively and efficiently contribute to the production of knowledge. The main purpose of this chapter is to briefly discuss cloud technologies, cloud-based networked spaces, and cloud learning spaces and to critically explore and examine the features and affordances of cloud technologies for pedagogical purposes focusing on the improvement and transformation of existing pedagogical practices (e.g., teaching, learning, training, and collaborative knowledge engagement in general). Similarly, this chapter captures the uses and impacts of cloud computing in teaching, learning, and engendering new types of student engagement opportunities. It also demonstrates how newer cloud- and crowd based pedagogical strategies function within networked community members and beyond in relation to collaborative knowledge building processes, and it exhibits how cloud- and crowd based pedagogy harnesses collective intelligence within networked learning communities and beyond.

This chapter opens up with the concept of cloud computing, cloud technologies, networked spaces, and learning spaces. Second, it discusses what cloud- and crowd-based networked pedagogy is in relation to classroom and workplace setting; it justifies why present sites and potentials of cloud-technologies and cloud- or crowd-based pedagogy is important within classroom and beyond. It primarily justifies how cloud tools are used to enhance students' inquiry, communication, discovery, and knowledge construction processes. This chapter reflects how students and/or networked community members write when they write and/or how they communicate when they communicate in the cloud; and it discusses what rhetorical strategies students and/or networked community members use when they compose in cloud- and crowd context. To illustrate cloud- and crowd based pedagogy, it explains how students and/or networked community members use cloud technologies to collaborate, cooperate, and create contents for their individual and networked community purposes in classroom (in the cloud) setting and beyond. Finally, it stresses how cloud-and crowd-based pedagogy promotes cross-cultural, inter-cultural, and inter-epistemic communication/knowledge from the local to global level. In nutshell, this chapter not only addresses why cloud- and crowd literacies are important and why we should harness cloud technologies for pedagogical purposes (both in academic institutions and social spaces), it also stresses epistemological, ontological, and axiological conceptualization of cloud pedagogies including critical analysis within socio-economic, cultural, political, and psychological terrains.

CLOUD COMPUTING, CLOUD TECHNOLOGIES, AND NETWORKED SPACES

Cloud computing in the simplest terms is the use of hardware and software to deliver services through the Internet, or the meaning of cloud computing is to store and access data, information, and so on over the Internet. In other words, in cloud computing, the networked community members or users can access data, files, or information from any device, any place, and any time as long as the users have the Internet access. So, cloud computing in general is a metaphorical term used for the Internet. Similarly, cloud technologies basically refers to networked-based cloud services; it is also a concept that involves a large number of cloud or computing devices and/or network devices (computers, smartphones, tablets, and iPods/iPads) connected to a synchronous as well as asynchronous communication network (Internet) (Limbu, 2014, p. 153). More importantly, the concept of cloud technology changes when there are multiple consumers and/or users as they bring cloud- and crowd-based technologies into actions such as in classroom, workplaces, and learning communities. The constant cloud- and/or crowd engagement becomes a newer contact zone (a digital and physical space where students from different cultural, linguistic, and geo-political locations meet) in which newer affordances, newer applications, and meanings are invariably in the making. Due to the newer affordances and newer applications, cloud computing has become one of the leading forces of cloud- and crowd-based digital communications since the first decade of the 21st century. In the cloud or crowd-based communication, innumerable participations usually from closed group and also beyond engage in discussions, considerations, and negotiations. Hence, cloud and crowd-based pedagogy refers to a huge mass of people who participate in the production of text and/or knowledge in the cloud. Similarly, cloud computing refers to Internet-based collaboration, document sharing, web publication, data syncing, and digital communication. Cloud computing tools in a plain language include Web 2.0/3.0, Google-based web spaces, vlogs, Wikis, Twitter, LinkedIn, Academia.edu, podcasting, dropbox, iCloud, browser-based apps, browser-based programming, and crowd-based mobile apps to mention a few.

According to Vouk (2008) "[c]loud computing predecessors have been around for some time now, but the term became 'popular' sometime in October 2007 when IBM and Google announced a collaboration in that domain.... Since then, everyone is talking about 'Cloud Computing'" (p. 235). Jaeger, Lin, and Grimes (2008) contend that cloud computing infrastructure resides in a large data center and is managed by a third party, who provides cloud computing resources as if it were a utility, such as electricity—accessible from anywhere by anyone with the Internet connection. Similarly, Scale (2010) contends that cloud computing "implies a service-oriented architecture, reduced information technology overhead for the end-user, greater flexibility, reduced total cost of ownership, on demand services and many other things" (p. 934). We personally and professionally have utilized cloud-based services in our day-to-day lives in multiple ways. At this point what we understand is that cloud computing is conceptualized, theorized, and utilized as the web-based hosting of software where we, end users, do not necessarily need to consider upgrading hardware or software because of the new releases (Knorr & Gruman, 2008; Limbu 2013, 2014); from this perspective, cloud technologies have significant impact in cloud-based networked pedagogy as well as in networked workspaces in the context of digitally connected global village.

Among many reasons why cloud computing is so popular both in writing classrooms and workspaces is that it virtualizes documents such as videos, sounds, images, and texts, and students and/or networked community members (those whoever are connected to the Internet and particular discussion group) such as local and global citizens share any information (videos, music, sounds, images, and texts) in the cloud. This setting conceptually, theoretically, and practically demonstrates that cloud information and/or cloud data are always mobile, transferable, and instantly accessible from anywhere, any device, and by anyone (as long as networked community members are connected to the Internet). From this point of view, cloud computing, in the 21st century networked communities, promises to collaborate, create, sync, and share information with friends and co-workers in the cloud. Or, cloud computing means having every piece of data that we need for every aspect of our lives are at our fingertips, and they (data) are always ready for sharing with local and global network communities. The portable and interactive potential of cloud computing is not only the ability to sync up data to several devices such as computer desktops, laptops, cell phones, iPads/iPods, tablets, and other small handheld devices, but also share them (data) with multiple collaborators in the cloud. The shared data in the cloud is the data that we access in the cloud from any place such as social networks, blogs, cloud spaces, shared data storage, and newsrooms.

As many cloud technologies are communicative, collaborative, and user-centered, they have unimaginable potentials to cultivate students' writing and communication skills in pedagogical setting. Because of such pedagogical potentials, instructors can use digital tools to observe cloud potentials such as what cloud computing is in the context of culturally and linguistically diverse classrooms, how cloud-or crowd-based networked writing enhances students' writing, how it enriches intercultural and cross-cultural communication skills, how both students and technologies (students and network devices) and/or students, technologies, and students interact to explore, produce, and/or discover newer meanings. Similarly, cloud-based pedagogies also create various setting in which instructors can observe how technologies and humans (students) coexist in symbiotic relationship in the context of 21st century digital world (also see Graupner, Nickoson-Massey, & Blair, 2009; Porter, 2007). Students, in cloud computing setting, both collaborate, cooperate, and create, and they save and sync them in the cloud storage such as Dropbox, Google Drive, Google Sites, and mycloud. In this pedagogical setting, by sharing documents or cultural and individual narratives in the cloud with peers, other local and global collaborators, and instructors, they stimulate to promote cross-cultural, intercultural, and global communication skills. In so doing, students from different cultures and different continents will be able to collaborate and create in the crowd, and they will also be able to share writing skills as well as develop global and local rhetorics, literacies, and communication strategies.

By making the knowledge so cheap and easily available to any person (unlike the past) and by making the network and communication easy, cloud-based technologies changed the networked global spaces/villages such as networked classrooms, networked workplaces, and networked learning communities that people never imagined just a decade ago (Limbu, 2012; also see James, 2014; Yu, 2014). Via these networked spaces such as Facebook, Twitter, Instagram, YouTube, and other interactive cloud spaces, people whoever are connected to the Internet constantly interact with other community members and/

or group members. The current cloud computing tools, which are rapidly shifting local and global networked communities in unpredictable ways, are almost walks of everyone's life such as in business, science, engineering, education, and politics. In other words, the mantra of cloud computing is always to become able to access shared data, collaborate, create, edit, and publish them from anywhere, any device, anytime, and by any person basis (Limbu, 2012). One of the most important elements of cloud computing, as implied earlier, is that it also indiscriminately facilitates cross-cultural, intercultural, and/or global communication strategies. In other words, by engaging and contesting in the crowd-networked spaces and/contact zones, people become better cross-cultural, intercultural, and global communicators. Additionally, after the advent of cloud technologies, digital contact zones and crowd engagement challenges the traditional concept of "contrastive rhetoric" (see Kaplan, 1966) and introduces intercultural, cross-cultural, and even micro inter-epistemic communication (discussed in detail later in this chapter).

WHY CLOUD TECHNOLOGIES AND CLOUD/CROWD PEDAGOGIES IN DIFFERENT LEARNING COMMUNITIES

Our knowledge is constantly shifting from analog literacies to digital literacies, industrial literacies to information societies, and mono-modal literacies to multimodal literacies due to the emerging technologies (see Limbu, 2012, 2013, 2014; Warschauer, 2011). The change in technologies has become a disruptive force in cloud pedagogy (teaching and learning) in the digitally networked global village. Although many of us may not know and may not have yet practiced cloud technologies in our classrooms and/or in workplaces, it has already transformed traditional paper/analog cultures into cloud digital ones and industrial world into information world. Because of the impact of such cloud- and crowd-centric epistemic shift, the world is constantly changing, and instructors should also address the epistemic shifts in the writing classes so that we can transform the traditional pedagogies, outdated classes, and outmoded universities into digital, information, and global networked communities. Since digital literacy is inescapable, we profoundly use digital technologies to classrooms and workplaces so that they can fit in 21st century networked education, business, science, and engineering (see Limbu, 2012, 2013, 2014). And, we should also push ourselves towards cloud writing so that our now students and future colleagues will be able to address the epistemic shifts according to the demands, needs, and expectations of their digitally networked communities and other global citizens.

As I implied earlier, the reason why instructors should use cloud technologies in the writing classes is that many cloud-technologies are cost-effective, accessible, and user friendly, and students can afford them. And since cloud-computing tools are user-friendly and user-editable, they offer students a freedom of composing in the cloud as they (cloud tools) allow them to work within their own cultural accounts and prior academic experiences (Hocks, 2008; Limbu, 2011a, 2012; Takayoshi & Selfe, 2007). In this pedagogy, students can create their cultural, linguistic, and individual identities/voices by sharing cultural materials and prior experiences. Since students' cloud spaces are always accessible, they also will be able to share other students' local linguistic codes and cultural conditions, which illuminate previously untapped cultural, linguistic, and geopolitical information. In this manner, cloud-based pedagogical landscape will prepare students to become digitally as well as culturally proficient critical and analytical communicators and writers. And gradually, they will be able to create their own worlds for themselves and for their community members in the context of the 21st century globlized world. This is one of the reasons why we should teach our students all available means of digital or cloud-based writing, all available means of rhetorical approaches (Selfe, 2009, p. 645; Takayoshi & Selfe, 2007, p. 8).

Cloud-based pedagogy creates crowd-based contact zones and/or crowd-based networked space where students exchange their texts, documents, sounds, and videos, which also provides students opportunities to share, contest, question, and learn from their peers who are in the network (but come from different cultures and continents of the world). In the cloud- and crowd-based contact zones, students tend to grasp elements of cross-cultural, intercultural, and/or inter-epistemic communication when they engage in the interactive cloud tools (also see Limbu, 2011b, 2012, 2013, 2014). As Warschauer (2011) states the use of digital media facilitates students' writing because in cloud-based pedagogy networked community member's writing becomes visible and/or accessible than in the traditional handwritten one. From a pedagogical perspective, cloud pedagogy makes students' writing more vibrant and dynamic since peers, colleagues, and other audience can read, edit, comment, share, and contribute to the production of documents (from anywhere, any devices, and any time basis).

In terms of the use of cloud technologies in academic spaces such as physical and online classes, we generally assume that students (who were born in digital era) are digital natives (Palfrey & Gasser, 2008), and they learn digital skills through actively engaging in practices, or they learn from their friends, online help systems, YouTube, and online supports. One of the important elements instructors invariably should keep in mind that though students seem to be digital natives, and they know much more about newer network technologies, they obviously do not have the digital and multimodal understandings and skills that our composition classes or our courses require and/or our academic communities demand. For instance, many students, in my writing classes, always tell me that the use of cloud technologies such as Facebook, WeChat, blogs, websites, Eli, and Google Sites to mention a few are very efficient and effective; they are better means to communicate, collaborate, cooperate, and create with peers. At the same time, students also admit that they have never used the cloud technologies, and/or cloud apps the way we use them in my class/es. Obviously, our students are digital citizens who understand the basic grammar, syntax, and language of digital community and understand gesture of digital culture, but they have not yet become the members of the digital academic community; therefore, they lack complex grammar, language, jargon, and practice that our academic cultures require. On the other hand, we (instructors of digital age) also should understand that although we advocate for the revolutionary use of cloud tools in writing classes, we can also testify how social networking spaces including digital devices tend to distract students both inside and outside of the classes. For instance, as students open their computers and other network devices in the class/es, the first things they usually tend to check are social networking spaces such as Facebook, Twitter, Instagram, and Google+; then they begin their work. Even when students are in the midst of the class discussion/other activities, they frequently tend to either communicate with their colleagues or glance their social networking spaces (Limbu, 2011b).

As I implied earlier, instructors should always remember that instruction on the use of different multimodalities, web creation, web publication, and online data storage in digital academic context is always essential because majority of students are not familiar with software, hardware, and other multimodalities (CCCC, 2013; Cook, 2005; Cooper, 2007; DePew & Lettner-Rust, 2009; Limbu, 2013, 2014; Selfe & Hawisher, 2004). Students also admit that they know some functionality of cloud tools and/or cloud apps such as social media including cloud-networking spaces, but they do not know affordances of cloud tools such as Google apps, Google sites, Eli, websites, blogs, web publishing, online data storage, and other multimodalities (that we use in the writing classes). Instructors should understand that students always "need help in framing their understandings critically so that they can question their own judgment and look at their work from the perspectives of audience" (Selfe & Hawisher, 2004, p. 209).

Cloud- and crowd-based pedagogy allows students and/or networked community members to introduce to newer venues, for networked community members interact with glocal (global and local) colleagues from different cultural, linguistic, and disciplinary backgrounds. Cloud- and crowd-based networked pedagogy provides an environment from where cloud- or crowd-members construct their cultural and linguistic spaces and identities; it potentially tends to make people understand affordances of cloud technologies. When students engage in digital dialogical environment, they also expand their various literacy skills by producing unpredictable texts that propel them towards their future goals. In digital pedagogical environment, students develop their ability to critically explore and understand uses of diverse cultural narratives, digital texts, and multimodal texts, and they also achieve confidence to appreciate and create multiple texts (texts, sounds, images, and videos) in effective and productive ways.

Writing and/or communicating in the cloud in the composition classes is like entering into the arena of intercultural, cross-cultural, and/or global communication setting. And obviously global citizens and/or networked community members constantly communicate in cloud spaces such as Facebook, Instagram, Twitter, LinkedIn, and blog by posting messages, writing their journals, updating their statuses, uploading images/videos, and chatting with their colleagues. Not only do students post contents on regular basis, but also use various cloud apps for various reasons and purposes. Due to students' constant digital engagement, cloud-and/or crowd-based communication tools become much better pedagogical tools with which students can communicate quicker and better than they do on traditional tools such as email because in crowd-based pedagogical tools networked community members role is not limited as consumer of the knowledge as it used to be, but they (networked community members) become prosumers (consumer and producer) of knowledge as I mentioned earlier in this chapter.

Better part of cloud pedagogy is that students' shared materials (documents, video, drafts, reviews, and responses) are always accessible and visible in the cloud spaces. Because of this possibility, students can access their peers' documents (essays, reading responses, drafts, reviews, and presentations) from anywhere, any device, and any time through which students who are a bit slow and shy learn how to research and write for themselves (Limbu, 2013). In other words, by seeing other students' strategic writing choices or by seeing their peers' rhetorical/strategic moves and/or by seeing diverse cultural rhetorical strategies, they learn how they should research, communicate, and write for themselves. Through this pedagogical setting, students learn how to engage in inquiry, communication, and discovery moves in the writing/composing processes. In cloud-based pedagogy, networked community members (whoever are in the group or even beyond) do not necessarily need their own computers/laptops to access the shared documents, data, and information, they can use any network devices, computers, iPads, iPods, and tablets (in library or computer lab), and they can also share their documents with their peers and instructors via these devices from any where and any device. This cloud-based networked pedagogy suggests that students (networked crowd members) always walk around with their data, files, and documents as well as with their colleagues' narratives, documents, and projects.

In terms of classroom practices, instructors can also save students' papers, responses, and digital documents on the cloud spaces such as dropbox, box.com, iCloud, Google Drive, OneDrive, mycloud, and institutional clouds and can have access to them from anywhere, any device, and anytime as long as they are connected to the Internet. For instance, instructors save their teaching materials and students' projects, responses, and progress records on online data storage (dropbox, OneDrive, and Google drive) when students ask about their papers, projects, and progress reports, they can share them instantly from their networked devices (computer and other mobile devices). Thus, saving most of the teaching materials, syncing them online and accessing and sharing them from anywhere and anytime makes cloud-based teaching and learning easier and more effective.

Cloud pedagogy also shifts the traditional teacher-centered pedagogy into student-centered one. In the traditional pedagogy, "[s]tudents mostly interact with their instructor by asking questions or submitting work, and they tend to have little correspondence with other peers" (DePew & Lettner-Rust, 2009, p. 174); and instructor also occupies the center space and is considered as the purveyor of absolute knowledge. The mantra of cloud- and crowd pedagogy is that the instructors are not the ones who occupy the center space in the writing class/es, but they are only one of the contributors, facilitators, reviewers, and learners in cloud- and crowd-networked community. The reason we should welcome cloud- and crowd-based pedagogy is that we (instructors) should not only romanticize the presence of culturally, linguistically, religiously, and geo-political diverse students in our classrooms (both face-to-face and online classes), but we, by theory and practice, should validate their voices and identities (Limbu, 2012; also see Marcelo, Yot, & Mayor, 2015; Montaghian, Hassanzadeh, & Moghadam, 2013). In other words, by inviting culturally and linguistically diverse students as ambassadors, ethnographers, and historians of their cultures, cloud pedagogy encourages them to bring their cultural narratives and individual voices to the center (Limbu, 2012; also see Harris, 1995). In this pedagogical procedure, students discuss the materials they bring in; they question and/or contest on the materials; and they tend to validate their colleagues' cultural and individual voices. In so doing, they learn to negotiate their spaces. Furthermore, since cloud pedagogy tends to be more democratic, students have freedom of expressing their thoughts and ideas in the center. In short, cloud pedagogy empowers students to play dominant roles in the writing classes, and it also creates settings through which cloud pedagogy challenge teacher-centered pedagogy (teacher as purveyor of knowledge and authority), it (cloud pedagogy) challenges traditional concept of monoculture, monolingual, and mono-centric pedagogy. In other words, cloud- and crowd networked pedagogy, as a dynamic and evolving pedagogy, challenges the traditional notion of "mono-centric" pedagogy by demonstrating how global literacy or global knowledge has changed over the past decade/s.

The other reason why we should welcome cloud- and crowd pedagogy is that it is student-centric where students are empowered. Besides, instructors do not always have to respond to each student's questions and concerns while working on students' inquiry questions, outline, drafts, and revision including other activities. In cloud pedagogy, students are connected via cloud networking spaces such as Google sites, Google docs, Google slides, Eli, WeChat, Facebook to mention a few, they themselves (or anyone from the crowd) do help; or in cloud- and crowd pedagogy, students always tend to help each other. Importantly, instructors have to create creative, constructive, and compelling rubrics, project guidelines, peer review guidelines, and other pedagogical instructions, and these elements should be much more open ended so that students do not feel constricted within the rubrics or parameters provided by the instructor. Other benefit of networked cloud pedagogy is that communication in the cloud never halts. Meaning, students ALWAYS stick with their network devices such as laptops, tablets, cell phones, tablets, and iPads, and if any student seeks for help, someone from that particular crowd (class) is always on the networking space and will immediately respond to his/her peer's questions and concerns (this particular student-online-help always amazes me). This pedagogical strategy makes networked cloud pedagogy much more student-centered where they can share their cultural literacies, prior literacies, and prior individual literacies. This particular setting leads our cloud-based pedagogy towards global pedagogy. This does not mean that instructors should remain idle all the time, but they, as contributors, facilitators, moderators, reviewers, as well as learners, have to observe how students are collaborating and cooperating, what and how students are writing, and how they are participating. Instructors should help students more often than not without intervening them because instructor's frequent intervention can be very intimidating; it can paralyze students' creativity and cloud participation (for which teacher's creating a safe contact zone is extremely important).

While using cloud technologies in the class, my students always reported that cloud discussions such as Facebook, WeChat, Eli, and Google docs were effective and efficient because students could interact with other students in the class or group how they are communicating, exploring, and creating, what strength they have in their paper, and what other elements prevented them from understanding their peer's paper. While using cloud technologies, students reported that cloud discussions were effective and efficient because students could make sure what classroom activities were going on, or what assignments were due. Likewise, students believed that Facebook discussion alone stood as the leader of class discussions and responses, while website and blog were the leader of peer review, and Google drive and Eli were the front-runners of group collaborations, peer reviews, and presentations. It demonstrates that Google Drive, Eli, and websites better assist students to interact, collaborate, cooperate, and create contents in multiple ways.

Cloud-based networked pedagogy has potentials to blur the boundaries between the virtual and physical classroom spaces because of its effective applications, such as chat app, video app, and so on. For instance, when students are absent in the class (for any reason), they can still participate in the classroom discussions from anywhere and any time in both synchronous and asynchronous settings. To illustrate it more evidently, in my writing classes, despite the fact that student/s are absent in the class, they can still collaborate and create with their group members who are in the class. Their cloud-based networked collaborative work and cloud discussion are as effective as they (absentees) are in the class. As a matter of fact, when we teach in the cloud environment, students, by being absent in the class, can also easily contribute and capture the information in the cloud such as what activities their classmates have done in the class, how these activities have been done, and who have participated for the discussion. This emerging cloud-based pedagogy is giving birth to many unimaginable global universities such as MOOCs, online courses, and online presentations.

Cloud-based pedagogy deconstructs the traditional notion of western writing because traditional western pedagogy is centered to just written texts; and cloud pedagogy allows students to use technologies to create unimaginable texts in multiple ways. In cloud-based pedagogy, students, other than traditional writing, create multimodal documents as a part of their projects/assignments in writing classes. Such multimodal texts, such as sound, image, graphics, and video always empower non-traditional students to precisely reflect their cultural narratives and to better articulate or rearticulate their ideas, rhetorical choices, and rhetorical strategies. In cloud-networked pedagogy, digital technologies become mediums through which multilingual and multicultural students, including monolingual students, can mediate their cultural, linguistic, and individual stories to construct their situated identities. In short, cloud pedagogy saturated by new media technologies engages students in different digital, multimodal, and cross-cultural writing tasks that not only offers them to create, name, and claim their identities, spaces, and voices in the center, but it also provides them valuable future career preparation (Limbu, 2012).

Cloud computing reinforces students to work as networked community members by collectively engaging them in the cloud. The cloud-based pedagogy provides them a safer space for slower and shy students, for they (slow and shy students) get opportunity to share what other students write, how they write, how they organize, and what rhetorical strategies or moves they use to compose; by seeing other students writing in the cloud and/or in the cloud discussions, they can write for themselves. From this perspective, cloud-networked pedagogy offers students opportunity to construct and globalize their local narratives and localize global narratives. In other words, in the process of working in cloud-networked spaces, students learn different multimodal skills (that could be much more non-western that they are familiar with), and they become good at communicating, exploring, and expressing themselves. Due to the multimodal-composing environment (non-traditional composing process) including traditional composing environment, cloud-based pedagogy also has unique potentials such as creating digital multicultural materials, diverse digital narratives including oppressed/suppressed indigenous stories/knowledge and publishing and sharing them with their peers in the cloud. Cloud pedagogy has probability to dialogically engage both monolingual and multilingual students so that they learn newer literacies and create newer texts in digital and physical spaces. Hence, "preparing students to communicate in the digital world using a full range of rhetorical skills will enable them to analyze and critique both the technological tools and the multimodal texts produced with those skills" (Handa, 2004, p. 3). Furthermore, "social networking sites provide an easy, accessible way to interact with peers and gather feedback. These opportunities may be particularly significant since peers are readily available online at almost any time, and the tools provided make communication easy to accomplish" (Pempek, Yermolayeva, & Calvert, 2009, p. 228). Such digital information and communication enriches students' learning processes by intensifying the sense of trust on their personal and professional development.

To further reiterate cloud potentials, cloud technologies are not only about communicating with colleagues, but more importantly the tools allow diverse group of students to question, contest, claim, and negotiate their identities and spaces. For instance, when students share their multimodal stories in the cloud environment, they, more often than not, question on the contents when they do not understand and/or when they disagree. In this pedagogical setting, at times, students agree or disagree, which makes them name claim their space, ideologically challenge each other by rhetorically supporting their arguments and/or by refuting their peers' claims. Such questioning and contesting, in networked pedagogy, has an immediate impact on students' (both traditional and non-traditional students') interests and lives that offer them ways to create newer rhetorical strategies (Clark, 2010). Cloud-based networked pedagogy extends students' understanding of communication, writing, and response in a larger scale; it also helps students connect their local materials and individual understanding to the global level and vice versa. Furthermore, many cloud technologies consist of a one-to-many communication styles, where information tremendously amplifies, and they reach to diverse audience at a time (Pempek, Yermolayeva, & Calvert, 2009, p. 234). In a nutshell, cloud pedagogy prepares students better critical, analytical digital collaborators, contributors, communicators, and writers who serve need and expectation of the 21st digital world.

CLOUD- AND CROWD-BASED NETWORKED PEDAGOGY AND ITS SIGNIFICANCE IN WRITING CLASSES

The emergence of cloud technology offers people newer ways of communication by conferring many user-friendly affordances such as cloud tools for sharing, collaborating, and creating contents within an identified cloud-based pedagogical environment (Panteli, 2009; Werstch, 1998). So, cloud-based technologies (such as Google docs, Eli, blog, and vlog) confer possibilities where students can collaborate, cooperate, compose, and comment on their peers' papers in the cloud. In this pedagogical setting, students become able to express their thoughts and ideas in digital contact zones. Since cloud-based technologies offer students more cross-rhetorical learning opportunities (meaning, they also learn by seeing peer's rhetorical moves in their writing strategies), they gradually become able to understand how research, writing, and communication functions in different cultures. In other words, via cloud- and/or crowd-based pedagogy, students learn and practice or become familiar with local as well as global cultural functionalities as they constantly communicate with peers, or as they see peer's writings from diverse cultural and linguistic backgrounds; and they (peers and/or networked community members) can also change our preconceived assumptions about (global) literacies (also see Vaidhyanathan, 2004, p. 21). From this perspective, cloud- and crowd-based pedagogy is perhaps explicitly global, intercultural, and cross-cultural communication medium through which students comprehend and create their own-networked paths as writers and readers (Aleman & Wartman, 2009; Limbu, 2011a, pp. 17-18; Purvis & Savarimuthu, 2009; Richardson, 2007; Thatcher, 2005). From this perspective, cloud computing has become a digital networking medium through which students can construct their cultural and individual identities by reframing the horizons of their cultural artifacts and cultural understandings (Heidegger, 1977; Lawson, 2008). In a nutshell, because of diverse cloud affordances, cloud-based networked pedagogy in linguistically and culturally diverse classrooms has become a convergence of self, global colleagues, and new media technologies in the context of 21st century digitized networked classrooms (Limbu, 2011a, p. 22).

Although composition theories/theorists advocate for empowering students in cloud writing classes, current writing pedagogy still informs teacher-centered pedagogical practices. For instance, writing instructors identify themselves as experts who still impart prescriptive forms and grammars to their students, and in such pedagogical approaches students are, more often than not, expected to demonstrate prescribed proficiencies (Berlin, 1984, 1987; Brereton, 1995). In other words, despite the fact that we advocate for the student-centered and/or student-networked pedagogy, we tend to implicitly support traditional prescriptive pedagogy. Although instructors attempt to practice student-centered pedagogy, their pedagogical practices still offer only one-on-one student and teacher relationship in which student writes paper, and teacher reads the paper, and gives feedback and grades on it. We (instructors) implicitly tend to practice pedagogical approaches and values that ignore students' cultural, linguistic, and prior experiences. Similarly, we, including writing administrators, also impose and/or create curricula, syllabi, and other activities such as projects, reading materials, discussions, presentations, and reflections without knowing a huge number of student populations and/or their cultural and linguistic backgrounds and their prior academic literacies. Such pedagogical attitude both does not value and/or valid students' cultural and linguistic literacies, and it also prevents them from sharing their narratives, stories, and experiences with their peers and other audience within their class and beyond. Or such pedagogy that we (many instructors) currently practice not only limits the significance of peer network (inside class and beyond), peer collaboration (both in physical and cloud contexts), and quality content production (from local and global audience perspective), but also confines cross-cultural, intercultural, and global aspects of communications in the age of digitally globalized world (Limbu, 2011).

Cloud-based pedagogy challenges the traditional notion of authority and authorship because human minds are now profoundly influenced by popular cultural activities, culturally produced and transmitted tools, including symbolic nature of language and social circumstances, from which we construe our situated rhetorical situations (also see Bazerman, 2008; Berlin, 1988, 1992; Vygotsky, 1978). Cloud-based networked pedagogy shapes networked knowledge communities in such a way that challenges the traditional notion of authority and reconstructs newer pedagogical strategies (student-centric pedagogy in the context of the 21st century digital world) such as when students write in the cloud environment, they, as authorities of their cultures, share a complex set of situated cultural rhetorical identities by informing their peers, instructors, and networked community members about their cultures, languages, geo-political situations, and individualities. In crowd-based pedagogy, instructor's role becomes a moderator or facilitator and students play principal roles to exchange, share, question, and contest on their prior- cultural, academic, and institutional knowledge.

Cloud-and crowd-based networked pedagogy allows students both to comprehend diverse local and global literacies and to become familiar with different rhetorical strategies people use to communicate in different cultures. Such knowledge sharing and knowledge critiquing processes more often than not becomes a site from where students know that whatever they were taught or were told in their local cultures (social institution) was a lie and/or it was only the politics of knowledge construction. For instance, Saudi female students often talk about women rights and identities in Saudi Arabia, and they (Saudi female students) find how they are portrayed in their culture is quite insensitive and meaningless. Through such local and global discussions in the cloud (as well as in the face-to-face classroom), they understand the body-graphic politics of knowledge construction and/or body politics of knowledge construction. Similarly, students also discuss and debate how they were taught "us" vs. "other" (always "other" as an inferior one), and they find the binaries quite futile because they do not find these constructed identities in the classrooms (where/when they meet people/students from different continents of the world). Through such cloud- and crowd based learning (because they feel free to express their thoughts, ideas, and experiences), students realize the politics of knowledge construction such as "us" vs. "them" or "superior" vs. "inferior" or "us" vs. "enemies"; they discover and/or understand the politics of divide and rule. Hence, cloud- and crowd-based networked pedagogy helps student individually and collectively explore politics of knowledge construction, and cloud- and crowd-based pedagogy provides all means of situations to unlearn what and how they were oriented in their mainstream social and academic institutions. Cloud- and crowd-based networked pedagogies thrive in collaboration and collective intelligence harnessed within the local and global learning contexts. This more often than not requires cross-cultural, multi-centric, trans-national, and global engagement that validates the presence and participation of the "crowd" representing the diverse local and global citizens and/or global learners. Cloud pedagogies play important roles to enhance learners' technological knowledge and skills that are highly relevant for preparing themselves as professionals, entrepreneurs, and/or global citizens in the digitally networked global village. Therefore, the application of cloud technologies and/or cloud-based networked pedagogies will be a timely call to explore the potentials of global classrooms to meet the needs, demands, and expectations of the 21st century's global citizens and global communities.

In the era of the webbed world, cloud technologies impact our daily activities and communication strategies, and when the media by and large sing the praises of the local and global communication, it becomes constructive element for those of us teaching writing (Arola, 2010, p. 13) because cloud technologies cultivate students' global and local professional writing skills, cross-cultural composition skills (communication strategies, writing strategies, and prior experiences), and critical and analytical understandings. The use of cloud-based networked pedagogy welcomes students from different cultural and linguistic backgrounds invites them as ambassadors of their cultures and geographical locations and lets them share their individual experiences and cultural assets (histories, narratives, social norms/values, and politics). In so doing, the cloud network pedagogy creates diverse classroom learning atmosphere from where students learn to understand other cultural, linguistic, and geo-political rhetorics. In this pedagogical process, students not only get abundant opportunities to share their prior academic, cultural, and individual literacies, but also get opportunities to compare, contrast, and construct realities for their purposes. In so doing, they become able to expose their identities and their realities from local to global level for which crowd sharing and learning becomes significant pedagogical element. Since students are constantly exposed to diverse cultural and geopolitical situation in the cloud-based networked pedagogy, they also gradually learn to question power, privilege, and difference (also see Berlak, 2008; Freire, 2001; Giroux, 1985; Kincheloe & McLaren, 2007). In a nutshell, the potential of cloud- and crowd-based pedagogy is not only to create and share contents with peers within the classroom, but contents are shared beyond classroom and network community, for knowledge sharing process in the cloud is just at the fingers tips; for instance, once you hit the button, contents and/or information is shared (around the world and beyond) with those who are connected to the Internet.

Additionally, cloud tools are also cost-effective and people from remote areas or from different parts of the world also can use the shared ideas (in the cloud) for their purposes. Additionally, cloud- and crowd pedagogy invites students including indigenous students and linguistic and cultural minority students to participate in academic discourse community where they share their transcultural experiences with other global and local citizens. Meaning, cloud pedagogy tends to create democratic, inclusive, and representation contact zone where students from different continents having different faiths, philosophies, and ideologies network and/or interact that cloud setting makes them globally well-informed citizens in the context of the 21st century global village. Through such digital (cloud) dialectical engagement, students from different cultures understand the dynamics of different geo-graphic, body-graphic politics, and/or multi-dimension of local and global societies; they also appreciate the contradictory phenomena, dynamic negotiation practices. By understanding such dynamics and dimension of different culture and/or dynamics of emerging cultural theories and practices, now students and future leaders, advisors, and political philosophers of the world can easily navigate what other cultural patterns, social institutions, and philosophies are, and how they function in local and global contexts. In so doing, they can also negotiate their spaces and identities for the peace, progress, and prosperity of the global village and global citizens. Or cloud- and crowd pedagogy creates contact zones where everyone can have their voices in which students and/or networked community members create and share together which directly or indirectly bridges local and global cultural experiences, narratives, and voices leading to the understanding of global literacies.

CROSS-CULTURALIZING STUDENTS' RHETORICAL APPROACHES IN THE CLOUD- AND CROWD PEDAGOGY

By engaging students in networked cloud spaces and by sharing their prior academic and cultural literacies, cloud pedagogy integrates cross-cultural conditions, cross-cultural rhetorical appeals, and cross-cultural writing strategies. Cloud networked pedagogical setting engages students to perceive diverse cultural narratives and process them from local to global understanding. In so doing, students from different cultural, linguistic, and geo-political backgrounds contest, negotiate, and process cross-cultural literacies and/or global literacies. In other words, through such pedagogical engagement, students learn to globalize their local literacies and vice versa. Cloud networked pedagogy reinforces students to challenge the traditional hegemonic boundaries such as the traditional notion of superior culture vs. inferior cultures, standard language vs. non-standard language, superior body vs. inferior bodies (body-graphic politics), and cloud-based networked pedagogy reinforces newer paradigms for students' own purposes. In so doing, cloud pedagogy aids students' settling-in process by promoting the existence of cloud-networked communities (Limbu, 2012; Madge, Meek, Wellens, & Hooley, 2009, p. 152) and by constructing their ingenuities in multiple forms in the cloud. In this process, students always provide digital cultural narratives, stories, descriptions, and elaborations, which are culturally reflexive and individually subjective (Knobel & Lankshear, 2008).

In the cloud- and crowd-based pedagogy, students conceptualize and frame and reframe digital narratives on their local social, political, and economic histories and/or narratives by gathering points of references; and when students bring such local narratives and/or histories for discussion, such dialogical engagement make them become cross-culturally pro-active, pro-creative, and transformative. This crowd-based networked dialogical process tends to generate cross-cultural and global cultural communications that operate interpretive syntheses and critical analyses of the realities in immeasurable ways, and possibly it can also transform student's and/or cloud-networked member's individual identity and social conditions through the shared narratives and stories (Bruner, 2002; Chavez Chavez, 2003). For instance, lately, I find many indigenous peoples and/or linguistic and cultural minority groups meet with other members from within their culture and beyond where they inquire, communicate, discover, and challenge about their identities and spaces. Since in such cloud-centric dialogical discussions, participants come from within and beyond their culture/s, they tend to share diverse political and ideological opinions, which make them much more cross-culturally pro-active and pro-creative. Through such dialogical engagement, crowd members in the cloud share different cultural theories and philosophies that motivate them (crowd members) to delink the local as well as global cultural, linguistic, and religious colonization and relink and/or cultivate their own indigenous knowledge. Or crowd interaction motivates them to effectively and efficiently discuss, research, and discover their identities. For instance, through innumerable cloud- and/or social spaces, Limbus (from Nepal, India, Bhutan, Burma, Thailand, UK, USA, and Canada to mention a few) network not only with Limbus, but also with other indigenous peoples and minorities, and they are constantly and consistently delinking Khas-Hindu, Indian, and western cultural and linguistic colonization, and are relinking Susuba Lilim or Kirat epistemologies.

When students and/or networked community members read any shared materials and write/read responses in the crowd contexts, they can capture diverse cross-cultural, inter-cultural, and inter-epistemic knowledge/understandings. For instance, in one of my first-year writing classes, students watched Dr. Martin Luther King JR's famous speech, "I Have a Dream"; then students wrote responses, followed by cloud- and crowd discussion. During the physical and virtual discussions, the way students understood, interpreted, and reflected it was different based on students' cultural, racial, sexual orientation, and geo-political locations. African American students, for example, interpreted it based on their cultural and historical backgrounds, which was different from the way Anglo-American students perceived and interpreted. The way Middle Eastern students processed and interpreted "equality," "rights," and "liberty" was different from the way Mexican, Chinese, Korean and, other students did. Similarly, the way Chinese students construed "freedom" was different from what American, Taiwanese, and South Korean students to mention a few did (also see Limbu, 2012). Obviously, students' interpretations and analyses also differed within homogenous cultures, or students' perspectives differed from culture to culture and person to person as well. This suggests that knowledge is not always local or only culturally situated, but it is also inter-epistemic, or perception different within mono culture, within single family, and within an individual being depending upon time and situation.

In one of my writing classes, though there were a great number of different opinions and interpretations, the way a Middle Eastern female student interpreted "women rights" was different from the majority of female students as well as male students did. Through such crowd-based networked engagement, students share and/or tell us what they already knew and what they learned from the dialogical engagements. In other words, students understand how the same content is understood, interpreted, and consumed in multilayered ways in various cultures. This dialogical engagement not only boosts up students' horizon of critical understanding of diverse cultures, but also encompasses their cross-cultural and/or inter-epistemic understandings in the local and global context. Students' exposition of local and global literacies based on race, gender, class, caste, and sexual orientation help students delink their dominant culture's colonization, suppression; for instance, Middle Eastern female students understand what it means to be a woman in that part of the world; and how conceptual, foundational, theoretical, and practical aspect of meaning of gender and rights is constructed. More importantly, in crowd-based pedagogy, students from indigenous cultures and minority group more often than not understand how knowledge is epistemic or inter-epistemic, and how it is constructed to meet the purpose of dominant culture. Through crowd- and cloud engagement, students can dissect politics of knowledge construction and/or how knowledge is created in the mainstream culture's lab such as body politics of knowledge, ego-politics of knowledge, colonization of souls and minds (in their own culture and across the world) (also see Mignolo, 2007). In other words, the cloud- and crowd-pedagogy prepares students as progressive intellectuals or dynamic and evolving local and global activists who learn to delink colonization and/or challenge the logics of local and global coloniality for their purpose and/or for their community- and community member's purpose. In so doing, via inquiry, communication, and discovery processes, they seek to explore and relink their true identities and agencies.

In the course of sharing, contesting, and interpreting their cultural materials and community histories/narratives, students gradually perceive how people from different cultural and geographical locations use different rhetorical strategies to create knowledge and to perceive and communicate realities. In other words, by engaging in the cloud- and crowd-based dialogues, students (from different continents and different cultural backgrounds) understand how culture and language can affect and shape human communication, understanding, and consideration, and they understand how knowledge is epistemic, political, and ideological and how knowledge is created to serve purposes. In a larger picture, sharing such a complex set of linguistic and cultural strategies tends to blur the traditional contrastive concepts of universalism vs. particularism, individualism vs. communitarianism, specificity vs. diffuseness, achieved vs. ascribed status, and inner direction vs. outer direction (see Hampden-Turner & Trompenaars, 2000; Limbu, Zeng, & McCool, 2013). In so doing, students in cloud-based writing tend to build complex inter-cultural and cross-cultural codes, for the networking and socialization supported by cloud pedagogy is in many respects a hybrid, replicating real-world social interaction alongside facilitating the formation of new contacts based on students' interests (Kreps & Pearson, 2009, p. 158). So, because of cloud- and crowd-based pedagogy, traditional cultural and linguistic boundaries become blurry; they become ambiguous and overlapping since there are not any wholly and virtually clearly defined benchmark between languages and cultures (Connor, 2008; Limbu, McCool, & Zeng, 2013; McCool, 2010; Thatcher, 2010).

By introducing various cultural materials, cultural narratives, socio-economic conditions, and geopolitical codes, cloud-based networked pedagogy expands the understanding and horizon of global cultures. Similarly, it also contributes to the construction, contestation, dissemination, and amplification of diverse cultural artifacts/materials, which are more feasible in cloud computing platforms, for digital global discourse can be steered in more democratic and socially equitable directions (also see Fairclough, 2006, p. 162). For instance, in cloud-based writing classes, students write on their cultural artifacts and prior cultural experiences such as women rights, minority or indigenous identities, and technologies. While working on these projects as I stated earlier, students post/share their inquiry questions, outlines, drafts, and reviews in cloud spaces; and other students get the opportunity to read their peers' questions and outlines that help them both understand diverse cultural conditions and inter-cultural or cross-cultural rhetorical moves and/or rhetorical choices. This pedagogical setting helps students expand their understanding of diverse local and global cultural communication moves or writing strategies. This pedagogical setting demonstrates how people from collective and individualistic culture tend to communicate (which is not universal, but it more often than tends to happen in oral and written communication). The cloud and crowd-based pedagogical landscape allows students to question, contest, challenge, and appreciate other cultural patterns and also gradually helps them develop newer cross-cultural understandings and also inter-epistemic communication (communication difference—culture-to-culture and person-to-person) at the micro-to-macro level.

The praxis of cloud-based pedagogy also offers students' cloud- and crowd engagement in non-linear ways of digital production (invention, inquiry, organization, revision, editing, and production). Meaning, cloud- and crowd-based writing provides students ample opportunities to compose, question, and revise in any portion of the text (in non-linear fashion) through discursive and recursive composing processes. In cloud pedagogy, since students utilize different cloud computing tools and/or apps, they tend to immerse in the make-up of the local and global networked communities within and beyond. For instance, in my writing class, students always do peer review at least four or five times on Google docs and/or Eli with their peers. I have also noticed that students request their friends and family members to read and comment on their essays, reading responses, presentation slides, and multimodal texts. Such cloud collaboration and contribution, within and beyond group members, tend to question and challenge their prior assumptions and our pedagogical assumptions in unimaginative ways. Or such diverse cloud- and crowd engagement or contribution to the production of texts introduces students to local, global, institutional, and non-institutional audience perspectives. Thus, in cloud- and crowd-based pedagogy, students more often than not tend to be familiar with global communication or cross-cultural moves and/or cross-rhetorical writing strategies. In this manner, cloud- and crowd pedagogy informs that cloud-based communication is a platform for diverse student populations from where they reduce adaptive unconscious cultural and geopolitical gaps; they illuminate invisible ideological blind spots, and they mutually challenge inequalities that had been invisible and undetectable in their local (social and academic) communities (Limbu, 2012, 2013). Thus, when students tell their stories and share them in the cloud, their learning has an immediate impact on their lives and interests that allow them to put their newer skills into play within their communities and beyond.

Cloud-and crowd based networked pedagogy not only empowers students to become ethnographers, historians, and ambassadors of their cultures, but this pedagogy also helps them become critique of their culture and global cultures. For instance, when students participate in the cloud as their community representatives, they bring their cultural narratives and/or they share their diverse historical, social, and political concept of knowledge and practices. In the similar fashion, via cloud- and crowd-based communication, they become able to discover their dominant culture's politics of knowledge construction, body politics of knowledge construction, and implicit ideological politics of coloniality (within their local as well as global culture/s). For instance, Chinese students who speak Cantonese advocate for Cantonese language, their culture, and their life styles/choices. Similarly, in such cloud- and crowd-based pedagogy, majority of students (who are minorities or indigenous peoples) discover the political and ideological concept of being, becoming, and belonging or ego-politics of knowledge construction, or they discover how (their) dominant culture/s created and/or creates knowledge that make them see their culture, language, and body through the lenses of dominant culture. For instance, as I implied earlier, Saudi female students research, communicate, and discover that women were/are not as weak as what their (dominant) culture portrayed them for a long time. Similarly, through the cloud- and crowd-based pedagogical engagement, students discover that how West labels the East (culturally, geographically, and body-graphically) is not true. Therefore, in cloud- and crowd-based pedagogy, cloud tools and crowd communication become mediums through which students mediate their cultural materials, economic conditions, and social situations. This mediation includes their own language, community, and learning that shape their identities, subjectivities, and conceptions of their cultural narratives and social conditions (Berlin, 1992, p. 26). While students share their cultural narratives, histories, and individual stories/experiences in the cloud, they grasp other global cultural conditions, global economic settings, and geopolitical situations. With such digital dialogical participations, by blurring the traditional boundaries (local vs. center, superior culture vs. inferior culture, and standard vs. non-standard English), cloud-based networked pedagogy cultivates and/or promotes students' cross-cultural communication skills that portrays their prior notion of language and culture fluid and arbitrary. Furthermore, while sharing, discoursing, and creating contents in the cloud- and crowd-based pedagogy, students realize that writing (written, oral, and multimodal texts) is not static and/or mechanical, but it is situated and dynamic and is always in the making. So, in the cloud pedagogy, students understand that truth is not "universal," but "pluri-versal." In other words, students understand that truths are multiple and are also cross-culturally and individually different; thus, truths are culturally and ideologically constructed (also see Berlin, 1988; Bruffee, 1986; Brummett, 1979; Limbu, 2011a; Scott, 1967). In the cloud-based writing, students recognize that writing, communication, and rhetoric is framed as opportunity for inquiry, communication, and discovery.

Additionally, particular cloud- and crowd-based pedagogy makes research and writing more accessible for them as it provides them opportunity to share their prior literacies, online experiences, and current works. In this process, as everyone is engaging in sharing, questioning, commenting, and negotiating processes, diverse student populations (such as students from different cultural, linguistic, and academic background) not only learn to validate diverse information, but they also learn to perceive, process, and circulate information. This process gradually makes them familiar not only with digital writing and digital publishing process, but it also familiarizes them with cross-cultural, intercultural, and inter-epistemic communication processes. In so doing, cloud pedagogy consequently makes students' research and writing activities seem less foreign (also see Purdy, 2010, p. 55) even though they are in the newer academic culture within their home country or in geo-politically newer academic spaces. Cloud- and crowd pedagogy leads monoculture, monolingual, and monolithic ideology to cross-culture or trans-culture, and cross-cultural or transcultural understanding leads us to creative, constructive, and co-operative global culture. These shifts help global citizens discover different local and global cultural practices, social assumptions, geo-political expectations, and academic/literacy practices. Cloud-based pedagogy facilitates cross-cultural knowledge, global and local communication skills and/or intercultural/cross-cultural communicative norms and values (through the cloud-based dialectic engagement). Cloud-based engagement familiarizes students with emerging digital technologies and their affordances, and cloud technologies familiarizes students digital skills to local to global network skills; cloud-based networked writing also exposes students what knowledge is, how knowledge construction happens as it happens, and how knowledge is maintained across the world. In other words, engaging and networking with students from different cultures, linguistic backgrounds, and geo-political locations, students or any discourse community members learn how their glocal peers/audience create and circulate newer knowledge in order to construct newer knowledge for their own purposes. In this pedagogical setting, cloud- and crowd-based cross-cultural contact zone/s becomes a space of opportunity for students/learners to become a globally well-informed critical and analytical communicator/writer.

As in cloud-based network pedagogy, students and/or any discourse community members gradually learn to engage in cloud technologies such as social media, web 2.0/web 3.0 spaces, which helps them produce quality text for their targeted audience. Cloud-based pedagogy offers students ability to find sources for purpose, to read for purpose, and write/process for purpose. In other words, cloud-based pedagogy offers students ability to connect, evaluate, and process materials for students' own purpose including their community and community member's purpose. As students constantly engage in the network contact zones, they also gradually achieve ability to write for specific audience and to arrange materials and process them with purpose. Cloud-based network pedagogy helps them become a member of their discourse community such as students learn what their field is and how it functions such as it promotes their ability to search materials, to create contents, upload them, download necessary contents, or find necessary information, evaluate them, and circulate them in their field as an emerging and contributing member of their fields.

Concerning the sociological, political, cultural, and economic aspects of any student's home country or culture, cloud-and crowd-based network pedagogy tend to unlock or delink networked community member's colonized knowledge. Meaning, majority of students tell us their stories that whatever they learned before they came to college and/or before they engaged in the cloud-and crowd-based learning (questioning, contesting, discovering, and constructing) was much more logo-centric pedagogy. Students more often than not tell us that their understanding of knowledge, people, and culture much more locally situated and often time misleading (see the examples above) because cloud- and crowd-based learning offers them opportunity for inquiry, communication, discovery, and re/construction. In the cloud- and crowd-based learning, students and/or other community members (at workplaces or communities) seem to discover the political sites of knowledge construction in their home countries; they see the sites of body politics of knowledge construction; they see politics of caste construction (such as Bahun, Chhetri, Baisya, and Sudra in Nepal and India). In the process or progress of cloud- and crowd engagement, students seem to delink or de-learn or challenge the prior knowledge such as politics of knowledge construction such as body-based politics, caste-based politics, gender-based politics, and language-based politics. Through the inquiry and communication, students and other community members learn that they are not truly who they are in terms of identity; so, they learn to research and relink their true knowledge such as who they are, who they were, and who they should be. This dynamic action primarily occurs when students or community members engage in cloud-based communication because cloud-network pedagogy or cloud communication tends to challenge our pre-supposition and pre-assumption and/or colonial pedagogy. This setting happens because cloud- and crowd based communication and discovery process do not function the way traditional pedagogy did a decade or two decades ago. Cloud- and crowd communication became a medium that implicitly or explicitly introduces newer grammar and language of democracy, inclusion, and representation in the context of the 21st century local and global context.

CONCLUSION

By understanding the dynamics of cloud computing in local and global context or within global or local networked communities, we should embrace the reality that cloud-based pedagogy is inescapable. So, we should embrace the digital social constructivism practice that devises active and self-regulatory learning practices by discoursing collaboratively within the networked knowledge communities. In the cloud-based pedagogy, students, by respecting and understanding other cultures, people, and languages, can also alter the traditional conservative boundaries because digital media are the primary social fields, and they have become powerful tools to mediate social elements (Silverstone, 1999; Thompson, 1995; Tomlison, 1999; Virilio, 1997). Consequently, digital interfaces are sites within which ideological and material legacies are constantly questioned, written, and rewritten along with more positive cultural legacies (Selfe & Selfe, 2004, p. 431). What is important about cloud pedagogy is that it opens up various venues from where students get opportunity to enter into other global networked communities and/or they get opportunity to expose themselves to complex intercultural, cross-cultural, and inter-epistemic communication atmospheres. Moreover, in cloud-based classes, whether students are from mainstream culture, or minority culture, or indigenous culture, they believe that their opinions are validated in the center and/or they are not prevented from bringing in their experiences to the center. Cloud pedagogy creates environments where students can explore how rhetorical traditions, cultural materials, and geopolitical conditions are changing, and how such epistemic shifts are influencing their roles as local as well as global citizens. Finally, cloud-based pedagogy lies as an agentive force in the fast changing global village saturated by digital technologies; and digitally literate students not only can communicate effectively with people from different cultures/continents, but also produce more effective, accurate, and high quality texts. It also informs us that we should engage students in different digital, multimodal, and other emerging writing spaces that will provide them valuable local as well as global future career skills and/or proficiencies. In this journey, we, along with our students, will continue to enact an epistemology of representation that will guide present pedagogical practice and will shape prospective pedagogical research inquiries. Finally, we do not perpetuate the traditional hegemonic and ideological pedagogy as they have always been practiced, but we will re/design and reform cloud and crowd-centric pedagogy as they will have been practiced in the future.

REFERENCES

Aleman, A. M., & Wartman, K. L. (2009). *Online social networking on campus: Understanding what matters in student culture*. New York, NY: Routledge.

Arola, K. L. (2010). The design of Web 2.0: The rise of the template, the fall of design. *Computers and Composition*, *27*(1), 4–14. doi:10.1016/j.compcom.2009.11.004

Bazerman, C. (2008). Theories of the middle range in historical studies of writing practice. *Written Communication*, *25*(3), 298–313. doi:10.1177/0741088308318025

Berlak, A. (2008). Challenging the hegemony of whiteness by addressing the adaptive unconscious. In V. Lea & E. J. Sims (Eds.), *Undoing whiteness in the classroom: Critical educultural teaching approaches for social justice activism* (pp. 48–66). New York, NY: Peter Lang.

Berlin, J. (1988). Rhetoric and ideology in the writing class. *College English*, *50*(5), 477–494. doi:10.2307/377477

Berlin, J. (1992). Poststructuralism, cultural studies, and composition classroom: Postmodern theory in practice. *Rhetoric Review*, *11*(1), 16–33. doi:10.1080/07350199209388984

Brereton, J. (Ed.). (1995). *The origins of composition studies in the American college* (pp. 1875–1925). Pittsburgh, PA: University of Pittsburgh Press.

Bruffee, K. A. (1986). Social construction, language, and the authority of knowledge: A bibliographical essay. *College English*, *48*(8), 773–790. doi:10.2307/376723

Brummett, B. (1979). *Three meanings of epistemic rhetoric*. Speech communication association annual convention, San Antonio, TX.

Bruner, J. (2002). *Making stories: Law, literature, life*. New York, NY: Farrar, Straus, and Giroux.

CCCC. (2013, March). *A position statement of principles and example effective practices for online writing instruction (OWI)*. National Council of Teachers of English.

Chavez Chavez, R. (2003). Our responsibility: A perspective on "Taking a stand". *Teacher Education and Practice*, *16*(2), 156–170.

Clark, J. E. (2010). The digital imperative: Making the case for a 21st –century pedagogy. *Computers and Composition*, *27*(1), 27–35. doi:10.1016/j.compcom.2009.12.004

Connor, U. (2008). Mapping multidimentional aspects of research. In U. Connor, E. Nagelhout, & W. V. Rozycki (Eds.), *Contrastive rhetoric: Reaching to intercultural rhetoric*. Philadelphia, PA: John Benjamins B.V. doi:10.1075/pbns.169.19con

Cooper, M. M. (2007). Learning digital literacies. In G. E. Hawisher & S. Selfe (Eds.), *Multimodal composition: Resource for teachers, new dimensions in computer and composition* (pp. 181–186). Hampton Press, Inc.

DePew, K., & Lettner-Rust, H. (2009). Mediating power: Distance learning interfaces, classroom epistemology, and the gaze. *Computers and Composition*, *26*(3), 174–189. doi:10.1016/j.compcom.2009.05.002

Fairclough, N. (2006). *Language and globalization*. New York, NY: Routledge.

Freire, P. (2001). *Pedagogy of the oppressed*. New York, NY: Continuum.

Giroux, H. (1985). Critical pedagogy, cultural politics and the discourse of experience. *Journal of Education*, *167*(2), 22–41.

Graupner, M., Nickoson-Massey, L., & Blair, K. (2009). Remediating knowledge-making spaces in the graduate curriculum: Developing and sustaining multimodal teaching and research. *Computers and Composition*, *26*(1), 13–23. doi:10.1016/j.compcom.2008.11.005

Hampden-Turner, C., & Trompenaars, F. (2000). *Building cross-cultural competence: How to create wealth from conflicting values*. New Haven, CT: Yale University Press.

Handa, C. (2004). *Visual rhetoric in a digital world: A critical sourcebook*. Bedford, MA: St. Martin's.

Harris, J. (1995). Negotiating the contact zone. In *Landmark Essays on Basic Writing* (pp. 27–42). Erlbaum.

Heidegger, M. (1977). *The question concerning technology*. New York, NY: Harper and Row.

Hocks, M. E. (2008). Understanding visual rhetoric in digital writing environments. In T. R. Johnson (Ed.), *Teaching composition: Background readings* (pp. 337–362). New York, NY: Bedford/St. Martin's.

Jaeger, P. T., Lin, J., & Grimes, J. M. (2008). Cloud computing and information policy: Computing in a policy cloud? *Journal of Information Technology and Politics, 5*(3). Retrieved from http://www.urniacs.umd.edu/~jimmylin/publications/Jaegeretal2008.pdf.

Kaplan, R. (1966). Cultural thought patterns in intercultural education. *Language Learning*, *16*(1), 1–20. doi:10.1111/j.1467-1770.1966.tb00804.x

Kincheloe, J. L., & McLaren, P. (Eds.). (2007). *Critical pedagogy in the twenty-first century: Evolution for survival*. New York: Peter Lang.

Knobel, M., & Lankshear, C. (2008). Introducing TPCK. In American Association of Colleges for Teachers (Ed.), Handbook of Technological Pedagogical Content Knowledge (TPCK) of Educators (pp. 3-27). New York, NY: Routledge.

Knorr, E., & Gruman, G. (2008, April 7). What cloud computing really means. *Infoworld.* Retrieved from http://www.infoworld.com/d/cloud-computing/what-cloud-computing-reallymeans-031

Kreps, D., & Pearson, E. (2009). Community as commodity: Social networking and transnational capitalism. In N. Panteli (Ed.), *Virtual Social Networks: Mediated, Massive, and Multilayers Sites* (pp. 155–174). Eastbourne, UK: Macmillan. doi:10.1057/9780230250888_9

Lawson, C. (2008). An ontology of technology: Artifacts, relations and functions. *Techne, 12*(1). Retrieved January 28, 2011 from http://scholars.lib.vt.edu/ ejournals/SPT/v12nl/pdf/lawson.pdf

Limbu, M. (2011a). *Cross-cultural-composition 2.0: Mapping/remapping spaces of Language minority students in the contact zones*. Berlin, Germany: LAMBERT Academic Publishing.

Limbu, M. (2011b). Processing first-year college writing via Facebook pedagogy in linguistically and culturally diverse first-year composition classes. *Journal of International Students.*, *1*(1), 59–62.

Limbu, M. (2012). Mapping "Bottom up" pedagogy in the age of digitally globalized world. *Nelta Choutari: Nepalese ELT practioners meet the world.* Retrieved August 25, 2012 from http://neltachoutari.wordpress.com/2012/03/01/mapping-bottom-up-pedagogy-in-the-age-of-digitally-globalized-world/

Limbu, M. (2013). *Emerging pedagogies in the networked knowledge society: Practices integrating social media and globalization*. Academic Press.

Limbu, M. (2014). *Digital rhetoric and global literacies: Communication modes and digital practices in the networked world.* Academic Press.

Limbu, M., McCool, M., & Zheng, X. (2013). Writing Across Cultures: Understanding and Teaching Writer Responsibility and Reader Responsibility Writing. *Journal of Global Literacies, Technologies, and Emerging Pedagogies*, *1*(2), 56–70.

Madge, C., Meek, J., Wellens, J., & Hooley, T. (2009). Facebook, social integration and informal learning at university: It is more for socializing and talking to friends about work than for actually doing work. *Learning, Media and Technology*, *34*(2), 141–155. doi:10.1080/17439880902923606

Marcelo, C., Yot, C., & Mayor, C. (2015). University teaching with digital technologies. *Media Education Research Journal*, *13*(45), 117–124.

McCool, M. (2010). Rethinking the problem of linguistic categorization for global search engines. *Rhetoric. Professional Communication and Globalization*, *1*(1), 60–76.

Mignolo, W. D. (2007). Delinking: The Rhetoric of Modernity, the Logic of Coloniality and the Grammar of Decoloniality. *Cultural Studies*, *21*(2), 449–514. doi:10.1080/09502380601162647

Motaghian, H., Hassanzadeh, A., & Moghadam, D. K. (2013, January). Factors affecting university instructors' adoption of web-based learning systems: Case study of Iran. *Computers & Education*, *61*(1), 158–167. doi:10.1016/j.compedu.2012.09.016

Palfrey, J., & Gasser, U. (2008). *Born digital: Understanding the first generation of digital natives*. New York, NY: Perseus Books Group, Basic Books.

Panteli, N. (2009). *Virtual social networks: Mediated, massive, and multilayers sites*. Eastbourne, UK: Macmillan. doi:10.1057/9780230250888

Pempek, T., Yermolayeva, Y. A., & Calvert, S. (2009). College students' social networking experiences on Facebook. *Journal of Applied Developmental Psychology*, *30*(3), 227–238. doi:10.1016/j.appdev.2008.12.010

Porter, J. E. (2007). Foreword. In H. A. McKee & D. N. DeVoss (Eds.), *Digital writing research: Technologies, methodologies, and ethical issues* (pp. ix–xix). Cresskill, NJ: Hampton Press.

Purdy, J. P. (2010). The changing space of research: Web 2.0 and the integration of research and writing environments. *Computers and Composition*, *27*(1), 48–58. doi:10.1016/j.compcom.2009.12.001

Purvis, M., & Savarimuthu, B. T. R. (2009). *Computer-mediated socialnetworking*. Springer. doi:10.1007/978-3-642-02276-0

Richardson, W. (2007). In my view: Teaching in a Web 2.0 world. *Kappa Delta Pi Record*, *43*(4), 150–151. doi:10.1080/00228958.2007.10516471

Scale, M.-S. E. (2010). Assessing the impact of cloud computing and web collaboration on the work of distance library services. *Journal of Library Administration*, *50*(7-8), 933–950. doi:10.1080/01930826.2010.488995

Scott, R. L. (1967). On viewing rhetoric as epistemic. *Central States Speech Journal*, *18*(1), 9–17. doi:10.1080/10510976709362856

Selfe, C., & Hawisher, G. (2004). *Literate lives in the information age: Narrative of literacy from the United States*. Mahwah, NJ: Erlbaum.

Selfe, C., & Selfe, R. J. (2004). The politics of the interference: Power and its exercise in electronic contact zones. In J. Johnson-Eilola & S. A. Selber (Eds.), *Central Works in Technical Communication* (pp. 428–445). New York, NY: Oxford University Press.

Selfe, C. L. (2009). The movement of air, the breath of meaning: Aurality and multilingual composing. *College Composition and Communication*, *60*(4), 616–663.

Silvertone, R. (1999). *Why study the media?* London, UK: SAGE.

Takayoshi, P., & Selfe, C. (2007). Thinking about multimodaligy. In G. E. Hawisher & S. Selfe (Eds.), *Multimodal Composition: Resource for Teachers, New Dimensions in Computer and Composition* (pp. 1–12). Hampton Press, Inc.

Thatcher, B. (2005). Situating L2 writing in global communication technologies. *Computers and Composition, 22*(3), 279–295. doi:10.1016/j.compcom.2005.05.002

Thatcher, B. (2010). Editor's introduction to first edition: Eight needed developments and eight critical contexts for global inquiry. Rhetoric, Professional Communication and Globalization, 1(1), 1-34.

Thompson, J. B. (1995). *The Media and Modernity*. Stanford University Press.

Tomlison, J. (1999). *Globalization and Culture*. Cambridge, UK: Polity Press.

Vaidhyanathan, S. (2004). *The anarchist in the library: How the clash Between freedom and control is hacking the real world and crashing the system*. New York: Basic Books.

Virilio, P. (1997). *Understanding pragmatics*. London, UK: Verso.

Vouk, M. A. (2008). Cloud computing—issues, research and implementations. *Journal of Computing and Information Technology, 4*(4), 235–246. doi:10.2498/cit.1001391

Vygotsky, L. S. (1978). *Mind in society: The development of higher psychological process*. Cambridge, MA: Harvard University Press.

Warschauer, M. (2011). *Learning in the cloud: How (and why) to transform schools with digital media*. New York, NY: Teachers College, Columbia University.

Wertsch, J. (1998). *Minds as action*. New York, NY: Oxford University Press.

KEY TERMS AND DEFINITIONS

Cloud Computing: Cloud computing in the simplest terms is the use of hardware and software to deliver services through the Internet, or the meaning of cloud computing is to store and access data, information, and so on over the Internet. In cloud computing, the networked community members or users can access data, files, or information from any device, any place, and any time as long as the users have the Internet access. So, cloud computing in general is a metaphorical term used for the Internet.

Cloud Pedagogy: The term "cloud" refers to mainly the off-premise computing services and facilities such as virtual storage(s), virtual machines, data-bases, and web-hosting services provided by big data centers, and teaching, learning, and writing activities done in such environment is cloud pedagogy.

Cross-Cultural Communication: It is the interaction of people from different cultural, linguistic, religious, and/or geo-political backgrounds in the 21st century networked global village. Skills in cross-cultural communication play key role to the success of global trade, education, and politics, etc. in today's world.

Crowd-Based Pedagogy: Crowd-based pedagogy focuses on the digital and/or engagement of students. In crowd-based pedagogy, students from different cultural, linguistic, religious, and geo-political backgrounds tend to challenge the traditional mono-culture and/or local culture because crowd-based pedagogy more often than not challenge other students pre-supposition about other cultures.

Digital Literacy: It is an ability to effectively and efficiently understand digital technologies (both software and hardware) and evaluate them, navigate them for specific purposes. Digital literacy is the knowledge, skills, and behaviors used in a broad range of digital devices.

Chapter 2
Cloud-Enabled Learning Environment:
Optimizing Collaborative Pedagogies, Bridging the Digital Divide, and Enhancing Inclusive Learning

Dilli Bikram Edingo
York University, Canada

ABSTRACT

The emergence of cloud computing has changed the ways of thinking, communicating, performing professions, and maintaining sociocultural and community relations. The capacious cloud storage and its amazingly growing facilities and capabilities in virtualizing human activities and the entire phenomenal entities and in synchronizing them with new digital cloud technologies such as laptops, tablets, smartphones or mobile phones, and personal computers (PCs) have not only increased human capabilities, but also added new creative dimensions to sociocultural, economic, political, epistemological, ontological, and educational fields. The ways of producing, sharing, and acquiring knowledge, teaching, and learning have been profoundly changed. So this chapter first defines what a cloud-enabled learning environment refers to and critically examines how cloud computing optimizes learning opportunities and transforms teaching and learning pedagogies. Then, it critically explores how cloud-enabled learning environments and cloud-based pedagogies can address the gaps in education caused by the digital divide, how cloud-assisted networks of local learning-hubs can contribute to the success of global literacy campaigns, and how cloud computing reaffirms the significance of distance learning or massive open online course (MOOC) and cloud-assisted practices of teaching self. The rapid shifts in pedagogical grounds from non-virtual paradigms into the virtual world or the cloud clearly indicate that in the future teaching and learning activities and pedagogies become more cloudocratic.

DOI: 10.4018/978-1-5225-1650-7.ch002

INTRODUCTION

The expeditious growth in the use of big data and the emergence of the cloud are the two most significant hallmarks of the twenty-first-century revolution in the field of information and communication technologies (ICTs) and digital technologies. Here the phrase "the cloud" is used as an umbrella concept that includes all of virtual machines, virtual storages, virtual platforms, and the Internet. Another important phrase alternative to "the cloud" is "cloud computing," which the National Institute of Standards and Technology ([NIST] 2011) defines as "a model for enabling ubiquitous, convenient, on-demand network access to a shared pool of configurable computing resources (e.g., networks, servers, storages, applications, and services) that can be rapidly provisioned and released with minimal management effort or service provider interaction" (p. 2). The cloud is used to generate, shape, and contain information, ideas, knowledge, and skills in order to globally share and communicate them through a communication system enabled by cloud technologies such as the Internet, the world wide web (WWW), PCs, tablets, smartphones, and mobile phones. The information, ideas, and knowledge about diverse human activities, skills, and all phenomenal entities have been increasingly being translated into the forms of digitized data—a new epistemological perspective. They have their parallel existence also in the virtualized digital world, alternative to the real world—a new ontological ground. The underlying urgency bolstered by the facts and arguments about the rapid growth in the acts of digitizing ideas, concepts, and knowledge about human activities and the phenomenal world is that there is a huge growth in need of high capacity disk-spaces in order to adjust the ever-increasing data. Consequently, big data centers such as Google Data centers, Facebook Data centers, Amazon Data centers, and Microsoft Data centers have been established. These big data centers offer facilities of high capacity disk-spaces which are made globally accessible and synchronous and called "virtual storages."

Along with the establishments of big data centers, local storages have been moved into global virtual storages, local networks into global networks, and on-premise settings into off-premise settings. The hardware and other physical facilities such as disk-space or storage device, random-access memory, and other in-house infrastructure that an end-user or a client computer requires to be run are moved into remote big data centers or the cloud. The virtual machines in the data centers built up in different locations are globally linked by the Internet.

The Internet works as a global conduit or router through which the global and synchronous process of storing big data into virtual storage/the cloud and accessing into it is always being securely and innovatively executed. Viewed broadly, the cloud implies a series of new concepts such as globally elastic virtual storage, a new virtual platform where human activities can be performed, a faster means of communicating data around the world, and an increased ability to perform creative works through collaborative global networks. The cloud is one of the most innovative dimensions of ICTs that has very lately added new innovative dimensions to economic, social, cultural, and educational efforts as well as to political practices.

The educational dimension of cloud computing provides a new form of physical and electronic foundation upon which a rapid increment of ability has been progressively witnessed in educational field. The attributes of the cloud have significantly changed the ways of thinking, communicating ideas, creating knowledge, and sharing as well as teaching and learning pedagogies. The cloud provides a virtualized data space where teaching-learning materials are re-/generated, re-/stored, re-/shared, re-/used, and communicated globally and instantly.

This chapter analytically explores innovative probabilities, expansions in horizons of learning opportunities, and new parameters of teaching and learning pedagogies in close association with cloud computing. It first defines what a cloud-enabled learning environment means and critically examines how cloud computing optimizes learning opportunities and transforms traditional teaching and learning pedagogies. Then, it critically explores how cloud-enabled learning environments and cloud-based pedagogies can address the gaps in education affected by digital divide, how cloud-assisted networks of local learning-hubs can contribute to the success of global literacy campaigns, and how cloud computing further reaffirms the usefulness of distance learning or MOOC and, additionally, of cloud-assisted practices of teaching self as well. It critically remaps the online teaching and learning activities on the capacious cloud space at large. In this chapter, the phrase "teaching and learning" is used broadly to include all formal and informal teaching and/or learning activities performed in cloud-assisted learning environments such as teaching and learning activities in local learning-hubs and formal schools and colleges or universities, as well as informal and free acts of teaching self or self-studies. The rapid shifts in pedagogical grounds from non-virtual paradigms into the virtual world or the cloud clearly indicate that in the future teaching and learning practices become more cloudocratic, inclusive, interactive, and participatory.

Cloud-Enabled Learning Environment as an Inclusive, Shared, and Collaborative Environment

A cloud-enabled learning environment refers to the kind of an inclusive learning environment, flexibly and adaptively scaled and strongly enabled by the Internet connection or the WWW, online (listening, speaking, reading, and writing) materials, online instructions and courses that are synchronized with various digital devices such as PCs, tablets, laptops, and mobile phones, and most importantly by capacious virtual storage. The cloud-enabled learning environment is a learning environment where credit-owning learning and cloud technologies get well-synchronized and where the latter adaptively supports the former. In such a learning environment, the most important element is the virtual storage, which is considered to imply a globally handy instrument, an innovative platform, and a dynamic process. The capacious cloud storage makes the processes of synchronization and virtualization possible.

Another emerging aspect associated with the idea of a cloud-enabled learning environment is the idea of networked and distributed system of teaching and learning management. It is managed and maintained by shared or collaborative efforts of participants or co-workers from around the world. For example, the protection of high-power disk space or virtual machine is maintained by engineers who work 24/7, say, in any of Microsoft Data center, or Google Data center, or in Amazon Data center. Cloud storage or virtual storage can be basically used in two ways. Clients can use cloud storage to store information, ideas, and various resources in the form of data such as iCloud and Dropbox and manage database themselves. Or, they can also use it with database functionality, creating cloud-database over the service provider site (Jain, Singh, & Shrivastri, 2015, pp. 596-597). In the second type, all the management and maintenance of (private, public, and community) clouds and databases that refer to a systematic management of all items or resources of knowledge and information we obtain through the Internet are carried out by information and technology (IT) experts who work in the cloud-hosting companies like Microsoft Cloud Service and Amazon Cloud Service or cloud service-provider companies like Dropbox and Amazon Cloud, or in web hosting companies like GoDaddy and WordPress. The cloud is impressively liable to benevolently give educators a creative freedom to use cloud storage to either create their own teaching and learning materials or use materials from the databases housed in big data centers. In this sense of a broader perspective, a teaching-learning class in a cloud-enabled learning environment is predicated on the shared responsibility and distributed management of IT experts and engineers, distant teachers, cloud service providers, learners as users of online resources, local educational departments or communities, and states. Cloud storages, virtual platforms, and virtualized/synchronized teaching and learning materials can be accessed even from remote corners of the world in order to educate learners dwelling in those parts. For this reason, the cloud-enabled learning environment is considered to be much more inclusive than any other technologically-enhanced learning environments.

Cloud Computing: Optimizing Learning Opportunities and Transforming Teaching Pedagogies

The most prominent innovation that plays a vital role in creating a cloud-enabled learning environment is cloud computing, which has profoundly changed the traditional ways of knowledge production and acquisition and parameters of teaching and learning within the topographical boundary of hallmarked educational institutions such as schools, colleges, and universities which have been unanimously accepted as the centers of learning for centuries. The traditional centers of learning for higher education are mostly found to have been established in urban centers. Only the certain people from geographically, economically, and educationally capable class have easy access to those learning centers mainly in the developing countries like Nepal, India, Pakistan, and Nigeria. As opposed to such tendencies in the localized centers of learning, the cloud provides a novel pedagogical ground to altruistically substantiate the argument that the propitious events of knowledge production, acquisition, and circulation can occur anywhere beyond the localized formal classrooms where expert agents' roles are expected to be vital in some ways. Teaching and learning activities have been earnestly expanded by the cloud from the centers of learning out to the socially and economically remote areas of the world (Gutari, 2013; Limbu, 2014, p. 67; Mitra, 2007; Radius Stories at the Edge, 2015). The cloud offers a virtual space where people generate and share knowledge and where disadvantaged learners are also given a handy chance to learn it. For example, people use social clouds like YouTube and software-as-a-service models of clouds such as eDhii, Learnopia, Odijoo, and Wikipedia as well as web hosting services such as WordPress and Google Sites to produce and share knowledge with a larger number of everyday digital learners around the world. The advent of the cloud has optimized the learning opportunities and processes of acquiring knowledge and made them more democratic by increasing the possibility of welcoming a larger number of previously disadvantaged learners from around the world.

The distinct attributes of cloud computing such as on-demand usage, ubiquitous access, multi-tenancy, elasticity/scalability, virtualization, and resiliency (Devi & Gaba, 2013, p. 1249; Lewis, 2010, pp. 3-4; NIST, 2011, p. 2; B. K. Rani, B. P. Rani, & Babu, 2015; Sunita & Prachi, 2013, p. 1400; WhatIsCloud.com, n.d.) have made teaching and learning processes more democratic, inclusive, and learner-friendly. Virtualized teaching and learning materials and performances predicated on on-demand usage and ubiquitous access become instantly available to multi-tenants or many learners and educators. Similarly, elasticity and resiliency make cloud-enabled teaching and learning more adaptive to diverse learners who have differing degrees of educational, economic, and intellectual abilities. The defining attributes of the cloud and their practical implications as such fairly uphold the argument that it has better democratized learning opportunities and teaching and learning pedagogies by globalizing and making them more inclusive and better approachable.

The on-demand usage of virtual storage, software services for teaching such as Knewton, Moodle, and Coursera, web browsing interfaces such as Chromosome and Firefox, virtualized platforms or web hosting services such as Google Sites and WordPress and synchronized instructions as well as teaching and learning materials including online library-resources are incorporated to create a virtual global school in the context of the twenty-first-century global education. The cloud technologies, online tools, and cloud platforms as such have been proved to be usefully new tools, participatory pedagogies, and global spaces for designing teaching-learning materials, sharing with students, and engaging them democratically and inclusively beyond the hurdles of geographical limitations. They can access them and interactively participate from around the world through web browsing interfaces. I myself had an opportunity to attend distance classes for the graduate certificate program, Career Development Practitioner (CDP), offered by Conestoga College. Though the students enrolled to the program were only from different provinces of Canada, the cloud-based pedagogical processes, tools, and methodologies adopted for the program can be successfully applied to any courses or programs that massively target global students who virtually exist anywhere in the world. We, the CDP students, had a great practical leverage to visit local offices, professional fields, colleges, immigration centers, community centers, and employment agencies for empirical knowledge and experience as well as for the placement or practicum opportunities; we conducted information interviews and attended workshops in the local offices, institutions, and agencies. Our learning environment was apparently enriched by prescribed asynchronous books and cloud-assisted synchronized materials, questions, interactive and collaborative forums, social clouds like Google apps, YouTube, Facebook, and LinkedIn and teleconferencing tools like Skype, Google Hangout, and GoToMeeting. We routinely participated in interactive, critical, and collaborative discussions on online forums where we shared and exchanged our views, ideas, knowledge, and experiences concentrating on the given topics and issues or current problems in the focused fields of the program. I found cloud spaces like Google docs, Wikipedia, and Prezi creatively useful for preparing PowerPoint slides and teleconferencing tools like GoToMeeting very effectively useful for conducting presentations and discussion-classes audio-visually. I further found social clouds like Facebook apps, Google docs, Skype, Windows Movie Maker, and Movie Maker Prezi very useful to accomplish various individual and group assignments; we practiced and discussed various types of interviews through Skype, Facebook apps, and Google Hangout; we completed our group-based writing assignments on Google docs and used the movie makers to produce short advocacy videos. Many of us uploaded videos on YouTube and shared their YouTube-URLs on discussion-forums for comments and feedback. Each of the students created his/her e-portfolio on one of various web hosting services. These learning performances supported by the cloud can be accomplished from anywhere across the globe. The cloud computing and cloud technologies have transformed the traditional pedagogies of teaching and learning into student-centred interactive, peer-oriented, and dynamic ways and have also moved the learning opportunities from localized centers to the globalized virtual world. The immensely capacious cloud storage has made it easier to virtualize all teaching and learning activities; such a virtualization process has transformed the entire world into a single global school, and has generously made learners global students. That is, the twenty-first-century teaching and learning activities abundantly occur in the global school in a more democratic, participatory, and interactive fashion in a cloud-enabled learning environment.

The virtual global school has ideally made every corner of the world a place where production and sharing of knowledge and activities of teaching-learning are possible. It is governed by the fundamentals of democratic norms such as flexibility or scalability, on-demand usage of virtual storage, and pay-as-you-go model of services. The Internet service, web hosting services such as DreamHost, GoDaddy, InMotion, and SiteGround and virtual storage such as Dropbox, Google drive, iCloud, and MEGA (https://mega.nz/#pro/mEY00QaS) are user-centred or user-friendly services and give clients a great freedom to use them as much as they need and as long as they want. The multi-functional cloud facilities as such are a great advantage to creative educators and learners because the former function as an online forum where the latter produce knowledge and express ideas, as a medium through which the latter communicate and share their creations, knowledge, and ideas globally, and as a virtual class where the latter learn any knowledge and skills from any place in the world. Learning materials for listening, speaking, reading, and writing practices and any other information stored in the cloud, in the form of big data overwhelmingly larger than ever before, can be displayed on the web browsing or user friendly interfaces on the cloud platforms such as iPads or tablets, iPhones, laptops, mobiles, PCs, and smartphones. These practices of teaching and learning enthusiastically prompted by the cloud are the recognizable and perceivable embodiments of a new form of learning opportunities possible in the virtual global space.

The virtual global pedagogical environment remarkably tends to put much emphasis on the better democratic pedagogies consummately conditioned by a priority to learning from a learner's point of view and a shift in pedagogical grounds from unidirectional and one-way method of delivering knowledge and skills to a cloud-based multidirectional interactive and collaborative method. The traditional classes within walls with a limited number of students have been moved out into the cloud that accommodates incomparably a large number of students. The increasing use of social clouds such as Facebook, Twitter, and YouTube as pedagogical tools indicates a pedagogical shift towards the extreme characterized by "a ubiquitous user-centric, user-content generated and user-guided experience" (Duffy, 2008, p. 119). This argument's underlying tone is that the cloud-based pedagogies inherit student-centric, student-content generated, and student-guided learning. For instance, as I mentioned earlier, the CDP students including myself used Facebook apps, Google docs, and YouTube in order to present different perspectives over assigned issues and problems on discussion-forums for interactive discussions and peer-devised solutions to them—an example of student-centered cloud-based pedagogy. Such student-centered cloud-enhanced pedagogies and tools can be beneficially practiced also by educationally, digitally, and geographically disadvantaged remote people of the world. Social clouds, like Facebook, Twitter, and YouTube, have further optimized teaching and learning processes and resources of knowledge. For instance, students share various relevant resources on Facebook, Twitter, and YouTube; even technical skills and knowledge about, say, creating personal web sites today can be learned through YouTube demonstrations. YouTube functions as an interactive space for sharing and exchanging comments and feedback (Limbu, 2014, p. 68) and also as an effective virtual medium through which knowledge is flexibly, easily, and globally delivered by educators to virtually global students/learners.

In short, cloud computing has better democratized knowledge and learning opportunities and introduced new ways of teaching and learning paradigms such as student-centred, self-motivated, interactive, and network-based collaborative paradigms. It has contributed greatly to the global emergence of inclusive, shared, and collaborative learning environments, or cloud-enabled learning environments, where interactive student-friendly teaching and learning pedagogies work best.

Cloud-Enabled Learning Environment: Bridging the Digital Divide

The cloud-enabled learning environment offers a better solution to the barriers to or gaps in the efforts of acquiring knowledge and skills salable in the current technology-dominated world of professional, educational, and economic activities. One of the main reasons predominantly responsible for engendering the barriers or the gaps as such is the digital divide, which Rogers (2001) defines as "the gap that exists between individuals advantaged by the internet and those individuals relatively disadvantaged by the internet" (p. 96). The creation of the gap, rather the hierarchy, between digital "haves" and "have nots" or the users and non-users of the Internet and digital technologies is determined by various factors such as gender issues, economic conditions or money flows, unequal distributions or global configurations of technologies, and spatial differences on the globe (Appadurai, 2008, p. 218; Barker, 2008, p. 347; Vie, 2008, p. 10). Viewed from a binary perspective on the global and the local scenarios, the digital divide still prevalently exists, for example, between the developed countries and the developing countries, between the urban centers and the rural areas, between the indigenous native people and elite ruling classes, and between the rich people and the poor. Focusing on the global scenario of the digital divide, Papert and Cavallo (2000) succinctly argue that "for all except the richest countries the technology is not quite ready at a feasible price point and in any case there are necessary lags between planning and achieving deep change" (para. 5). The underprivileged and remote people of developing countries and indigenous ethnic peoples have faced more hindrances to their career success in comparison to those of the digital "haves" and been long deprived of good education (Gutari, 2013, para. 3; Mitra, 2007, 2013). The emergence of the cloud in its present form in the beginning of the twenty-first century tends to progressively prompt new strategies and independent/online as well as remotely assisted learning pedagogies in order to bring the educationally disadvantaged parts and people of the world into the stream of better education and current knowledge and skills. The cloud-enabled learning environment can be created even in economically and geographically remote parts for the digitally and educationally disadvantaged people who participate in the learning activities through the Internet using digital devices. Now relevant questions may promptly arise, such as: is the cloud-enabled learning environment affordable in the remote corners and people of the world? How can it be economically and physically managed to make it really an inclusive advantage to the disadvantaged indigenous people?

One of the defining features of the cloud is that it significantly reduces the expenditure by shifting the in-house hardware and other on-premise infrastructure that are required to manage databases and maintain their durability and security into off-premise cloud. Therefore, the idea of opting for the teaching and learning in the cloud-enabled learning environment sounds to be an economically most appropriate choice mainly for those rural people who are deprived of educational and technological achievements in developing countries. Traditional systems of school management are the localized systems. The localized systems of managing classrooms, teachers, libraries, and other infrastructure are expensive and burdensome. Such localized management systems can now be distributed globally through a network for sharing contents from the databases in the cloud known as online libraries and collaborative efforts through cloud-enhanced platforms such as GoToMeeting, Skype, Google apps, and social clouds. Educational institutions or organizations both in the public and the private sectors form a network of classes in remote locations globally connected by cloud-based web portals such as MySpace, Baidu, Wikipedia, Blogger, Windows Live, Facebook, YouTube, Yahoo, and Google apps. This argument is strongly supported also by what educationist Mitra (2007, 2013; CUE Powerful Learning, 2015) found out of his experiments in slums and remote areas of India where he left children with computers, downloaded resources in compact disks, and/or Internet connections to learn something by themselves. The children were found to have learned a lot.

By setting virtual classrooms, in certain selected rural locations where having computers and Internet facilities individually might be impossible, the problems of inadequate numbers of well-trained and experienced teachers and lack of infrastructures as well as economic resources can be better solved because such classes can be conducted using online learning materials, synchronous instructions, and, if required, with the help of best teachers and professors from distant schools, colleges, and universities. The cloud-assisted networks and shared or distributed management systems make educational efforts not only more economic and faster than ever before, but also "substantially reduce their load, leveraging efficiencies across the nationwide or statewide school network" (Sourya, 2011).

Cloud technologies and their global networks have linked the local spaces of the remote parts and the poor people with the global virtual store of resources, knowledge, instructions, and materials. The hurdles and burdensome responsibilities in a local place has been transformed into the kind of school management that can be globally shared and collaborated. Such a shared and distributed system of school management is more economic than the localized systems. These native or inherent features of a cloud-enabled learning environment have made it economic and hence play a significant role in bridging the digital divide.

A MOOC as a Functional Subset of the Cloud-Enabled Learning Environment

In order to further elaborate how the cloud can be used to render educational efforts more successful, it is necessary to critically examine what relation a MOOC bears with the cloud in general and with the cloud-enabled learning environment in particular. MOOCs are hosted on the cloud. MOOCs are conducted within the cloud-enhanced learning environment. Actually the cloud, as a whole, is an indefinitely and capaciously elastic virtual space where various socio-cultural, economic, political, and educational functions are carried out. The sociocultural, economic, and educational functions performed on the cloud are considered to form different categories of virtual subspaces. Accordingly, MOOCs further form one of the applied/functional subsets within educational space at large.

MOOCs have emerged out of the cloud elements, e.g., virtual storage, cloud-based platforms or tools like Moodle, RCampus, Caroline, Peer 2 Peer University (P2PU), and Udemy, and synchronization facilities. Indeed, there is a higher potential for achieving a better success in endeavors to educate learners through MOOCs in the cloud-enabled learning environment or cloud-assisted networks of learning. Instead of limiting the teaching and learning activities only on Dropbox-based "desire to learn" (D2L) forums for interactions and submissions of assignments, the maximum use of the software-as-a-service model of clouds such as Facebook, YouTube, Wikis, and Google docs make MOOCs more fruitful to learners and also bring virtual activities very close to non-virtual class events. For instance, learners use the chat-apps of Facebook for democratic and interactive discussions and sharing knowledge, ideas, and information (Limbu, 2012), which are very close to our non-virtual class performances characterized by non-verbal/paralinguistic features of communication. They engage themselves in collaborative works on cloud technology-tools or virtual spaces such as Wikis, Google docs, Facebook, and YouTube, where they as peers also share their own audio-visual and individual writing practices among themselves so as to exchange feedback for collective improvements and knowledge-achievements (Beldarrain, 2006, p. 148; Czerniewicz, Deacon, Fife, Small, & Walji, 2015, p. 2; Limbu, 2012, 2014). With these practical evidences, it can be contended that MOOCs are a particularized and creatively defined functional zone on the cloud. As the cloud-enabled learning environment sets forth a kind of learning environment for implementing MOOCs, the former is a broader concept inclusive of the latter itself.

There have been debates on pros and cons of MOOCs, which delineate some kind of digital divide. For example, Czerniewicz, Deacon, Small, and Walji (2014) contend that "MOOCs offer opportunities but are also pose the danger of further exacerbating existing educational divisions and deepening the homogeneity of global knowledge systems" (p. 1); MOOCs are conducted on a hierarchical pattern that supports the argument that a delivery of knowledge and skills is accomplished from traditional centers of learning like universities of developed countries. Summarizing people's negative reactions to MOOCs, Knox (2014) also opines that the massive emergence of MOOCs have made people very anxious about how individual learners are positioned in relation to an external and superior force, a kind of external threat to both the individuals and the expectations of organizations and disciplines in various educational settings (p. 168). Similarly, Christensen, Steinmetz, Alcorn, Benett, Woods, and Emanuel (2013) argue that MOOCs seem to better serve those who are "well educated, and employed, with a majority from developed countries" (para. 1) than any other population category. They find the skills, knowledge, and experience gained from taking MOOCs very helpful to build up the advantaged people's careers. The underlying emphasis of these arguments is that MOOCs apparently lack a potential of creating any revolutionary changes that would work to concurrently optimize and democratize educational systems, knowledge creations, and sharing so as to upgrade the global literacy in support of the disadvantaged people or those digital "have nots." Concentrating on such gaps or lacks closely associated with MOOCs, what can be imperatively proposed is that the cloud, by its inherent nature, tends to work more on the side of digital "have nots," by opening up new ways of cloud-based global networks of learning and pedagogies.

One undeniable fact about the cloud is that it has now become inevitable parts and parcels of the current educational culture. As the cloud has increasingly become a crucial virtual space which is quintessentially related to various human activities, there has also reciprocally been rapid expansions of Big Data centers to provide more virtual storages and platforms. The expansions on virtual storages and platforms as such make online activities and resources considerably cheaper and comparatively easier to be accessed even by the poor people of geographically, economically, and technologically remote areas. The findings of a survey conducted by Zhenghao, Alcorn, Christensen, Eriksson, Koller, and Emanuel (2015) also seem to highlight such inclusive attributes of cloud platforms and technologies; their findings show that "people from developing countries more frequently report benefits from taking MOOCs and, also in developing countries, people with lower socioeconomic status and with less education are more likely to report benefits" (para. 3). The evidences clearly indicate that strategies of learning and knowledge production and deliveries have been changed; learning practices and knowledge have been better democratized.

Cloud-Assisted Networks of Learning: Mapping of the Cloud's Positive Impact on Teaching and Learning Efforts

The active participants in a cloud-assisted network can be broadly categorized into three types. The first type includes those digitally, economically, and educationally disadvantaged learners. The second type includes those current students in the centers of learning such as schools, colleges, and universities. And, the third one includes those who have earned degrees but require to be constantly updated with current knowledge and new skills. This section attempts to show how educational and digital gaps associated with the underprivileged people of the remote parts of the world can be addressed by forming local learning-hubs and connecting them with the Internet, how cloud technologies complement the credit-bearing formal education, and how cloud-enabled learning helps to update various professional and general knowledge and skills. Cloud-enabled learning environments can be equally helpful to all of geographically, economically, educationally, and digitally underprivileged learners in remote parts of the world, current and prospective students in traditional centers of learning, and informal and free learners such as various professionals and job-seekers who adopt the "teach-yourself pedagogy." The cloud and cloud technologies have equally optimized teaching-learning opportunities and pedagogies for all categories of educators and learners as illustrated by the elaboration of following ideas and evidences.

Linking Local Learning-Hubs as a Part of Global Literacy Campaign

A global literacy campaign for the digitally, economically, geographically, and educationally disadvantaged learners can be better conducted by forming cloud-assisted virtual networks of learning-hubs. Papert and Cavallo (2000) precisely describe learning-hubs as conditions that create "communities of like-minded people to think with, diverse forms of knowledge to fuel the thinking, and real-world experiences to keep the thinking under control" (para. 3). Types and formations of learning-hubs is relatively dependent on the purposes, contexts, needs, and types of active participants: for example, learning-hubs of children, learning-hubs of graduates, and learning-hubs of creative writers who form their own coteries. Learning-hubs can be created either for formal education or informal learning. They can also be divided into two further categories defined by the types of participants and their locations: local learning-hubs and global learning-hubs.

Local learning-hubs are made up of local students characterized by a set of definite identities such as familiarity, features of physical proximities, and fixed locations with well-equipped infrastructures like computers, tables, and large screens. The local learning-hubs are also characterized by the paralinguistic features of here and now. Contrarily, as global learning-hubs tend to depend much on virtual networking spaces, they are not necessarily enhanced by the paralinguistic features of here and now and physical proximities. Participants can virtually exist anywhere in the world and involve in interactive and collaborative performances on social clouds. So, global learning-hubs refer to issue-bound groups of people connected only by social clouds and technologies of teleconferencing such as telephone, Skype, Google Hangout, and GoToMeeting. The primary focus of this paper is placed on the local learning-hubs in a cloud-enabled learning environment because they can better benefit the geographically, economically, and technologically underprivileged learners or students of remote parts of the world.

In order to further elaborate the concept, the very local learning-hubs that are run in a cloud-enabled learning environment are known as cloud-enabled local learning-hubs. The notion of cloud-enabled learning-hubs is "a technology-rich learning environment with both physical and virtual components" (Selinger, 2013, p. 4), where a group of active educators and/or learners or groups of peers who share locally centralized digital devices and resources obtained from virtual storages, and are essentially connected by the Internet or the WWW. Cloud-enabled local learning-hubs and their networks can be formed in any part of the world. Such ubiquitous attributes of the cloud-assisted learning-hubs and the networks offer better opportunities to launch literacy programs in the economically, educationally, and digitally disadvantaged remote places around the world. In remote areas of many developing countries, to mention few, like Nepal, Bangladesh, Pakistan, Uruguay, India, and Paraguay, it is still difficult for learners to have PCs individually; the ideal notion of virtual classrooms, "with students attending class in their own homes on their own computers" (Sourya, 2011, para. 4), cannot be rendered into a feasible reality. Therefore, the processes and patterns of teaching and learning adopted so far in implementing MOOCs may not work in rural areas of the world. States, educational departments, and community organizations are required to set up local physical class-settings equipped with computers for groups of learners so that the digital devices can be shared by digital "have nots." Such learning-hubs from different locations get connected by the Internet to both virtual and non-virtual resources. As a learning-hub refers to a digitally equipped local center of learning set up for technologically and economically disadvantaged people, it is a concept different from that of the traditional centers of learning where usually the students from rich economic, technological, and educational backgrounds entertain the urban learning environments.

The "seven schools in the cloud," five of which have been established in India and two in England and run in cloud-enabled learning environments initiated by educationist Sugata Mitra (CUE Powerful Learning, 2015), illustrate how cloud-enabled local learning-hubs can be created for economically, geographically, and technologically underprivileged children. The schools intimately reflect a purposeful plan designed in integrity with experimenting the cloud-assisted learning and cloud technologies in diverse climate, temperature, and ethnic communities covering different geographic and socioeconomic areas of India and England. The schools have been established in the middle class urban location of England like Killingworth, the urban center of India like Kalkaji of New Delhi, the remote places like Phaltan of Maharastra and Gocharan of Bengal, India, the remoter village like Chandrakona of Bengal and the remotest village like Korakati of India. The students in the schools engage in self-organized group activities and peer teaching without any teacher or supervisor, and they themselves maintain the learning environment, which Mitra calls self-organized learning environment (SOLE). They sometimes are connected by cloud-supported platforms like Skype, Google Hangout, and GoToMeeting with some senior ladies working as volunteer-manipulators or encouragers from different countries like Britain and Australia. Mitra calls such a pedagogy "The Granny cloud" (CUE Powerful Learning, 2015). The schools are the examples of how local learning-hubs can be created in cloud-enabled learning environments in remote parts of the world. As a probable model of creating new and inclusive learning opportunities, cloud-enabled local learning-hubs hopefully embody new potentials of bridging gaps created by the digital divide.

In any discourse on concepts like learning-hubs, cloud-enabled learning environments, and SOLEs, one of the most essential components is the Internet. So an inevitable question that might be relevantly raised here is: how can facilities of the Internet be managed in those remote corners of the world? An immediate answer to this question would be that this is the age of cloud computing, remote control, and Wi-Fi or wireless communication. Of the latest ICTs, Wi-Fi has not only been a great support in endeavors for connecting local area networks, but has also proved itself to have been the handiest tool in connecting the technologically underprivileged people of remote corners with the global systems of learning, communication, and resources. For instance, the cloud-enhanced school in Korakati village in the area of the Sunderbans, India, has been connected with the global network of information and communication system by consuming the energy obtained from solar-power panels and using a wireless Internet receiver (Wi-Fi?) placed at the height of forty-five feet supported by bamboos (CUE Powerful Learning, 2015). Another enlightening example is Nepal Wireless Networking Project (NWNP) initiated by IT engineer Mahabir Pun in order to provide economically, geographically, and technologically underprivileged people of remote Nepal with the Internet facilities based on high power Wi-Fi technology. One of the driving objectives of the project is to increase "the quality and educational opportunities in rural communities by creating tele-teaching programs and by making e-learning materials accessible to students, teachers, and villagers through online and offline e-libraries" (NWNP, 2014a, para. 4). Altogether 15 districts and 175 remote villages of Nepal have been connected with the Internet so far (NWNP, 2014b, para. 17). Though the Internet service predicated on Wi-Fi as such is not powerful enough to individually connect every household, it is obviously powerful enough to create a cloud-enabled learning environment and networks of learning-hubs in the geographically, economically, and technologically underprivileged rural areas.

While launching educational programs and projects in distant rural corners, educational planners, policy makers, and educators have to design local or national context-specific course-contents appropriate to the needs and abilities of local students (Czerniewicz et al., 2014, p. 124). For this, the cloud has offered them a new option for buying a virtual storage and operating expertise from cloud service providers such as Microsoft or Amazon in order to create national context-specific course contents and implement them through a network of learning-hubs on their own virtual private cloud. Both the virtualized local contents and other globally useful online resources can equally and adaptively benefit the local learners who are hubbed in comfortable local centers. The online platforms such as Moodle and Caroline can also be used to link and engage many learning-hubs under one national or regional or district management.

The Cloud and Credit-Owning Learning as Complementary Concepts

The prospective and the current college and university students require to equally depend on both synchronous and asynchronous materials, virtual and non-virtual resources, and in-campus and off-campus performances. Cloud technologies and their uses have become an inevitable pedagogical tool, ancillary to the credit-owning formal teaching and learning activities as a means of fast communication, a cloud-based interactive forum for sharing ideas, and a virtual storage for storing and distributing subject-specific materials and instructions. For instance, cloud-based technologies like emails work as an essential means of communication, a synchronous online storage like Dropbox, and an interactive online forum such as D2L commonly used by faculties and students in colleges and universities have become important components of current academic culture. Similarly, most frequently used cloud-based means for exposing or sharing knowledge, skills, and expertise in various workshops and seminars on various occasions including formal and informal or closed and open classes are Google docs, Wikis, and Prezi. Cloud-based collaborative forums such as Google docs and Wikis and social clouds like Facebook have been proved as very helpful pedagogical tools to accomplish assignments, creating and editing papers as well as group projects (Changchit, 2014; Limbu, 2012). The rapid growth in the use of cloud technologies as such make credit-bearing learning a great success by multiplying the chances of accessibility, retaining students, and improving their performances (Limbu, 2012; Lewin, 2013; Morris, 2013, p.252). These facts about blended learning in credit-owning courses and localized on-campus classes manifestly indicate that cloud-technologies have been significant tools or pedagogical components in rendering the credit-owning courses successful in the traditional centers of learning. Here, the notion of credit-bearing/owning learning is used to imply a broad concept, inclusive of both on-campus or in-class courses and formal online courses such as MOOCs.

Long outdated have become the tendencies of depending only on on-campus instructors, asynchronous instructions, prescribed materials, and in-class performances due to the revolution in the field of ICTs and procurements of new virtual platforms like the cloud. The prospective and the current college and university students are required to spend a quite adequate amount of time in either informally exploring and reading online resources or taking formal MOOCs in order to gain academic excellence. For instance, the findings of a research on usefulness of MOOCs conducted by Zhenghao et al. (2015) show that 88% of "educational seekers" who are prospective college or university students found MOOCs to have been an educational advantage. Such complementary endeavors on the cloud occurs at both individual and institutional levels. Students always individually consult with cloud-based online resources and online libraries any time at home or school and from anywhere they want in order to increase their knowledge, skills, and abilities required to complete their courses for attaining degrees. Similarly, universities offer free and paid online courses in certain areas of study because many undergraduates arrive on universities and campuses needing remedial work, and graduate students also require to develop more skills such as proposal writing, research methods, and statistical analysis (Lewin, 2013; Czerniewicz et al, 2015, p. 4). The underlying idea in these facts is that the cloud and credit-owning learning function as complementary factors and are blended to make a learning process and its environment more adaptively flexible because they offer students abundant opportunities for re-visiting tutorials and other resources communicated by their instructors through a Dropbox or D2L, emails, Google apps, platforms like Moodle and Peer 2 Peer University (P2PU), and social clouds such as YouTube and Facebook. That is, viewed broadly, a blended learning pedagogy incorporates the uses of free online resources obtained from google search engine and credit-owning courses. The contribution of blended pedagogy as such proves itself to have been a great support in avoiding or substantively minimizing the high rates of school dropout (Montgomery, Hayward, Dunn, Carbonaro, & Amrhein, 2015).

The programs that blend cloud-supported online studies and credit-owning learnings can be launched at a broad regional or national level of networks. Indeed, a cloud storage is a creative space where educators and institutions can design course-contents as per their needs. For example, my daughter is in grade two and her district board of education has created really excellent cloud-assisted tutorials for different subjects such as mathematics, social studies, English, stories, and many more for all K-1-10 students. I myself enjoy watching my daughter do with the materials and various exercises stored and managed with a great potential of re-usability in the virtual private cloud named UG2GO. All the students in the schools under her district board of education, Upper Grand District School Board, are provided with individual usernames and passwords so as to allow them to access the resources at home or outside. I witness that the cloud-based tutorials work best in a way supportive to the betterment of her on-premise formal studies/classes.

The Cloud-Enabled Learning for Updating Knowledge and Professional Skills

The cloud and cloud technologies have further enriched the online self-learning environment which offers job seekers—who have earned degrees in certain fields of their specialization—and diverse professionals an opportunity for teaching themselves adaptively without teachers and beyond physical limitations. Only the attainment of formal degrees is not enough in the current competitive job market because the globalization and advancements of ICT or digital technologies have greatly changed the ways and parameters of learning skills and acquiring professional expertise as well as urgencies of newer skills and knowledge. Both the job seekers and diverse professionals are required to constantly update themselves with new skills and knowledge in the career-fields of their choices. The virtual space, online platforms or software such as the Internet, the WWW, and other cloud-computing technologies such as PCs, tablets, and smartphones are incorporated to globally provide the career seekers with a virtual learning environment and a virtual class as alternatives to non-virtual classes and localized learning centers. There is always a high potential of performing the act of teaching-self adaptively, increasing professional ability immensely, and widening the horizon of new knowledge and skills on a cloud-enabled virtual learning environment without physical barriers beyond limitations of a number of desks and walls (Limbu, 2014, p. 67; Sorensen, 2014). All human activities including professional transactions, collaborated production of knowledge, communication, and sharing of knowledge are recognizably and reliably executed on the cloud or in the cloud-assisted virtual world in a way parallel to their existence in the real/non-virtual world. That is why, the endeavors for updating professional skills and knowledge have empirically become helpful in career efforts. This fact is also supported by the findings of the research conducted by Zhenghao et al. (2015) that, of all the career builders interviewed, 87% found online course a career benefit of some kind: "tangible career benefits – getting a raise, finding a new job, or starting a new business – as well as intangible ones such as enhancing skills for a current job or improving their ability to get a new job" (para. 8).

The intuitive strengths like self-efficacy and confidence are fairly considered as the intangible career benefits enhanced by the cloud-enabled learning environment and virtual self-learning that intimately welcome the democratic assumptions and practices of learners by allowing them to carry out their studies from their own perspectives and in integrity with their own beliefs and needs. Such a learning from an insider's point of view increases learners' self-efficacy and confidence which work as important boosters for students in their academic performances and job seekers as well as professionals in their career efforts.

Due to globalization and revolution in digital technologies and ICTs, the skills and knowledge gained three years before and, in many professional fields such as in ICT, gained even three months before become outdated. Here, it would be fairly pertinent to refer to the question which is said to be asked as an ultimate question in job interviews mainly in highly competitive job markets in megacities like Toronto and New York: "What did you learn last week?" (JIBBER JOBBER, 2014, para. 2). As a student in Career Development Practitioner program at Conestoga College, I was fortunate to participate in a discussion about this question. The main motif of bringing in the reference of the question here is to convey the sense of urgency that students, career seekers, and various professionals require to constantly update their skills and knowledge. The capacious cloud offers them new opportunities for self-study and inexhaustibly reusable resources, interactive forums or social networking spaces, and handy media to learn new skills and knowledge and constantly update them as well.

CONCLUSION AND FUTURE DIRECTION

Cloud computing has further expanded the horizons of learning opportunities beyond the traditional centers of learning, better democratized knowledge, and introduced new trends and parameters of creating knowledge in both formal and informal ways and in both academic and non-academic sectors. The traditional unidirectional method of teaching and learning have been transformed into a cloud-assisted multidirectional interactive, learner-centered, and collaborative method. Very strongly bolstered by the capacious virtual storage where abundant resources and teaching-learning materials can be stored, shared, accessed, and re-/used from any part of the world through the Internet, cloud-enabled learning environments offer educators, learners, and educational policy-makers new visions and grounds for addressing the educational gaps created by the digital divide. Cloud-assisted networks of local and global learning-hubs empirically promote action-oriented endeavors that work with a clear predilection for transforming education or literacy rate of geographically, economically, educationally, and technologically disadvantaged people of remote areas. Similarly, the cloud-based online learning that includes formal credit-owning MOOCs and informal practices of teaching self proves itself to be a significant pedagogy in multiple ways; for instance, it works as remedial for prospective and current students and as the virtual school for career seekers and professionals to acquire new knowledge and skills and then constantly update them

The cloud computing technologies such as the Internet, the WWW, PCs, tablets, smartphones, mobiles, and cloud based means of communication such as emails, D2L/Dropbox, blogs, and online resources including online libraries have increasingly been inextricable parts and parcels of educational/learning culture. These emerging technologies including social clouds such as Facebook, Twitter, and YouTube provide a virtual global space where an interactive, democratic, and student guided learning is possible. They transform the entire world into a virtual global school that welcomes all including disadvantaged people of remote parts.

The inexhaustibly capacious attribute of cloud storage has moved local storages into global virtual storages, local networks to global networks, and on-premise settings to off-premise settings. These events of shifting human performances including teaching and learning activities from non-virtual world into the cloud through the processes of virtualization and synchronization clearly indicate that in the future teaching and learning activities and pedagogies grow more cloudocratric. The notion of cloudocracy refers to the preponderant dominance of cloud computing and cloud technologies that can be observed in all fields of daily human activities. As capacious cloud storage can generate and store more resources of knowledge and listening, speaking, reading, and writing materials, cloudocracy obviously is marked by more inclusive and fruitful learning events and characterized by better democratic and participatory practices and technology-optimized opportunities.

REFERENCES

Appadurai, A. (2008). Disjuncture and differences in the global cultural economy. In S. During (Ed.), *The Cultural Studies Reader* (pp. 216–226). New York: Routledge.

Barker, C. (2008). *Cultural Studies: Theory and Practice*. Los Angeles, CA: Sage Publication.

Beldarrain, Y. (2006). Distance Education Trends: Integrating new technologies to foster student interaction and collaboration. *Distance Education*, *27*(2), 139–153. doi:10.1080/01587910600789498

Changchit, C. (2014). Students' perceptions of cloud computing. *Issues in Information Systems*, *15*(1), 312–322. Retrieved from http://iacis.org/iis/2014/60_iis_2014_312-322.pdf

Christensen, G., Steinmetz, A., Alcorn, B., Bennett, A., Woods, D., & Emanuel, E. J. (2013). The MOOC Phenomenon: Who Takes Massive Open Online Courses and Why? Working Paper. *Social Science Research Network*. doi:10.2139/ssrn.2350964

CUE 2015 Annual Conference. (n.d.). Retrieved from https://www.youtube.com/watch?v=y-e9WRMWcdI

CUE Powerful Learning. (2015). *Sugata Mitra: The Future of Learning* [Video file]. Author.

Czerniewicz, L., Deacon, A., Fife, M., Small, J., & Walji, S. (2015). Introduction to MOOCs: definition and characteristics. *MOOCs: CILT position paper*. Retrieved from http://docplayer.net/13741959-Moocs-introduction-to-moocs-definition-and-characteristics-cilt-position-paper.html

Czerniewicz, L., Deacon, A., Small, J., & Walji, S. (2014). Developing world MOOCs: A curriculum view of the MOOC landscape. *Journal of Global Literacies, Technologies, and Emerging Pedagogies*, *2*(3), 122–139. Retrieved from http://joglep.com/files/7614/0622/4917/2._Developing_world_MOOCs.pdf

Devi, P., & Gaba, T. (2013). Cloud Computing. *International Journal of Advanced Research in Computer Science and Software Engineering, 3*(5), 1246–1251. Retrieved from http://www.ijarcsse.com/docs/papers/Volume_3/5_May2013/V3I4-0494.pdf

Duffy, P. (2008). Engaging the YouTube Google-Eyed Generation: Strategies for Using Web 2.0 in Teaching and Learning. *The Electronic Journal of e-Learning*, *6*(2), 119 – 130. Retrieved from http://www.ejel.org/volume6/issue2

Gutari, F. (2013). Can Children Teach Themselves? *Scientific American*. Retrieved From http://blogs.scientificamerican.com/observations/can-children-teach- themselves/

Jain, M. K., Singh, R., & Shrivastri, S. (2015). Privacy Preservation and Authentication Method in Cloud Computing. *International Journal of Advanced Research in Computer Science and Software Engineering*, *5*(12), 596–600. Retrieved from http://www.ijarcsse.com/docs/papers/Volume_5/12_December2015/V5I12-0251.pdf

Jibber Jobber. (2014). *The Ultimate Interview Question #JobSearch* [Blog post]. Retrieved fromhttp://www.jibberjobber.com/blog/2014/11/12/the-ultimate-interview-question-jobsearch/

Knox, J. (2014). Digital culture clash: "massive" education in the E-learning and Digital Cultures MOOC. *Distance Education*, *35*(2), 164–177. doi:10.1080/01587919.2014.917704

Lewin, T. (2013, April 30). Colleges Adapt Online Courses to Ease Burden. *The New York Times*. Retrieved from http://query.nytimes.com/gst/fullpage.html?res=9E02E5D7163BF933A05757C0A9659D8B63&ref=tamarlewin

Lewis, G. (2010). *Basics About Cloud Computing*. Retrieved from http://resources.sei.cmu.edu/asset_files/WhitePaper/2010_019_001_28877.pdf

Limbu, M. (2012). Teaching Writing in the Cloud: Networked Writing Communities in the Culturally and Linguistically Diverse Classrooms. *Journal of Global Literacies, Technologies, and Emerging Pedagogies*, *1*(1), 1–20. Retrieved from http://joglep.com/files/7613/5174/0862/ML.pdf

Limbu, M. (2014). Emerging Pedagogies in the Networked Knowledge Communities: Interweaving and Intersecting Global Communities in the 21st Century Global Village. In M. Limbu & B. Gurung (Eds.), *Emerging Pedagogies in the Networked Knowledge Society: Practices Integrating Social Media and Globalization* (pp. 61–86). Hershey, PA: IGI Global Publishing. doi:10.4018/978-1-4666-4757-2.ch003

Mitra, S. (2007, February). Kids can teach themselves. *Ted Talk* [Video file]. Retrieved fromhttps://www.ted.com/talks/sugata_mitra_shows_how_kids_teach_themselves?language=en

Mitra, S. (2013, February 28). Build a School in the Cloud. *Ted Talk* [Video file]. Retrieved from http://www.ted.com/talks/sugata_mitra_build_a_school_in_the_cloud#t-27842

Montgomery, A. P., Hayward, D. V., Dunn, W., Carbonaro, M., & Amrhein, C. G. (2015). Blending for student engagement: Lessons learned for MOOCs and beyond. *Australasian Journal of Educational Technology*, *31*(6), 657–670. doi:10.14742/ajet.1869

Morris, L. V. (2013). MOOCs, Emerging Technologies, and Quality. *Innovative Higher Education*, *38*(4), 251–252. doi:10.1007/s10755-013-9263-2

National Institute for Standards and Technology (NIST). (2011). *The NIST Definition of Cloud Computing*. Retrieved from http://nvlpubs.nist.gov/nistpubs/Legacy/SP/nistspecialpublication800-45.pdf

Nepal Wireless Networking Project (NWNP). (2014a). *Mission*. Retrieved from http://www.nepalwireless.net/content.php?id=27

NWNP. (2014b). *Our Story*. Retrieved from http://www.nepalwireless.net/content.php?id=48

Papert, S., & Cavallo, D. (2000). *Entry Point to Twenty First Century Learning: A Call for Action at the Local and Global level*. Retrieved from http://learning.media.mit.edu/learninghub.html

Radius Stories at the Edge. (2015). *Leveraging Cloud to Transform Education in Remote Areas of the World*. Retrieved from http://www.vmware.com/radius/leveraging-cloud-transform-education-remote-areas-world/

Rani, B. K., Rani, B. P., & Babu, A. (2015). Cloud Computing and Inter-Clouds - Types, Topologies and Research Issues. *Procedia Computer Science, 50*, 24-29. Retrieved from http://www.sciencedirect.com/science/article/pii/S1877050915005074

Rogers, E. M. (2001). The Digital Divide[Abstract]. *Convergence (London)*, *7*(4), 96–111. doi:10.1177/135485650100700406

Selinger, M. (2013). *Learning Hubs Where Learning Takes Place in a Digital World*. Retrieved from http://www.cisco.com/c/dam/en_us/about/ac79/docs/ps/Learning-Hubs.pdf

Sorensen, C. (2014). Classrooms Without Walls: A Comparison of Instructor Performance in online. *MERLOT Journal of Online Learning and Teaching*, *10*(4), 569-576. Retrieved from http://jolt.merlot.org/vol10no4/Sorensen_1214.pdf

Sourya, B. (2011). *Can Cloud Computing Help In Education?* Retrieved from http://cloudtweaks.com/2011/02/how-can-cloud-computing-help-in-education/

Sunita & Prachi. (2013). Introduction to Cloud Computing. *International Journal of Advanced Research in Computer Science and Software Engineering*, *3*(5), 1399–1401. Retrieved from http://www.ijarcsse.com/docs/papers/Volume_3/5_May2013/V3I5-0346.pdf

Upper Grand District School Board. (n.d.). *Parent Involvement Committee*. Retrieved from http://www.ugdsb.on.ca/pic/parentresources.aspx?id=17113#top

Vie, S. (2008). Digital divide 2.0: Generation M and Online social networking sites in the composition classroom. *Computers and Composition*, *25*(9), 9–23. doi:10.1016/j.compcom.2007.09.004

WhatIsCloud.com. (n.d.). *Basic Concepts and Terminology*. Retrieved from http://whatiscloud.com/basic_concepts_and_terminology/index

Zhenghao, C., Alcorn, B., Christensen, G., Ericksson, N., Koller, D., & Emanuel, E. J. (2015). Who's Benefiting from MOOCs, and Why. *Harvard Business Review*. Retrieved from https://hbr.org/2015/09/whos-benefiting-from-moocs-and-why

Chapter 3
Teaching and Learning in the Cloud:
"Anywhere, Anytime." Anybody, Too?!

Anita August
Sacred Heart University, USA

ABSTRACT

Knowledge is no longer produced exclusively in the traditional class-based learning environment. For twenty-first century learners, digitally networked classrooms are the new social spaces where innovative learning perspectives are cultivated. However, like traditional class-based learning environments, digitally networked classrooms need to be sensitive to the social forces of race, gender, and class that will inescapably invade digital cultures. Therefore, even in the cloud, this chapter argues, "difference" as a concept is always already embedded as a contributing feature under which knowledge is constructed and constructing. To this end, this chapter suggests that a consideration of "difference" and its signifying effect on cloud pedagogy is a useful lens to explore the phrase "anywhere anytime" to the term "anybody" in the digitally networked classroom. Finally, this chapter proposes that the model "anywhere, anytime, anybody" must become part of the basic structure of a democratic and collaborative knowledge building community to democratize teaching and learning in the cloud.

INTRODUCTION

The only real voyage of discovery consists not in seeking new landscapes, but in having new eyes. —— Marcel Proust, In Search of Lost Time

With the ever-increasing reliance on web-based learning environments such as Google Drive, Dropbox, iCloud, Web 2.0 tablets, twitter, and podcasts, knowledge building is being shaped and determined by people who may never meet in traditional class-based learning environments. For the twenty-first century, this is increasingly the rule, rather than the exception. As an interactive epistemic space, digitally networked classrooms have the potential to democratize learning by enabling all voices to share in

DOI: 10.4018/978-1-5225-1650-7.ch003

knowledge building. Unlike traditional class-based learning environments where teaching and learning are still considered the best method for knowledge building, the social forces of race, gender, and class, still create imagined boundaries of difference between self and others. Although digitally networked classrooms have "positive effects that extend beyond the exact conditions of initial learning" (Bransford & Schwartz, 1999), what is overlooked are the social forces that function outside the cloud, which, I argue, will have some mediating effect on the social forces inside the cloud.

However, while I believe the notion of an "imagined community" (Anderson, 1983) in the cloud is quite possible, we must remain open to what, how, and why some groups are "imagined" into digitally networked learning communities and other groups are not. To be sure, this involves questions of power and agency (Foucault, 1982). For example, despite bodies being physically absent and invisible in the cloud, "issues of marking, racial and otherwise, are unavoidably part of [digitally networked classroom communities] signifying practices" (Nakaruma, Kolko, & Rodman, 2000), which will infect any notion of a collaborative knowledge building community. Therefore, the shift to teaching and learning "anywhere anytime" inevitably beckons more questions regarding knowledge building environments and particularly for digital natives (Palfrey & Grasser, 2008), whose social identities and mode of learning are the most constructed in digital cultures.

With this in mind, digitally networked classroom learning communities, like the cloud, are networked sites of conversation and conflict. To be sure, questions of pedagogy are involved given they are conceptual frameworks where teaching and learning is *constructed and constructing*. This is important since the "anywhere anytime" notion of learning is the new mantra in secondary and post-secondary education institutions. However, for some groups, the digital divide is a material reality and exclusionary practices are present despite the cross-cultural, multi-centric, trans-national, and global engagement initiatives that will continue to shape twenty-first century teachers and learners. In light of this, this chapter will address the role of cloud pedagogies as being blind to "difference" in digitally networked classroom learning communities. A stance, I believe, is counterintuitive to the collaborative intelligence goals and objectives. In fact, difference (in any form), is arguably one of the defining features of digitally networked classroom learning communities, since unlike encountering sameness, encountering difference asks teachers and learners to take part in "the reality of other possibilities, as well as the possibility of other realities" (Kessler & McKenna, p. 164).

This chapter, divided into three sections with the overarching goal of providing an alternate pedagogical account of digitally networked classroom learning communities and their power to democratize with "difference" as a salient feature in the cloud will shape the discourse in this chapter. The first section begins with an examination of current conceptual and theoretical notions of cloud pedagogy, which is important on two fronts. First, by individually exploring the terms "cloud" and "pedagogy" a critical analysis of their connection will give a clearer understanding of the implications and the presuppositions of the two terms when combined and adopted as "cloud pedagogy." Second, it is important to demonstrate that pedagogies, such as "cloud pedagogies" are constructed; and therefore, imbue all of the failures of the social forces that mediate constructed notions of knowledge.

For example, what does racial, gender, sexuality and disability "difference" mean in a digitally networked community, if it means anything at all. Is this the new frontier of difference blindness? Accordingly, in the second section, I consider and characterize knowledge building in digitally networked classroom learning communities, and consider how difference is a counternarrative and yet despite difference as mediating collaborative intelligence, grand possibilities of transformation to difference are conceivable and achievable. The third section explores cloud pedagogies as a discursive site where knowledge making is recursive; and thus, problematizes the phrase "anywhere anytime" to determine if it functions through "anybody" or just some bodies? That is, bodies of "difference" that are marked by race, gender, sexuality, and disability. I conclude with some broader thoughts on how cloud pedagogies affect the ontology of digitally networked classroom learning communities, when visual "difference" is invisible but imagined to promote a collaborative knowledge building community.

Cloud Pedagogy: An Introduction to a Curiously Cloudy Term

Despite the escalating use of the term "cloud computing" in secondary and post-secondary educational settings, the term "cloud" remains cloudy with no clear or coherent understanding for a global culture of expert and non-expert users obsessed with the internet and new technologies. To tack on the oft-used secondary and post-secondary phrase "pedagogy" behind the term "cloud" to form "cloud pedagogy" continues to veil any lucid conceptualization of the term. However, if we bracket the terms and meanings of "cloud" and "pedagogy" we may start to get a sense of how they mediate any notion of semiotic suggesting when combined as "cloud pedagogy." With this in mind, our focus on how teaching and learning in this twenty-first century Wide Area Network (WAN) occurs is a great reference point for a comprehensible notion of the term cloud pedagogy in secondary and post-secondary educational settings.

As noted in the introduction, the term "cloud computing" is notoriously opaque. While vague and incomprehensible technical terms are often common for the computer sciences, given the daily use of cloud computing by non-experts in the field, a utilitarian understanding of the term is needed. Again, as noted in the introduction, when "cloud computing" is combined with "pedagogy"—another opaque and confusing term in academe—and adopted as "cloud pedagogy"—both experts and non-experts struggle for an enabling conception of the term. Therefore, clarifying the use of the term, at least in this chapter, is important before its application as a framework for examining its connection to the notion of "anywhere anytime anybody." With this in mind, it is not the intention of this chapter to cover the term "cloud computing" exhaustively or comprehensively, but only to characterize its role as a concept in the sphere of digitally networked classroom learning communities.

For instance, what is most curious about the term "cloud computing" is that a United States government organization, National Institutes of Standards and Technology (NIST), formulates the nature of its meaning rather than academics. In "Cloud Computing Explained," Jared Carstensen, Bernard Golden, and JP Morgenthal write regarding cloud computing is "there are more definitions" they argue "than there are stars in the sky" (p. 24). Although the term "cloud computing" is unusually dense and linear with no hardened attempt to locate the term, it is not that the term is meaningless. What is most interesting about the term is that it is rooted in power and agency, which tacitly undermines any notion for clarity. That "cloud computing" is situated in the dialectical space of government where obscurity of meaning privileges the expert rather than the non-expert is important, given the use of the term is evaluated and understood only in its practice by the experts. In short, the experts dialogically trap the non-expert as a developmental social and cultural use of the term occurs, since neither the expert nor the non-expert has adequately expressed the nature of the term.

While the inability to locate the rhetorical function of the term in its expressivity privileges the expert, it is problematic for the non-expert. The non-expert is often held accountable to the instrumental meaning of the term only when its application is located within social systems managed by the government and situated in such a way that indicts government bureaucratic agencies or the State as *irrelevant or irreverent* to civil liberties. This is not a modern dilemma between the State and the individual where the continuities between liberty and rights are often blurred when a new regime of thought occurs, like the Internet and new technologies, which challenges and transforms notions of existing socio-political and cultural systems. For as Karl Marx warns, "The limits of political emancipation appear at once in the fact that the *state* can liberate itself from constraint without man himself being *really* liberated; that a state may be a *free state* without man himself being a *free man*" ("On the Jewish Question" p. 32). As a result, the interpretation of the term by the non-experts may indeed have insurgent ambitions since the production and expansion of the network society are redefined and recontexualized by the "enduring grip of "difference" in the public imagination, and the genuine social and economic conflicts over what difference comes to mean over time" (Minow p. 201). Without question then, "cloud computing" as a shared telecommunications system *has to become* and *has the potential to become* a dialectical process of communication where indeed "anywhere, anytime, and anybody" is more than just a slick Aristotelian sophistic approach of rhetorical inclusivity. As a concept, then, "cloud computing" may remain rhetorically constituted in the political interests of the experts, since very few non-experts have the specialist knowledge to empty the term of its obscurity. Furthermore, although the term "cloud computing" is not exclusionary in terms of the "anytime anywhere" philosophy that shapes it. The rhetorical deficiencies are that "cloud computing" does not advocate for the transformation of its governing principles for "anybody" both in its theory and in practice.

However, when the term "cloud" is rhetorically tethered to "pedagogy" the dialectical expressivity of the term "cloud pedagogy" is discursively amplified which exposes the weaknesses in its use by the experts as a heuristic device to create hierarchies. To be sure, in its modern rhetorical encasing, pedagogy is a highly social and political term and in a narrow conceptualization, pedagogy can cause more harm than good. Constructivist theorist Jerome Bruner believes that students learn best when current and past knowledge(s) come into active dialogue with one another to construct new frameworks for learning. However, Bruner notes "Pedagogy is never innocent" because he argues, "it is a medium that carries its own message" (p. 63), which is imbued with cultural, political and social meaning and experiences. Bruner's theory is important since once non-experts employ the term "cloud pedagogy" they use it as a rhetorical tool to dismantle structural inequities. The subversive claim of the term reconstituted by those without expert training, criticize, and release the term from its canonical and rhetorical hold by the experts to explore the dialogical socio-political expressivity of the term. "Cloud pedagogy" is not exclusively situated like the term "cloud computing" within a canonized and formal setting with its meaning and function conceptualized by the experts. For once claimed by marginalized groups and dislodged from its rhetorical hold by the experts, the expressivity of "cloud pedagogy" in the Networked Knowledge Society (NKS), for example, is no longer linear and situated. "Cloud Pedagogy," then, becomes fluid, open-ended, and imbued with rhetorical possibilities for civic action.

In *On Critical Pedagogy*, radical educator and provocateur Henry Giroux has developed one of the most robust reframings of pedagogy called "critical pedagogy" to give the term a complex and multifaceted meaning tied to social justice in the classroom. For Giroux, the classroom and society should not be viewed as separate ideological entities but as coexisting dialectics. By shedding light on socio-political injuries to civil liberties in educational settings Giroux believes entrenched orthodoxies of power that overwhelmingly support dominant groups and mainstream ideologies in the social order are unmasked and replaced with alternative and egalitarian forms of democratic learning environments. For Giroux, then, if regimes of thought that clearly favor the elites and dominant modes of discourse are "outed" in educational settings, student are less likely to tolerate and fall in lock-step with structural forms of oppression in the social order. Giroux writes:

My view of critical pedagogy developed out of a recognition that education was important not only for gainful employment but also for creating the formative culture of beliefs, practices, and social relations that enable individuals to wield power, learn how to govern, and nurture a democratic society that takes equality, justice, shared values, and freedom seriously. I began to see how pedagogy is central to politics in that it is involved in the construction of critical agents and provides the formative culture that is indispensable to a democratic society. (Giroux, Ch. 1, Kindle location 66, 4519)

Giroux's statement is particularly relevant to digitally networked classroom learning communities, I argue, because it does not advocate as noted earlier, a separation of classroom learning from the socio-political order. Not only is Giroux's philosophy a conceptual model for the term "cloud pedagogy," it also functions as theory to inform the transformative potential in the digitally networked classroom. Difference as an ontological argument in the digitally networked classroom, shapes and is shaped by, the epistemological coding in "cloud pedagogy." That is, student's social and political realities are a synthesis of their ontological arguments and the epistemological coding in the digitally networked classroom learning communities. Therefore, to participate in a "melting pot narrative" where all is the same defiles the emancipatory role that "difference" plays in the digitally networked classroom. This is important since more than ever, social interaction is taking place in the "cloud," which, in turn, influences and or transforms any notion of "pedagogy" in the digitally networked classroom. "Cloud Pedagogy," then, is not so cloudy when one considers that the term is constantly "evolving" to mean something new when it encounters issues related to students' social and political realities that are not *lived in* the digitally networked classroom, but most certainly *lived out in* the digitally networked classroom. That is, a new dimension of reality breaks out through collective discourse, without any consideration to the socio-political hierarchical structure outside the digitally networked classroom.

Therefore, the next section will take into account how knowledge producing in the digitally networked classroom is re-defined through rhetorical examination of the material world with difference being an organizing feature of the collective discourse.

New Knowledge Cultures and the Digitally Networked Classroom

Henry Jenkins' concept of participatory culture is widely known from his influential book *Convergence Culture: Where Old and New Media Collide*. In his introduction to this important work, Jenkins appears just as baffled as everyone about the participatory culture where in the socio-political hierarchical structure privileges provide rank, power, and agency. In a participatory culture, like the digitally networked classroom, however, the space "the cloud" is heterogonous and homogenous—not hierarchical. Jenkins' participatory culture view, now well known, is still worth repeating because he sounds the alarm for proposing any sustainable research paradigms for establishing any core methods for analysis. Jenkins explains:

The term, participatory culture, contrasts with older notions of passive media spectatorship. Rather than talking about media produces and consumers as occupying separate roles, we might now see them as participants who interact with each other according to a new set of rules that none of us fully understands. (p. 3)

Although Jenkins' definition of participatory culture has erased the notion between the dichotomy of privilege and rank during the construction of knowledge producing, it also muddies his own term by suggesting that not all differences "are created equal" (p. 3). As Jenkins notes, "Corporations—even individuals within corporate media—still exert greater power than any individual consumer or even the aggregate of consumers. And some consumers have greater abilities to participate in this emerging culture than others" (p. 3). The key feature of Jenkins' analysis is that "collective meaning-making" is not specifiable to one disciplinary form of knowledge. Rather, as Jenkins notes participatory culture, like digitally networked classroom, "within popular culture is starting to change the ways religion, education, law, politics, advertising, and even the military operate" (p. 4). Therefore, a master narrative is highly unlikely in a digitally networked classroom since there is no foundationalist center. Rather, "cloud pedagogy" will never become fixated like canonical texts that seem to code human expressivity despite insurgent rhetorical discourse by Othered groups. Jenkins seems to echo this view by stating there is no definite or fixed view on knowledge making. Rather, Jenkins posits, "I explore how collective meaning-making within popular culture is starting to change the ways religion, education, law, politics, advertising, end even the military operate" (p. 4).

Although Jenkins' participatory culture definition was and still is an insurgent idea, Jenkins is quick to note that his ideas are a mish mash of Pierre Levy's notion of "collective intelligence," articulated in his seminal monograph *Collective Intelligence: Mankind's Emerging World in Cyberspace* which gestures towards a break with knowledge that rests on the head of one shoulder. For Levy, in the new knowledge culture everything depends on everybody because, "No one knows everything, everyone knows something, all knowledge resides in humanity" (pp. 13-14). Levy's epistemological break with canonized ways of knowledge producing is a particularly welcome discourse in "cloud pedagogy" since as he notes, "nothing is fixed" (p. 17). This lack of fixity or permanence in Levy's notion of the new knowledge culture does not mean that ideas have no relationship or relevance to the social order. Levy suggests, and I concur, actors shift the discourse in the new knowledge culture or the digitally networked classroom, to reflect their encounter(s) with the social order. Actors reject cleavages to systematized pedagogy validated by the socio-political hierarchical structure, in favor of allegiance to ideas that promote a more inclusive pedagogical structure. In this way, everyone participates in new knowledge cultures like the digitally networked classroom, which dethrones the rubrics of a text-bound pedagogy with a monologist view of knowledge.

It is important to underscore the revolutionary nature of the new knowledge culture in the digitally networked classroom since the idea that the actors define and defend their pedagogy rather than the instructor, reflects the transgressive nature of pedagogy that Giroux and Jenkins endorses, breaks with the rigid system of secondary and post-secondary knowledge making systems. Like Giroux and Jenkins, Levy argues for a similar releasing of totalitarian control of knowledge making to produce more inclusive voices and ways of knowing in what he calls cosmopedic knowledge, which he argues "brings us closer to the lived world" (p. 216). Levy's definition of cosmopedic knowledge is worth citing in full since it is a complex heuristic for political action in a democratic technological space. Levy maintains,

The characteristic principle of the cosmopedia, and that which makes it worthwhile, is its non-separation. For collective intellects, knowledge is a continuum, a large patchwork quilt in which each point can be folded over on any other. The cosmopedia dematerializes the boundaries between different types of knowledge. It dissolves the differences between specializations, as separate zones of power, and leaves behind regions with fluid borders, structured by concepts of variable significance and objects that are continuously being redefined. In place of the fixed organization of knowledge into discrete and hierarchical disciplines (typical of territorial space)—or the chaotic fragmentation of information and data (typical of the commodity space)—there now exists an unbroken, dynamic topology. (p. 217)

Levy's cosmopedia does not allow any one discourse to take rhetorical hostage of other discourses. This is an important concept and alien to modern secondary and post-secondary educational environments where every few years a new representational college education emerges and renders others irrelevant. For example, the academic disciplines of science, technology, engineering and mathematics or STEM, are the new representational college education. In a cosmopedia setting, however, like the digitally networked classroom, a STEM education would have no more rank and privilege than a liberal arts education. In the cosmopedia, all types of knowledges when they intersect and interact will, by a radical opposition to a hierarchal form of knowledge making will inevitably create new discourses. Levy's cosmopedia theory, then, suggests that new knowledge cultures like the digitally networked classroom are spaces where knowledge making is endlessly being produced and reproducing without any totalitarian control or hierarchy. Thus, the notion of a representative education in the digitally networked classroom is constrained since there is no valorization of one discourse over another. Although Giroux, Jenkins, and Levy make tacit gestures towards difference in new knowledge cultures, some cultural theorists make theirs explicit. This is important since multiple literacies are not produced mechanically—they are produced out of a multicultural society where "difference" is the norm, and properly understood and engaged in a digitally networked classroom, "difference" should not be viewed as undermining but as a transforming feature of pedagogy.

Difference as a Social Movement in the Transgressive Space of the Digitally Networked Classroom

In his influential book, *Networks of Outrage and Hope: Social Movements in the Internet Age*, Manuel Castells argues, "networks of power in various domains of human activity" (p. 7) are important components for expressing insurgent ideas which are "intimately linked [and possess] "extraordinary power" to transform socio-political cultures by uniting diverse ideologies. Like most individual systems of ideology coerced into networks of power despite trying to sustain their own identity, Castells warns, they often "do not merge" (p. 8). Castells is suggesting that "meta-networks of power" (p. 7) within a technological movement do not organically explain, clarify, and confirm, the nature of its teaching—that is, it's pedagogical ethos. Rather, as Castells suggests, networks of power "control the capacity of defining the rules and norms of society through a political system that primarily responds to their interests and values" (p. 8) are derivatives of a social movement. Castells believes that programmers and switchers are the two groups that "holds power in the network society" (p. 8) and to shift this power dynamic, Castells argues is by "switching power" (p. 8).

Castells approach is interesting because while articulating an idea for an expansive view of technological networks, Castells technological manifesto also constitutes the core principles of equality and justice for everyone, which echoes and reflects historical and modern reform movements. Within secondary and post-secondary digitally networked classrooms, Castells' new concept is particularly engaging since it places the transformation of public power in the hands of ordinary citizens. As Castells notes,

Digital social networks offer the possibility for largely unfettered deliberation and coordination of action. However, this is only one component of the communicative process through which social movements relate to society at large. They also need to build space by creating free communities in the urban space. (p. 9-10)

Castells seems to suggest that like race and gender, class and education are also hindrances to a democratic digital social network. Urban spaces, then, where underprivileged raced and gendered people reside, are also from the underclass and typically undereducated. These are all structural and institutional systems of injustice that most societies try to confront and change typically by a distributive system of justice with goods and services. However, Castells argues for public spaces as a conceptual form of justice as well so that "anywhere anytime," will include "anybody." Furthermore, Castells recognizes that even in public spaces that appear to have democratic tendencies or ambitions, the social group disparity still hinders any notion of a technological inclusive framework. For Castells, although the primary goal of an institutional public space was to erase the boundaries where power and hegemony convene, the dominant elite often maintain a successful advantage and thus maintain their privilege and rank. Castells' social justice position with technology sounds strikingly similar to Jenkins and Levy's. However, Castells goes a step further with his challenge to democratize technology by criticizing the space it occupies. Institutional public space, Castells argues, are often an obstacle that adds to the bifurcation of learning, which creates power divisions. Castells writes:

Since the institutional public space, the constitutionally designated space for deliberation, is occupied by the interests of the dominant elites and their networks, social movements need to carve out a new public space that is not limited to the Internet, but makes itself visible in the places of social life. This is why they occupy urban space and symbolic buildings. Occupied spaces have played a major role in the history of social change, as well as in contemporary practice. (p.10)

For Castells, "togetherness, symbolic power, and political space" (pp. 10-11) characterize the new public space which is a stark reversal of institutional public space, which he argues, exists mainly for the perpetuation of power controlled by dominant elites. In the new public space, however, justice is the overarching philosophy with the wider concepts of agency and power being part of the paradigm. Castells' gesture is more than just token inclusivity—it motions towards a radical rethinking of what inclusivity means and how restructuring inclusivity inescapably involves agency and power in the new public space. For Castells,

The critical matter is that this new public space, the networked space between the digital space and the urban space, is a space of autonomous communication. The autonomy of communication is the essence of social movements because it is what allows the movement to be formed, and what enables the movement to relate to society at large beyond the control of the power holders over communication power. (p.11)

Like Castells, cultural theorist bell hooks call for a radical transforming of space, which, for hooks, decenters institutionalized paradigms of agency and power albeit in the classroom. Despite hooks' generalized view of the classroom, I would like to identify "space" as the digitally networked classroom in both secondary and post-secondary environments. Moreover, I would like to tether Castells' alternate new public space and hooks' suggestion of "transformative pedagogy" (p.36) to my earlier representation of "cloud pedagogy" since pedagogically, both embody a radical departure from current systemized notions of knowledge producing. The result, I argue, is epistemological and ontological: epistemologically, it reorders the origin and nature of who constitutes knowledge and the space (s) where knowledge is constituted. Ontologically, it considers the nature of knowledge and its relations to human agency, particularly when rhetorically situated within totalizing discourses and spaces of power. For hooks, then, in *Teaching to Transgress*, the classroom,

[On] all levels, from elementary to university settings—we must acknowledge that our styles of teaching may need to change. Let's face it: most of us were taught in classrooms where styles of teachings reflected the notion of a single norm of thought and experience, which we were encouraged to believe was universal. This has been just as true for nonwhite teachers as for white teachers. Most of us learned to teach emulating this model. As a consequence, many teachers are disturbed by the political implications of a multicultural education because they fear losing control in a classroom where there is no one way to approach a subject—only multiple ways and multiple references. (pp. 35-36)

It is interesting to note that both hooks and Castells have political identities. hooks' socio-cultural theory as a raced and gendered person is representative of her identity, which is central to her engagement with her students in the classroom. Castells as a raced Hispanic person orients his view and encounter with being different across borders of language, culture, and ethnicity within spaces of power. Taking into account hooks and Castells' story, then, identity politics are important to generating alternative practices of cloud-based pedagogies.

If we are to create a *new public space,* as Castells argues, and "teach in a manner that empowers students" (p.15) as hooks encourages, the notion of "anywhere, anytime, anybody" is not a rhetorical exaggeration of transformative human agency and power. Thus, the concept of "anywhere, anytime, anybody" within a cloud pedagogy that embodies emancipatory possibilities will emerge. My vision of "cloud pedagogy" after all may not appear as alien as previously noted. "Cloud pedagogy," then, is an evolving process, which we should not surrender to attitudes that pedagogically appear key to shaping our technological destinies in secondary and post-secondary digitally networked classrooms.

CONCLUSION

This chapter began with a discovery of what it means to intertextualize the term "cloud" to "pedagogy" within a secondary and post-secondary digitally networked classroom. However, before this rhetorical tethering, the vision of the term "cloud computing" was examined to understand its epistemological impact on "cloud pedagogy" in the digitally networked classroom. Pedagogy, according to Bruner and Giroux is major driving force of scholasticism in both secondary and post-secondary learning environments. However, for Jenkins and Levy, unless and until these environments are participatory without rank and privilege, any learning is unsuccessful—that is for the masses. Castells and hooks' emphasis on the empowerment of space is particularly important since they argue space is both creative, transformative, and filled with possibilities for autonomy and transgressive behavior. The emphasis on both technology and its pedagogical impact is especially important given they both aim to realize the possibility of "anywhere, anytime, anybody." While this utopian ideal may appear lofty and especially naïve in a society that values an Aristotelian logos centered mode of thought. We must remember that radical skepticism in the sphere of the digitally networked classroom is not about undermining "cloud pedagogy" but simply to underscore its service to reforming the spatial politics where all voices, despite their complication by identity of difference are in large part the beginning of a less divided society on difference.

REFERENCES

Anderson, B. (1983). *Imagined Communities. Reflections on the Origin and Spread of Nationalism.* London: Verso.

Bransford, J. D., & Schwartz, D. L. (1999). Rethinking Transfer: A Simple Proposal with Multiple Implications. *Review of Research in Education, 24*, 61–100.

Bruner, J. (1996). *The Culture of Education.* Cambridge, MA: Harvard UP.

Carstensen, J., Golden B., & Morgenthal JP. (2012). Cloud Computing Explained. In *Cloud Computing* (pp. 23-56).

Castells, M. (2012). *Networks of Outrage and Hope: Social Movements in the Internet Age.* Cambridge, UK: Polity Press.

Foucault, M. (1982). The Subject and Power. *Critical Inquiry, 8*(4), 777–795. doi:10.1086/448181

Giroux, H. (2011). *On Critical Pedagogy.* New York, NY: Continuum.

hooks, b. (1994). *Teaching to Transgress: Education as a Practice of Freedom.* New York: Routledge.

Jenkins, H. (2012). *Convergence Culture: Where Old and New Media Collide.* New York: New York University Press.

Kessler, S., & McKenna, W. (1985). *Gender: An Ethnomethodological Approach.* New York: Wiley.

Kolko, B., Nakamura, L., & Rodman, G. (2000). *Race in Cyberspace.* New York: Routledge.

Lévy, P. (1997). *Collective Intelligence: Mankind's Emerging World in Cyberspace.* New York: Plenum Trade.

Marx, K. (1978). On the Jewish Question. In R. Tucker (Ed.), The Marx-Engels Reader (pp. 26-46). New York: Norton and Company.

Minow, M. (1993). From "Justice Engendered". In P. Smith (Ed.), The Nature and Process of Law (pp. 201-218). New York: Oxford University Press.

Palfrey, J. G., & Urs, G. (2008). *Born digital: Understanding the first generation of digital natives.* New York: Basic.

ADDITIONAL READING

Castells, M. (2009). *The Information Age: Economy, Society, and Culture* (Vol. 1). Massachusetts: Blackwell.

Kress, G. & van T. Leeuwen, T. (2001). *Multimodal Discourse: The Modes and Media of Contemporary Communication.* London: Edward Arnold.

Kress, G. (2003). *Literacy in the New Media Age*. London: Routledge. doi:10.4324/9780203164754

Selfe, C. (1999). *Technology and Literacy in the Twenty-First Century: The Importance of Paying Attention*. Carbondale: Southern Illinois University Press.

Warschauer, M. (2011). *Learning in the Cloud: How (and Why) to Transform Schools with Digital Media*. New York: Teachers College Press.

KEY TERMS AND DEFINITIONS

Anywhere Anytime Anybody: This view is representative of the 24 hour seven days a week available of technology and the transactions that can occur across any geographical, land or techno-spatial borders. In short, the terms imply that everyone has the capability in any context to participate in any community or transaction without any false border.

Cloud: Despite its contested meaning, most often the term refers to a datacenter connected to servers that are connected to the internet. A cloud is either public, private, local or global which is referred to as a Wide Area Network (WAN), or contained within a specific business or organization, Local Area Network (LAN). The pliability in the use of the term no doubt contributes to the terms lack of preferred meaning.

Cloud Computing: Refers to a combination of software and hardware services that are in the "cloud" and available for use through the internet.

Cloud Pedagogy: Describes the knowledge that is specific to teaching about the theories and methods of the cloud.

Pedagogy: Although this is a fluid and open ended term, in its most ideal interpretation, pedagogy is the art, theory, science and practice of teaching.

ENDNOTES

1 At best, this statement is utopian with the understanding that lived reality will trump any notion of a fairytale utopianism imbued with 'willful blindness' where one intentionally refuses to see and listen beyond what is clear and present before them.

2 Although Giroux resists the label of being one of the architects of Critical Pedagogy philosophy, he is most definitely one of the original framers of the term along with Paulo Freire.

Chapter 4
Genres in the MOOCology of Writing:
Understanding Cloud-Based Learning through a Genre-Activity Analysis

Jason Chew Kit Tham
University of Minnesota, USA

ABSTRACT

With constant emergence of cloud services and platforms for learning at a global scale, the field of education is in the midst of exploring and adapting to new pedagogical features afforded by these environments. Among the most debated is the development of MOOCs, short for massive open online courses, which pose questions to the traditional brick-and-mortar teaching model and implore new ways for instruction and learning. While some studies have looked at the effectiveness of MOOCs as a mode of delivery, there still lacks a genre approach to analyzing MOOCs as socio-rhetorical systems that have complex relationships with other social entities in the larger ecology of learning. With an eye toward how writing is taught and learned in the MOOC context, I investigate the kinds of course genre invented or reimagined by the cloud technologies and pedagogies afforded by MOOCs, and how those affordances facilitate writing instruction. Specifically, I use Activity Theory to highlight the genre activities specific to two composition MOOCs. By situating these MOOCs as activity systems, I offer an informed observation on the genre components affecting how students learn about writing in MOOC settings. These insights lead to numerous pedagogical implications, including the need to treat MOOCs as an emerging learning ecology that is different from conventional models.

INTRODUCTION

MOOCs, short for massive open online course, had all the rage from all around the world when Stanford computer scientists Sebastian Thrun and Peter Norvig, along with their instructional team, designed a tuition-free artificial intelligence course, taught over the web to hundreds of thousands of students in 2011 (Leckart, 2011). More recent hype began in the fall of 2011, when over 450,000 students signed up for

DOI: 10.4018/978-1-5225-1650-7.ch004

a computer science course offered at Stanford University. Within months of the Stanford experiments, a few start-up companies debuted in the name of giving "everyone access to the world-class education that has so far been available to a select few" (Coursera.org, 2015). Coursera, a for-profit educational technology enterprise founded by Andrew Ng and Daphne Koller from Stanford University, is among the several "social entrepreneurship" companies that partner with "top universities in the world" to offer free online courses (Coursera.org, 2015). Other massive open course providers include Udacity, edX, Khan Academy, Peer-to-Peer University (P2PU), Udemy, and NovoEd, just to name a few.

Amidst the media's continued representation of MOOCs as both opportunities and disruption to higher education systems, scholars and researchers in rhetoric and composition have taken interests to further understand MOOCs as communities of learning (Krause & Lowe, 2014). Of particular interest to writing specialists is research suggesting that learning to write in the digital environment is complex in ways that go beyond texts and students' learning abilities. For instance, at Michigan State University, researchers in the WIDE (Writing in Digital Experience) research center study ways in which learning takes place in digital, informal learning spaces have identified different types of rhetorical moves that take place in those spaces and moments of change as expressions of participant learning (Matrix, 2015).

In 2013, the MOOC Research Initiative (MRI) was founded to advance MOOC-related research. Funded by the Bill and Melinda Gates Foundation, MRI seeks to further evaluate MOOCs and how they impact teaching, learning, and education in general. In its inaugural year, MRI offered a total of $400,000 grants to interested academic institutions to examine the efficacy of early MOOC models for various learner audiences and in a wide variety of contexts (MOOC Research, 2015). More than 20 reports were produced at the international conference MRI hosted at the University of Arlington, Texas, in December 2013, most of which compared various learning models—traditional, online, hybrid or blended models—to the MOOC model. An area in learning assessment that was of particular interests to most of these studies are participant engagement. For example, John Witmer and his team at Mt. San Jacinto College was interested in what engages students in a remedial English Writing MOOC. Similarly, Bruno Poellhuber has led a team of researchers to survey the relationships between participants' attitudes, their motivation to learn, and engagement level in a MOOC. Duke scholars Denise Comer and Dorian Canelas, on the other hand, have conducted a multidisciplinary inquiry into peer-to-peer interaction through writing using discussion forum and peer assessment data in two MOOCs.

Picking up from the momentum of these studies, I seek to complicate the notion of online open writing instruction from a different perspective—through an analysis of the genre components within the MOOC setting and how they mediate learning activities in those contexts. For the purpose of this edited collection, I argue that MOOCs are cloud-based learning environments wherein students and instructors utilize interactive features from anywhere, anytime, any device, and anybody, for pedagogical purposes. With communicative functions such as discussion forums and peer-to-peer assessment interfaces, MOOCs enact digitally networked learning communities that are unprecedented by any learning environments before. I have playfully coined the term "MOOCology" in the chapter title to call our attention to the notion of learning ecology as enacted by a cloud-based environment like MOOCs. Underpinning the present study is such acknowledgment and the curiosity for ways a genre analysis might inform us of writing and learning in these emergent settings.

With an eye toward how writing is taught and learned in the MOOC context, I investigate the kinds of course genre invented or reimagined by the technologies and pedagogies afforded by MOOCs, and how those affordances facilitate writing instruction. To do so, I use Activity Theory to highlight the genre activities specific to two composition MOOCs. In this chapter, I first outline the MOOC model of instruction that will be useful in understanding how learners (henceforth participants) situate themselves in the open online learning environment. Then, I offer an autoethnographic account of being a participant in two postsecondary-level writing MOOCs and devise a MOOC activity system that elucidates aspects of MOOCs to better understand the nature of open online writing instruction and analyzes how the parts of the system work together to help participants achieve their needs and goals. Finally, I identify the difficulties inherent in such massive online learning environment and argue that MOOCs call for new ways of teaching and learning—particularly how the learning community facilitates a participant's enculturation as a member of the community of practice. By situating these MOOCs as activity systems, I offer an informed observation on the genre components affecting how students learn about writing in MOOC settings. These insights lead to numerous pedagogical implications, including the need to treat MOOCs as an emerging learning ecology that is different from conventional pedagogical approaches.

LITERATURE REVIEW

What Is a MOOC?

To tease out the relationship between MOOCs and writing instruction, I first attempt to map out the pedagogy of MOOCs that serve as the foundation for teaching and learning of writing. MOOCs are built on the characteristics of massiveness, openness, and a connectivist philosophy. The four descriptive letters in the acronym of MOOC make up the fundamental features of MOOCs:

- **Massiveness:** MOOCs easily accommodate hundreds of thousands of students. As noted in the introduction section, Coursera has reached more than one million users in August 2012 and the number of new users is still on the climb. "From a pragmatic perspective, MOOCs provide access to large numbers of people who might otherwise be excluded for reasons ranging from time, to geographic location, to formal prerequisites, to financial hardship" (McAuley et al., 2010).
- **Openness:** Openness involves several key concepts: software, registration, curriculum, and assessment; communication including interaction, collaboration, and sharing; and learning environments. Osvaldo Rodriguez of Universidad del CEMA, Argentina, further discusses that

The software used is open-source, registration is open to anyone, and the curriculum is open (perhaps loosely structured and it can even change as the course evolves), the sources of information are open, the assessment processes (if they exist) are open, and the learners are open to a range of different learning environments. (Rodriquez, 2013)

McAuley et al. (2010) have reiterated the concept of openness as any learner can take a MOOC and, as are result, exclusion from higher education opportunities is not an issue.

- **Online:** The key distinction between MOOCs and their precursors is that MOOCs are conducted online and therefore do not share some of the common challenges correspondence and broadcast courses face: time and space separation. As such, MOOCs capitalize on the ability to reach their students synchronously and asynchronously via online platforms, where students can pace their own learning.

- **Course:** Similar to existing classroom-based learning, MOOCs allow their participants to acquire a structured curriculum of knowledge and skills, and to develop shared practices and understanding around a specific topic, such as Public Speaking, Cryptology, Greek Mythology, Business Writing, Medical Humanities, etc. This also implies that there are some traditional conventions of how a course operates, such as requiring enrollment, a start and end date, instructor-developed content delivered to the learner, and some means of assessment.

Despite the attributes of free and open curriculum, the general completion rate for MOOCs remain around 10% (Lewin, 2013). Such a low completion rate raises eyebrows among pedagogues and instructional designers, calling for further investigation into participants' expectations and learning behaviors, thus providing an exigence for a study such as this to scrutinize MOOCs not just as a learning technology but social activities constructed by signifying practices. I outline this urgency for inquiry in the following section.

The Need for Inquiry

Changes in instructional media have always caused debates about how education and participation in education is threatened or liberated. These debates usually revolve around the values of technology and material culture that influence how we perceive education in general. In the search for an appropriate frame of analysis for MOOCs, James Porter suggests that we first ask if a MOOC is a course or a courseware. Early open educational resources such as the MIT OpenCourseWare project and Yale Open Courses provide online instructional materials for free under a Creative Commons open access license. This allows students to share, redistribute, and remix the course materials any way they like, as long as they credit the source and license the new materials they create with the same kind of license. However, these open-access courseware projects are not courses themselves; they simply publish free course materials such as syllabi, readings, and assignments to the web and let users learn at their own pace. What make MOOCs different from open-access courseware are the added elements that constitute a more course-like experience: the delivery, the performance, class discussions, the instructor, the students, the students' contributions (including writing)—the unfolding action of a course in time.

Hence, to learn from a MOOC means to participate actively in a structured set of activities designed to help participants achieve their needs and goals. While a rhetorical analysis can be helpful in identifying the course features and the rhetorical situation of learning on MOOCs, there are many things it may fail to recognize. For example, a rhetorical may not reveal who does what tasks pertaining to the teaching and learning in MOOCs: does only one instructor teach the course? Do participants work in teams? Why do some participants become more engaged in the course activities and others do not? A rhetorical analysis also won't show the evolution of genres within a specific learning context such as the MOOC, or suggest that the researcher explores whether the features of genres as embodied in MOOCs are uncontested.

To get to the questions above, as well as to understand the relationships among participants in MOOC activities, the tools they use to accomplish their activities, and the goals they have for the activities, I turn to Activity Theory as my theoretical lens in this study.

THEORETICAL FRAMEWORK AND METHODS

Entering Activity Theory

A cultural-historical theory of activity initiated by Russian psychologists in the early 20th century, Activity Theory was originally a psychological theory that "sees all aspects of activity as shaped over time by people's social interactions with each other and the tools they use" (Kain & Wardle, 2014). Activity Theory provides a helpful lens for understanding how people in different communities carry out their activities. It provides specific aspects of context for researchers to look at as they consider the various factors that influence and change the approaches to accomplishing a given activity—such as learning to write.

The most basic unit of analysis in Activity Theory is the activity system, defined as "a group of people who share a common object and motive over time, as well as the wide range of tools they use together to act on that object and realize that motive" (Kain & Wardle, 2014). Yrjö Engeström, an Activity Theory proponent, has devised a model that is useful for understanding how a wide range of factors work together to impact an activity (see Figure 1). Engeström's principles highlight mediation and development. In mediation, Activity Theory emphasizes that human activities are mediated by tools in a broad sense. Tools are created and transformed during the development of the activity itself, and carry with them a particular culture. So, the use of tools is an accumulation and transmission of social knowledge. Tool use influences the nature of external behaviors and the mental functioning of individuals. Second, in Activity Theory, development is concerned with the formative evaluation of changes in participant behaviors and activities. Ethnographic methods are common in Activity Theory studies to track the history and development of a practice.

In his article, "Rethinking Genre in School and Society," David Russell describes an activity system as "any ongoing, object-directed, historically conditioned, dialectically structured, tool-mediated hu-

Figure 1. Activity System Triangle
Adapted from Engeström (1999)

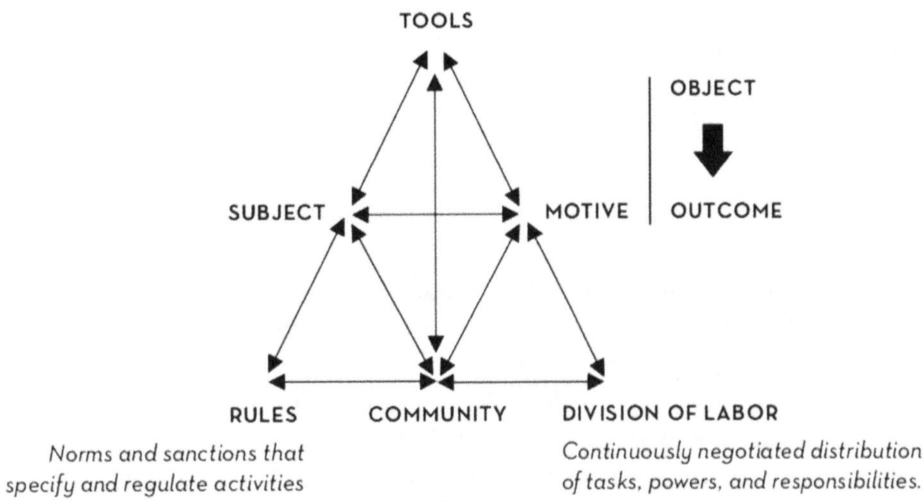

man interaction" (1997). Besides these elements, activity systems are also concerned about divisions of labor and rules. For instance, when Russell analyzed the university as an activity system, he points out that labor is divided among the participants – students are responsible for completing assignments, instructors are responsible for grading assignments; administrators are responsible for making sure grades appear on students' transcripts (Kain & Wardle, 2014). Additionally, all these participants also operate within a set of rules for classroom participation and learning. The rules in many aspects are mutual agreement about how the activity should be carried out so all participants could progress toward the desired outcome of learning.

In this study, I use Activity Theory to study how participants engage in different kinds of activities in the MOOC learning environment. Particularly, I investigate the kinds of genre emerging from MOOCs, including meta-genres, genre sets, and genre systems in MOOCs that inform and affect the MOOC as activity system. To do so, I present my autoethnographic narratives as a participant in two writing-related MOOCs, namely *Crafting an Effective Writer: Tools of the Trade* (offered by Mt. San Jacinto College on Coursera, January 30 through March 8, 2015) and *High-Impact Business Writing* (offered by the University of California, Irvine, on Coursera, April 6 through May 7, 2015). I first identify the major genre components in these MOOCs, and then illustrate these MOOCs as systems of activity where participants learn to write by using the various tools and technologies afforded by the courses, including rules and conventions set around the courses as well as the motives and outcomes made deliberate through the learning objectives of these course.

Specifically, my study is guided by these two questions:

1. What are the genre components, i.e., meta-genres, genre sets, and genre systems, in the MOOCs analyzed in this study?
2. How do these genre components help the respective MOOC participants learn about writing in an activity system?

In the following section, I showcase the types of tools and genres employed in the two courses above, and demonstrate how these genres are utilized to further goals of learning in these courses.

FINDINGS AND DISCUSSIONS

Genres in MOOCs

Based on my participation and observation in the two Writing MOOCs studied in this project, I have identified over 20 genre items that a student would typically interact with to achieve the learning goals set in these MOOCs. The following table outlines these items by comparing the two MOOCs observed in this study. I have also organized the genre items based on where and when they appear during the MOOCs, i.e., before, during, and after the course.

Comparing the genre items found in both MOOCs, I realize that not all MOOCs are created equal, so to speak. Based on my previous experience as a MOOC participant (I have taken more than 10 MOOCs and completed four prior to this project), I notice that the CEW-MOOC represents a more "traditional" MOOC than the HBW-MOOC with items that are familiar to me. Genre items such as the course guide, modular cover page, weekly announcements, peer assessment systems, and discussion forums are common to Coursera's MOOCs regardless of the course subject.

The HBW-MOOC, on the other hand, seems like a new interface that I have not experienced before. Nevertheless, both MOOCs were provided and hosted by Coursera (see Figures 2 and 3 for screenshot comparisons) at the time of this project. It's surprising to me how different the two interfaces are. My speculation is that the HBW-MOOC was a part of a "specialization track" where participants would complete a series of four to five courses to earn a "specialization certificate," and thus it was made to look different from a more traditional, free-standing MOOC such as the CEW-MOOC.

To begin evaluating MOOCs as an activity system, I first identify the meta-genres, genre sets, and genre systems present in such environment. Meta-genres, genre sets, and genre systems are important with regard to social action and interact to further the goals of a community. In the following sections, I model after Bazerman's method in analyzing the genre systems in classrooms and in the US patent application process (Bawarshi and Reiff, 2010, p. 88) to examine how these genre components help MOOC students like myself to engage with and complete the courses.

Figure 2. Screenshot of CEW-MOOC's course management page

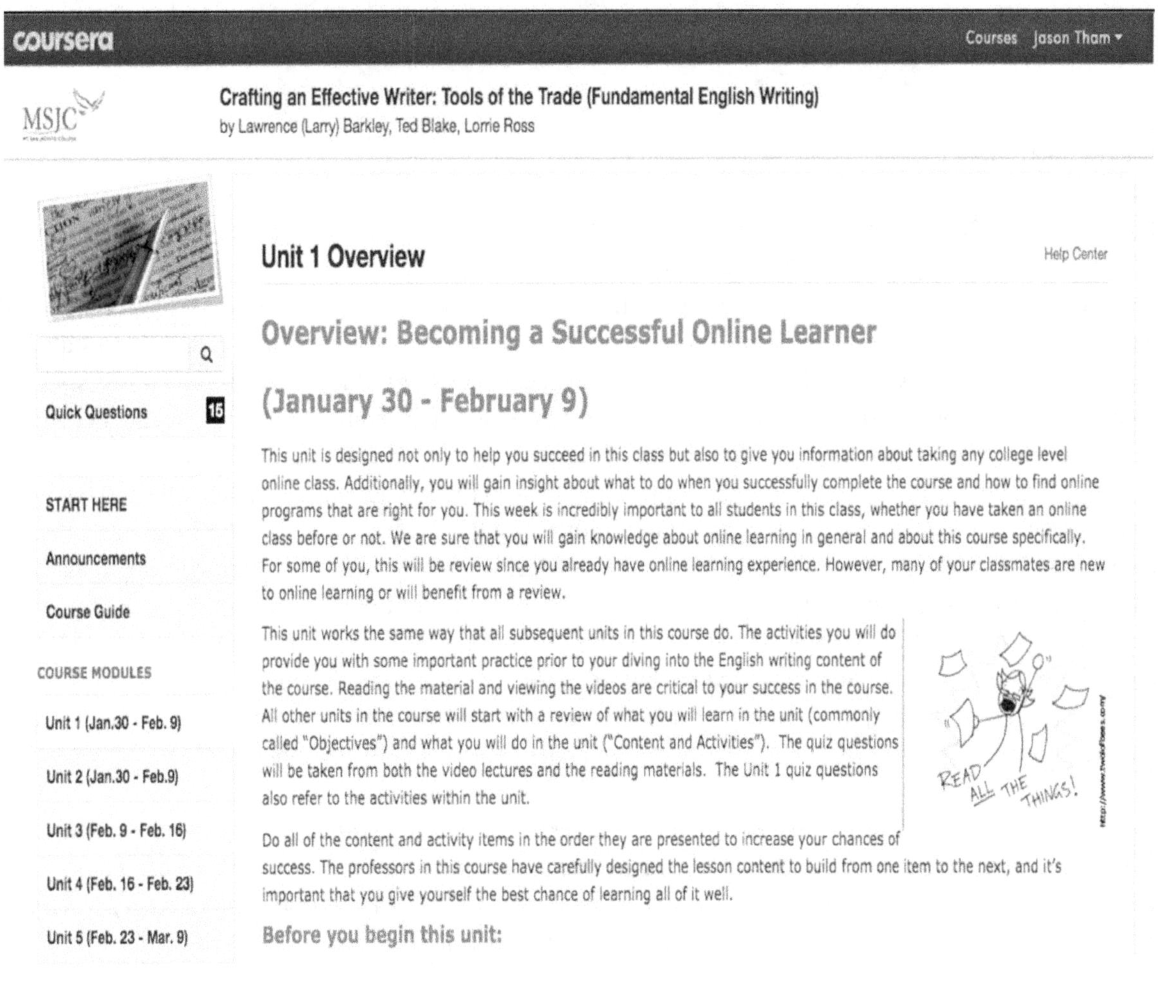

Figure 3. Screenshot of HBW-MOOC's course management page

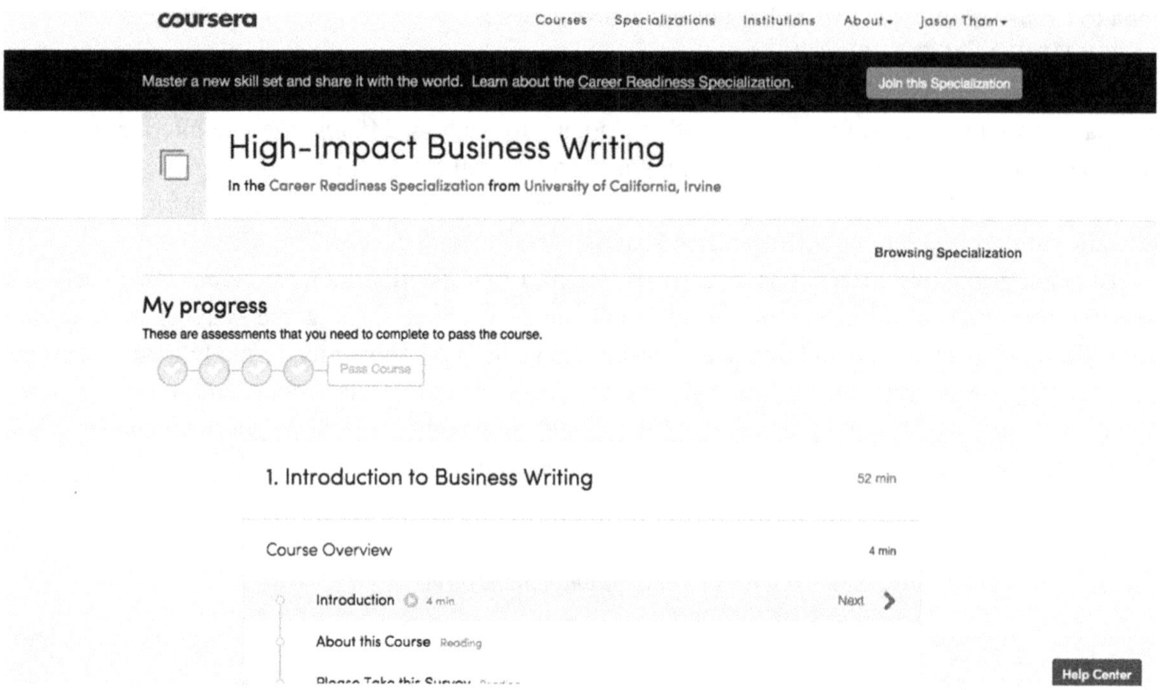

Meta-Genres

Janet Giltrow introduces the term meta-genre to describe "situated language about situated language" (2002, p. 190). More generally, she describes meta-genres as "[A]tmospheres of wordings and activities, demonstrated precedents or sequestered expectations" that surround a genre and indicate how readers and writers should appropriately take it up" (Giltrow, 2002, p. 195). Meta-genres serve to teach and stabilize uptakes (Bawarshi & Reiff, 2010, p. 94). They teach users how to produce and use genres in a specific context—genres about genres. As such, a syllabus in a MOOC can be considered a meta-genre because it teaches participants how to navigate the course, use the various tools and interfaces, as well as to create a shared vocabulary for talking about the subject matters—which in our case are academic and business writing. Another example of meta-genre found in the MOOCs I have studied is the Frequently Asked Questions (FAQs) page. According to Bawarshi and Reiff, meta-genres form uptake knowledge and shape "how we navigate genre systems and their genre sets in order to enact meaningful, consequential actions" (2010, p. 94). The FAQs in a MOOC serve to reinforce tacit knowledge about being a MOOC participant and thus may affect participants' buy-in on the credibility of the course and how they would engage with the particular community of (MOOC) discourse. In some ways, these meta-genres—both the syllabus and FAQs—also signal insider and outsider status. As Giltrow observes,

meta-genres flourish at those boundaries, at the thresholds of communities of discourse, patrolling or controlling individuals' participation in the collective, foreseeing or suspecting their involvements elsewhere, differentiating, initiating, restricting, inducing forms of activity, rationalizing and representing the relations of the genre to the community that uses it. (2002, p. 203)

Explicit meta-genres like the syllabus and FAQs, as I will demonstrate later, provide the foundation to operationalize the constellations of genres in activity systems and serve to mediate tensions participants experience within and between activity systems.

Genre Sets and Genre Systems

To identify and describe the complex ways in which genres enable their users to perform consequential actions, rhetorical genre scholars have developed useful concepts, namely genre sets and genre systems, to observe and explain these actions. A genre set, as defined by Charles Bazerman, is a group of several genres that predictably recur inside a domain-specific community (Honig, 2010, p. 91). Genre sets are "associated through the activities and functions of a collective" under a limited range of actions (Devitt, 1993, p. 57). Loosely defined, genre sets are a repertoire of genres that seek to enable the accomplishment of a particular action—such as learning about a new concept in the Writing MOOCs. For instance, in CEW-MOOC, the course guide, weekly announcements and instructor's notes, and emails/e-blasts are a genre set that work together to coordinate a participant's learning of the MOOC course structure, pedagogical objectives, and timely (weekly) updates relevant to the course materials. Bounded by specific functions, this genre set is housed in the in-course category (see Table 1) because it embodies a limited range of intentions and actions.

Another example of a genre set is one that enables MOOC participants to interact with one another during the course of learning. This genre set includes the discussion forums, peer assessments interface, and an interactive world map that lets participants submit their current location and see where their peers are taking the course from. Although MOOCs in general are perceived as a social learning platform and that such genre set is common in Writing MOOCs, this genre set is omitted from the HBW-MOOC as shown in Table 1. This creates an interesting evidence for counter-arguments against those who insist that MOOCs have to be inherently social. Comparing my experiences in both MOOCs, I find that the exclusion of a social-networking platform in a MOOC does not hinder my learning of the subject matter (in HBW). Though, the readily available forums and peer-to-peer connection tools in a MOOC did enrich my learning experience as I was curious to learn about other participants and their respective cultures. So, the decision to include or exclude such a genre set is seemingly based on the pedagogical intentions the instructors have for the course. In return, it impacts the behaviors of the participants—either learning in isolation or in connection with others—and influences the works of other genre sets in a larger picture, the genre system.

A genre system, as Amy Devitt puts it, is a "set of genres interacting to achieve an overarching function within an activity system" (Bawarshi & Reiff, 2010, p. 87). More importantly genre systems "involve the interaction of users with different levels of expertise and authority, who may not all have equal knowledge of or access to all the genres within the system" (Bawarshi & Reiff, 2010, p. 88). Figure 4 shows an example of genre system found in the CEW-MOOC.

As one could tell almost immediately, a genre system is adapted from a Russian activity system triangle and focuses on the subject(s), mediational means (or tools and genres), and object/motive(s). The genre system highlights how genre sets operationalize the micro-level activities—such as weekly modules and assignment instructions—that together activate the macro-level activities—such as peer assessments and instructor's feedback—in the MOOC. As discussed earlier, the meta-genres inform participants of the genre knowledge in the MOOC learning environment and guide uptakes. The arrows in Figure 4 show the uptake relations within a genre set and between genre sets in the genre system. For instance,

Table 1. A comparison of genre items between CEW-MOOC and HBW-MOOC

Genre Items	CEW	HBW
Pre-Course Items		
Surveys	✓	✓
Course description	✓	✓
Course syllabus & materials	✓	✓
Introduction video	✓	
Course at a glance	✓	✓
Frequently asked questions (FAQs)	✓	
Statement of certification	✓	✓
In-Course Items		
Course guide	✓	
Honor code	✓	
Modular cover page (weekly descriptions and instructions)	✓	
Modular video lectures and in-video textual content	✓	✓
Instructor's weekly announcement	✓	
Quizzes	✓	✓
Student writings / texts	✓	✓
Peer assessments	✓	
Discussion forums	✓	
Participant's location map	✓	
Resource page	✓	
Emails / e-Blast announcements	✓	✓
Help center	✓	✓
Post-Course Items		
Follow-up / Next steps	✓	
Course certificate	✓	✓

CEW = Crafting an Effective Writer MOOC
HBW = High-Impact Business Writing MOOC

the genre set containing student writings, modular videos, and assignment instructions will activate the genre set of assessments, which contains peer assessments and instructor's comments.

Ostensibly, genres operationalize not only the activity within a genre system, but also between genre systems. For instance, instructors of both CEW and HBW-MOOCs are not only operating within the said MOOCs, but also acting and responding to other entities such as external funders, the hosting universities, the course management systems, etc., all of which consist distinctive and overlapping genre systems. Russell, in his analysis of the writing classroom as an activity system, calls this phenomenon "intertextuality" (qtd. in Bawarshi & Reiff, 2010, p. 98), where genres are linked within and between genre systems. When these genre systems are situated in a larger learning ecology, a MOOC can be visualized as an activity system that organizes the learning (and teaching) experience.

Figure 4. Two example genre sets in CEW-MOOC creating a genre system

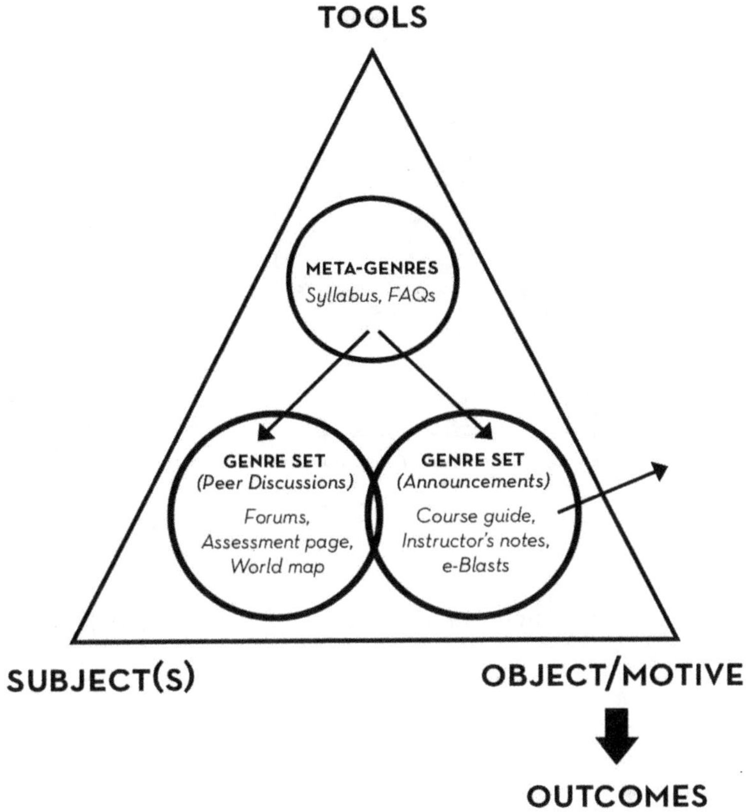

MOOCs as an Activity System

As a conceptual and analytical tool, the activity system allows researchers to map out the dialectical relationship between genres, activities, and contexts. Using the elements of Activity Theory, combined with various genre relations found in a genre system, I have constructed an activity system triangle to illustrate the common organization of CEW-MOOC and HBW-MOOC.

In addition to the interactions between meta-genres, genre sets, and genre systems, the activity systems present how these relationships are enacted in meaningful contexts. The inclusion of rules/norms, community, and division of labor complicates a participant's MOOC-taking experience. The rules/norms make explicit the implicit regulations, social norms, and conventions that guide or restrict a participant's behavior in the MOOC. For example, when writing to other participants in the discussion forums, CEW-MOOC participants seem to follow the conventions of email writing (see example in Figure 6 below) by including a name to address (such as "Hi Philip), a body text (usually a brief response to a question), and a sign-off (like "Best, Larry"). Such "rule" of writing in the discussion thread was not stated explicitly in any of the course guide or instructional materials, but are assumed by most MOOC participants. This infers that learning is not only confined in the formal modules of the course but could also happen in the interactions among participants on a social environment such as the forum.

Figure 5. CEW-MOOC and HBW-MOOC as an activity system
Created by Tham (Forthcoming)

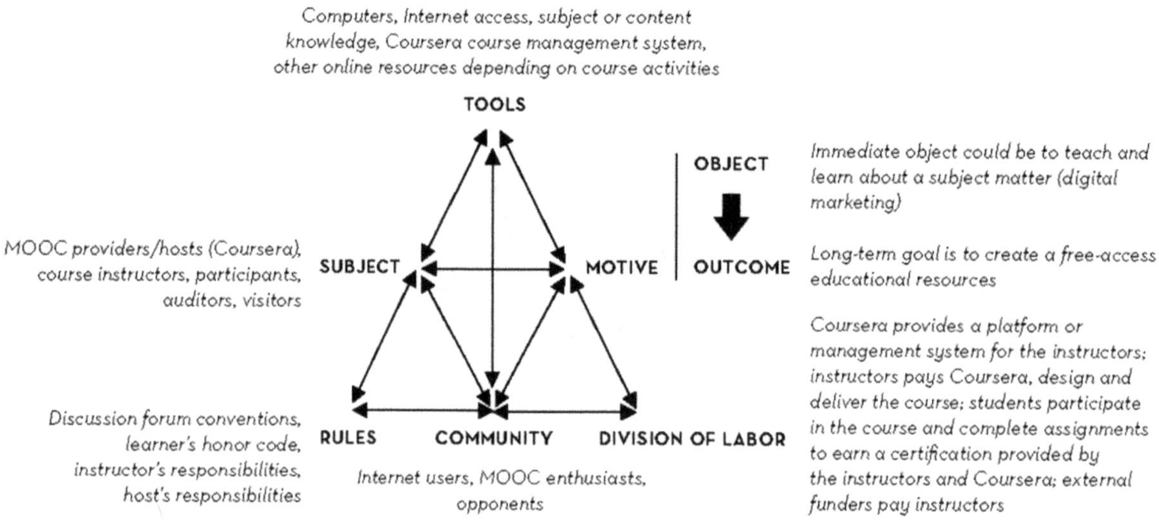

Figure 6. Screenshot of a conversation thread in the CEW-MOOC discussion forums

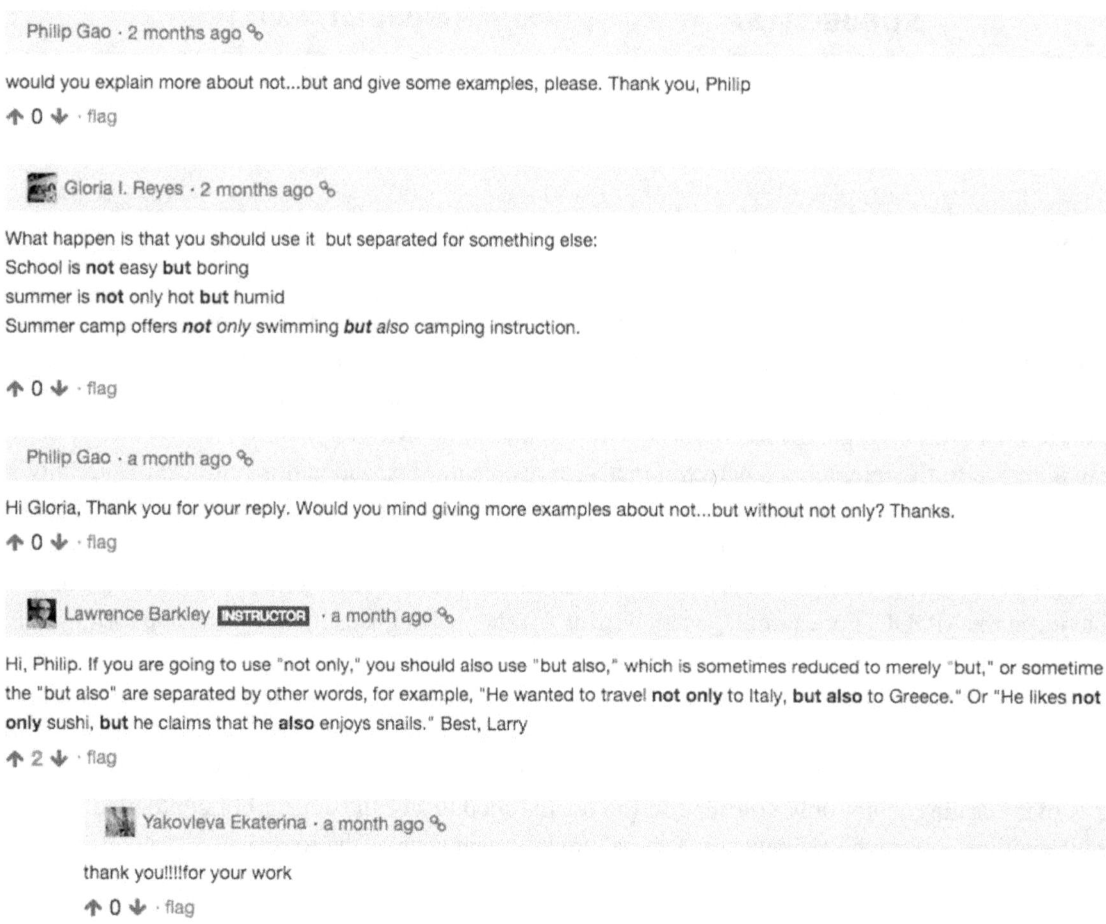

Community comprises multiple individuals and/or groups who have similar objectives but distinguish themselves from other communities. The groups of individuals could be active participants/students, instructors, and those who are simply auditing the course but not intending to complete or get certified by neither the MOOCs observed in this study. Lastly, division of labor refers to both the horizontal distribution of tasks among members of the community and the vertical division of power and control that mediate and stabilize ways of acting and interacting that subjects use to achieve the goals of their activities.

As Bazerman's "Genre and Cognitive Development" (2009) demonstrates, activity systems can help scholars to trace individual and group cognitive developments as these are mediated by genres specific to certain activity systems. Thus, we may also analyze MOOCs as socio-rhetorical systems for writing instruction. In the last section below, I make the connections between the genres specific to CEW-MOOC and HBW-MOOC and the activity systems representing the organization of MOOCs above to conceptualize MOOCs as a virtual learning ecology that demands learning behaviors different from the physical classroom, while at the same time offering new learning experiences.

CONCLUSION

MOOCs as a New Networked Learning Ecology

Students cannot simply duplicate their traditional learning habits onto the MOOC learning environment because the genres they might use on a MOOC platform can differ greatly from the genres employed in brick-and-mortar classrooms. To succeed in achieving the goals set in each MOOC, whether individually or collectively, participants need to familiarize themselves with the meta-genres, genre sets, and genre systems within the MOOC they take so they can navigate the course effectively—as opposed to merely signing up for a course, watching the videos, and taking the quizzes. Based on my experience in this project, a successful learning experience requires the participants to understand how the video modules work, how to use the peer assessment interface, when to take the quizzes, how to submit writing assignments, how to participate in the discussion forums, how to get feedback, and where to find resources for better understanding the subject matter or getting assignment done, just to name a few. These micro-level activities, as I have discussed in the previous section, operationalize macro-level activities such as receiving feedback on writing or getting a grade at the end of the course. And these operationalizations are different compared to the ones many participants are used to experiencing in the traditional writing classroom. This is due to the different genre sets and genre systems functioning in the MOOC ecology of learning.

Some participants may recognize the object/motives but may not know which mediational means (genres or genre sets) to use for accomplishing the task at hand, or they may not feel comfortable with the requisite authority they have in the MOOC learning environment versus the traditional distribution of power in a typical classroom. Additionally, the virtual presence of thousands of participants in a course also changes the dynamic of learning in the social setting; and recognizing that kind of dynamic is also key in a positive MOOC experience. Therefore, to ensure the success of the MOOC participants—and arguably retain more participants by improving their MOOC-taking experience—the activity system-specific genres need to be made clear and comprehensible to the participants. Such is an area that is lacking in current MOOCs.

Toward a New Learning Experience

The proliferation of MOOCs in higher education and among Internet users from different parts of the world presses an urgency to develop a rich body of research to evaluate how MOOCs impact teaching and learning. As we consider bold new approaches to teach writing, how might we (re)imagine an ecology of learning that best facilitate writing activities? To echo Cindy Selfe and Richard Selfe, it is prudent to acknowledge the complications and contradiction inherent in understanding MOOCs as complicated spaces for learning (p. 82). As cited by these authors, Terry Winograd and Fernando Flores point out, we must take on the responsibility of continuing to "work towards unconcealment… and let our awareness guide our actions in creating and applying technology" (1986, p. 179).

In this study, I have investigated the kinds of genre emerging from MOOCs, including meta-genres, genre sets, and genre systems in MOOCs that inform and affect the MOOC as activity system. Future studies should consider the issues with diversity and globalization of education through MOOCs, with regards to access issues, representations, and student engagement online—and how these issues could be enlightened or overcome by cultivating rhetorical genre knowledge and awareness. For MOOC developers and designers, it is important to consider the implications of the specific genre items they decide to embed into the course system have on student learning. As evident in this study, every genre component affects certain behaviors and decisions made by the learners. For teachers, it is crucial to pay attention to the infrastructure of the learning management system and not merely accept all functionalities created by the course provider. Scholars and researchers alike should continue to influence the design and development of emerging learning systems such that the interests of the students are always put at the forefront.

REFERENCES

Bawashi, A. S., & Reiff, M. J. (2010). *Genre: An introduction to history, theory, research, and pedagogy* (C. Bazerman, Ed.). Anderson, SC: Parlor Press.

Bazerman, C. (2009). Genre and cognitive development: Beyond writing to learn. In C. Bazerman, A. Bonin, & D. Figueiredo (Eds.), *Genre in a Changing World*. West Lafayette, IN: The WAC Clearinghouse and Parlor Press. doi:10.4000/pratiques.1419

Coursera.org. (2015). *About Coursera*. Retrieved 4 April 2015 from http://www.coursera.org

Devitt, A. (1993). Generalizing about genre: New conceptions of an old concept. *College Composition and Communication*, *44*(4), 573–586. doi:10.2307/358391

Giltrow, J. (2002). Meta-genre. In R. Coe, L. Lingard, & T. Teslenko (Eds.), *The rhetoric and ideology of genre: Strategies for stability and change* (pp. 187–205). New York, NY: Hampton Press.

Hornig, S. (2010). What do children write in science? A study of the genre set in a primary science classroom. *Written Communication*, *27*(1), 87–119. doi:10.1177/0741088309350159

Kain, D., & Wardle, E. (2014). Activity theory: An introduction for the writing classroom. In Writing about writing (2nd ed.). Boston, MA: Bedford/St. Martin.

Krause, S., & Lowe, C. (2014). *Invasion of the MOOCs*. Anderson, SC: Parlor Press.

Leckart, S. (2011). The Stanford education experiment could change higher learning forever. *Wired*. Retrieved 20 March 2015 from http://www.wired.com/2012/03/ff_aiclass/

Lewin, T. (2013). Universities abroad join partnership on the web. *New York Times*. Retrieved 5 April 2015 from http://www.nytimes.com/2013/02/21/education/universities-abroad-join-mooc-course-projects.html

Matrix Center for Digital Humanities and Social Sciences. (2015). Facilitating Learning in Digital Spaces. *Matrix.msu.edu*. Retrieved 4 April 2015 from http://www2.matrix.msu.edu/portfolio-item/facilitating-learning-in-digital-spaces/

McAuley, A. (2010). The MOOC model for digital practice. *Elearnspace.org*. Retrieved 4 April 2015 from http://www.elearnspace.org/Articles/MOOC_Final.pdf

MOOC Research. (2015). *Reports*. Retrieved 4 April 2015 from http://moocresearch.com

Rodriquez, C. O. (2013). *MOOCs and the AI-Stanford like courses: Two successful and distinct course formats for massive open online courses. European Journal of Open, Distance, and E-Learning.*

Russell, D. (1997). Rethinking genre in school and society: An activity theory analysis. *Written Communication, 14*(4), 504–554. doi:10.1177/0741088397014004004

Selfe, C., & Selfe, R., Jr. (2008). The politics of the interface: Power and its exercise in electronic contact zone. In Computers in the composition classroom: A critical sourcebook. New York, NY: Bedford/St. Martin.

Tham, J. (Forthcoming). Audience, user, producer: MOOCs as activity systems. In E. Monske & K. Blair (Eds.), *Writing and composing in the age of MOOCs*. Hershey, PA: IGI Global.

Winogard, T., & Flores, F. (1986). Understanding computers and cognition: A new foundation for design. Reading, MA: Addison.

KEY TERMS AND DEFINITIONS

Activity System: A collective, systemic formation of behaviors within a complex, mediational social structure.

Activity Theory: A conceptual and methodological framework for studying individual subjects and the social reality they reside within through socio-cultural examinations of the mediating activities.

Autoethnography: A method of social research that involve the researcher's self-reflection and writing that explore the researcher's personal experience and observation during the period of study.

Genre Analysis: An analytical framework used to study how situated language is used to mediate behaviors and activity goals within a particular context.

Genre Set: A recurring set of associated genres that work together to enact particular behaviors in a community.

Genre System: Sets of genres that interact with one another to accomplish an overarching function within an activity system.

Learning Ecology: A learning habitat wherein participants coexist in relative interdependence with specific conventions for using, creating, and regulating resources within the habitat. A learning ecology in the 21st century is typically mediated by technological tools—cloud- or ground-based instruments—that underpin learning processes within the ecology.

Meta-Genre: Genre about genre(s); situated language or activities that teach and stabilize uptake of certain genres.

MOOCs: Short of massive open online courses, MOOCs are structured courses that are delivered online through a provider who manages that learning platform and interface. These courses are typically free to anyone with internet access across the world and are taught by instructors from credible institutions.

Section 2

Chapter 5
3Ds of Integrating Cloud Technologies into Classrooms:
Digital Identity, Competencies, and Self-Efficacy

Binod Gurung
New Mexico State University, USA

ABSTRACT

Cloud technologies offer many pedagogical possibilities for collaboration, ubiquitous learning, and documenting student engagement activities through learning analytics among others. However, effective integration of cloud technologies demands a complex set of teachers' theoretical and conceptual understandings and digital competencies. Furthermore, the teachers also need to re-examine their critical internal barriers such as the lack of digital self-efficacy. A closer look reveals that there is an undergirding notion – the teachers' digital identity – that enables them to develop their conceptual and practical digital competencies and self-efficacy. In this chapter, I critically explore and examine new pedagogical possibilities of integrating cloud technologies into classrooms within the triadic interplay of digital identity, competencies, and self-efficacy (3Ds).

INTRODUCTION

Effective integration of technology into classrooms involves a complex process. The teacher, whether as a sage on the stage or a guide by side, plays central role in blending technology into teaching and learning processes. Customarily, teachers' digital competencies followed by their technology beliefs and attitudes (referred to in this chapter as digital self-efficacy) are considered the most important factors for successful integration or blending of technology into classrooms (e.g., Ertmer, Ottenbreit-Leftwich & York, 2006; Hew & Brush, 2007; ISTE Standards for Teachers, 2016). However, many teachers face enormous challenges to develop their digital competencies and maintain a positive digital self-efficacy in the context of ever evolving technological advancements. This is even more challenging when it comes to using emerging technologies such as social media, educational apps, learning games, and cloud computing. As result, technology makes little, if any, inroads to the classrooms.

DOI: 10.4018/978-1-5225-1650-7.ch005

Although digital competencies and self-efficacy are essential, I argue that there is a little explored third factor – the teachers' digital identity, which is at the core of their technology-mediated pedagogical practices. Developing a strong, solid digital identity, I argue, empowers teachers to explore emerging technologies and build their digital competencies and self-efficacy accordingly. In this chapter, I seek to critically explore and examine new pedagogical possibilities of integrating cloud technologies into classrooms within the triadic interplay of digital identity, competencies, and self-efficacy (3Ds).

Cloud Technologies for Education

The diffusive nature of digital technology has made it pervasive in our everyday lives and classrooms impacting on how we interact, socialize, learn, and live. Digital devices such as smartphones, tablets, gaming consoles, and computers are now personal and household gadgets and regular types of educational technology equipment in classrooms. More recently, those digital devices are being powered by an emerging technology, called cloud computing, that has the capacity to transform the existing physical computing resources and tools into online environments.

Cloud computing has already gained significant attraction in the field of teaching and learning. Of the many useful cloud affordances, teachers and learners can utilize its data storage capacity along with the other features such as creating content, sharing, and interacting online. Moreover, new features and functionalities are progressively being added to cloud technology making it viable for educational engagement more than ever. Cloud's features and affordances resonate with the teacher and learners because they carry potentials of pedagogical imaginaries of collaboration, anytime anywhere learning, and documenting the learning processes and outcomes through the implementation of learning analytics. Yet, cloud technology is available on-demand and at affordable costs ranging from free and basic, to customizable, and systemwide purchases. As result, many teachers around the world use cloud technologies such as Google drive, Edmodo, iCloud, and Onedrive to facilitate teaching and student learning engagement in more dynamic ways. The teachers harness those tools to facilitate their ongoing pedagogical practices and also to design new types of learning environments such as flipped classrooms and social learning platforms.

What Is Cloud Computing?

Cloud computing is basically the virtualization of computing resources such as servers, data, software, and applications. The National Institute of Standards and Technology (NIST) states that cloud computing has three major service capabilities including infrastructures as a Service (IaaS), platform as a Service (PaaS) and, software as a Service (SaaS) (Mell & Grance, 2011). For education, PaaS and IaaS are mainly designed to meet the large scale computing needs and resources such as at the institutional levels (e.g., colleges and universities) as those cloud services provide on-demand services for massive scale applications, storages, and servers.

SaaS, on the other hand, is designed for small business and individual or small group consumers. Teachers and learners can harness some of the limitedly free SaaS based cloud services such as Google Drive, OneDrive, and Edmodo. Those cloud services and tools offer new and more efficient pedagogical affordances. Perhaps the single most important advantage of using cloud over the traditional computer-based hardware and software is to move everything online – folders, files, documents, and the whole learning engagement. Traditionally, files and folders are shared via emails and course management systems purchased by the colleges and universities (e.g., Blackboard).

Once the learning resources are online in the cloud, there appear numerous previously unseen learning engagement opportunities. Now with cloud technology, learning is a ubiquitous phenomenon, a portable and on-demand entity, and a social process transgressing the traditional classroom boundaries, fixed-time schedules, and one-size-fits for all type of instruction. Students can have on-demand access to courses, learning resources, peers, teachers, and content experts at anytime from their personal gadgets and computers. Similarly, collaboration opportunity and feedback are available online and in an instant manner (e.g., using Google doc). Utilizing the reports from learning analytics, students might easily self-monitor, customize, and even optimize their learning engagement.

The current generation of learners, often termed as digital natives or digital learners, are quite familiar with these features, mediational means, and affordances of cloud and online technologies. However, the digital technology including cloud computing remains limited at the periphery of the core academic practices with minimal, sporadic, and often ill-structured uses (Gurung & Rutledge, 2014). Why does it happen so? What are the critical barriers that preclude the successful integration of technology? Why do not such seemingly powerful affordances of technology make sense to teachers and students in the way it is envisioned? Or do we, as teachers and learners, have to necessarily run after and embrace emerging technologies such as this one?

Critical Barriers and Enablers of Technology Integration

The historical trend of "underuse" and ill-structured use of digital technology continues to persist in the classrooms (Cuban, 2001). Cloud technology, despite its powerful potentials for so called 21st century education, is no exception. When the first microcomputers were introduced to schools in the 1970s and 1980s, external barriers such as inadequate technology resources, time, and training were considered the major obstacles to technology integration (Means & Olson, 1997). Meanwhile, as the computers were "oversold" but "under used" (Cuban, 2001), it was increasingly becoming apparent that not only the external barriers, but also internal barriers such as teachers' technology competencies, beliefs, and attitudes were contributing factors to the failure of successful technology integration (Ertmer, 1999).

Over the past two decades, both of these barriers have been extensively explored through research and practice. When external barriers are considered to have been resolved as most US schools have access to digital technologies (see Gurung & Rutledge, 2014), internal barriers are still the recurring issues. Lately, internal barriers have been addressed through different terms such as teachers' digital competencies (Hew & Brush, 2007; ISTE Standards for Teachers, 2016), technological pedagogical content knowledge (Mishra & Koehler, 2016), computer self-efficacy beliefs (see Moos & Azevedo, 2009), attitudes towards using technology (see Hsu, Hung, & Ching, 2013), pedagogical intention (e.g., Asing-Cashman, Gurung, Limbu, & Rutledge, 2014), technology acceptance (e.g., Teo, Lee & Chai, 2008), and digital and online identity (Licona & Gurung, 2011; Moje & Luke, 2009; Turkle, 1995) among others. In a review of extensive literature spanning over the past three decades in the field of educational technology (Hsu, Hung, & Ching, 2013), acceptance or attitude toward technology was one of the three major research clusters (other two being technology integration and learning environments) of research and publication. More recently, the notion of "enablers" (Prensky, 2010; Ertmer, Ottenbreit-Leftwich & York, 2006; Ertmer, Ottenbreit-Leftwich, Sadik, Sendurur & Sendurur, 2012) has been used as a counter-concept so as to avoid negative connotations associated with the term "barriers" about the teachers' technology knowledge, skills, and attitudes they possess.

While I consider both the external and internal barriers are equally crucial, I posit that teachers' digital identity performs as a primal enabler to overcome these barriers. In the next section, I revisit the notion of digital identity in general and move onto discussing how a strong, solid digital identity of teachers enable them to understand and exploit digital structures and resources for successful blending of technology into pedagogy.

Digital Identities of Teachers

Digital identity is the mediated online presence of a person representing his or her autobiographical projection of multiple selves and also a publicly observable image established through collective, socially constructed discourses (e.g., biographical wikis). Digital identity is also closely associated with the ownership of technology gadgets, tools, and apps; and how they interact with them. Reflecting upon their knowledge, skills, and attitudes, people willfully project even portray their multiple selves on the Web as bloggers, programmers, hackers, professionals, fashion designers, socialites, and so on. The autobiographical projections essentially capture what people do, think, and believe who they are in their real life and physical worlds. Since digital identity is largely an interest-driven construct instigating both real and unreal selves, there is likelihood of presenting both "masked" (unreal) and "unmasked" (real) online identities (Licona & Gurung, 2011).

An online search reveals plenty of information created by people on the other people's life, work, and activities. Thus, digital identity becomes fluid and emergent as it goes through "dynamic and shifting constructions and presentations of self" in the public digital spaces (Coiro, Knobel, Lankshear, & Leu, 2008, p. 526). A teacher's digital identity is also interest-driven and complex, embodying the characteristics described above and other added attributes. Responsive to newer pedagogical contexts that continue to surface, teachers' digital identity is an emergent and trans-border phenomenon (i.e., across physical and online spaces and also interdisciplinary) routinely augmented by the diverse knowledge bases of pedagogy and technology, ever-expanding digital skills, and in-the-making technology attitudes. Furthermore, as the notion of identity has been a sociopolitical and ontological construct, digital identity is also a cultured construct enmeshed in the intersectionalities of individual interests, professional obligations, and institutional policies and practices that speak to larger socio-political conditions and institutional structures.

Provided the complexity of teacher's digital identity, I will not be able to treat it fully in the limited space of this chapter to the extent it deserves. Nonetheless, I will focus my discussion on the professional aspects of digital identity as an "enabler" to teachers' knowledge, skills, and attitudes that are necessary for successful technology integration into pedagogy. I will herein, at the same time, touch upon some of the major technology related theoretical constructs – i.e., structure, agency, and mediational means – as an effort to put digital identity into perspective within the micro- and macro-contexts of educational technology. Central to the argument is that teachers' digital identity determines how they deal with structures of external factors such as technology tools and resources available in the schools, curricular requirements, student learning needs, and instructional policies (i.e., structure); how they act with and by technology (agency); and how and what types of technological affordances they appropriate for the pedagogical purposes they intend to pursue (i.e., using technology as mediational means).

First, structures are the resources and rules that are "recursively" put into practice for routine reproductions of the existing systems and practices (Giddens, 1984; Sewell, 1992). Structures also denote, although outside the discussion of this chapter, the larger socioeconomic, political, and cultural contexts of using technology such as digital divide, technological consumerism, and engagement in networked knowledge communities (see Gurung, 2013). In the given structures, the notion of identity manifests as a performative and cultural construct that regulates and constrains the individuals' discourses and practices (Butler, 1993; Giddens, 1991; Goffman, 1973); so is the digital identity because it is an extension of such "real" identity. In other words, the digital identity, similar to that of the real identity, performs, regulates, encumbers, or expands the norms, means, and appropriations of digital structures and resources.

For teachers, structures are the "biotic" and "abiotic" resources (Orlikowski, 2000; Zhao & Frank, 2003) that are available in the school's ecosystem, for example, digital technologies in the classrooms, mentor teachers and fellow colleagues, shared pedagogical knowledge, curricula, institutional policies and so on. As structures have "transformative powers" to change realities (Giddens, 1984), digital technologies within the school's ecosystem should be viewed creatively and critically as tools and resources to improve and change pedagogical practices. For instance, teachers might seek to access, manage, evaluate, and manipulate classroom and school resources for pedagogical transformations, in our case, leveraging the powers of technology. However, effective utilization of digital resources demands teachers to have critical agency – the informed capacity of teachers to transcend the constraints of the structures and ability to take risks for pedagogical innovations – that can be developed by strengthening or solidifying their digital identity.

Second, as Sewell (1992) states that everyone has "a capacity for agency – for desiring, for forming intentions, and for acting creatively" in a given structure (p. 20), teachers with their agency, will also have the capacity to imagine and realize technology-mediated pedagogical potentials of their own. Teachers' agency can be invoked and exercised to explore, understand, and exploit technologies for enhancing and transforming their pedagogy. However, it is important to understand that the power of agency is qualified (e.g., limited and delimited) by the undergirding structures. To unleash the transformative powers, therefore, the teachers need to develop critical agency by reinvigorating their digital identity, which is also building up their digital competencies, beliefs, and attitudes. In so doing, the teachers will have to re-construct their digital competencies, beliefs, and attitudes that are relevant to their pedagogical imaginaries and intentions. I will describe those digital competencies, beliefs, and attitudes in the next section.

Third, the notion of "mediational means" attends to the instrumental aspects of digital identity. Mediational means involves both agent and instrumentality to produce a mediated action (Wertsch, 1998; Vygotsky, 1978). In terms of digital identity, mediational means involves the teachers' critical agency (i.e., agent) within the given "structures" to mediate their pedagogical actions using digital technologies (i.e., mediational means). Let's take a look at Wertsch's (1998) description of mediational means and mediated action below.

1. Mediated action is characterized by an irreducible tension between agent and mediational means;
2. Mediational means are materials;
3. Mediated action typically has multiple simultaneous goals;
4. Mediated action is situated on one or more developmental paths;
5. Mediational means constrain as well as enable action;
6. New mediational means transform mediated action;
7. The relationship of agents toward mediational means can be characterized in terms of mastery;

8. The relationship of agents toward mediational means can be characterized in terms of appropriation;
9. Mediational means are often produced for reasons other than to facilitate mediated action; and
10. Mediational means are associated with power and authority. (p. 25)

Indeed, teachers and digital technologies as mediational means have complex tension, such as functional relationships, influencing each other's capabilities. Digital technologies as mediational means are constrained or leveraged depending on how the teachers appropriate them to mediate their teaching and student engagement activities, for instance, an online course or discussion. In a deeper sense, mediational means is a bridge connecting digital structures and agency to materialize the structures into creating new and innovative pedagogical designs and delivery. To better understand how a mediational means functions, one might look into the "activity theory" (Engeström, 1990), which is based on the social constructivist theory of learning pioneered by Vygotsky (1978) and Leont'ev (1978). I will describe this theory in greater details in the latter section.

Re-Constructing Teachers' Digital Competencies

Meaningful technology integration into classrooms requires the teachers' theoretical and practical understanding of multiple competencies and skills. While the notion of digital competencies remains a moving goal, there exist some comprehensive frameworks and theories that capture the foundational aspects of developing digital competencies by the teachers. Below, I will briefly describe some of the major frameworks and theories of educational technology including the ISTE Standards for Teachers (Standards*T - 2016), technological pedagogical content knowledge or TPACK" (Mishra & Koehler, 2006), and theories of educational communications and technology (Spector, Merrill, Merrienboer & Driscoll, 2008).

The ISTE's Standards*T, previously known as the National Technology Standards for Teachers (NETS*T), outlines a comprehensive framework pertaining to the teachers' essential digital knowledge and skills. The "Standards*T" emphasizes on enabling teachers to design and develop digital age learning experiences for their students by creating digital learning environments to enhance student creativity, innovation, and thinking.

Mishra and Koehler (2006) have developed a framework called "technological pedagogical content knowledge" (TPACK) establishing the knowledge bases for using technology in teaching. This framework offers theoretical insights into "what knowledge teachers must have to integrate technology into teaching and how they might develop this knowledge" (Schmidt et al., 2009). As shown in Figure 1, interweaving the three foundational concepts including the knowledge of technology (TK), pedagogy (PK), and content (CK), TPACK derives a new set of advanced knowledge as follows:

- **Pedagogical Content Knowledge (PCK):** It encompasses the knowledge of connecting pedagogy with content such as how to teach a particular curricular content.
- **Technological Content Knowledge (TCK)**: It covers the knowledge about how and what types of technology can be harnessed to teach particular types of content.
- **Technological Pedagogical Knowledge (TPK):** It is the knowing of how technology mediates the teachers' pedagogy that they intend to implement in their classrooms.
- **Technological Pedagogical Content Knowledge (TPACK):** This knowledge provides a conceptual basis for teachers to blend technology with pedagogy and content. This conceptual understanding, at the same time, is derived within the complex interplay of PCK, TCK, and TPK.

Figure 1. TPACK Framework
Source: Mishra & Koehler (2006)

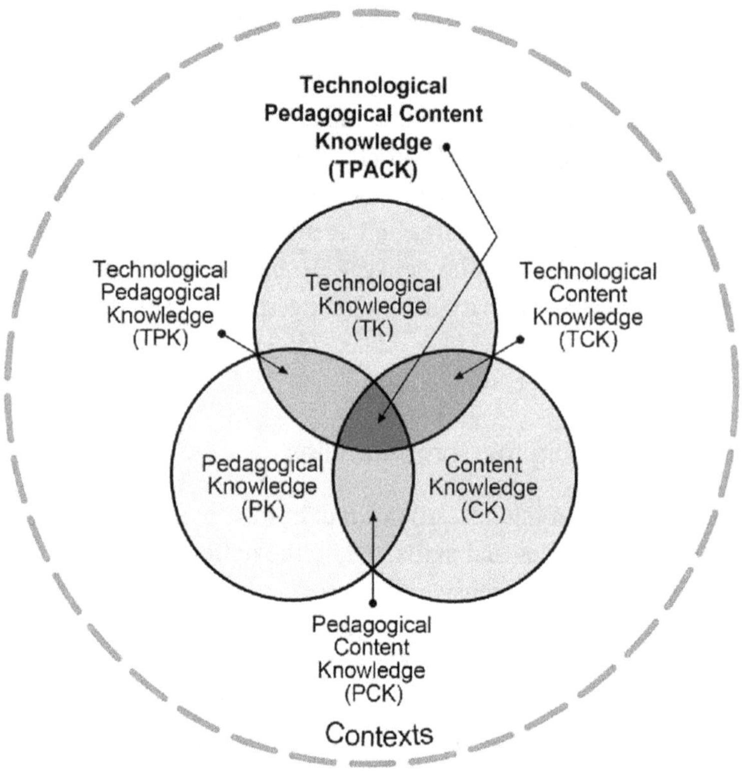

While TPACk is built on Shulman's (1986, 1987) historical notion of "pedagogical content knowledge," there is another important theoretical trend oriented toward educational implementation of information and communications technology. Perhaps in a most comprehensive way, Spector (2008) outlines four major theoretical foundations for research in educational communications and technology: psychology of learning, communications theory, human-computer interaction, and instructional design and development. Briefly, psychology of learning delves into "how we think" (Dewey, 1910) and "how we/people learn" in a given learning context using their brain, mind, and experiences (Bransford et al., 2000). Since Dewey, psychology of learning has evolved from behaviorism (e.g, Skinner 1938), to cognitivism (Piaget, 1929), constructivism (e.g., Bruner, 1986), and more recently to neuroscience or brain-based learning (Caine & Caine, 2011). Although behaviorism could still be useful to teach some particular content and skills, currently technology mediated teaching and learning are more geared toward utilizing cognitivist, constructivist, and brain-based learning principles.

Communications theory in educational technology research is based on the idea that language, human interaction, and thinking are in a complex interplay to shape up one's learning experiences (Vygotsky, 1978). Language and communication are used to express and share one's thoughts and experiences. In educational technology, researchers, instructional designers, and teachers explore and seek to implement how pedagogical messages or content can be transferred to learners in more effective and meaningful ways.

Human-computer interaction (HCI) looks into the nature and processes of human interactivity with computing devices and also the psychological aspects associated with it. HCI is concerned with the user experiences of the leaners that how and where they interact with technology to learn. Furthermore, HCI focuses on user-friendliness and aesthetics of instructional designs. In sum, HCI focuses on the creation of simple and "intuitive interaction designs" (Bannon, 2011) which allow teachers and learners to easily create, share, and discuss.

Finally, theories of instructional design and development refer to "the systematic and reflective process of translating principles of learning into plans for instructional materials, activities, information resources, and evaluation" (Smith & Ragan, 2005, p. 4). Instructional design is at the core of pedagogical practice within educational technology because it is the process of creating "blueprints for effective, efficient, and engaging instruction" (Merrill, Barclay, & Schaak, 2008, p. 173). Instructional designs include an array of technology-integrated pedagogical models such as problem-based, task-centered, cognitive, and collaborative among many others.

Enmeshed in these theoretical and conceptual frameworks described above, the development of digital competencies for teachers is a multi-layered endeavor. First, they might begin with building basic digital literacies (see Lankshear & Knobel, 2008) and then move toward exploring critical digital literacies (e.g., Watulak & Kinzer, 2012). Pursuing a continuous reflective pedagogical practice and professional development, the teachers can utilize these two literacies and make sense for "meaningful integration of technology" in designing those learning activities that are intentional, active, constructive, cooperative, and authentic (Howland, Jonassen & Marra, 2012). Although the phenomenon of digital literacies is dynamically evolving, Bawden's (2008) identification of four interrelated and inter-functional components of digital literacies are always useful to consider:

1. **Underpinnings:** Basic computer and ICT literacies required as in workplace and the everyday lifeworld;
2. **Background Knowledge:** Knowledge about the online information and digital resources to be used;
3. **Central Competencies:** Basic skills and knowledge to be able to read and understand information in digital and non-digital formats, knowledge assembly, media literacy, create and communicate digital information, etc.; and
4. **Attitudes and Perspectives:** Ability to perform independent learning and maintain moral and social literacy while engaging in the digital world.

The theory of critical digital literacies (CDL), in correspondence with digital literacies, seeks to examine the use technology from critical and sociocultural perspectives. Watulak and Kinzer (2012) posit that CDL promotes the "Understanding cultural, social, and historical contexts of technology use, including ethical and appropriate practices; critical thinking and analysis; reflective practice; and functional skills with digital technologies" (p.135). Nonetheless, this description of CDL is just a mere beginning. CDL is a praxis -- an ever going cyclical process of practicing, reflecting, and devising improved new practices-- that goes beyond the justification of digital utilities to critical investigation of how digital technologies perpetuate the ongoing socio-technological issues such as equity issues of accessibility and affordability (e.g, digital divide), commercialization of media content and the Internet, net neutrality, intellectual property, and so on.

Teachers are always able to advance their CDL by incorporating critical pedagogies and multicultural education theories (Freire, 2000; Sleeter & McLaren, 1995) in order to investigate such socio-technological issues. I believe that acquiring CDL and digital literacies will help teachers to kick start their projects of pedagogical designs and delivery in the advent of technology. The teachers' digital competencies are further consolidated by actively aggregating and manipulating an array of technology standards and benchmarks (e.g., ISTE Standards), theories of educational technology (e.g., TPACK and Instructional design), and technology integrated pedagogical models (e.g., flipped classrooms, mobile learning, and Webquest).

Teachers' Digital Self-Efficacy

The other constitutive element of teachers' digital competencies is their "digital self-efficacy" consisting of beliefs, values, and attitudes toward using technology in the classrooms (Asing-Cashman, Gurung, Limbu & Rutledge, 2014; Moos & Azevedo, 2009). Digital self-efficacy is grounded in the sociocognitive theory (Bandura, 1986), which maintains that individuals are proactive, self-reflective, and self-regulating for their behavioral adaptation. Certainly, digital self-efficacy is not a stand alone construct lying in the workings of one's inner minds, but it is resulted by the "triadic reciprocality" between environmental, behavioral, and personal influences within existing external and internal structures (Bandura, 1986; Moos & Azevedo, 2009).

The teachers construct their digital self-efficacy over time through learning by doing and reflections. Positive digital self-efficacy empowers teachers to grapple with the "situational demands" (here, pedagogical needs) because it helps them to elevate the current states of their motivation, course of actions needed, and cognitive resources (Wood & Bandura, 1989). When teachers feel empowered, they are more likely to refine and increase their pedagogical motivation, goals, and digital competencies. Having the positive digital efficacy, teachers are, thus, well equipped to activate their agency for a change in their pedagogical practice; to realize the digital structures available in the classrooms; and to proactively formulate goal-directed pedagogical interests of blending technology into practice.

Given the primacy of teachers' digital self-efficacy in enhancing their pedagogical practices with and by technology, it is important to see how it is formed. Studies suggest that both behavioral and psychological factors are associated with digital self-efficacy (Moos & Azevedo, 2009). Therefore, teachers might explore and reinvigorate behavioral factors such as augmenting their exposure and frequency of using technology. Psychologically, they might strive for developing positive attitude and curiosity to explore new digital tools and resources for pedagogical possibilities. These kinds of positive behavioral and psychological experiences of teachers will reinforce the growth of their efforts to build digital self-efficacy and eventually to reconstruct their digital identity.

Re-Conceptualizing Cloud Technology for Pedagogy

Building upon the cloud affordances and the notions of 3Ds -- i.e., teachers' digital identity, competencies, and self-efficacy, I present a conceptual framework for integrating cloud technologies into pedagogy. Briefly, cloud affordances include digital tools and resources for catering more dynamic teaching and learning engagement such as online collaboration, anytime anywhere learning, self-paced content delivery, and efficient and effective monitoring of student engagement via learning analytics tools.

As mentioned earlier, I argue that developing a solid digital identity is the basic and fundamental process toward re-conceptualizing technology integration into pedagogy. A solid identity enables the teachers, at least in the three fronts: to exploit digital structures and resources for improving and transforming pedagogical practices; to reconstruct their digital agency for devising technology-mediated pedagogical potentials of their own; and to implement agency and structures into practice by conceptualizing technology as mediational means.

The way we (re)conceptualize technology determines its functions and affordances for mediating our practice of pedagogical design, development, and delivery. So, it is important to understand the basic concepts involved, for instances, what technology is and how it works for intended pedagogical purposes. A concepetual framework lays out the essential concepts, where concepts are the set of abstract or generic ideas about "what something is or how it works from particular instances[1]"-- and also explains how such a conceptual approach facilitates the process of transforming the functions and features of cloud technologies into pedagogical designs, development, and delivery. Prevailing educational uses of technology suggest that it can be conceptualized at four different levels, ranging from simple to complex: a) as a digital tool or instrument to facilitate the traditional pedagogies; b) as a cognitive tool or mindtools to enhance student learning; c) as a mediational means to mediate and generate new pedagogical opportunities; and d) as digital learning environment to transform the existing pedagogical practices as a whole, ecologically.

First, using cloud technologies as tools is the simplest form of technology integration, for instance, digitizing the face-to-face classroom activities and "hard copy" learning resources. This is a technically neutral and simplistic transferring, often termed as "instrumental" functions of technology (Feenberg, 1991; Habermas, 1970), of hard materials (e.g., traditional lecture notes and posters) into soft materials (e.g., PowerPoint presentations via Google Slides and Prezi) using cloud tools. Some other types of more complex classroom activities, for instance, group discussions also can be conducted using online discussion tools such as Blackboard discussion boards, Google docs, and Wikispaces.

Second, generally speaking, well-designed educational software, apps, learning games, and Webquest function as cognitive partners, also called "mindtools." Jonassen (2005) describes computers as mindtools that enhance the cognitive powers of learners for analytical thinking, critical thinking, and scaffolding. The mindtools are used to engage learners in metacognitive processes such as thinking, problem solving, scaffolding, and learning in general. Within this concept of cognitive tools, technologies have constructive functions in which the teachers facilitate the learning processes while the learners interact with digital tools and resources to construct meaning of the content. Cloud technology such as Wikispaces and Google Drive tools (e.g., docs, slides, and drawing) can be easily transformed into mindtools. Wikispaces, Google docs, and Google drawing are useful tools to create mind map, organize information, and manage acquired knowledge. Google forms can be used as a scaffolding tool to survey learner's background knowledge, to assess understanding, and to reinforce learning. More interestingly, a vast number of cloud-based add-on apps and widgets that function as mindtools can be easily integrated into Google drive for use.

Third, conceptualizing technology as a mediational means has expansive and transformative functions. A mediational means extends the instrumental and cognitive functions of technology and helps to generate new pedagogical possibilities. This is where the sites of pedagogical innovations and creativities emerge. It is a turn to a social constructivist practice of using technology where learning becomes a collaborative endeavor situated within a community or social group of practice. Fluidity and multiplicity of learning activities are made possible by the mediational means engendering multiple perspectives through thick discussions and contested knowledge creations.

One of the most important theories on blending technology as mediational means into practice is the "activity theory" (Engeström, 1990; Gurung & Chavez, 2011; Kuutti, 1996; Leont'ev, 1978). As shown in Figure 2, the activity theory captures the essence of learning as a collaborative, social, and cultural practice mediated by technological, psychological or sociocultural tools (Gurung & Chavez, 2011). This theory also clearly defines rules, outcomes, and roles and responsibilities for learning engagement. Furthermore, this type of mediated learning engagement can be made intentional and rigorous by defining or designating specific learning goals (i.e., object/outcome), assigning specific tasks for individual students from the group (i.e., division of labor), and so forth. To note, what activity theory does something important is the re-conceptualization of learning as a mediated action. As Wertsch (1998) and others (e.g., Gurung & Chavez, 2011) argue that when technology (e.g., cloud) is used as a mediational means to "mediate" learning, the learners will have the easy access to learning opportunities for collaboration, co-construction of knowledge, building multiple perspectives, and scaffolding that would otherwise difficult or impossible in many ways.

Needless to say that cloud tools afford the collaborative learning opportunities online, synchronously and asynchronously. For example, Wikispaces is a useful tool for creating collaborative group projects and online discussions. Another example, Google docs is highly efficient for group writing projects to be completed in the classroom or elsewhere at their preferred time and place.

Finally, digital learning environment (DLE) culminates the former three concepts and holds the capacity to transform pedagogies ecologically altogether. Learning environment can be described as the learning spaces where students, individually or in groups, interact with tools, materials, and resources to develop their knowledge and skills (Jonassen, 2006; Zhao & Frank, 2003). All types of biotic and abiotic structures and resources within a school and the community become integral parts of a "learning ecology," where it is viewed as "the accessed set of contexts, comprised of configurations of activities, material resources and relationships, found in co-located physical or virtual spaces that provide opportunities for learning" (Barron, 2004, p. 6).

Figure 2. Activity Theory
Based on Engeström's Activity Theory (1990)

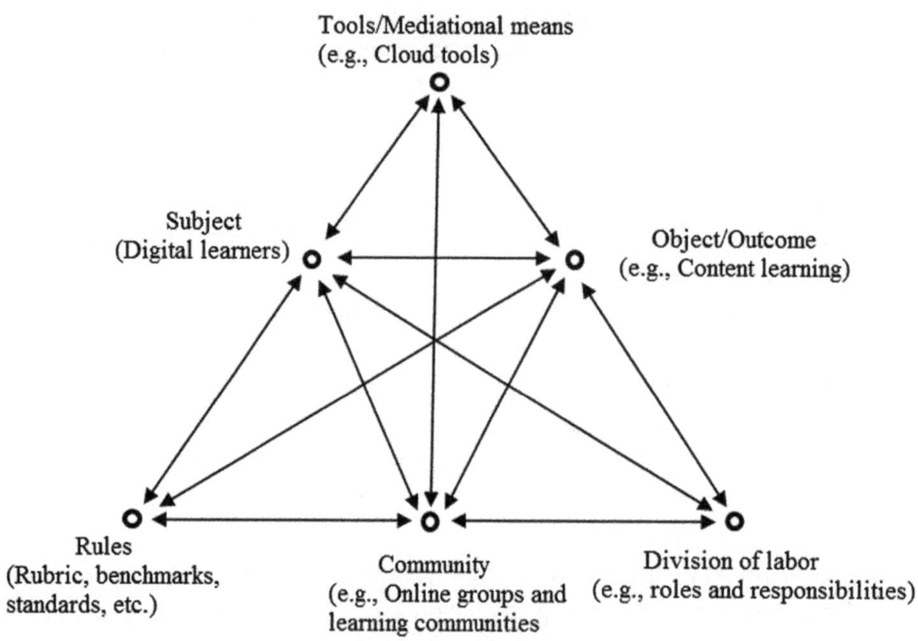

Developing a DLE is a complex, interactive, and systemic process of blending technology into pedagogy. So, designing a DLE entails a complex understanding of pedagogical components and educational technology contexts, both of which are constantly evolving. Briefly, pedagogical components cover the knowledge bases described in TPACK above, whereas pedagogical contexts are the larger structures of educational technology such as sociocultural, economic, political, and technological conditions. As I have argued elsewhere (see Gurung, 2013), the pedagogical essence of this changing components and contexts is to re-think teaching and learning as a dynamic process, what I have called is the practice of "emerging pedagogies." In so doing, the teachers are sought to reflect continuously on what it means to teach in the currently evolving networked society and how to leverage technologies to mediate such emerging pedagogies.

Developing and designing DLEs demand higher level of pedagogical and technological knowledge and skills. Therefore, substantive pedagogical intention, motivation, and persistence are essential constructs. These constructs are enabled when teachers have a set of strong 3Ds including their solid digital identity, positive digital self-efficacy, and substantive digital competencies. Having these strong 3Ds, the teachers are empowered to unleash *anew* transformative powers of technology for creating DLEs. The teachers unleash the transformative powers of technology by re-imagining technology as an instrument, a cognitive tool, and mediational means. By means of transformative powers, DLEs should unfold many envisioned and emergent teaching and learning opportunities listed below, but not limited to:

- DLEs should address "multiple intelligences" (Gardner, 2001) through technologies that offer multimodality in learning, for example, images, videos, apps, and learning games;
- DLEs address digital equity issues such as accessibility and affordability;
- DLEs facilitate teaching and learning processes grounded in the sound learning theories such as cognitive- and social-constructivist theories, social cognitive theory, multicultural education, and critical pedagogies;
- DLEs should be informed by best-evidence practices of instructional and learning designs;
- DLEs diversify learning experiences through individualized learning experiences (e.g., customization, autonomy, and flexibility);
- DLEs should enrich and diversify content;
- DLEs capture the cutting edge technological affordances such as mobility, interactivity, interoperability, and user-centric designs of learning spaces and resources;
- DLEs interlink classrooms with local and global learning communities, workplaces, and society (e.g., networked knowledge society);
- DLEs should provide easy and effective access to learning analytics for increased learning motivation and (self)monitoring);
- DLES should afford "unbound possibilities" with many alternatives for all possible aspects of technology integration (e.g., the alternatives for tools of engagement, courses or curricula, learning platforms, scaffolding tools, and learning support);
- DLEs are conceived of creating learning ecologies by adding new structures and resources all the time;
- DLEs should allow collaboration among teachers, learners, and the community to author content, deliver instruction, and design learning spaces; and much more.

Studies (e.g., Ding, Xiou & Leu, 2014) show that carefully designed DLEs offer ubiquitous learning opportunities, rich and diverse learning resources, collaborative knowledge construction and learning, and learning support such as online tutors, pedagogical agents, and instructional videos. Simply speaking, DLEs should allow the teachers and learners to immerse themselves within the technology-mediated learning ecologies, where they autonomously interact, collaborate, and build knowledges in a ubiquitous fashion (e.g., pursuing leaning engagement on-demand from anywhere and at anytime).

Cloud technologies are quintessentially applicable for designing DLEs. Cloud technologies provide the affordances to develop and design pedagogical models that are "learner centered, knowledge centered, assessment centered, and community centered" (see Bransford, Brown & Cocking, 2000). However, it is suggested that teachers conceptualize cloud technologies to be exploited at all of these four levels based on their pedagogical needs. In fact, it will be more practical to begin at level one and move upward progressively.

CONCLUDING REMARKS

As cloud technologies have proliferated into the digital worlds, we are fascinated by the pedagogical possibilities offered by those technologies. Cloud affordances, as I have outlined above, can be re-conceptualized and harnessed as simple tools or instruments, cognitive tools, mediational means, and digital learning environments. In other words, cloud offers a range of possibilities for teaching and learning, at least in four different levels, from simple use as instruments or tools (e.g., Powerpoint), to mindtools, to mediational means, to highly complex as DLEs. The teachers might harness cloud at any of these four levels depending on their students' learning needs and purposes. However, I argue that, for a successful integration of cloud at all these level, the teachers need to explore and examine the 3Ds -- that is, their digital identity, digital competencies, and digital self-efficacy -- and the complex triadic interplay between them.

Traditionally teachers' digital competencies and self-efficacy are considered as the most influential factors when it comes to integrating technology into the classrooms. But a closer look reveals an underlying deep structure – i,.e., the teachers' digital identity -- exists as a foundational component. The digital identity is the understructure because the teachers' efforts to develop their competencies and self-efficacy are rooted in their beliefs, values, and positions they hold for the real and perceived usefulness of technology. However, digital identity must not be mistaken as the overarching force as such to guide everything about technology integration, but as an anchoring component within the triadic interplay of the 3Ds. Developing the digital identity is a threshold that every teacher must meet and cross over, just to begin the act of using technology in teaching and learning. As the threshold, the digital identity functions as a springboard or foundation for technology implementation in classrooms, but not as an end target. Therefore, the teachers need to constantly re-construct their digital identity through reflective teaching practice of blending technologies into their classrooms while continuing to build up their digital competencies and self-efficacy.

REFERENCES

P21. (n.d.). *Framework for 21st century learning*. Retrieved April 11, 2016 from http://www.p21.org/about-us/p21-framework

Asing-Cashman, J., Gurung, B., Limbu, Y., & Rutledge, D. (2014). Pre-service teachers' computer self-efficacy beliefs in using free and open source tools (FOSTs): An empirical investigation. *International Journal of Teaching and Learning in Higher Education*, *26*(1), 66–77.

Bannon, L. (2011). Reimagining HCI: Toward a more human-centered perspective. *Interaction*, *18*(4), 50–57. doi:10.1145/1978822.1978833

Barron, B. (2004). Learning ecologies for technological fluency: Gender and experience differences. *Journal of Educational Computing Research*, *31*(1), 1–36. doi:10.2190/1N20-VV12-4RB5-33VA

Bawden, D. (2008). Origins and concepts of digital literacy. In C. Lankshear & M. Knobel (Eds.), *Digital literacies: Concepts, policies, and practices* (pp. 17–32). New York: Peter Lang.

Bransford, J. D., Brown, A. L., & Cocking, R. R. (Eds.). (2000). *How people learn: Brain, mind, experience, and school*. Washington, DC: National Academy Press.

Bruner, J. (1986). *Actual minds, possible minds*. Cambridge, MA: Harvard University Press.

Butler, J. (1993). *Bodies that matter: On the discursive limits of "sex"*. New York: Routledge.

Caine, R., & Caine, G. (2011). *Natural learning for a connected world: Education, technology and the human Brain*. Teachers College Press.

Coiro, J., Knobel, M., Lankshear, C., & Leu, D. (2008). Central issues in new literacies and new literacies research. In J. Coiro, M. Knobel, C. Lankshear, & D. Leu (Eds.), *The Handbook of Research on New Literacies* (pp. 1–21). New York: Lawrence Erlbaum.

Engeström, Y. (1990). *Learning, working and imagining: Twelve studies in activity theory*. Helsinki: Orienta-Konsultit Oy.

Ertmer, P. A., Ottenbreit-Leftwich, A., Sadik, O., Sendurur, E., & Sendurur, P. (2012). Teacher beliefs and technology integration practices: A critical relationship. *Computers & Education*, *59*(2), 423–435. doi:10.1016/j.compedu.2012.02.001

Ertmer, P. A., Ottenbreit-Leftwich, A., & York, C. S. (2007). Exemplary Technology-using Teachers: Perceptions of Factors Influencing Success. *Journal of Computing in Teacher Education*, *23*(2), 55–60.

Feenberg, A. (1991). *Critical theory of technology*. New York: Oxford University Press.

Freire, P. (2000). *Pedagogy of the oppressed*. New York: Continuum.

Gibson, J. (1979). *The ecological approach to visual perception*. New York: Houghton Mifflin.

Giddens, A. (1984). *The constitution of society: Outline of the theory of structuration*. Berkeley, CA: University of California Press.

Goffman, E. (1973). *The presentation of self in everyday life*. Woodstock, NY: The Overlook Press.

Gurung, B. (2013). Emerging pedagogies in networked knowledge communities. In M. Limbu & B. Gurung (Eds.), *Emerging Pedagogies in the Networked Knowledge Society: Practices Integrating Social Media and Globalization* (pp. 1–24). Hershey, PA: IGI Global.

Gurung, B., & Chávez, R. C. (2011). Transformative multicultural engagement on a web 2.0 interface. In G. Kurubacak & T. V. Yuzer (Eds.), *Transformative online education and liberation: Models for social equality* (pp. 15–46). Hershey, PA: IGI Global. doi:10.4018/978-1-60960-046-4.ch002

Gurung, B., & Rutledge, D. (2014). Overlapping of personal and educational digital engagement. *Computers & Education*, *77*, 91–100. doi:10.1016/j.compedu.2014.04.012

Howland, J. L., Jonassen, D. H., & Marra, R. M. (2012). *Meaningful learning with technology* (4th ed.). Boston, MA: Pearson Education.

Hsu, Y. C., Hung, J. L., & Ching, Y. H. (2013). Trends of educational technology research: More than a decade of international research in six SSCI-indexed refereed journals. *Educational Technology Research and Development*, *61*(4), 685–705. doi:10.1007/s11423-013-9290-9

ISTE Standards for Teachers. (2016). Retrieved April 1, 2016 from http://www.iste.org/standards/iste-standards/standards-for-teachers

Jonassen, D. H. (2006). *Modeling with technology: Mindtools for conceptual change* (3rd ed.). Columbus, OH: Merrill/Prentice Hall.

Kuuti, K. (1996). Activity theory as a potential framework for human-computer research. In B. A. Nardi (Ed.), *Context and consciousness: activity theory and human-computer interaction* (pp. 17–44). Cambridge, MA: MIT Press.

Lankshear, C., & Knobel, M. (Eds.). (2008). *Digital literacies: Concepts, policies, and practices*. New York: Peter Lang.

Leont'ev, A. N. (1978). *Activity, consciousness and personality*. Englewood Cliffs, NJ: Prentice-Hall.

Licona, M., & Gurung, B. (2011). Online multicultural education discussion: Praxis retained. *Multicultural Education*, *9*(1), 2–8.

Means, B., & Olson, K. (1997). *Technology and education reform: Studies of education reform*. Washington, DC: U.S. Government Printing Office.

Mell, P., & Grance, T. (2011). *The NIST Definition of Cloud Computing (NIST Special Publication 800-145)*. Gaithersburg, MD: National Institute of Standards and Technology.

Merrill, M. D., Barclay, M., & van Schaak, A. (2008). Prescriptive Principles for Instructional Design. In J. M. Spector, M. D. Merrill, J. van Merrienboer, & M. P. Driscoll (Eds.), *Handbook for research on educational communications and technology* (3rd ed.; pp. 173–184). New York: Lauren Erlbaum Associates.

Mishra, P., & Koehler, M. J. (2006). Technological pedagogical content knowledge: A framework for integrating technology in teacher knowledge. *Teachers College Record*, *108*(6), 1017–1054. doi:10.1111/j.1467-9620.2006.00684.x

Moos, D. C., & Azevedo, R. (2009). Learning with computer-based learning environments: A literature review of computer self-efficacy. *Review of Educational Research*, *79*(2), 576–600. doi:10.3102/0034654308326083

Orlikowski, W. J. (2000). Using technology and constituting structures: A practice lens for studying technology in organizations. *Organization Science*, *11*(4), 404–428. doi:10.1287/orsc.11.4.404.14600

Piaget, J. (1929). *The Child's Conception of the World*. New York: Harcourt Brace Jovanovich.

Schmidt, D. A., Baran, A., Thompson, A. D., Mishra, P., Koehler, J., & Shin, T. S. (2009). Technological Pedagogical Content Knowledge (TPACK): The Development and Validation of an Assessment Instrument for Preservice Teachers. *Journal of Research on Technology in Education*, *42*(2), 123–149. doi:10.1080/15391523.2009.10782544

Sewell, W. H. Jr. (1992). *A theory of structure: Duality, agency, and transformation*. *American Journal of Sociology*, *98*(1), 1–29. doi:10.1086/229967

Shannon, C. E., & Weaver, W. (1949). *The mathematical theory of communication*. Urbana, IL: University of Illinois Press.

Shulman, L. S. (1986). Those who understand: Knowledge growth in teaching. *Educational Researcher*, *15*(2), 4–14. doi:10.3102/0013189X015002004

Sleeter, C., & McLaren, P. (Eds.). (1995). *Multicultural education, critical pedagogy, and the politics of difference*. Albany, NY: SUNY.

Teo, T., Lee, C. B., & Chai, C. S. (2008). Understanding pre-service teachers' computer attitudes: Applying and extending the technology acceptance model. *Journal of Computer Assisted Learning*, *24*(2), 128–143. doi:10.1111/j.1365-2729.2007.00247.x

Zhao, Y., & Frank, K. A. (2003). Factors affecting technology uses in schools: An ecological perspective. *American Educational Research Journal*, *40*(4), 807–840. doi:10.3102/00028312040004807

KEY TERMS AND DEFINITIONS

Cloud Technology: The technology that virtualizes computing resources such as servers, data, software, and applications.

Critical Barriers: Factors that impede or preclude the effective use of technology.

Digital Agency: The teachers' informed capacity to transcend the constraints of the structures and ability to take risks for pedagogical innovations.

Digital Competencies: Knowledge bases of technology and its affordances to be harnessed for specific purposes.

Digital Identity: Digital identity is the online presence of a person representing his or her multiple selves. It is also a publicly observable image established by the people themselves or somebody else through collective discourses. Digital identity also denotes the ownership of technology gadgets, tools, and apps; and how they interact with them.

Digital Learning Environments: The technology mediated learning spaces where leaners interact with tools and resources to develop their knowledge and skills.

Digital Self-Efficacy: Beliefs, values, and attitudes toward the effectiveness of using technology.

Digital Structures: All types of biotic and abiotic resources available in a given learning ecology.

Enablers: Factors that empower or encourage users to blend technology into their actions.

Mediational Means: A tool or means that mediate an action generating new possibilities for the action.

ENDNOTE

1 http://www.merriam-webster.com/dictionary/concept_

Chapter 6
Critical Cloud Pedagogies:
Using Network Diagrams to Name and Visualize Learning Networks

Jack Hennes
Michigan State University, USA

ABSTRACT

Many students will soon enter high-tech workplace environments that utilize cloud technologies and systems, yet they must be critical of the technologies and infrastructures they use on the cloud. More approaches are needed, however, to facilitate learning environments where students both use cloud technologies and have opportunities to critically reflect on their rhetoricity. The author argues that new vocabularies are needed to describe the use of cloud technologies, especially those used in our pedagogical practices. Utilizing vocabularies and methods informed by actor network theory, instructors can easily identify and diagram the networks that students compose in pursuit of their learning goals. To demonstrate, the author offers network diagrams representing two different writing courses taught in the United States, in turn presenting how instructors can engage in similar diagramming practices and even use the "cloud" and "networks" as crucial points of inquiry for students.

INTRODUCTION

In the not-so-distant past, writers would need to save their files and data on a local hard drive. However, cloud technologies have quickly transformed the way writers compose, shifting from a hardware-driven logic to a network-driven, cloud logic. In addition to the hardware-to-network shift, writers have also experienced a new age of asynchronous collaboration previously impossible in the past. Everyday literacies are now mediated by a range of web-based applications that work from the cloud logic, such as word processors (i.e., Google Docs, Etherpad, TitanPad), data storage and management (i.e., Dropbox, Google Drive, Box), and social media platforms (i.e., Twitter, Facebook, Tumblr). The shifts of 'hardware to network' and 'individual to collaborative' are not just shifts in logic, but they are also profound shifts in our orientation to technologies and the affordances they provide.

The shift from an industrial to an information age has shaped the context for distributed work teams. According to Michael Hardt and Antonio Negri (2000), "In the passage to the informational economy,

DOI: 10.4018/978-1-5225-1650-7.ch006

the assembly line has been replaced by the network as the organizational model of production, transforming the forms of cooperation and communication within each productive site and among productive sites" (qtd. in Meijas, 2013, p. 4). Work in this information economy is now mediated by collaborative tools on the cloud, helping facilitate network-driven knowledge production in new, dynamic ways. To further highlight the context of knowledge work mediated through cloud technologies, high-tech work environments are increasingly global, with workers distributed across geographical and geopolitical borders. Robert Reich (1992) coined the phrase symbolic-analytic work, which describes how workers in an information economy are problem solvers who utilize computers for their everyday work activities. Symbol analysts, who primarily analyze and arrange symbols for their daily work activity, can often telecommute and are granted with more mobility for their careers. Now nearly two decades since the Reich outlined the work activities of symbol analysts, a new creative class has emerged, including a new culture of innovators and entrepreneurs. Institutions of higher learning continue to play a key role in preparing new members of this information economy.

However, in this era, perhaps more than any other in history, a failure to consider and confront the power relationships represented and enacted by technologies is vital. Students, many of whom will enter high-tech workplace environments that utilize cloud technologies and systems, must be critical of the technologies and infrastructures they use on the cloud. There is lack of methods to engage students in critical cloud pedagogies, however. More approaches are needed to facilitate learning environments where students both use cloud technologies and have opportunities to critically reflect on their rhetoricity.

In light of the challenges that the cloud presents, important delineations are needed. "The cloud", the way I utilize it here, refers to the sociotechnical imaginary that has now provided a new logic for knowledge work in an information economy. Cloud technologies are social web-based tools that allow users to perform, participate, and engage in networks on the cloud. Following these terms--and in the interest of this collection-- "cloud pedagogy" refers to teaching and learning that utilizes cloud technologies and sometimes even engages students in the topic of the cloud itself.

The shifts in logic and orientation have been facilitated by development of the cloud. Still, the cloud is difficult to grasp. It is at once technological and cultural, both imaginary and artefactual. The shift to the cloud has happened so quickly, and has so rapidly permeated our everyday literate practices, that we are still attempting to make sense of it. The difficulty in making sense of the cloud logic and its influence on everyday writers is, primarily, a lack of vocabulary to describe it.

In this chapter, I argue that new vocabularies are needed to describe the use of cloud technologies, especially those used in our pedagogical practices. In order to address this, I suggest that actor network theory can provide both a vocabulary and a modeling method for cloud pedagogy. Utilizing vocabularies informed by actor network theory, instructors can name and visualize the networks that students engage in for their learning goals. Network models are especially beneficial for critical reflection and course planning, especially courses in which students utilize multiple cloud technologies to facilitate their learning. When utilizing actor network theory, including its vocabularies and methods, instructors are better situated to afford students with more agency and, ideally, provide learning environments where students can achieve learner autonomy and grant themselves with more agency. Cloud pedagogy, when informed by the sensibilities of actor network theory, has an opportunity to shift to a network-focused pedagogy that values relationality of people and things, avoiding technology-driven pedagogies and curricula. Actor network theory methods can also help facilitate rhetorically-focused pedagogies that utilize cloud technologies. I first begin by highlighting the metaphorical underpinning of the *cloud* and the *network*, examining how these terms operate rhetorically. I then provide an overview of actor network theory and the vocabularies it can offer for cloud pedagogies. Finally, I demonstrate how actor network theory modeling serves as a useful technique to engage students with the rhetoric of the cloud and networks.

Metaphors of the Network and the Cloud

The information economy has experienced a shift in orientation from linear assembly to distributed networks of labor. However, the network has also been used to regard everyday social life as well. The network, then, has operated metaphorically in a number of powerful ways. The network operates as a "model or template for organizing society", in other words, as a guiding heuristic for the production of technologies and infrastructures (Meijas, 2013, pg. 3). But the network also serves as an epistemic construct, one that organizes knowledge and participation in the context of 21st century, technologically-mediated work and social life (Mejias, 2013). As an episteme, "the network" allows people to see and understand the world in terms of networks, "even to things that are not networks" (Mejias, 2013, pg. 3). While networks have indeed been present long before technological tools began to facilitate social networking, online social networking platforms have accelerated the use of the network metaphor in guiding the understanding of the world in terms of nodes and links. The metaphor of the network has also found its way into teaching and learning, and the use of a personal learning network (PLN) in curricula is not uncommon. Students and professionals are constantly reminded by how networking—utilizing a range of materials, methods, and tools to build a professional social network—is vital to achieve their professional goals. In order to network, students and professionals utilize social networking platforms to build links and relationships to people, organizations, and resources. Networking, then, represents how one must utilize social and technological networks to achieve professional success.

The metaphor of the network is strikingly similar to the metaphor of the cloud. Both metaphors can refer to a larger, sociotechnical orientation to the way that technologies are guiding the social world. However, the both the cloud and the network have a tendency of amplifying inequalities. In *A Prehistory of the Cloud*, Tung-Hui Hu presents an important perspective on "the cloud" and its implications in postmodern, technologically-mediated, connected life. He draws an important parallel that helps illustrate the context of the cloud as we know it today. Victorian cities, according to Hu, were constructed with the ensuing fear of risk. In a "risk society," cities are constructed to minimize and prevent threats to economic prosperity, such as attacks and environmental disasters. In drawing a comparison, Hu states that the cloud is constructed on the same principles of risk—in turn giving rise to "gated communities" that optimize safety and "seal off encounters between those at different ends of the socioeconomic curve" (pg. 65). The risk society has indeed shaped the cloud, and the cloud has a tendency of amplifying disparities. For instance, many people do not have access to the cloud at all. Not everyone possesses the literacy skills--whether language or technological literacies--to engage in the cloud. Language distribution (and even the left-to-right order of reading and orientation to web design) used and represented on the cloud is uneven and unequal, and users with visual impairments are often an afterthought if considered at all. Many communities do not have access to internet speeds fast enough to run a large number of websites and browser-based applications. The translation from city to sociotechnical infrastructure has, in essence, successfully extended the same power relations and hegemony onto the cloud. This translation also provides a useful frame for understanding the cloud metaphor and its construction as an oppressive space. It's a space that represents the unequal infrastructure of cities and natural resources, one where an unequal distribution controls who has access and who does not, who can make significant contributions and who cannot, and who can break and resist that infrastructure and who cannot. The inequalities created by the cloud are often overlooked, however, perhaps because the network appears to be a better provider of equality and opportunity than alternatives, such as oppressive social institutions or the state (Mejias, 2013, p. 8). This masking of inequality represents how rhetorically successful the cloud has been in creating a narrative of democratization.

The cloud has given rise to a cultural fantasy, one that purports that it provides an endless and inexhaustible resource. To Hu, this is similar to any other myth that a natural resource is inexhaustible, such as the air "as the abode of the endless: inexhaustible, limitless, invisible" (Connor qtd. in Hu, p. 66). Of course, all natural resources are indeed exhaustible and have their own limits, and the cloud is no different. On the surface, the cloud provides a new realm for interactivity, collaboration, and engagement using web-based applications with data, information, and exchange stored on the cloud. Below the surface lies an entire sociotechnical economy with mass amounts of server space and personnel required to maintain, secure, and improve cloud-based tools. Further, social interaction and exchange is now silently and easily commodified on cloud platforms. While users may be convinced that these platforms are affording them with new democratizing ways to share and express their opinions and participate in social and civic life, their data is being catalogued, stored, and sold.

There are seemingly infinite metaphors that describe the cloud, including its vast, interconnected, and endless ability to connect and democratize the world. However, the cloud and its democratizing rhetoric is a cultural fantasy. The cloud has its limits, and the cloud is far from being an equal, democratizing space. Instead, it represents and amplifies hegemony, unequal power structures, control of the subaltern, and a space for corporate-led, large-scale order of the masses. It's the largest and most efficient economic marketplace in the world. In terms of scale, it's easily the largest network of knowledge in the history of humankind—and it's production was so rapid that sensationalizing metaphors about connectedness and democracy have been hastily assigned, whereas critical metaphors about it's hegemonic construction and imprisonment have not found their way into everyday vocabularies.

While the metaphors of "network" and "cloud" are now pervasive, it remains vital that we problematize these metaphors. Rhetorical approaches to the network and the cloud are needed to analyze, critique, and unveil how these terms operate to organize the social world. Networks and the cloud increasingly mediate students' everyday literacies. It is vital that students are provided opportunities to critically analyze these terms, the tools they use, and consider their rhetorical power. But in order to combat the rhetoricity of these terms, study them, understand them, teach them, and inform our own pedagogies, a vocabulary is needed to guide this work.

History and Context of Actor-Network Theory

Actor Network Theory (ANT) is often said to have originated in the work of Bruno Latour (1996), John Law (1992), and Michel Callon (1986). According to Potts (2008, 2009), this work was then furthered by Annemarie Mol and John Law (1994). Mol (2011) has stated that ANT is not, in fact, a theory at all. Instead, ANT is anything but a coherent framework as it serves as a set of terms and sensibilities (Mol, 2011). To Moreira (2010), "ANT is a malleable set of conceptual tools and methodological strategies that enable researchers to investigate and organize empirical materials and helps us understand the dynamics of actions involving key actors" (pg. 8). Despite its supposed promise of offering conceptual tools, ANT is antithetical to coherence and strives to playfully explore and complicate instead of seeking order out of things. Mol (2011) has called ANT a "wild and creative intellectual tradition" and for good reason.

Actor Network Theory (ANT) is a theory of contradictions. It is as provocative as it is playful, as complicated as it seems overly simple. The origin of the theory can be traced to 30 years ago, in the work of the sociology of science. To date, the theory has been applied widely across the social sciences and humanities, from business to public health to urban planning. In recent years, the theory has been applied to the field of rhetoric and writing. Spanning sub-fields from composition studies to technical and professional communication, ANT has presented itself as much more than a trend or boutique theory, lending itself to valuable conversations about pedagogy and the social world. At the same time, however, rhetoric and writing scholars are still only beginning to explore the applicability of the theory and its ideological impact.

ANT attempts to explain how material-semiotic networks come together and act as a unified whole. Networks are constantly moving, are being made, and re-made. A network is considered an *actant*, and is made from a series of *actors*. Actors can be either human or nonhuman, and controversially, both human and nonhuman actors are imbued with an equal amount of agency in any network. When Latour playfully and provocatively claimed that both humans and nonhumans have equal agency, he resisted major western intellectual traditions in sociology of science and science and technology studies. This facet of the theory continues to draw criticism and speculation, however, it is this perspective that has provided a landscape for scholars to analyze and understand the way humans interact with complex technologies.

Latour (1990) is interested in agencies, and in fact, he identifies that the origin of science studies emerged from the impossibility of differentiating between the agencies of the natural, the social, and the semiotic. In brief, ANT is interested in accounting for both the social world as well as the essences of societies and natures. ANT claims that modern societies cannot be described without recognizing them as fibrous in character--and is never quite understood by looking at it in terms of territories, spheres, categories, structures, and systems (Latour, 1990, p. 3). To Latour, ANT is also a change of metaphors to describe essences: instead of surfaces one gets filaments (Latour, 1990, p. 3). The introduction of these metaphors presents a new frame for understanding the complexities of technologically-mediated, everyday life. ANT, then, was developed to invent a vocabulary to describe the situation of agencies. According to Latour, the word network has its origin in the work of Diderot and was used by Diderot to describe matter and bodies (in order to avoid the Cartesian divide between matter and spirit). Further, the origin of the word, to Latour, has a strong ontological component (Latour, 1990). ANT also presents a change in topology, and "Instead of thinking in terms of surfaces—two dimension—or spheres—three dimension—one is asked to think in terms of nodes that have as many dimensions as they have connections" (Latour, 1990, p. 3). As a result, ANT presents a new set of metaphors, vocabularies, and ontologies to guide the analysis of networks and the agents that help tie those networks together.

Latour famously outlined how ANT treats human and nonhuman actors equally. This has interesting contributions to cloud pedagogues, who engage students in innovative and engaging learning experiences with technologies. However, it begs the question of how things can have the same amount of agency as a human being. Latour takes a view that anything that modifies a state of affairs or makes a difference is an actor, or if it does not yet have a figuration, an actant (Latour, 2005, p. 71). Latour asks a guiding question about any agent: "Does it make a difference in the course of some other agent's action or not?" He then provides examples of trials, such as: hitting a nail without a hammer, turning on a TV without a remote, keeping track of an inventory without a list, and more. To those who subscribe to Latour's thing-oriented vision for actors, the things involved in these examples are all actors. More precisely, however, they are all participants in the course of actions (Latour, 2005, p. 71). This view, however, seems to suggest that things always determine actions, however, Latour does not claim that objects do things *instead of* human actors. To Latour, "no science of the social can even begin if the question of who and what participates in the action is not first of all thoroughly explored, even though it might mean letting elements in which, for lack of a better term, we would call non-humans" (Latour, 2005, p. 72). ANT, then, presents the vocabularies and sensibilities to understand "the who" and "the what" participating in any action.

Jason Swarts (2008) demonstrates an example of coordinated activity guided by the agencies of people and things. In many cases, multiple authors contribute to the production of an object. In addition to multiple authors, the production of an object may also originate from information fragments offered by both human (engineers, technicians, etc.) and nonhuman (machine interfaces, testing instruments, etc.) sources. These information fragments, Swarts (2008) argues, "may be held together firmly in a familiar genre form or tentatively by the cognitive efforts of those who use the information" (p. 302). Humans, nonhumans, texts and technologies engage in a kind of coordinated conversation. In other words, knowledge and expertise are offered by a number of agents, and when assembled together, produce what Swarts calls a discursive object. The resulting discursive objects that Swarts describes then help coordinate activities on a larger scale, such as issuing an air quality permit or designing an airplane. In short, Swarts demonstrates that ANT provides an interpretive frame for understanding the agencies of technology and people. The theory helps describe how human actors organize and orient themselves to ecologies of knowledge work. When considering the terms actant and actor, in addition to the agencies between people and things, ANT presents a useful vocabulary for analyzing and interpreting the way networks form and operate. To illustrate the vocabularies I outlined above, I model how ANT can be used as a method to critically reflect on the cloud technologies used in two different writing courses taught in a higher education setting.

ANT Diagramming as a Critical Pedagogical Method

Actor network theory offers a method, a vocabulary, and a sensibility to technologies, networks, and agencies. Those employing ANT as a method have used it as a means to analyze communication systems and problems. ANT methods have also been used to inform the design of communication systems, such as researching user experiences and activities. In this sense, ANT methods are manifest through the drafting of ANT diagrams, simple sketches or illustrations that identify the actant and all the actors in any moment of interaction. In an ANT diagram, symbols such as arrows help identify relationships between and across actors, thus illustrating the exchange of information, ideas, or goods.

ANT diagramming has also been used as a tool to research communication systems and understand how those systems can be better designed to be truly user-centered. Liza Potts (2008) demonstrates how ANT can operate as a method to understand interactivity in communication systems. Potts (2008) explains how traditional software architecture diagrams can be augmented with diagrams inspired by ANT to account for all of the participants involved in a communication system. Traditional Use Case Diagrams, to Potts (2008), can help document the actions that take place in communication systems, while ANT diagrams encourage "designers to see a wider spectrum of use and users" (p. 3). Potts (2008) then offers a three-stage sequence to engage in ANT diagramming:

1. Identifying an actor network (actant),
2. Naming people, places, and things (actors), and
3. Highlighting temporary relationships among actors (pp. 3-5).

Identifying temporary relationships on an ANT diagram is especially useful when looking at how users utilize communication systems. ANT diagramming is also beneficial to understand the context of students using cloud tools for learning. Below, I offer brief and informal ANT diagrams that represent the learning networks composed in two different writing courses.

First-Year Writing Course

I outline two courses previously taught by myself at Michigan State University in the department of Writing, Rhetoric, and American Cultures. The first is a thematic first-year composition course consisting of mainly first-year students entitled "Writing in Science & Technology" (WRA 110). The thematic course, fulfilling the university-wide undergraduate writing requirement for all majors at the university, attracts students representing intended majors across science, technology, engineering, and mathematics (STEM) fields. Like many other first-year writing courses, students engaged in the writing process to produce a range of documents and artifacts, both alphabetic and multimodal. Because the professional and intellectual interests of the students in the course, I placed particular emphasis on critical perspectives of technologies. As a major semester-long project, students created personal learning networks (PLNs) that aligned with their disciplinary and professional goals. The PLNs were then followed by an investigative research paper on the role of writing and communication in their intended career paths. During their learning processes, students engaged in a number of tools, platforms, and resources to facilitate learning. In Figure 1, I identify all the technologies utilized by students in the course in pursuit of their learning and engagement in the course.

The ANT network diagram in Figure 1 represents an actant, that is, a learning network composed by a typical student in the course. The actors in the network were influenced by both instructor and student goals. For instance, actors such as Google Docs, the course website, Eli Review, and Camtasia Relay were

Figure 1. An actor network theory diagram representing a student's learning network in a thematic writing course for undergraduate students

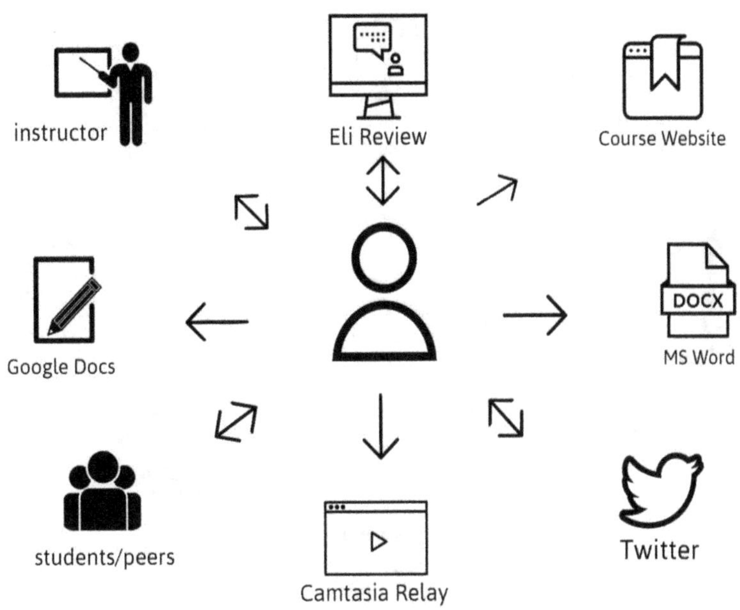

all introduced by the instructor to facilitate a learning experience for all students. Actors such as Twitter and Google Docs represent an individual students' agency in shaping the network for their learning. In the diagram, one-way arrows indicate that the student regularly consulted an actor for its role as a tool or resource. The two-way arrows indicate that student had a relationship in which they not only consulted that actor(s), but that actor(s) also informed their decision-making in the process of their learning. As the ANT diagram in Figure 1 indicates, the actant is composed of both human and nonhuman actors. For instance, throughout the semester students and peers provided ongoing feedback and ideas to fellow students in the course, which was mediated by the nonhuman actor, Eli Review. Some actors work in concert with nonhuman actors to exchange ideas and information, while others more generally inform the learning process in the actant.

Professional Writing Course

The second course I outline is entitled "Web Authoring" (WRA 210), a required course for professional writing majors at Michigan State University. Emphasizing a rhetorical approach to authoring on the web, the course covers HyperText Markup Language (HTML) and Cascading Style Sheets (CSS) in addition to topics such as information architecture, usability testing, and iterative design. As a major project in the course, students engage in the production of their own professional portfolio websites from the ground up. A number of artifacts are created during this process, such as low and high-fidelity sketches, wireframes, and design comps. As a result, the production of their websites and the technologies they used were both traditional (i.e., pencil and engineering paper) and advanced (i.e., Adobe Photoshop). During their process, students form work teams that utilize both face-to-face and online communication to share resources, goals, and ask questions. Figure 2 represents the range of technologies students used during their learning process in the course.

Figure 2. An actor network theory diagram representing a student's learning network in a web authoring course designed for undergraduate professional writing majors

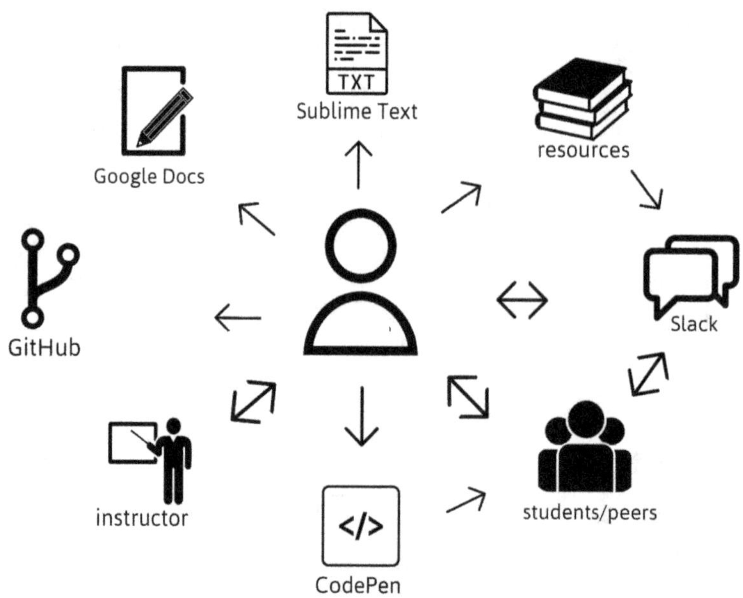

In Figure 2, the actant represents a dynamic learning environment that employs a range of cloud-based technologies. Utilizing a range of cloud-based tools and resources, students demonstrate that cloud-based technologies can help facilitate dynamic group work and distribute knowledge amongst different students instead of the instructor serving as the source of knowledge. To facilitate the communications between and across actors, the cloud-based communication tool Slack was used. Using Slack, I encouraged students to identify key skill areas that they would offer their work teams, such as writing and editing, graphic design, and usability. Because students in the class had a range of goals and interests beyond their undergraduate education, such as technical writing, user experience design, writing for nonprofit organizations, editing and publishing, and even marketing, encouraging students to identify themselves as experts allowed them to claim that identity when interacting with their peers. Students then composed work teams that represented a range of skills in each, with each team utilizing their unique communications channel on Slack.

Students were able to exchange information between and across actors, both human and nonhuman, to establish identities as experts. For instance, a student with expertise in web design is easily able to consult an online resource for CSS, utilize the ideas from that resource and compose a simple navigational menu on CodePen, a cloud-based tool that allows graphic designers to save and share code snippets. The student then shares a link to CodePen with human actors, such as her fellow students and peers. Students then have the option of creating their own "pen" on CodePen, which represents their own transformation and adaption of the navigational menu produced by the original actor, their fellow student.

As the ANT diagram in Figure 1 and Figure 2 demonstrate, activity can be easily illustrated and described using terminology from ANT to examine how classroom-based human and nonhuman interactions are fostered through cloud technologies.

Outcomes for Cloud Pedagogies and Agencies

The ultimate goal of ANT, using this approach to classroom analysis, can help instructors identify the agencies of tools and students. As a result of this focus on agencies, instructors can then approach future classrooms with the goal of affording students with more agency though the selection of cloud-based tools. Perhaps the goal, then, is to facilitate learning environments where students compose their own learning networks, through their own choices of cloud-based tools. Marilyn Cooper (2011) has stated that "students (as rhetors) are always productive agents" (pg. 423). In that sense, much of the perspectives on agency as a commodity, as I have outlined for most of this chapter, may be flawed. However, in order to begin to understand the agencies of students in their learning practices, identifying the actants and actors involved in their learning process is a useful reflective practice for teachers. When students are asked to diagram their own learning networks, they are effectively asked to identify, name, and map the actant and the actors involved in their learning processes—in turn, allowing them to critically reflect on their own agencies in those learning networks.

Providing a space for students to compose and arrange all the actors in their learning networks can be a challenge, however, there are a number of ways to encourage students to engage in this practice. First, instructors can provide students an opportunity to create ANT diagrams that represent their everyday literacy practices. This practice is especially valuable for students to situate themselves in the context of the cloud and its broader information economy. Second, instructors can encourage students to be agents of their own networks by providing them with tool and resource-building moments. For example, students can have moments in class to gather and identify sets of tools, people, technologies, and systems and then share their findings to a class-wide, collaborative document or space (i.e., Twitter hashtag or Slack channel). During these moments, instructors should allow students to be critical of their use of these tools by encouraging them to think deeply about the rhetoric of networks and the agencies of tools. Students should also be encouraged to think critically about their own agency in relation to the tools they use during their learning process. Finally, instructors can use ANT diagrams to visualize the networks that students use in the classroom. This is most useful for post-semester reflection or for planning upcoming classes, especially courses that will utilize cloud technologies for student engagement and learning.

ANT diagrams, including the vocabularies and sensibilities to agencies that the theory provides, serve as important tools for practicing teachers to make sense of the dynamics and networks that emerge when students utilize cloud tools, especially multiple cloud-based tools. ANT diagrams, as a result, allow teachers to critically reflect on their cloud-based pedagogies in a verbal (utilizing vocabularies) and visual (utilizing diagrams) ways. In that sense, ANT allows for descriptive pedagogical practices for understanding how learning networks best can be facilitated through cloud-based tools, especially for the unique demographics, interests, and literacy practices of students. The rhetoric of the cloud and the network has presented a number of promises for democratization. However, as pedagogues we have the responsibility to use the cloud and the network as critical points of inquiry in our pedagogy and as reflective practices. Network diagramming, informed by ANT methods and vocabularies, presents a means through which students can not only name and visualize their roles in a sociotechnical system, but also to critically reflect on their agencies in that system as writers.

REFERENCES

Callon, M. (1986). Some elements of sociology of translation: Documentation of the scallops and the fishermen of St. Brieuc Bay. In J. Law (Ed.), *Power, action, & belief: A new sociology of knowledge?* (pp. 196–229). London: Routledge.

Cooper, M. (2011). Rhetorical agency as emergent and enacted. *College Composition and Communication, 62*(3), 420–449.

Hardt, M., & Negri, A. (2000). *Empire*. Cambridge, MA: Harvard UP.

Latour, B. (1987). *Science in action: How to follow scientists and engineers through society*. Cambridge, MA: Harvard UP.

Latour, B. (1990). Om aktor-netvaerksteroi. Nogle fa afklaringer og mere end nogle fa forviklinger. *Philosophia, 25*, 47–64.

Latour, B. (1996). *Aramis. Or the love of technology* (C. Porter, Trans.). Cambridge, MA: Harvard UP.

Latour, B. (2005). *Reassembling the Social: An Introduction to Actor-Network-Theory*. Oxford: Oxford UP.

Law, J. (1992). Notes on the theory of the actor-network: Ordering, strategy and heterogeneity. *Systems Practice, 5*(4), 379–393. doi:10.1007/BF01059830

Mejias, U. A. (2013). *Off the network: disrupting the digital world*. Minneapolis, MN: University of Minnesota Press. doi:10.5749/minnesota/9780816678990.001.0001

Mol, A. (2011). Actor-Network Theory: Sensitive terms and enduring tensions. *Kölner Zeitschrift für Soziologie und Sozialpsychologie*, *50*(1), 253–269.

Mol, A., & Law, J. (1994). Regions, networks and fluids: Anaema and social topology. *Social Studies of Science*, *24*(4), 641–671. doi:10.1177/030631279402400402 PMID:11639423

Moreira. (2010). Actor-network theory. In *Encyclopedia of Science and Technology Communication*. SAGE Publications.

Potts, L. (2008). Diagramming with Actor Network Theory: A method for modeling holistic experience. *Proceedings of the 2008 IEEE International Professional Communication Conference*. doi:10.1109/IPCC.2008.4610231

Potts, L. (2009). Using Actor Network Theory to trace and improve multimodal communication design. *Technical Communication Quarterly*, *18*(3), 281–301. doi:10.1080/10572250902941812

Reich, R. (1992). *The work of nations: Preparing ourselves for 21st century capitalism*. New York: Alfred A. Knopf.

Swarts, J. (2008). Information technologies as discursive agents: Methodological implications for the empirical study of knowledge work. *Journal of Technical Writing and Communication*, *38*(4), 301–329. doi:10.2190/TW.38.4.b

Swarts, J. (2010). Recycled writing: Assembling actor networks from reusable content. *Journal of Business and Technical Communication*, *24*(2), 127–163. doi:10.1177/1050651909353307

KEY TERMS AND DEFINITIONS

Actor Network Theory: A methodological strategy for researchers to understand and research interactions that involve key actors.

Agency: An emergent property of individuals to act independently and make their own choices. Agency can refer to individuals' ability to make an affect on the world without being fully aware of how or what.

Cloud Pedagogy: Teaching and learning that utilizes cloud technologies and, sometimes, even critically engages students in the topic of the cloud as an area of study.

Knowledge Work: Labor in which the main capital is knowledge.

Network Diagramming: The practice of drawing simple sketches or illustrations that identify the actors in any moment of interaction. Symbols such as arrows help identify relationships between and across actors, thus illustrating the exchange of information, ideas, or goods.

Chapter 7
Pervasive Pedagogy:
Collaborative Cloud-Based Composing Using Google Drive

Maury Elizabeth Brown
Germanna Community College, USA

Daniel L. Hocutt
University of Richmond, USA

ABSTRACT

Cloud-based services designed for educational use, like Google Apps for Education (GAFE), afford deeply collaborative activities across multiple applications. Through primary research, the authors discovered that cloud-based technologies such as GAFE and Google Drive afford new opportunities for collaborative cross-platform composing and student engagement. These affordances require new pedagogies to transform these potentialities into practice, as well as a reexamination of contemporary theory of computers and composition. The authors' journey implementing Google Drive as a composing and communication environment required continually remediating content, relationships, practices, and their own identities as they interacted with students in the cloud. This chapter addresses how GAFE and Google Drive engage students in the composition classroom, redefine and transform pedagogical and curricular concepts, and improve students' experience and learning.

INTRODUCTION

Using personal cloud-based storage has become a way of life for many. Whether it's Dropbox or Google Drive, Microsoft OneDrive or Apple iCloud, free and low-cost personal cloud storage is readily and inexpensively available, enabling users to access their files and content from any networked device (Duffy, 2014). With a networked device, internet connection, and an account, files can be saved and backed up online, shared, and downloaded on demand. This new way of accessing, managing, and sharing information is transforming the tech industry, the workplace, and our personal relationship to technology. Increasingly, cloud-computing plays a role in education, as students use applications located

DOI: 10.4018/978-1-5225-1650-7.ch007

in the cloud, and store and share a variety of media with classmates and faculty. Institutions -- including colleges and universities -- that implement storage and sharing using cloud technology must consider the way that it transforms access, communication, interaction, and relationships between and among the institution and its constituents.

File storage and file sharing, however, only scratch the surface of the potential that cloud-based technologies offer. Cloud-based services designed for educational use, like Google Apps for Education (GAFE), afford deeply collaborative activities across multiple applications. Google Drive and Google Docs, two of the applications in GAFE and the focus of this chapter, work in tandem to provide shared folders (through Drive) for exclusive, password-protected file sharing among class members and free web- or app-based word processing (in Docs). Google Docs also offers the opportunity for synchronous or asynchronous collaborative use. Granular sharing levels enable strict or loose limits on the way partners or groups can collaborate in a document or among multiple documents. With appropriate sharing permissions, collaborating can take the form of typing in the same document at the same time, typing in the same document at different times, and suggesting and accepting changes at the same time and different times. Asynchronous commenting, threaded and labeled by user, enables users to post comments, respond to comments, and mark comment threads as resolved. Synchronous chats are also built into the document as a sidebar or separate window, enabling brainstorming sessions and communication related to, but outside of, the primary composition space. Multimedia can be embedded, and this functionality can be extended to voice and video collaboration by using other GAFE applications like Google Hangout. GAFE offers this level of collaborative affordances in Docs (word processing), Sheets (spreadsheets), Slides (presentations), Forms (web-based forms connected to Sheets), and Drawings (drawing) applications, all of which can be combined and shared through Drive. Other third-party apps, such as mindmapping, can be added to this standard suite to extend the functionality and collaboration possibilities of GAFE, and Google encourages developers to create new apps.

These collaborative cloud-based affordances offer composition studies the opportunity to rethink not only our pedagogy but also key "givens" in the field, such as drafts, process, peer review, and authorship. In this chapter, the authors present their combined efforts to revise and rethink teaching composition with/in the cloud using GAFE in two different first-year composition situations: rural campuses of a community college serving a mix of traditional students and working professionals, and the continuing education unit of a suburban private liberal arts college serving working professionals. The authors integrated GAFE for student composing, collaboration, and communication, requiring work to be completed using GAFE collaborative applications and shared with peers and their instructor using Google Drive folders. Students completed invention, drafting, revision, review, and submission activities in Google Drive; they produced no printed compositions. Although the authors used their institutions' learning management systems (LMS) to post grades, students submitted assignments to the LMS as Google Doc URLs, and instructors annotated and assessed (without grading) assignments within the Google Doc. After observing student interaction during both face-to-face class sessions and within the online documents, the authors surveyed students about their experience using GAFE in the composition course.

Through primary research, the authors discovered that cloud-based technologies such as GAFE and Google Drive afford new opportunities for collaborative cross-platform composing and student engagement. These affordances require new pedagogies to transform these potentialities into practice, as well as a reexamination of contemporary theory of computers and composition. The authors' journey implementing Google Drive as a composing and communication environment required continually remediating content, relationships, practices, and their own identities as they interacted with students in the cloud. Using theory and praxis from online writing instruction (OWI), information communication technology (ICT), and rhetoric and composition studies, this chapter will address how GAFE and Google Drive engage students in the composition classroom; redefine and transform pedagogical and curricular concepts; and how these transformations improve students' experience and learning.

Literature Review

One reason cloud computing is so attractive to scholars, instructors, and students is its 24/7 availability and ubiquity. Twenty-first century students in higher education represent a shifting demographic, one that includes far more part-time students who fit school around other schedules, including work and family obligations (Schuetze & Slowey, 2002). The rise of online learning and the readily-available Web 2.0 online interfaces demand that composition pedagogy and practice, among other educational experiences, be flexible and available beyond traditional "classroom" space (James, 2014). With an inexpensive netbook, tablet, smartphone, or other mobile networked device, students and teachers can access educational activities and engage in collaborative composing and reviewing. This ubiquity, especially supported by pervasive wifi across vast swaths of urban and suburban centers (Yu, 2014), makes collaborative cloud computing more accessible[1] and reliable for instructional use.

This interest in using cloud-based technologies in composing practice responds to Yancey's (2004) call for composition scholars and educators to study and incorporate technological and multimodal affordances in our composition practice and instruction. Our field has responded with many studies exploring the relationship between the digitally-mediated composing environment and writing outcomes. Several aspects of this relationship have received critical attention. For example, Cook (2005), Depew & Lettner-Rust (2009), and the "Position Statement of Principles and Example Effective Practices for Online Writing Instruction" (CCCC, 2013) call on teachers to privilege pedagogy over technology; to develop composition courses around sound pedagogy first, then select technologies that successfully implement pedagogical decisions. Focusing more directly on technologies for specific composing tasks, Halasek et al. (2014) and Porter (2014) seek to explore the potential benefits and drawbacks of using MOOCs for composition classes or as media for composing texts, while Breuch (2005) encourages teachers to utilize the affordances of the online environment (while recognizing and adapting to its constraints) when planning and leading peer review sessions in synchronous and asynchronous sessions. In seeking to examine ways technology can be used to better facilitate summative assessment of composing practices, Barrett (2006), Clark (2010), Davis and Yancey (2014), and Tulley (2013) pay critical attention to the development and use of eportfolios. McKee and DeVoss (2013) edited an online collection titled *Digital Writing Assessment and Evaluation* that offered several different scholars' perspectives and ideas on ways assessment needs to adapt to the online digital composing space and its artifacts.

The new ways of interacting and new implications for digital composing provided by cloud-based applications and Networked Knowledge Communities (NKCs) require new pedagogical approaches, as several scholars have explored. Boyd (2007) demonstrates the importance of digital media to young people for idea sharing and creativity, and how they participate in a variety of small and large, local, and global networks in their daily lives outside of educational contexts. Gee and Hayes (2011) note that new forms of digital media engage students in alternative ways of learning and advocate bringing them into the classroom and improving teachers' awareness of and facility with them as new pedagogies. Limbu (2013) explores how networked technologies and web 2.0 applications affect multiple literacies -- traditional, digital, and global. Gurung (2014) considers the conceptual and theoretical aspects of emerging pedagogies in Networked Knowledge Communities, emphasizing their pedagogical implications and teachers' knowledge base. Echoing Gurung (2014), DePew, Spangler & Spiegel (2014) note that few instructors have been trained to critically examine technological programs' affordances to determine how they affect the relationship between students, the instructor, and course content despite the importance of this critical awareness in developing pedagogies designed for networked spaces. Brown & Hocutt (in press) look specifically at issues related to institutional policy, transparency expectations, trust, surveillance, composing practices, and pedagogies that instructors and institutions must consider when implementing GAFE.

Other scholars have thoughtfully considered how specific digital tools can be used in composition classes: For example, Reid (2008) examines iTunes U as LMS and encourages teachers to integrate formal and informal composing practices in mobile learning pedagogy on such a platform; Bowie (2012) examines ways podcasts can be effectively used in composition classes; and Robins (2008) examines Second Life for its potential as a space for composition teaching, learning, and practice. Focusing on the social nature of composing, Danowski (2006), Neff and Whithaus (2008), and Warnock (2008) encourage composition teachers to use digital network affordances to encourage and facilitate composing as a collaborative activity. Noting that "nearly all composition is digital composition," Eyman and Ball (2014) call for the composition studies field to engage more deeply with the "very rapid shift in modes, genres, and media of textual production" which they argue is critical for building literacies and expanding research in the field (p. 114). Cloud-based computing is is a frontier in composition studies, and represents a growing site for research into composing practices, engagement, literacy, and new pedagogies that capitalize on its unique affordances.

Despite studies like these that examine the relationship between various technologies and composing practice and pedagogy, little critical attention focuses on the use of cloud-based tools for collaborative composing. Use of cloud-based tools in classroom settings has not yet become widespread, partially due to institutional privacy concerns in cloud-based technologies and potential FERPA implications of using third-party applications like GAFE or Dropbox. As a result, despite its no-cost ease of access and extensive collaborative affordances, little research focuses on the use of Google Drive for collaborative cloud-based composing. Two recent international studies (Cuestas & Fazzi, 2012; Rowe, Bozalek, & Frantz, 2013) addressed pedagogical implications of using Google Drive and concluded that implementing GAFE enabled pedagogical transformations in critical thinking, power relationships, and students' perception of learning, but they did not address composition specifically. This chapter seeks to begin the work of closing that gap by providing data on the effects using cloud-based technologies such as Google Drive has on student composing and engagement, as well as on pedagogical practice, in two different classroom environments.

Collaborative composing is a term the authors use to mean two separate but related ways of thinking about composing with others. The first generally refers to the use of specific technological affordances to enable multiple users to compose together; the second refers more abstractly to the social production of meaning through composition, "a writing process that grows out of the very nature of language" (Fontaine & Hunter, 2006, p. 12). The authors understand technological affordances as the means to collaborating, of working together to solve a problem with language. As a result, the authors recognize collaborative composing as rooted in writing's social aspects (Bazerman, 1994, 2004; Gaillet, 2009; Miller, 1984, 1994). Collaborating in the same document, on the same assignment, as part of an intentional community of learners, replaces the writer/reader binary and its corollary, the solitary, discipline-bounded writer expressing a single idea at a given moment (J. Rice, 2006) with a far more social actor in a complex, networked space (Latour, 2005). When Bezemer & Kress (2008) consider current and future understandings of "text" and "genre" in composition studies, they invoke the social dimension of composing in multimodal texts. Collaborative composing is a networked activity (Bazerman, 2004), and using GAFE and Google Drive, networked activity among class members and instructor can easily become networked activity among other classes and instructors (also functioning within networks) that are seeking to address common critical approaches and composing outcomes. The nesting of networks within networks, and collaborative activity beyond the brick and mortar classroom, beyond the course in a single semester, beyond the campus, and indeed beyond other geographic borders also makes cloud computing and collaborative composing in GAFE all the more relevant and transferable to situations both within and outside of higher education.

Throughout the article the authors make reference to CCCC Principles for Online Writing Instruction (OWI). The courses the authors taught and reference in this article were not online. They were a variety of options of face-to-face courses as described below. However, when one uses a cloud-based computing interface which requires students to interact online, the principles of OWI are not only relevant, but crucial. In using GAFE with students, the course becomes online writing no matter the modality assigned to it by the institution or the presence of face-to-face interaction that occurs between instructor and students.

Methods

In first-year composition (FYC) at two different institutions -- rural campuses of a mid-size Virginia community college and the professional and continuing education division of a private Virginia liberal arts college -- the authors integrated GAFE for student composing, collaboration, and communication. The courses operated independently and students in one course did not interact with each other, although the GAFE interface does make that possible and such cross-course and cross-institutional collaboration is an avenue for future research.

Brown used Google Drive for two sections of College Composition I and one section of College Composition II. The Composition II course was taught twice per week during the day in a computer classroom at a regional center. Students ranged in age from dual-enrolled in high school to early 60's. One Composition I section was taught twice per week during the day in a traditional classroom at the campus primarily serving allied health students, and contained students in a similar age range. The other Composition I section met once per week in the evenings in a computer classroom, and contained two high school students along with adults who worked full-time during the day. Hocutt used GAFE for one section of Critical Research and Writing I in the continuing studies school of a small liberal arts college. Students ranged in age from twenty-something employees to fifty-something mid-level professionals, meeting once weekly in the evening on the university campus.

Data were collected in three ways:

1. Ethnographically, via instructor as a participant/observer in the respective classrooms;
2. Via traces left within the Google Drive environment itself; and
3. Via a mixed-methods survey instrument administered anonymously at the end of the semester to gauge student perceptions of the usefulness and application of Google Drive to their personal, academic, and professional lives.

The instrument is an original survey design which was constructed as a Google Form and made available only to students in these composition sections. Students were asked to complete the surveys at the end of the semester, either in class following the final exam, or on their own time. Student survey responses were confidential. The survey instrument consisted of a total of 28-questions, broken down into four sections: Access to and Use of Google Drive, Function and Utility of Google Drive, Effectiveness of Google Drive, and Attitudes Toward Google Drive. Survey questions used standard Likert and Likert-Type scales to measure attitudes and values along the negative-positive dimension.[2] At the end of the instrument, participants were asked demographic data that allows for segmentation and comparative study. In addition to the quantitative questions described above, the instrument also contained narrative questions to allow students to elaborate on their ranked choices and to make open-ended comments regarding their experience using the interface in the composition classroom.

Brown's classes consisted of 66 students at two campuses, both serving a rural and suburban commuter population. Hocutt's class consisted of 14 students attending evening classes on the main campus. Of these 80 students, 56 voluntarily responded to the survey, a 70 percent response rate. In the combined student population, 73 percent of students were in the "traditional" college age group of 18-24, 13 percent ages 25-34, 13 percent ages 35-54 and less than 2 percent age 55 or older. We used the standard US Census codes to determine student demographic characteristics. The combined student population was 68 percent female and 31 percent male. Fifteen percent of students identified as Hispanic, 18 percent Black, 5 percent Asian, 5 percent American Indian, and 2 percent Native Hawaiian/Pacific Islander; the remainder identified as White.

Different Implementations

Google Drive and Google Apps for Education allow for customized implementations, depending on the instructor's curricular goals and pedagogical style, as well as the needs of students. This affordance enables instructors to maintain control over their pedagogical implementations, upholding instructor professionalism and classroom autonomy in line with OWI Principle 5 that promotes instructors being able to "retain reasonable control over their own content and/or techniques for conveying, teaching, and assessing their students' writing" in their classrooms (CCCC, 2013). The primacy of instructor control available in GAFE was important to the authors, as each followed different strategies for setting up shared Google Drive folders. The authors each created a series of shared folders on their own Google Drive accounts that they shared with their students. Brown required students to create their personal folders within the shared class folder (see Figure 1), while Hocutt required students to share their own folders with members of their writing and peer review groups (see Figure 2). Brown's method required students to share their composing practices with the rest of the class from the earliest stages, while Hocutt's method required students to share all folders with the instructor early in the process, but to share composed drafts at later stages of development with a smaller group of students.

One of the strengths of GAFE is its flexibility to adapt to different teaching and learning styles without compromising collaborative affordances. Brown's method reflected her desire to co-create classroom activities and outcomes with students, while Hocutt's methods reflected his desire to maintain a level of control over folder structures and shared content. Despite these different strategies and the philosophical positions they reflect, the authors experienced similar results among our students.

Figure 1. Brown's shared folders, one for each course section, owned and shared by the instructor for the length of the class

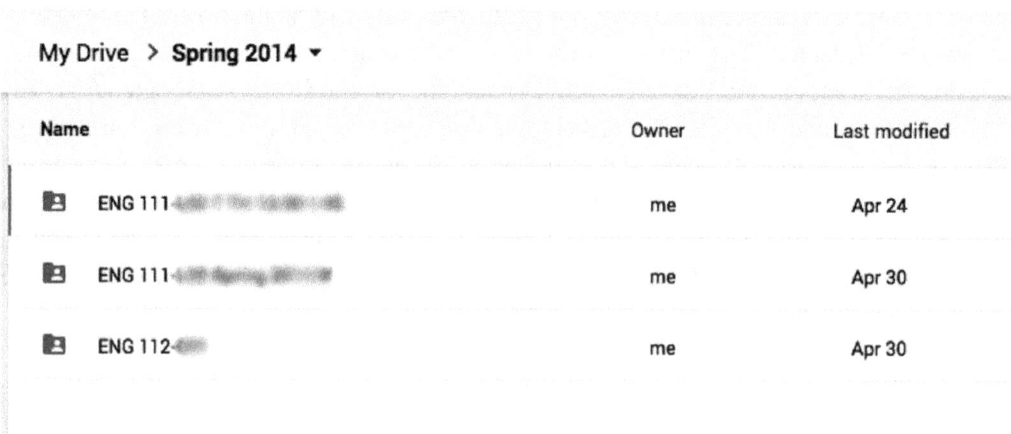

Figure 2. Hocutt's student folders, owned by the students and shared selectively as assigned

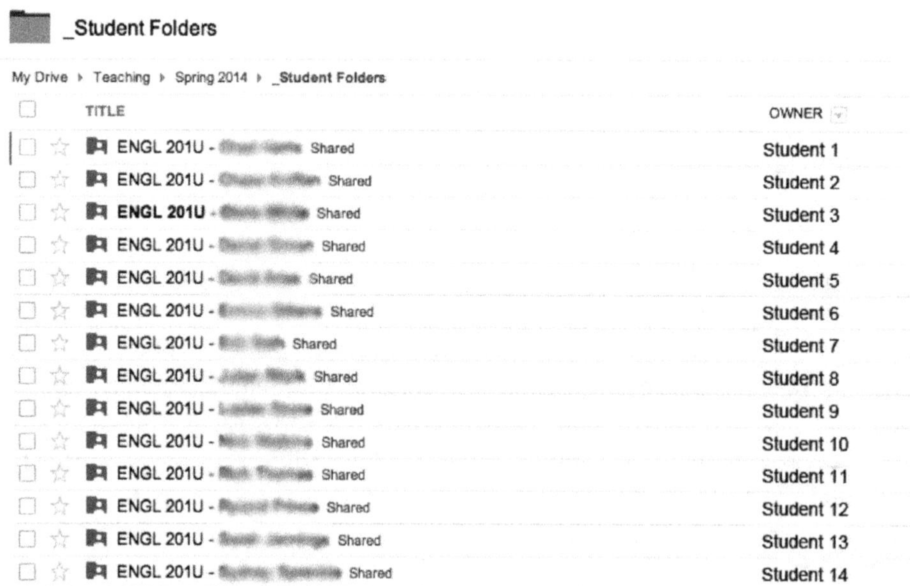

Results and Discussion

Although implementation of the composing platform differed at the two sites, the authors discovered that Google Drive engages students in the composition classroom; redefines and remediates traditional concepts of artifacts, processes, and places; transforms students' experience and learning; and requires new pedagogies to align the technology with composition theory and praxis.

Because of their pervasive nature and cross-platform capabilities, cloud technologies redefine the classroom. "Classroom" now can mean the wider world, as it is not bound by time and space to the 2.5

hours per week face-to-face session. These results suggest the cloud-based ubiquity of GAFE allowed engagement to occur beyond the classroom environment, and even beyond the virtual classroom environment into the shared composing environment of the cloud-based technology itself. While access to course content 24/7 is not unusual in today's higher education environment where professors create a course web page or use a LMS to deliver content, much of that "interaction" is top-down: the delivery of information from the instructor to the students. Items such as course syllabi, assignment sheets, handouts, or even recorded lectures and multimedia items can be viewed by students from any device with an internet connection. The GAFE environment is fundamentally different from these interfaces that allow for information dissemination and submission, or asynchronous interaction through discussion board posts.

Google Docs allows students to interact simultaneously and iteratively. Rather than a static discussion board post that another student replies to, students interacting in a Google Doc can leave comments on specific paragraphs, sentences, or even individual words. These comments can then be replied to, and ultimately an action on the comment is taken by the document owner (the student writer) when s/he decides how to resolve the comment. That could mean taking the advice of the commenter, rejecting it, or a nuanced middle ground in which the writer considers the feedback and makes his/her own revisions to address the concern raised in a way that feels authentic to their voice and purpose. This back-and-forth is not done a single time, but can be done multiple times as the document evolves, and done with nested levels of specificity, related to a single comment, idea, or phrase. This composing process among collaborators is accomplished within the same document, without downloading or re-uploading, as a dynamic conversation in networked space (see Figure 3). The writing is transformed as the prior, less polished prose is overwritten, and evidence of this transformation is captured and archived in GAFE through revision history.

We found that students engaged with their documents beyond the class session. While some of that is unsurprising -- students must work on their papers outside of class -- there was a change in their writing process in terms of when, where, and with whom they wrote. Students accessed GAFE at all times of the day and evening, weekdays and weekends, and using a multitude of platforms, including their personal desktop/laptop (91%), their work desktop/laptop (17%), college computer during class (81%), college computer outside of class (40%), their smartphones (38%), and their tablet devices (15%). Throughout these disparate spaces and places, they were engaged in the composing process, not merely downloading or uploading content. Since students had access to the technology -- and thereby their drafts -- 24/7, they often participated in small "doses" of composing or editing when it was convenient for them, or as ideas occurred to them, accessing GAFE from multiple devices and platforms, including their phones and tablets. GAFE becomes a space of interactivity and creativity, of recursive collaborative composing and not the transaction-based use of an LMS.

The fundamental difference between GAFE and other cloud-based applications such as an institutional LMS is that GAFE easily allows and encourages students to work together *as they are completing the assignment*, as part of the composing process, rather than enabling students to respond to another's composition *after it's already been submitted* to a discussion forum or digital drop box. Students can "meet-up" in a Google Doc, from a distance or in person, and work together synchronously using the chat feature to ask questions, develop ideas, socialize, and build community. Later, students can return to that document and leave comments for peers to read and review. GAFE allows students to move seamlessly between synchronous and asynchronous interactions. What is ultimately produced by an individual student following this process is a text that was socially composed, with iterative feedback and input from peers provided as it developed. The social composing can also be traced by looking at the

Figure 3. Sample comments written by classmates on an invention assignment. each blurred entry represents a commenter. This figure reflects a synchronous in-class review session.

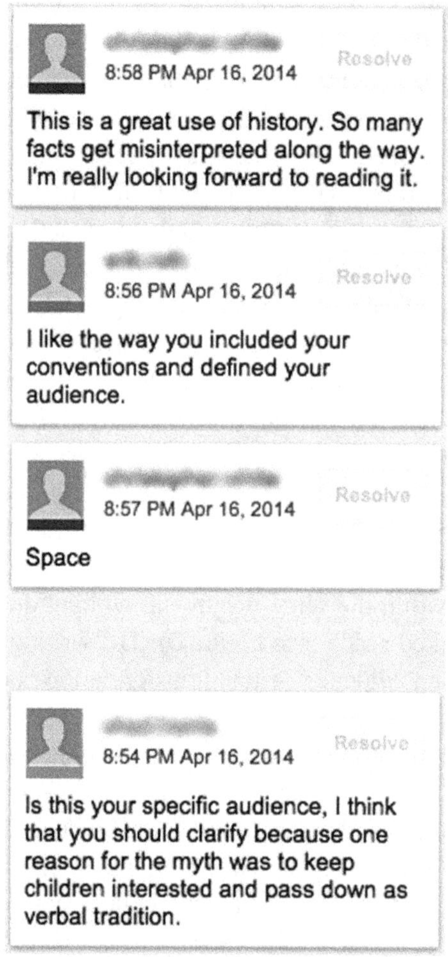

Doc's revision history (see Figure 4), where comments and replies to them (but not chats) are archived in addition to revisions to the document itself.

The authors' implementation of GAFE applications enacted the tenets of OWI Principle 3, which calls for teachers to develop "appropriate composition teaching/learning strategies... for the unique features of the instructional environment" (CCCC, 2013). The authors taught their classes in synchronous face-to-face sessions, so they were able to immediately gauge engagement in the classroom space. Because the authors could also see what their students were doing any time they reviewed the contents of students' shared folders, they could tell when and how students were engaged. The survey focused on student attitudes toward GAFE, and the authors were particularly interested in whether student use would change attitudes and expectations of both the use of technology and the composing practice. The authors asked students to evaluate how using Google Drive affected their expectations about several classroom activities and functions on a 5-item Likert-like scale: better than expected, somewhat better than expected, matched my expectations, somewhat worse than expected, and worse than expected. The

Figure 4. Sample Revision history from a student paper (left) and this chapter you are reading now (right). In the student paper's revision history (left), each blurred entry represents a collaborator's contribution. In this chapter's revision history (right), timestamps reflect asynchronous individual work and synchronous collaboration.

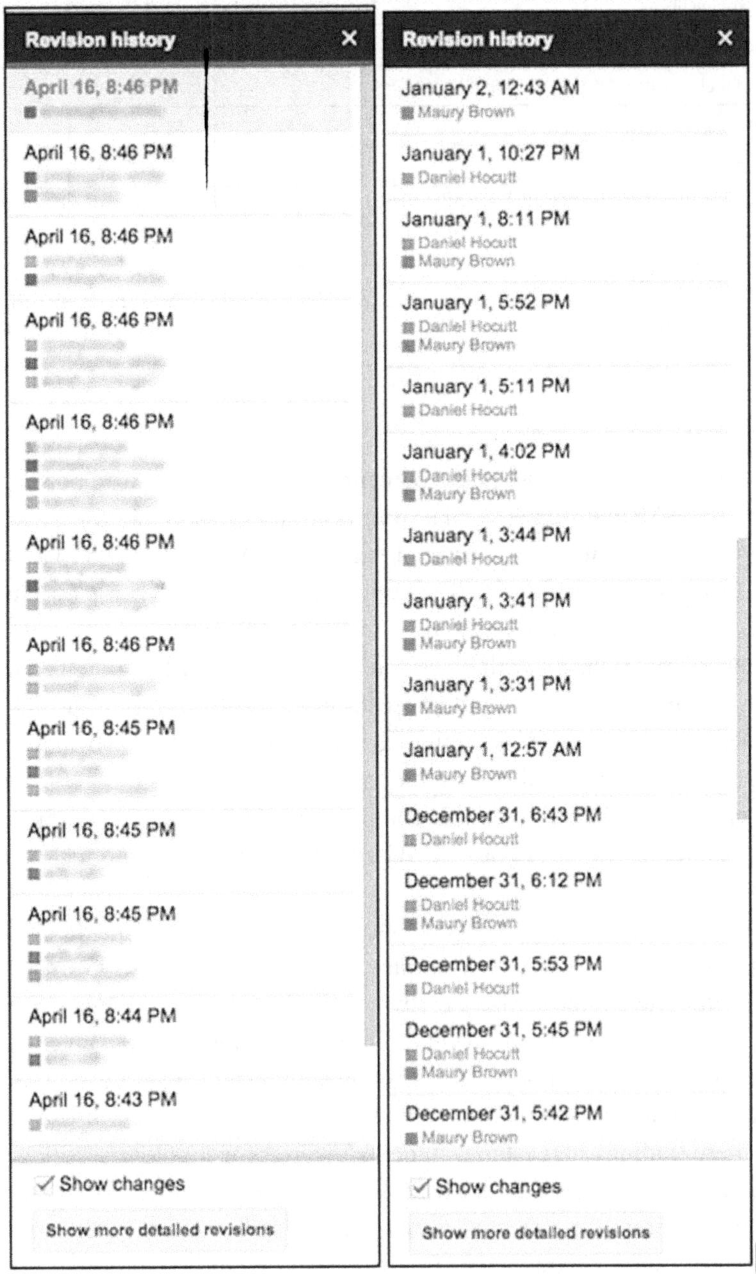

majority of students found the classroom activities and functions involving Google Drive were better than expected or somewhat better than expected. These results, focused on how using Google Drive exceeded expectations about class activities and functions, are listed in Table 1.

Table 1. Percentage of students who found using Google Drive in classroom activities and functions exceeded expectations

Activity or Function	Better	Somewhat Better	Overall
In-class activities and assignments	48%	30%	78%
Instructor/student relationships	39%	29%	68%
Your relationship with your classmates	41%	29%	70%
Your involvement in the class	46%	28%	78%
Your writing or composing process	44%	27%	71%
Your revising process	44%	27%	71%
Peer review	51%	19%	80%
Writing/composing together	45%	28%	73%
Submitting assignments for grading	42%	18%	60%
Grading/assessment	39%	17%	56%

Of particular interest in these results is the percentage of students who reported that using Google Drive exceeded their expectations related to classroom activities that do not directly engage technology, namely class involvement (78%, itself a measure of engagement) and relationship with classmates (70%) and teacher (68%). One student noted that, "Realizing that people could come into my paper at anytime was a little intimidating, but it also gave me a push saying 'you can do it,'" a comment that demonstrates positive involvement and relationship with classmates. By using GAFE, students are no longer solitary individuals composing on individual computers, seeking advice (if at all) after their paper is finished. One student affirmed, "I spent more time planning what I wrote before I write and I also spent more time reviewing my work. Because of the constant communication I spent more time interacting than I usually do." Another confirmed that the GAFE composing environment "made me look my paper over multiple times and ask people to peer review it. When I use to write I would just be like 'whatever', no one will see this."

More importantly, students engaged with one another in their writing practices and appeared to appreciate the opportunity to do so. The overwhelming majority of students (95%) considered the ability to share documents with one another either somewhat (20%) or very (75%) useful. Students found the opportunity to comment on others' compositions and to receive comments from classmates useful: 65% found this function very useful, 28% found it somewhat useful. And students also found useful the ability to create collaborative documents with others: 63% found this function very useful, while 30% found it somewhat useful. These findings suggest that students found the technology's collaborative affordances and its cross-platform ubiquitous availability useful for composing in the digital environment.

These quantitative findings are reflected in qualitative feedback from students, such as: "I expect myself to be working in groups of people in the future and to perhaps have multiple people edit my works. Google Docs makes that easily done." Other students wrote, "It has made it tremendously easy to share documents with other students and professors"; "I liked seeing other classmates opinions"; and "The ability to share each other's documents allows not only for feedback from other students but also allows people to get an idea of what other people have written." These comments, and others they represent, demonstrate the value students found in the collaborative affordances of GAFE in their composition practice. They also reflect OWI principle 2, which calls on writing classes to focus not on teaching the technology but on teaching writing skills (CCCC, 2013). GAFE collaborative affordances are intuitive enough that, even for the most fearful or hesitant student, the technology quickly fades from being an obstacle or learning curve to becoming a useful and meaningful composing tool.

As a result of using Google Drive for composing, the students' relationship to the instructor, to each other, to the writing process, and to the technology changed in significant ways, creating a more collaborative and transparent composing process. One simple example addresses students being prepared for class with paper drafts. Previously, as any composition instructor has experienced, multiple students would come to class without a draft for workshop, or with a severely anemic one. Somehow, on days when papers were due, many students would experience hard drive crashes, disappeared documents, locked up computers, lost or broken flash drives, failures to save documents, or drafts left on a different computer or at another location. There was little an instructor could do in the face of these impediments to the day's lesson plan: the choice was generally between telling the student to leave class since they were not prepared, or asking them to give feedback on another student's paper despite not having their own. The student without a draft would miss out on critical feedback to develop a draft to a more polished product and was also "successful" at thwarting instructional attempts to engage in the writing process. There was little accountability to the student -- perhaps a zero on a homework grade or the chagrin of a small number of classmates working with the student in a writing pair or group. Students who resisted drafting and reviewing their work have developed sophisticated ways to get out of doing it, keeping with their method of writing a single draft at the last minute before the final paper is due. The authors found that using GAFE changed these patterns by making the drafting process transparent and eliminating many of the common excuses students use to avoid it.

Since all drafts in Docs are automatically saved, there was never a problem with typing out a draft and forgetting to save or having a computer accidentally shut down and the document be unrecoverable. Students found this GAFE function liberating since it relieved the worry of losing work; one student wrote that "You don't have to worry if you forget to save. It automatically saves everything you type." But it also introduced a measure of transparency and accountability. Work done in Docs is automatically saved, *and time-stamped, and visible, and can be restored through revision history*. With GAFE, there is no "I forgot it at home" or "my flash drive is corrupt." Google Docs are available from any computer or mobile device with an internet connection. Thus, the student can simply log in and pull up his or her draft from a classroom or campus computer and participate in the workshop. If a student attempts to use former fail-safe strategies for not having a draft, the failure to complete the draft would be immediately apparent and compounded with their untruth about its whereabouts. As a result, students tended to have at least a basic draft posted in the Google Drive folder for workshop days. Instructors noticed a decrease in the number of students who came to class unprepared with drafts, while students themselves reported that they found peer review more valuable than their previous experiences.

With Google Docs the instructor can tell when and what a student types and can witness drafts as they progress. Simply by pulling up revision history (see Figure 4), the instructor can see -- and show to other students -- how a document changed over time, including who made the change, what change was made, how substantial that change was and whether it was in response to a comment from the instructor or a peer. In fact, the authors modeled this feature many times, pulling up documents on the podium computer and projecting them onto the screen for the class to see. Students began to expect that the authors were interested in, and did, indeed review, the revisions they made to their documents. They could no longer change a word or two, or increase the margins of a paper, to make it appear that they had made revisions from a "rough" to a "final" draft. In fact, the concept of a static rough and final was transformed by using GAFE as well. In a composing environment where multiple authors and respondents contribute comments, revisions, and texts at different times, few traditional clues exist to delineate a rough draft from a final draft other than due dates as chronological markers. A peer reviewer's suggestion might prompt revisions that occur after the posted due date for a specific draft. And even after due dates, students are able to comment on others' work and review instructor feedback, itself posted in comments related to content and style, not grades or formal assessment. The composing process *as collaborative process* could be the focus of student and instructor feedback and commentary. The work came to be more about the revision of the document and not about having a deliverable at a deadline.

The collaborative affordances of Google Drive clearly positively affected students' expectations of the experience of peer review (80%), an important aspect of the social nature of composing. Students made connections between the ease of peer review and the effect on their relationship with classmates: comments such as "I liked seeing other classmates opinions" and noting that Google Drive provides an easy way for those opinions and feedback to be shared. In Brown's classes, documents were housed in a shared folder for each assignment, making each student's draft available to all other students in the class. In Hocutt's class, students shared specific assignment folders with a peer review group and the instructor. These pedagogical practices had several positive results. First, in both instructional settings, students were accountable to each other for turning in their drafts. It was obvious, at a glance, whose paper was in the folder and whose was not. Students tend to care about what their peers think (Nelson & DeBacker, 2008), and are also crafting a classroom persona. The knowledge that a student was accountable to their peers, and not just the instructor, for posting a quality draft, was a powerful motivator for many students. They did not want to look bad in front of their peers, so they ensured they had something posted that was acceptable. One student echoed others' sentiment by saying that "the ability to share each others documents allows not only for feedback from other students but also allows people to get an idea of what other people have written." Students were viewing each others' documents as part of their own learning process, and this awareness of practice helped them to be more accountable to each other.

Our different implementations of Google Drive sharing -- Brown's with instructor-owned folders shared with all students, Hocutt's with student-owned folders shared with a peer editing group -- allowed students to both comment on any other student's paper, as well as read the comments posted by others on their papers. This transparency required a large amount of vulnerability and trust on the part of the students. In response, the authors both sought to prepare students for "the unique technological components" of technology-facilitated peer review as encouraged by OWI principle 10 (CCCC, 2013), and carefully modeled peer review in Google Docs through whole class discussion and individual and collective student practice. The authors continued to model and direct peer review throughout the semester, through the tenor of their comments in student papers in Google Docs and in their replies to other students' comments they had offered to their peers. The fact that other students could read comments given to them by a peer or the instructor -- something that was previously private between the peer reviewer and instructor or student -- caused many students to take immediate interest and action in the comments they received. For a few students, it was not uncommon for them to read, reflect on, and respond to comments given on their papers within hours of receiving them. They simply did not want the evidence of their possible shortcomings remaining visible in their document. And some simply didn't like the "mess" of the comment streams with their talk bubbles and different colored texts marring their document. Their urge to organize and clean up caused them to revise their document, engaging them in the writing process as a result of their interaction with the GAFE interface. The comments on their document were distributed to them via an email to their college Gmail account. For many, these emails appear as notifications on their mobile devices. The prompting of the notification urged the student to take action, in much the same way as they might reply to a Facebook post or comment on an Instagram photo.

Since all student drafts were either already available to all classmates (Brown's implementation), or easily shared with specific classmates (Hocutt's implementation), from a single interface, the instructors could assign spontaneous writing workshops, organizing students into heterogeneous groups based on previously demonstrated strengths and weakness, or on interests and topics that complemented each other. Students could work with a recurrent writing group, but then obtain a second peer review from another classmate. This practice allowed students to obtain a diversity of opinions on their drafts, while also having the ability to develop a closer relationship with a core group of peer reviewers they could work with assignment to assignment. This practice also fostered OWI principle 11, which calls on teachers and institutions to "develop personalized and interpersonal online communities to foster student success" (CCCC, 2013). While this can be done with printed copies of a paper draft and students circulating in a classroom, with Google Docs, the comments become visible to others, and those comments became ideas that the next peer reviewer can also interact with (see Figure 3). Reviewer 1's comments may agree or disagree with Reviewer 2's thoughts. Reading Reviewer 1's comments may cause Reviewer 2 to consider something s/he would not have on his/her own. The two reviewers enter a conversation with each other and with the primary writer. Multiple reviewers can comment on a document using a word processing program such as Microsoft Word, but in such programs only one person can view and comment on the document at a time. Reviewer 2 would have to wait until Reviewer 1 finished commenting and exited the document. The original author would have to wait until both Reviewers were finished to read and respond to any comments made using track changes. In GAFE, both R1 and R2 can simultaneously review a piece, and the original author can choose to watch responses unfold. This creates a much more dynamic interface and a sense of immediacy with the writing process. The review and revision happens before the writer's eyes. One student remarked, "I like to get comments when I am not done so I can see what to change, look over or just to hear a 'good job.'"

Pervasive Pedagogy: Composition Transformed

Using GAFE remediates the composing experience by shifting from computer-based, individually licensed, and often expensive software to free, cloud-based, pervasive composing and collaboration tool. This remediation of the composing experience accomplishes the work encouraged by OWI principle 4, which calls on teachers and WPAs to migrate and adapt "appropriate onsite composition theories, pedagogies, and strategies" to the online -- or, in this case, to the cloud-based pervasive composing -- environment (CCCC, 2013). This remediation occurred in several different ways.

First, a digital networked environment through cloud computing allows students to collaborate not only when they are together in space and time, but also when they are available and have access to the required technology and internet access. Furthermore, while face-to-face groupwork can also require collaboration outside of class, the students we teach at open-access commuter campuses, particularly those who are considered "non-traditional," have an even more difficult time coordinating schedules around family and work responsibilities. Since GAFE is a web-based service that requires only a network device connected to the internet along with a browser or mobile app, using the GAFE apps expands the temporal and spatial limits of our classroom beyond our allotted class time, shifting agency for participation from instructor and school schedule to student. Being able to work beyond the standard class time breaks the learning environment out of the classroom, into the lived experience of the students, including home and workplace, among other possibilities. The Google Docs interface is replicated in the various physical environments students inhabit and is a constant familiarity, a standard "place" to go and meet peers. The familiar interface and functionality across platforms represents the universal and accessible character of GAFE, important pedagogical affordances that reflect the call of OWI principle 1 for instruction to be "universally inclusive and accessible" (CCCC, 2013). The GAFE free, collaborative composing environment is available 24 hours a day, seven days a week, without scheduled downtime, which allows for an anywhere/anytime opportunity for learning.

Second, as visualized above, GAFE reveals processes and retains traces of the entire composing process. Each file contains a comprehensive revision history that includes both changes made and the identity of the account making the change. Comments are also archived; even when comments are resolved, the entire history of the comment, including any discussion made about the comment, remains available for review. These traces encourage accountability among students and instructors alike, to themselves and to the other members of the class, for their full engagement in the collaborative composing process. Students and teachers alike can access existing and previous work, enabling all to review the entire composing process. Teachers are offered a unique opportunity to view composing practices in real time, to coach when needed and model as appropriate. Teachers can interact with students during any moment of the process of composing, not just during class time or during a review session or in comments on a rough draft or final submission. As importantly, other students can view these same processes and traces, extending their learning beyond their own compositions. Access to the entire composing process makes the experience explicitly social, transparent among members of the class and/or peer review group. We can integrate metacognitive reflection on their own and others' composing processes as part of the social learning experience. Reviewing the traces of the composing process offers students and teachers access to procedural patterns. A metacognitive focus on these traces (facilitated and modeled at first by the teacher) enforces and reinforces the iterative nature of composing.

Being able to see revision history makes grading process, rather than a product, much more viable. Danowski (2006) and Warnock (2008) reiterate the importance of low-stakes composing exercises for successful digital composition instruction. By developing low-stakes checkpoints within the same document or shared folder -- like an invention submission and peer responses to the invention; an incomplete draft and corresponding peer and instructor responses; a full draft for review and multiple reviews of others' drafts; a full revision with peer and instructor feedback; and a final version for grading that incorporates peer and instructor responses -- instructors shift the focus of review and assessment from the various products submitted throughout a semester or term to the iterative process of composing. Low-stakes assessment and review checkpoints throughout the entire process, made possible in a single interface in Google Docs, relieve the pressure of high-stakes final drafts and the inconvenience of multiple submissions throughout a term. Although digital writing assessment is a practice whose implications and procedures remain in flux (McKee & DeVoss, 2013), the ability to view and provide feedback on all parts of the composing processing is a powerful affordance that encourages new methods for formal and informal assessment practices and methods.

Third, the performative and collaborative nature of activity in GAFE is explicitly visible: all users synchronously accessing the file are listed with avatars at the top of each file, and all activity in the comments archive, chats, and revision history are identified by user account. All of the activities in which students participate, from invention strategies to graded drafts, are designed to be socially accomplished, in collaborative spaces with one or more people from the class (students or instructors).

The longer students use Google Docs in collaborative composing, the more comfortable they become with the idea that writing is social. The GAFE explicitly visible account avatars, along with archiving features, remind students that they are never writing for themselves. This exemplifies the social turn in composition, but we contend that awareness of others in collaborative composing, whether synchronous or asynchronous, goes beyond traditional understandings of composition's social turn and replaces the experience of the lone writer with the experience of a writer within a supportive composing community. As students compose in a collaborative environment, they continually navigate social tensions, engage in knowledge making and undergo habituation through repeated and iterative processes. The GAFE collaborative interface enables students and teachers alike to participate in dynamic social relationships. In groups and as a class, students work on composing processes that alternately call upon strengths of different members of the groups and class. The dynamism of participants means habits and processes can't be static. In order to complete composing assignments, students and teachers must engage with different group members, participate in different scaffolded activities, and navigate the process of reaching consensus when working in a group. As a collaborative networked space, students are continually navigating the power relationships inherent in classroom environments (e.g. self-perceived stronger and weaker writers, non-native and native language users, teacher and student) through their composing activities. Although such navigation is also present in f2f classes, Google Drive-mediated composing relies almost entirely on written text as the primary mode of communication, further reinforcing the rhetorical nature of composition and the need for carefully considered and composed prose.

Last, GAFE enables teachers to step aside, to avoid being a bottleneck in the teaching and composing processes. Instead of students performing for the teacher -- which, given the political dynamics of the classroom, is somewhat unavoidable -- students are performing with and for one another in a shared situation toward a common goal. As instructors, we are free to flip the instructional focus from "sage on the stage" to "guide on the side," to join the composing processes as participants, as facilitators, as coaches and cheerleaders. With agency in the hands of the students, they are free to engage in creating knowledge collaboratively, regardless of whether the instructor is facilitating the process.

CONCLUSION

This primary research demonstrates that cloud-based technologies such as GAFE afford new opportunities for collaborative cross-platform composing and student engagement, and that new pedagogies are required to transform these potentialities into practice. GAFE is easily adapted to multiple instructional environments. Although our experience largely represents f2f instruction, we also experimented with blended, asynchronous, and synchronous online class sessions and found GAFE equally capable and relevant. In fact, Hocutt found GAFE far more reliable during a synchronous online session than the institution's LMS, while Brown maintained instructional continuity while traveling overseas using GAFE's pervasive and continuous accessibility. Affordances are also easily adapted to instructor teaching styles and data control preferences, as reflected in the different folder sharing implementations Brown and Hocutt enacted in their classrooms. And because GAFE is easily adapted to teaching styles, it's also easily adapted to the institutionally mandated and/or instructor and students' preferred location of teaching and learning, whether it be the traditional classroom, a computer/technology lab, an off campus location, or the online environment.

The Google Drive interface enables several collaborative affordances, including synchronous chat within the file -- meaning conversations can be held parallel to, but not outside of, the primary composing space, the "page" on the screen. The same composing space can also contain selection-specific or file wide commenting, tracked by user and even threaded to a limited extent. These comments can be responded to and resolved, allowing composers to engage one another about general or specific aspects of their compositions. Commenting is available in synchronous or asynchronous modes, so time and space are not factors in commentary. This enables teachers to shift peer reviewing to an asynchronous mode, if they wish. Google Drive also tracks all changes and allows file sharers to view those changes. Finally, GAFE includes features that extend the composing environment, including Google+ Hangouts. In Hangouts, up to six people can network by telephone or video feed simultaneously, and they can open Google Drive files and other Google products (like Blogger or Google search) in the Hangouts interface to collaborate on the document while video chatting. The result is that GAFE combines the affordances of several technologies: threaded discussion forum, office suite (including word processor, spreadsheet, presentation, and drawing applications), video chat, real-time SMS chat, and word processor revision tracking and recording.

Students who used GAFE were able to interact with the technology, the instructor and each other beyond the 2.5 hours per week of the f2f classroom, and reported doing so from a variety of devices and locations. The single interface of GAFE made the composing, communication, and collaboration process simple, ubiquitous, transparent, and continuous. Students reported more interaction with their drafts, and more attention to revision based on comments from peers and instructors. Through engagement with the technology, students engaged with the course content, each other, and the writing process, reporting that their experiences with the course content, activities, peers, and instructors were better than they expected. In implementing this technology, instructors created and used a Collaborative Cross-Platform Cloud-Based Pedagogy that was based in theory and praxis from Online Writing Instruction (OWI), Interactive Computer Technology (ICT), and rhetoric and composition studies. More research is needed to further support the ways this pedagogy, enabled and enacted through GAFE, benefits student learning within and beyond the traditional boundaries of a composition classroom or course.

The authors have not promoted specific practices that can or should be implemented in the face of the remediated composing experience afforded by GAFE. This has been intentional. Their experiences and pedagogical decisions were influenced by personal and professional preferences, institutional policies and procedures, student capabilities and access to technology, and a host of additional local considerations too numerous to include. These are the situational variables of our profession, and each teacher must develop practices in response to these variables. What we discovered, and what we promote in this chapter, is that GAFE -- and potentially other pervasive cloud-based collaborative composing tools that are in development and will be released in the future -- fundamentally changes the way we and our students think about composing. This fundamental change requires an equally fundamental response in composition theory and composing praxis. Grounded in OWI principles and careful attention to the primacy of pedagogy over technology in the composition classroom, and supported with the results of primary research, the authors imagine this chapter as a theoretical foundation for scholars and teachers to begin the process of developing pedagogical practices and assessment tools that take full advantage of pervasive collaborative composing using cloud-based tools. The authors, too, commit themselves to this task, taking to heart the encouragement to conduct "ongoing research into their programs and courses" found in OWI principle 15 (CCCC, 2013).

AUTHORS' NOTE

Google Apps for Education was renamed G Suite for Education as this volume was going to press.

REFERENCES

Barrett, H. C. (2006). Using electronic portfolios for formative/classroom-based assessment. *Classroom Connect Connected Newsletter, 13*(2). Retrieved from https://electronicportfolios.org/portfolios/ConnectedNewsletter.pdf

Bazerman, C. (1994). Systems of genre and the enactment of social intentions. In A. Freedman & P. Medway (Eds.), *Genre and the new rhetoric* (pp. 79–104). London, UK: Taylor & Francis, Ltd.

Bazerman, C. (2004). Speech acts, genres, and activity systems: How texts organize activities and people. In C. Bazerman & P. Prior (Eds.), *What writing does and how it does it: An introduction to analyzing texts and textual practices* (pp. 309–340). New York, NY: Routledge.

Bezemer, J., & Kress, G. (2008). Writing in multimodal texts: A social semiotic account of designs for learning. *Written Communication, 25*(2), 166–195. doi:10.1177/0741088307313177

Bowie, J. L. (2012). Rhetorical roots and media future: How podcasting fits into the computers and writing classroom [Audio podcast]. *Kairos, 16*(2). Retrieved from http://technorhetoric.net/16.2/topoi/bowie/index.html

boyd, d. (2007). Why youth (heart) social network sites: The role of networked publics in teenage social life. In D. Buckingham (Ed.), *Youth, Identity, and Digital Media*. Cambridge, MA: The MIT Press.

Brandt, J. E. (2012). Google Apps for Education and accessibility: Review of research. *Maine CITE*.

Breuch, L. K. (2005). Enhancing online collaboration: Virtual peer review in the writing classroom. In K. C. Cook & K. Grant-Davie (Eds.), *Online education: Global questions, local answers* (pp. 141–156). Farmingdale, NY: Baywood.

Brown, M. E., & Hocutt, D. L. (in press). All composition is local, even in the Googleverse: Glocalizing the composition classroom with Google Apps for Education. In R. Rice & K. St.Amant (Eds.), *Thinking globally, composing locally: Rethinking online writing in the age of the global internet*. Boulder, CO: University Press of Colorado.

CCCC. (2013, March). A position statement of principles and example effective practices for online writing instruction (OWI). *National Council of Teachers of English*. Retrieved from http://www.ncte.org/cccc/resources/positions/owiprinciples

Clark, J. E. (2010). The digital imperative: Making the case for a 21st-century pedagogy. *Computers and Composition, 27*(1), 27–35. doi:10.1016/j.compcom.2009.12.004

Cook, K. C. (2005). An argument for pedagogy-driven online education. In K. C. Cook & K. Grant-Davie (Eds.), *Online education: Global questions, local answers*. Farmingdale, NY: Baywood Publishers. Baywood's Technical Communications Series.

Cuestas, A., & Fazzi, V. (2012). The use of ICTs in the English class: An enriching experience. *Puertas Abiertas,* (8). Retrieved from http://www.memoria.fahce.unlp.edu.ar/art_revistas/pr.6019/pr.6019.pdf

Danowski, D. (2006). Anyone? Anyone? Anyone? Leading discussions in cyberspace: e-Journals and interactivity in asynchronous environments. In J. Alexander & M. Dickson (Eds.), *Role Play: Distance Learning and the Teaching of Writing* (pp. 97–108). Cresskill, NJ: Hampton Press.

Davis, M., & Yancey, K. B. (2014). Notes toward the role of materiality in composing, reviewing, and assessing multimodal texts. *Computers and Composition, 31*, 13–28. doi:10.1016/j.compcom.2014.01.001

DePew, K. E., & Lettner-Rust, H. (2009). Mediating power: Distance learning interfaces, classroom epistemology, and the gaze. *Computers and Composition, 26*(3), 174–189. doi:10.1016/j.compcom.2009.05.002

DePew, K. E., Spangler, S., & Spiegel, C. L. (2014). Getting past our assumptions about Web 2.0 and community building: How to design research-based literacy pedagogy. In M. Limbu & B. Gurung (Eds.), *Emerging Pedagogies in the Networked Knowledge Society: Practices Integrating Social Media and Globalization* (pp. 120–143). Hershey, PA: IGI Global. Retrieved from.

DeVellis, R. F. (2012). *Scale development: Theory and application* (3rd ed.). Los Angeles, CA: Sage Publications, Inc.

Duffy, J. (2014, April 2). *The best cloud storage solutions*. Retrieved August 30, 2014, from http://www.pcmag.com/article2/0%2c2817%2c2413556%2c00.asp

Eyman, D., & Ball, C. E. (2014). Composing for digital publication: Rhetoric, design, code. *Composition Studies, 42*(1), 114–117.

Gaillet, L. L. (2009). A socially constructed view of reading and writing: Historical alternatives to "Bridging the Gap.". In L. Ostergaard, J. Ludwig, & J. Nugent (Eds.), *Transforming English studies: New voices in an emerging genre* (pp. 163–178). West Lafayette, IN: Parlor Press. Lauer Series in Rhetoric and Composition.

Gee, J. P., & Hayes, E. (2011). *Language and learning in the digital age*. New York: Routledge.

Google Apps Help. (2014). Google Apps user guide to accessibility. *Google Apps Help Center*. Retrieved from https://support.google.com/a/answer/1631886?hl=en&ref_topic=3035040

Gurung, B. (2014). Emerging pedagogies in the networked knowledge communities. In M. Limbu & B. Gurung (Eds.), *Emerging Pedagogies in the Networked Knowledge Society: Practices Integrating Social Media and Globalization*. Hershey, PA: IGI Global. doi:10.4018/978-1-4666-4757-2.ch001

Halasek, K., McCorkle, B., Selfe, C. L., DeWitt, S. L., Delagrange, S., Michaels, J., & Clinnin, K. (2014). A MOOC with a view: How MOOCs encourage us to reexamine pedagogical doxa. In Invasion of the MOOCs: The promises and perils of massive open online courses (pp. 156-166). Anderson, SC: Parlor Press.

James, R. (2014). ICT's participatory potential in higher education collaborations: Reality or just talk. *British Journal of Educational Technology, 45*(4), 557–570. doi:10.1111/bjet.12060

Latour, B. (2005). *Reassembling the social: An introduction to actor-network-theory*. Oxford, UK: Oxford University Press. Clarendon Lectures in Management Studies.

Limbu, M. (2013). Digital and global literacies in networked communities: Epistemic shifts and communication practices in the cloud era. In G. Verhulsdonck & M. Limbu (Eds.), *Digital Rhetoric and Global Literacies: Communication Modes and Digital Practices in the Networked World*. Hershey, PA: IGI Global. Retrieved from.

McKee, H. A., & DeVoss, D. N. (Eds.). (2013). Digital writing assessment & evaluation. Logan, UT: Computers and Composition Digital Press/Utah State University Press. Retrieved from http://ccdigitalpress.org/dwae

Miller, C. R. (1984). Genre as social action. *The Quarterly Journal of Speech*, *70*(2), 151–167. doi:10.1080/00335638409383686

Miller, C. R. (1994). Rhetorical community: The cultural basis of genre. In A. Freedman & P. Medway (Eds.), *Genre and the new rhetoric* (pp. 67–78). London, UK: Taylor & Francis, Ltd.

Neff, J. M., & Whithaus, C. (2008). *Writing across distances & disciplines: Research and pedagogy in distributed learning*. New York, NY: Lawrence Erlbaum Associates.

Nelson, R. M., & DeBacker, T. K. (2008). Achievement Motivation in Adolescents: The Role of Peer Climate and Best Friends. *Journal of Experimental Education*, *76*(2), 170–189. doi:10.3200/JEXE.76.2.170-190

Porter, J. E. (2014). Framing questions about MOOCs and writing courses. In Invasion of the MOOCs: The promises and perils of massive open online courses (pp. 14-28). Anderson, SC: Parlor Press.

Reid, A. (2008). Portable composition: iTunes University and networked pedagogies. *Computers and Composition*, *25*(1), 62–78. doi:10.1016/j.compcom.2007.09.003

Rice, J. (2006). Networks and new media. *College English*, *69*(2), 127–133. doi:10.2307/25472197

Robins, S. (2007, October 24). *Second Life in education* [Video file]. Retrieved from http://youtu.be/ueAcz7ZyFpM

Rowe, M., Bozalek, V., & Frantz, J. (2013). Using Google Drive to facilitate a blended approach to authentic learning: Authentic learning and Google Drive. *British Journal of Educational Technology*, *44*(4), 594–606. doi:10.1111/bjet.12063

Schuetze, H. G., & Slowey, M. (2002). Participation and exclusion: A comparative analysis of non-traditional students and lifelong learners in higher education. *Higher Education*, *44*(3/4), 309–327. doi:10.1023/A:1019898114335

Tulley, C. (2013). Migration patterns: A status report on the transition from paper to eportfolios and the effect on multimodal composition initiatives. *Computers and Composition*, *30*(2), 101–114. doi:10.1016/j.compcom.2013.03.002

Warnock, S. (2009). *Teaching writing online: How & why*. Urbana, IL: National Council of Teachers of English.

Yancey, K. B. (2004). Made not only in words: Composition in a new key. *College Composition and Communication*, *56*(2), 297–328. doi:10.2307/4140651

Yu, R. (2014, May 2). Cable companies expand public Wi-Fi for customer loyalty. *USA Today*. Retrieved August 29, 2014, from http://www.usatoday.com/story/money/business/2014/04/30/cable-wifi/8525347/

KEY TERMS AND DEFINITIONS

24/7 Availability: In general, refers to continuous uptime of network services and users' ability to access network-based resources at any time.

Affordances: Capabilities or uses offered by a design element or technology and perceived as beneficial by the user. Based on the work of James Gibson and Don Norman.

Cloud-Based: Internet-based storage solutions accessed using a secured login, often via web browser. Files are stored on servers not owned by the individual, organization, or institution using the files and are accessible to the user at any time from a variety of platforms and devices.

Collaborative Composing: Use of multi-user technology to accomplish synchronous and asynchronous writing or creation among a group of users.

Constraints: Limits to use available in a design element or technology. Generally opposed to affordances. Based on the work of James Gibson and Don Norman.

Google Apps for Education (GAFE): The suite of cloud-based applications available from Google for educational use. Although this chapter focuses on Docs and Drive, other applications include Sheets, Slides, Forms, Gmail, Hangouts, and more. In October 2016, GAFE was renamed G Suite for Education.

Learning Management System (LMS): The Web-based tool used by educational institutions to manage instructional tasks and services. Among often-used systems are Blackboard and Canvas.

Networked Knowledge Communities (NKC): Sometimes referred to as a community of practice or a virtual community of practice, Networked Knowledge Communities are distinguished from a social network of individuals by a shared responsibility and outcome(s). Members collaborate together to create and construct knowledge.

Non-Traditional Student: A growing population of students in higher education, these students are often age 25 and up, non-residential, part-time, working a full-time or part-time job, supporting a family, or a combination of these.

Pervasive Pedagogy: Instruction that is not constrained by the confines of classtime, classroom space, or a particular hardware or device, but that is available and provided at any time, from multiple platforms.

ENDNOTES

1 We echo the CCCC's "A Position Statement of Principles and Example Effective Practices for Online Writing Instruction (OWI)" in seeking universal accessibility for instructional technology. GAFE is not universally accessible, but we have recently seen Google make efforts to address this concern. Brandt (2012) notes that "Google has expressed some willingness to achieve success in

terms of accessibility of the product and continues to work in that direction," while Google Apps Help (2014) offers accessible affordances for each of its Apps. In this case, we are referring more specifically to the affordances widespread wifi, browsers, devices, and applications offer users to access GAFE applications and services.

2 We chose two different Likert-type scales to reflect the different kinds of questions we posed. As advocated by DeVellis (2012), questions regarding preference used an even number of options on the Likert and Likert-Type scales to avoid a default to the middle, rather than making a choice. However, when asking participants about how their expectations matched their experience, we chose a five-point scale with a mid-point value -- "matched my expectations" -- that fell directly between the "better than expected" or "worse than expected" values. We chose a five-point scale rather than a three-point scale to provide students the opportunity to make nuanced distinctions between the declarative "worse than expected" or "better than expected" values and the less distinct "somewhat worse or better" values.

Chapter 8
New Media and Technology:
How Do They Change the Notions of the Rhetorical Situations?

Ramesh Pokharel
University of Toronto, Canada

ABSTRACT

New media and technology have an overall impact in our lives including the way we write and read a text, and teach writing. By altering our literacy practices, new media and technology always create a new situation, and require the users to use it in a defined way, and "to explain what a tool [technology] is and how to use it seems to demand narrative" (Nye, 2006, p. 5). In this chapter, the author creates a narrative that tells stories how new media and technology have created a new situation to redefine/reexamine/remap/revive the existing notions of the rhetorical situation. The author begins by offering a definition of new media and technology, and the impact of new media and technology in changing the notions of the rhetorical situation. The author then discusses how new media and technology has changed the notions of the rhetorical situation.

INTRODUCTION

Humans had technologies before they invented language. For example, humans had skills or tools for hunting food before they learned to use human language systematically. People have used technology as a medium to do something in a better way and communicate across space and time from time immemorial, as Nye (2006) says, "One way to define 'technology' is in terms of evolution" (p. 1). Technology is so much attached with evolution that it is "not foreign to 'human nature' but inseparable from it" and "technologies have been used for social evolution" (Nye, 2006, p. 2). Technologies are characterized as social evolution, and as an ever-changing, ever-advancing site, because they always facilitate human lives with the supply of tools and methodologies to meet their necessities, which humans continually redefine to suit their needs (Nye, 2006, p. 2). However, there are mutual relationships between necessity and technology: most of the time necessity engenders technologies, and sometimes technologies (tools) generate necessity. So, "Technologies are not just objects but also the skills needed to use them"

DOI: 10.4018/978-1-5225-1650-7.ch008

(Nye, 2006, p. 4), hence both object and process. The ancient Greeks used the word "techne" instead of technology which had to do with skills in the arts that meant rational faculty used in making something, and a productive quality exercised in combination with true reasoning.

Over time, technology has advanced and become more complex thereby making human consciousness more complex. Consequently, linear media such as print failed to capture the structure of our thought. As an intellectual predicament of the second half of the twentieth century, we experienced flickering focus, a deferral of meaning between the signifier and the signified. On this backdrop, geared up by advanced technology (digital technology), new media, as a new medium of human expression, was born as "a sign of our current confusion about where these efforts are leading and our breathlessness at the place of change" (Murray, 2003, p. 3). Though communication scholar, Marshall McLuhan, first used the term "new media" in 1953, "the term really emerged in the late 1990s when it began to be used as an all-encompassing description for emerging and digital technologies" (Smith & Hendricks, 2010, p. 4). So, new media is usually associated with the spread of information digitally that is characterized by computer-mediated forms of production, distribution and communication. Smith and Hendricks (2012) argue that new media surpasses just digital communication and just the technology that made it possible. For them:

It has become associated with converged, computerized, networked, interactive and compressible technologies and information. If we go with this all-encompassing definition, we are primarily talking about only the technology that truly makes it new media. For many, the definition goes even further. It is not just the technology, but it is the way in which we interact with the technology that truly makes it new media. (Smith & Hendricks, 2012, p. 5)

Like Smith and Hendricks, Kember and Zylinska (2012), in *Life after New Media,* extends the definition of new media even further. They make a significant shift in the way new media is perceived and understood "as a set of discrete objects…to understanding media [new media] predominantly in terms of processes of mediation" (p. xiii). For them, new media as processes of mediation "is a complex and hybrid process that is simultaneously economic, social, cultural, psychological, and technical" (Kember & Zylinska, 2012, p. xv). This can be a big debate on new media scholarship, but I am not going to explore this issue here because of my research limitation. I will define new media only in terms of its technological feature that could be useful in our discipline.

We cannot move along without new media and technology because new media and technology is inevitable in our lives, and has so much impacted our lives that we have become cyborg both physically and mentally. As a powerful means to master the complexity of life, new media has enabled us to understand complex world around us, and, thus, helped us to "refigure our bodies, our cultures, ourselves in hopeful ways" (Murray, 2003, p. 5). Many scholars have felt the need to define new media and technology. So, there have been many efforts to define and explain new media and technology. However, "[e]fforts to understand, explain, and analyze the new media are demanding and endlessly complex" (Dennis, 1998, p. xi), because, as Lievrouw and Livingstone (2002) believe, new media has been defined in terms of technological, economic, behavioral, and critical/cultural issues that deal with system features and services, industry structure and ownership, psychology of media users, and content and forms, respectively. I divide this chapter into two broad parts: definition of new media and technology, and the impact of new media and technology in changing the notions of the rhetorical situation. While in the first part, I delineate the definitions of new media primarily in terms of technology, in the second part, I discuss how new media and technology has changed the notions of the rhetorical situation.

DEFINING NEW MEDIA AND TECHNOLOGY

When we define new media in terms of the technological aspect, it refers to a number of system features and services new media inherently has. Lister, Dovey, Giddings, Grant, and Kelly's (2009) list that sums up the features of new media can be useful to define it. According to them, new media refers to the following: new textual experiences (new kind of genre and textual form); new way of representing the world; new relationships between subjects (users and consumers) and media technologies; new experiences of the relationship between embodiment, identity and community; new conceptions of the biological body's relationship to technological media; new pattern of organization and production; computer-mediated communication; new ways of distributing and consuming; virtual 'realities'; a whole range of transformations and dislocations of established media (pp. 12-13). From these enumerations of the characteristics of new media, they derive some defining concepts that are essential qualities of new media: digital, interactive, hypertextual, virtual, networked, and simulated (Lister, Dovey, Giddings, Grant, & Kelly, 2009, p. 13). In what follows, I will define new media and technology under some headings, and discuss and explain these essential qualities.

Computerization: The Heart of New Media and Technology

As Lievrouw and Livingston (2002) argue, "Undoubtedly, most definitions of new media and ICTs [information and communication technologies] to date have focused on their technological features" (p. 5), computerization in particular and technology in general is the pivotal force to give birth to new media. New media (the Internet, Web sites, computer multimedia, computer games, CD-ROMs, DVD, and electronic books, for example) is usually defined as something that created a massive transformation of the old media (television, film, and publishing) on the basis of computer-based production, storage, and distribution of information. The basis for this transition to computer-based production, storage, and distribution is technology. Dizard's (2000) statement reconfirms the argument that computerization is the heart of new media and technology:

This new media pattern is qualitatively different from earlier ones [old media] in several ways. One technology—computerization—is now the module for all forms of electronic information: sound, video, and print....Computers are forcing a massive restructuring of older media services and, at the same time, creating a new set of competing services. (p. 28)

Computer-mediated forms of production, distribution, and communication as a massive restructuring agent of a new media has changed the face of old media in such a way that it has transformed television sets "from passive receivers of distant pictures into multimedia interactive instruments, capable of handling all types of video, print, and sound services" (Dizard, 2000, p. 28). Manovich (2001) also believes that the use of computers for distribution and exhibition of information and communication is what identifies a new media, different from old media, as a new media. He explains the difference between old media and new media with *examples in this way:*

...texts distributed on a computer (Web sites and electronic books) are considered to be new media, whereas text distributed on paper are not. Similarly, photographs that are put on a CD-ROM and require a computer to be viewed are considered new media; the same photographs printed in a book are not. (Manovich, 2001, p. 19)

New media has, thus, revolutionized the production, distribution, and communication of information more profoundly than the previous ones, and it is able to do this with the use of computer thereby affecting all stages of communication (acquisition, manipulation, storage, and distribution), and all types of media (texts, still images, motion picture, sound, and spatial construction). In the center of these changes that new media brought is its ability for networking, and using all forms of computing. Further defining new media, Manovich (2003) says, "new media are the cultural objects which use digital computer technology for distribution and exhibition. Thus, Internet, Web sites, computer multimedia, computer games, CD-ROMs and DVDs, virtual reality, and computer-generated special effects all fall under new media" (pp. 16-17), and, for mass exhibition and distribution, it uses digital data that could be manipulated by software based on the principle of numerical representation, modularity, automation, variability, and transcoding.

It is necessary, here, to talk about how new media uses digital data—known as digitization—to store, process, transmit, and retrieve the data in more advanced way that in non-digital (analogue) text. Goggin (2012) explains digitization in very lucid way:

Simply put, the stuff of media [new media]—words, texts, images, sounds, sensations and design—can be converted to a stream of ones and zeros (binary code). This fundamental encoding of what otherwise is non-digital...into digital form has profound implications. It allows media [new media] to be stored, transmitted, communicated, retrieved, inspected and enjoyed across what were thought to be previously distinct areas of the media [new media]. (p. 14)

As mentioned above, new media use digital data that make mass exhibition and distribution of information possible. It involves conversion, processing and storing of all input data in numbers which "are 'dematerialized'; ...can be compressed into very small spaces; ...can be accessed at very high speeds and in non-linear ways;... can be manipulated far more easily than analogue forms" (Lister et al., 2009, p. 18). Thus, by assigning numerical value to phenomena, the data is decoded and received as screen displays and as sound. However, without intending to discount the value of digitality in the making of new media, Wysocki (2004) defines new media in terms of materiality instead of digitality in order to give justice to the importance of materiality in new media, because she believes "to look at texts only through their technological [digital] origin is to deflect our attentions from what we might achieve mindful that textual practices are always broader than the technological" (p. 19). For her, materiality of texts comprises of the making process and the contexts which makes the texts easily accessible not only for its composers but also the readers. It is materiality that helps "readers/consumers/viewers stay alert to how any text... doesn't function independently of how it is made and in what context" (Wysocki, 2004, p. 15). Thus, any text that has been designed with sufficient focus on the context and process of making thereby not effacing its materiality can count as new media. For Wysocki (2004), materiality is important aspect of new media also because it gives agency to the reader as she asserts it "helps us see where openings for agency are within the new media texts we compose" (p. 15), because the various materialities of new media help the readers understand how it is read and understood, and how the compositing process, how words and visual representation, for example, function and relate. As discussed above, computerization as a primary feature of new media that distinguishes it basically from old media, and defines its inherent qualities, also contributes to its definition as a multimodal site which I discuss next.

Multimodality

Since new media uses the most advanced technology in processing, storing, distribution, and exhibition of digital data controlled by software, it is natural to expect that it will fully obey the principles of modularity, variability, and automation. However, it does not always do so; it can be seen as a multimodal site that combines both traditional and modern means of presenting data and genres. In this context, Manovich (2003) stresses this mix: "new media today can be understood as the mix between older cultural conventions for data representation, access, and manipulation and newer conventions of data representation, access, and manipulation" (p. 19). This mix is possible also because new media is fundamentally multimodal.

Selfe (2004a) believes that new media is "created primarily in digital environments, composed in multiple media (e.g., film, video, audio, among others), and designed for presentation and exchange in digital venues" (p. 43). Sorapure (2006) echoes Selfe, Kress, van Leeuwen, and Ball, when she talks about multimodality of composing in new media, "composing in new media usually involves bringing together multiple modes—text, image, sound, animation, and/or video—in order to convey a meaning or create an effect" (p. 4). While so doing, new media challenges containment of alphabetical systems of the print (old media) which privileges only reading thereby making the readers only receivers of information thereby demanding the multiple literacies of seeing, listening, writing, and even allowing readers to manipulate the information. The physical/material/aesthetic characteristics of new media make it appealing, because, as Selfe (2004a) says, "they are often richly textured with combination of visual elements, sound, and words; they are interactive and often hypertextual, and they can be aesthetically pleasing…" (p. 44). Unlike old media, new media, thus, attaches more importance on visuals and sound and makes it richly textured. While so doing, it demands visual literacy from both the authors and readers. By visual literacy, Selfe (2004b) means:

the ability to read, understand, value, and learn from visual materials (still photographs, videos, films, animations, still images, pictures, drawings, graphics)…as well as the ability to create, combine, and use visual elements (e.g., colors, forms, lines, images) and messages for the purpose of communicating. (p. 69)

Multimodality better expresses the mode of communication today, because it can express various modes and communicative experiences in a most truthful way, and visual literacy is one color we cannot ignore to make communication complete. In this context, both Kress (1999) and Hocks (2003) value the importance of visual rhetoric in new media. Like Hocks (2003) says, "Its [visual rhetoric] importance has been amplified by the visual and interactive nature of native hypertext and multimedia writing" (p. 629), Kress (1999) also suggests the increasing emphasis on the visual presentation of information, and the challenge to alphabetical texts by visual text in new media:

The visual is becoming more prominent in many domains of public communication. From a different perspective this is to realize that written language is being displaced from its hitherto unchallenged central position in the semiotic landscape, and that the visual is taking over many of the functions of written language. (p. 68)

Visual literacy has become an essential aspect of new media and technology (Selfe, 2004a; Selfe, 2004b; Kress, 1999; Costanzo, 1994; and Reynolds, 2004), and, in her article "The Movement of Air, the Breath of Meaning: Aurality and Multimodal Composing," Selfe (2009) adds a dimension in multimodality, i. e. aurality, while talking about "the need to pay attention to *both* writing and aurality, *and* other composing modalities, as well" (p. 618). While Costanzo (1994) argues that "the visual composition of a message, whether a movie or an advertisement, represents a large part of its meaning" and "computers seem to reinforce this notion by drawing more attention to the visual aspects of text" (p. 15), Reynolds (2004) asserts that "new technologies are generating more attention to visual culture" (p. 63). Reynolds (2004) also talks about how new media and technology has contributed to the ubiquity of visual literacy as "screen culture:"

The terms visual literacy or visual rhetoric are becoming more common as well; that is, the ability to "read" images critically, analyze the way they work, and choose or design images that communicate effectively....There's a direct correlation, of course, between the rise of (visual-based) electronic technologies—screen culture—and the scholarly or pedagogical interest in visual literacy. (p. 64)

New media and technology, thus, creates a differently configured communicational world by making it so much inherently multimodal that "[e]ven visual modes, such as television and billboards, are interwoven with speech, writing and sign" (Aitchison & Lewis, 2003, p. 1). This new communicational world provides many choices to design new media text in any mode, genre, ensembles of modes and genres in any occasion. This flexibility opens up "new possibility of arrangements, the new grammars of multimodal texts" (Kress, 2003, p. 117). In this way, new media and technology has liberated only mono-modal traditional text thereby making it multimodal, as Kress (2003) says:

Where before, up until twenty or thirty years ago, writing carried all the communicational load of a message, and needed to have grammatical and syntactic structures that were equal to the complexities of that which had to be represented in that single mode, now there is a specialization, which allows each of the modes to carry that part of the message for which it is best equipped. (p.117)

In this way, new media uses alternative, blended, diverse, mixed, or experimental discourses, and makes it hybrid, and intertextual essentially thereby overlapping or intersecting print with digital, and multimodal text.

Thus new media and technology have ruptured the traditional notion of genre by creating a multimodal genre in mixed genre mode. Even in predominantly written mode in new media, the question of genre no longer rests, because there is always a shift from one genre to another, which I call "genre-switching" or "mode-switching," and mixing of many genres (modes) that breaks the traditional norms of writing mode. And through this mix, new media enhances plural perspectives in reader. In this context, Brooke (2009) argues that:

one of the things that new media interfaces do stylistically is to help us from the abstracted, single perspective of the reader of a static text or the viewer of a painting to the multiple and partial perspectives necessary for many forms of new media. (p. 114)

The possibility of mixing traditional and modern means of presenting data in new media, and its composition putting up together multiple media like print, speech, still images, video, and sounds rhetorically, materially, or technologically thereby making it a multimodal site also inherently makes it an interactive space, which I discuss below. Whereas the writers discussed above talk about the technical aspects of multimodality in new media, Janice Lauer (1993) details its contribution to rhetoric and composition as a discipline to enrich with heuristic power, epistemology, and questioning capability. She asserts:

Multimodality gives rhetoric and composition heuristic power, creating dialogic inquiry that enables the field to raise new questions about writing in our time. Such a rhetoric as an art is radically democratic because it redistributes the knowledge of social practices that characterize act of insiders, thus enabling both the critical examination of culture and the invention of new social possibilities. (p. 44)

However, Shipka (2001) wants to liberate multimodal definition of new media and technology from its association only with the "terms like *multimodal, intertextual, multimedia,* or *media-rich* as synonyms for digitized products and processes" (p. 10), and, thus, broadens it "to include everything from conventional essays, to painting, photographs, video, *and hybrid that we have yet to imagine"* (p. 11). She believes that new media and technology's association only with the terms listed above limits its scope to "text that can be composed, received, and reviewed onscreen" that risks "missing or undervaluing the meaning-making and learning potentials associated with the uptake and transformations of still other representational systems and technologies" (Shipka, 2001, p. 11). Palmeri (2012) also buys Shipka's views on incorporating "old" technologies to design multimedia text in new media. With the introduction of more and more advanced technology, new media has ever been using more advanced computerized technology, has been able to make it multimodal in more advanced way resulting into making it more interactive and participatory in a creative way. So, Yancey (2004) says new media and technology "bring us together in new ways" (p. 100). In the heart of this advancement and change there is motional quality of new media. It is because of its motion toward ever-burgeoning advancement; new media can be seen as a motional site, which I will discuss in what follows.

Interactivity

By nature, humans have tendency to engage with new technologies, and try to see what they can do to make life easier by making new media and technology more participatory in such a way that we push them beyond their limits. Tribe (2001) rightly captures the participatory ability of Internet here, "The Internet is particularly ripe with the potential to enable new kinds of collaborative production, democratic distribution, and participatory experience" (p. xi). As a result, new media technology has made communication and information mass communication and mass information in real sense of the term, and interactive because it has made communication and information more easily accessible for the mass. Murray (2003) argues that "the awe-inspiring representational power of the computer derives from its four defining qualities: its procedural, participatory, encyclopedic, and spatial properties" (p. 6), which fundamentally defines new media. The most obvious property of new media is its encyclopedic capacity that enables it store enormous data at a location, both actual and, more importantly, symbolic (as on a Web site), available for random access. Murray (2003) believes that:

This spatializing quality is based upon the other two properties of the digital medium, the two most basic and defining attributes: its processing power, which allows us to specify procedures which will be not merely recorded but executed; and its participatory quality, which will allow it to receive input, to allow manipulation of its process and data by the user. (pp. 6-7)

The procedural and participatory attributes of new media are what defines "interactivity" as the fundamental experience of new media. The spatial feature of new media as represented by a Web site, specially, provides participatory experiences with so much ease of availability and interactivity that "it will allow us to say more complicated things to more people with greater understanding" (Murray, 2003, p. 11) thereby being "a pool of human knowledge, which would allow collaborators in remote sites to share their ideas and all aspects of a common project" (Berners-Lee, Cailliau, Luotonen, Nielsen, & Secret, 2003, p. 792).

Wysocky (2004), talking about new media texts, also takes "interactivity" as "a buzzword for describing something about readers and digital texts" though "not as an isolated property inherent to digital texts" (p. 17). She believes that it is "interactivity" that makes online texts [new media] different from print texts [old media] apparently, and "interactivity" for her speaks to the relations readers have with new media, which is fundamentally different from the readers' relations with old media, because readers have linear relations with old media while they have recursive interaction with new media as the role of readers might change in the process of interaction with new media. While Selfe (2004a) stresses on new media's fundamental nature of interactivity, Lister, Dovey, Giddings, Grant, and Kelly (2009) discuss ideological aspect of interactivity in new media. For them, "the term [interactivity] stands for a more powerful sense of user engagement with media texts, a more independent relation to sources of knowledge, individualized media use, and greater user choice" (Lister, Dovey, Giddings, Grant, & Kelly, 2009, p. 21) that liberates users from author centered old media text thereby making new media "user-centered" technology, where users have ability to directly intervene in and change the content as they wish, as Johnson (1998) says "technologies are constantly tested and refigured by those who use them" (p. 10) in order to fit them in changed context and users. While explaining the user-centered approaches, Johnson (1998) says:

[u]ser-centered approaches should rethink the user as being an active participant in the social order that designs, develops, and implements technologies. Users as producers have the knowledge to play an important role in the making of technologies; users as practitioners actually use the technologies and thus have a knowledge of the technologies in action; users citizens carry user knowledge into and arena of sociotechnological decision making. (p. 64)

Johnson's examination of user-centered technology thus very much rightly expresses the notion of interactivity in new media, and because of interactivity, "the audience for new media becomes a 'user' rather than the 'viewer' of visual culture, film and TV or a 'reader' of literature" (Lister et al., 2009, p. 22).

New media and technology highly values online interactivity "primarily as an attribute of technological functions of the medium such as hypterlinking, activating media downloads, filling in feedback forms and playing online games" (Warnick & Heineman, 2012, p. 51). It helps sequencing and reciprocal communication in the context in which communication occurs and functions as a significant rhetorical appeal thereby engaging and activating user responses rhetorically. So, Warnick and Heineman (2012) assert, "Online interactivity…functions as a means of activating user responses and as a mode of address that can influence users and can itself be rhetorical in its effects" (p. 53), which, in turn, make the responses persuasive.

Sally J. McMillan (2002) developed taxonomy of three types of online interactivity that have enabled analysts to identify communication patterns in online exchanges: user-to-user, user-to-system, and user-to-document (p. 174). Very importantly, we can see the users in the center of all these online exchanges having a kind of crucial role in making the interactivity possible. Users' engagement here is also possible, because intertextuality "offers a wide repertoire of ways to engage attention, such as the use of embedded hyperlinks to external resources, as readers become complicit in constructing the meanings of the text they encounter" (Warnick & Heineman, 2012, p. 77).

Hypertextuality also enhances interactivity in new media by allowing "a web of connection which the user explores using the navigational aids of the interface design" (Lister et al., 2009, p. 26). Johnson-Eilola (1994) defines hypertext as "a computer-based organizational scheme that allows them [writers and readers] to move from one section of text…to related sections of the text quickly and easily" that "consists of a network, or web, of multiply connected text segments" (p. 197) that resonates Ted Nelson's original definition of hypertext as nonsequential writing. However, Rice (2006) argues that "web-based developments over the last few years have shifted Ted Nelson's original definition of hypertext as non-sequential writing to a more multimedia method of expression centered around HTML tags" (p. 151). While Johnson-Eilola's (1994) definition of hypertext is associated primarily with textual experience related to writing and reading, and Bolter's (2001) defines it as an only linking, "hypertext consists of discrete units—pages, paragraphs, graphics—and the link between them" (p. 29), Rice's (2006) definition of hypertext is a departure from both Johnson-Eilola and Bolter, as he believes "technology…has outgrown the vision of hypertext as only linking" (p. 151). In this context, Catherine F. Smith (1994) adds a dimension to Johnson-Eilolo's definition by defining hypertext "as intellectual experience" (p. 266) thereby providing an alternative view of hypertext. She views:

hypertext as mental activity and examines it in relation to the philosophy of mind, the cognition of comprehension, and the computational modeling of discourse processes…it is a technology for defining meaningful units of information (nodes) and making meaningful connections (link) among them. (Smith, 1994, p. 267)

This definition broadens the scope and meaning of hypertext from just a textual experience to cognitive experience or human thinking, whereas Dryden (1994) further extends it to an expanded notion of literacy, "Hypertext…by virtue of its associative, multilinear branching and linking, offers a powerful medium for an expanded notion of literacy" (p. 285) that integrate electronically the media of print, video, and sound and provides space for a rich interplay of text, which I will discuss in some paragraphs below.

Braaksma, Rijlaarsdam, Couzijn, and van den Bergh (2002) buy Dryden's view of hypertextuality as multilinear linking. While talking about the composing process of hypertext, they mention that it is a *hierarchicalization* process that makes it distinct from the *linearization* process of the composition of linear text. Johnson-Eilola's (1997) postmodern definition of hypertext truly captures the essence of hypertextuality, "The text [hypertext] is no longer a linear or hierarchical string of words…but now an explicitly open space of text that can apparently be entered, navigated, deconstructed, reconstructed, and exited in nearly infinite ways" (p. 147).

Defined as connected through webs or pathways, hypertext can be seen also as an interaction between and among texts, because through a number of pathways to other units of text, hypertext allows different texts to interact with each other in non-linear fashion. This non-linear connection as a fundamental quality of hypertext makes it sophisticated that differentiates it from computer and networks, as Selfe and Hilligoss (1994) argue, "Unlike computers and networks, hypertext is not a physical thing but a sophisticated idea developed in a number of widely available computer programs" (p. 5). The digital technology as discussed earlier makes it possible to access the texts from different pathways instantaneously and recursively. Lister et al. (2009) says "Such technology offers the idea that any data location might have a number of instantly accessible links to other locations built into it. Equally the many interventions and manipulations enabled by this facility create the qualities of interactivity" (p. 26). In this way, hypertext as a multifarious notion is the essence of new media. Johnson-Eilola and Hea (2003) truly captures its meaning in the following lines:

Hypertext has always been a multiple and conflicted term, shifting and configuring at the nexus of local tendential forces. Hypertext coalesces, it seems, around a wish of what we want text to be—contingent, anchored, slipping, caught in net, Disappearing. In this time and in this place (themselves slipping away), we use hypertext as a deconstructive hinge, as an opening into which we find (and lose) ourselves. For although we want to avoid claiming a foundation or core truth for hypertext, we also want to make a space that can help us think about the future of hypertext as well as its past. (p. 416)

Since "hypertext binds together a variety of positions, tones, voices, authors, and context" (Brooke, 2009, p. 4), it creates space for multiple interactions of these entities thereby causing symptomatic "broader changes in the range of informational, communicative, and expressive potentials embodied in new media" (p. 5). This idea of hypertext contributes to other qualities of new media, i.e. networked and collaborative. Because new media and technology facilitates group writing, conferencing, and peer review, it is highly networked and collaborative. While Costanzo (1994), in this connection, gives the example of *interactive fiction* as perhaps the most fascinating instance of collaboration between the user and the computer, which I will explore more in the second part of this chapter, Zeni (1994) talks about a new hypertext environment, *Storyspace,* that "supports planning, organizing, and collaborative response to work in progress," in which, "Students create writing windows with links to other texts….play with organization by rearranging these spaces and design paperless essays for readers to navigate" (p. 81).

As a networked tool, users use new media and technology to collaborate and promote active learning. Duin and Hansen (1994) see "computer networks as a means for students to acquire literacy," because "[a]s students write, interpret, and negotiate texts via computer networks, they are participating within a context that promotes active learning" (p. 89). While Duin and Hansen (1994) call the literacy learnt this way "situated literacy," because it is "situated within the computer network" (p. 89), Forman (1994) names it *computer-supported literacy,* and defines it as "the ability to work in groups effectively, to learn collaboratively, to create a high quality written product, and to make intelligent choices and uses of technology that assist in collaborative composing" (p. 132). In the heart of both the words and definitions, there exists the notion of collaboration and networks. Duin and Hansen (1994) define computer networks in this way:

Computer networks are no more than electronically linked computers through which users can readily share, send, and receive files. Yet they can liberate students, who discover new ways of sharing and receiving information, of reacting and responding to their own texts and those of others. (pp. 89-90).

Digital technologies have also created an interactive space known as virtual space. Virtual space refers to "an alternative or parallel space—a space that it is believed that *we* or *they* inhabit for some, or most of the time" (Gillen & Merchant, 2013, pp. 9-10). Gillen and Merchant believe "this space is variously conceived of as an extension of the 'real world' or an unhelpful, distracting, or even perilous escape from it" (pp. 9-10). Though, of course, we create a virtual world similar to the world described here through our creative imagination while watching a movie or reading a literary piece, the world created thus cannot be a virtual world because there is no interactivity. Virtual world created as a product of computer-based simulation allows the users to interact with the computer as a both way traffic, which, unlike the world we experience by reading literature, is interactive in true sense of the term. By quoting Hayles (1990), Gillen and Merchant (2013) make an interesting point about virtuality:

'Virtuality is a negotiation between materiality and information' through interactions between people and technology—at least in the sorts of virtual environments.... [that] is actually constructed from bits of data, or 'information,' the material affordances of the computer and screen allow these users to see, inhabit, and often to modify that world—and in doing so they become material. (p. 11)

New media technologies produce virtualities of different kinds. Virtual reality (VR) is "produced by immersion in an environment constructed with computer graphics and digital video with which the 'user' has some degree of interaction" (Lister et al., 2009, p. 36). Users' immersion in an environment created by their engaged interaction with the new media creates a microcosmic world (virtual reality) that replaces the real world. It also "refers to the space where participants in forms of online communication feel themselves to be" (p. 36). It is also used to mean retrospective contemplation that one experiences while watching film and television, reading books or contemplating photographs and paintings.

Unlike its old use to mean 'almost' or 'as good as,' "it now suggests and alternative to the real and, maybe, 'better than the real'" (Lister et al., 2009, p. 36). "Cyberspace" is alternative and generic word that is used to mean VR. Alexander (2006) defines cyberspace as a large textual universe, "Cyberspace is a textual artifact of immense size, developed at an historically unprecedented pace, and including a rich variety of audiences, authors, discourses, and narrative production" (p. 27). Cyberspace's ability to include a rich variety of audiences, authors, discourses, and narrative production interests me here, which I will explore in the second part of this chapter. To go back to the notion of virtuality with which this paragraph began, "Virtual" has close association with "simulation," which means "artificial, synthetic and fabricated, but...not 'false' or 'illusory'" (Alexander, 2006, p. 38). The multimedia mix is another advanced output of computerization technology of new media. Virtual reality (VR) programming (a new kind of human-computer interface), as a model of multimedia mix, has made new media more interactive by allowing the user "to create and experience fantasy situations that are generated by computers filled with interactive software" (Dizard, 2000, p. 41). More than a science fiction game, its application in business, online shopping, research, planetary exploration, education and training field also contribute to the changes in the notions of rhetorical situation, which I will discuss in part two of this chapter later.

All the qualities discussed above make new media different from old media, but we cannot find all these qualities necessarily present in an example of new media at a time. Here, Lister, Dovey, Giddings, Grant, and Kelly (2009) aptly express this idea in the following lines:

The characteristics [of new media]...should be seen as part of a matrix of qualities that we argue is what makes new media different. Not all of these qualities will be present in all examples of new media—they will be present in differing degrees and in different mixes. (p. 44)

And what characteristics will be present in what degree and in what mixes in new media also depends on how new media and technology evolves. It is very customary to say that everything in the world changes. However, it is imperative to talk about new media and technology as a dynamic and evolving space as its inherently qualifying characteristics. In what follows, I will discuss this feature of new media and technology.

A Dynamic and Evolving Space

There is a joke about new media and technology: the moment you define what new media and technology is, it will already be old. Due to continuous innovation and reinvention, new media and technology is always in flux as Haas and Neuwirth (1994) say, "technologies are continually evolving; they are not static but shaped subtly and constantly by the uses to which they are put and by the discourse that accompanies those uses" (p. 324).

By birth and by nature, new media is a motional site because it maintains its qualifier ("new") by changing, and modifying itself thereby incorporating recent advanced technology, and also by inventing new technology to make it always new. In this context, Jenkins (2003) says:

The media never rest. Their various modes are in perpetual circulation. Consulted, scanned and read in every country and on every continent, they are a vital means of communication in the modern world. Sometime criticized or even abused, they are also refreshed and renewed as they accomplish multiple tasks. (Foreword)

Lister, Dovey, Giddings, Grant, and Kelly (2009) also buy Jenkins's (2003) view and admit that new media is always in the state of constant flux: "such media had continually been in a state of technological, institutional and cultural change or development; they never stood still" (p. 10). New media can be seen as an agent of globalization of all kinds by dissolving "national states and boundaries in terms of trade, corporate organization, customs and cultures, identities and beliefs, in which new media are seen as a contributory element" (Lister et al., 2009, p. 11). As Tribe (2001) believes "New Media represents a constantly shifting frontier for experimentation and exploration" (p. xii), it does not simply keep up with the changing environs around it, rather it leads the change thereby doing experimentation with the new technology, and exploring new technology that could be useful to motor the change. As a motoring agent of new technology as well as cultural change or development, new media keeps on changing and generating changes in the society thereby always causing of epoch-making phenomena of some sorts with the emergence of new media. Lister, Dovey, Giddings, Grant, and Kelly (2009), in this context, rightly observe, "the emergence of 'new media' as some kind of epoch-making phenomena, was, and still is, seen as part of a much larger landscape of social, technological and cultural change; in short, as part of a new technoculture" (p. 11).

In what preceded, new media and technology are seen as evolutionary pivoting forces to effect global changes in the world, because it has an imperative push and pull tendency that keeps us doing some sorts of activities to bring changes in both technology and society. Miller's (2010) idea about technology is very pertinent here, "Technology, like rhetoric, can both push and pull at us....Technology pushes or manipulates us by requiring us to do certain things and in certain ways" (p. ix). What I find interesting and touching in these lines of Miller is technology's ability to push or manipulates us. People generally take for granted that they use technology to use it or as a means to do things, without ever being aware how technology shapes them both physically and psychologically. It is the push-pull tendencies of new media and technology that constantly shape new media and technology and is shaped by them thereby making it a motional site forever. The Web can be seen as a most fertile site for new developments in information technology. Berners-Lee, Cailliau, Luotonen, Nielsen, and Secret (2003) illustrate the point how the Web orchestrates innovation and invention of new media and technology:

The W3 [World Wide Web] initiative occupies the meeting point of many fields of technology. Users put pressure and effort into bringing about the adoption of W3 in new areas. Apart from being a place of communication and learning, and a new market place, the Web is a show ground for new developments in information technology. (p. 797)

New media and technology as a motional and evolutional site is seen as something that evolution happens for some better reasons because it is believed to bring some sort of hopes and claims to make the life easier than before. I conclude this section by citing Lister, Dovey, Giddings, Grant, and Kelly's (2009) optimistic lines in this regard, "New media appear, as they have before, with claims and hopes attached; they will deliver increased productivity and educational opportunity and open up new creative and communicative horizons" (p. 11). In what preceded, I briefly discussed on overall impact of new media and technology in human life physically and psychologically, and in what follows, I will discuss how new media and technology particularly change the notions of the rhetorical situation.

HOW DO NEW MEDIA AND TECHNOLOGY CHANGE THE NOTIONS OF RHETORICAL SITUATION?

New media and technology have an overall impact in our lives including the way we write and read a text, and teach writing, because as Selfe and Hilligos (1994) argue, "Technology changes us, redirects our thinking about the primary tasks of teaching reading and writing" (p. 1). William Costanzo (1994) extends Selfe and Hilligoss's idea on technology further, "computers are altering the way many of us read, write, and even think. It is not simply that the tools of literacy have changed; the nature of texts, of language, of literacy itself is undergoing crucial transformations" (p. 11). By altering our overall literacy practice, new media and technology always creates a new situation, and require the users to use it in a defined way, and "to explain what a tool [technology] is and how to use it seems to demand narrative" (Nye, 2006, p. 5). For this matter, here, I will create a narrative that tells stories how new media and technology has created a new situation to redefine/reexamine/remap/revive the existing notions of the rhetorical situation. New media and technology have moved us at least some distance away from the familiar realm of paper, ink, and books, and thus affected the locus of reading, writing, and interpreting texts thereby enabling us to understand the new interfaces through which most of the communication are done these days. How new media does it is rightly observed by Brooke (2009) in these lines, "new media invites us to rethink (or reinvent) the canons of classical rhetoric, understanding them as practices that might, in turn, be used to understand the proliferation of interfaces that surround us" (p. xiii). Selber (2010) also buys Brooke's idea as to how new media and technology helps us to reinterpret the canons of classical rhetoric. As Selber (2010) says, "Their [technologies] increasingly widespread integration into all facets of culture has encouraged scholars and teachers to reinterpret (yet again) the traditional cannons of rhetoric" (p. 2), given the impact of new media and technology, the traditional notions of the rhetorical situation has to be reinterpreted in order to incorporate the changing/changed social and cultural milieu as a product of overall impact of new media and technology. In the part that follows, I will first discuss how new media and technology has caused overall changes in the notions of the rhetorical situation, and then examine the changes in particular components of rhetorical situation (writers, readers, and text, for example) in terms of how some characteristics of new media and technology discussed above impact the change as an agent.

General Impact

Digital composition as an inherent qualifier of new media and technology has impacted not only the way we write and read a text, but also the way how we perceive the constituents of the rhetorical situation—writers, readers, text—and their relationships as a product of overall impact of new media and technology that has changed the notions of the rhetorical situation. Whereas Johnson-Eilola (1997) sees this radical disruption of the connection situated in print media in this way, "The links between author and text, sign and signified that were reinforced by the physical and social structure of book discourse seem to come radically unglued" (p. 171), Takyoshi and Selfe (2007) believe that digitization that played crucial role to revolutionize new media has challenged overall existing literacy practices in general and the nexus between the constituents of the rhetorical situation in particular. In this connection, they argue, "It is fast becoming a commonplace that digital composing environments are challenging writing, writing instruction, and basic understandings of the different components of the rhetorical situation (writers, readers, texts) to change" (p. 1). Like Johnson-Eilola, and Takyoshi & Selfe, Marilyn M. Cooper (2010), in her essay, "Being Linked to the Matrix," "reimagines the basic structures of the rhetorical situation, offering a view that embraces dynamic interaction, negotiation, and coordination as major elements" (cited in Selber, 2010, p. 6). Likewise, new media and technology has the potential to "bring us together in new ways" (Yancey, 2004, p. 100), to "change the way students write, read and think," and to "cultivate multiple literacies, to blur the writer/reader boundary and to broaden notions of 'composing'" (Zoetewey & Staggers, 2003, p. 135). New media and technology have impacted our lives so much that "[c]omputers change the ways in which we read, construct, and interpret texts. In doing so, technology forces us to rethink what it means to be human" (Selfe & Hilligoss, 1994, p. 1). New media and technology, thus, have broken the linear relationship between writer and audience, performer and viewers. As a result, readers can act like writers in many ways, and writers sometimes have to behave like readers. In this sense, it has changed some existing notions of the rhetorical situation as something static, linear, real, genuine, and objective. This situation influences and shapes our understanding of the rhetorical situation, because the writers and readers now do not act like traditional writers and readers. They have a changed role: the writers do not have so much authority on the text/message while readers have been empowered to take author-like roles.

Impact of Multimodality

The traditional notion of the rhetorical situation treats readers only as passive receivers of information thereby limiting the scope of readers. But, as a multimodal and interactive space, new media challenges containment of alphabetical systems of the print (old media) which privileges only reading thereby making the readers only receivers of information, and demands the multiple literacies: seeing, listening, writing, and allows readers even to manipulate the information. Multimodality in new media and technology thus produces new possibilities for the existence of different rhetorical situations, because it creates a new site where writer, reader, and text crisscross. This fact gets expressed in Williams's (2007) lines below:

We should instead regard the ability to use multiple modalities of communication as a call to examine how new ways of conceiving of literacy and composing produce new possibilities for different rhetorical situations. The multiple purposes and audiences for which we write demand multiple approaches for communicating our message. (p. xi)

While so doing, new media changes the role of a reader and dismantles the lines between reader and writer, which breaks the linear notions of the rhetorical situation.

Since new media and technology stresses much on the use of visuals, and visual literacies, the traditional notions of "author" and "reader" as perceived in Bitzer's notion of the rhetorical situation are changing or taking new meaning of "composer/designer" and "viewer" respectively. As Lauer (1993) points out, "Multimodality represents, if we're using Bakhtin's term, a dynamic diversity of modes grounded in different points of view on the world, in diverse forms for conceptualizing the world, each characterized by its own objects, meanings, and values" (p. 45), it fosters polyvalent, multiple, and plural messages, hence breaking the traditional notion of message "out there" designed by the author. Ball (2004) talks about how multimodal text operates to make meaning by placing readers in the center of meaning making process, unlike in traditional text, which privileges author. She says:

Without the reader choosing clips to include on the timelines, this new media text would not be able to perform its intended argument....The reader must participate by dragging the still, audio, or text clips that she wants to the timelines. For the fullest understanding of the text's meaning, all three timelines must be used, and then the reader must click the play button on the viewer to see the composed collage. No matter which selection and arrangement of clips the reader makes, the argument she constructs will be a smaller version of the whole, perhaps made to lesser or greater strengths depending on the combination of clips chosen" (Ball, 2004, p. 417).

Hocks (2003) also opines that multiple modalities enhanced by communication and information technologies allow ongoing dialogue and negotiations among the constituents of the rhetorical situations—writers, audiences, and text—thereby making multiple meanings possible. Her view that "digital rhetoric describes a system of ongoing dialogue and negotiations among writers, audiences, and institutional contexts, but it focuses on the multiple modalities available for making meaning using new communication and information technologies" (p. 632) echoes Kolb's (1994) argument how the roles of author and reader change in multimodal text and how it makes difference in meaning, "the roles of author and reader begin to shift as the being of the text changes" (p. 323). All these points made above about the contribution of multimodality to shifting the roles of reader and writer, empowering readers unlike in traditional texts, allowing ongoing dialogue among writers, readers and text, and creating plural message orchestrate how the notions of the rhetorical situations have changed and how the traditional notions cannot necessarily function in today's world that has been so much influenced by new media and technology. Thus new media and technology break the traditional version of the rhetorical situation as they blur the distinction between the reader and writer, question the existence of exigencies in their palpable forms, and decontextualize the context as perceived in the traditional notions.

Impact of Hypertext

The idea of author being in the center of traditional texts ("books") and reader being in the center of hypertexts gets expression when Selber (2004) compares books and hypertext: "Books are static, linear, hierarchical, author-centered, and dialogic, why hypertexts are dynamic, non-linear, non-hierarchical, reader-centered, and polylogic" (p. 20). Like Hilligoss and Selfe (1994) say "[w]ith hypertext, teachers and researchers have also blurred the boundaries between writing and reading" (p. 337), hypertext also has blurred the boundaries between the two constituents of the rhetorical situation—writers and readers. What interests me in the views expressed above is the reversal of author-reader role in making meaning that shifts not only the role per se, but it also changes the value attached to one of the constituent of rhetorical situation, i.e. readers, in traditional notions of the rhetorical situation, because it allows users to collaborate more substantially in the act of writing and making meaning that complicates traditional notions of authorship. In relationship to the rhetorical situation, hypertext creates a space for readers in such a way that it empowers them, and frees them from their subservient role unlike the ways they are perceived by Bitzer and many other scholars who believe that readers are only recipient of messages always passively waiting for the authors to solve the exigencies through the rhetorical discourses.

The use of hypertexts in new media has complicated the linear notion of writer and reader, because it "has potential to change fundamentally how we write, how we read, how we teach these skills, and even how we conceive of text itself" (Charney, 1994, p. 239). In hypertext, a non-linear, computer supported text, "the common distinctions between 'writer' and 'reader' begin to collapse in a way that has long been theorized for print text but not realized in such visible form" (Johnson-Eilola, 1994, 195). Unlike print text, readers have very important role in hypertext, because the sequence of reading, which is fundamentally nonsequential, is determined by readers' navigational interest which involves selecting parts of the hypertext and deciding which other parts they want to navigate. So, "Within hypertext the reader can become something of a co-author because the order of a nonsequential document is determined only at the time of reading" (Carter, 2003, p. 4). The nonsequential and fluid nature of hypertext, reader's increased ability to make meaning, and author-reader role shift get expressed when Claire Lauer (2009) says:

The notion of the author as a single, solitary voice communicating to his or her audience through the finished product of the book has been transformed as communications media have opened up the possibilities for textual production to be non-linear, hypertexual, continuously revisable, and interactive. As writing becomes an increasingly screen-based activity, the ways in which we write (from the grammar we use to the style, tone, appearance, and structure of our words, sentences, paragraphs, and pages) necessarily make more fluid and transitory the role we occupy as "author" of a text. This change in the relationship of author to text, and thus in the way in which meaning can be communicated through text, was facilitated by technological advancement that allowed for a shift from the static medium of the page to the more fluid medium of the screen. (p. 227)

This notion of hypertext has contributed to the creation of hyperfiction which has broken the spatio-temporal concept of the beginning, middle, and end of fiction. This gets pronounced in Pavlik (1998), "Writers are even venturing into a new form of non-linear text known as hyperfiction, in which notions of beginning, middle and end have little meaning and the reader enters the realm of story creator" (p. xii). Hypertext opens up a space for "fundamental alterations in the roles of the writer, the reader, and the text" (Johnson-Eilola, 1994, p. 196) thereby collapsing the distinction between writer and reader. Thus, hypertext allows two-way multiple interactions between writer and readers, because "[h]ypertext writers set up multiple connections between nodes of a text, and readers choose which links to follow, which nodes to read, and which nodes to skip" (Johnson-Eilola, 1994, p. 197). The readers have so much freedom to read the text in any way they like based on their interest that allows them to create the meaning of their own.

This opens up possibilities for the readers to assume the role of a writer. It changes and fuses the role of writer and reader, "Using hypertext, people are neither solely readers nor solely writers—users take the two roles simultaneously and visibly" (Johnson-Eilola, 1994, p. 206). Unlike traditional readers as only the recipient of message, the hypertext readers are creator and manipulator of message, likewise unlike "writer-controlled" traditional text, hypertext is also "reader-controlled," which, in turn, problematizes also the notion of message and text. Hypertext requires both readers and writers to participate in making the text and, thus, become "co-learners" (Joyce, 1988, p. 12) who influence each other to make the text, and derive meaning from it. In this way, new media and technology problematize the whole traditional notions of rhetorical situation by collapsing the lines between the authors and readers, empowering the readers unlike they are perceived in the traditional notions of the rhetorical situation, and allowing readers access the text in any way they like. This situation creates the possibilities of the existence of not only the plural rhetorical discourses, but also of multiple messages, and readers and writers hence revision of the traditional notions of the rhetorical situation.

New media and technology has, thus, used hypertext "as a means to liberate readers (as well as writers) from the constraints of text boundaries, freeing them to wander through and array of connected texts, graphics, and commentary, to explore and create topical paths of association at will" (Charney, 1994, p. 240) thereby making it an open-ended text in true sense of the term, where readers, text, and writers engage in multiple mutual interaction constantly. Allen (2000) powerfully expresses this multiple author-text-reader interaction while concluding his theories of intertextuality, "hypertext makes author, text, and reader into joint participation of a plural, intertextual network of significations and potential significations" (p. 202). While so doing, hypertext breaks the linear relationships between the constituents of the rhetorical situation, and thus impacts the traditional notion.

While talking about why hypertext is fundamentally different form of text, Dryden (1994) makes an interesting point about the authorship of hypertext. He believes that authorship is fundamentally different in hypertext, because "the reader chooses how to navigate through the text; in some hypertext, the reader can also choose to add to the text, perhaps in a way that makes his or her additions indistinguishable from the original" (p. 309). The writers and readers both affect each other and are affected by the text, hence symbiotic relationships between writers, readers, and texts, unlike discrete relationships between the constituents of traditional notions of the rhetorical situation. In this context, Johnson-Eilola (1997) believes writing and reading activities are affected by the concerned community's ideology, "Hypertext provides vivid examples of the ways in which the activities of writing and reading are transformed and appropriated by widely divergent communities, each of which reconstructs general characteristics of hypertexts in relationship to that community's goal" (p. 7). Hypertext has transformed/revolutionized writing and reading spaces in such a way that it allows "writers and readers the capability for productive, purposeful, empowering action in a range of text types and social situations" (Johnson-Eilola, 1997, p. 25). Here, readers can assume the role of writer, and, thus, problematizes the linear relationships between them, hence questioning the traditional notions of the rhetorical situation.

By borrowing Deleuze and Guattari's (1987) notion of rhizome, hypertext is like a "rhizome as an ever-shifting organism that challenges the 'root-book'" (Johnson-Eilola, 2003, p 422). Rhizomatic tropes defines hypertext in terms of its "connections, heterogeneity, multiplicity, asignifying rupture" (Johnson-Eilola, 2003, p. 423) that acknowledge that no writers or readers are in control of meaning of a text, which is rather determined by rhizomatic relationships between readers, writers, and the text, as Johnson-Eilola (2003) says:

In this trope, hypertext is about a constant making and remaking....In the play of the rhizomatic, we are asked to hold all our sacred beliefs about readers and writers, text and meaning against the larger systems that reify traditional power dynamics. Without a rigid structure to reject, deny, or even hold on to, we read rhizomatic hypertext as a means to challenge binary logics that separate ways of living in language, that occlude other connections and multiplicities. (p. 423)

By summing up what hypertext contributes to literary theories, poetry and creative writing, technical writing, and our perception about writing and reading, Johnson-Eilola and Hea (2003) say:

For literary theorists, hypertext provided the true weapon for assassinating the author: Readers wrestled control of the text away, kicked the author in the head a few times for good measure, and skipped off into the down of a new day. For poets and creative writers, hypertext provided the foundation for erecting a space for free exploration and innovation, unburdened by the repressive limits of the line. For technical writers, hypertext provided a method for dealing with individual users in varying situations—rather than force users to tediously thumb through manuals, hypertextual online help would bring the right information (and only the right information) directly to the user, when the user needed it, and not a moment sooner or later. And, for a few bold writing instructors, hypertext provided the means to challenge the preferred genre of the first-year composition course: the traditional, linear, "logical" print-based essay. From its most conservative to its more iconoclastic enactments, hypertext set about shifting our perceptions of writing and reading. (pp. 416-417)

By the same token, hypertext in particular and new media and technology in general changes our conceptions about the notions of the rhetorical situation by breaking the traditional meanings of reader, writer and text. We can, thus, describe hypertext as breaking the lines or jamming code, or whatever it does, it primarily frees "the word from the page, the text from the line, the writer and reader from their separateness" (Johnson-Eilola & Hea, 2003, p. 417). What interests me most in hypertext here is its ability to free the writer and reader from their separateness. The traditional notions of the rhetorical situation clearly separate writer and reader by drawing a demarcation line between them, perhaps keeping them in two different watertight compartments, thereby assigning two different set of roles to them. Very interestingly, hypertext, guided by postmodernist tendencies, has broken this modernist containment in defining the constituents of the rhetorical situation, and freed the writer and reader from their separateness thereby allowing them to cross the border. I will discuss a postmodernist reading of how new media and technology dismantled the linear relationship between readers, writers, and text later in this chapter. Now, I will examine how interactivity as a product of new media and technology in general and hypertext in particular has impacted the changes in the traditional notions of the rhetorical situation.

Impact of Interactivity

By making new media and technology a truly collaborative site where both readers and writers collaborate via writing and reading the text to manipulate it in their own way, interactivity as one of the qualifying features of new media and technology has also contributed to the change in traditional notions of the rhetorical situation. While so doing, interactivity allows change in the role of writers and readers, and performers and viewers in such a way that the boundaries between them collapse. Here is an example of how new media and technology has dismantled the traditional linear relationship between performer and viewers, two of constituents of the rhetorical situations by extension:

Families in test communities in California are playing Jeopardy! via computer in simultaneous competition with the competitors seen on television each evening. Viewers in Montreal, Canada, are selecting stories of their own choice each evening on nightly newscasts and playing armchair director during telecast of Montreal Canadian hockey games, choosing camera angles and instant replays as they desire. (Pavlik, 1998, p. xii)

In this context, Pavlik (1998) says "These new technologies are radically transforming almost every aspect of how we communicate and with whom, as well as just about any other dimension of our lives, from dating to making money to health care" (p. 1). New media and technology is revolutionizing some aspect of human communication in one way or the other, and thus extending communication well beyond text-based communication, and transforming all forms of human communication thereby blurring lines between writer and reader.

The Internet as a legitimate product of new media and technology has given birth to web 2.0 tools which are so much fundamentally social and interactive that "[e]ven aspects of the Internet that do not seem particularly social, such as business sites, online magazines and information services, have integrated social opportunities such as chat spaces and bulletin board into their sites" (Baym, 2002, p. 62), and has made them synchronously and asynchronously interactive. This highly interactive feature of the Internet blurs the traditional relationship between writer and reader that can be characterized as fluid and slippery because they change their role so quickly that we cannot perceive them as static.

Sally J. McMillan (2002) talks about three types of online interactivity that have enabled analysts to identify communication patterns in online exchanges: user-to-user, user-to-system, and user-to-document (p. 174). Very importantly, we can see the users in the center of all these online exchanges having a kind of crucial role in making the interactivity possible that overpowers readers, unlike in print media. For example, in user-to-system interactivity, "the user activates a technical capacity of the system, and the system responds" (Warnick & Heineman, 2012, p. 56). While user-to-user interactivity naturally focuses on users, because they have very prominent role in making communication possible, Warnick and Heineman argue that the users' role is crucial and equally important in user-to-document interactivity, because:

users become active co-creator of the messages when they customize site content, vote in online polls, submit questions to be answered on the site, or post messages and photos that become part of the Web site text. In this sort of exchange, the Web site invites users to submit content; uses send in materials; and then those materials are posted to the site for others to read. And even more frequent form of user-contributed cross-reference is when respondents on political blog posts include hyperlinks that can be further pursued by those readers who are interested in viewing the recommended content. (Warnick & Heineman, 2012, p. 56).

Intertextuality also allows some sorts of interactivity not simply by making readers to partake actively in the design of the text in new media; it allows readers to become "complicit in constructing the meanings of the texts they encounter" thereby offering "a wide repertoire of ways to engage attention, such as the use of embedded hyperlinks to external resources" (Warnick & Heineman, 2012, p. 77). Interactivity created in this way makes readers prominent by allowing them to create text, construct the meanings, and collaborate with writers and other readers in full potential, hence assuming author like role. Interactivity is also enhanced and exemplified by defining new media as a virtual space, which I will talk in the part to follow.

Impact of Virtual Space

The Web as a legitimate product of new media and technology has created a virtual space as an interactive site where users and writers interact in such a way that line between the constituents of the rhetorical situation is blurring, and the sense of location as perceived in traditional notions of the rhetorical situation is lost. As in *Nostalgic Angels,* Johnson-Eilola (1997) states:

In online information systems, users inhabit and navigate a virtual space," and "the concept of location becomes less physical and more mental... as they move from 'place' to 'place' electronically, they see and manipulate information in and as a space that spans the entire earth" (p. 93),

new media creates the illusion of space within a machine through its navigational commands which blurs our notion of space, and supplants it with "cyberspace," "it is so fundamental to the way we experience the world, and so desirable a means of representing the world, that we have to think about it as a property in itself" (Murray, 2003, p. 6) thereby blurring the distinction between the constituents of the rhetorical situation. As Manovich (2003) believes "it [new technology] will destroy the 'natural relationship between humans and the world' by 'eliminating the distance' between the observer and the observed," (p. 19), new media and technology has ruptured the linear notions of the rhetorical situation. The idea of blurring the writer/reader boundary gets more vividly expressed in Costanzo's (1994) example of *interactive fiction* as a most fascinating instance of collaboration between the user and the computer, where readers can manipulate the story so much that:

Everything depends on the reader. Readers move through the story by typing in commands or questions from the keyboard....Much of the appeal of interactive prose lies in readers' leaning about their fictional characters, discovering the characters' goals, overcoming conflicts, and exploring imaginary worlds.... The story is a collaborative creation of the author and the reader. (pp. 16-17)

The notion of cyberspace and virtual world as mentioned in the first part of this chapter interests me here because it also contributes to change the traditional notions of authors, readers, discourses and narrative production. As Alexander (2006) clearly points out while defining cyberspace as "a textual artifact of immense size" that includes "a rich variety of audiences, authors, discourses, and narrative production" (p. 27), it reconceptualizes the notion of plural authors, audiences, discourses, and narrative production by interrogating the traditional notions of constituents of the rhetorical situation that is inherently singular. The notions of cyberspace as perceived above actually breaks the border between writers and readers because it allows readers to play the role of writers and make writers to act also like readers sometimes, hence diminishing the authorship of writers and increasing the writer-like role of readers. Likewise, virtuality makes users very powerful in modifying the virtual world. In virtual world, "the material affordances of the computer and screen allow these users to see, to inhabit, and often to modify that world—and in doing so they become material" (Gillen & Merchant, 2013, p. 11). The notions of hypertext, cyberspace, and virtual world as discussed above can be seen as a postmodern concept, because they enhance the notions of plural authors (or death of the authors), multiple audiences in author's voice, participatory discourses (texts), and petit narratives, which essentially blurs the boundaries between them. In the following part, I will do postmodern reading of what the prominent qualifying features of new media and technology have to offer in relation to the notions of the rhetorical situation, and how it does so.

Postmodern Reading

I have mentioned above that new media and technology has the tendency to blur the lines between reader, writer, text, and their relationship, which is verisimilitude with postmodern rupture. New media and technology in general and the Web in particular helped hypertext accelerate its postmodernist tendencies to blur the distinction between the writer and reader by "turning the reader into a voracious, consuming mouseclick" (Johnson-Eilola & Hea, 2003, p. 417). Hocks (2003) extends this argument to include digital text that contributes to making new media inherently postmodern, when she says, "Interactive digital texts can blend words and visuals, talk and text, and authors and audiences in ways that are recognizably postmodern" (pp. 629-30).

In postmodernist perspectives, hypertext ruptures the boundaries between writer, reader, and society as it totalizes and fragments them on computer screen. In this connection, Johnson-Eilola (1997) argues:

[H]ypertext may end by affording only a postmodernist forum, in which everything (writer, reader, and society) becomes simultaneously totalized and fragmented, simulated on the computer screen and in magnetic memory. We should not be surprised at this condensation of agents, objects, and subjects: The collapse of subject, method, object, and interpretation is immanent from a poststructuralist standpoint. (p. 137)

Hypertext as a multifaceted space, thus, fosters intertextuality (multitextuality); problematizes the social construction of knowledge and the roles of readers and writers; and enhances indeterminacy of context and meaning and the formation of subjectivity, and the multiplicity of discourses, which, in turn, breaks down the traditional notions of rhetorical situation. Johnson-Eilola's (1997) views, in this connection, are worth-mentioning:

One of the most striking features of space and subject hypertext is the way in which the technology apparently breaks down the distinctions between writer and reader, especially the commonsense notions of these roles as polar opposites. Theorists see the blurring of the line between writer and reader as extending recent theoretical positions in literary theory—hypertext, in this articulation, makes visible something that has long been theorized. (p. 143)

This explicit postmodern blurring of the lines of responsibility between reader and writer, as expressed by Landow (1992), "Hypertext blurs the boundaries between reader and writer" (p. 5), and postmodern rupture of the notions of texts, message and interpretation in hypertext open up the possibility to theorize the rhetorical situation from a new thread of line, because hypertext complicates traditional notions of authorship and text's authority, "the original author or text's authority seems to evaporate under the force of the readers' movements: Readers not only choose among the options offered by the original text, but may also add their own paths or even texts" (Landow, 1992, p. 145). Though some websites still characterize modernist notions of space as linear and hierarchical, apparent as in the ordered list of information, "information-rich screens" as pointed out by Johnson-Eilola (1998), which is enriched by a hypertext, "ask users to understand things in multiple, contingent spatial structures rather than in serial and chronological orders" (Reynolds, 2004, p. 67). The creation of postmodern spaces in hypertext allows readers more freedom to perceive the meaning in any way they like and thus assigns them authorship of meaning thereby empowering them over the authors themselves. These postmodern spaces created by hypertexts get more clearly characterized in Johnson-Eilola's (1998) lines:

these spaces can be navigated and negotiated from a simultaneous, surface perspective that does not attempt to find single facts or linear structures but has learned to process information along parallel lines without relying on a single focal point or goal....In learning to understand communication in terms of simultaneous, contingent streams and structures, users also lose the ability to anchor themselves anywhere with certainty. (p. 205)

The increasingly widespread integration of new media and technology in any communicative practice today has made writers and communicators "anticipate reader control with modular hypertext that can support multiple interpretive pathways and that can invite textual transformations and revision" (Selber, 2010, p. 2).

Snoddy (2003) anticipated the pervasiveness of new media and technology, and its impact in bringing up the world together by dismantling the notion of distance:

Technology will one day be so pervasive and so inexpensive that everyone...will have the ability to call up on the move every image and tact to a portable device that will combine the characteristics of a computer, television set and telephone. This will of course amount to The Death of Distance. (p. 18)

Brooke (2009) expresses similar idea about new media and technology's ability to break the spatial conception of geography. But while asserting this fact, he also mentions that new media and technology both connects and separates us: it connects us with the world at distance, while it separates us from more immediate, local connection. In this context, he says, "Online networking might enable us to forge new connections with concern for geography, but those connections may come at the cost of our more immediate, local connections" (Brooke, 2009, p. xv). Thus, new media and technology complicates the notion of distance by providing us with connections with the world around us, and also distancing us from more immediate world, which, in turn, problematizes also breaks the linear notion of the constituent of the rhetorical situation: audience, constraints, and exigence.

The conception of audience, constraints, and exigence is based on the idea of immediacy, and urgency. Audience, by and large, is associated with the immediacy of the targeted people whom the message is intended to address. But new media and technology distance the immediate audience around the author, and connect with the audience far and beyond. Likewise, constraints are loaded with urgency and immediacy that is defined as some hurdles that influence the decision and action of the rhetor, and expectation of the audience. New media and technology dilute the immediacy and urgency of constraints by distancing the rhetor and audience. So is the case with exigence. Bitzer (1968) defines exigence as "an imperfection marked by urgency; it is a defect, an obstacle, something waiting to be done, a thing which is other than it should be" (p. 6). However, new media and technology divert the rhetor's attention from the immediate urgency, imperfection and a defect that need to be solved. For example, you might be donating and helping to make the lives of the poor people better somewhere in the world, without paying attention to the poverty most immediately around you.

CONCLUSION

Though there are many socio-political implications of new media and technology both as a motoring agent to gear up economic, scientific and educational advancement, and as a debacle of social values and humanity, my concern here is to discuss about it as a tool, an approach, an insight, a pedagogy, a philosophy, and an overall guiding principle in relations to Rhetoric and Writing Studies that significantly prioritize the use of new media and technology. In this context, I want to conclude this essay only by talking about what is new media and technology, and how it has changed the notions of the rhetorical situation, and literacy. To sum up the points I already made, as an ever burgeoning use of new media and technology in any communicative practice, new media and technology is redefining both how we write, think and read, and the older notions of the rhetorical situation, and so subtly changing the way we conceive of the linear and distinct constituents of the rhetorical situation. Its contribution to writing is vividly expressed in Zoetewey and Staggers's (2003) lines, "new media writing affords students new opportunities to reassemble the world outside the linear constraints of the print paradigm and make things fit in new ways" (p. 135). While they particularly talk about the impact of new media and technology in writing practice, Haas and Neuwirth (1994) relate it to the overall literacy practices, "The new media technologies for literacy are such a powerful force that simply introducing them to writers or in writing classrooms will change writing and reading for the better, supplanting completely the old pen-and-book technologies" (p. 323).

Because of its powerful force to affect all, and to effect change in literacy practices, new media and technology is so omnipresent (and perhaps omnipotent?) in our lives that we have interfaces everywhere. Brooke (2009) rightly expresses this phenomenon when he says, "We encounter interfaces as a part of our individual media ecologies, and those interfaces each serve as ecologies of rhetorical practice, where cannons shifts, overlap, intermingle, and combine, sometimes as a direct result of our choices and sometimes despite them" (p. xiii). By being so ubiquitously present, especially in our rhetorical practices, as ecologies, new media challenges the structuralist binary oppositions and boundaries that we have inherited from the classical canons. Brooke's (2009) view in this regard is pertinent to mention, "new media occupy an increasingly relevant focus within the disciplinary ecology of rhetoric, challenging traditional binaries and boundaries, some of which we have retained since rhetoric's inception" (p. xiii).

However, new media and technology's unequivocal emphasis on "medium is the message" is sometimes problematic because it diverts its focus from audience and purpose, which are some of the most important concerns of all rhetorics including new media rhetorics. While the new media text's singular focus on the medium is said to have ignored the audience and purpose to some extent, "we now must deal with the fact that choice of medium influences audience expectation" (Rabkin, 2006, p.136). I argue that new media does not ignore audience and purpose; it only changes the way audience and purpose are treated by offering new possibilities to examine author, audience, purpose, discourse and interactivity between them. Nevertheless, it is true that "the set of expectations an audience has about any of these new media is necessarily more contingent than those raised by book culture" (Rabkin, 2006, p. 136). Here, I would argue that an expectation of an audience of new media is more contingent upon the medium than the expectation of an audience of print media. As Rabkin (2006) suggests that digital media often breaks down the boundaries between "the finality of composition, the identity of the author, the role of the audience, and the unity of purpose" (p. 137), new media and technology contributes to the changes in the traditional notions of the rhetorical situation because now "we live and work in an inherently collaborative infosphere" (Rabkin, 2006, p. 137).

The underlying structure of new media and technology hitherto discussed is its user-centered quality that separates it from traditional text which makes it an inherently collaborative infosphere, where, as Rice (2006) says, "Users not only can create, but also (re)distribute, recommend, and evaluate content" (p. 1). However, the absence of skill provides a bleak image about it, because it pushes users into the conundrum of definitions, from where no solution can be obtained, and thus there is no way to get out from the labyrinth of knowledge. In this context, Murray (2003) provides an optimistic note when she says, "We will not be mere prisoners of the labyrinth, nor even trail-blazers: we will be the makers of the labyrinth, the gods of our own machine" (p. 11). I conclude this essay with Withrow's (2004) pragmatic lines, "The challenge is to use the right technology at the right time. Technology should never be used just for the sake of technology. Technology should increase the learning experience for the learner" (p. 42).

REFERENCES

Aitchison, J., & Lewis, D. M. (Eds.). (2003). *Introduction. New media language.* New York, NY: Routledge.

Alexander, B. (2006). A threat to professional identity? The resistance to computer-mediated teaching. In M. Hanrahan & D. L. Madsen (Eds.), *Teaching, technology, textuality: Approaches to new media* (pp. 27–35). New York, NY: Palgrave Macmillan. doi:10.1057/9780230523302_3

Allen, G. (2000). *Intertextuality.* London: Routledge.

Arthur, W. B. (2009). *The nature of technology: What it is and how it evolves.* New York, NY: Free Press.

Ball, C. F. (2004). Show, not tell: The value of new media scholarship. *Computers and Composition, 21*(4), 403–425. doi:10.1016/S8755-4615(04)00038-6

Baym, N. K. (2002). Interpersonal life online. In L. A, Lievrouw & S. Livingstone (Eds.). Handbook of new media: Social shaping and consequences of ICTs (pp. 62-76). London: Sage Publication.

Berners-Lee, T., Cailliau, R., Luotonen, A., Nielsen, H. F., & Secret, A. (2003). The world-wide web. In N. Wardrip-Fruin & N. Montfort (Eds.), *The new media reader* (pp. 791–798). Cambridge, MA: The MIT Press.

Bitzer, L. (1968). The rhetorical situation. *Philosophy & Rhetoric*, *1*, 1–14.

Bolter, J. D. (2001). *Writing space: Computers, hypertext, and the remediation of print* (2nd ed.). Mahwah, NJ: LEA.

Braaksma, M. A. H., Rijlaarsdam, G., Couzijn, M., & van den Bergh, H. (2002). Learning to compose hypertext and linear text: Transfer or interference? In R. Bromme & E. Stahl (Eds.), *Writing hypertext and learning: Conceptual and empirical approaches* (pp. 15–37). Boston, MA: Pergamon.

Brooke, C. G. (2009). *Lingua Fracta: Toward a rhetoric of new media*. The University of Michigan: Hampton Press.

Carter, L. (2003). Argument in hypertext: Writing strategies and the problem of order in a nonsequential world. *Computers and Composition*, *20*(1), 3–22. doi:10.1016/S8755-4615(02)00176-7

Charney, D. (1994). The effect of hypertext on processes of reading and writing. In C. L. Selfe & S. Hilligoss (Eds.), *Literacy and computers: The complications of teaching and learning with technology* (pp. 89–112). New York, NY: MLA.

Cooper, M. (2010). Being linked to the matrix: Biology, technology, and writing. In S. A. Selber (Ed.), *Rhetoric and technologies: New directions in writing and communication* (pp. 15–32). Columbia, SC: University of South Carolina Press.

Costanzo, W. (1994). Reading, writing, and thinking in an age of electronic literacy. In C. L. Selfe & S. Hilligoss (Eds.), *Literacy and computers: The complications of teaching and learning with technology* (pp. 11–21). New York, NY: MLA.

Dennis, E. E. (1998). Foreword. In J. V. Pavlik (Ed.), *New media technology* (2nd ed.; pp. ix–x). Boston, MA: Allyn and Bacon.

Dizard, W. (2000). *Old media and new media: Mass communications in the information age* (3rd ed.). New York, NY: Longman.

Dobrin, D. N. (1994). Hype and hypertext. In C. L. Selfe & S. Hilligoss (Eds.), *Literacy and computers: The complications of teaching and learning with technology* (pp. 305–315). New York, NY: MLA.

Dryden, L. M. (1994). Literature, student-centered classrooms, and hypermedia environments. In C. L. Selfe & S. Hilligoss (Eds.), *Literacy and computers: The complications of teaching and learning with technology* (pp. 282–304). New York, NY: MLA.

Duin, H., & Hansen, C. (1994). Reading and writing on computer networks as social construction. In C. L. Selfe & S. Hilligoss (Eds.), *Literacy and computers: The complications of teaching and learning with technology* (pp. 89–112). New York, NY: MLA.

Gillen, J., & Merchant, G. (2013). From virtual histories to virtual literacy. In G. Merchant, J. Gillen, J. Marsh, & J. Davies (Eds.), *Virtual literacies: Interactive spaces for children and young people* (pp. 9–26). New York, NY: Routledge.

Goggin, G. (2012). *New technologies and the media*. London: Palgrave Macmillan.

Haas, C., & Neuwirth, C. M. (1994). Writing the technology that writes us: Research on literacy and the shape of technology. In C. L. Selfe & S. Hilligoss (Eds.), *Literacy and computers: The complications of teaching and learning with technology* (pp. 319–335). New York, NY: MLA.

Hilligoss, S., & Selfe, C. L. (1994). Studying literacy with computers. In C. L. Selfe & S. Hilligoss (Eds.), *Literacy and computers: The complications of teaching and learning with technology* (pp. 336–340). New York, NY: MLA.

Hocks, M. E. (2003). Understanding visual rhetoric in digital writing. *College Composition and Communication*, *54*(4), 629–656. doi:10.2307/3594188

Jenkins, S. (2003). Foreword. In J. Aitchison & D. M. Lewis (Eds.), *New media language*. New York, NY: Routledge.

Johnson, R. R. (1998). *User-centered technology*. New York: State University of New York Press.

Johnson-Eilola, J. (1994). Reading and writing in hypertext. In C. L. Selfe & S. Hilligoss (Eds.), *Literacy and computers: The complications of teaching and learning with technology* (pp. 89–112). New York, NY: MLA.

Johnson-Eilola, J. (1997). *Nostalgic angels: Rearticulating hypertext writing*. Norwood, NJ: Ablex Publishing.

Johnson-Eilola, J. (1998). Living on the surface: Learning the age of global communication networks. In I. Snyder (Ed.), *Page to screen: Taking literacy into the electronic era* (pp. 185–210). New York, NY: Routledge. doi:10.4324/9780203201220_chapter_9

Johnson-Eilola, J., & Hea, A. C. K. (2003). After hypertext: Other ideas. *Computers and Composition*, *20*(4), 415–425. doi:10.1016/j.compcom.2003.08.014

Joyce, M. (1988, November). Siren shapes: Exploratory and constructive hypertexts. Academic Computing.

Kember, S., & Zylinska, J. (2012). Introduction. In S. Kember & J. Zylinska (Eds.), *Life after new media: Mediation as a vital process* (pp. xiii–xx). Cambridge, MA: The MIT Press.

Kolb, D. (1994). Socrates in the labyrinth. In G. P. Landow (Ed.), *Hyper/text/theory* (pp. 323–342). Baltimore, MD: Johns Hopkins University Press.

Kress, G. (1999). "English" at the crossroads: Rethinking curricula of communication in the context of the turn to the visual. In G. Hawisher & C. Selfe (Eds.), *Passions, pedagogies, and 21st Century technologies* (pp. 66–88). Logan, UT: Utah State University Press.

Kress, G. (2003). *Literacy in the new media age*. New York, NY: Routledge. doi:10.4324/9780203164754

Landow, G. P. (1992). *Hypertext: The convergence of contemporary critical theory and technology.* Baltimore, MD: Johns Hopkins University Press.

Lauer, C. (2009). Contending with terms: "Multimodal" and "Multimedia" in the academic and public spheres. *Computers and Composition, 26*(4), 225–239. doi:10.1016/j.compcom.2009.09.001

Lauer, J. (1993). Rhetoric and composition studies: A multimodal discipline. In T. Enos & S. C. Brown (Eds.), *Defining the new rhetoric* (pp. 44–54). Newbury Park, CA: Sage.

Lievrouw, L. A., & Livingstone, S. (Eds.). (2002). *Handbook of new media: Social shaping and consequences of ICTs*. London: Sage Publication.

Lister, M., Dovey, J., Giddings, S., Grant, I., & Kelly, K. (2009). *New media: A critical introduction* (2nd ed.). New York, NY: Routledge.

Manovich, L. (2001). *The language of new media.* Cambridge, MA: The MIT Press.

Manovich, L. (2003). New media from Borges to HTML. In N. Wardrip-Fruin & N. Montfort (Eds.), *The new media reader* (pp. 12–23). Cambridge, MA: The MIT Press.

McMillan, S. J. (2002). Exploring models of interactivity from multiple research traditions: Users, documents, and systems. In L. Lievrouw & S. Livingston (Eds.), *The handbook of new media* (pp. 163–182). Thousand Oaks, CA: Sage.

Miller, C. R. (2010). Foreword. In S. A. Selber (Ed.), *Rhetoric and technologies: New directions in writing and communication* (pp. ix–xii). Columbia, SC: University of South Carolina Press.

Murray, J. H. (2003). Inventing the medium. In N. Wardrip-Fruin & N. Montfort (Eds.), *The new media reader* (pp. 3–10). Cambridge, MA: The MIT Press.

Nye, D. E. (2006). *Technology matters: Questions to live with.* Cambridge, MA: The MIT Press.

Palmeri, J. (2012). *Remixing composition: A history of multimodal writing pedagogy.* Carbondale, IL: Southern Illinois University Press.

Pavlik, J. V. (1998). *New media technology* (2nd ed.). Boston, MA: Allyn and Bacon.

Pavlik, J. V. (1998). Preface. In *New media technology* (2nd ed.). Boston, MA: Allyn and Bacon.

Rabkin, E. S. (2006). Audience, purpose, and medium: How digital media extend humanities education. In M. Hanrahan & D. L. Madsen (Eds.), *Teaching, technology, textuality: Approaches to new media* (pp. 135–147). New York, NY: Palgrave Macmillan. doi:10.1057/9780230523302_11

Reynolds, N. (2004). *Geographies of writing: Inhabiting places and encountering difference.* Carbondale, IL: Southern Illinois University Press.

Rice, J. (2006). The rhetoric of new media: Teaching a rhetoric of hypertext. In M. Hanrahan & D. L. Madsen (Eds.), *Teaching, technology, textuality: Approaches to new media* (pp. 148–161). New York, NY: Palgrave Macmillan. doi:10.1057/9780230523302_12

Rice, R. E. (2013). Preface. In F. L. F. Lee, L. Leung, J. L. Qiu, & D. S. C. Chu (Eds.), *Frontiers in new media research* (pp. 1–5). New York, NY: Routledge.

Selber, S. A. (2004). *Multiliteracies for a digital age*. Carbondale, IL: Southern Illinois University Press.

Selber, S. A. (2010). Introduction. In S. A. Selber (Ed.), *Rhetoric and technologies: New directions in writing and communication* (pp. 1–11). Columbia, SC: University of South Carolina Press.

Selber, S. A. (Ed.). (2010). *Rhetoric and technologies: New directions in writing and communication*. Columbia, SC: University of South Carolina Press.

Selfe, C. L. (1999). *Technology and literacy in the twenty-first century: The importance of paying attention*. Carbondale, IL: Southern Illinois University Press.

Selfe, C. L. (2004a). Students who teach us: A case study of a new media text designer. In *Writing new media: Theory and applications for expanding the teaching of composition* (pp. 43–66). Logan, UT: Utah State University Press.

Selfe, C. L. (2004b). Toward new media texts: Taking up the challenges of visual literacy. In *Writing new media: Theory and applications for expanding the teaching of composition* (pp. 66–110). Logan, UT: Utah State University Press.

Selfe, C. L. (2009). The movement of air, the breath of meaning: Aurality and multimodal composing. *College Composition and Communication*, *60*(4), 616–663.

Selfe, C. L., & Hilligoss, S. (1994). Introduction. In C. L. Selfe & S. Hilligoss (Eds.), *Literacy and computers: The complications of teaching and learning with technology*. New York, NY: MLA. doi:10.1300/J054v02n01_01

Shipka, J. (2011). *Toward a composition make whole*. Pittsburgh, PA: University of Pittsburg Press.

Smith, C. F. (1994). Hypertextual thinking. In C. L. Selfe & S. Hilligoss (Eds.), *Literacy and computers: The complications of teaching and learning with technology* (pp. 264–281). New York, NY: MLA.

Smith, S., & Hendricks, J. A. (2010). New media: New technology, new ideas or new headaches. In J. A. Hendricks (Ed.), *The twenty-first century media industry: Economic and managerial implications in the age of new media* (pp. 3–22). Plymouth, UK: Lexington Books.

Snoddy, R. (2003). Modern media myths. In J. Aitchison & D. M. Lewis (Eds.), *New media language* (pp. 18–20). New York, NY: Routledge.

Sorapure, M. (2006). Between modes: Assessing student new media composition. *Kairos*, *10*(2), 1–15.

Takayoshi, P., & Selfe, C. L. (2007). Thinking about multimodality. In C. L. Selfe (Ed.), *Multimodal composition: Resources for teachers* (pp. 1–12). Cresskill, NJ: Hampton Press, Inc.

Tribe, M. (2001). Foreword. In L. Manovich (Ed.), *The language of new media*. Cambridge, MA: The MIT Press.

Warnick, B., & Heineman, D. S. (2012). *Rhetoric online: The politics of new media* (2nd ed.). New York, NY: Peter Lang.

Williams, B. (2007). Foreword. In C. L. Selfe (Ed.), *Multimodal composition: Resources for teachers*. Cresskill, NJ: Hampton Press, Inc. doi:10.1016/B978-0-7506-8368-5.50002-0

Withrow, F. B. (2004). *Literarcy in the digital age: Reading, writing, viewing, and computing*. Lanham, MD: Scarecrow Education.

Wysocki, A. F. (2004). Opening new media to writing: Openings and justifications. In *Writing new media: Theory and applications for expanding the teaching of composition*. Logan, UT: Utah State University Press.

Wysocki, A. F., Johnson-Eilola, J., Selfe, C., & Sirc, G. (2004). *Writing new media: Theory and applications for expanding the teaching of composition*. Logan, UT: Utah State University Press.

Yancey, K. B. (2004). Looking for sources of coherence in a fragmented world: Notes toward a new assessment design. *Computers and Composition*, *21*(1), 89–102. doi:10.1016/j.compcom.2003.08.024

Zeni, J. (1994). Literacy, technology, and teacher education. In C. L. Selfe & S. Hilligoss (Eds.), *Literacy and computers: The complications of teaching and learning with technology* (pp. 11–21). New York, NY: MLA.

Zoetewey, M. W., & Staggers, J. (2003). Beyond current-traditional design: Assessing rhetoric in new media. *Issues in Writing*, *13*, 133–157.

Chapter 9
Translingual and Digital Ecologies:
A Cloud Pedagogy for Second Language Classrooms

Jialei Jiang
Indiana University of Pennsylvania, USA

ABSTRACT

Scholarship in cloud pedagogy has provided intriguing lenses through which researchers enhance pedagogical approaches for digital composition classrooms. However, there is a lack of discussion on how cloud pedagogy could be employed to benefit second language learners of writing. Scholars in both digital and translingual areas of research have touched on conceptualizing their theories through multimodal, collaborative, and ecological perspectives of writing. Therefore, this article looks into the theories and practices of translingualism, and explore how translingual writing can be merged and integrated into the multimodal applications of cloud-based learning. Following and expanding the practices of digital composition, this paper aims to argue for an ontological shift to a translingual view of cloud-based writing and examine how it informs second language learning.

INTRODUCTION

With the growing population of international multilingual learners in English speaking countries, the issue of student mobility has been propelled into the limelight. As classrooms in U.S. colleges are becoming increasingly globalized and multifaceted, researchers and teachers are faced with the challenge on how to better address the needs of diverse populations of second language learners. As second language students move across national and cultural borders, they are no longer confined by fixed definitions and dispositions of the places and cultures from which they come. International students' mobility has also contributed local knowledge to the process of globalization, challenging the structure of extant forms of education (Collins, 2012).

DOI: 10.4018/978-1-5225-1650-7.ch009

Through this lens, writing is no longer bounded by predefined norms and locations. Rather, it encompasses joint networks of local and global encounters. As international students move across their home and target language and cultures, their local knowledge could be utilized for translingual and multimodal practices to co-construct meaning in digital composition. A cloud pedagogy from the angle of translingualism may enhance students' inquiry into language and culture, endorse the collaborative nature of translingual and multimodal writing, and enact both human and non-human resources in the learning process. Cloud pedagogy therefore is closely linked with translingual perspectives that manifested critical resistance to the dominant ideologies and modes of representations through encouraging multilingual students to utilize multiple semiotic resources (Kress, 2010; Van Leeuwen, 2005), or socially-made and every-changing means of meaning making, from their diverse linguistic and cultural backgrounds. The use of diverse semiotic resources leads to students' engagement with writing on an ecological scale. The translingual and digital ecology builds the connection between students' living experience of their local cultures and study-abroad environments.

Scholarships in digital composition and translingualism thus have a shared understanding on the multimodal, collaborative, and ecological aspects of writing. This being said, however, translingual and digital multimodal studies exist mainly as two separate areas of research, despite a few scholarly efforts to conflate and combine these research interests. For instance, Horner and Selfe (2013) stress that "despite their common points of origination, discussions of modality have remained largely separate from discussions of translingualism, to the impoverishment of both" (p. 2). In other words, the two conceptual frameworks in general have not benefited much from a collaborative work. For this reason, there is a need to bridge the theoretical orientations of translingualism and multimodality through exploring the complexity and diversity of translingual cloud-based learning. Following and expanding the practices of digital composition, this chapter aims to argue for an ontological shift to a translingual view of cloud pedagogy and examine how it provides pedagogical implications for second language learning.

The argument of this chapter will be presented in four sections. First, cloud pedagogy in second language writing will be discussed, in terms of three types of learning opportunities enacted through the cloud pedagogy; namely, multimodal affordances, collaborative affordances, and ecological affordances. Secondly, the framework of translingualism will be presented and discussed through the lenses of translingual writing and translingual ecology. The next section will focus on the pedagogical implications of translingualism for cloud-based second language writing. Special attention will be paid to the themes of bridging print and digital modalities, negotiating linguistic and cultural differences, and conflating human and non-human ecologies. Finally, the chapter offers general thought on future research directions for using translingualism and cloud pedagogy in second language writing classrooms.

CLOUD PEDAGOGY IN SECOND LANGUAGE WRITING

Scholarship in cloud technologies has been under the influence of theories in multimodality. Cloud pedagogy incorporates cloud technologies in classroom teaching, including but not limited to Facebook, Google docs, wikis, blogs, Twitter, and mobile apps that have been shown to facilitate second language writing. Current literature demonstrates that cloud technologies have empowered the voice for second language learners, and provided the opportunity for cross-cultural communication (Lantz-Andersson, Vigmo & Bowen, 2013; Lee et al., 2016; Limbu, 2013; Mitchell, 2012; Nelson, 2006). Lying at the heart of such benefits is the use of cloud pedagogy to meet the needs of linguistically and culturally diverse students. The next section will focus on three types of "affordances," or resources to be enacted (Canagarajah, 2016) by cloud pedagogy in second language classrooms, namely multimodal affordances, collaborative affordances, and ecological affordances.

Multimodal Affordances

Cloud technologies and multimodal networks have expanded the existing literature on face-to face communication and language learning by formulating "new social spaces, linguistic and semiotic practices" (Lam, 2006). For instance, multimodality emerges from the New Literacy Studies' theory of multiliteracies (New London Group, 1996) that redefines literacy as a social practices related to the negotiation of multi-faceted cultural and linguistic differences, and proposes that five modes of meaning can be generated in literacy education, i.e., linguistic, visual, audio, gestural, and spatial ones. Kress (2010) further interprets multimodality as the design to organize these different modes into a multimodal "ensemble," or the combination of "a plurality of signs in different modes into a particular configuration to form a coherent arrangement" (p. 162). Through examining the combination of various modes, including verbal and non-verbal modes of meaning, the multimodal orientation, including the use of digital technologies, therefore questions the boundaries between languages and other modalities. This definition of multimodality is key to rethinking the ontological basis of language, writing, and technology.

Digital technologies including cloud computing contribute to the development of multimodal literacy. Through encompassing multiple modes of communication, multimodal literacy blurs the boundary established by traditional print-based texts that prioritize linguistic modes. Horner and Selfe (2013) note,

While print texts have always mixed some modalities of expression (words and visual information, for instance), digital environments allow for different kinds/varieties of mixing. Here, I'm thinking of the ways in which print text and video/audio texts can be juxtaposed/combined in a single composing environment. (p.10)

In other words, while print texts intermingle the linguistic and visual modes of meaning making, digital media open the door to a nexus of multiple modalities. Just as Kress (2005) points out, in the print media writing still remains its dominance and privilege over other modes, such as limited use of images and pictures. Therefore, traditional print-based materials create a binary between linguistic modes and other modalities of writing. Digital spaces incorporate and accommodate more varieties of modes, serving to deterritorialize the prevalent use of language in paper-based texts. Research in digital writing and multimodality hence has problematized and challenged the divide between different modalities of meaning making.

Furthermore, multimodal means of communication is also salient in informing second language writing and developing writers' voice and identities (Lam, 2006; Lotherington & Jenson, 2011; Nelson, 2006; Shin & Cimasko, 2008). Digital and cloud-based studies have been conducted to explore the interconnection between different modes of communication, and the use of multimodalities in second language pedagogy (Lotherington & Jenson, 2011). Looking into the synesthesia of multiple modes in second language writers' digital storytelling, recent research suggests that multimodal communicative practices could amplify second language learners' voice and authorship when the learners have acquired a semiotic awareness of multimodal composition (Nelson, 2006). In this sense, the multimodal affordances of cloud pedagogy grant second language writers the freedom to negotiate meanings beyond the limits of the linguistic modes and their language competency. Through investigating the "interactivity" among the interconnected networks of modes for second language learners of English, researchers have also found that non-linguistic modes of communication are used by second language writers to maintain their national and cultural identities (Shin & Cimasko, 2008). In a nutshell, recent research in digital and cloud pedagogy focuses on conceptualizing different modes of expression as multi-faceted and intermingled, working together as a synthetic amalgamation to facilitate second language learning.

Collaborative Affordances

Cloud pedagogy also allows for interpersonal collaboration and intercultural communication (Lantz-Andersson et al., 2013; Lee et al., 2016; Mitchell, 2012). As the "multimodal affordances" undermine categorizations of language and technologies, the 'collaborative affordances' challenge distinctions between individual writers and speakers. Cloud technologies facilitate knowledge sharing and collaborative learning in second language learning. Language learners' dynamic social media have made it possible to bridge school and home learning through creating spaces for collaborative learning activities. Drawing from the sociocultural model of collaborative learning mediated by social practice, scholars have contended that cloud technologies such as social networking sites formulate platforms through which young people mediate their learning (Lantz-Andersson et al., 2013). Social networking sites such as Facebook create spaces for extended collaborations both in both formal learning contexts and everyday technological use. Mobile learning has also been shown to assist in the development of collaborative skills for second language learners. Through mobile serious games, students have developed collaborative skills in the process of solving problems with their group mates (Lee et al., 2016). In this sense, collaboration is achieved through learners' interaction with other members of the learning community. Cloud technologies also function as an avenue for intercultural communication. Research has found that second language learners are motivated to acquire cultural knowledge when engaging in Facebook communication (Mitchell, 2012). It has been suggested that part of the reasons why second language students join Facebook is the need for cultural learning. The students who have joined Facebook are able to share their local cultures and learn about American culture through the social networking site. Through this lens, cloud technologies have generated collaborative affordances to stimulate interpersonal and intercultural collaboration.

Additionally, cloud-based learning contributes to the exchange of values and ideas across the spectrum of local and global interactions. Cloud computing "connects people globally with those who have similar as well as dissimilar social, cultural, and political beliefs" (Limbu, 2013, p. 138). In this light, cloud pedagogy thus provides a space for global citizens to exchange local and global perceptions and ideologies. For second language writers, cloud pedagogy creates a network of social encounters. Cloud computing expands the literal meaning of learning space to denote metaphorically a nexus of sociopolitical events and practices. In today's digital and multimodal world, learning is mediated and actualized through the joint networks of local and global encounters. The collaborative affordances of cloud pedagogy thus are also manifested by transnational collaborations.

Ecological Affordances

Before discussing the ecological affordances of cloud and digital pedagogy, it is necessary to review the ecological modal of writing in composition studies. The ecological modal of writing emerges from the works of composition scholars such as Marilyn Cooper, Sidney Dobrin, and Christian Weisser. Debunking Flower and Hayes' cognitive view of composition that isolate writers from the social world, Cooper (1986) espouses an ecological model of writing that moves beyond individual writers and their writing contexts. Rather, the ecological model examines "dynamic interlocking systems" of social activities contributing to the writing process. She further maintains that "writing…is seen to be both constituted by and constitutive of…ever-changing systems, systems through which people relate as complete, social beings…" (Cooper, 1986, p. 373). In this sense, the writing process itself is emergent and fluid, undergoing changes relative to the transformations of ecological and social systems in which composition takes place. Drawing from Cooper's (1986, 2011) ecological model of writing, Dobrin and Weisser (2002) illustrate a dialectic relation between discourse and environment. Compositionists make inquiries into the process in which discourses shape places and environments just as nature and environments influence discourses (Dobrin & Weisser, 2002, p. 573). In other words, writing constitutes part of the materiality in the same way that material environment shapes the construction of linguistic meanings. Both discourses and materiality play an agentive role in responding to and acting upon each other. This ecological view of composition essentially sheds light on a reciprocity between human beings and ecological environments.

Challenging human centrality and dominance has also become salient in recent works of ecological and digital writing. Guattari's (1989) "The Three Ecologies" has been cited by scholars to displace human intentionality in human and non-human ecological systems. This theory maintains that there are three registers of ecologies, namely social ecology, mental ecology, and environmental ecology. The theory thus postulates an "ecosophy" that delves into the interrelations between the natural environment, social relations, and human subjectivity. Building on Guattari's "The Three Ecologies," Dobrin (2011) maintains that his ecological theory complicates the notion of subjectivity, thereby serving as a critique of the "learner-as-designer" metaphor salient in research on multimodality. Dobrin holds that the dichotomy between nature and culture oversimplifies ecological relationships. Instead, with the emergence of computer-aided subjectivity and the new media, it is time to disrupt and extend the current knowledge of writing system by way of examining the interconnection between the three registers of ecology. Morey (2012) also draws on Felix Guattari's philosophy of ecosophy to illustrate that the boundary between human and non-human agents is porous. Citing Guattari, Morey seeks to build the connection between Guattari's ecosophy and digital ecologies. He has used the metaphor "digital ecologies" to denote the inseparability of natural and digital worlds. For instance, Morey (2012) argues that composition "is also digital and has digital effects where it interacts with nature; the two create an ecological relationship" (p. 114). This view of composition therefore delves into the complex ecologies that evoke both partial and holistic, both heterogeneous and homogeneous notions of natural and social environments, challenging the division between human and non-human systems in the digital multimodal ecologies of learning. Similarly, DeVoss, McKee, and Selfe (2009) delve into the technological ecology of writing. It has been pointed out that a complex ecology emerges out of the interaction between computerized writing artifacts and human beings utilizing and supporting the technologies (DeVoss, McKee, & Selfe, 2009). The researchers conceptualize digital composition as similar to ecological systems in which human beings and the material technologies formulate a network of interaction. In this sense, the sustainable system of composition classrooms and programs is constructed and maintained by both human and technological agents. The ecological affordances of cloud pedagogy, therefore, recognize the interactions between human and non-human subjects in second language writing.

TRANSLINGUALISM

Given that digital technologies could provide multiple affordances for writing learners, digital and multimodal composition has not been explored exhaustively to benefit second language writers. The framework of translingualism that addresses the needs of linguistically and culturally diverse groups of students, in this sense, may infuse new vigor to the application of digital writing in second language classrooms. Recent years have witnessed an interest in translingualism among composition scholars (Domahue, 2016; Gonzales, 2015; Kiernan, 2015; McCorkle, Halasek, Clinnin, & Selfe, 2016; Shipka, 2016). However, although being a novel trend in language learning, translingual practice is faced with pedagogical challenges to meet the needs of second language students. One critique on translingualism lies in its limited capacity to inform writing pedagogy and classroom instruction. For instance, translingual writing "has not widely taken up the task of helping L2 [second language] writers increase their proficiency" (Atkinson et al., 2015, p. 384). Translingualism has also been under the criticism of lacking viable pedagogical applications for improving multilingual learners' proficiency in English (Mastuda, 2014). This section contends that through bridging the gap between translingual research and digital composition, translingual scholars may be able to address the scholarly debate on the pedagogical application of translingual practices in second language teaching and learning.

Translingual Writing

Translingualism has its root in the concept of the "the contact zone." In "Arts of the Contact Zone", Pratt (1991) coins the term "contact zones" to denote the social spaces in which dominant and subordinate cultural concepts and beliefs are in confrontation with and conflict against each other. The term demythifies the illusion of "a unified and homogenous social world" through the juxtaposition of difference with authority and heterogeneity with ubiquity, which is then exemplified by indigenous rewriting of Christian history, as well as by students' resistance against dominant institutions (Pratt, 1991). This contact, therefore, brings about ideological shifts, whereby diverse power groups question and challenge the legitimacy of the norms established by the authoritarian communities.

Drawing from Pratt's concept of the "contact zone," translingual theories promote "an engagement with diverse languages and cultures," which is manifested in the mixing of language resources (Canagarajah, 2013a; 2013b; 2014a). Mixed forms of academic learning have been equated with a "contact zone," which creates the space for negotiation of meaning for translingual performance. The boundaries between linguistic and cultural modes have also been problematized. Rather, language has been redefined as "a demarcation of a far more complex ecology of practices" (Horner & Selfe, 2013, p. 9). Subsuming languages into clearly defined categories oversimplifies the complexity of the relations between different languages and cultures.

Debunking the monolingual and nativist assumptions of second language learners, translingualism launches a scholarly debate on standardized English. Standardized English has been questioned for "the immutable set of rigid rules implied by designating it as "standard" (Bizzell, 2014a, p. 134). In contrast, the concept of global Englishes has expanded geographic regions in which English is conventionally and historically has been adopted as the native form of language (Bizzell, 2014a). The local has also been conceptualized as a space of "enactment" and "recontextualization," (Pennycook 2007, p. 111), or a form of critical resistance to homogeneity and assimilation, blurring the boundaries between English as a local and global language. Creating a space for negotiation among different varieties of English challenges the pre-established cultural and political categories in support of a view of language that positions English as a living and changing language.

Thus, translingual writing illuminates a new avenue for understanding language differences through a focus on learner agency and intercommunity negotiation. Debunking the monolingual and "English only" view of composition, scholars espouse the translingual paradigm to consider the power relations in writing classrooms and empower multilingual and second language writers' agency of learning (Canagarajah, 2013a; Horner & Selfe, 2013; Horner et al., 2011; Lu & Horner, 2012). For instance, student writers could draw on their repertoires of linguistic and cultural resources to bring diversity into the standardized forms of language and culture (Horner, Lu, Royster & Trimbur, 2011; Domahue, 2016). In a similar vein, translingual practice has been posited as "the work of creative and active social agents" who engage with the different and sometimes conflictual systems of language and thought (Canagarajah, 2013a, p. 32). In this sense, the translingual paradigm has prioritized writers' subjectivity and agency in language practices. Translingualism also highlights inter-community negotiations (Canagarajah, 2013b, 2016). It is through negotiation of ideas and identities that language learners generate new knowledge and formulate group solidarity. Negotiating "diverse languages, symbol systems, and modalities of communication," (Canagrajah, 2013b, p. 41), translingual learning thus debunks the notion that students from a learning community should act according to pre-established norms of communication, especially the norms under the disguise of monolingualism. Instead, through inter-community negotiations and collaborations, second language students generate new norms and achieve communicative goals with their group members.

Translingual Ecology

Scholars of translingual research have envisioned writing as embedded in the interactions between multifaceted systems and ecologies of learning. This can be exemplified by the growth of research interests in language and ecologies. Canagarajah (2013b) conceptualizes translingual practices through the lens of ecological writing. According to him, ecology and environment provide a wealth of affordances that learners could draw on to co-construct meaning in dialogues. He further contextualizes text as a not only a constituent of local ecologies but also as affordance of diverse resources for meaning making, generated through "the interplay of participants, objects, spatiotemporal contexts, and the ecology of semiotic resources, not words in isolation" (Canagarajah, 2013b, p. 62). For this reason, discourse and environment are not separate systems of learning, but overlap and interact with each other. Horner and Selfe (2013) also acknowledge that language should be understood as demarcating a "complex ecology of practices" (p. 9). That is to say, the interplay between language and other semiotic modes generates an ecological network encompassing multiple forms of practices.

Additionally, scholarships in translingualism also orient toward viewing composition as a fluid and dynamic process, one of the key notions in ecological composition. Translingual studies have adopted "an expansive, holistic, and plural orientation" to espouse the ecological orientation to English teaching and learning that interprets writing as embedded in changing ecological and multimodal environments (Canagarajah, 2014a; 2014b). Due to the unpredictability of class and the change of students' predilection, teachers are supposed to reorient pedagogical activities through negotiations with students in the classroom (Canagarajah, 2014b). The fluidity and changeability of learning environment is also manifested in the envisioning of classroom ecology as permeated with semiotic resources that students can transform into affordances, of which teachers may not be consciously aware (Canagarajah, 2016).

Through this lens, translingual scholarship embraces the unpredictability of the ecology through which the production of texts along with semiotic resources occurs in tacit and subtle forms.

Albeit that translingual scholars have touched on the social and fluid aspects of ecological writing, they remain centralizing human beings as agents taking active control of the writing process, a concept that has been problematized by recent studies in translingualism and materiality. Recent compositionists inaugurate a reworking of translingual theories in a material and ecological direction. Jordan (2015) taps into the ontological and ethical questions underlying the ideology of translingualism. Through questioning the overemphasis on human agency and subjectivity, he situated translingual practices into the framework of the neo-materialistic and ecological philosophies. That is to say, translingualism should take into consideration the complex ecologies of teaching and learning that shape the interplay between human and non-human agents. Additionally, the ecological model of learning expands the translingual framework of language practice. Performativity moves writing from language representation to discursive practice, focusing on the "production of the matter of bodies" (Barad, 2003, p. 807-808). The ecological model is therefore linked with translingual learning in that translingual theories are rooted in language learning as practice-based (See Canagarajah, 2014b). At the same time, however, the ecological concept of practice broadens the "practice" nature of translingualism to underscore not only practices of human subjects, but also non-human bodies and matters. This sense of practice is linked with the notion of materiality. Micciche (2014) writes that collaborations between human and non-human agents should be construed as "partnerships that involve the merging of various forms of matter" (p. 498). The key concept, therefore, lies not so much in who should be dominating the classroom ecology manifested in both teacher-centered and student-centered orientations, as in how human beings perform translingual practices through interacting with non-human materials. Drawing from Micciche's notion of materiality, Shipka (2016) notes that the collaboration between the translingual and multimodal (including digital) orientations also is manifested in the intermingling of human and non-human resources. This notion of materiality correlates with the ecological affordances of cloud pedagogy, which will be further elaborated in the next section.

INCORPORATING TRANSLINGUALISM INTO CLOUD PEDAGOGY

What is left to be explored, then, is how the ontological interpretation of translingualism could benefit cloud pedagogy. Translingualism has provided intriguing lenses through which researchers enhance pedagogical approaches for teaching second language students in U.S. academic writing classrooms. Scholars in both digital and translingual areas of research have touched on conceptualizing their theories through a multimodal, collaborative, and ecological perspective of writing (Canagarajah 2014a, 2016; Dobrin et al., 2012). Through tracing the similarities between translingual and digital writing, this section explores the theoretical and pedagogical implications incorporating translingualism into digital composition. For this reason, this section also seeks to examine the ontology of translingualism that allows multilingual learners to utilize their diversified repertoires of linguistic and cultural knowledge. Furthermore, the section proposes addressing the research gap of digital and translingual literacy practices by examining the theoretical framework of translingualism and the function of translingualism in facilitating cloud pedagogy. This being said, however, there is a lack of empirical research looking into the collaboration between translingualism and cloud pedagogy, which awaits exploration by future researchers.

Bridging Print and Digital Modalities

Translingual scholars have tapped into the dialectical relations between different varieties of languages and modalities. The distinction between an array of modes and languages misinterprets disparate languages as having specific effects and oversimplifies the complexity of human experience associated with different senses (Horner and Selfe, 2013). In other words, the compartment of single languages and modalities does not accurately reflect human experience related to various sensations. Rather, the nomenclature of "translingualism" attests to the ontological move blending multiple modalities of meaning. For instance, the prefix of "trans" in translingualism denotes the tendency to incorporate other forms of semiotic resources beyond language, including color, image, and symbols (Canagarajah, 2013b, p. 41). Thus, scholars in translingual research challenge the notion to categorize and isolate disparate modes of communication, including linguistic modes and non-linguistic resources. From this perspective, translingualism not only includes the mixing and mingling of different languages but also suggests the crossing and bridging of semiotic boundaries. This translingual orientation thus bears a resemblance to digital and multimodal research in that both of the two trends aim to question the boundaries between languages and modalities. Scholars tend to recognize the complexity and diversity of translingual and digital spaces.

The mixing of semiotic resources can be seen in recent compositional research. Gonzales (2015) has conducted a rhetoric genre study on the use of translingualism in multimodal composing practices of second language writers. Gonzales (2015) utilizes multimodal and translingual theories to conduct a focus-group analysis on linguistically diverse students at two large public state universities. The researcher explores how the students' approaches and conceptions of writing shift when composing print and multilingual genres. The researcher looks into both verbal and gestural means of communication to gain knowledge about the students' perception of how they approach different genres of writing. Through analyzing the video data coded through ELAN, the researcher finds that students' use of gestures, "in conjunction with their verbal discussions, suggest a limited, linear perception of conventional print genres" (p. 12). Different from the discussions on print-based texts, during the focus group discussion of digital projects, the majority of second language students have utilized words, wavy gestures, and other semiotic resources to convey concepts that they may have found difficult in expressing through words alone. In this sense, the study recommends a translingual approach in digital composition that may potentially benefit second language writers.

Constituting part of the multimodal research, cloud computing provides various modalities and resources for second language students. However, there is a shortage of studies examining how cloud technologies could potentially bridge print and digital modalities in language learning. In this light, compositionists can look into various forms of modalities being adopted in cloud-based writing classrooms. For instance, writing instructors can ask students to describe their use of technological tools such as Google docs and the influence of the technologies on their digital learning. By way of inviting students to describe their experience, the instructor as well as the students can explore the multiplicity of cloud-based practices enacted through a heterogeneity of modalities including but not limited to words, pictures, figures, PowerPoints, and videos that could be shared via cloud technologies. Discussions can also focus on how digital tools such as social networking websites change student writers' engagement with classroom activities. Key questions to consider include the following: how will multilingual learners benefit from the interactions between multiple modes of communication? How will composition teachers assess students' writing cross multiple linguistic and symbolic modalities? In this sense, future research needs to look into how cloud-based learning takes place among the interactions of translingual individuals and the impact of these interactions on the writers' digital activities.

Negotiating Linguistic and Cultural Differences

Transligualism confirms and expands the notions of interpersonal collaboration and cross-cultural communication in cloud pedagogy. Cloud technologies have provided a platform for collaboration. The framework of translingualism enriches the collaborative affordances of digital tools by examining the needs of linguistically and culturally diverse populations of students. From the translingual point of view, linguistic and cultural norms are not pre-established, but rather negotiated through the interaction and collaboration of language learners.

Culturally-based collaborative activities have been draw upon to facilitate second language writers' translingual and multimodal learning. Kiernan (2015) explores the role of cultural sharing through multimodal and translingual classroom practices, specifically food culture, in developing critical thinking and writing skills for college second language learners. The study also aims to use culturally-based pedagogical approaches for bridging translingual and multimodal ideologies of composition. A discourse analysis is conducted on second language learners in a preparatory writing class who are asked to complete a print-based writing assignment on food culture and a digital-based video project on the same topic. The findings suggest that that the culturally-based activities have contributed to the students' intellectual growth and promoted translingual and multimodal ideologies within pedagogies.

Translingual collaboration can also be actualized in online instructional settings. McCorkle et al. (2016) have discussed the use of a World English approach in the context of a Massive Open Online Course (MOOC) that encourages students to negotiate language differences. MOOC has been configured as an instructional tool to facilitate language learning for second language writers. Highlighting peer feedback as exchange of ideas, cloud computing thus moves away from the power imbalances between native speakers and second language students and the nativist assumptions of the culturally diverse groups of learners. Instead, a World English approach that foregrounds cross-cultural negotiation, in tandem with the translingual ideology, has been utilized to disrupt monolingual norms and standardized English and encourage multilingual and translingual students' participation in the online instructional context.

While these studies discussed the use of a translingual paradigm highlighting cross-cultural negotiation in general, translingualism has not been adopted widely in cloud-based writing research. In composition classrooms, this recognition of negotiation can be used for promoting cloud pedagogy. Writing teachers could invite students to have collaborative writing and peer feedback activities that empower second language students' interpersonal and inter-community interactions. Culturally-based activities can also be incorporated into the cloud-based learning. Despite current research's focus on the benign aspects of negotiating languages and meanings in online practices of writing, there exist potential challenges that second language learners may face. For instance, students with pre-established monolingual ideologies may be less motivated to negotiate meanings with their peers. Students with limited exposure to digital tools may also find it challenging to communicate meaningfully and effectively through cloud-based platforms. To explore these issues, composition researchers can empirically examine how teachers, learners, and technologies interact with each other in cloud-based practices, and how to deal with learners' struggle with technological devices. To further explore the issue, future research is needed to investigate in a greater depth into the pedagogical gap between cloud technologies and translingualism.

Conflating Human and Non-Human Ecologies

The pedagogical implications is also less explored regarding a synthesis of translingual and digital ecologies in cloud-based practices. Scholars of digital and translingual research have envisioned writing as embedded in the interactions between multifaceted systems and ecologies of learning. In this light, recent translingual scholarship correlates with digital and multimodal research in terms of their shared understanding that writers are situated within an ecological learning environment permeated with a multitude of semiotic resources and modalities. Digital and translingual ecology thus encompasses the interactions of both human and non-human subjects.

Conflating human and non-human ecologies has been a focus in recent compositional works. Fraiberg (2010) elaborates on the need to expand the existing frameworks in multimodal and multilingual composition, and to bridge the boundaries between human beings and non-human objects. Using a high-tech company in Israel as an example, the researcher illustrates the mixing of Hebrew and English on the company's website. The article hence recommends incorporating multimodal and multilingual texts from everyday language practices into composition classes and writing research. It has also been pointed out that non-human materials provide an analytical tool for literacy practices. Through examining the company's websites, blogs, emails and other ecologies, the researcher has garnered useful cultural information about the company's rhetorical practices. As Fraiberg (2010) writes, "human actors are no longer in dialogue only with one another, but also with other texts and tools" (p. 107). From this perspective, composition teachers and students also engage with the material tools including textbooks, assignments, and websites. It is thus significant to investigate the translingual and technological aspects of the writing ecology.

This being said, however, it is worth nothing that the ecological move of translingualism does not run contrary to the "learner-centeredness" in translingual and cloud-based pedagogy. Rather, the ecological theorization of translingualism moves beyond "learner-centered" teaching to incorporate both human and non-human agency. In other words, both human beings and material objects not only constitute part of the composing practices but also serve as agents to take active control of the writing processes. This ontological move sheds light on the classroom application of the translingual digital ecologies.

The pedagogical implication for compositionists is the recognition of material objects, including digital and print-based learning tools, as agents that facilitate translingual and digital learning for second language writers. Composition teachers could ask students to reflect on the material tools they use to construct or interpret translingual texts. Students can also discuss how they engage with cloud technologies through multimodal projects such as designing a wiki page to illustrate their writing or collaborating on Google Doc to write an essay. Classroom activities may focus on various forms of cultural artifacts such as food, clothing, and rites, and examine how these material artifacts of language and culture provides the opportunity for cross-cultural negotiation. Additionally, future composition scholars could look into the interactions between different human and non-human subjects in digital and translingual ecologies, with an eye on the complex system of learning when students interact with digital and material artifacts to negotiate meanings.

CONCLUSION AND FUTURE DIRECTION

This chapter has elaborated on using translingualism to inform cloud pedagogy. The review of literatures focuses on three aspects of translingual and multimodal writing that are most germane to enhancing composition pedagogy for second language learners, namely bridging print and digital modalities, negotiating linguistic and cultural differences, and conflating human and non-human ecologies. These three aspects of digital writing shed light on the agentive role played by both print and digital modes of writing, both native speakers and second language learners, and both human and non-human agents in cloud-based composing practices. Albeit that recent compositionists have theorized translingualism as conducive for digital learning, there are few empirical studies examining the use of translingualism to benefit cloud pedagogy and digital composition. In this light, this article has argued for more studies to be conducted to explore the pedagogical implications of translingualism in composition classes.

The theoretical framework of translingualism aligns with the digital and multimodal research agenda to provide a cloud pedagogy for second language students Translingualism aligns with digital and multimodal scholarship in switching the focus away from monomodality, monolingualism, and human subjectivity. To this end, scholars in translingual and digital writing have problematized and complicated the fixed, clear, and static definitions of languages and modalities. These concepts may all be explored in interesting ways through the lens of multilingual and second language students' life and study in the United States. Future researchers need to look further into how to design pedagogical activities that embody the values of a cloud-based writing ecology reflecting both translingual and digital practices.

REFERENCES

Atkinson, D. et al. (2015). Clarifying the relationship between L2 writing and translingual writing: An open letter to writing studies editors and organization leaders. *College English*, *77*, 383–386.

Barad, K. (2003). Posthumanist performativity: Toward an understanding of how matters comes to matter. *Signs (Chicago, Ill.)*, *28*(3), 801–831. doi:10.1086/345321

Bizzell, P. (2014a). Toward "transcultural" literacy. In B. Horner & K. Kopelson (Eds.), *Reworking English in rhetoric and composition: Global interrogations, local interventions* (pp. 131–149). Carbondale, IL: Southern Illinois University Press.

Bizzell, P. (2014b). We want to know who our students are. *PMLA*, *129*(3), 442–447. doi:10.1632/pmla.2014.129.3.442

Canagarajah, S. (2013a). English as translingual. In *Translingual practice: Global Englishes and cosmoplitan relations* (pp. 56–75). London: Routledge.

Canagarajah, S. (2013b). Negotiating translingual literacy: An enactment. *Research in the Teaching of English*, *48*(1), 40–67.

Canagarajah, S. (2014a). In search of a new paradigm for teaching English as an international language. *TESOL Journal*, *5*(4), 767–785. doi:10.1002/tesj.166

Canagarajah, S. (2014b). *Clarifying the relationship between translingual practice and L2 writing.* Paper presented at The 2014 Maryland Conference on Academic and Professional Writing, University of Maryland, MD. Retrieved September 4, 2016, from https://www.academia.edu/16051926/Clarifying_the_Relationship_between_Translingual_Practice_and_L2_Writing

Canagarajah, S. (2016). Translingual writing and teacher development in composition. *College English, 78*(3), 264–272.

Collins, F. L. (2012). Researching mobility and emplacement: Examining transience and transnationality in international student lives. *Area, 44*(3), 296–304. doi:10.1111/j.1475-4762.2012.01112.x

Cooper, M. (1986). The ecology of writing. *College English, 48*(4), 364–375. doi:10.2307/377264

Cooper, M. (2011). Rhetorical agency as emergent and enacted. *CCC, 62*(3), 420–449.

DeVoss, D., McKee, H., & Selfe, R. (Eds.). (2009). *Technological ecologies and sustainability* [PDF e-book]. Retrieved September 4, 2016, from http://ccdigitalpress.org/tes/TES_COMBINED.pdf

Dobrin, S. I. (2011). *Postcomposition.* Southern Illinois University Press.

Dobrin, S. I., & Weisser, C. R. (2002). Breaking ground in ecocomposition: Exploring relationships between discourse and environment. *College English, 64*(5), 566–589. doi:10.2307/3250754

Domahue, C. (2016). The "trans" in transnational-translingual: Rhetorical and linguistic flexibility as new norms. *Composition Studies, 44*(1), 147–150.

Fraiberg, S. (2010). Composition 2.0: Toward a multilingual and multimodal framework. *College Composition and Communication, 62*(1), 100–126.

Gonzales, L. (2015). Multimodality, translingualism, and rhetorical genre studies. *Composition. Forum*, 31.

Guattari, F. (1989). The three ecologies. *New Formations, 8*, 131–147.

Horner, B., Lu, M., Royster, J. J., & Trimbur, J. (2011). OPINION: Language difference in writing: Toward a translingual approach. *College English, 73*(3), 303–321.

Horner, B., & Selfe, C. L. (2013). *Translinguality/trasmodality relations: Snapshots from a dialogue.* Unpublished working paper, University of Louisville. Retrieved September 4, 2016, from http://louisville.edu/workingpapers/doc/self-horner-working-papers-version

Jordan, J. (2015). Material translingual ecologies. *College English, 77*(4), 364–382.

Kiernan, J. E. (2015). Multimodal and translingual composing practices: A culturally based needs assessment of second language learners. *Journal of Global Literacies, Technologies, and Emerging Pedagogies, 3*(1), 302–332.

Kress, G. (2005). Gains and losses: New forms of texts, knowledge, and learning. *Computers and Composition, 22*(1), 5–22. doi:10.1016/j.compcom.2004.12.004

Kress, G. (2010). *Multimodality: A social semiotic approach to contemporary communication.* London: Routledge.

Lam, E. (2006). Re-Envisioning language, literacy, and the immigrant subject in new mediascapes. *Pedagogies*, *1*(3), 171–195. doi:10.1207/s15544818ped0103_2

Lantz-Andersson, A., Vkigmo, S., & Bowen, R. (2013). Crossing boundaries in Facebook: Students' framing of language learning activities as extended spaces. *International Journal of Computer-Supported Collaborative Learning*, *8*(3), 293–312. doi:10.1007/s11412-013-9177-0

Lee, H., Parsons, D., Kwon, G., Kim, J., Petrova, K., Jeong, E., & Ryu, H. (2016). Cooperation begins: Encouraging critical thinking skills through cooperative reciprocity using a mobile learning game. *Computers & Education*, *97*, 97–155. doi:10.1016/j.compedu.2016.03.006

Limbu, M. (2013). Digital and global literacies in networked communities: Epistemic shifts and communication practices in the cloud era. In G. Verhulsdonck & M. Limbu (Eds.), *Digital rhetoric and global literacies: Communication modes and digital practices in the networked world* (pp. 131–153). Hershey, PA: IGI Global.

Lotherington, H., & Jenson, J. (2011). Teaching multimodal and digital literacy in L2 settings: New literacies, new basics, new pedagogies. *Annual Review of Applied Linguistics*, *31*, 226–246. doi:10.1017/S0267190511000110

Lu, M., & Horner, B. (2012). *Translingual literacy and matters of agency*. Unpublished working paper, University of Louisville. Retrieved September 4, 2016, from http://writing.uncc.edu/sites/writing.uncc.edu/files/media/docs/Min-Zhan_Lu_and_Bruce_Horner_Translingual_Literacy_and_Matters_of_Agency(1).pdf

Matsuda, P. K. (2014). The lure of translingual writing. *PMLA*, *129*(3), 478–483. doi:10.1632/pmla.2014.129.3.478

McKorkle, B., Halasek, K., Clinnin, K., & Selfie, C. L. (2016). Negotiating world Englishes in a writing-based MOOC. *Composition Studies*, *44*(1), 53–71.

Micciche, L. R. (2014). Writing material. *College English*, *76*(6), 488–505.

Mitchell, K. (2012). A social tool: Why and how ESOL students use Facebook. *CALICO Journal*, *29*(3), 471–493. doi:10.11139/cj.29.3.471-493

Morey, S. (2012). Digital ecologies. In S. L. Dobrin (Ed.), *Ecology, writing theory, and new media* (pp. 106–121). London: Routledge.

Nelson, M. E. (2006). Mode, meaning, and synesthesia in multimedia L2 writing. *Language Learning & Technology*, *10*(2), 56–76.

New London Group. (1996). A pedagogy of multiliteracies: Designing social futures. *Harvard Educational Review*, *66*(1), 60–92. doi:10.17763/haer.66.1.17370n67v22j160u

Pennycook, A. (2007). Language, localization, and the real: Hip-hop and the global spread of authenticity. *Journal of Language, Identity, and Education*, *6*(2), 101–115. doi:10.1080/15348450701341246

Pratt, M. L. (1991). Arts of the contact zone. *Profession*, *91*, 33–40.

Selfe, C. (2009). The movement of air, the breath of meaning: Aurality and multimodal composing. *CCC*, *60*(4), 616–663.

Shin, D., & Cimasko, T. (2008). Multimodal composition in a college ESL class: New tools, traditiaonl norms. *Computers and Composition*, *25*(4), 376–395. doi:10.1016/j.compcom.2008.07.001

Shipka, J. (2016). Transmodality in/and processes of making: Changing dispositions and practice. *College English*, *78*(3), 250–257.

Van Leeuwen, T. (2005). *Introducing social semiotics*. London: Routledge.

KEY TERMS AND DEFINITIONS

Cloud Pedagogy: The use of cloud technologies in classroom teaching, including but not limited to Facebook, Google docs, wikis, blogs, Twitter, and mobile apps.

Contact Zone: Social space in which dominant and subordinate cultural concepts and beliefs were in confrontation with and conflict against each other.

Multimodal Composition: Writing projects that incorporate various modes of communication, including but not limited to the use of texts, images, sounds, videos, and digital tools.

Second Language Writers: Writers who write in a language that is not their first language or mother tongue.

Semiotic Resources: Social, cultural, and material resources that have the potential of meaning-making.

Translingualism: The language practice that repudiates the monolingual ideology in support of code-meshing and language mixing across social and cultural contexts.

Writing Ecology: The notion of writing as emergent and fluid, undergoing changes relative to the transformations of ecological and social systems in which writing takes place.

Chapter 10
The Digital Third World, Digital Democracy, and Cloud Pedagoy:
Learning from Multilingual Bloggers

Dhruba Neupane
University of Waterloo, Canada

ABSTRACT

Cloud computing and Cloud technology has generated teachers' and scholars' attention as a viable alternative to traditional education. However, the discourse and rhetoric around Cloud—computing, education, pedagogy—seems to romanticize the potential of Cloud technology, ignoring, consequently, questions about language, power, and ideology. This chapter reintroduces those issues. Then it discusses blogs by multilingual writers that not only provide teaching materials free of access but also show how language, translation, and transnational exchanges get mediated. I show connection between the digital Third World, issues of equality and access that constitute part of the discussion around Cloud education, and offer a few takeaways from blogs as a democratic exercise. Finally, I discuss what Cloud pedagogy can learn from recent discussion in translingualism.

THE (DIGITAL) THIRD WORLD, DIGITAL DEMOCRACY, CLOUD PEDAGOGY AND BLOGGING

This paper will draw attention to what I am calling rather loosely and descriptively the digital Third World in connection with access to digital resources and what has recently been popularized as cloud pedagogy. When I say descriptively I do not mean that description is apolitical, un-ideological, and neutral— in fact all descriptions are discursive products and highly implicated in disciplinary practices and the politics that shape their language and discourse. Cloud pedagogy—if we can use this term to mean the pedagogy

DOI: 10.4018/978-1-5225-1650-7.ch010

that makes use of cloud technology, for example, by using resources like YouTube videos, blogs, and podcasts—has been hailed as a positive development that has the potential to democratize education. In this paper, I argue that while this possibility remains, those working to develop cloud technology to the aid of cloud pedagogy as an alternative to traditional institutional teaching need from the very beginning to account for such questions as who develops the materials, for whose benefit, who decides what counts as important, what cultural, linguistic, class, gender and racial factors play roles in such pedagogy, questions that have remained at the heart of critical engagement for scholars across various disciplines.

That instructors, students and institutions around the world have benefitted from accessible media platforms, software and virtual spaces in not new anymore. Cloud technology has recently been known to offer new possibilities for education. Writers invested in cloud computing have consistently pointed out that virtualized resources such as cloud technology can have significant impact on the educational future. Ercan (2010), for example, claims that cloud is "an excellent alternative for educational institutions … under budget shortage" (p. 939). Stein, Ware, Laboy, and Schaffer (2012) also speak positively; that cloud computing offers an opportunity to improve pedagogy: "the Cloud can deliver services such as remote access to learning tools in a cost effective manner to school systems struggling with reductions in local and state funding" (p. 235). This and similar discussions, however, tend to focus more on technological aspects than on what I have underscored above, such questions as who decides what counts, for whose benefit and so on.

When I say the Third World in the title, I mean it to work as a critique of what can be called the Third Worldism/Wordism, both as a desire to homogenize diverse energies and impulses within the Third World and then to subsume those into the dominant in the name of globalization of everything. This paper therefore is a critique of the desire and anxiety of the traditional centers to create homoginizable *Others* as static, unwilling to change, develop, or progress (to be connected, netted, or wired in the digital sense), and by the same token, frontier, virgin or unexploited land, space, and mind, to be colonized. In that spirit, I will use the term "Third World" in so far as it carries the sense of energy of resistance and decolonizing spirit, not in the sense of an insular or strategic third world nationalism, not even in the sense of Western Marxism, which conceals, in its preoccupation with economism, internal rifts, fissures and contradictions.

Also the philosophical and idealistic category "democracy" has now assumed the political and metanarrative sense of Euro-American democracy modeled after Enlightenment rationality, which roughly carries the meaning of some fundamental principles or set of rules of governing people. This form of democracy is increasingly functioning more as a panoptical machine to normalize and contain human actions and relations rather than allowing an unprecedented, unlegislated set of relations and actions to emerge. A democracy that does not allow *other* systems that it deems undemocratic deserves criticism. By digital democracy I mean real diversity and plurality in thinking, believing, valuing, and interacting. In discussing cloud computing and other resources such as blogging, I will be interested in exploring how these resources could potentially democratize learning spaces. The pedagogical democracy I am looking at basically relates to access and equality and is concerned with the material and the linguistic.

This chapter forms part of my plan to work on a book length project in which I wish to analyze the language matters of the multilingual speakers based both in the metropolis and the periphery but realized in a common space of blogosphere. Blogs have lately been hailed as democratic sites of knowledge sharing and knowledge making, allowing people to self (publish), share ideas, and most importantly campaign for a cause, social action and movement (check, for example, Idle No More). With its popularity and ease of access, many traditional print media such as news and journals have started adopting it as an alternative, with an increasing number of journals and news media at least offering some blog platforms. The idea of access and democratizing knowledge spaces is what ties cloud computing and my discussion of blogs. With that in mind, in this chapter, I will focus solely on how the Third World diasporic writers who are currently residing in the first world, and by virtue of their location, have mediated their languages and cultures and epistemologies. The blog posts I have considered for discussion are by South Asian students, writers and scholars currently residing in the USA, Canada, and the U.K. I have considered them for four important reasons. Firstly, all writers are multilingual speakers from the so-called Third World now resigning in the so-called First World, which will have an interesting implication when scholarship around language plurality and translingualism (Horner, Lu, Royster, Trimbur, 2011) is surging. With a varying degree of mixing and mashing, these writers have crossed languages. By the time this paper started, three bloggers were in the process of completing graduate studies in the U.S. Secondly, as these writers have traversed languages, cultures and nationalities and are in the roles of interpreters or translators, their play the role as communicators and mediators can be challenging at times, and this should be interesting for us to see. As Ashcroft, Griffith, and Tiffin (2002) contend, an interpreter always emerges from the dominant discourse. An interpreter

acquire(s) the power of the new language and culture in order to preserve the old, even while it assists the invaders in their overwhelming of that culture. In that divided moment the interpreter discovers the impossibility of living completely through either discourse. ...The role of the interpreter is like that of the post-colonial writer, caught in the conflict between destruction and creativity. (p. 79)

I find this truism particularly illuminating in analyzing the blogs entries in question. As Royster (1996) confesses after her experience "When the first voice you hear is not your own," the writer's "'subject' position is really everything" (p. 29). Writer's subject is especially important when considering border-crossing rhetorical and communicative acts involving negotiation of identities, converging of dialectical perspectives. Thirdly, the compositions we are examining include as diverse genres as creative nonfiction, poetry, memoir, and multilingual practices. Auto-ethnographic and autobiographical elements have strong presence. Autobiographical texts are theories and philosophies on their own, and blogs provide spaces and affordance for "new expressionism" (Jameson, 1991, p.1) of publishing oneself into being. Finally, these writing do the work that blogs do, *alt-ac* and counterdiscursive.

In what follows, I will discuss digital divide and the rhetoric around it, criticizing the tendency of Third Worlding/Wording. Implicit in such rhetoric, as I see it, is also a capitalistic, expansionist desire to reach out to the rest of the world that cloud computing and similar developments should be aware of. Many technologies that were previously expensive or unavailable are now becoming more accessible. This is true for most web sites, blogs, video sharing, music sharing, social sharing, collaboration software, presentation and publishing, and computing platforms in the "cloud."

The Rhetoric of Digital Divide

The discourse around digital divide or the rhetoric around digital (shall we call it digitalism?) has more often than not focused too narrowly on whether or not and which world is developed. Such a focus only re-creates world division rather than challenging it. The first obvious sign of the will to world is the Third Worlding/Wording. The Third Worlding/Wording has more recently taken the form of the rhetoric of digital divide, wherein the rhetoric of digital divide is mostly framed around the idea of the availability, or unavailability thereof, of materials in the Third World. The global digital divide is widely measured by international institutions in terms of the number of persons with individual access to those technologies. Consider, for example, the Geneva-based International Telecommunication Union's (ITU) reports every year (https://www.itu.int/net4/ITU-D/idi/2015/). The general tone of the digital divide discourse is that the world without ICT is illiterate, dark, slow, irrational, nonfunctioning, isolated and unconnected. ICT liberates; it's freedom from poverty and backwardness. While cloud computing, digital humanism and similar conversation should be aware of the material situations in disadvantaged parts of the world, it should try, precisely for this reason, to come up with less technologically, linguistically and culturally divisive ways to reach out to educate the larger number of world population.

Within the so-called First World, there has been a growing concern, along with the digital turn, that digital technologies have not equally benefitted all sections of people. In addition to class and race, gender complicates what would have looked to be neutral world technology. We know all clearly now that science and technology has been a field in which vulnerable and marginalized people and women feel uncomfortable and unprepared to go simply because of the dominance of males in these fields, with consequences on who designs technologies and how, for whose benefit, with whose values and so on. Besides, social class plays a role in deciding who gets to go in such fields. As a result, what gets produced is in favor of those who produce. A discussion such as this challenges us to think about technology not above and beyond divisive potential. I argue here that more of this kind of discussion, especially when cloud computing is being celebrated and advocated as a liberating possibility, should focus on the so-called Third World's material conditions, without recreating world division.

Even within the context of the so-called First World, William Pannapacker (2011) is concerned, for example, about the "divide between the builders and theorizers and coders and noncoders" (#4). Pannapacker is worried that digital humanities will foster an inclusive/exclusive divide reminiscent of the culture of Big Theory of the 80s and 90s. Apparently, the assumption that the digital now liberates us from the despotic, undemocratic, unenlightened print past then is cast in the vein of "Enlightenment meta-narratives of humanism" (Lister et al. 2009, p. 220). Stanley Fish's (2011) article "The Old Order Changeth" joins this concern. Fish is critical of digital humanities' supposedly prophetic promises, which he believes have in common with the postmodern celebration of the possibility of disestablishing every imaginable power. Recounting the general tone that characterized the postmodern theoretical turn, Fish observes:

In theory's wake, everything would have to change. Old questions were revealed to be based on a mistaken belief in the stability of texts and the self-identity of authors; rock-solid procedures and methodologies were shown to rest on the shifting sands of history; canonical authors were dislodged from their pedestals and exposed as racists, misogynists and apologists for empire; the canon itself was condemned as an artifact of patriarchal politics; and the practitioners of traditional criticism (yesterday's stars, today's relics) were denounced for being complicit with every evil known to humankind.

Fish (2011) draws further parallels between the digital humanism and postmodernism. Just as postmodernism was once understood to cover everything under the sun; digital humanities is used as an umbrella term for topic as diverse as

the organization and administration of libraries, the rethinking of peer review, the study of social networks, the expansion of digital archives, the refining of search engines, the production of scholarly editions, the restructuring of undergraduate instruction, the transformation of scholarly publishing, the re-conception of the doctoral dissertation, the teaching of foreign languages, the proliferation of online journals, the redefinition of what it means to be a text, the changing face of tenure—in short, everything.

The totalizing force that digital humanities is increasingly becoming or is aspiring to be, as Fish notes, deserves fresh attention, and I also share his and others' concern that this field has reintroduced the question of "who's in" and "who's out", as in "the early theory days when those who were in the know used language confidently and prophetically, while those who were not in the know of the language were made to feel ignorant, passed by, left behind, old". The takeaway of this discussion is that cloud pedagogy should constantly watch itself against the possibility of it becoming one of those exclusionary practices. I think that we need to rethink the uncritical embracing of any technology, including cloud, and the politics around the digital writ large. In our frantic move to go digital at this digital turn, we need to be skeptical of the idea that print and mass media are naturally authoritative and linear and thus at the service of the imperialistic, capitalistic office, but more importantly the idea that technology is a neutral medium. In this regard, Selfe and Selfe (1994) remind us that digital sites should not be taken for granted; they need to be seen as sites where oppression, including sexism, racism, colonialism, and homophobia are reproduced, to which I will turn after a brief digression. Following these scholars, I am interested in asking again and again "Whose interest are we serving in equating the revolution in online with 'egalitarian and democratic new humanism'?" What is political about presentation of the digital as the liberator?

The celebratory rhetoric of going digital or going cloud in this context—that just going digital or going cloud is a sufficient indication of the democratization of knowledge—loses sight of the various subtle ways the dominant reshapes itself into new forms and realizations. The new can be used to re-inscribe the old; for example, the use of blog as a pedagogical tool or medium where students are made to do things they would otherwise do on paper. The democratizing potential of blogs is here reduced, intentionally or unintentionally, to reproducing the traditional hierarchical relationships rather than to diffuse them. Deploying new social media and interactive space should be attended by the questions concerning power, agency, ownership, and labor underlying the production knowledge and meanings.

That is why we need to invoke time and again Selfe's (1999a) cautions. In her essay "Lest We Think the Revolution is a Revolution" Selfe (1999) discusses three totalizing narratives about digitality: (a) The "Global Village" and the "Electronic Colony" Narratives, (b) The "Land of Equal Opportunity" and the "Land of Difference" Narratives, the narrative of America as a land of opportunity and free access— which mirrors the ideology of American dream framed around the idea that those who work hard, play by the rules of fair game, and value innovation, individualism and competition will succeed—and finally (c) the narrative of technology as gender free zone or "the Un-Gendered Utopia" and "The Same Old Gendered Stuff" Narratives. The narrative of global village flattens out all relationships of hierarchies and differences and misrepresents the false ideal of the world as one common space, without accounting for the unequal power relations among the world villagers. That the American dream is a myth needs no further explanation when we are all too aware of America's treatment to its own racial others and minorities. Moreover, if anything is very sexist, it is this digital world. Technology is the area that has attracted few women as its designers and researchers with a consequence the male-dominated field reproduces gender hierarchies because more likely than not it creates a world on its own image.

What can be called digital colonialism carries with it image of pioneers, frontiers, tourists, and adventurers. 'America' considers itself to be the leader in this regard and assumes the role of an expansionist in search of uncharted, fresh, wild, unwired, unconnected population that it touts as 'isolated' from the rest of the world. Thus, the turn to digital needs to be alternatively seen as a technological missionary or a new form of colonialism: cyber colonialism led by representatives of multinational companies and "cyber capitalists" (Selfe, 1999b, p. 295). In "Technology and Literacy: A Story about the Perils of Not Paying Attention", Selfe (1999b) again provides us the context of the US education's turn to digital literacy. The point in this provocative essay is that any discussion of the digital should not forget various political and economic motives and motivations that have introduced the digitality in the first place. In particular Selfe wants us to remember the rhetoric of opportunity, access, and equity are more complicated than how it is narrativized. Below I reproduce Selfe's points which cast doubt on the liberatory claims and narratives of digital literacy:

- Digital "literacy myth" is a belief that literacy and literacy education lead autonomously, automatically, and directly to liberation, personal success, or economic prosperity (Selfe, p. 420).
- Race and socioeconomic indices/axes that are largely ignored in such narratives.
- Digital literacy education is a political act.
- **Expansionism:** Technologically sophisticated workers and technology specialist reach new global markets and export more American manufactured equipment and specialized technology services to the rest of the world. Technicians are trained in the deployment and use of American technology and American-designed operating systems.

Some scholars based in metropolis want to argue in favor of simply transplanting and transferring the digital metropolis to the worlds as if that satisfies most local literacy and pedagogical needs. What this transference argument ignores is digital literacy is not a singular, undifferentiated monolith that has the same impact across the globe. I argue that:

1. We need to understand local educational and pedagogical needs so that people don't feel that their mind is colonized (the aim should be decolonizing the mind);
2. We should promote local participation in curricular design and development so that people's culture, belief systems and values are represented and acknowledged;
3. Englishes that these students use and create should be actively promoted.

This finally brings me to the demonstrative part of the essay, related to language, multilingual, transcultural, transnational, diasporic (and local) negotiation and the difficult role of the interpreter and the difficult site of translation. What we are going to see in what follows is translational and transnational features that complicate rootings and attend to routing (Gilroy, 1995) and enact interstitiality and liminality (Bhabha, 1994).

Appropriation

The choice of language (an appropriate language at that) is clearly difficult one, and this topic has inspired numerous comments from scholars all around, particularly among postcolonial writers. As early as 1938, Raja Rao said this in his preface to *Kanthapura*:

The telling has not been easy. One has to convey in a language that is not one's own the spirit that is one's own. One has to convey... a certain thought-movement that looks maltreated in an alien language. I use the word 'alien', yet English is not really an alien language to us. It is the language of our intellectual make-up. We are all instinctively bilingual, many of us writing in our own language and in English. We cannot write like the English. We should not. We cannot write only as Indians. We have grown to look at the large world as part of us. Our method of expression therefore has to be a dialect which will some day prove to be as distinctive and colorful as the Irish or the American. Time alone will justify it. (vii)

The difficulty of conveying "the spirit of one's own in a language that is not one's own" (my reversal) is understandable. The syncretic, monistic cosmic belief that Rao is alluding to, and the responsibilities that come along with world citizenship, is worth noting here. Rao's recommendation that writers who straddle different worlds choose a dialect—I take "dialect" both in the sense of language dialect and in the sense of dialectic, mediation and interaction, as a "method of expression"—is meaningful. His speculation that the dialectic will attain a "distinctive" status has proven true along with time as more and more world population engage with their *own* (both as adjective and as a verb) englishes.

In postmodern and postcolonial writing, there has now been a tradition of appropriation of language. Echoing the concerns of Rao above, Okara adds,

There are ... versions of English. All of them add vigour to the language while reflecting their own respective cultures. Why shouldn't there be a Nigerian or West African English which we can use to express our own ideas, thinking and philosophy in our own way? (cited in Thiong'o, 1994, p. 9).

And Achebe adds,

Is it the right that a man should abandon his mother tongue for someone else's? It looks like a dreadful betrayal and produces a guilty feeling. But for me there is no other choice have been given the language and I intend to use it (cited in Thiong'o, 1994, p. 7).

Achebe writes very insightfully that for the English language to "carry the weight of my African experience… it will have to be a new English, still in in full communion with its ancestral home but altered to suit new African surrounding" (p. cited in Thiong'o, 1994, p. 8). I will refrain from going into the world of socio-linguistics and applied linguistics for lack of space. Also the discussion around world English(es), English as a Lingua Franca, Lingua Franca English, and so on deserve a separate space.

The ideas behind appropriation are that:

1. Appropriation is not mimicking and aping of the privileged and the dominant language and culture, but devising a localized and contextualized version of it in a way that what is imitated and repeated does not remain the same the moment it is appropriated; thus,
2. Appropriation is a process of localization, recontextualization and indigenization;
3. Appropriation allows partial agency as it is a site of mixing, mashing, and meshing, hybridity and cross-fertility;
4. However, appropriation is a challenging job.

The appropriation by the periphery of the center can be realized in various ways. Ashcroft et al. (2002) discuss:

1. Glossing, untranslated words;
2. Interlanguage and interculture, a term that Nemser (1971) and Selinker (1972) popularized (Interlanguage is "the utterance of a second-language learner are not deviant forms and mistakes, but rather are part of a separate but genuine linguistic system"; (
3. Syntactic fusion; and
4. Code switching (in Ashcroft et al., 2002, p. 66).

While the four textual features of appropriation that Ashcroft et al. pointed out is insightful, it is not comprehensive enough to cover a more complex phenomenon of appropriation, namely code-meshing, which its advocates argue is a more deliberate and agentive way of appropriating (V. Young, 2005). In analyzing the blogs, I will discuss the relevant appropriative moments and then will link it to "translingual approach" (Horner et al. 2010) to pedagogy scholars such as Canagarajah, Horner and others have actively written about.

In the first blog I am considering, the writer recounts his memory of the past when he used to attend a popular local *melaa* (festival gathering). Recounting a festival song the blogger writes, in the middle of that memoir,

Gai kote kote, ma budho hoina hai dant matrai thote
(The cows in their sheds, don't call me an oldie, for I am only toothless)
He lai lai Mai beni mela, sauteni bhanera nagara hela
(The Mai River Fair, don't look down upon me just because I am your step son)
Rote linge ping, basaunla bhanthen hai aigo hidne din
(Bamboo and wooden swings for swinging, I wish I could stay longer, but alas, my days are done) (Blogger's translation)

In this song, after each line the writer glosses and translates Nepali in English. The script is not Nepali Devanagarik but 'Romanized' (e.g., "ping" = swinging rope, which in Devanagarik would be ~ पगि) version of English. This creative non-fiction piece came out of a class that linked creative non-fiction genre with pedagogy, and was primarily written for English audience (course instructor and peers). When it moved to blog, the writer added images from of the festival site, meant both for English speaking audience and Nepali audience, primarily I would say Nepali audience. Considering the fact that the readers would now be primarily from his community, the writer could have added Devanagarik script while retaining the Romanized and translated version to retain wider audience. The entire blog has no apparent code switching.

In the second blog entry I am discussing, there are striking similarities in terms of audience and genre. But there is an obvious difference in the way the writer reproduces the verse from a rather locally circulated among mature women for a specific purpose, namely Rateli, a festival night in Nepal marking the departure of bridegroom to bring home his bride. As the blogger explains, Rateli provides a moment for sexually (gender-ly) repressed women to express themselves:

The women unbound, the 'obscene' tribe at present, away from the gaze of the systems of 'discipline and punish,' the male Panopticon machine, were practicing a ritual which would save them from being 'mad women in the village' throughout the year. To the accompaniment of the madal, Rateli dance, a slow tempo at first, gradually mounts to an exciting climax when spirited women participants sing and dance with the whole body pulsating to a fast rhythm. And this was an occasion to reenact their first nights, to renew their past glory, to feel fresh again. Again, this was the venue to witness the repressed in the semiotics of their songs and dances about exploitation, domination, and repression; about pathos, conflict, poignancy, fantasy, and symbolism all intricately woven together. It was letting loose what was kept fettered in society.

So sang one woman:

ऐंसेलुको पातमा कान्डो छैन

आज जाने दुलाको *डो छैन

मेरा बादुरे *डो छैन

[No thorn on the berry leaf, no penis in today's groom.]

There is in this entry Nepali (Devnagarik) script but the song also is glossed for English readers. But still, there is no code-switching and code-meshing happening in these instances. Part of the reason in the previous blogger's choice of not choosing heritage script can be explained in terms of the writer trying to be accessible to outside audience. This blog has the heritage script but the writer also glosses. We need not link this to the writer exercising his agency. But we can at least say that these are unique engagements typical of diasporic writers. Of course more complex examples appear in Rushdie's "chutnification", the mixing, meshing and mashing of language and cultures in ways that they cross-fertilize each other in a syncretic way.

Let us consider the last blog in discussion. The blogger has given it a title "जीवनको प्यानोरोमा" translated as "Panorama of Life." The second word in this title is English sound (not the meaning) translated into Nepali. The blog entry sentence reads: "जब म लभिरपुल स्ट्रीट ट्रेन स्टेशनमा सेन्ट्रल लाइनको ट्युबबाट सरकल लाइन परविर्तन गर्न दौडरिहेको थएँ, भीडमा एउटा परचिति अनुहार पनि दौडरिहेको देखें" (Sapkota, 2012), and has predominantly sound-translated and "invited" words in Nepali, called आगन्तुक शब्द. Of course, the audience in mind is both diaspora or nondiasporic insider community, not English audience. The amount of time it takes to typing in the heritage language from the keyboard that has no such script is quite telling. However, the writer takes the labor and does what I would consider to be an effective mixing of language in a way that seems characteristic of world speakers who mix and switch between languages.

Translation, Transnation, Translingualism

Translation is a world on its own. It is in the labor of translation that we will be able to best acknowledge the fact that no technology has been created equally for all. The labor of translators and interpreters is complicated by the fact that there are no easy tools for translation when it comes to less worldwide, less circulated, and minority language. Part of the reasons that the bloggers under discussion have not meaningfully exploited code-switching and code-meshing (of which code-switching is less preferable option for those who would want to remix languages in ways that goes beyond the false idea of language use as discrete) opportunities is this difficulty of translation and crossing brought about by transnational migration and exchanges. Aside from this literal meaning of translation and the difficulties of doing translation from one language to another when the tools are not created equally and are not accessible to all, I wanted to invoke the broader implication of translation by invoking Pennybook's (2008) idea that all languages, including English, are always in translation in that they evolve over time as they move and migrate, get adapted and appropriated. The work we examined are the result of precisely this translation and demands a treatment to viewing English not as a language onto to itself, but as something that gains its significance when it enters into the "global traffic of meaning" (p. 33). This idea of translation pays attention to the diversity of meanings (semiodiversity) as well as the diversity of forms (glossodiversity). The idea of translingual approach becomes relevant precisely at this point.

A translingual approach that scholars such as Pennycook (2008), Horner et al. (2011) and Canagarajah (2013) starts with the premise that there are differences in and across all languages, that language and language varieties are fluid, and that language differences and fluidities "are resources to be preserved, developed, and utilized" (Horner et al. p. 304), that all variations of English are accented including the so-called standard variety and subject to change and modification. Translingual approach makes us aware of the history, origin, and later development of English and its heterogeneity as evidenced in new "word formations, the developments of World Enlgishes, and shifting conventions" (p. 311). In addition,

> *a translingual approach rejects discrimination on the basis of language identity and use.... It also rejects the view that so-called English language learners are the only ones in need of language development. Instead, it supports efforts to increase the number of languages and language varieties that students know, and to deepen their knowledge of these.... It supports efforts to increase English monolingual students' repertoire of language and to award academic credit for such learning. A translingual approach to language differences is aligned with multilingual education insofar as that education aims to develop and broaden the repertoire of students' linguistic resources and to honor the resources of all language users. (p. 308)*

The translingual and local practice orientation to language can be a point of departure from the available options including multilingualism. The translingual perspective has us as teachers and scholars shift our focus from helping students achieve mastery of one language or more, each taken in isolation and with the ideal native speaker as the ultimate model, to developing and promoting communicative repertoire, in which all linguistic abilities are considered holistically. Finally, a translingual approach also can take us beyond the current debate between monocentric and pluricentric perspectives of English because it recognizes that English has multiple, heterogeneous, and simultaneous points of origins (Pennycook, 2011)—both across time and space. It allows creativity, deviation, and ambiguity to be part of student writing. (Examples include Lu's, 1994, close reading of a student's use of "can able to" and Canagarajah's, 2016, analysis of Buthainah's code-meshing.) These scholars have stressed the importance of linguistic variation from norms as productive of meaning and indicative of writers' agency, and the cultural underpinning. Translingual approach, therefore, has us daring enough to face ambiguity, contradiction, and incomprehensibility as part of the meaning-making process rather fear and avoid them, or simply persist with our monolinguistic obsession with correctness and immediate clarity. In one way or another, the blogs I examined are meaningful from a translinguistic standpoint, with implication on teachers, policy makers, and global citizens in general.

CONCLUDING REMARKS

In closing, I would like to bullet-point some of the issues that we can derive from the discussion above and continue to pay attention to in an increasingly porous linguistic world we are inhabiting.

- Rethink the discursive impact of the third worlding rhetoric of digital divide.
- Understand that technology is not neutral; rather, it is interested.
- Understand that translation involves a complex work and there has not been enough focus going on in this area at least in terms of technological equality.
- Reconsider global and local boundaries in light of this possibility and difficulty of translation, disrupt center/periphery, and acknowledge internal fissures and disjunction.
- Cloud education can benefit from the conversation in translingual scholarship if it wants to account for linguistic and cultural plurality and include materials that express language and cultural crossing.

Overall, this paper situates blogs as a site wherein to encounter routes, passages, movements, contamination, translation, infection and inflection (Gilroy, 1993; Freiberg, 2012). Multilingual writers' language traverses different worlds and reaches out to a wider variety of audience as well as retain their own, to which cloud pedagogy should pay more attention. Examples we saw suggest that English is appropriated by writers to serve their rhetorical needs. These examples illustrated, along with previous studies, a variety of appropriation, ranging from, if we were to call forth Ashcroft et al. (2002), heritage words with translation, heritage words Romanized and further translated in English, a reverse sound-translation of English into heritage language. These examples are by no means ideal examples for someone who is interested in seeing more complex code meshing that we can find in Rushdie's *Midnight's Children* (1981) and *The Satanic Verses* (1988). The examples studied came either from creative nonfiction genres with a certain level of freedom and agency trusted upon writers or from personal writing not for evaluation purpose. Writing done for more rigid genres and for more rigorous evaluative environment would obviously reflect a different degree of language engagement. However, these examples are good examples for instructional purposes in so far as they make a statement that that the focus on language use has to be how language is *practiced.*

From a pedagogical standpoint, the examples we saw illustrate the point that language is increasingly used today to cross boundaries rather than preserve them. The implication of this for teaching is be that educators need to respect and even actively encourage writers to draw on their multiple resources rather than requiring them to conform to a prescribed set of standards and rules. More importantly the rhetoric and practice of cloud pedagogy should constantly aware itself against the possibility of its glossing the divides. Cloud pedagogy in both the "developed" and "underdeveloped" places must be in the service of people who do not have access to knowledge and should strive to maximize the possibility of their participation in knowledge making.

REFERENCES

Ahmad, A. (1987). Jameson's rhetoric of otherness and the 'national allegory. *Social Text*, *17*(17), 3–25. doi:10.2307/466475

Ashcroft, B., Griffiths, G., & Tiffin, H. (2002). *The empire writes back: Theory and practice in post-colonial literatures* (2nd ed.). London: Routledge.

Bhabha, H. K. (1994). *The location of culture*. London: Routledge.

Canagarajah, S. (2002). *A geopolitics of academic writing*. Pittsburgh, PA: Pittsburgh UP.

Canagarajah, S. (2016, January). Translingual writing and teacher development in composition. *College English*, *78*(3), 265–273.

Donahue, C. (2009, December). 'Internationalization' and composition studies: Reorienting the discourse. *CCC*, *61*(2), 212–243.

Fish, S. (2011, Dec 26). The order of things changeth. *The New York Times*. Retrieved 15 February 2015 from http://opinionator.blogs.nytimes.com/2011/12/26/the-old-order-changeth/

Fraiberg, S. (2010, September). Composition 2.0: Toward a multilingual and multimodal framework. *CCC*, *62*(1), 100–126.

Gilroy, P. (1993). *The black Atlantic: Modernity and double consciousness*. Cambridge, MA: Harvard UP.

Horner, B., Lu, M., Royster, J., & Trimbur, J. (2011). Language difference in writing: Toward a translingual approach. *College English*, *73*(3), 303–321.

Lamsal, T. (2013). *Fleeing Mai Fair: Bye bye Guddusingh*. Retrieved 15 June 2014 from http://tikalamsal.com/2013/10/

Lu, M.-Z. (1994, December). Professing multiculturalism: The politics of style in the contact zone. *CCC*, *45*(4), 442–458.

Neupane, D. (2011). *Memories*. Retrieve 12 August 2013 from https://dhrubazdiary.wordpress.com/2011/08/16/memories/

Pannapacker, W. (2012). Digital humanities triumphant? In *Debates in the digital humanities*. Minneapolis, MN: U of Minnesota P. Retrieved 16 March 2013 from http://dhdebates.gc.cuny.edu/debates

Pennycook, A. (2008). English as language always in translation. *European Journal of English Studies*, *12*(1), 33–47. doi:10.1080/13825570801900521

Pennycook, A. (2010). *Language as a local practice*. London: Routledge.

Rao, R. (1938). *Kanthapura*. London: George Alen and Unwin Ltd.

Royster, J. (1996). When the first voice you hear is not your own. *College Composition and Communication*, *47*(1), 29–40. doi:10.2307/358272

Rushdie, S. (1981). *Midnight's children*. London: Penguin Group.

Rushdie, S. (1988). *The satanic verses*. London: Penguin Group.

Selfe, C. (1999a). Lest we think the revolution is a revolution: Images of technology and the nature of change. In G. E. Hawisher & C. Selfe (Eds.), *Passions, pedagogies, and 21st century technologies* (pp. 292–322). Logan, UT: Utah State UP.

Selfe, C. (1999b, February). Technology and literacy: A story about the perils of not paying attention. *College Composition and Communication, 50*(3), 411–436. doi:10.2307/358859

Selfe, C., & Richard, S. (1994, December). The politics of the interface: Power and its exercise in electronic contact zones. *College Composition and Communication, 45*(4), 480–504. doi:10.2307/358761

Spivak, G. C. (1999). *A critique of postcolonial reason*. Cambridge, MA: Harvard UP.

Thiong'o, N. W. (1986). *Decolonising the mind: The politics of language in African literature*. Portsmouth: Heinemann.

Young, R. (2004). *White mythologies: writing history and the west* (2nd ed.). London: Routledge.

Young, V., & Martínez, A. Y. (Eds.). (2011). *Code-Meshing as world English: Pedagogy, policy, performance*. Urbana, IL: NCTE.

Section 3

Chapter 11
Doctoral Learning and Cognitive Apprenticeship:
Technology Tools for Emerging Scholars

Katherine Emmons
Walden University, USA

ABSTRACT

This chapter discusses the role of cloud technology tools in helping build mentoring relationships in online doctoral programs, drawing on examples and experiences observed in the author's 15 years as a PhD dissertation chair. Ideas of cognitive apprenticeship and learning communities together provide a framework for identifying methods and skills that are helpful in the development of emerging scholars. The author describes the steps of modeling, coaching, scaffolding, articulation, reflection, and exploration in the context of helping doctoral learners through to completion. Practical implications of using cloud technologies such as web conferencing, folder and file sharing, scheduling tools, and learning management systems are discussed through examples. The author also considers online strategies for fostering of one on one mentoring relationships for doctoral research and writing, as well as establishing and maintaining communities of doctoral peer groups.

INTRODUCTION

This chapter discusses how cloud technologies provide tools to help build the mentoring relationships that are needed for doctoral students to become scholars in their own right. I draw on observed examples and experiences to discuss a model of cognitive apprenticeship as first described by Collins, Brown, and Newman (1986) and Collins, Brown, and Holum (1991). This model is helpful for understanding the required relationships and commitments in online doctoral learning, especially between mentors and doctoral students. When these relationships are formed early in the process of dissertation research, progress in the degree program can be encouraged, and is more likely to culminate in timely completion (Kumar, Johnson, & Hardemon, 2013). As noted by Lyons, Scroggins, and Rule (1990), "It is clear that doctoral students who had experienced a close working relationship with a faculty member had a fuller education

DOI: 10.4018/978-1-5225-1650-7.ch011

than their counterparts who did not" (p. 284). Technology can foster these relationships, particularly for doctoral students who study at a distance, including those enrolled in online programs. I discuss my own experiences of using technology in online programs spanning over 15 years, as well as the entry of helpful cloud tools for conferencing, folder and file sharing, scheduling, and community building.

As occurs with any innovation, the availability and growth in online doctoral programs has not come without its challenges. For individual students, the challenges include a geographically dispersed community of learners and a mentor who is accessible only from a distance. Learning at a distance can be a lonely and isolating experience (Erichsen & Bolliger, 2011), especially for doctoral students who may become disengaged when the demands of careers and families keep them from interacting regularly in a community of scholars. Doctoral learners in online programs also work with dissertation chairs and committee members whom they may have never met in person. With no regularly scheduled seminars or classes, both student and mentor need to find other ways to engage proactively for progress to occur. The idea of cognitive apprenticeship provides a useful framework with which to discuss cloud technology tools that facilitate the mentoring of doctoral students in an online program.

Elements of cognitive apprenticeship are modeling, coaching, scaffolding, articulation, reflection, and exploring (transfer of learning) (Austin, 2009). Embedded within these methods of cognitive apprenticeship are also the building of trusting relationships and the importance of writing feedback. The benefits of cognitive apprenticeship necessarily extend beyond graduation for new scholars. Ideally, they will be able to conduct research without the close mentoring that was provided during the dissertation process.

Online Doctoral Programs

The growth in enrollments in online degree programs in the last 10 or 15 years is well documented (Allen & Seaman, 2015), and doctoral programs have been part of that growth. With access to online learning, individuals may no longer see the need to relocate, change employment status, or even postpone plans for family to pursue graduate studies. In addition, many private online universities have relatively open enrollment and admission criteria, which further increase accessibility. As some have pointed out, doctoral learning is no longer just for an elite group (Johnson, 2014), as it has become available to a wider spectrum of people across the world (Engels-Schwarzpaul, & Peters, 2013; Metcalf, 2006). Others (deMeyer, 2013; Preston, 2014; Radda, Cross, & Holbeck, 2012) have advocated for a shift away from "traditional" PhD programs to those that are more applied, and more amenable to students who are already working in their fields and could attend professional doctoral programs at a distance. Nerad (2012) has mentioned the increasing globalization of the PhD, which points to the need for tools that nurture important academic relationships across language, cultural, and geographical boundaries. My PhD students have lived in various regions of the United States, as well as in Africa, South America, and Europe. When one of my students conducted her final oral defense, she and her committee members called in from four different continents. The number of doctoral learners in the USA alone may be approaching 400,000 (Walker, Golde, Jones, Bueschel & Hutchings, 2008), which necessitates the use of all available technology to help them achieve their goals. Cloud technologies have emerged to facilitate the needed cognitive apprenticeships within geographically dispersed learning communities.

Cloud technologies were in their infancy when I began teaching online in 2000. While online learning technology was initially transformative in its capacity to connect learners in different parts of the country and world, most learning management systems (LMS) were also rudimentary and text-based. For many years, online graduate-level classes used (and many still use) the same basic technology: content rendered from HTML text and JPEG graphics, accompanied by online discussion areas and locations for assignment uploads. Over time, links to multimedia were included in many course offerings, but good quality resources required considerable investment in their development (Lam & McNaught, 2006). In the last several years, new educational technologies, including cloud technologies, have allowed for expanded opportunities for learning (Denton, 2012), even beyond what Ghefaili (2003) initially suggested could be used in a cognitive apprenticeship framework. Cloud technologies may have specific application for doctoral programs as they can help foster scholarly learning communities where modeling, coaching, and scaffolding can occur.

Scholarly Communities

Cognitive apprentices are developing experts who gain practice in their roles as emerging scholars by providing expertise to peers as part of a learning community, most likely with the leadership of a mentor. Without tools for interaction, doctoral students would otherwise struggle to find what Lave and Wenger (1991) might describe as scholarly communities of practice, and what (Austin, 2009) suggested is critical for their development as scholars. Without effective means for professional communication, geographically dispersed doctoral learners would work in isolation. In some cases they may have only occasional communication with faculty and other students in the program (Janta, Lugosi, & Brown, 2014). In the absence of face to face office hours, doctoral seminars, visiting scholar talks, public dissertation defenses, and teaching or research assistantships, online doctoral students often work in solitude. Technology makes it possible to establish and facilitate the mentor as the point of contact in a community of scholars, regardless of the geographical locations of the community members.

In a cognitive apprenticeship (Collins et al., 1991), an instructor can model complex tasks. Opportunities for scaffolding and coaching occur at various steps within them. While cognitive apprentices in doctoral learning may benefit from a larger community of mentors, advisors, and instructors (Kwan, 2008), typically there remains one faculty member who is the primary mentor. This mentor serves as doctoral chair, and is a point of contact for specific students who are assigned under his or her supervision. On the surface, this model is not unlike the traditional master-apprentice model in doctoral learning, whereby a guiding relationship between the doctoral chair and the PhD student must be fostered. However, with cognitive apprenticeship, there is a focus on specific tasks that the mentor can explicitly observe (Austin, 2009), as well as practices that foster learning communities (Maher, Gilmore, Feldon, & Davis, 2013). I would also critique Ghefaili's (2003) suggestion that the technology tools themselves could be mentors in a cognitive apprenticeship, because this idea may not be particularly useful in the context of doctoral learning. At a minimum, the first steps in cognitive apprenticeship (modeling, coaching, and scaffolding) should be facilitated by a human mentor, using technology to assist if appropriate. The later steps (articulation and reflection) occur as the process of "fading" strengthens and the mentor steps back while the student gains expertise (Collins et al., 1986). The technology tools may continue to facilitate the learning but the expert individuals remain behind them, especially as learners seek out others with similar expertise, and explore avenue to broaden their scholarship. The final step, exploration or learning transfer, might be accomplished by the learner independently and with appropriate tools. But for this step to be linked with scholarship, the learner must eventually integrate with a community.

THE COGNITIVE APPRENTICESHIP METHODS

The core of cognitive apprenticeship teaching methods are modeling, coaching, and scaffolding. These "help students acquire an integrated set of skills through processes of observation and guided practice" (Collins, Brown, & Holum, 1991. p. 13). Articulation and reflection are a means for students to focus on problem solving. They identify and describe problems, and can begin to address them with strategies that they have already observed as practiced by the mentor or peers (Collins, Brown, & Holum, 1991). Exploration, also described by Austin (2009) as transfer of learning, is the final method in which learners can demonstrate their autonomy. My doctoral learners who have reached the point of successful exploration feel confident in their expertise and define themselves as scholars. These six methods are described more fully below.

Modeling

In cognitive apprenticeship a mentor can provide the doctoral apprentice with the opportunity to observe the performance of tasks. In doing so, the mentor explicitly teaches the processes that might otherwise remain internal (Collins, Brown, & Holum, 1991). A doctoral learner will often require clear instruction on how to format a research proposal, for example, or how to articulate the procedures for data collection. To facilitate observation of such tasks, as well as the externalization of the processes involved, I provide mentees with examples of dissertations, both completed and in progress. While I am not able to model the process of dissertation research and writing all at once due to the size and complexity of the task, examples provide a tangible reference for discussion of each of the parts, as well as overall alignment in the research and writing. I use several cloud technologies to model various steps in the overall process, including Dropbox, which provides an easily accessible repository for completed works, and Adobe Connect, which allows web conferencing around specific dissertation tasks. These tools, and others, are discussed more fully later in the chapter.

Coaching

Coaching allows an instructor to observe the student as he or she completes a task. A key aspect of my coaching in doctoral learning is approaching sections of writing in "chunks." I provide feedback on these, and target any areas of weakness as Austin (2008) suggested. Helping my mentees break the writing process down into smaller, observable tasks allows me to provide feedback on each component. It also helps the learner observe integration of that piece of writing into a whole. For example, a doctoral learner may be working on research questions in the proposal, and be struggling with alignment between research problem, research purpose, and research questions. Cloud technology allows for the one-on-one discussion of those portions of a document in real time, allowing mentor and student make and observe specific edits that relate to key changes in language. While this type of coaching is not always practiced as a real time conference, the process should nevertheless always be iterative (Caffarella & Barnett, 2000). Any changes that take place in the writing between each draft are thus observed closely.

Scaffolding

Scaffolding is a key component of cognitive apprenticeships, and applications for doctoral writing and advising are described in the literature (Austin, 2008; Hasratti, 2005; Wolff, 2010; Swanson, West, Carr, & Augustine, 2015). A study by Maher and others (2013) suggested that when scaffolding is not provided, PhD research assistants will not feel a sense of "purposeful 'upward movement'" in their learning (p. 18). Scaffolding refers to the supports that the mentor provides, and comprises the modeling and coaching is described above.

The associated concept of fading has particular relevance to cognitive apprenticeships, and refers to steps the mentor takes to gradually remove the supports (Collins et al., 1986). Sometimes, the mentor will need to continue to step in at various points and provide heavy support, so the process of fading can happen very gradually for some tasks and more rapidly for others. I have found that I offer extensive and repeated comments on writing for the Introduction and Literature Review sections of a dissertation. I will review multiple drafts and hold several sessions, depending on the writing skills of the student in the beginning and the effort that he or she has applied so far. After the research has been completed, intensive writing support is rarely needed. Our meetings will focus instead on how to express synthesis, and how to structure the findings. As with all stages in the research and writing process, I will continue to point to available examples of completed works.

Articulation and Reflection

Articulation allows doctoral learners to share what they have learned by making their learning or thought processes known to others. In an interesting articulation of his own experiences with coaching, one of my mentees told me "now when I read my own work, I hear your voice in my head, and it is easier for me to see my mistakes." Doctoral learners also gauge their own learning through reflection, and by comparing themselves to experts or to peers to are directly ahead of them in the process (Austin, 2009). As part of articulation, learners ask questions, seek clarification, and make decisions. Some of their decisions require quite a bit of thought; the student is expected to respond to my own questions in a way that helps reveal the path forward. Because I expect my students to be emerging (if not actual) experts on their topics, we may, for example, engage in important discussions about how they understand and view the purpose of their research, the functionality of the research questions, or the clarity and alignment of theoretical or conceptual frameworks.

Within the process of reflection the learners become skilled at accepting and responding to writing feedback, and ideally become more capable at self-correction (Wolff, 2010). The most obvious articulation is with the final product itself, and the dissertation serves as a primary communication tool for what the student has learned and discovered through the PhD research. In the process of writing it, students compare their work to published doctorates. This focused reflection helps students consider questions such as: How am I doing? Where am I in this process? Where should I be? Does this meet expectation? and, Am I almost done? Once the dissertation has been published, the student becomes officially part of a community of scholars. The research is made available for the process to continue with students who come later, not to mention with the wider community of scholars. Reflection also helps learners see the limitations of me as their mentor, and also helps them see that acknowledging these gaps is useful: what I do *not* know is as important to my mentoring as what I *do* know. I can make it explicit to mentees when I'm confident in my advice, as well as admitting to gaps in my own knowledge. As we discuss and brainstorm, learners come to know that even my gaps do not necessarily comprise rigid limits to my mentorship. But if they do, our acknowledgement allows the learners to seek answers on their own, as is demonstrated in the next step, exploration.

Exploration

Exploration in a cognitive apprenticeship helps a doctoral learner practice skills independently and in new situations. Austin (2008) interpreted the exploration step as a transfer of learning, and in my students I see this as an import aspect of them becoming "experts." Key to the transition from student to scholar is for students to:

1. Gain confidence as experts on their topics,
2. Interact with other scholars at conferences and in online forums, and
3. Seek opportunities to broaden experience as professionals and scholars.

They practice the stages of exploration as doctoral learners by reviewing the literature, by re-articulating a problem statement in response to critical reading, and by considering various research designs and procedures with which to approach the identified problem.

In a transfer of learning, new scholars are able to consider applying familiar research methodology to new research topics. They may expand their learning by engaging in related studies, and by collaborating with others, including as a primary researcher themselves. As Collins, et al. (1991) noted, exploration is not only the natural culmination of fading in support from a mentor. It is also a fading from known and comfortable settings, and represents venturing into new territory. A similar notion was termed as independence and emancipation (Lee, 2008). Skills in research methods and conceptualization, as well as in writing, literature search, collaboration, and time management all carry over from the student phase to the independent scholar phase. I've noticed also what Hazratti (2005) identified as a new phase in the mentor-learner relationship, which eventually takes a bi-directional form. I tell my mentees that my idea of a good relationship with them is one that could be "flipped" should the occasion ever arise. Sometimes it does: for example, my students sometimes read new methodology resources before I do, and can provide recommendations and comparisons for their peers and me.

THE CLOUD TOOLS

Cognitive apprenticeship in doctoral learning is facilitated through online technologies. My PhD mentees and I regularly make use of several cloud technology tools, particularly folder and file sharing, web conferencing, scheduling, and online forums. Some tools are proprietary or behind pay walls, while others are free or have free versions available for educational purposes.

Shared Folders

Shared folders and files allow for the cognitive apprenticeship methods of modeling and coaching. Examples of shared folders are Dropbox, which is available at Dropbox.com, and Google Drive. My PhD students have access to an extensive library of resources related to the doctoral learning process, including previously published dissertations in Dropbox folders. There are also examples doctoral works in progress that include editorial comments and conceptual feedback (shared with the permission of the authors). These examples provide emerging scholars with examples of both the process and product of dissertation research. Most of the shared documents are from students with whom I have previously worked as either chair or committee member. I know the works well and can interpret them as needed, which makes them especially helpful models and scaffolds for my mentees who are still learning the processes. When feedback from other reviewers is shared (IRB, research review, etc), current and future tasks and steps are demystified and become tangible. When a mentee experiences a block at a certain step, I can provide examples related to content area or methodology by suggesting specific dissertations as models. Students often have difficulty conceptualizing their research within a body of theory, and I can also provide specific examples of how previous mentees integrated theory into their research topics, discussing specific processes involved and even the innovations of previous students. For example, one mentee was able to place three contrasting theories in a graphic organizer within her literature review. In her final discussion chapter, she added another aspect that integrated her own findings into the previous theoretical ideas. With easy access to her work, my other mentees are able to learn from her model as they organize and display their own conceptual ideas.

Web Conferencing

There are some aspects of mentor guidance that are particularly complex and require more than written feedback within a document, and more than coaching through a telephone conversation. In such cases I can meet my mentees in a web conference and we can together view a document in real time. Such meetings can be hosted by Adobe Connect conferencing software, which in my case is offered as a resource by the university. Similar conferencing tools include Zoom, Team Viewer, Goto Meeting, and others. Conceptual process discussion can be more explicit in such sessions, which I sometimes call "workshops." Such meetings may last an hour or more as we discuss problem statements or research questions, or struggle together through a issue in the methodology section.

The *record meeting* feature in Adobe Connect can be used to capture these real-time conferences between my student and myself, capturing both voice and screen. One obvious advantage of recordings is that the student can view and listen to the feedback more than once. The record feature ensures that Adobe Connect is a useful tool even when a real-time web conference is not possible due to scheduling conflicts or other reasons. In such cases I can record a "walk through" of written feedback that I already made in a document, and additional verbal feedback can be included without the student being present. A link to the recording is then sent for the student to view in his or her own time and learners see the writing revisions modeled as the document is being discussed. This feature makes feedback more personalized, and it can provide a softer approach for newer doctoral students who may be more sensitive to written feedback than those who are more familiar with iterative processes. It can be made particularly clear, for example, where heading levels are not consistent with an expected writing structure, or where a main point is at the bottom of a paragraph and needs to be closer to the top.

Because of the capability for Adobe Connect to capture and share the mentor's or student's computer screen, it is particularly useful for providing coaching on those aspects of dissertation work that require deep thinking and discussion. One of the most helpful aspects of coaching happens early on in the mentoring relationship, when the student needs to formulate a research problem out of his or her interests, passions, and (hopefully) prior work and readings. In such sessions, I guide mentees through a series of five or six questions to help conceptualize their research problems, prompting them to speak from their hearts (i.e. "what is the problem--educational/social/etc.--that you feel needs to be addressed?"). The mentee thinks, but not for too long, and then articulates the problem in no more than three short sentences. I stop the learner there, and we document what was said. In doing so, we quickly establish the heart of what interests the learner both personally and professionally. When we record those few sentences verbatim, the mentee avoids over-thinking or any false sophistication in the writing, which is often present with new doctoral learners who aren't sure how to express their thoughts. The discussion progresses to another question (i.e. "what is happening, or will happen, when this problem is not addressed?" or "what is the extent of this problem?), and the process continues until the learner has a rudimentary, yet aligned idea of what he or she wants to study. After this process is complete, we discuss where the sections of the dissertation fit into those thoughts: the study purpose, the research questions, the literature review, and the methodology. Because the conversation can be recorded in Adobe Connect the learner can review it to write a short prospectus or basic research plan that forms the basis for what will eventually become a full-fledged study.

Adobe Connect is also helpful for group meetings. When I occasionally ask a mentee to present work or offer assistance to peers, we can also do this in Adobe Connect, and record the meeting for those who were not able to attend. Because I have mentees at all stages of dissertation writing and research, it is very helpful to ask a "senior" among them to discuss their own research procedures, provide advice, and answer questions. In such meetings, I adjust the tool setting so that the presenter can share his or her own screen and chair the meeting.

Scheduling Tools

For a cognitive apprenticeship to develop, mentor and mentees need a time and place to communicate. A first step for coaching sessions is for my student and myself to find a time to meet. A new cloud tool allowed my mentees to see my available times, and the frequency of our conversations increased almost overnight. I had previously tried a number of different tools to aid the scheduling of telephone conferences and eventually found Teamup to be accurate and efficient (I had previously tried Doodle, Google Calendars, and others). My students reside in various time zones in the USA and internationally, and I cannot keep track of the work schedules of everybody. I am also a frequent traveler, and I quickly abandoned an attempt to hold regular office hours and drop-in times because they were not attended. The free tool provided by Teamup offers excellent capability for Calendar management, integration into Google Calendars, iCal links, and time zone support. My mentees can make an appointment by viewing the calendar in their own time zones, and then I can view it in mine time zone without either of us having to worry about conversion. In the beginning there remained some time zone confusion, due mostly to our previous habits of adding or subtracting hours to scheduled meetings. Once it was clear that this conversion was no longer needed, the confusion was resolved quickly. Now, when students make appointments, I get an email alert and can then confirm the time or suggest an alternative. I am able to change the color of confirmed appointments, which tells the students that they can count on me to attend. I also note times and days where I am not available, which allows students to view my schedule in advance and plan accordingly.

Document Sharing and Editing

Cloud tools offer additional tools for coaching, and these provide flexibility for helping doctoral learners with writing. A number of other authors have suggested that the doctoral writing process might benefit from both cognitive apprenticeship (Maher et al., 2013; Swanson et al., 2014; Wolff, 2010) and the idea of scholarly community models (Aitchison, 2009; Hasrati, 2005; Johnson, 2014). Google Docs, together with a telephone connection, allows real-time shared review and editing of documents. This can allow for a mentor to quickly share a simple editing fix for a problem that appears to be fossilized in a learner's writing. As Bean (2011) suggested, fixing a writing or a citation problem for the students may not be the best strategy for holding them responsible for their writing. It is more beneficial to have the learners find their own errors. But I find that a coaching process can help them see errors that they originally may overlook, and can include strategies for finding repeated errors. We can correct a few errors together, which hopefully helps learners remember when and how to prevent future instances. Technologies integrated into word processing enable iterations, including commenting, editing, and tracking features in Microsoft Word. Most of these features are visible when a document is uploaded into Google Docs.

Google Docs also provides a quick alternative if conference software cannot be used due to bandwidth problems or needed updates. For example, a mentee might call into a conference telephone line, but not be able to join the web conference. In such cases, I can quickly upload the student's file into Google Docs, send her the link, and allow us both to view, discuss, and edit the document online and in real time.

Learning Management Systems (LMS)

LMS tools such as Moodle and Blackboard provide a virtual venue to a community of emerging scholars. Through them, learners can communicate and share progress, experiences, suggestions, frustrations, and celebrations. While they are guided where appropriate by the mentor, they also learn from each other by providing tips and inspiration, asking questions, and discussing barriers they encounter along the way. In doctoral learning coaching extends beyond the academic, and cloud tools ease opportunities for social and emotional processes of encouragement to take place. These include the specific (i.e. "I need to get my time management under control") and the general or even philosophical (i.e. "what does this all mean, anyway?" or "how badly do I want this degree?").

LMS tools also often serve a primary purpose for the university of showing learners' attendance and participation in the program, including proven contact with an instructor. Such proof is typically needed for requirements such as accreditation and financial aid. Because the universities provide these forums, and because students and faculty are required to use them, they provide a convenient asynchronous location for weekly check-ins, questions, announcements, and discussions about dissertation process and progress.

Online forums provide a helpful venue for establishing new relationships between mentor and mentees, and also for establishing a learning community with a group of mentees. A new mentee will find herself enrolled in my Blackboard forum at the start of the term. Upon logging in, she will see a welcome post and a greeting, as well as introductions from other members of my mentee group. One institution requires that mentors greet learners with a "warm welcome" video, which gives new mentees a quick introduction to my personal and professional interests. Others might receive a text-based message with the same general information, accompanied by my photo.

The forums available in LMS course tools provide opportunities for building trust between mentor and mentees, as well as building community among mentees and attending to their social and emotional needs. An active mentee forum is a place for learners to communicate as a group, and helps reduce loneliness and isolation in the process. In his research on metacommunication between graduate students and supervisors, Baltzersen (2013, p. 135) described the "importance of an open and transparent communication style." In the forums, both mentees and mentor can report their current steps in the research process or the outcomes of committee review. They also observe the mentoring of others within the group. There is frequent mention, for example, of scheduled meetings (i.e. "Angie, I see we are going to talk on Tuesday, I look forward to that!"). Such discussion is a way of gently establishing routines and expectations for the whole group. Those who have fallen out of communication can reassess their progress within the group and remember to make an appointment on my schedule. Baltzersen (2013) recommended that supervisor and students should openly discuss their expectations for communication, including how, when, and how often communication takes place, as well as the format and function of feedback. One of my mentees did this on his own initiative when he began a discussion with the subject line "how did you choose a mentor?" As his peers responded, it provided me with an opportunity to discuss some of my mentoring habits and preferences as well as reflect on my own mentoring style. For example, I might have shared, "I really rolled up my sleeves when I helped you with your literature review. It was probably painful at times, but the work has paid off. Your other committee members thought it was great!" Such a comment not only reinforces to a mentee that his or her hard work had a successful outcome, but it also sends the message to all mentees that they will likely face hard work, receive lengthy feedback, and ultimately find success.

The online forums provide a place to practice the fading that necessarily must occur with scaffold support. Those who are farther along in the process might see me share a message that indicates to others how I might gently remove some of these supports. For example, I could comment to a specific mentee: "Your chapter four was one of the best first drafts I've seen in a long time. You only have a few changes to make." That learner might remember sending me 15 drafts of their first dissertation chapter, and may then reveal to the group that the latest success was not a first draft at all, but was instead the culmination of applying all the skills learned with mentorship throughout all the drafts of the previous chapters. The practice of fading can also be demonstrated to the group when learners ask questions that they or others have asked before, or when they ask questions that are at a basic level. The forum provides me with an opportunity to be present and supportive, and to set the mentees on the right track without doing the whole task for them. I might also do a quick search in Google Scholar on a learners' topic, for example, and provide the link to the search in the forum, along with a quick lesson on using different phrase combinations and moving quotations marks around to narrow and broaden a search. Others in a similar position can learn from the exchange, and all then can rely less on my support for their own work.

Research Tools

Exploration at the doctoral level necessarily requires skill in using other available cloud tools for the research process. Emerging scholars should be able to conduct literature searches not only within their own online academic libraries, but within Google Scholar as well. Abstracts and journal article previews are increasingly available in the cloud without requiring a full download, which greatly speeds the research process. There are tools for citation in APA and other formats, including quick links to RefWorks or EndNote. Additional tools within Google Scholar put information at my mentees' fingertips, and they should not miss out on their value. When I was a doctoral learner in the early 1990s, I had to access complex volumes in the library to find "cited by" information on publications. Articles of interest had to be ordered through interlibrary loan if I could not find them on the shelf. I welcomed the innovation of ERIC abstracts on CD ROM. We were allowed to use them with library computers, and they were accompanied by files and files of microfiche articles that could only be viewed on special machines. Google Scholar achieves many of these functions with a couple of clicks. Even older articles are now available in PDF, and searching using key words and other search criteria can be quick and powerful.

Drawbacks and Challenges of Cloud Technology

There are disadvantages to relying on technology for building cognitive apprenticeship with doctoral learners, but these can be partly mitigated by coaching and by finding alternatives. Coaching helps ensure that everybody benefits from the use of cloud technology. Experience and comfort in using technology varies greatly, and among my mentees I have both digital natives and digital immigrants (see Prensky, 2001). Some mentees were already using some of the cloud technologies before I introduced them, but others have struggled. I have used Adobe Connect screen sharing to demonstrate to one learner how to make appointments using Teamup, and to another learner how to access Dropbox folders. Of course, they first needed to successfully be able to use Adobe Connect.

Alternatives are usually available when the tools fail, or when there are user errors. If my mentee is not able to download the Adobe Connect plug-in right before a meeting, then we can quickly shift to Google Docs. It that also fails, the meeting can still occur, provided there is a telephone connection. Integrating audio with Adobe Connect is not always easy, and on more than one occasion I forgot to record a session after promising a mentee that I would. In meetings with more than one mentee, it is more difficult to provide everybody with voice connection, due to possible background noises, echoing, and different volume levels. Encouraging participants to use the chat feature for questions and comments is one way to keep a meeting running smoothly while still ensuring all can participate

Sharing folders via Dropbox also has its risks. Dropbox allows users to store shared files in their local computers as well as in the cloud, and the local folder is synched whenever changes are made. Sometimes, mentees will reorganize a folder on their personal computer, forgetting that I'm sharing the folder with them and as many as 20 other current and former mentees. Files can be deleted, overwritten, or moved. Fortunately, Dropbox can alert me to file changes and I can always revert to or restore an original version. Similarly, the Teamup scheduling tool provides open access to all, and until I provided clear instructions, some mentees were inadvertently changing or deleting appointments made by others in the process of creating their own.

Finally, there is always the risk that mentees resist using any of the available cloud tools. These individuals may join the online forum only once a month or so, and it may take them weeks and months to send me updated drafts of their work via email or Blackboard. In such cases the task iterations are so far apart that we loose the thread of our conversation about their work. Coaching then needs to start near the beginning with each conversation, as it is difficult for me to remember each mentee's specific struggles when weeks or months have passed since the last iteration. To avoid the problem of lapsed communication, I require my mentees to check into the LMS forum every week. If they are absent for 2 weeks or more, I contact them with a reminder and a request for an update. Kumar et al. (2013) found that doctoral learners preferred it when their mentors facilitated a structured communication environment, and this included structuring the communications with their peers. It is possible that some will resist required inclusion in the learning community, but I have found that insisting on a minimal level of participation does help establish the relationship needed to build a healthy cognitive apprenticeship.

FINAL THOUGHTS

Many doctoral students struggle to complete their degrees. I have encountered those who are not prepared for the task and who need to greatly improve their writing, critical reading, and research skills to productively engage in the dissertation process. There are others who progress quickly, and who come with a good basis in skills, yet struggle with time management or have personal issues and life events that impinge on their time. I tell my students that there may be times when the dissertation needs to go on the "back burner" due to demands of family, job, or health; but it will never be completed if it does not regularly get rotated to the front where it gets immediate and lengthy attention.

The process of doctoral study is well-suited to cognitive apprenticeship methods, and these are in turn greatly enriched by cloud technology tools when the members of a learning community are located at a distance from each other. But a PhD or professional doctorate is not just a process; it is necessarily a product as well. To complete a satisfactory product, students need the modeling, coaching, and scaffolding that are designed to show them precisely how to meet that target. Yet cognitive apprenticeship methods are not designed for reaching basic standards only. My students also know that I want them to exceed far beyond the minimum target, and I communicate these expectations to them in our first meeting. I may begin the conversation with "this is the kind of mentor I am…" so that they know what to expect from me. They also find ways teach me, either through their content writing or through their feedback and communication. My own mentoring techniques have adapted for the better as a result.

The relationship between doctoral mentors and their apprentices needs to be a trusting one. Sometimes this trust is built through a sort of trial period in which the mentee considers "I will see how it goes," knowing that in a large online university, there are other mentors out there. When I bring them into a community of emerging scholars at various stages, my new mentees gain a sense that things are moving along for others through scaffolding and coaching. These interactions are models in and of themselves, and they aid in building that initial trust in new mentees. I can reassure them that even if they don't see the whole "map" of the dissertation process ahead, I usually can. My job is to keep track of the map so I can guide them along it to completion. In each final oral defense--the culmination of my mentee's work--a committee member will invariably ask, "what will you do next with your work?" The responses always provide evidence that the (almost) graduate is ready to explore, and that he or she has confidently gained the skills required to transfer the learning to new scholarship or other professional endeavors. The apprenticeship may be officially over as the graduate leaves my small community of learners, but a larger community of scholars awaits.

REFERENCES

Aitchison, C. (2009). Writing groups for doctoral education. *Studies in Higher Education, 34*(8), 905–916. doi:10.1080/03075070902785580

Allen, I. E., & Seaman, J. (2015). *Grade level: Tracking online education in the United States.* Babson Survey Research Group and Quahog Research Group. Retrieved from http://onlinelearningconsortium.org/read/survey-reports-2014/

Austin, A. E. (2009). Cognitive apprenticeship theory and its implications for doctoral education: A case example from a doctoral program in higher and adult education. *The International Journal for Academic Development, 14*(3), 173–183. doi:10.1080/13601440903106494

Baltzersen, R. K. (2013). The importance of metacommunication in supervision processes in higher education. *International Journal of Higher Education, 2*(2), 128. doi:10.5430/ijhe.v2n2p128

Bean, J. C. (2011). *Engaging ideas: The professor's guide to integrating writing, critical thinking, and active learning in the classroom.* John Wiley & Sons.

Caffarella, R. S., & Barnett, B. G. (2000). Teaching doctoral students to become scholarly writers: The importance of giving and receiving critiques. *Studies in Higher Education, 25*(1), 39–52. doi:10.1080/030750700116000

Collins, A., Brown, J. S., & Holum, A. (1991). Cognitive apprenticeship: Making things visible. *American Educator: The Professional Journal of the American Federation of Teachers, 15*(3), 6-11, 38-46. Retrieved from: http://elc.fhda.edu/transform/resources/collins_brown_holum_1991.pdf

Collins, A., Brown, J. S., & Newman, S. E. (1986). *Cognitive Apprenticeship: Teaching the Craft of Reading, Writing, and Mathematics* (No. BBN-6459). BBN Labs Inc. Retrieved from: http://eric.ed.gov/?id=ED284181 (ERIC Document Reproduction Service No. ED 284181)

DeMeyer, A. (2013). The future of doctoral education in business administration. *Journal of Management Development, 32*(5), 477–486. doi:10.1108/02621711311328264

Denton, D. W. (2012). Enhancing instruction through constructivism, cooperative learning, and cloud computing. *TechTrends, 56*(4), 34–41. doi:10.1007/s11528-012-0585-1

Engels-Schwarzpaul, A. C., & Peters, M. A. (Eds.). (2013). *Of Other Thoughts: Non-Traditional Ways to the Doctorate: A Guidebook for Candidates and Supervisors.* Springer Science & Business Media. doi:10.1007/978-94-6209-317-1

Erichsen, E. A., & Bolliger, D. U. (2011). Towards understanding international graduate student isolation in traditional and online environments. *Educational Technology Research and Development, 59*(3), 309–326. doi:10.1007/s11423-010-9161-6

Ghefaili, A. (2003). Cognitive apprenticeship, technology, and the contextualization of learning environments. *Journal of Educational Computing, Design & Online Learning, 4*(1), 1-27. Retrieved from: https://wss.apan.org/jko/mls/Learning%20Content/Aziz%20-%20Cognitive%20Apprenticeship.pdf

Hasrati, M. (2005). Legitimate peripheral participation and supervising Ph.D students. *Studies in Higher Education*, *30*(5), 557–570. doi:10.1080/03075070500249252

Janta, H., Lugosi, P., & Brown, L. (2014). Coping with loneliness: A netnographic study of doctoral students. *Journal of Further and Higher Education*, *38*(4), 553–571. doi:10.1080/0309877X.2012.726972

Johnson, E. (2014). Toward the building of a cross-disciplinary doctoral research and writing culture. *Journal of University Teaching & Learning Practice*, *11*(1), 4. Retrieved from http://ro.uow.edu.au/jutlp/vol11/iss1/4

Kumar, S., Johnson, M., & Hardemon, T. (2013). Dissertations at a distance: Students' perceptions of online mentoring in a doctoral program. *International Journal of E-Learning & Distance Education*, *27*(1). Retrieved from http://ijede.ca/index.php/jde/article/view/835/1481

Kwan, B. S. (2009). Reading in preparation for writing a PhD thesis: Case studies of experiences. *Journal of English for Academic Purposes*, *8*(3), 180-191. DOI:10.1016/j.jeap.2009.02.001

Lam, P., & McNaught, C. (2006). Design and evaluation of online courses containing media-enhanced learning materials. *Educational Media International*, *43*(3), 199–218. doi:10.1080/09523980600641403

Lave, J., & Wenger, E. (1991). *Situated learning: Legitimate peripheral participation*. Cambridge University Press. doi:10.1017/CBO9780511815355

Lee, A. (2008). How are doctoral students supervised? Concepts of doctoral research supervision. *Studies in Higher Education*, *33*(3), 267–281. doi:10.1080/03075070802049202

Lyons, W., Scroggins, D., & Rule, P. B. (1990). The mentor in graduate education. *Studies in Higher Education*, *15*(3), 277–285. doi:10.1080/03075079012331377400

Maher, M. A., Gilmore, J. A., Feldon, D. F., & Davis, T. E. (2013). Cognitive apprenticeship and the supervision of science and engineering research assistants. *Journal of Research Practice*, *9*(2), Article M5. Retrieved from http://jrp.icaap.org/index.php/jrp/article/view/354/311

Metcalfe, J. (2006). The changing nature of doctoral programmes. *Wenner Gren International Series*, *83*, 79. Retrieved from: http://www.portlandpress.com/pp/books/online/fyos/083/0079/0830079.pdf

Nerad, M. (2012). Conceptual approaches to doctoral education: A community of practice. *Alternation*, *19*(2), 57-72. Retrieved from: http://alternation.ukzn.ac.za/Files/docs/19.2/04%20Ner.pdf

Prensky, M. (2001). Digital natives, digital immigrants part 1. *On the horizon*, *9*(5), 1–6. doi:10.1108/10748120110424816

Preston, J. C. (2014). Online Doctoral Programs: Can They Produce the Business Scientists and Leaders Needed for the 21st Century? *International Journal of Leadership and Change*, *2*(1), 5. Retrieved from http://digitalcommons.wku.edu/ijlc/vol2/iss1/5

Radda, H., Cross, T., & Holbeck, R. (2012). Learning together: Perceived cognitive and behavioral outcomes of learners in a nontraditional, professional doctoral program. *Journal of Instructional Research*, (1). Retrieved from https://cirt.gcu.edu/ jir/documents/2012-v1/raddapdf

Swanson, K. W., West, J., Carr, S., & Augustine, S. (2015). Supporting Dissertation Writing Using a Cognitive Apprenticeship Model. In V. C. X. Wang (Ed.), *Handbook of Research on Scholarly Publishing and Research Methods*, (pp. 84-104). Information Science Reference, IGI Global.

Walker, G. E., Golde, C., Jones, L., Bueschel, A. C., & Hutchings, P. (2008). *The formation of scholars: Rethinking doctoral education for the twenty-first century*. San Francisco, CA: Jossey-Bass.

Wolff, L. (2010). Learning through Writing: Reconceptualising the Research Supervision Process. *International Journal of Teaching and Learning in Higher Education, 22*(3), 229-237. Retrieved from: http://files.eric.ed.gov/fulltext/EJ938558.pdf (ERIC Document Reproduction Service No. EJ 938558)

Chapter 12
Phases, Scaffolds, and Technology:
Cloud-Based Student Collaboration Model for Online and Blended Course Design

Julia Parra
New Mexico State University, USA

ABSTRACT

With ubiquitous Internet and the related tools, including computational devices and cloud-based technology, has come public access to a world of information literally at one's fingertips. This has led to the increased use of cloud-based student collaboration as a key strategy for engaging students as responsible, creative, and productive participants in the learning process. For the purpose of this qualitative study there are three objectives: 1) update and revise a course design model for cloud-based student collaboration that uses phases and scaffolds, and includes an optimal cloud-based collaboration toolkit identified by graduate students, 2) describe an online course wherein this model has been applied, and 3) share exemplar course materials including guides, learning plans and directions, and content scaffolds in the form of templates, that support this model and can be repurposed by anyone using cloud-based student collaboration in higher education.

INTRODUCTION

In the last twenty years, with the advent of the Internet and the development of computational devices for the general public, the world began to change. In the past 6-10 years, the fast forward button for change was pressed as smart phones started a path to ubiquity. With ubiquitous Internet and related tools has come public access to a world of information literally at their fingertips. If information resides "in the human mind as knowledge" (Liew, 2007, Section 2, para. 8) and if "knowledge is power" (Annan, 2000), then at no time ever before this time period, have people had so much potential for power. This power is available to education and the New Media Consortium Horizon Reports (Cummins, Johnson,

DOI: 10.4018/978-1-5225-1650-7.ch012

& Adams, 2012; Johnson, Becker, Estrada, & Freeman, 2014) note trends impacting higher education including the technologies we use becoming increasingly cloud-based and the increasingly collaborative nature of work environments driving changes in the way student projects are structured leading to shift of students as consumers to creators and to new education paradigms that include online, hybrid, and collaborative models. Nace (2015) notes the need in education for supporting the development of "change skillsets." For this, a curriculum of change and innovation is needed. Change is needed but change is hard, and rapid innovative change seems near to impossible. To support a more rapid approach for development of "change skillsets" and curriculum of change and innovation, it is imperative that educators share viable models and resources. For the purpose of this qualitative study using case study methods and auto-ethnographic methods, there are three objectives, 1) update and revise a course design model for cloud-based student collaboration that uses phases, scaffolds, and an optimal cloud-based toolkit, 2) describe a graduate level online course wherein this model has been applied, and 3) share exemplar course materials including guides, activity plans and directions, and content scaffolds in the form of templates.

BACKGROUND

As previously noted, work environments are becoming increasing collaborative, new educational paradigms include online, hybrid, and collaborative models, technologies we use are becoming increasingly cloud-based, and student roles are shifting from consumer to creator. Thus, cloud-based student collaboration is increasingly becoming an effective strategy for teaching and learning, and includes a beneficial set of skills for students to develop. Further, many cloud-based collaboration tools are available to support student collaboration in a variety of forms such as student group work, the focus of cloud-based student collaboration in this study.

Cloud-Based Student Collaboration

Conrad and Donaldson (2004) remind us that "Bruner, Vygotsy, and Piaget all embraced the philosophy that humans do not learn in a vacuum but rather through interaction" (p. 4), and Pallof & Pratt further discus collaboration as an integral component and "the 'heart and soul' of an online course or, for that matter a course that bases its theoretical foundation in constructivism" (Pallof & Pratt, 2005a, p. 6). When students are engaged in learning groups within a learning community they "have the opportunity to extend and deepen their learning experience, test out new ideas by sharing them with a supportive group, and receive critical and constructive feedback" (Pallof & Pratt, 2005b, p. 1). Collison, Elbaum, Haavind and Tinker (2000) further note the importance of collaboration and collective inquiry:

A process that involves inquiry confronts the unknown and relies on personal or collective resources to resolve questions. The online environment in which inquiry can flourish is gradually built by collaborative and collective contributions. Such collaboration efforts are likely to result in better outcomes, designs, practices, or products. (p. 30)

With the increasing development of cloud-based technologies, elements for the development of learning community and for class collaborations have also moved to the cloud. Such elements include student-ways of communication and document sharing (Fichter, 2005), student reflective activities (Lin,

Wen, Jou, & Wu, 2014), collaborative writing (Blau, & Caspi, 2009) brainstorming and teamwork/group work (Herrick, 2009). This study focuses on these elements as cloud-based student collaboration particularly in support of student group work.

Developing Skills for Cloud-Based Student Collaboration

Pedagogically, there are many benefits of cloud-based student collaboration such as the development of critical thinking skills, co-creation of knowledge and meaning, reflection, and transformative learning (Pallof & Pratt, 2005a). But along with the benefits of collaborative group work, there are of course, challenges that increase when collaborative group work is taken into online or blended courses. Lack of online technology skills, time conflicts, differences in team member participation, and logistics of teamwork, are just a few, and because of these challenges, students often end up unhappy with the process (Kim, Liu, & Bonk, 2005; Koh & Hill 2009).

In order "to maximize the benefits and minimize the challenges, students should be supported in the development of skills with the use of relevant (often emerging or Web 2.0) online technologies" (Parra, 2013) alongside the development of skills related to collaboration and group work. This is applicable for all courses and learning environments but especially important for online courses. There are a variety of strategies for developing skills for cloud-based student collaboration course that can be used including, for this study, Salmon's 5-Stage Model (2004, 2013), Conrad and Donaldson's Phases of Engagement (2004, 2011, 2012), and the use of content scaffolds (Su & Klein, 2010). Of note, these are strategies that are particularly important for online course design but equally valid for hybrid or blended course design.

Gilly Salmon's 5-Stage Model provides the stages and pacing for instructors of online courses as they navigate the support of student skills in the use of technology. Salmon's five stages include, access and motivation, online socialization, information exchange, knowledge construction and development. Similar to Salmon's "stages," Conrad and Donaldson created a model of phases with a focus on developing learner engagement in online courses. The current, revised Phases of Engagement model (2012) is an "instructional strategy for guiding students through levels of increased collaborative engagement" (Chapter 2, para. 1). Their four phases evolved into five phases and include Connect, Communicate, Cooperate, Collaborate, Facilitate, and Continue. Finally, content scaffolds, such as the group project templates used in this study, can be used to support students as they develop both technology and collaboration skills in preparation for collaboration and group work (Cho & Jonassen, 2002; Su & Klein, 2010).

Technology for Cloud-Based Collaboration

To facilitate cloud-based student collaboration, cloud-based tools like wikis, collaborative documents, webconferencing, online forums, and project management tools are available. There are so many cloud-based tools for group work and collaboration available that the biggest problem for students working collaboratively really ends up being agreeing on which tools to use. A sampling of popular and useful tool types and specific tools is provided and discussed. For the process of online and blended course design and long-term discussion, the type of tool is what is important. For actual implementation of cloud-based student collaboration tool use, the specific tools become important. Types of tools sampled here are used by the described online course in this study and include learning management systems, small group and 1-1 web conferencing, large group and class web conferencing, collaborative document/product creation, wikis and blogs, and microblogging tools.

Learning Management Systems (LMS)

Learning management systems (LMSs) are used to contain online course content, interactions, and assessments. Institutions provide LMSs via on-premise servers or they have them hosted via a cloud-based service. LMSs have integrated tools that support student communications, interactions, and collaborations and usually have specific group areas that can be designated for students to collaborate. Most LMSs provide discussion areas for groups and group projects in that allow private group communications with the ability to send group messages, chat or conferencing tools to communicate synchronously, and areas to store or collaborate on files. Additionally, LMSs are working to integrate third-party tools. For example, the researcher's current cloud-based LMS, Canvas, integrates easily with Adobe Connect, Google Docs, Twitter, and more.

Small Group and 1-1 Web Conferencing

Small group and 1-1 web conferencing tools such as Skype and Google Hangout support synchronous communication and collaboration for 1-1 study partners and small to medium-sized groups. Both Skype and Google Hangouts are considered cloud-based tools and are mostly used synchronously (where participants are participating at the same time) unless a recording is generated, in which case the recording may be used as an asynchronous resource (participants are using at a different time than the resource was created). Skype started with "peer-to-peer (P2P) architecture but became so ubiquitous that it had to move to a "cloud-based system" (Skype, n.d.). Currently, Skype allows up to 25 people in a voice-only conference and Google Hangout supports a video chat with up to 10 people with the option to broadcast to the world, however, this is a feature subject to change. Additionally, tools like Skype and Google Hangout allow for text, audio, and video chat along with other features including screen sharing, file sharing and a variety of other collaboration features. Skype and Google Hangout are emphasized here because they include free options and are cross-platform. Additionally, Skype is very popular for personal use thus a good option for student use and Google Hangout is quickly gaining ground with its ease of use and evolving features.

Large Group and Class Web Conferencing

Large group and class web conferencing tools such as Adobe Connect and Blackboard Collaborate support synchronous communication and collaboration on a larger scale than the small group and 1-1 web conferencing tools. As with LMSs, these tools can be either provided on-premise or via hosting in the cloud. These tools can support 100 or more participants with a rich array of features including PowerPoint and other document display, chat, audio, video, application and screen share, whiteboards, breakout rooms, recording, and more. Adobe Connect and Blackboard Collaborate are cross-platform but they are not free. They are, however, becoming prevalent at institutions that offer online education.

Collaborative Document/Product Creation

Collaborative document and product creation tools such as Google Drive include effective tools for collaboratively creating documents, spreadsheets, presentations, and even movies. For example, using Google Docs is just like using MS Word except that everyone in a group can edit the same document online synchronously, asynchronously, and from any Internet connected computer. A tool like Google Docs along with a web-conferencing tool like Skype or Google Hangout, can support groups or teams with effective and efficient communication and collaboration as they engage in and complete group-based activities. Reyna (2010) provides an extensive list of advantages of using Google Docs, including PC and Mac cross platform compatability, automatic saving every 15 seconds, accessible from almost any Internet-connected device (sometimes an app is needed, i.e. for phones, phablets, and tablets), student work can be monitored in real-time and revision history allows for easy determination of which students actually contributed, documents can be exported in a variety of helpful formats such as PDF, MS Word, etc. and finally, Reyna (2010) notes that "Google Docs do[es] not claim ownership or control over submitted content. For documents you expressly choose to share with others, Google Docs ha[s] the proper license to display those documents to your selected users" (p. 2 of download, p. 1567 of proceedings).

Wikis and Blogs

Wiki tools like PbWorks and Wikispaces and blogs like Blogger and WordPress are great tools for group work, collaboration, and collaborative publishing. Wikis are different from Google Docs in that only one person can create or edit at a time. Wikis and blogs are most helpful for group work if a polished end product is required.

Microblogging Tools

Microblogging tools like Yammer and Twitter are engaging tools for asynchronous communication and collaboration. Where Twitter is a free and global microblogging tool, Yammer is an organization-focused microblogging tool with free and paid for components. By using the mobile notifications, a group could stay on top of group activities. The researcher has personally experienced this strategy recently and found it a fun and timely way to accomplish group activities.

A CLOUD-BASED STUDENT COLLABORATION MODEL FOR COURSE DESIGN

Context

The researcher is an assistant professor at New Mexico State University in the College of Education, Department of Curriculum Instruction. She teaches online and blended courses about learning design and technology with a focus on online and blended course design and is a Quality Matters[1] Peer Reviewer with two Quality Matters Recognized online courses. In 2011, after four years of teaching mostly online courses, she realized a gap in the field of online course design. She was using several models and strategies to design for cloud-based collaboration including, 1) Conrad & Donaldson's Phases of Engagement model (2011) introducing phases of student engagement in a 16-week online course as related to group work and collaboration; 2) Gilly Salmon's 5-Stage Model (2004) providing the stages and steps for instructors of online courses as they navigate the support of student skills in the use of technology; and 3) the strategy of using content scaffolds to support student project teams (Su & Klein, 2010). However, there was no model that combined all three of these elements. Thus, the author developed and published one, titled, the Phases and Scaffolds for Technology Use & Collaborative Group Work model (Parra, 2013). After several more years of implementation and the evolution of cloud-based terminology, this qualitative study is conducted wherein, the Phases, Scaffolds, Technology & Collaboration model is updated, revised and newly titled, Cloud-Based Student Collaboration (CBSC) model.

Purpose

The first goal for this chapter is to update and revise a course design model for cloud-based student collaboration that uses phases and scaffolds, and an optimal cloud-based student collaboration toolkit as identified by graduate students in an online course designed using the CBSC model. The second goal of this auto-ethnographic study is to describe an online course wherein this model has been applied. Finally, the author shares exemplar course materials including guides, activity plans and directions, and content scaffolds in the form of templates.

Data Collection

Field Notes

The author uses ADDIE (analysis, design, development, implementation, and evaluation) as a basic process for online and blended course design. As part of evaluation, the author uses Google Docs to keep field notes including observations related to course design, conversations between instructor and students in live synchronous class meetings regarding course design, and archives of course activities. The field notes are used to address course revisions and revisions for the course design model in this study.

Online and Blended Course Archives

The author keeps archives of online and blended courses. Course archives provide further data for course revisions, for updating the course design model, and for accessing course materials considered successful for supporting students in the process of cloud-based collaboration.

Survey

The author used Survey Monkey to design an end-of-course survey to identify an optimal cloud-based student collaboration toolkit based on student perceptions. The survey was sent by email after the conclusion of a fully online course.

An Optimal Cloud-Based Student Collaboration Toolkit

There are a plethora of tools and tool types that currently exist and continue to be developed. However, it is also important to keep things manageable for optimal learning and learning design. Therefore a strategy of selecting a set of tools or a toolkit that is manageable and proven to be effective is recommended. To support the identification of a currently effective and optimal toolkit, the researcher used 1) field notes and course archives to provide auto-ethnographic perspective and 2) designed and conducted a survey for graduate students (Parra, 2013) that included the following questions (see Appendix 1 for question design):

- What tools were most helpful to you in conducting your group work?
- How satisfied were you with the [following] tools you used to complete your [group project]?
- How did the [following] tools you used to complete your [group project] impact your overall learning?
- How did the [following] tools you used to complete your [group project] impact your success?

The use of [group project] indicates a specific group project referred to in one of the author's courses. The use of [following] is to imply the list of tools graduate students could choose from as follows:

- Adobe Connect
- Skype
- Blackboard Discussion
- Blackboard Chat
- Blackboard Mail
- Gmail
- Google Docs or other collaborative document
- PBWorks or other wiki tool
- Yammer
- Twitter
- Other

The data analysis based on this inquiry verified that the tools most beneficial and valued by students for group work and collaboration in an online class were, in fact, Skype, Google Docs, and Adobe Connect (Parra, 2013). Of note, the combination of synchronous discussion with a tool like Skype and product development with a tool like Google Docs, supports highly effective and efficient collaboration.

It is also key to point out, that these tools are important for the categories they represent, in this case these tools include: class web conferencing tools; 1-1 and small group web conferencing tools; and collaborative document creation tools.

Based on this inquiry, the researcher's field notes, and course archives, for the near future in online course design and development, the following are the recommended tool types for optimal cloud-based student collaboration toolkit.

- The LMS, wherein synchronous and asynchronous features and interactions are contained along with course content;
- Large group and class web conferencing system such for class activities including course orientation, class meetings, discussions, Q&A, and presentations;
- 1-1 and small group web conferencing tools for dyad and small group collaboration as well as student-instructor interaction; and
- Collaborative document creation tools such as Google Docs and other Google Drive tools such as Spreadsheets and Presentation. As noted by one student in the survey inquiry "having access to the shared docs in Google docs was a great benefit as we could all edit and change things as suggestions were made."

The author's current supported cloud-based student collaboration toolkit includes:

- Canvas
- Adobe Connect
- Skype
- Google tools including, Gmail, Google Drive (Docs, Slides, etc.)
- PBWorks
- Twitter

Cloud-Based Student Collaboration Model

The Cloud-Based Student Collaboration (CBSC) model uses a process of phases including content and metacognitive scaffolding to support students in in the development of skills for cloud-based collaboration. This model can be applied to courses with any type of content and can be used for blended courses as well. Table 1 provides an easy to use guide for the design of CBSC into a 16-week course. Note that the researcher has used a modification of this model for a 1-week workshop and a 5-week mini-semester course. Items with asterisks are course materials and scaffolds and will be further discussed and shared later in this study.

Cloud-Based Student Collaboration Model Applied to an Online Course

The author applies the Cloud-Based Student Collaboration (CBSC) model to any online or blended course that includes collaborative group work. These courses are designed using a learning management

Table 1. Cloud-based student collaboration (CBSC) course design model

Phases	Instructor Roles	Recommended Student Activities	Scaffolds and Technology
Phase 1: Preparing for CBSC (Weeks 1-2)	• Community Leader • Role Model • Master Learner • Coordinator • Motivator	1. Attend course orientation; CBSC tools are demonstrated. 2. Participate in course introductions 3. Develop optimal CBSC Toolkit 4. Prepare for CBSC	1. Class web conferencing 2. Discussion forum 3. Getting Started Guide*; small group CBSC tools such as Skype, Google Drive, etc. 4. Google Doc for students self-assigned grouping and Group Work Guide*
Phase 2: Practicing CBSC (Weeks 3-5)	• Leader • Role Model • Master Learner • Coordinator	1. Complete a group contract 2. Complete a fun, low risk group activity	1. Group Contract template* 2. Activity instructions and template*
Phase 3: Participating in CBSC (Weeks 6-12)	• Role Model • Counselor • Mediator • Motivator	1. Participate in group projects 2. Submit artifacts or progress reports 3. Attend synchronous class meetings for related course content and Q&A	1. Small group CBSC tools such as Skype, LMS discussion, Google Drive, etc. 2. LMS assignment tool 3. Class web conferencing
Phase 4: Presenting CBSC Projects (Weeks 13-16)	• Master Learner • Counselor • Mediator • Coordinator	1. Submit final products (slides, site, documents, etc.) 2. Practice presentations 3. Present in synchronous class meeting	1. LMS assignment tool 2. Class web conferencing 3. Class web conferencing

system (LMS) and all course content is added using modules. The following is the structure for an online graduate course titled, Fostering Online Learning Communities that is part of a 5-course series in the Online Graduate Certificate in Online Teaching and Learning, thus the content is about teaching people to teach online. Elements of Cloud-Based Student Collaboration model are annotated with (CBSC).

1. **Module 1:** Course Materials
    a. Syllabus
    b. Live Synchronous Meeting Schedule
    c. Course & Tech Help
    d. Additional materials added as needed
2. **Module 2:** Adventure 1-Getting Started
    a. Adventure 1 Overview
    b. Course Orientation Meeting Information (CBSC)
    c. Program Orientation Meeting Information
    d. Getting Started Quiz
    e. Introductions (CBSC)
    f. Setup Your Collaboration Toolkit (CBSC)
    g. Reflection
3. **Module 3:** Adventure 2-Set Up for Collaborative Group Work (CBSC)
    a. Adventure 2 Overview
    b. Google Doc for Setting up Groups
    c. Collaboration and Group Work Guide
    d. Group Contract
    e. Fun Group Activity
4. **Module 4:** Adventure 3-Designing for Online Learner & Community Success
    a. Adventure 3 Overview
    b. Discussion: Online Learner & Community Success
    c. Discussion: Supporting Online Learners
    d. Discussion: Online Learning Community
    e. Assignment: Design Your Draft Getting Started Materials
5. **Module 5:** Adventure 4-Navigating the Roadblocks in Online Learning Communities
    a. Adventure 4 Overview
    b. Review the Quality Matters Rubric (Part 1 and Part 2)
    c. The Great Debates (Part 1 and Part 2)
    d. Summarize the Great Debate
6. **Module 6:** Midpoint Learner Assessment
    a. Midpoint Learner Assessment
    b. Focus Essay-Course Rationale Draft
    c. Learning Design Vocabulary Assessment
    d. Concept Map or Infographic for Learning Communities
7. **Module 7:** Adventure 5-Designing your Syllabus and Learning Objectives
    a. Adventure 5 Overview
    b. Design, Share, and Revise Your Draft Syllabus
8. **Module 8:** Adventure 6-Designing Learning Activities

   a. Adventure 6 Overview
   b. (Collaborative Group Activity) Design a Learning Activity for this Course (CBSC)
   c. (Individual) Create and Share a Learning Activity for Your Online Course
9. **Module 9:** End of Course Learner Assessments
   a. End of Course Learner Assessments Overview
   b. Present Collaborative Group Activity (CBSC)
   c. Focus Essay: Revised Course Rationale
   d. Final Reflections
   e. End of Course Survey for OTL Program

Exemplar Course Materials

The exemplar course materials shared below, include guides, learning plans and directions, and content scaffolds in the form of templates that support this model and can be repurposed by anyone using cloud-based student collaboration in higher education. These course materials are from the most current version of the graduate course discussed earlier and titled, Fostering Online Learning Communities.

Getting Started Materials

A Getting Started Guide or Getting Started module in an online or blended course is a highly recommended practice and strategy and is discussed in Phase 1 of the CBSC Model. The Getting Started module in this case includes a Getting Started Overview (see Appendix 2) and an activity to Set Up Your Collaboration Toolkit with mini-tutorials for any key technologies used the course (see Appendix 3). This can lessen student confusion and lessen the amount of questions received by the instructor.

Collaboration and Group Work Roles Guide and Group Contract Template

The researcher has developed resources to guide students as they are forming and starting their groups and collaborations. The Collaboration and Group Work Guide (see Appendix 4) provides students with a rationale and overview of collaboration and support the development of groups and group roles. The Group Contract Template (see Appendix 5) is part of Phase 2 in the CBSC Model.

Fun and Low Risk Group Activities and Templates

A fun, low risk (low points) activity is provided early in the course (Phase 2) to prepare for the more complex, higher risk (high points) activity later in the course (Phase 3). This fun, low risk activity helped students to understand their group dynamics and further practice cloud-based collaboration skills. This activity, the Twitter Top 5 (see Appendixes 5 and 6), also supports student development of personal learning networks and can be modified to address different content areas.

FUTURE RESEARCH DIRECTIONS

The Cloud-Based Student Collaboration model for course design can be used for designing online and blended course in support of a variety of class collaborations, in this study the focus was on student group projects. However, cloud-based collaborations can be used and further investigated for additional areas emphasis and future research is recommended, including:

- The impact of scaffolding on cloud-based student collaboration.
- The impact of cloud-based collaboration on actual student cognitive and affective growth.
- Cloud-based collaboration for sharing power between instructor and students including course co-design and class co-creation and publication.

CONCLUSION

The rapid changes occurring with technology and globalization is making it necessary for educators to re-envision how teaching and learning is done. One of the great things about technology, globalization and the topic of this chapter – cloud-based student collaboration – is that educators have the ability to easily share what they are doing. As noted by Araujo, Carmona, Parra, & Chávez (2014):

The top-down approach of educational reform focused on a standardized change model is clunky, time-consuming, and difficult to implement. A grass-roots, bottom-up approach of sharing new forms of education and learning design, thereby updating focused areas of curriculum is a non-threatening approach and completely doable. (p. 17)

This chapter represents one instructor/researcher's attempt to participate in a grass-roots, bottom-up approach to educational reform by sharing successful strategies, models and resources for use in online and blended courses when designing for cloud-based student collaboration.

REFERENCES

Annan, K. (2000). *We the peoples: The role of the United Nations in the 21st century*. New York: United Nations.

Araujo, B., Carmona, J. F., Parra, J., & Chávez, R. C. (2014). Digital Explorations Along the Borderlands: Transfronterizo Youth, Testimonio and Personal Learning Networks. *International Journal of Information Communication Technologies and Human Development*, *6*(2), 16–31. doi:10.4018/ijicthd.2014040102

Blau, I., & Caspi, A. (2009). What type of collaboration helps? Psychological ownership, perceived learning and outcome quality of collaboration using Google Docs. In *Proceedings of the Chais conference on instructional technologies research* (Vol. 12).

Cho, K. L., & Jonassen, D. H. (2002). The effects of argumentation scaffolds on argumentation and problem solving. *Educational Technology Research and Development*, *50*(3), 5–22. doi:10.1007/BF02505022

Collison, G., Elbaum, B., Haavind, S., & Tinker, R. (2000). Facilitating Online Learning: Effective Strategies for Moderators. Atwood Publishing.

Conrad, R. M., & Donaldson, J. A. (2004). *Engaging the online learner. Activities and resources for creative instruction*. San Francisco: Jossey-Bass.

Conrad, R. M., & Donaldson, J. A. (2011). *Engaging the online learner. Activities and resources for creative instruction (updated version)*. San Francisco: Jossey-Bass.

Conrad, R. M., & Donaldson, J. A. (2012). *Continuing to engage the online learner: More activities and resources for creative instruction* (Vol. 35). John Wiley & Sons.

Cummins, M., Johnson, L., & Adams, S. (2012). *The NMC horizon report: 2012 higher education edition*. The New Media Consortium.

Fichter, D. (2005). The many forms of e-collaboration: Blogs, wikis, portals, groupware, discussion boards, and instant messaging. *Online*, *29*(4), 48–50.

Gasser, U., Palfrey, J., & Becker, M. B. (2012). *Mapping Cloud Interoperability in the Globalized Economy: Theory and Observations from Practice.* NCCR Trade Regulation Swiss National Center of Competence in Research.

Herrick, D. R. (2009, October). Google this!: using Google apps for collaboration and productivity. In *Proceedings of the 37th annual ACM SIGUCCS fall conference: communication and collaboration* (pp. 55-64). ACM. doi:10.1145/1629501.1629513

Jacobs, H. H. (Ed.). (2010). *Curriculum 21: Essential education for a changing world*. Alexandria, VA: Association for Supervision and Curriculum Development.

Johnson, L., Becker, S., Estrada, V., & Freeman, A. (2014). *The NMC horizon report: 2014 higher education*. The New Media Consortium.

Kim, K. J., Liu, S., & Bonk, C. J. (2005). Online MBA students' perceptions of online learning: Benefits, challenges, and suggestions. *The Internet and Higher Education*, *8*(4), 335–344. doi:10.1016/j.iheduc.2005.09.005

Koh, M. H., & Hill, J. R. (2009). Student perceptions of groupwork in an online course: Benefits and challenges. *International Journal of E-Learning & Distance Education*, *23*(2), 69–92.

Liew, A. (2007). Understanding data, information, knowledge and their inter-relationships. *Journal of Knowledge Management Practice*, *8*(2). Retrieved from http://www.tlainc.com/articl134.htm

Lin, Y. T., Wen, M. L., Jou, M., & Wu, D. W. (2014). A cloud-based learning environment for developing student reflection abilities. *Computers in Human Behavior*, *32*, 244–252. doi:10.1016/j.chb.2013.12.014

Mircea, M., & Andreescu, A. I. (2011). Using cloud computing in higher education: A strategy to improve agility in the current financial crisis. *Communications of the IBIMA, 2011*, 1–15. doi:10.5171/2011.875547

Moore, J. (2005). *The SLOAN Consortium Quality Framework and the Five Pillars*. SLOAN-C. Retrieved January 5, 2015 from http://sloanconsortium.org/publications/books/qualityframework.pdf

Nace, F. (2015). *Messaging the mindset: An intelligent approach to systemic change in education*. Washington, DC: Rowman & Littlefield Publishers.

Palloff, R., & Pratt, K. (2005a). *Collaborating Online: Learning Together in Community*. San Francisco: Jossey-Bass.

Palloff, R., & Pratt, K. (2005b). Learning Together in Community: Collaboration Online.*Proceedings 20th Annual Conference on Distance and Teaching and Learning*. University of Wisconsin.

Parra, J. L. (2013). Developing technology and collaborative group work skills: supporting student and group success in online and blended courses. *Cutting-Edge Technologies in Higher Education, 6*, 287-337.

Reyna, J. (2010). Google Docs in higher education settings: A preliminary report. In *Proceedings of World Conference on Educational Multimedia, Hypermedia and Telecommunications 2010* (pp. 1566-1572). Chesapeake, VA: AACE. Retrieved January 13, 2015 from http://jorgereyna.weebly.com/publications.html

Salmon, G. (2004). *E-moderating: The key to teaching and learning online*. Psychology Press.

Salmon, G. (2013). *E-tivities: The key to active online learning*. Routledge.

Skype. (n.d.). *What is the cloud?* Retrieved January 13, 2015 from https://support.skype.com/en/faq/FA12381/what-is-the-cloud

Su, Y., & Klein, J. (2010). Using scaffolds in problem-based hypermedia. *Journal of Educational Multimedia and Hypermedia, 19*(3), 327–347.

Sultan, N. (2010). Cloud computing for education: A new dawn? *International Journal of Information Management, 30*(2), 109–116. doi:10.1016/j.ijinfomgt.2009.09.004

Tout, S., Sverdlik, W., & Lawver, G. (2009). Cloud computing and its security in higher education. *Proceedings of ISECON, 26*.

KEY TERMS AND DEFINITIONS

Asynchronous: Asynchronous tool use implies that participants are not participating in an activity or with a tool at the same time as other participants. Examples include email and discussion forums.

Blended Learning: Blended learning is learning that occurs both online and face-to-face. This can relate to the content, the technology, or the students.

Collaboration: Collaboration occurs when individuals work together to achieve a common goal.

Online Learning: Learning that occurs via the Internet. Can be formal or informal.

Phablets: Smartphones that are very large and verge on tablet size such as iPhone 6+ or Samsung Galaxy S®5.

Scaffolding: In education, scaffolding is an instructional strategy that supports students during the learning process. Metaphorically, scaffolding provides learners with stepping-stones or a ladder to success.

Synchronous: Synchronous tool use implies that participants are participating in an activity or with a tool at the same time as other participants. Examples include a phone call and a live web conferencing meeting.

ENDNOTE

1 Quality Matters (QM) defines itself as an international organization whose "quality assurance processes have been developed to improve and certify the design of online and blended courses." (see www.qualitymatters.org)

APPENDIX 1

Survey Questions Design

Of the following tools, which tools were most helpful to you in conducting your group work in EDLT 528/628?

Didn't use l Not helpful l somewhat helpful l helpful l very helpful

- Adobe Connect
- Skype
- Blackboard Discussion
- Blackboard Chat
- Blackboard Mail
- Gmail
- Google Docs or other collaborative document
- PBWorks or other wiki tool
- Yammer
- Twitter
- Other

Comments

How satisfied were you with the tools you used to complete Project #2 in EDLT 528/628?

Didn't use l unsatisfied l somewhat unsatisfied l somewhat satisfied l satisfied

- Adobe Connect
- Skype
- Blackboard Discussion
- Blackboard Chat
- Blackboard Mail
- Gmail
- Google Docs or other collaborative document
- PBWorks or other wiki tool
- Yammer
- Twitter
- Other

Comments

How did the tools you used to complete Project #2 impact your overall learning in EDLT 528/628?

negative impact l neutral or no impact l positive impact

- Adobe Connect
- Skype
- Blackboard Discussion

- Blackboard Chat
- Blackboard Mail
- Gmail
- Google Docs or other collaborative document
- PBWorks or other wiki tool
- Yammer
- Twitter
- Other

Comments
How did the tools you used to complete Project #2 impact your success in EDLT 528/628?
negative impact | neutral or no impact | positive impact

- Adobe Connect
- Skype
- Blackboard Discussion
- Blackboard Chat
- Blackboard Mail
- Gmail
- Google Docs or other collaborative document
- PBWorks or other wiki tool
- Yammer
- Twitter
- Other

Comments

APPENDIX 2

Getting Started Overview

It is very helpful and recommended for students to have immediately obvious and available Getting Started instructions. In fact, one of your projects in this course is to create your own Getting Started instruction and activities. In many courses it is helpful to spend the first week on getting started activities and introductions so that is what we will do! This module addresses the course overarching learning objectives as follows:

1. You will begin to experience the key concepts and strategies related to successful online learning and knowledge building communities.
2. You will immediately have ideas to help you later when you develop key online course elements including Getting Started, Syllabus, Schedule, and Learning Activity with Assessment that meet QMR standards.

Learning Objectives and Mini-Checklist for the Getting Started module:

1. Successfully attend or review the recording of the Program Orientation or successfully review the recording.
2. Successfully attend or review the recording of the Course Orientation.
3. Complete the Getting Started Quiz with a perfect 10/10 score.
4. Get to know each other with an Introductions discussion and experience the initial stages of online learning community building.
5. Set Up Your Collaboration Toolkit.
6. Create a Reflection on where you stand on online learning community.

If you have any problems with any of the technology, you can get assistance by either posting a message to Course & Tech Help discussion. Everyone should feel free to help anyone who needs assistance - in fact, I encourage it!

APPENDIX 3

Set Up Your Collaboration Tool Kit

For this class, there are a few tools that you should become familiar with right away. These tools are some of my favorites for communication, collaboration, and personal learning network (PLN) development.

Make sure you have read my Online Identity resource post.

There are five (5) tools for you to get started with.

Tool #1: Create a Skype Account & Chat w/ Instructor

What is it?

Skype is an instant messenger, audio conferencing and much more technology.

Why use it?

To communicate with me and your small groups, a must have tool in every EdTech Tool Kit!

Directions:

1. Go to Skype to download the software. See the Help for Windows users or Help for Mac users if you need help. during the installation process, you'll be asked to create a Skype user name and to add contacts to your contact list. Later, you will add student colleagues that you know to your contact list - their skype IDs will be listed on the class communications survey spreadsheet posted as a link in the Group Work Module. Don't stress about this, what is most important for this step is to have Skype and your Contact ID.
2. If you need help, post a message in Course Help discussion topic.
3. When you can, begin a text chat with me when you see me online so I will know that you were successful in installing and using Skype. I also have important information for you! My Skype contact is desertjul. Note that two contacts come up for me, 1) Doc Julz and 2) I'M MOVING TO desertjul. Doc Julz is the correct account.

Tool #2: Create Google Account

What is it?

It's The Google and includes Gmail, Gdocs, Calendar, Sites, Scholar, and MUCH MORE. You need this account to use the Canvas Collaborations tool.

Why use it?

It's THE GOOGLE for heaven's sake! Need I say more?

Directions:

1. If you already have an account, skip to where you send me a Gmail message.
2. Go to http://gmail.com and click "Create an account" on the right, follow the directions.
3. Send me a Gmail message.

Tool #3: Join Twitter and create an update with #NMSUOTL

1. Join Twitter at http://twitter.com.
2. Create a post and at the end add #nmsuotl, you have a maximum of 140 characters. See an example of a Twitter account at http://twitter.com/desertjul. Don't freak out, just do this. If you don't like it, after the course, you can delete it.

Tool #4: Canvas Profile

1. Set up your Canvas Profile and make sure to set link up your collaboration tools- see Canvas Student Orientation Resources if you need help.

APPENDIX 4

Collaboration and Group Work Guide

Overview

Group work or teamwork is an important strategy for teachers and students to know about. Here are just a couple of reasons:

- Collaborating with others provides us with other perspectives besides our own, increasing the potential for knowledge gained and products created. Thus, increasing learning.
- For some students, teamwork provides the social presence needed to be successful. Especially in an online course.
- Living and working in today's "flat world" means we have to know about working online with others.

Of course, there are challenges to address and potential roadblocks to avoid, especially in online and blended learning environments. As we are finding out, there are many ways to arm ourselves with knowledge and solutions so that the challenges and roadblocks disappear...

So get the challenges out of the way first. This guide provides resources and examples to help you and your group address the challenges and start out on the right track in the development of your collaborative product.

Please note that in my classes, the most important part is the process. It is through the process that learning, collaboration, knowledge sharing, etc. occurs. Treat each other with kindness and do your best to include everyone. oh yeah, and have fun!

Establishing Group Policies and Procedures

As a group you will need to consider:

- How you plan to get the work done,
- Communication/meeting plans,
- Timelines/Deadlines,
- Goals/Milestones,
- Individual roles Problem/Conflict resolution.

If you establish organizational strategies and roles in the beginning, then it's much easier to get your group organized and headed in the right direction. I suggest a synchronous group meeting using your learning management system (LMS) chat tool or Skype to discuss the Group Contract. To get work done I recommend continued use of Skype if possible and using your LMS Group area for asynchronous and synchronous discussion. For actual product development, tools I find helpful are cloud-based collaboration tools such as those in Google Drive or a wiki page as in PBWorks. A fun new tool to try out is the Google Hangout, but you need to be in Google + to use Google Hangout.

Collaborative Tools

There are so many collaboration tools available that the biggest problem for groups really ends up being agreeing on which tools to use. Here are my recommendations.

- **LMS Group Tools:** In your groups, you have access to asynchronous and synchronous group tools including discussions, conferences, chat, and more.
- **Skype:** This is great for FREE synchronous collaboration allowing text, audio, and video chat. Sharing files and large chunks of text are excellent features of Skype.
- **Google Docs:** This is a great tool for online collaborative writing. It's just like using MS Word and everyone in your group can edit the same document online at anytime. If you have a gmail account, you may already have Google Docs as a feature when you log in to your gmail account. And nice for us, Canvas has a nifty Collaborations feature that integrates with Google Docs.
- **PbWorks:** PbWorks is a great tool for collaboration. It's different from google docs in that only one person can edit a page at a time. You can create your own or use the class wiki.

Further Information Resource Links

Use the following resources to learn more about online collaborative group work. If you find any other great resources, let me know so I can add them to the list. I have also provided two articles that I am working on in this module, indented under this resource.

Online Resources Include:

- Group Projects: Organizing and working with groups in projects accessible at http://www.studygs.net/groupprojects.htm
- Working in Groups accessible at http://isites.harvard.edu/fs/html/icb.topic58474/wigintro.html
- A Definition of Collaborative vs Cooperative Learning accessible at http://home.capecod.net/~tpanitz/tedsarticles/coopdefinition.htm

Make sure to go complete the Group Contract!

APPENDIX 5

Group Contract Template

How to use this document:

- Copy the below information into your own google doc that you created in Canvas Collaborations.
- Share your group document with all members of your group, there is a Share button in the upper right. Add the group member gmails to the add people box. Alternately, the Canvas Collaborations has this capacity built in.
- Fill in the blank side on the right. Everyone needs to add your own name in the group roles section and use a different color. Whenever you contribute, use your color.
- When you have completed this activity, share your group document with your instructor using her gmail account; alternately, Canvas Collaborations has this capacity built in.
- When you have completed this activity, use the share feature to share your group document with your instructor using her gmail.
- Post a link to your Group Contract in the Group Contract discussion tool. View each others' Contracts, you will learn a lot!

Table 2.

Group Name	
Group Members & Roles List the Names of your group members and their roles. Roles are helpful to build on the strengths of the team/group members. There are many models for teams and roles. One model includes: • leader - strength in organizing, may organize the Skype meeting, create an agenda, facilitate the conversation, etc. • recorder - strength in typing and summarizing, takes notes about what is discussed, makes sure notes are added to group space, keeps on top of group's shared knowledge, etc. • editor - strength in grammatical areas and how documents/presentations work, makes sure that group's product is grammatically correct, follows the guidelines, etc. • connector - strength in networking people, ideas, etc., helps leader keep track of team, keeps track of time, submits assignments to the instructor, etc. You are not bound to this model. It's just an example. I just recently used - Organizer, Document Specialist, Research Specialist, etc.	
Participation Members must share information, resources, and their unique ideas and perspective. Every member is responsible to participate in any weekly meetings or complete postings by a specific deadline for threaded discussions. How will you handle situations where a member is not participating?	
Communication What tools will your group be using to collaborate? How often will you be getting together virtually or (face-to-face for blended and local students)? It's a REALLY good idea to compare schedules and set up meeting times right away.	
Decisions How will the group make decisions? Will the group be polled and differences explored? When is a high level of agreement needed and appropriate? When should the group ask for instructor input or help?	
Conflicts How will the group handle differences of opinion and conflicts?	

Table 3. Another example of roles using google tools roles

Google Doc Manager	This person will be the manager of all of the google docs and any other documents, presentations, and or learning objects created by this workshop. Responsible for adding links to these documents or uploading these as attachments and overall formatting.
Google Jockey	Responsible for searching up relevant topics on Google and linking us to only the best of resources.
Google Note Taker	Records as best as possible the most important points from the content of the workshop.
Google Reflector	Adds reflections to the Note Taker's notes about how this relates to our classroom practice.
Google Thinkers	Offer constructive comments; add your own reflections as you feel comfortable.

APPENDIX 6

Twitter Top 5 Learning Plan

Overview and Learning Outcomes

Twitter is not just a tool to talk about Justin Bieber! No offense Beliebers:) Twitter can be a powerful tool for building your professional and personal learning network and being on top of current information in the areas that are meaningful to you. One of the most important things to understand is that it all starts with "who" you follow. Eventually, maybe, who follows you becomes important.

In this collaborative group activity, you will:

- Communicate and collaborate (using collaborative tools like Google Docs and Skype) to complete this learning activity.
- Search for and analyse online resources with concepts, and strategies related to microblogging, specifically, for the tool Twitter, and identify the 5 best resources.
- Participate in the Twitter global community and collaborate to create a top five list of who to follow in Twitter.
- Collaborate to identify the one best account in each of your top five lists to follow based on your top 5 lists.
- Reflect on and share learning by creating a minimum of two reflective tweets.
- Expand your opportunities for continuous professional development and lifelong learning by developing your PLN.

Instructions

1. Groups should already be created as part of completing the Group Work module.
2. One group member needs to use Collaborations (see course menu on the left), to create the group Google Doc and add group members and the instructor, to the document.
3. Everyone needs to add your own name in the group roles section and use a different color. Whenever you contribute, use your color.
4. Upon completion of this activity, have one group member share your collaborative worksheet document in the Fun Group Activity discussion. View each others' worksheets, you will learn a lot!

APPENDIX 7

Twitter Top 5 Worksheet Template

How to use this document:

- Copy the below information into your own google doc that you created in Canvas Collaborations.
- Share your group document with all members of your group, there is a Share button in the upper right. Add the group member gmails to the add people box. Alternately, the Canvas Collaborations has this capacity built in.

- When you have completed this activity, share your group document with your instructor using her gmail account; alternately, Canvas Collaborations has this capacity built in.
- Post a link to your Group Contract in the Group Contract discussion tool. View each others' Contracts, you will learn a lot!

Twitter Top 5 Activity Worksheet

Remember your class hashtag for using Twitter

Group Member Names:

Group/Team Name:

Part 1: Getting Started Readings

Note: If you can't click the links, you can Google these resources.

Social Media Resources

- Socialnomics 3
- What is Social Media in Plain English?
- Why Social Media is Critical in Schools

Twitter Resources You Should Explore Prior to Group Work

- What is Twitter in Plain English?
- Online Identity
- What is Twitter?
- The Beginners Guide to Twitter (2012, Mashable)
- The Twitter Guide Book (Mashable)
- How to Get Started Using Twitter (2011, CNET)
- Twittering, Not Frittering: Professional Development in 140 Characters

You want more? Of course, I've got more!

- What I Wish I Knew Before I Started Twitter
- Much more as needed - Five-Minute Film Festival: Twitter in Education
- Bundlr Resource - http://bundlr.com/b/learning-environments-twitter
- A rubric for assessing use of Twitter for instructional assignments.
- Twitter Directory for Higher Education
- A-Z Education Hashtags
- Popular Education Hashtags on Twitter
- 100 Ways To Use Twitter In Education, By Degree Of Difficulty

Part 2: Collaborative Group Work Set Up

1. Create a Group Name:
2. Create your Twitter accounts and list them here:

Part 3: Learning About Twitter Together

3. As a group, do some research about Twitter and add five new resources that you find here:
4. As a group, choose the one resource about Twitter you would recommend the most here and explain what makes it your recommendation. You can use the resources provided in this worksheet or it can be from the five new resources you find as a group:
5. Every person should post a reflection to Twitter about this part of the activity. Copy your posts here:

Part 4: Twitter for Class Content and Developing Your Personal Learning Network

6. As a group search for the best people or accounts you can find to follow in the area of educational technology. List the Top 5 people or hashtags to follow in the area of educational technology here:
7. As a group, identify the one account or hashtag, you think is the best of the five, create and tweet it with a very brief explanation of why it is the best and add your class hashtag. Copy your tweets here:

Part 5: Assessment and Get Your Grade!

8. Ponder and answer these questions here - 1) how can we use Twitter to expand our personal and/or professional learning networks? 2) how can we use Twitter for learning (consider digital literacy)?
9. Follow the instructions in the course to share this activity.

Chapter 13
Digital Literacy:
Dilemma for EAL Parents

Byanjana Sharma
Monash University, Australia

ABSTRACT

In the context of the practice of digital literacy in western classrooms, this book chapter explores the views of six newly arrived English as an additional language (EAL) parents and four Australian primary government school teachers on digital literacy. The EAL parents came to Australia from India, Indonesia, Nepal and the Philippines. The data used here are drawn from a PhD study which explores parents' and teachers' perspectives on the literacy learning of EAL children at a primary school in Victoria. Qualitative data include a questionnaire, focus group interviews, individual interviews, classroom observation and emails. The findings indicate that the teachers are positive towards digital literacy whereas the parents express mixed views. Most of the negative comments from the parents have come from their misunderstanding about how digital literacy is included in the school curriculum.

INTRODUCTION

Digital literacy is an essential part of classrooms, especially in western countries these days. It emerged simultaneously with a view of literacy as a social practice. This view emphasizes the understanding of literacy practices in their social and cultural contexts (Street, 2009). It is understood that literacy practices are context-dependent (Freebody, 2007; Street, 1993).

Digital literacy is a part of new literacies, which are associated with screen-based technologies (Snyder, 2001), and emerged in the 1980s with the digital revolution. During that period there was a huge public uptake of computers. Then in the 1990s there was a rise of the Internet and the use of hypermedia. More recently, there has been the emergence of a networked information economy (Brockmeier & Olson, 2009; Dobson & Willinsky, 2009). Thus, new literacies are connected to the Internet and other information and communication technologies (ICTs), according to Coiro, Knobel, Lankshear, and Leu (2008). In contemporary western society, literacy looks beyond mere print literacy (Cope & Kalantzis, 2000) to mean visual texts, symbolic texts, electronic texts along with print texts (Campbell & Green,

DOI: 10.4018/978-1-5225-1650-7.ch013

2000). Today's children experience childhood receiving information multimodally through television, the computer screen, and electronic games (Vincent, 2006).

EAL Parents and Views of Literacy Teaching

English as an additional language (EAL) parents usually have an understanding that literacy is taught as a set of skills (Huh, 2006; Li, 2006 & 2007) which is underpinned by the view of literacy as a cognitive ability (Luke & Freebody, 1997). On the other hand, it is taught as a social practice in English-speaking countries, such as Australia (Freebody, 2007). According to this view, literacy is not treated as an isolated cognitive ability and a property of individual minds (Barton & Hamilton, 2000). Instead, it emphasises the understanding of literacy practices in their social and cultural contexts (Street, 2009).

This difference may lead to misunderstandings in EAL parents while dealing with the Australian education system, where digital literacy is an important part in the school curriculum. Research studies show that parental involvement can improve children's learning and increase their achievement level (Barnard, 2004; Ford & Amaral, 2006; Rogers, Theule, Ryan, Adama, & Keating, 2009), regardless whether they are EAL or English-speaking parents. Sheldon and Voorhis (2004) also support family and community partnerships with schools to improve students' literacy practices. They emphasise developing high quality programs, such as the organisation of different workshops for parents, more extensive distribution of newsletters or organisation of interactive homework (between parents and children), to encourage more parental participation. This could particularly help the new EAL parents to understand the literacy pedagogy at their children's school.

Digital Literacy

As mentioned above digital literacy is related to screen-based technologies. Screen-based literacies are regarded as "new" to distinguish them from "old" print-based literacy, but interestingly among many rapidly emerging screen-based literacies, those which should be regarded as "new" can also be questioned. For example, until the emergence of instant text messaging, email was "new," but in comparison to instant text messaging, email can be treated as "old" literacy (Coiro et al., 2008). Similarly, with the appearance of social networks such as Facebook, instant text messaging has also become "old." However, for the purpose of this study, it is good to consider all technology-based literacies as "new literacies," as opposed to old print-based literacy (Cope &Kalantzis, 2000). From this perspective, literacy practices related to television, radio or telephone can also be regarded as "new" literacy practices to distinguish them from the print-based literacy. Since the focus of this chapter is digital literacy, radio and telephone have been excluded because they are not screen-based.

Traditional print literacy is still the most important part of school literacy practices (Hall, 2004). However, unlike in the past, print literacy, is not enough for those who live in contemporary developed western society. School literacy practices are influenced by the vast development in communication technology in the world. Children of the 21st century are surrounded by different sorts of technological devices in and outside school. According to Prensky (2001):

Today's students – K through college – represent the first generations to grow up with this new technology. They have spent their entire lives surrounded by and using computers, videogames, digital music players, video cams, cell phones, and all the other toys and tools of the digital age. (p. 1)

This means that schools have a responsibility to strengthen children's digital literacy that they are exposed to in and outside school. Computer literacy is an essential part of literacy lessons in schools. Teachers use online texts while teaching literacy, multimodal texts are common in the classrooms. Literacy lessons now require the Internet (Lankshear&Knobel, 2006; Poynton, 2005). Current research shows that 92% of primary school children are confident users of the Internet (Valcke, Bonte, Wever, & Rots, 2010). Among the many examples given by Prensky (2001) of electronic equipment that children come into contact with, the computer is most widely used in schools.

Snyder (2001) however states that digital implications for education has been taken positively as well as negatively. According to her:

Enthusiasts openly embrace the technologies, claiming they offer a panacea for educational problems, enhance communication, empower users and democratise classrooms. By contrast, demonisers express cynicism about the technologies' apparent powers, either dismissing them as new instructional and communication tools or rejecting them as yet a further form of social control. (pp. 117)

As mentioned above new technologies may neither be a "panacea" for all educational problems nor are they a form of "social control." What research has shown us that their use in the classroom strengthens children's learning. For instance, Hartley (2007) reviewed the literature on the use of new technology in teaching and learning, and concluded that the digital devices are effective particularly in giving direct and adjunct instruction. Furthermore, they are helpful in facilitating the skills of learning, such as reading, writing and thinking. They seem to be effective in facilitating students' social skills too. Not only this, the use of technology widens learners' horizons. For example, television does this by taking the viewer out of the classroom. It is said that over 60% of children have access to home computers. Obviously, parents purchase computers partly for their educational potential (Hartley, 2007).

Similarly, Sutherland-Smith (2002) points out that technology or computer skills are essential for survival in the 21st century. Therefore, students and teachers must be competent and, more important, comfortable with the medium. She argues that the Internet technology has had a significant impact upon reading strategies. According to her, the World Wide Web offers teachers and students an opportunity to enrich and expand concepts of literacy.

The web invites a nonlinear, interactive, nonsequential approach to reading by students, and the multimedia elements add to the visual literacy skills they require. Web literacy requires a rethinking of the skills needed by the literate being in the 21st century. The Internet provides a gateway to content, and web literacy represents the digital bridge that will reshape our teaching of reading skills in this new millennium. (Sutherland-Smith, 2002; pp. 668)

Whether writers oppose (Birkerts, 1994; Postman, 1995; Stoll, 1995) or support (Hartley, 2007; Lankshear & Knobel, 2006; Poynton, 2005; Sutherland-Smith, 2002) digital literacy, it has been incorporated in the school curriculum in the western countries. As mentioned above, the EAL parents understand literacy as a set of skills, where digital literacy has no place. Therefore, it is important to understand how they view digital literacy being practiced in their children's school in Australia, and if their views would match with the teachers' views on the same.

The Study

This study was informed by the sociocultural theory of literacy teaching/learning, according to which literacy is understood as social practice, as mentioned earlier. Since the sociocultural theory of literacy itself is very broad, only its aspect of "digital literacy" is considered in this chapter to analyse the data related to this aspect and generated from the six EAL parents and four mainstream primary school teachers in Victoria, Australia.

The study followed a qualitative research approach (Charmaz, 2006; Gay & Airasian, 2003; Knobel & Lankshear, 1999) to identify parents' and teachers' opinions on and experiences of digital literacy. It was based on a case study research design (Brown & Rodgers, 2003; Knobel & Lankshear, 1999), which involved one mainstream primary state school as a single case. The school was located in the South Eastern Region of Melbourne, Victoria, and assigned with the pseudonym, Paterson Primary School. At this school, six parents of Years 3/4 and Years 5/6 students, four English teachers, and the school principal volunteered as research participants.

This school was chosen for several reasons. The first and most important is that it had many students from diverse communities, speaking many languages. According to the *Paterson Primary School Information Handbook* (2009), 65% students of the total students in school were from an EAL background. Languages spoken included Bengali, Chinese, Greek, Hindi, Indonesian, Marathi, Nepali, Punjabi, Tagalog, and others. The researcher, therefore, thought that her chances to capture EAL parents' multiple perspectives were high in this school and she would be able to compare and contrast their perspectives within the parent group and with Australian teachers.

It was likely that teachers teaching in such a school might also have much to share. Another typical feature of Paterson Primary School was that there were a lot of EAL students whose parents were post-graduate students. This was a practical advantage, which increased my chances of finding parents who could communicate with me in English. However, this may have biased the data sample in favour of more educated parents than is typical in state primary schools in Victoria. The third reason for choosing this school was that my son was studying there at the time of planning my data collection. Therefore, I hoped to gain access to this school more easily. As is usual in any mainstream school, in Paterson Primary School, there were students from both English-speaking and non-English-speaking backgrounds and they were taught together in all classrooms.

Purposive sampling was used in the selection of parent participants. The selection criteria were

1. Their length of residence in Australia was between six months and two years;
2. Their children were in Years 3 to 6 and, above all;
3. The participants were able to communicate with the researcher in English because the researcher could not afford the high translation and interpretation costs.

The EAL parents whose stay in Australia was not more than two years were termed as "newly arrived" parents in this study. This group of "newly arrived" parents was chosen because, being new, they were aware of differences in literacy teaching in Australian schools. Parents of Years 3 to 6 were selected because these children were taken to have had adequate exposure to schooling in their home countries. In other words, spending a few years at school they were familiar with all four language skills – listening, speaking, reading and writing; and more importantly, they were exposed to a lot of reading and writing activities in English. Thus, their parents could make a comparison between literacy teaching in their home countries and Australia.

Two Indonesian, two Indian, One Filipino and one Nepali parents agreed to take part in this research. They chose or were given pseudonyms Lily, Dewita, Nita, Tara, Sharon and Binod. Among them the Indonesian (Lily, Dewita), Filipino (Sharon) and Nepali (Binod) parents could communicate in English, whereas the Indian parents (Nita, Tara) could understand English but were not comfortable speaking it. These Indian parents were chosen purposefully because the researcher could communicate with them in Hindi. This group of parents were educated; they were from postgraduate to Year 12 pass. This aspect was important for the researcher as she thought these parents could be able to elicit rich, valuable and more authentic data.

Two focus group interviews (three participants in each group) and six individual in-depth semi-structured interviews were used to gather data, each of which lasted for about an hour. These interviews allowed the researcher freedom to ask the participants questions to draw rich data (Patton, 2002). Before organising the individual interviews, focus group interviews (Morgan, 2004) were organised to capture the participants' broader experiences. In addition, the focus group interview stimulated responses through discussion.

At the time of data collection, there were composite classes at Paterson Primary School, with three groups of Years 3/4 and three groups of Years 5/6. To recruit the teacher participants, the principal advised me to see them on their planning days when they did not have their regular classes. Accordingly, I approached all six teachers in Years 3/4 and Years 5/6. I explained my study orally to them. Although all teachers expressed an interest in taking part in the study, four teachers, two from Years 3/4 and two from Years 5/6 were selected as research participants. These teachers were chosen to keep a balance in number between Years 3/4 and Years 5/6 teachers, and to include some gender balance as well. Among them, three were female and one was male (the only male class teacher in the school at that time). These teachers were also given pseudonyms. The three female teachers were given the names Alice, Amber, and Ann and the male teacher was given the name Andrew. All of them described themselves as monolingual speakers of Australian English.

Individual interviews and classroom observation were used to elicit data from the teachers, and an interview was conducted to gather data from the principal. Teacher interview questions were divided into three sections. They were

1. General questions which asked about teachers' experience with new EAL students,
2. Lesson-related (the lessons were observed before scheduling interviews) questions, and
3. EAL parent-related (especially newly arrived) questions.

In addition to teacher interviews, classroom observations and emails were used to gather data from the teachers. This was to help me to broaden my understanding of literacy teaching/learning in Victorian classrooms, and to give me an opportunity to compare what teachers did in the classroom and what they said during the interview, although this comparison was not a primary focus of the research. Altogether 16 one-hour lessons were observed in the school Term 4, 2009. All the data related to the parents, teachers and principal were collected between October 2009 and February 2010. The data were analyzed using thematic analysis discussed by Creswell (2008) and Roulston (2010). For instance, the parents' data were analysed in terms of the literacy areas where they expressed satisfaction and dissatisfaction. Their

Table 1.

Areas of Satisfaction	Areas of Dissatisfaction
Literacy pedagogy	Literacy pedagogy
Multiliteracies	Multiliteracies
Home-school partnerships	Home-school partnerships
Teachers' role	Teachers' role
Children's improvement in literacy	Student engagement at home
	Education system
	Curriculum
	Cultural differences

expressions of satisfaction were classified into five broad themes; and the expressions of dissatisfaction were presented into eight themes which are given in Table 1:

The data related to digital literacy were elicited either under the theme of literacy pedagogy, multiliteracies or student engagement at home. What parents expressed regarding digital literacy in discussed below.

Parents' Views on Digital Literacy

The participating parents said that they did not know how exactly literacy was being taught in the classroom because they did not see any "textbook" being used there. They had considered the prescribed "textbook" as their only reference which their children did not have. Therefore, the parents were unable to say how teachers were teaching literacy. However, on the basis of their general observation they all agreed that in the context of Australia, their children could not be considered as fully literate if they learned print literacy alone. For instance, according to Binod:

When I came here I realised that literacy is not only reading and writing. Something else is there because we are also learning culture here. We're from different culture. We are from another culture! I think if you come here, learn culture. Where is culture? On TV. (Binod, Focus Group 2, p. 14)

Observing his son's literacy development, Binod started to be aware that literacy learning is not limited to reading and writing print texts alone. Other parents agreed with him that alongside print literacy their children must also know other forms of literacy, such as digital literacy. All of the six parents realised the importance of computers and the Internet to enhance their children's learning. They found them especially useful for their children to complete their project work. Tara said:

I asked him whatever information you need [to complete the project work], you go and find on the Internet. He first wrote his work in his notebook, then typed afterward. (Tara, Individual Interview, p. 19)

In response to a question about whether the Internet was useful for her daughter, Sharon answered:

Yes. Now, yes, because if they are researching, very helpful. She is the one doing the research about her project and I just check it if all the ideas and the facts are there. (Sharon, Individual Interview, p. 10)

All of the parents agreed that TV could be helpful for their children to develop English literacy. As Lily said:

Actually I allow them to watch TV. I know it's also exposure for them to English. So to me "that's another learning," quotation mark [gesture]. (Lily, Individual Interview, p. 13)

On the one hand, these parents seemed to be supportive of their children's use of digital devices and on the other hand they expressed their strong view that excessive watching of TV and excessive use of the Internet or other types of digital games could be harmful for their children as the following quotes show.

Now I try to minimise my children's TV watching time. I'm afraid they will get addicted to watch TV. In Indonesia they rarely watch TV, maybe watch TV only one hour per day but now more than one or two hours. Electronic games are also distracting their focus from individual studying at home. (Lily, Individual Interview, p. 10)

Likewise, Tara also said that computer or the Internet does not help in her son's learning. According to her:

Computer is for playing. It does not have a lot of study materials. We can find such materials in books (emphasis). Therefore children do not need to browse the Internet for study purpose. There is a danger that their interests can divert to other unnecessary things and they cannot pay attention to their studies. (Tara, Individual Interview, p. 20)

What Dewita found strange was that her son could collect a lot of information via the Internet to complete his project work but when she asked particular questions about the topic he could not answer. She said:

But what so strange is he collect all these information about Ned Kelly (project work) but he doesn't read that! He browse on the Internet and find the piece of information. He doesn't really read them! He just copy and pasted on his PowerPoint. So if I say, "What do you know about Ned Kelly?" He goes, "Oh, he is a bush ranger!" "What else?" I ask and he says, "Umm..." He doesn't know much because he doesn't read the text. (Dewita, Individual Interview, p. 15)

In Binod's experience his son used to read and write a lot when his family did not have home computer or other digital devices in the earlier days of their arrival in Australia. But later his child's attention moved towards the digital gadgets from the books. According to him:

Especially we (parents) encourage him to read. We go to public library. Bring a lot of books. He read almost one or two books in a day initially and he started writing. He contributed three or four stories in an online magazine in Nepal. It got published as well. But later he started giving more time to television. When we buy a Nintendo for him, he spent more time for Nintendo. When we got a computer, he spent his time in playing computer games, so time is divided. He doesn't have much time for reading and writing. (Binod, Individual Interview, pp. 1-2)

These responses indicate that the parents were not so sure whether their children were involved in actual literacy learning via digital devices. However, they expressed limited advantages of such materials to assist their children's literacy development. All of their positive comments on the use of the Internet, computer or television came from their own observation of their children's engagement at home while doing their project work. None of them said they saw teachers using digital devices in classroom teaching. They attached more value to print literacy as Tara pointed out that the computer does not have a lot of study materials. For them, such electronic devices relatively had more entertainment value. They wanted their children to spend more time reading and writing at home, not watching television or playing computer games. In the interviews all of these parents strongly emphasized that their children must have got "textbooks" as a source of learning material. Mainly, their dissatisfaction on literacy teaching was related to their unawareness of how teaching learning activities were done inside the classrooms.

Teachers' Views on Digital Literacy

As mentioned above literacy is taught as a social practice in Australia. So with emergence of the information technologies in the broader society they obviously got entry into schools. As a result digital literacy had been embedded in school curriculum of literacy education at Paterson Primary School. The computer was vital part of literacy teaching. Each teacher had a laptop on their class desk. This was used for the interactive whiteboard and for retrieving Internet texts. Apart from this, in Years 3/4 and 5/6 each classroom had four computers, the ratio of computer use being five children to one computer. All teachers had a computer group as one of their rotating reading and writing groups. The students in the computer group were encouraged to explore information on their own, especially to complete their project work. Students were expected to produce their final version of writing in a typed form, not a hand-written one. In addition, these teachers used text materials from websites. Amber pointed out:

With websites for teaching, we find them ourselves. However, we share them with each other. Julie has set up a web page where we can add useful resources we find for others to access. (Amber, Email, 19/11/2009)

Alice also agreed with Amber that the teachers would share the useful websites among them. According to her:

Within the school we share websites that we found a lot, but also I do a lot of searching, I would type in a particular thing, I'm searching for website activities to do with punctuation, and then I'll have a look over the weekend, I'll look at the particular websites to see whether they're really valuable, whether they're interactive enough'cause the children don't particularly like websites that they just look at, they like the ones where they get to do something or participate with um... that Jenny Eatheris the one that's been referred to me because it's really simply laid out what they need to do. Spelling City is a site that got referred to us from the ICT manager for our region. (Alice, Interview, p. 10)

What the teachers said during the interviews regarding the use of websites was confirmed in the classroom observation. For example, in Alice's class students were engaged in an individual writing task, which was followed by the teacher's explicit teaching and joint teacher-student construction of text. She was teaching the Modern Cinquain, a 5-line poem organised on a word count of 1, 2, 3, 4, 1, with words used from a particular word class. The structure of this poem is: Line 1, a noun; Line 2, two adjectives; Line 3, 3 verbs in –ing form; Line 4, four descriptive words to describe the noun in the Line 1; and Line 5, another noun for the noun used in Line 1. To clarify this structure, Alice displayed the following Cinquain from the website of *Jenny Eather*:

House
Tiny, snug
Protecting, warming, welcoming
The family I love
Home
(Classroom Observation 1)

When I observed Andrew's lessons his students were engaged in their project work which was report writing on 'Australia.' They were expected to write a report about anything Australian, e.g., Australian animals or famous Australian landmarks, following a certain structure of a report writing style. In the interview Andrew clarified how he selected the content to serve his purpose of teaching report writing in the following way:

...Say we're doing Australia. It's very broad but from week to week we'll concentrate on one aspect of Australia, and then we'll find websites accordingly for the kids to use. We always go on and we're looking and looking to find something that's appropriate and also is going to work for us and is going to be worthwhile for the kids to use. Then we put them on the student home page. We make a link for them to access those. So they don't search for them. (Andrew, Interview, p. 14)

Unlike the EAL parents the school teachers considered digital literacy an essential aspect to develop children's literacy learning. For them, it was an integral part of literacy education. They were guided by the philosophy of literacy as a social practice rather than a set of skills. Their curriculum had also integrated print and digital literacies together. Therefore, they used different websites as useful resources.

DISCUSSION AND CONCLUSION

Even though the notion of "digital literacy" used at Paterson Primary school was new for the parents, they were aware of its importance in their children's lives. For example, they were all familiar with computers from their home countries, so when their children started using them for literacy learning at school, the parents were pleased. Based on their own observations, the parents had realised that in order for their children to succeed in the Australian school, print literacy alone was not sufficient. Instead, the children should also be equipped with digital literacy. Their positive comments on this form of literacy align with Sutherland-Smith (2002). However, all six of the parents expressed dissatisfaction with how their children spent time at home. In contrast to their expectations of more reading and writing, the children spent a large amount of home time in playing digital games or watching television. The parents did not see much information in them to strengthen the children's learning as Vincent (2006) has pointed out. This created a conflict between the parents' expectations and what they perceived to be the school's expectations. In their opinion the use of the Internet or websites would not help develop students' reading and writing as Dewita and Tara indicated above. The parents' negative comments on digital literacy are based on their understanding of literacy as a cognitive ability (Luke & Freebody, 1997) which emphasises that literacy should be taught as a set of skills (Huh, 2006; Li, 2006 & 2007), so they strongly opposed digital literacy (Birkerts, 1994; Postman, 1995; Stoll, 1995). All six parents agreed that they did not know how teachers teach inside the classroom. This view has an implication that they were unaware of how teachers used, handled or encouraged digital literacy in their lessons.

On the contrary, teachers were pretty aware that literacy should be taught as a social practice (Freebody, 2007), so they included digital literacy in their teaching as an inseparable part. They often used computers and the Internet along with print-based text materials. For example, the Internet was used to read online texts, and students in all classes were asked to write and publish texts on the computer. Teachers' interview and classroom observation data confirmed the views of Hartley (2007), Lankshear and Knobel (2006), Poynton (2005) and Sutherland-Smith (2002) on the use of computers and the Internet. The teachers spent a significant amount of time to research about the useful websites for their students. They believed digital literacy would strengthen students' learning.

As indicated above this group of newly arrived EAL parents came from a traditional literacy teaching background, underpinned by a theory of literacy as a cognitive ability, activated when all children learn the content, usually prescribed in textbooks. This philosophy did not match that of mainstream Australian teachers. These teachers considered literacy as a social practice and believed that literacy teaching/learning materials were better found in real texts available in real society, no matter whether they were print or online materials. This created a gap between the parents' and teachers' views on whether the students should be given a chance to use digital devices to practise literacy. This gap mainly arose due to the weak home-school partnership (Sheldon & Voorhis, 2004). The parents had less communication with their children's teachers so they could not realise how seriously digital literacy was in practice at Paterson Primary School. So they found it as a distraction for learning most of the time. In addition, they could not involve themselves in their children's literacy development journey (Barnard, 2004; Ford & Amaral, 2006; Rogers, Theule, Ryan, Adama, & Keating, 2009) as they had expected because they lacked knowledge about how literacy was taught inside classrooms.

To make the newly arrived EAL parents better understand the underpinning theories and practice of digital literacy in Australian schools the first step would be to improve home-school partnerships. For this, they should explicitly be invited in the classrooms to observe literacy lessons. Besides classroom observations, a special curriculum night program or at least a dedicated session (Sheldon & Voorhis, 2004) for newly arrived EAL parents could be organised to address all the issues related to literacy pedagogy, which obviously would include digital literacy. This would help parents to involve in their children's literacy learning more.

REFERENCES

Barnard, W. M. (2004). Parent involvement in elementary school and educational attainment. *Children and Youth Services Review*, *26*(1), 39–62. doi:10.1016/j.childyouth.2003.11.002

Barton, D., & Hamilton, M. (2000). Literacy practices. In D. Barton, M. Hamilton, & R. Ivanič (Eds.), *Situated literacies: Reading and writing in context* (pp. 7–15). London: Routledge.

Birkerts, S. (1994). *The Gutenberg elegies: The fate of reading in an electronic age*. Boston: Faber & Faber.

Brockmeier, J., & Olson, D. R. (2009). The literacy epesteme: From Innis to Derrida. In D. R. Olson & N. Torrance (Eds.), *The Cambridge handbook of literacy* (pp. 3–21). Cambridge, UK: Cambridge University Press. doi:10.1017/CBO9780511609664.002

Brown, J. D., & Rodgers, T. S. (2003). *Doing second language research*. London: Oxford University Press.

Campbell, R., & Green, D. (Eds.). (2000). *Literacies and learners: Current perspectives*. Prentice Hall.

Charmaz, K. (2006). *Constructing grounded theory: A practical guide through qualitative analysis*. London: SAGE Publications.

Coiro, J., Knobel, M., Lankshear, C., & Leu, D. J. (2008). Central issues in new literacies and new literacies research. In J. Coiro, M. Knobel, C. Lankshear, & D. J. Leu (Eds.), *Handbook of research on new literacies* (pp. 1–21). New York: Taylor & Francis Group.

Cope, B., & Kalantzis, M. (Eds.). (2000). *Multiliteracies: Literacy learning and the design of social futures*. London: Routledge.

Creswell, J. W. (2008). *Educational research: Planning, conducting, and evaluating quantitative and qualitative research*. Pearson Education, Inc.

Dobson, T. M., & Willinsky, J. (2009). Digital literacy. In D. R. Olson & N. Torrance (Eds.), *The Cambridge handbook of literacy* (pp. 286–312). Cambridge, UK: Cambridge University Press. doi:10.1017/CBO9780511609664.017

Ford, L., & Amaral, D. (2006). Research on parent involvement: Where we've been and where we need to go. *BC Educational Leadership Research*, *3*(March), 1–20.

Freebody, P. (2007). *Literacy education in school: Research perspectives from the past, for the future*. Australian Council for Educational Research.

Gay, L. R., & Airasian, P. (2003). *Educational research: Competencies for analysis and applications*. Pearson Education Inc.

Hall, K. (2004). *Literacy and schooling: Towards renewal in primary education policy*. Aldershot, UK: Ashgate Publishing Limited.

Hartley, J. (2007). Teaching, learning and new technology: A review for teachers. *British Journal of Educational Technology*, *38*(1), 42–62. doi:10.1111/j.1467-8535.2006.00634.x

Huh, K. (2006). Korean mothers' perspectives of schooling in the United States. *Primary English Education*, *12*(2), 337–361.

Knobel, M., & Lankshear, C. (1999). *Ways of knowing: Researching literacy*. Sydney: Primary English Teaching Association.

Lankshear, C., & Knobel, M. (2006). *New literacies: Everyday practices and classroom learning*. Berkshire, UK: Open University Press.

Li, G. (2006). What do parents think? Middle-class Chinese immigrant parents' perspectives on literacy learning, homework, and, school-home communication. *School Community Journal, 16*(2), 27–46.

Li, G. (2007). Second language and literacy learning in school and at home: An ethnographic study of Chinese Canadian first grades' experiences. *Literacy Teaching and Learning, 11*(2), 1–31.

Luke, A., & Freebody, P. (1997). Shaping the social practices of reading. In S. Muspratt, A. Luke, & P. Freebody (Eds.), *Constructing critical literacies: Teaching and learning textual practice* (pp. 185–225). Cresskill, NJ: Hampton Press, Inc.

Morgan, D. L. (2004). Focus groups. In S. N. Hesser-Biber & P. Leavy (Eds.), *Approaches to qualitative research: A reader on theory and practice* (pp. 263–285). New York: Oxford University Press.

Paterson Primary School Information Handbook. (2009). Melbourne, Australia: Paterson Primary School.

Patton, M. Q. (2002). *Qualitative research and evaluation methods*. Thousand Oaks, CA: SAGE Publications.

Postman, N. (1995). Virtual students: Digital classroom. *Nation (New York, N.Y.), 26*, 377–382.

Poynton, T. A. (2005). Computer literacy across the lifespan: A review with implications for educators. *Computers in Human Behavior, 21*(6), 861–872. doi:10.1016/j.chb.2004.03.004

Pressley, M. (2002). Effective beginning reading instruction. *Journal of Literacy Research, 34*(2), 165–188. doi:10.1207/s15548430jlr3402_3

Rogers, M. A., Theule, J., Ryan, B. A., Adama, G. R., & Keating, L. (2009). Parental involvement and children's school achievement: Evidence for mediating processes. *Canadian Journal of School Psychology, 24*(1), 34–57. doi:10.1177/0829573508328445

Roulston, K. (2010). *Reflective interviewing: A guide to theory and practice*. Los Angeles, CA: SAGE Publications. doi:10.4135/9781446288009

Sheldon, S. B., & Voorhis, F. L. V. (2004). Partnership programs in U.S. schools: Their development and relationship to family involvement outcomes. *School Effectiveness and School Improvement, 15*(2), 125–148. doi:10.1076/sesi.15.2.125.30434

Snyder, I. (2001). A new communication order: Researching literacy practices in the network society. *Language and Education, 15*(2-3), 117-131.

Stoll, C. (1995). *Silicon snake oil*. New York: Doubleday.

Street, B. V. (1993). *Literacy in theory and practice*. Cambridge, UK: Cambridge University Press.

Street, B. V. (2009). Ethnography of writing and reading. In D. R. Olson & N. Torrance (Eds.), *The Cambridge handbook of literacy* (pp. 3–21). Cambridge, UK: Cambridge University Press. doi:10.1017/CBO9780511609664.019

Sutherland-Smith, W. (2002). Weaving the literacy web: Changes in reading from page to screen. *The Reading Teacher*, *55*(7), 662–669.

Valcke, M., Bonte, S., Wever, B. D., & Rots, I. (2010). Internet parenting styles and the impact on Internet use of primary school children. *Computers & Education*, *55*(2), 454–464. doi:10.1016/j.compedu.2010.02.009

Vincent, J. (2006). Classroom writing: Multimodality and assessment in the writing classroom. *Literacy*, *40*(1), 51–57. doi:10.1111/j.1467-9345.2006.00426.x

Chapter 14
Scaffolding Agency and Responsibility in Cloud-Based Collaborative Writing

Kate Fedewa
Michigan State University, USA

Kathryn Houghton
Michigan State University, USA

ABSTRACT

Although most students regularly interact online for social reasons, many are uncomfortable collaborating for academic work, even work utilizing familiar cloud technology. Because collaborative writing in digital spaces is becoming commonplace in work and academic environments, composition teachers must help students to recognize their individual agency within group work and to develop strategies for a shared writing process. How can we scaffold online writing experiences so that our students' ability to collaborate emerges as a strategic and still-developing part of the learning process? In this chapter we discuss strategies for scaffolding a collaborative writing process using Google Docs in the composition classroom. We describe four sample activities appropriate for undergraduate writing courses: anonymous invention, group annotated bibliographies, group agendas and project plans, and peer review. We suggest best practices for developing individual agency and shared responsibility for group writing in the cloud.

INTRODUCTION

In a 2013 editorial for *The Chronicle of Higher Education* David Helfand challenged the individualized model of higher education:

The brains of today's undergraduates—a product of a million years of hominid evolution—are instinctively collaborative, innately cooperative, and structurally wired for small-group interaction mediated by language and an awareness of the intentionality of others. What might happen if we structured our educational system to take advantage of these natural attributes?

DOI: 10.4018/978-1-5225-1650-7.ch014

As undergraduate writing instructors, we ask a similar question when we consider how we might transform our pedagogy to engage with the collaborative writing our students are already doing online. But how can teachers scaffold "interaction mediated by language and an awareness of the intentionality of others" toward learning? And how can cloud technology be best utilized toward knowledge building? Collaboration, regardless of its instinctive or innate relationship to the human mind, is difficult and takes practice. Collaboration, like writing, is an activity that must be taught, learned, and practiced, not just required.

Background Information

As teachers we are accustomed to the collective groan that often follows an announcement about an upcoming group project. We believe such resistance is indicative of a widespread frustration among students: they are expected to work together, to create collaboratively, but often have not learned the tools necessary to make such work positive as well as productive. This situation can be compounded when collaboration occurs via digital spaces for two reasons. First, students are being asked not only to collaborate but also to use online tools in new ways, thus increasing the amount there is to learn.[1] Second, cloud technology is marketed as necessarily collaborative, which can mask the need to provide instruction in appropriate ways to collaborate within such spaces.

The frustration our students have expressed in connection with collaborative assignments has led us to question how we can scaffold experiences that will help our students thrive in cloud collaboration and in writing classrooms. How can we scaffold online writing experiences so that our students' instinctive ability to collaborate emerges as a strategic and still-developing part of the learning process? How might we use cloud technology to help students identify and reflect on the specific decisions and attitudes that contributed to a collaborative experience? We hope to encourage careful attention to these broad questions by focusing here on a single, fundamental aspect of collaborative writing: fostering a sense of individual student agency and shared responsibility. This chapter offers practical suggestions for cloud-based activities that identify, develop, and nourish individual contribution to group collaboration. We believe these activities can be adapted for use in first-year writing, writing across the curriculum, and professional writing classrooms.

Student Responsibility in Collaboration

Building off the work of Haring-Smith (1994), Kittle and Hicks (2009) identified collaboration in the writing classroom as a process requiring co-authorship and a sense of shared responsibility for a text. They write that:

Genuine collaboration involves a number of tasks beyond simply getting along and adding one part: giving ideas and feedback, creating content, debating the merits of an overall argument for the paper, writing and revising a particular section, researching information for that section, sharing one's writing by raising questions for peers about content and style, editing all parts of the document, taking a risk as a writer by sharing all of this publicly, and encouraging one's group members to engage in all of these tasks. In short, when a collaborative writing group produces a text, its members share full responsibility for the final product. (p. 527)

Collaboration, they note, is not simply "getting along;" it requires contributions to invention and drafting, self and peer critique, risk-taking, and civic engagement. What interests us most about Kittle and Hicks' description is that it provides specifics regarding the ways in which collaboration is "mediated by language and an awareness of the intentionality of others" (Helfand, 2013). So often in popular writing, collaboration is portrayed as a single moment or as a monolithic activity. Even in scholarly literature about cloud technology, collaboration is discussed as a starting point or an outcome. We follow Kittle and Hicks in recognizing collaborative writing as a dialogic process of negotiation—negotiation of authority, ownership, creation, and revision, not to mention the negotiation of the text itself. In identifying the movement back and forth between the work of the individual and the work of the group in collaborative writing, Kittle and Hicks stress the individual agency of each author and the sense of "full responsibility" that is shared across all these tasks.

Collaborative writing requires students to practice individual agency and shared responsibility. When students feel their voices are valuable and valued, they are more likely to take ownership for their work, which in turn fosters a sense of responsibility and a recognition of value. This sense of agency or authorial identity is often complicated by students' relationship with their educational environment. Lunsford et al. (2013) argue,

Students come to understand that most college writing attains value insofar as it accepts the structures and strictures of academic literacy, a message transmitted most directly through curricular and pedagogical practices. In this context, as students gain proficiency in expert discourses, they learn also to surrender their writing and writerly identifications—in the form of intellectual property and intellectual property rights—to the workings of a largely hidden curriculum that equates literacy achievement with public conformity to its laws. (p. 471)

Encouraging students to engage in authentic ways, to value their own authority, is key to student-centered teaching. Best practices toward this end are still a matter of debate, especially—as we will discuss below—when compounded with issues of digital identity and authorship. To foster student agency within collaborative writing, students are often asked to self-assess strengths and assign tasks based on that self-assessment. Students must also feel that they are confronted with real choices, choices in which their decisions have weight, and they must feel capable of completing assigned tasks. This self-actualization fosters an investment in the project and an increased sense of responsibility: if coupled with regular attention to the group's collective work, an individual's personal sense of agency and responsibility can encourage a feeling of ownership over the whole.

In productive collaboration, individual agency functions symbiotically with collaborative creation and critique. The group works together, validating each writer's contributions toward a whole that any one writer could not have authored alone. A shared responsibility for the larger whole is the basis for the other collaborative tasks. In non-cloud collaboration, the roles of collaborators are, by necessity, more static: if one group member holds group files or papers, or if group members are divided into specific, project-long roles, it difficult for group members to gain an accurate sense of the whole. What's more, ownership becomes unequal, since responsibility and physical possession of the group's documents shift between group members. Cloud technology has the functionality to transform this. All members can access and contribute to all drafts of the document, so ownership and authorship can be more equal. The process itself becomes more transparent and roles can be more fluid.

Collaboration with Cloud Technology

Cloud technology offers new ways for writers to collaborate and for instructors to engage students in meaningful dialogues. Such technology is designed to require interaction. Limbu (2012) explains that "the mantra of cloud computing is to always become able to access shared data, collaborate, cooperate, edit, and publish them from anywhere, any device, anytime, and by any person" (p. 2). This is not to say that cloud technology assures successful collaboration; it does, however, compel users to participate and to view themselves as part of a network.[2] Cloud technology is often described using a rhetoric of community and social interaction, which appeals to young adults looking to create their own identities and affiliations. Cloud pedagogy capitalizes on the mindset of technology users to open conversations about authorship, collaboration, agency, and responsibility.

The work of sharing, collaboration, and co-authorship is essential to the ethos of the digital writer. The idea of authorship in the cloud is significantly different from the idea of authorship tied to print texts.[3] A writer's digital identity is simultaneously the sum of that writer's digital output and of digital output about that writer—that is, everything that comes up in a search—and also a changeable, emergent identity (re)created at every instance of the writer's interaction within Web 2.0 spaces. Writing in the cloud often means dialogic interaction with and contributions to the ideas of authors, via a platform created by yet someone else.[4] Users can also create groups, initiate group chats, and contribute to group-wide critique; Web 2.0 provides users an opportunity to take on fluid, public roles within communities. These roles are defined by access and timeliness: any user with a smart device can contribute at any time and from anywhere. As such, group dialogue in the cloud can be—or at least feel—decentralized, organic, and urgent. Users must receive alerts and pay attention to notifications or risk being left out or uninformed. This may increase the sense of a user's responsibility to a community. Even while cloud technology encourages self-expression and gives users a platform and a sense of agency, it also positions users as always already collaborative.[5]

Digital environments are familiar to most American undergraduates and have shaped their understanding of digital communication, at least for social purposes. Our unique challenge as twenty-first century educators is to help students to see connections between the writing they do for social purposes and the writing they are asked to complete within the classroom. Students value academic, professional, and social communication differently. Instructors must scaffold collaborative learning to help both students and educators recognize and value the contributions students can make to learning communities, even— or perhaps especially?— those facilitated by cloud technology. Students' online social writing can inform their ethos as academic writers and practice in and reflection on the academic work of collaboration and composition might deepen their understanding of authorship and communication more broadly. The importance of collaborative writing, however, has heightened with the rise of cloud technology. In her article "The Digital Imperative," Clark (2010) provides a concise statement of a larger sentiment when she argues that "In an emerging Web 2.0 culture that privileges community and collaboration, we need to work together to encourage our writing programs to develop extensive curricular reviews that address digital literacy in the 21st century" (p. 35). Any collaboration in a writing classroom should help students to acquire knowledge and skills toward these ends.

Activities in Google Docs that Scaffold Student Agency and Responsibility

To further examine the potential for scaffolding the development of student agency within the cloud, we turn to Google Docs as a model. The cloud-based word processor is a "productivity tool" within the Google Apps for Education suite. It is designed to be collaborative and includes a range of features meant to foster interaction:

- A "share" button, which allows the author of a document to allow others to view or edit that document via an email or a link.
- A "comments" feature, which allows a document's editors to leave notes about specific textual details for themselves or each other, and to respond to those notes.
- A tagging feature within "comments," so that writers can send a notification via email to another writer about a recommended change.
- A "see revision history" view, which allows all editors to look back at earlier moments in the drafting process and even to note which editor made changes in that moment.
- A "chat" feature, which allows group members to instant message each other while working on the same document without closing the document or writing in the document itself.
- Three different modes of interacting with the document ("Editing," "Suggesting," and "Viewing") which allow editors to shift between making direct changes, tracking changes as suggested edits, and presenting a more finished product.

Google Docs can also be modified by downloading "add-ons" that provide further collaborative capability, but even the most basic version of the app affords levels of access and transparency for collaboration that surpass standard word processors and even face-to-face collaborative writing.

In this section we discuss activities in Google Docs that teachers can use to scaffold individual student agency and shared responsibility within the scope of collaborative writing. In other words, these activities are designed to not only help students with their collaborative projects but specifically to help them understand their own individual roles, responsibilities, and importance within a larger collaborative project. We have ordered these activities so that they build upon each other. The anonymous invention activity fosters individual agency by highlighting individual contributions in a low-stakes setting. The annotated bibliography activity moves students step-by-step through a sequence of collaborative roles designed to familiarize them with the app's functionality. The project plans and agendas encourage students to view their work as a fluid but cohesive whole and to demonstrate an investment in that whole by claiming specific responsibilities. The peer review pushes students to take responsibility for the whole project while also demonstrating the value of their individual contributions.

Performing Anonymous Invention in Google Docs

One thing many teachers (and students) of the collaborative assignment struggle with is challenge of getting all group members to feel comfortable contributing to the group. A variety of issues may contribute to students' discomfort: a distrust of or lack of familiarity with academic modes of discourse, a prior history of "failure" in academic writing and/or group projects, complexities tied to speaking or writing in a second language or dialect, a shy or quiet personality, etc. We find that encouraging students to assume anonymous online identities early in a collaborative process helps students transition from the discomfort they feel contributing in academic group work toward a sense of self-expression they often associate with their social writing online. The activity can be as simple as having the students brainstorm a list of things they like, but we prefer to scaffold it as part of a larger collaborative assignment—for instance by having the students complete collaborative note-taking as preliminary research.

Having the students brainstorm anonymously allows the students to share their ideas in a low-stakes way. Students who may feel uncomfortable speaking up in a full-classroom environment (or even within their smaller groups) can add their voice to the discussion without ceremony and without drawing all eyes. Students can also make mistakes—either with the technology or with the activity—without having those mistakes attached to their student identities. In other words, while each student knows what he or she contributed, the document as a whole becomes the work of the full class. And because the document is available for the whole class to see in the cloud, we can praise specific details in such a way that validates every student: because the contributions are made anonymously, students must view each other as possible contributors, as valuable voices, for each detail.

Letting the students contribute to an activity anonymously, especially earlier in the semester, also models an environment of play and curiosity that we hope students will maintain in later work for the course. When the students enter a document that has been set up to hide their identities, Google Docs assigns each student an animal avatar, such as Anonymous Hippo or Anonymous Axolotl. When our students see this, they almost invariably spend the first few minutes of the activity trying to figure out which anonymous animal has been assigned to them, and they'll seek out the assistance of those seated around them. While allowing this activity may seem, at first, to counteract the benefit of having the students compose anonymously, we have not witnessed such an outcome. We have observed our students trying to discover their own identities but not the identities of those around them—at least not without being asked to. Instead, the students' amusement and curiosity with the avatars prompts them to interact with their peers and the technology in a way that feels fun and natural to them.

A sample process for an anonymous invention activity could be as follows:

1. Create a new Google Docs document and set the permissions so that anyone with the link can edit it.
2. Add a prompt to the top of the document. If you have a large group working on the document, you may want to provide a few prompts for the students to respond to so that they aren't all trying to type in the exact same area at once.
3. Share the document with the students by providing them with the link.
4. Give the students time to respond to the prompts in the Google Docs document.
5. Review their contributions as they compose, and use their responses to help them think more deeply, such as by pointing out contributions that are similar in nature or those that lead to further questions or possible synthesis.
6. As the students complete their responses, review the results as a full class. Ask students to identify the ideas they found most interesting and/or best suited to further inquiry.

Creating a Group Annotated Bibliography in Google Docs

We want the students to view themselves as authors with individually meaningful contributions to co-authored texts, and to view their other group members as co-collaborators with varied strengths and weaknesses. As our students become more involved in their collaborative assignment, we encourage these perspectives by having our student groups compile, revise, and reference collaborative annotated bibliographies in Google Docs. We see this activity as an introduction to the fluid roles students will assume while collaborating in the cloud and to the specific affordances of the Google Docs app.

Having a group of students engaged in a collaborative project maintain an annotated bibliography on Google Docs rather than in a non-cloud word processing program affects students' access and ownership. First, it removes ownership of the document from a single student and gives it to the group as a whole, allowing all members continuous access to the bibliography as well as the right and responsibility to add to or revise the bibliography as needed.[6] This in turn makes it easier for all group members to shape the direction of the research. Even when groups divide the research tasks among members, as we often see in our own classes—for example, assigning each group member a different subtopic to research—the accessibility of the document allows students to view the group's research as whole, and individual students will often identify and fill in research gaps.

The collaborative nature of an annotated bibliography in Google Docs also allows both students and teachers to critique and comment on the document, and for the feedback to be viewed by all group members, not just the individual student who found each source. We require that our students share their bibliographies with us, and we use our access to the documents to provide feedback on the suitability of the sources, the ways they might be used in the students' writing, the structure and format of the bibliography, etc. This feedback, while attached to issues in individual students' work (as students generally find sources individually), is available and addressed to all group members, making any necessary changes the responsibility of the group as a whole. And indeed, we see the students sharing this responsibility for revisions and have observed that students do not work on revisions only for the sources they, personally, contributed.

Finally, because we introduce the annotated bibliography early in our group projects, the assignment also allows students a low-stakes opportunity to navigate and explore the affordances of the technology itself. We require the students to input text and links, use the commenting and editing features, discuss group work using Google Docs' instant messaging, and reflect on the document's history. Students are encouraged to try things out and to help each other navigate each task. By requiring a reflection conversation at the end of the process, we also provide time to discuss group dynamics and technology possibilities early in the collaborative process.

A sample process for this assignment could be as follows:

1. Assign groups the task of creating an annotated bibliography and require that each group member contribute a minimum number of sources to the document. If there is time, model this work by creating an annotation for a resource on correct citation together.
2. Once each student has contributed sources, have the students in each group familiarize themselves with the full range of sources compiled by their group members.
3. Ask each group member to peer review their group's annotated bibliography, leaving feedback with the Comments and Suggested Edits features.
4. Review each group's annotated bibliography, responding to peer-to-peer suggestions and leaving any necessary additional feedback.
5. Have the groups discuss the suggestions (both those they themselves formulated and those received from the professor) via the chat feature. Students should decide upon a process and timeline for implementing necessary changes.

6. Once students have revised the document, discuss the entire writing and revision process. Use the Revision History feature to highlight specific examples of successful comments and revisions. Reflect on the individual strengths each student brings to the assignment as well as the strengths and weaknesses of the technology as a collaborative platform.

Creating Group Agendas and Project Plans in Google Docs

Collaborative assignments require students to juggle not only their own individual tasks, but also the tasks of the group as a whole. Each student must understand his or her own responsibilities while also understanding the status of the other project elements as well. One way we have helped students to navigate shared responsibility is through the requirement of project plans and weekly agendas.

We introduce the idea of a project plan early on in the group project by providing a set of things for each group to consider: What tasks and subtasks need to be completed? When should each tasks be completed by? How much time will each task take? What are the group members' individual strengths and weaknesses? We then ask the groups to break down the various tasks and compose a project plan in Google Docs where it can be accessible to the entire group. They are asked to update the plan throughout the course of the project by adding information on when each task was completed and who completed it as well as information on further tasks that might have arisen throughout the course of the project (such as another draft or another round of feedback).

Requiring the groups to compose and maintain their project plans in Google Docs not only ensures that all group members are on the same page and share responsibility for being aware of various completion dates, it also gives group members a quick and easy way to communicate their progress on various assignment components. For instance, instead of sending emails or text messages to update the group on any progress that has been completed, students post their progress in the project plan, allowing both their group members and the instructor to monitor project completion in one centralized place.

A sample process for a project plan assignment in Google Docs could be as follows:

1. Create a template for the project plan that includes the major tasks of the assignment, any interim due dates you have defined for the students (such as dates drafts must be completed for peer review), and any other plan structure you would like to provide.
2. Post the project plan template to Google Docs.
3. Have each group copy and paste the template into their own document in Google Docs and make sure it is shared with the instructor and all group members.
4. Brainstorm with the full class what other tasks (ones you have not listed for them) they will need to complete during the course of the project. You can either complete this brainstorming activity on a whiteboard or can use a different Google Doc.
5. Have each group fill out the project plan template with specific details on what needs to be completed, when each task needs to be completed by, and which group member (or members) will be responsible for completing each task.
6. Discuss the project plans as a full class by having the groups share the various ways they broke down the project tasks.
7. Have each group discuss and document how group members will let the group know when individual tasks have been completed.

8. Check in on each group's progress with the project plan at regular intervals during the assignment. Encourage groups to treat the plan as a living document, one that can be added to or revised as seems appropriate.

Our agenda assignment works in many of the same ways as the project plan, though on a much smaller scale. One element we have added to many of our collaborative projects is regular meetings between the group and the instructor, and we require each group to prepare an agenda in advance of each meeting. While we do not require that the students compose the agenda in Google Docs, we have seen many advantages to those agendas that were composed in the cloud. First, it allows all group members to see and revise the agenda, such as by filling in which tasks were completed and lists of questions they have moving forward. Second, during the meeting, students can type directly into the agenda to update their progress with or understanding of the work they are being asked to complete.

A sample process for an agenda assignment in Google Docs could be as follows:

1. Create a template for the agenda that includes basic agenda formatting and the sections you would like the agenda to contain. Our agendas contain sections for an objective, a report on work completed to date, any questions the group has, plans for the future, new business that needs to be discussed, and a list of meeting attendees.
2. Post the agenda template to Google Drive.
3. Have each group copy and paste the template to their own Google Drive and make sure it is shared with all group members.
4. Have each group discuss who will be responsible for completing each agenda. Will the full group contribute to the agenda for every group meeting or will specific students be assigned specific agendas based on the work they are currently completing for the assignment?
5. Have the students complete the agenda. This can be done in class but the agendas tend to be more useful if completed a day or so before the group meeting and so our students often complete them outside of class.
6. Have all group members review the agenda prior to the group meeting to update or add to the agenda based on the work each individual has completed.
7. At the group meeting, require each student to have the agenda pulled up on his or her own computer so that all group members can view and add notes to the document as needed.

Performing Peer Review in Google Docs

Peer review is a regular and essential component of the writing classroom, both with projects done individually by students and those done in groups, where peer review becomes less of a one-time class assignment and more of a recursive practice in the creation of the final product. We scaffold peer review activities only after we have provided opportunities for students to develop their own identity and a sense of shared responsibility within the group, so that their peer review seems more akin to contributions to a group on a social network than to anonymous trolling. We also stress to the students that the very act of peer review is one of collaboration in which students must trust themselves and their peers to be givers of useful feedback.

While we use peer review with a variety of Cloud and non-Cloud technologies in our classroom, having the students peer review each other's work in Google Docs has several advantages, particularly in terms of helping students find their own agency. In addition to repeating some of the other benefits we have discussed in terms of other activities (tracking contribution, allowing students to contribute with written language instead of spoken language, etc.), Google Docs allows students to build off of each other's feedback using the Comments feature, particularly by allowing students to see and reply to comments left by other students. In this way, students can have virtual discussions about the pros and cons of any suggested change, and the author can respond to any comment with a question or a request for additional explanation. For this latter use, Google Docs allows students to direct comments at a particular user (or at a set of particular users) by placing a plus sign (+) before another contributor's email address. This tags the specified user and generates an email to that student, drawing his or her attention to the ongoing discussion. In this way, additional discussion on the document does not go unnoticed by students who have already completed the peer review.

Peer review in Google Docs makes it easier for instructors to enter the documents and leave feedback of their own, creating a model of effective peer review and collaboration. Unlike a face-to-face peer review in which a professor can only work with one group at a time, the third-space nature of Google Docs allows the professor equal presence in each peer review and, through features like Revision History, increased access to the peer review process. What's more, the time stamps on the comments allow other group members and the instructor to see how long each individual actually spent leaving comments, which in turn provides a glimpse into how deeply each student engaged with the activity. Because this level of transparency is there not only for the instructor but also for the students, using Google Docs for peer review can increase each peer reviewer's sense of personal responsibility to the activity as a whole.

A sample process for a peer review assignment in Google Docs could be as follows:

1. Split the class into peer review teams and make sure each peer review team has access to the other team members' email addresses.
2. Work with the full class to define a set of peer review criteria. For instance, what things should the students be looking for? Will students be required to leave (or respond to) a particular number of comments? How much time should the students expect to spend on each paper?
3. Have each student (or each group for collaborative papers) share his or her document with the other members of the peer review team.
4. Have the students complete the peer review. This can happen inside or outside of class.
    a. If you have a complex set of criteria for the students to respond to, you could use Google Forms (available in Google Drive) as well.
5. If you would like to encourage extensive collaboration in terms of the students responding to other students' feedback, you could require a second, mini peer review in which the students re-enter the document at a later time to read and respond to other pieces of feedback.
6. Discuss with the full class what went well with the peer review and what could have been more helpful in order to inform future peer reviews.

CONCLUSION

Cloud-based technologies, such as wikis, Facebook, Twitter, and Google Apps for Education, have been praised for their potential to use peer-to-peer interaction to disrupt traditional classroom hierarchies and move marginalized voices to the center of the knowledge-sharing process (See, for example, Vie &

DeWinter, 2009; Clark, 2010; Limbu, 2012). Cloud technology also has the potential to foster transparent, effective collaboration, but such collaboration must be carefully scaffolded if it is to be optimized. If group members work with attitudes of agency and responsibility, cloud technology can facilitate efficient, convenient, and consensus-driven collaboration. Because authorial identity is itself collaborative in the cloud, cloud pedagogy can create useful discussions regarding intellectual property, agency and responsibility in communication, and the ethics of collaboration. It is our responsibility, then, to scaffold group work so that these attitudes and discussions can emerge.

REFERENCES

Caeton, D. A. (2009). Agency and Accountability: The Paradoxes of Wiki Discourse. In M. Barton & R. Cummings (Eds.), *Wiki Writing: Collaborative Learning in the College Classroom*. Ann Arbor, MI: University of Michigan Press; doi:10.3998/dcbooks.5871848.0001.001

Clark, J. E. (2010). The Digital Imperative: Making the Case for a 21st-Century Pedagogy. *Computers and Composition*, *27*(1), 27–35. doi:10.1016/j.compcom.2009.12.004

Connelly, L. (2015, April). *Technology in the Classroom: Google Drive*. Poster presented at Undergraduate Research and Arts Forum at Michigan State University, East Lansing, MI.

Duggan, M., Ellison, N., Lampe, C., Lenhart, A., & Madden, M. (2015). *Social Media Update 2014*. Pew Research Center. Retrieved from http://www.pewinternet.org/2015/01/09/demographics-of-key-social-networking-platforms-2/

Google. (n.d.). Productivity Tools. *Google for Education*. Retrieved from https://www.google.com/edu/products/productivity-tools/

Haring-Smith, T. (1994). *Writing Together: Collaborative Learning in the Writing Classroom*. New York: Harper Collins College.

Helfand, D. (2013, July 8). Watering the Roots of Knowledge through Collaborative Learning. *The Chronicle of Higher Education*.

Kittle, P., & Hicks, T. (2009). Transforming the Group Paper with Collaborative Online Writing. *Pedagogy*, *9*(3), 525–538. doi:10.1215/15314200-2009-012

Limbu, M. (2012). Teaching Writing in the Cloud: Networked Writing Communities in the Culturally and Linguistically Diverse Classrooms. *Journal of Global Literacies, Technologies, and Emerging Pedagogies*, *1*(1), 1–20.

Lunsford, A. A., Fishman, J., & Liew, W. (2013). College Writing, Identification, and the Production of Intellectual Property: Voices from the Stanford Study of Writing. *College English*, *75*(5), 470–492.

Maranto, G., & Barton, M. (2010). Promise and Paradox. *Computers and Composition*, *27*, 36–47. doi:10.1016/j.compcom.2009.11.003

Ritter, K. (2005). The Economics of Authorship: Online Paper Mills, Student Writers, and First Year Composition. *College Composition and Communication*, *56*(4), 601–631.

Vie, S., & DeWinter, J. (2009). Disrupting Intellectual Property: Collaboration and Resistance in Wikis. In M. Barton & R. Cummings (Eds.), *Wiki Writing: Collaborative Learning in the College Classroom*. Ann Arbor, MI: University of Michigan Press. doi:10.3998/dcbooks.5871848.0001.001

ENDNOTES

1 A recent survey of the 53 students in our first year writing class indicated that over 60% had used Google Docs, the key cloud technology of our course, prior to the course itself, though very few reported using the app for academic purposes (Connelly, 2015). Other cloud technology is even more ubiquitous: in 2014 87% of online adults between the ages of 18 and 29 were on Facebook, 53% used Instagram, and 37% used Twitter (Duggan et al., 2015). It isn't technology that is unfamiliar to students, but specific functionalities of technology.

2 In explaining the "social" nature of Facebook, Maranto and Barton (2010) wrote that "collaboration, is (of course) the bedrock of social networking sites. The whole point is to work with others, and nearly every aspect of the interface is based on communicating and sharing with others. Although there are certainly some mean-spirited and hateful profiles on Facebook, it's strange to call any of them 'anti-social.' A true recluse would never create a profile in the first place" (p. 44).

3 For excellent discussions of students' ideas of authorship within print texts, especially in academic settings, see Lunsford et al, 2013, and Ritter, 2005.

4 In fact, because profiles within cloud apps often ask users to create identities by selecting items from a list of specific options, both the user's identity and the user's position as an author already coded by the app developer. A user's profile is co-authored from the start (Maranto & Barton, 2010). What's more, sites like Facebook and Twitter grant users the power to share another's work toward the creation of the user's own identity and to tag images and text so that the user participates in authoring others' personae. The practice of trolling allows particularly bellicose writers to critique everything from grammar to content behind a shield of (seeming) anonymity. Although the cloud technology we focus on in this chapter, Google Docs, does not have this same attention to a user's profile, this larger social context shapes our students' understanding of authorship in digital spaces.

5 Identity can be experienced by users in other ways as well. Caeton (2009) describes online identity formation as a process of "perpetual negotiation" and quotes Mark Poster's argument that "the individual in a virtual object [is in] an unfinished, contingent state where identity is temporary … [and occupying a] subject position that is 'never before' rather than 'always already'" (Poster, 2001, p. 167-70 quoted in Caeton, 2009, p. 133).

6 Of course, one person is responsible for the initial creation of the document and for making that document shared. We have not yet, however, seen any difference in students' feelings of ownership in regard to which group member created the document itself.

Chapter 15
Using the Hybrid Interactive Rhetorical Engagement (H.I.R.E.) Metrics to Analyze the Effectiveness of E-Learning Websites

Yowei Kang
Kainan University, Taiwan

ABSTRACT

The rapid development of Web-based learning technologies has become a global phenomenon that affects higher education institutions. Both developing and developed countries are eager to take advantage of the multi-modal and asynchronous technical capacities that Web 2.0 can provide to college students. The "E-learning Phenomenon" has also prompted the development of different types of learning tools, ranging from commercially-developed Blackboard, open-source learning platform Moodle, or less popular platform developed by individual universities around the world. This study applied a theoretical concept, Hybrid Interactive Rhetorical Engagement (H.I.R.E.), and a series of quantitative metrics derived from H.I.R.E., to assess the Digital Learning Website developed at Kainan University, Taiwan. Exploratory empirical findings help college instructors to understand whether H.I.R.E. serves a good system design concept explain and predict users' learning behaviors and can be used to assess a variety of web-learning technologies in the market.

INTRODUCTION

Impacts of Web 2.0 on Education

Web 2.0 is often defined as a set of Internet-based tools, ranging from email, blogs, social networking service (SNS), web applications, Wikis, etc (Ehlers, 2009; Wan, 2010). These tools enable collaborative Internet applications to facilitate communication between organizations and individuals (Sendall, Ceccucci & Peslak, 2008). Web 2.0 is claimed to derive from "the collective intelligence of crowds to

DOI: 10.4018/978-1-5225-1650-7.ch015

create value" (O'Reilly, 2005, para. 25, cited in Barassi & Treré, 2012, p. 1270). Scholars have also claimed that Web 2.0 is a potentially effective tool to engage students in their own learning (Echeng, Abel & Grzegorz, 2013) because students are able to contribute to the creation of "knowledge repository" (Orchovacki, Gran & Kermek, 2013). The capabilities of Web 2.0 technologies to allow students to share educational and personal information also make these applications instrumental to teachers (John, 2013). This technology and its many emerging applications have attracted scholars' attention because of its interactivity, ease of use, and wide availability (Karunasena, Deng & Kam, 2013). Therefore, Krelja Kurelovic, Tomljanovic and Ruzie-Baf (2012) concluded that Web 2.0 is characterized by its attributes such as collaboration, collective intelligence, interactivity, openness, and social networking. These technical features are in line with contemporary teaching practices and are helpful to the development of e-education 2.0 (Krelja Kurelovic et al., 2012). Orchovacki et al. (2013) also observed that Web 2.0 also enables teachers to communicate with students, comment on students' shared artefacts, evaluate students' e-activities, and publish lecture materials. Researchers have empirically tested the impacts of e-learning technologies on the effectiveness of learning. For example, Karunasena et al. (2013) found that e-learning via Web 2.0 technologies is beneficial to students' instructional support, knowledge management, collaboration, and management of learning resources. Considering the promises provided by Web 2.0 technologies, Ehlers (2009) envisions the rise of *E-learning 2.0*, defined as "using social software and learning services, which can be combined according to individual needs" (p. 297).

The Emergence of Web-Based E-Learning Technologies

The rapid development of the Web-based E-learning technologies has become a global phenomenon (Esnault, 2008). Web 2.0 technologies and many emerging applications (e.g., chat room, tele-conferencing, e-mails, etc.) have increasingly gaining momentum in many classrooms (Jones & Vollmers, 2008; Murray & Jackson, 2009). For example, the integration of these technologies has become popular among Australian universities (Gosper, McNeili, Woo, Phillips, Preston & Green, 2011). Similar technologies have been used in the U.S. college classrooms (Jones & Vollmers, 2008).

From a business perspective, according to a 2013 report by *E-learning Industry*, it was estimated that, in 2011, about $35.6 billion was spent on self-paced E-learning across the globe (Pappas, 2013). Its market size is estimated to double by 2015 and shows no signs of slowing (Pappas, 2015). Pappas (2015) reports that about 46% college students have taken at least one online course and it is estimated by 2019, around half of all college classes will be based on a variety of E-learning platforms. The applications of E-learning technologies have been extended to a corporate setting. It is reported that about 41.7% of Fortune 500 companies use education technologies to train their employees (Pappas, 2015). E-learning has been found to grown in countries such as Malaysia and Vietnam and many regions around the world (Pappas, 2015). In Asia, the E-learning market has grown at 17.3% annually in the past five years, while in the Middle East, the number is at 8.2% (Pappas, 2015). The revenue of E-learning is estimated to grown to $8.1 billion by 2015, at the growth rate of 5.8% annually (Pappas, 2015).

Derived from past digital game research and its applications in various educational contexts (Gee, 2007a, 2007b), well-developed E-learning systems are also expected to generate positive student learning outcomes. However, while ample human-computer interaction research has extensively examined the use of game design and game elements in non-game contexts (Deterding et al., 2011), theory-based measurements derived from the persuasive manipulations between E-learning systems and their users to assess the effects on user experience and learning outcomes is scarce in the existing literature. Therefore, in this book chapter, the author proposes a newly-developed theoretical concept, *hybrid interactive rhetorical engagement* (henceforth, H.I.R.E.) (Kang, 2011) that can be used to study E-learning systems through the analysis of user experience in an educational setting.

Objectives of the Study

Given the potential of E-learning technologies and their foreseeable impacts on education, the author used the E-learning system at Kainan University, Taiwan as an example to discuss how H.I.R.E. metrics help assess the effectiveness of this Web-based system to demonstrate their current state, potential impacts, opportunities and challenges. The author attempts to present a preliminary assessment on the emerging importance and growing interests of the E-learning system and to validate the usefulness of H.I.R.E. metrics as a feasible analytical tool to assess the effectiveness of E-learning systems that have been implemented or are currently at their beta phases. Like other emerging Web-based online learning tools, the case study will provide H.I.R.E.-derived empirical data to better assess the education, research, and practices of E-learning technologies. However, what is lacking in the existing E-learning literature is an experience-based assessment of E-learning's current state, the types and the extent of impacts on various stakeholders, professional practices, and strategies to address its opportunities and challenges in an educational setting.

Therefore, the objectives of this book chapter aim to online learning educators, practitioners, and researchers to understand the emergence of Web-based E-learning technologies and to develop an experience-based H.I.R.E. metrics to assess the successful implementation of these increasingly popular E-learning platforms. This book chapter explores, beyond a simple system design perspective, to examine what constitute an effective E-learning system through the H.I.R.E. metrics by examining the interactions with the system that will generate different user experiences in the learning process. The study employed Kang's (2011) experience-based assessment metrics, "hybrid interactive rhetorical engagement" (H.I.R.E.), and empirically tested whether the concept can be a useful analytical tool to assess existing the E-learning system at Kainan University in particular, and other E-learning technologies in general. In particular, this study attempts to answer the following research questions:

RQ1: Will a high level of H.I.R.E. lead to students' usage behaviors with the system?
RQ2: Will a high level of H.I.R.E. lead to students' more favorable assessment with the system functions?

BACKGROUND

The Concept of H.I.R.E.

The concept of "hybrid interactive rhetorical engagement" (H.I.R.E.) (Kang, 2011) was originally developed to study gameplay experiences with MMORPGs. This term refers to gameplay experiences that are the results of the experiential outcome of persuasion during gameplay with digital games such as MMORPGs. Most gamers experience H.I.R.E. when interacting with game design elements (such as symbols, avatars, and narrative settings) and other gamers through the understanding, interpretation, and interaction with their rhetorical manipulation (Kang, 2011). Similar to other scholars in the E-learning literature (Hui et al., 2007; Pan, Zhang, Rhalibi, Woo & Li, 2008), the author reasons that E-learning systems are very similar to a digital game system, because of its dependence on computer and networking technologies.

The concept of H.I.R.E. attempts to understand the persuasive process that gamers experience in digital games. H.I.R.E. is situated within the rhetorical tradition that examines how various rhetorical elements (e.g., aural, visual, textual, and kinetic) affect the processes of entertaining, educating, informing, and persuading gamers. "Hybrid" refers to the multimedia capacities which advanced game technologies can provide by offering their users aural, visual, textual, kinetic in-game design elements during gameplay (Kang, 2011). In MMORPGs, gamers constantly exchange textual, aural, and visual messages to collaborate on completing their tasks during gameplay to generate gratifying experiences (Juul, 2005; Kang, 2011; Vorderer & Bryant, 2006). Technological advancements such as broadband connection, blue-ray PS3 game devices, virtual reality glove, and real-time voice chat/communication also provide players enriched and intensive gameplay experiences.

The concept of interactivity as an important theoretical dimension of the H.I.R.E. refers to the process that a gamer can modify, based on the context and characters involved, the state and happening in a digital game by some action through an interface (Grodal, 2003). Interactivity embedded in digital game devices and gaming environments allow gamers to conduct real-time communication, modify gaming spaces, and navigate the digital game environment (Ryan, 2001). For example, gamers are capable of exploring and responding to the gaming environment by interacting with the game interface, type in chats to converse with other gamers, and enjoy the pleasure of terminating an enemy by similar motor actions (Kang, 2011).

The concept of engagement, on the other hand, refers to are both the motivation and the sought result that prompt gamers to play MMORPGs. Engagement is defined as a psychological concept that refers to how and whether gamers are satisfied with their gameplay experiences (O'Brien & Toms, 2007). The level of engagement constitutes an important part of their persuasive gameplay experiences in digital games (Kang, 2011). Many digital game researchers thus have often characterized a gaming environment as engaging (Humphreys, 2003; Pickering, 1995). For example, Sony's *EverQuest* was also called "EverCrack" in the gaming community because of its addictive qualities (Burrill, 2005). As such, the concept of engagement can be defined as the interpretive, sympathetic, and interactive engagement with all game design elements that gamers are exposed to that have the purposes of educating, informing, entertaining, and persuading them (Tavinor, 2005). This important dimension of H.I.R.E. can therefore be extended to examine interactive engagements between students and instructor in E-learning systems.

On the basis of discussions above, H.I.R.E. will be a useful theoretical concept to study the interaction process between students and instructor in an E-learning context. H.I.R.E. is also a useful analytical tool help develop theory-based metrics to study online interactions to better assess students' online learning experiences. Furthermore, the concept of H.I.R.E. aims to capture the multiplicity of educational experiences by examining the role of participating students (audiences) and their active role in co-creating and shaping their own learning experiences in E-learning systems. To summarize, H.I.R.E. refers to a state of engaging and interactive experiences when interacting with other users, design elements, and the instructor in E-learning systems. H.I.R.E. properly characterizes students' learning experiences and is produced by a combination of multimodal persuasive interactions such as textual, aural, visual, and even kinetic interactivities, as well as socio-psychological gratifications as a result of participation and interactions with other students involved in E-learning systems.

The E-Learning System at Kainan University, Taiwan

The successful implementation of E-learning systems have been claimed to generate the following outcomes: to "improve student engagement, retention, and ultimately completion rates in higher education" (Heider, 2015, p. 183). With these objectives in mind, the Web-based E-learning system at Kainan University is open to all students who register a class where the instructor has developed a dedicated course E-learning system. Similar to other E-learning systems (such as Blackboard or Moodle), students are able to access various course contents provided by the instructors once they login the system. Figure 1 shows a screen-shot of the E-learning system. The first column on the left asks students to login the system with their user names and passwords. In the central column, daily updates of the courses are provided. The column on the right is the monthly calendar (See Figure 1).

MAIN FOCUS OF THE CHAPTER

In this book chapter, the author employed a survey method to examine and discussed whether H.I.R.E. metrics can be used to assess the effectiveness of the E-learning system at Kainan University, Taiwan.

This book chapter aims to empirically test the H.I.R.E. metrics that were developed to measure and assess user experiences in this E-learning system. The H.I.R.E. metrics will enable the developers of E-learning systems to better assess the processes and their effects at various learning phases and for future E-learning system improvements. In particular, the author discussed user experiences from the E-learning educational context. The author reasons that user experiences in digital game research resemble those in any E-learning system. Therefore, through the development and validation of the H.I.R.E. metrics,

Figure 1. E-learning system
(Source: Kainan University, Taiwan)

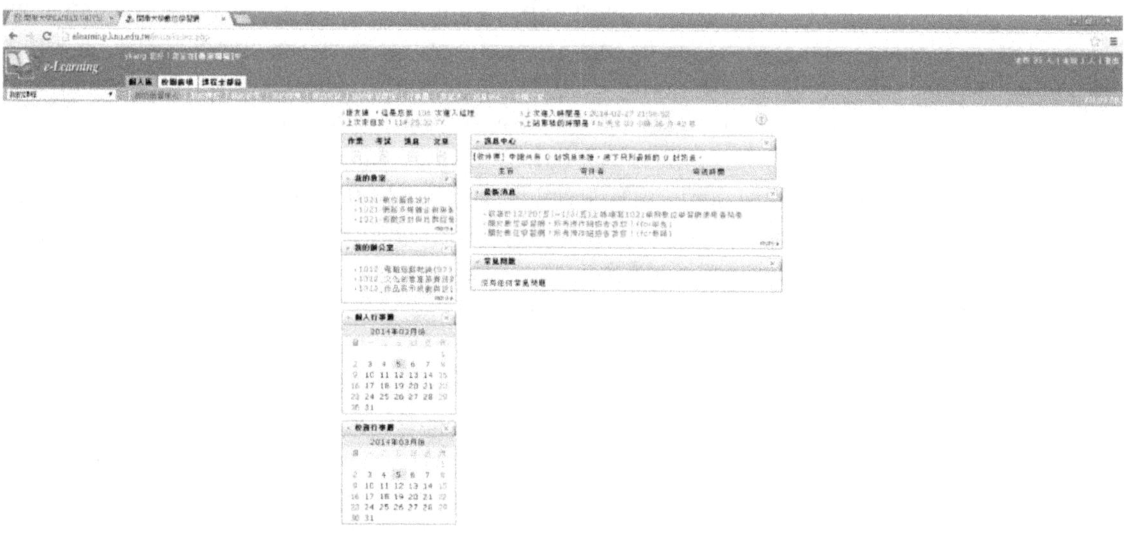

E-learning researchers and practitioners can explain, analyze, and assess these systems/applications to better understand their effects on students' learning process.

Factors Affecting the Success of E-Learning Technologies

In spite of the popularity of E-learning technologies, there have been a lot of factors determining their successful implementation on campus. As a result, recent developments of Web 2.0-based E-learning technologies have increasingly integrated students into the design process to make sure students' needs are included (Rahimi, van Den Berg & Veen, 2015) in the system development process. Rahimi et al. (2015) discussed Web 2.0 Personal Learning Environment (PLE) and argued that students' engagement and learning can be greatly enhanced by including student-controlled dimensions, student-centric instructional approaches, the learning potential of Web 2.0 tools and services, and technology-enhanced learning activities in the design. Empirical data collection from 29 student participants support that PLE helps to engage students in constructing their own learning environment, enhancing a sense of ownership, and generating communication among both students and the instructors.

However, to develop a successful E-learning system requires the understanding of the perspectives of all participants in the learning process. On the basis of the literature (Pahl & Donnellan, 2002; Thowfeek & Salam, 2014), problems with E-learning technologies were generally categorized into five key areas of research: system, instructors, students, organization, and communication. First, the study of system-level issues is most related to how E-learning systems are designed to accommodate different needs (Rahimi et al., 2015). Minović, Štavljanin, Milovanović, and Starčević (2008) studied the issues related to usability in mobile E-learning platforms due to its portability, social interactivity, connectivity, and individuality features. Their study found that the development of E-learning system needs to have learners/students at the center of the system development. Thowfeek and Salam (2014) conducted a survey among final year students in a Sri Lanka university and their findings confirmed that the usability attributes of E-learning web sites are essential to students' natural and spontaneous interactions with the technologies.

Secondly, issues related to instructors' adoption are also found to be important to the success of E-learning systems (Marcelo, Yot, & Mayor, 2015; Motaghian, Hassanzadeh, & Moghadam, 2013; Rhoden, 2014; Thowfeek & Hussin, 2008). Hue and Jalil (2013, cited in Marcelo, 2015) found that the frequency of integrating technologies into teaching depends on instructors' attitudes. Rhoden (2014) used the unified theory of acceptance and use of technology (UTAUT) model to examine factors determining the adoption of E-learning systems in Jamaica. In his dissertation, Rhoden (2014) investigated whether instructors' attitudes (such as performance expectancy, effort expectancy social influence, and facilitating conditions) affect their behavioral intention to adopt E-learning technologies. Motaghian, Hassanzadeh, and Moghadam (2013) also employed an integrated model of technology adoption to examine whether instructors' attitudes as measured by perceived usefulness, perceived ease of use and system quality would increase their intention to use web-based learning systems. The survey of 115 university instructors confirmed the attitudinal variable (i.e., perceived usefulness) affects their intension to use and actual usage the E-learning systems. The importance of college instructors' attitudes are also supported in Thowfeed and Hussin (2008) that they found that positive attitudes and supportive mindset of the instructors are essential to the successful implementation of E-learning systems at many tertiary education institutes.

Thirdly, Fichten et al. (2009) explored the influence of students' perceptions and attitudes on E-learning adoption. They surveyed 223 students with disabilities from Canadian colleges and universities and found a list of problems with E-learning systems, ranging from accessibility of digital audio and video, fixed time limits to take online exams, formats of course materials, lack of adaptive technologies, problems with downloading and opening files, and poor utilization of the system by instructors. Given the amount of difficulties encountered by students, Echeng et al. (2013) developed a predictive model to examine whether facilitating condition, motivation to use, perceived usefulness, perceived ease of use, performance expectancy, prior knowledge, and social factors would be able to explain students' intention to use Web 2.0 technology in learning. Empirical data collected from 270 respondents support that there are statistically significant relationships among users' perceptions and intention to use Web 2.0 technologies in a higher educational setting.

In addition to problems related to E-learning systems, other factors are likely to affect their successful implementation (Hartnett, George, & Dron, 2011; Nehme, 2010). Student motivation is one of the most researched factors (Hartnett et al., 2011; Nehme, 2010). Students' learning style and study habits can also be influential of their online learning success (Çakıroğlu, 2014). For example, students with low motivation (Nehme, 2010) or bad study habits and style (Çakıroğlu, 2014) may affect the successful implementation of E-learning systems. Without the routine structures of a traditional class, students may get lost or confused about course activities and deadlines. Students may feel isolated from the instructor and classmates. Prior experiences with E-learning technologies are likely to affect the success of the implementation (Shih, Munoz, & Sanchez, 2006). Shih et al. (2006) recruited 120 university undergraduate students to take part in a pre- and post-test experiment involved a Web-based course. Their study found that prior E-learning experiences contribute to their ability to organize online activities more effectively. Those participants who have more experience with Internet tools were found to spend less time and visit fewer pages when organizing their works in the virtual classroom (Shih et al., 2006). However, prior experience did not affect their assessment of Web-based learning (Shih et al., 2006).

In conclusion, student acceptance has been found to be an important factor to determine the success of E-learning technologies (Murray & Jackson, 2009).

Fourth, scholars claimed that E-learning has been recognized as an essential supportive practice of on-the-job learning (Cheng, Wang, Moormann, Olaniran, & Chen, 2012). Their study has identified several organizational characteristics (e.g., employees' characteristics, technological attributes, managerial support, job support, organizational support, and training design elements) on employees' motivation to adopt the technologies (Cheng et al., 2012). Keramati, Afshari-Mofrad & Kamrani (2011) studied the intervening role of readiness factors in E-learning outcomes in an organizational setting. Their study examined three types of organizational readiness factors (i.e., organizational, social and technical aspects) among 96 teachers at Tehran high schools where E-learning systems were implemented (Keramati et al., 2011). Hierarchical regression analysis also found that organizational readiness factors play a moderating role in the relationship between E-Learning factors and outcomes.

Finally, in terms of the communication process, Pahl and Donnellan (2002) pointed out that the virtual forms of teaching and learning often result in the depletion of direct contact and communication between students and teachers. Schertler and Bodendorf (2002) emphasized the important role of communication support to enhance the technical advantages of many E-learning systems. Schmieder (2008) reviewed existing literature to demonstrate the importance of effective collaborative tools in developing an atmosphere to encourage students' engagement in their online learning process.

In conclusion, the main focus of this book chapter is to employ the H.I.R.E. metrics to help E-learning researchers and practitioners to assess what makes effective systems and applications and how to assess their effectiveness as demonstrated in students' learning outcome and experiences. H.I.R.E. metrics were developed and empirically tested to the examination of user experience when taking part in any digital contents to accomplish outcomes as a result of their interactions with an E-learning system.

Effective E-Learning Technologies and Learning Outcomes

To identify what outcome measures should be included to assess whether an E-learning technology is effective, the author relied on the ample amount of the existing interdisciplinary literature on this topic. For example, Eom (2010) employed path analysis to investigate the relationships between E-learning systems and students' satisfaction with university online courses. His study focuses on system-related variables, such as computer self-efficacy, information quality, self-regulated learning behaviors, and system quality, and explores whether these predictors account for students' learning outcomes. The study also confirmed that information quality and system quality significantly predict students' satisfaction and actual system usage (Eom, 2010). Similarly, Ho (2009) studied high school students in Taiwan to examine how internal and external factors will affect their learning behaviors online. The study explores the relationships between E-learning system quality and technology readiness on students' learning outcomes and learning behaviors. The empirical data collected from 376 high school students in Taiwan were analyzed using structural equation modeling and confirmed the significant impacts of E-learning system quality and technology readiness on learning behaviors and learning outcomes. Despite the dominant themes in the existing literature emphasized the importance of system-related factors, Song (2010) instead studied students' perception of online courses in hospitality programs in Florida, Iowa, Nevada, Virginia, and Texas. A web-based survey was used to investigate the relationship between system-related variables, interaction-based factors, and students' learning outcomes. The study found that perceived interaction quality variables are more important than system-related variables in predicting students' satisfaction and learning outcomes. Song's (2010) study lent support to the H.I.R.E. metrics in this book chapter because these metrics also measure user experiences with E-learning systems.

SOLUTIONS AND RECOMMENDATIONS

Using H.I.R.E. Metrics to Analyze the E-Learning System at Kainan University, Taiwan

The H.I.R.E. metrics were developed to help E-learning scholars and practitioners in terms of what to study and how things work to create positive user experiences and learning outcomes among students in an educational setting. To measure these effects, the author relied on past empirical studies to develop the H.I.R.E. metrics to examine user experiences (Calvillo-Gámez, Cairns & Cox, 2011; Zagal, Chan, & Zhang, 2010). Calvillo-Gámez et al.'s *Core Elements of the Gaming Experience Questionnaire (CEGEQ)* (2011) particularly provides a very useful foundation to develop similar experiential metrics to assess user experience in any E-learning systems. Although *CEGEQ* offers an objective measurement of user experience in digital games (Calvillo-Gámez, Cairns, & Cox, 2009), these statements can be adapted to develop the H.I.R.E. metrics to better study the emerging E-learning phenomenon. On the basis of the 38-item scales, the author developed a set of H.I.R.E. metrics to capture user experiences in E-learning systems. These H.I.R.E. statements will be used to ask participants to respond, after interacting with the E-learning system at Kainan University, by indicating their agreements through 10 five-point Likert

Table 1. The 10-item H.I.R.E. metrics

	SD	D	N	A	SA
The e-learning system has textual design elements.	1	2	3	4	5
The e-learning system has aural-visual design elements.	1	2	3	4	5
The e-learning system is rich in its various design elements.	1	2	3	4	5
The e-learning system is interactive.	1	2	3	4	5
I enjoyed using the e-learning system.	1	2	3	4	5
I feel frustrated when using the e-learning system.	1	2	3	4	5
I was in control of the e-learning system.	1	2	3	4	5
I would use the e-learning system again.	1	2	3	4	5
The e-learning system is easy to use.	1	2	3	4	5
I liked the way the e-learning system was designed.	1	2	3	4	5

scales with 1 representing "strongly disagree," 2 representing "disagree," 3 representing neutral, 4 representing "agree," and 5 representing "strongly agree" (See Table 1).

In term of scale reliability, Cronbach alpha coefficient for these ten statements is.88 and the H.I.R.E. instrument is considered to be highly reliable. Participants' quantitative assessment scores were analyzed through various descriptive or inferential statistical procedures to assess the effectiveness of this E-learning system. A composite H.I.R.E. score was computed and used for later statistical analyses. Descriptive statistics of these metrics were reported in Table 2.

Students' usage behaviors were measured by two questions, asking students about their frequency of using the E-learning system per week and the amount of time of using the system each time. On the basis of the empirical data, students logged in the E-learning system 2.08 (S.D.=.77) per week, while an average of 22.85 minutes (S.D.=21.58) was spent on the system each time.

Table 2. Descriptive statistics of H.I.R.E. metrics

	Mean	S.D.
The e-learning system has textual design elements.	3.79	.77
The e-learning system has aural-visual design elements.	3.11	.83
The e-learning system is rich in its various design elements.	3.33	.93
The e-learning system is interactive.	3.28	.97
I enjoyed using the e-learning system.	3.15	.88
I feel frustrated when using the e-learning system.	3.08	.93
I was in control of the e-learning system.	2.97	.85
I would use the e-learning system again.	3.38	.99
The e-learning system is easy to use.	3.05	.94
I liked the way the e-learning system was designed.	2.99	.98
H.I.R.E. Composite Index	3.23	.62

Table 3. Descriptive statistics of students' assessments of various system functions

	Mean	S.D.
I can use the e-learning system to check handout and practice files.	3.54	.94
I always login the e-learning system to check new course materials.	3.31	.98
I will inform other students who are absent to check the e-learning system.	3.10	1.14
I feel the e-learning system is a convenient location to store my course materials	3.31	1.13
The e-learning system is much more flexible than other learning platforms.	3.51	.91
I am aware that the e-learning system offers online discussion forum function.	3.10	1.07
I am satisfied with all functions available on the e-learning system.	2.95	.94
I am satisfied with the group discussion function on the e-learning system.	2.95	.97
I am satisfied with course update function on the e-learning system.	3.26	1.14
I am satisfied with the learning assessment area on the e-learning system.	3.26	1.14
Assessment Composite Index	3.23	.87

Students' assessment of various functions of the E-learning system was measured by ten 5-point Likert statements (See Table 3). Reliability was assessed by Cronbach alpha coefficient for these ten statements (α=.95). Therefore, the function assessment instrument was also considered to be highly reliable.

Statistical Analysis

A total of 39 undergraduate students were conveniently recruited to take part in this study from the class that an E-learning system was developed and implemented as part of the course requirement. To provide empirical data to answer two research questions proposed earlier, "Will a high level of H.I.R.E. lead to students' usage behaviors with the system?" and "Will a high level of H.I.R.E. lead to students' more favorable assessment with the system?", the author conducted both linear regression and correlation analyses to examine whether H.I.R.E. level can predict students' usage behaviors and favorable system function assessment.

The first research question asks whether students' H.I.R.E in the E-learning system predicts how they will assess various functions of the system. Linear regression analysis was used to analyze empirical data collected from the student users. In the linear regression model, the level of H.I.R.E. was found to positively predict students' assessment of the E-learning system ($ß=.85$, $t=9.63$, $p<.001$). The results indicate that the more favorable students have experienced when using the E-learning system, the more favorable they would assess the functionality of the system. This H.I.R.E. factor also predicted how many minutes, student participants have spent on the E-learning system once they have logged in ($ß=.38$, $t=2.51$, $p<.05$). The results suggest that the higher level of H.I.R.E. when students have experienced using the E-learning system, the longer they will spend on the system once they log in. However, the frequency of checking the E-learning system was not affected by the level of H.I.R.E. ($ß=.04$, $t=.23$, $p>.05$) (Refer to Table 4).

Table 4. Linear regression models

Linear Regression Tests	*β*	*t*
Model 1: F=92.76, df=1/37, p<.001		
H.I.R.E. Index (R^2 =.72, Durbin-Watson=1.86)		
Assessment of the E-learning System Functions	.85***	9.63***
Model 2: F=.05, df=1/37, p>.05		
H.I.R.E. Index (R^2 =0.00, Durbin-Watson=1.49)		
Frequency of Logging in the E-learning Website	.04	.23
Model 3: F=6.28, df=1/37, p<.05		
H.I.R.E. Index (R^2 =.15, Durbin-Watson=1.49)		
The Amount of Time Using the E-Learning Website		1..38* 2.51*
(in Minutes)		

Note:
[a]*** represents p<.001; ** represents p<.01, * represents p<.05

CONCLUSION

This book chapter was written to address the gap in the existing literature to better study user experiences with E-learning systems. This chapter also aims to providing a preliminary assessment of the current state, impacts, challenges, and opportunities of E-learning technologies in higher education institutions. The author paid particular attention to how the H.I.R.E. metrics can function as a conceptual and analytical tool to explain students' usage behaviors and subsequently to contribute to develop more engaging and effective E-learning systems. The author employed a quantitative survey method to collect data from undergraduate students conveniently recruited from a course that has integrated a web-based system into the pedagogy.

As demonstrated in the empirical results, the H.I.R.E. metrics serve as a good predictor of students' assessment of the E-learning system and also partially explain students' usage behaviors. The concept of H.I.R.E. has been found to be as a measure of users' experiential dimensions leads to more holistic system usage experiences, but not a rational assessment of each function. The partial predictive power of the HIRE metrics is likely to because actual usage behaviors may be contingent on many factors (Pahl & Donnellan, 2002; Thowfeek & Salam, 2014). For example, whether instructors require students to check the E-learning website regularly as a part of the course requirement might account for the frequency of accessing the technology. Other factors are likely to be whether students are interested in the course, whether students are familiar with the E-learning system, and whether instructors incorporate the E-learning system fully into the instructional process.

The advent of Web 2.0 and its applications has placed a lot of emphasis on creating "a user-centred design and interactive information sharing" (Cheung & Dubey, 2011, p. 387). As a result, digital learning scholars have increasingly advocated the importance of integrating students' needs in the design process, so user-friendly Web 2.0 applications can be developed in an educational context (Cheung & Dubey, 2011). The H.I.R.E. metrics, derived from the rhetorical study of user experiences in digital games (Kang,

2011), could be an important component of the E-learning research and will have significant theoretical and methodological implications. First, the exploration of user experience through the H.I.R.E. metrics will generate new experiential data that can be analyzed in empirical research to assess the effectiveness of any E-learning system. Similar experiential data were collected and reported in Ho's study (2009) in Taiwan where experiences with an E-learning system significantly correlated with perceived learning outcomes. Despite the breadth of E-learning research as an interdisciplinary academic endeavor, the foci of conventional approaches generally seem to ignore the experiential dimension of using these technologies in the educational setting. However, because the creation of user experience in these E-learning systems is often based on intense interactions between system designers, student users, and instructors, what students really experience are essential to develop better and more effective E-learning systems.

Secondly, the study of user experience in E-learning systems as a result of their encounters with persuasive design elements in the instructional process is the area worthy of digital learning scholars' attention. Insights from digital game research will be helpful to better understand user experience and interaction in these systems and applications. The experience includes the interactions with other users, with ample design elements by designers, and numerous persuasive acts by all participants in the instructional process. Through these interactions, new research data can be generated to better understand various issues related to the learning process occurring in any E-learning systems. Design elements embedded in these learning systems and applications can be argued as equivalents of rhetorical discourses produced by a rhetor, so users can be persuaded to take part in these systems in their educational process. The study of user experience with these E-learning systems helps educational scholars focus on the persuasive nature in the interaction process as demonstrated in the H.I.R.E metrics.

Thirdly, the H.I.R.E. metrics, developed from the line of rhetorical research, also offer a potentially powerful assessment instrument to examine the persuasive interactions critical to understanding what student users have experienced with E-learning systems. As a concept, H.I.R.E. is comprehensive enough to cover all key characteristics of E-learning systems. At the same time, H.I.R.E. examines one important aspect of user experiences; that is, being persuaded to interact with the design elements and with other participants' symbolic actions as conceptualized by Burke (1966). Because of E-learning systems and applications constantly change due to the interactions and manipulations of users using symbols to persuade and convince other users, the rhetorical approach of E-learning systems and applications as H.I.R.E. intends to investigate will help advance E-learning theories by examining the persuasive manipulations during interactions with the E-learning system as an important component of this line of research.

While this exploratory study lends support to the usefulness and rigor of the H.I.R.E. metrics in the educational context, the empirical results are constrained by the small and conveniently recruited student sample. Therefore, future research directions should include more classes that cover students' various HIRE experiences when using E-learning systems. Future research will help assess different E-learning system may also help validate and refine the H.I.R.E. scales. Furthermore, research using a mixed method to produce both qualitative and quantitative data will also help assess the emerging applications of many Web 2.0-based learning applications.

REFERENCES

Barassi, V., & Treré, E. (2012). Does Web 3.0 come after Web 2.0? Deconstructing theoretical assumptions through practice. *New Media & Society*, *14*(8), 1269–1285. doi:10.1177/1461444812445878

Burke, K. (1966). Language as symbolic action: Essays on life, literature, and method. Berkeley, CA: The University of California Press.

Burrill, D. A. (2005). Out of the box: Performance, drama, and interactive software. *Modern Drama*, *48*(3), 492–512. doi:10.3138/md.48.3.492

Çakıroğlu, Ü. (2014). Analyzing the effect of learning styles and study habits of distance learners on learning performances: A case of an introductory programming course. *The International Review of Research in Open and Distributed Learning*, *15*(4). Retrieved from http://www.irrodl.org/index.php/irrodl/article/view/1840/3004

Calvillo-Gámez, E. H., Cairns, P., & Cox, A. L. (2011). Assessing the core elements of the gaming experience. In R. Bernhaupt (Ed.), *Evaluating user experience in games: Concepts and methods* (pp. 41–71). London: Springer.

Cheng, B., Wang, M., Moormann, J., Olaniran, B. A., & Chen, N.-S. (2012, April). The effects of organizational learning environment factors on e-learning acceptance. *Computers & Education*, *58*(3), 885–899. doi:10.1016/j.compedu.2011.10.014

Cheung, C. K., & Dubey, A. (2011). Enhancement and expansion of language education in the internet era role of web 2.0 technologies. *Journal of Current Issues in Media and Telecommunications*, *2*(4), 387–403.

Deterding, S., Dixon, D., Khaled, R., & Nacke, L. (2011b). *From game design elements to gamefulness: Defining "gamification"*. Paper presented at the MindTrek '11, Tampere, Finland. Retrieved November 27, 2014 from https://www.cs.auckland.ac.nz/courses/compsci747s2c/lectures/paul/definition-deterding.pdf

Echeng, R., Usoro, A., & Majewski, G. (2013). *Acceptance of Web 2.0 in learning in higher education: An empirical study of a Scottish university.* Paper presented at the IADIS International Conference Web-Based Communities and Social Media 2013, Prague, Czech Republic.

Ehlers, U. D. (2009). Web 2.0 - e-learning 2.0 - quality 2.0? Quality for new learning cultures. *Quality Assurance in Education*, *17*(3), 296–314. doi:10.1108/09684880910970687

Eom, S. (2010). *Relationships between e-learning systems and learning outcomes: A path analysis model.* Paper presented at the 2010 IEEE 10th International Conference on Advanced Learning Technologies (ICALT), Sousse, Tunisia. doi:10.1109/ICALT.2010.147

Esnault, L. (2008). Web-based education and pedagogical technologies: Solutions for learning applications. Hershey, PA: IGI Global. doi:10.4018/978-1-59904-525-2

Fichten, C. S., Ferraro, V., Asuncion, J. V., Chwojka, C., Barile, M., & Nguyen, M. N. et al. (2009). Disabilities and e-learning problems and solutions: An exploratory study. *Journal of Educational Technology & Society*, *12*(4), 241–256.

Gee, J. P. (2007a). What video games have to teach us about learning and literacy? (Rev. and updated ed.). New York: Palgrave Macmillan.

Gee, J. P. (2007b). *Good video games + good learning: Collected essays on video games, learning and literacy*. New York: Peter Lang.

Gosper, M., McNeili, M., Woo, K., Phillips, R., Preston, G., & Green, D. (2011, November). Web-based lecture technologies and learning and teaching: A study of change in four Australian universities. *Journal of Asynchronous Learning Networks, 15*(4), 84–95.

Grodal, T. (2003). Stories for eye, ear, and muscles: Video games, media, and embodied experiences. In M. J. P. Wolf & B. Perron (Eds.), *The video game theory reader* (pp. 129–155). New York, NY: Routledge.

Hartnett, M., George, A. S., & Dron, J. (2011, October). Examining motivation in online distance learning environments: Complex, multifaceted, and situation-dependent. *Examining Motivation in Online Distance Learning Environments: Complex, Multifaceted, and Situation-Dependent, 12*(6). Retrieved October 5, 2015 from http://www.irrodl.org/index.php/irrodl/article/view/1030/1954

Heider, J. S. (2015, July). Using digital learning solutions to address higher education's greatest challenges. *Pub Res Q, 31*(3), 183–189. doi:10.1007/s12109-015-9413-8

Ho, L. A. (2009, Autumn). The antecedents of e-learning outcome: An examination of system quality, technology readiness, and learning behavior. *Adolescence, 44*(175), 581–599. PMID:19950871

Hui, K.-c., Pan, Z., Chung, R. C.-k., Wang, C. C. L., Jin, X., Göbel, S., et al. (2007, June 11-13). *Technologies for e-learning and digital entertainment.* Paper presented at the Second International Conference, Edutainment 2007, Hong Kong, China. doi:10.1007/978-3-540-73011-8

Humphreys, S. (2003). Online multi-user games. *Australian Journal of Communication, 30*(1), 79–91.

John, N. A. (2013, March). Sharing and web 2.0: The emergence of a keyword. *New Media & Society, 15*(2), 167–182. doi:10.1177/1461444812450684

Jones, N., & Vollmers, G. (2008). Using web-based technologies for transformative hybrid distance education. In L. Esnault (Ed.), Web-based education and pedagogical technologies: Solutions for learning applications (pp. 37-55). Hershey, PA: IGI Global. doi:10.4018/978-1-59904-525-2.ch003

Juul, J. (2005). Games telling stories? In J. Raessens & J. Goldstein (Eds.), Handbook of computer game studies (pp. 219-226). Cambridge, MA: The MIT Press.

Kang, Y. W. (2011). *Hybrid interactive rhetoric engagements in Massively Multiplayer Online Role-Playing Games (MMORPGs): Examining the role of rhetors and audiences in generative rhetorical discourses.* (Dissertation). The University of Texas at El Paso. Ann Arbor, M.I. UMI.

Karunasena, A., Deng, H., & Kam, B. (2013). *Investigating the enabling role of Web 2.0 technology for interactive e-learning in Australia.* Paper presented at the 24th Australasian Conference on Information Systems, ACIS2013, Melbourne, Australia.

Keramati, A., Afshari-Mofrad, M., & Kamrani, A. (2011, May). The role of readiness factors in e-learning outcomes: An empirical study. *Computers & Education, 57*(3), 1919–1929. doi:10.1016/j.compedu.2011.04.005

Krelja Kurelovic, E., Tomljanovic, J., & Ruzie-Baf, M. (2012). *The use of Web 2.0 tools in education from the point of view of future teachers.* Paper presented at the MIPRO 2012 - 35th International Convention on Information and Communication Technology, Electronics and Microelectronics, Opatija, Croatia.

Marcelo, C., Yot, C., & Mayor, C. (2015). University teaching with digital technologies. *Media Education Research Journal, 13*(45), 117–124.

Minović, M., Štavljanin, V., Milovanović, M., & Starčević, D. B. (2008). Usability issues of e-learning systems: Case-study for Moodle learning management system. In R. Meersman, Z. Tari, & P. Herrero (Eds.), *On the move to meaningful internet systems: OTM 2008 Workshops* (pp. 561–570). Berlin, Germany: Springer. doi:10.1007/978-3-540-88875-8_79

Motaghian, H., Hassanzadeh, A., & Moghadam, D. K. (2013, January). Factors affecting university instructors' adoption of web-based learning systems: Case study of Iran. *Computers & Education, 61*(1), 158–167. doi:10.1016/j.compedu.2012.09.016

Murray, M., & Jackson, P. (2009). *Web 2.0 in the classroom: The possibilities.* Paper presented at the Proceedings of the 2009 International SIGED: IAIM Conference, Phoenix, AZ.

Nehme, M. (2010, October29). E-learning and students' motivation. *Legal Education Review, 20*, 223–239.

O'Brien, H. L., & Toms, E. G. (2007). What is user engagement? A conceptual framework for defining user engagement with technology. *Journal of the American Society for Information Science and Technology, 59*(6), 938–955. doi:10.1002/asi.20801

Orchovacki, T., Granic, A., & Kermek, D. (2013, December). Evaluating the perceived and estimated quality in use of web 2.0 applications. *Journal of Systems and Software, 86*(12), 3039–3059. doi:10.1016/j.jss.2013.05.071

Pahl, C., & Donnellan, D. (2002). *Data mining technology for the evaluation of web-based teaching and learning systems.* Paper presented at the E-Learning 2002 World Conference on E-Learning, Montreal, Canada.

Pan, Z., Zhang, X., Rhalibi, A. E., Woo, W., & Li, Y. (2008, June 25-27). *Technologies for e-learning and digital entertainment.* Paper presented at the Third International Conference, Edutainment 2008, Nanjing, China.

Pappas, C. (2013, December 1). *Top 10 e-Learning statistics for 2014 you need to know.* Retrieved from http://elearningindustry.com/top-10-e-learning-statistics-for-2014-you-need-to-know

Pappas, C. (2015, May 26). *Top LMS Statistics and Facts For 2015 You Need to Know.* Retrieved September 18, 2015 from http://elearningindustry.com/top-lms-statistics-and-facts-for-2015

Pickering, A. (1995). The mangle of practice: Time, agency, & science. Chicago, IL: The University of Chicago Press.

Rahimi, E., Van Den Berg, J., & Veen, W. (2014). Facilitating student-driven constructing of learning environments using Web 2.0 personal learning environment. *Computers & Education, 81*, 235–246. doi:10.1016/j.compedu.2014.10.012

Rhoden, N. S. (2014). *A study of factors affecting the adoption of e-learning systems enabled with cultural contextual features by instructions in Jamaican tertiary institutions.* Colorado Technical University.

Ryan, M.-L. (1999). Immersion vs. interactivity: Virtual reality and literary theory. *SubStance*, *28*(2), 110–137. doi:10.1353/sub.1999.0015

Schertler, M., & Bodendorf, F. (2002). *Supporting communication processes in e-learning networks.* Paper presented at the International Conference on Computers in Education (ICCE 2002), Auckland, New Zealand. doi:10.1109/CIE.2002.1185924

Schmieder, E. J. (2008, March). Communication: The tool to interact with and control your online classroom environment. *International Journal of Instructional Technology and Distance Learning*, *5*(3). Retrieved from http://www.itdl.org/journal/mar_2008/article2003.htm

Sendall, P., Ceccucci, W., & Peslak, A. (2008). *Web 2.0 matters: An analysis of implementing web 2.0 in the classroom.* Paper presented at the Information Systems Education Conference 2008, ISECON 2008, Phoenix, AZ.

Shih, P.-C., Munoz, D., & Sanchez, F. (2006, November). The effect of previous experience with information and communication technologies on performance in a web-based learning program. *Computers in Human Behavior*, *22*(6), 962–970. doi:10.1016/j.chb.2004.03.016

Tavinor, G. (2005, April). Videogames and interactive fiction. *Philosophy and Literature*, *29*(1), 24–40. doi:10.1353/phl.2005.0015

Thowfeek, M. H., & Hussin, H. (2008). Instructors' perspective on e-learning adoption in Sri Lanka: A preliminary investigation. *Communications of the IBIMA*, *6*, 124–129.

Thowfeek, M. H., & Salam, M. N. A. (2014, August). Students' assessment on the usability of e-learning websites. *Procedia: Social and Behavioral Sciences*, *141*, 916–922. doi:10.1016/j.sbspro.2014.05.160

Vorderer, P., & Bryant, J. (2006). *Playing video games: Motives, responses, and consequences*. Mahwah, NJ: Lawrence Erlbaum Associates.

Wan, L. (2010). *Application of Web 2.0 technologies in e-learning context.* Paper presented at the 2010 International Conference on Networking and Digital Society, ICNDS 2010, Wenzhou, China.

Zagal, J., Chan, S. S., & Zhang, J. (2011). *Measuring flow experience of computer game players.* Paper presented at the AMCIS 2010. Retrieved October 10, 2015 from http://aisel.aisnet.org/amcis2010/137

ADDITIONAL READING

Aarseth, E., Smedstad, S. M., & Sunnanå, L. (2003). *A multi-dimensional typology of games.* Paper presented at the Level Up: Digital Games Research Conference Proceedings, Utrecht, the Netherlands: Universteit Utrecht.

Alfaro, M. J. M. (1996, December). Intertextuality: Origins and development of the concept. *Atlantis*, *18*(1/2), 268–285.

Ang, C. S. (2006, September). Rules, gameplay, and narratives in video games. *Simulation & Gaming*, *37*(3), 306–325. doi:10.1177/1046878105285604

Bogost, I. (2007, July). *Persuasive games: The expressive power of videogames*. Cambridge, M.A.: MIT Press.

Coffee, E., Koenig, J.-P., Poornima, S., Ossewaarde, R., Forstall, C., & Jacobson, S. (2012). Autunm). Intertextuality in the digital age. *Transactions of the American Philological Association*, *142*(2), 383–422. doi:10.1353/apa.2012.0010

D'Angelo, F. J. (2010). The rhetoric of intertextuality. *Rhetoric Review*, *29*(1), 31–47. doi:10.1080/07350190903415172

Elverdam, C., & Aarseth, E. (2007, January). Game classification and game design: Construction through critical analysis. *Games and Culture*, *2*(1), 3–22. doi:10.1177/1555412006286892

Haverila, M. (2011, June). Prior e-learning experience and perceived learning outcomes in an undergraduate e-learning course. *MERLOT Journal of Online Learning and Teaching*, *7*(2), 206–218.

Kafai, Y. B. (1995). *Minds in play: Computer game design as a context for children's learning*. Hillsdale, N.J.: Lawrence Erlbaum Associates.

Kiousis, S. (2002). Interactivity: A concept explication. *New Media & Society*, *4*(3), 355–383. doi:10.1177/146144480200400303

Klabbers, J. H. G. (2003, November 4-6). *The gaming landscape: A taxonomy for classifying games and simulations*. Paper presented at the LEVEL UP: Digital Games Research Conference, University of Utrecht, The Netherlands.

Myers, S. A., & Goodboy, A. K., Members, of, & 600, C. (2014, January-March). College student learning, motivation, and satisfaction as a function of effective instructor communication behaviors. *The Southern Communication Journal*, *79*(1), 14–26.

Reeves, B., & Read, J. L. (2009). Total engagement: Using games and virtual worlds to change the way people work and businesses compete. Cambridge, M.A.: Harvard Business Press.

Salen, K., & Zimmerman, E. (2005). Game design and meaningful play. In J. Raessens & J. Goldstein (Eds.), Handbook of computer game studies (pp. 59-79). Cambridge, M.A.: The MIT Press.

Song, S. M. (2010). *E-learning: Investigating students' acceptance of online learning in hospitality programs*. Unpublished doctoral dissertation, Iowa State University, Ames, Iowa.

Turkle, S. (1984). *The second self: Computers and the human spirit*. New York, N.Y.: Simon and Schuster.

Yates, S. J., & Littleton, K. (1999, December). Understanding computer game cultures: A situated approach. *Information Communication and Society*, *2*(4), 566–583. doi:10.1080/136911899359556

KEY TERMS AND DEFINITIONS

Digital Game: Known as video games or computer games. According to *DiGra*, digital games or video games refer to a game which users play through audio-visual platforms with contents on the basis of a story. The concept of digital games as represented in existing game studies literature focuses on game itself, narrative (story), interactivity, and play.

E-Learning: The term is defined as a method of learning, supported by the use of information-communication technologies. Educational scholars often claim that E-learning is capable of transforming how teachers teach to improve learning.

Engagement: Engagement is a psychological construct that refers to how and whether individuals are satisfied with and immersed in the interaction process with E-learning systems.

Game Genre: A term that refers to how digital games can be categorized by examining various types of gameplay interactions, instead of classifying the games on the basis of narrative and visual differences. The classification of game genre is often based on challenges, plot, characters, settings, etc., in a digital game.

Gameplay: This term refers to how players interact with textual, non-textual, and contextual in-game design elements in digital games. This term often refers to a set of behavioral patterns as programmed by the embedded procedural rules that allow players to interact with each other and with the game through audio, visual, textual, and kinetic in-game design elements during gameplay.

H.I.R.E: The term is abbreviated from *hybrid interactive rhetorical engagement* and coined as a concept and analytical unit to examine the gameplay process as experienced by the gamers. The examination of gameplay experiences when gamers take part in any digital game. H.I.R.E. refers to a state of engaging and interactive gameplay experiences when interacting with other gamers in MMORPGs.

Hybrid: A concept describing a variety of in-game design elements such as audio, visual, textual, and kinetic messages. Also known as multi-modal or multi-platforms.

Interactivity: A term commonly used in information science, computer science, human-computer interaction, communication, and digital humanity research. The concept of interactivity refers to the capability of the information-communication technologies to allow two-way interaction among participants in a communication process.

MMORPGs: Abbreviated from Massively Multiplayer Online Role-Playing Games that encompass role-playing functions and enable multiple players at various locations to compete in a virtual world. MMORPGs refer to any computer network-mediated games where thousands of gamers are role-playing simultaneously in a graphical and 3-D environment. Popular subscription-based MMORPGs include *Ultima Online*, *EverQuest*, *World of Warcarft*, and *Second Life*. Free MMORPGs are also available to the public. Some of the top MMORPGs are *Neverwinter*, *Aura Kingdom*, *Tera Rising*, *Planet Calypso*, *Albione Online*, etc.

Perceived Ease of Use (PEOU): An important belief component in the technology acceptance models (such as TAM and TAM2). The term is defined by Davis (1989) as "the degree to which a person believes that using a particular system would be free from effort."

Perceived Usefulness (PU): A key belief component in the technology acceptance models (such as TAM and TAM2). The term is defined by Davis (1989) as "the degree to which a person believes that using a particular system would enhance his or her job performance."

Rhetorical Engagements: Referring to a series of rhetorical events made possible by the interactivity, immersion, interconnectivity, and role-playing functions abundant in MMORPGs.

The Unified Theory of Acceptance and Use of Technology (UTAUT) Model: A revised model proposed by Venkatesh et al. (2003) to examine information technology acceptance and use. The model is composed of eight significant user acceptance of new information technology to predict user behavioral intention and usage. These factors include performance expectancy, effort expectancy, attitude toward using technology, social influence, facilitating conditions, self-efficacy, and anxiety.

User Experience (UX): The concept refers to how an individual's attitudes, behaviors, and emotions are influenced through interaction with a particular product, system, or service. This term is commonly used in the human-computer interface (HCI) literature to describe the affective, meaningful, experiential, and practical aspects of human experiences.

Web 2.0: A term was coined during a conference brainstorming session between O'Reilly and MediaLive International. Web 2.0 refers to the latest developments of online technology when compared with the earlier applications of the Web. Web 2.0 applications are characterized by greater user interactivity and collaboration. Their applications also refer to more omnipresent network connectivity and improved communication channels.

World of Warcraft (*WoW*): A popular MMORPG product that was created in 2004 by Blizzard Entertainment. Various versions have been developed as part of the *WoW* franchise.

Chapter 16
Challenges in Using Cloud Technology for Promoting Learner Autonomy in a Spanish Language Course:
Reshaping Pedagogical Design

Jaya Kannan
Sacred Heart University, USA

Pilar Munday
Sacred Heart University, USA

ABSTRACT

In a digitally networked classroom, the learner connects with peers, instructors, and open resources, be they human experts or online resources in non-linear combinations. As a result, the learner must navigate a complex web of associations and pathways. Thus the teacher practitioner who uses the networked medium as the platform for facilitating language learning has the challenge of developing methodologies, task-based activities, and a selection of tools to frame a learning ground that will provide maximum opportunity for the student to strengthen learning. This chapter will present a case study of a teacher practitioner's pedagogical design process in an online undergraduate course, "Advanced Grammar and Culture through Social Media." The main focus of this case study is to identify key challenges for pedagogical design and offer the rhizomatic approach as a model to promote learner autonomy.

INTRODUCTION

Empowering language learning students to develop autonomously seems more attainable today than ever before because of networked environments using cloud technology tools. These tools have the innate ability to create connected learning communities and to place language learning within a global-

DOI: 10.4018/978-1-5225-1650-7.ch016

ized sociocultural context. This should be an immense advantage to educators in promoting autonomy. Learners could take charge of their learning (Holec, 1981, p.3) by framing thier own language learning gaols and sculpting their individualized paths to develop autonomously. Merely situating students with a networked environment, however, cannot guarantee the emergence of autonomy. Pedagogical design also has a crucial role to play in shaping student participation and attitudes, and in providing accessible opportunities. Pedagogical design is defined by Romiszowski as "any systematic choice and use of procedures, methods, prescriptions, and devices in order to bring about effective, efficient, and productive learning" (as qtd. in Halttunen, 2011, p. 62). In a digitally networked classroom, the learner connects with peers, instructors, and open resources, be they human experts or online resources in non-linear combinations. As a result, the learner must navigate a complex web of associations and pathways. Thus the teacher practitioner who uses the networked medium as the platform for facilitating language learning has the challenge of developing methodologies, activities, and a selection of tools to frame a learning ground that will provide maximum opportunity for the student to strengthen learning. Formulating this design and arriving at such an optimal template can pose several challenges for course design. (For a review about the importance of networked learning, see Goodyear et al., 2004).

Even before this age of digital disruption, foreign language teaching has been at the forefront of autonomy studies for more than four decades, starting with the publication of *Autonomy and Foreign Language Learning* by Holec in 1979. According to Little (2003), "if language learning depends crucially on language use, learners who enjoy a high degree of social autonomy in their learning environment should find it easier than otherwise to master the full range of discourse roles on which effective spontaneous communication depends."

The learning space within the digitally networked classroom is non-linear by default. The inability to predict what the next nodal connection will bring to the student's learning path is the norm, not the outlier. Under these conditions, how can the teacher practitioner, who is working within a formal education system that imposes the boundaries of a Learning Management System (LMS) space and semester-based timelines, design a course that truly promotes autonomy?

This chapter will present a case study of a teacher practitioner's pedagogical design process in an online undergraduate course, "Advanced Grammar and Culture through Social Media." The main focus of this case study is a professional development exercise in which the teacher practitioner went through one cycle of planning, piloting, reflecting on results, and identifying key challenges.

There were three main pedagogical objectives for integrating cloud technologies in this course: the first was to innovatively use an assemblage of cloud technology tools in order to build a suitable learning environment for the students in a way that cannot usually be achieved in face-to-face settings. The second objective was to map out a methodology for exposing students to the sociocultural components available in a global setting via cloud technology tools. The third objective, in keeping with the decades of foreign language research in autonomy studies, was to use multiple pathways of learning as an avenue for the development of learner autonomy.

The final assignment in the course was for each student to create his or her own personal learning network (PLN) for the continuation of their Spanish studies. Students were required to do this using cloud technology tools such as Google+ communities, Google Hangouts, Tackk, and Instagram. Each student creating a PLN with these cloud technology tools employed a unique process to arrive at a final product, and was expected to autonomously enhance his or her Spanish language competency. Warschauer and Liaw's (2011) evaluation of emerging technologies validates the potential of emerging technologies for language learning in such contexts. They "provide flexible means to develop language and literacy skills through authentic communication, collaboration, networking and scaffolding. They represent autonomous learning tools that can be placed in the hands of each individual learner, thus offering excellent ways to meet the needs of diverse students" (Warschauer & Liaw, 2011, p.116).

In examining the results from the case study, it became evident that there were gaps between the intended pedagogical design of promoting learner autonomy and learning outcomes. The limitations shown by the study can help to identify pedagogical challenges relating to access, participation, and learner attitude.

Through the lens of these key challenges, this chapter will explore this fundamental question: even with the establishment of networked learning environments, does adherence to a rigid approach to facilitating learning prevent students from growing as autonomous learners? Some researchers already seem to think this is the case (Hurd et al, 2001; Sasser, 2012).

An important next step in refining the pedagogical design for the next iteration was to consider an alternate theoretical framework for addressing the challenges. One such framework is the rhizomatic approach. The basic idea of this approach as posited by Deleuze and Guatarri (1987) is to view connected learning as essentially non-linear and unstructured. A 2004 study by Lian exploring the suitability of a rhizomatic approach for technology-enhanced language learning summed up the strength of the rhizomatic approach in this way: "The strength of the system lies not only in each of its parts, but particularly in the high level of connectivity between its parts" (Lian, 2004. p.1). "In a learning structure, it means that learners are able to connect from any activity or information point to any other activity or information point according to perceived need. A rhizomatic structure should not be thought of as chaotic, but rather as a self-regulating structure responsive to the learners' needs as determined by the mechanisms in place (human or otherwise) for determining such needs" (Lian, 2004, p.5). This chapter will conclude by considering the rhizomatic approach as an important theoretical framework that could provide a practical solution to the challenges faced in this case study.

CASE STUDY

Course Description

Summary Description of the Course

We will examine the case study of an online course in an undergraduate Spanish language curriculum. Fourteen students of varying language competencies attended this course, most of them Spanish majors or minors. The Foreign Languages and Cultures Department piloted this course in the fall 2014 semester as a pioneering attempt at the University to integrate multiple cloud technology tools for language learning. The course used Blackboard, the standard Learning Management System (LMS) at the institution mainly for the administrative purpose of information dissemination. The LMS was the place where students could view weekly announcements (which were also sent to students by e-mail), find modules and grammar units, and also see their grades in the Gradebook function. Keeping the Blackboard LMS as the central core, several activities using cloud technology tools were built around it.

Course Objectives

The title of the course was Advanced Grammar and Culture through Social Media. Here is a short description of the three main learning objectives (L.O): L.O. #1: The student will achieve a higher level of proficiency in Spanish by reviewing advanced grammar topics, which will be practiced via social media. L.O. #2: The student will identify some key concepts related to digital citizenship, such as digital footprint, content curation, privacy, and ethics, and will develop their own personal learning network to be used to augment their knowledge of the culture and language of the Spanish-speaking world. L.O. #3: The student will learn how to create a blog where he/she will be able to reflect on both the advanced grammar as well as the social and cultural aspects learned throughout the course. These explicit learning objectives are tied to the implicit objective of autonomy, which will be part of the discussion in this chapter.

As a final project for the course, each student had to create a Personal Learning Network (PLN) to strengthen Spanish language competency and foster learner autonomy within a learning community. During the semester and leading up to the final project, students were required to use several cloud technology tools, among them Google Apps (including Google+ communities, Slides and Hangouts), Blogger, Tackk, and Instagram. Each student had to create the final project (PLN) using these and other cloud technology tools, thus taking on the role of co-creator, contributor, and negotiator of learning. Each student had to come up with their own process for developing a customized PLN, and apply this PLN for enhancing their Spanish language competency.

Student Profile

The students attending the course were a very heterogeneous group in many respects: their ages ranged from 19 to 65 (two were older female students); half were commuters and half lived on campus; three were native speakers of Spanish who were Spanish majors; most had not taken an online course before; and most were not particularly comfortable or competent with cloud technology tools. For example, one of them did not have a smartphone (although she bought an iPad in the middle of the semester to complete some of the tasks), and at least half of the class had never taken a screenshot before.

Macro and Micro Levels of the Course

At the macro level, the pedagogical design for the entire course will be summarized to highlight the many variables of networked learning. At the micro level, a single activity, namely that of teaching the subjunctive, will be discussed as a subset of the larger complex pedagogical design.

Macro Level: Connected Tools Used in the Course

In this section, the focus will be the pedagogical design of the course, including the creation of connected learning spaces. It will show how these spaces are relevant to the use of cloud technology tools throughout the course.

Because this course was about learning through social media, with the ultimate goal of having students create their own PLN, it was imperative for the design of the course itself to contain networked elements. Although there was conceptually a potential for networked learning within Blackboard, it was very limited in scope and structurally inadequate for the academic vision envisaged by the instructor.

As an LMS, Blackboard is in fact not an ideal place for cloud-based networked learning. As Velestianos et al. (2013) pointed out in their review of the literature, "LMS have been described as tools that fail to provide users with the individual social presence necessary for more robust and valuable networking experiences that are essential for learning" (p. 257). Indeed, we found it advisable to follow Dalsgaard's schema. According to Dalsgaard, "a student-centered approach to e-learning is approached by: 1) using a management system for administrative issues, 2) offering students personal tools for construction, presentation, reflection, collaboration, etc., 3) facilitating networks between students within the same course, and 4) facilitating networks between students and other people working within the field." Blackboard therefore complied with the University's standards by serving as the core platform for administrative communications only. Several cloud technology tools were then integrated and linked to Blackboard to build a more robust networked framework. With this in mind, the following tools were incorporated into this class in addition to the LMS, which was used mainly for administrative issues as described above.

The integration of several social media networks such as Google+ community, Google Hangout, and Instagram provided an outer circle for enriching digital interactions. To meet the institution's course standards, the Blackboard LMS remained the core within which most of the social media networks could be combined. This expanded the horizons for digital discourse in a number of ways – a) it helped to move out of the confines of the Blackboard learning space, allowing access to resources and Spanish language users by building an outer circle of cloud-based Spanish learning resources, b) it connected the students with native speakers of Spanish for language learning, c) it provided alternate networked platforms for building on the power of peer learning, and d) it provided alternate channels of feedback from the instructor to the students.

To create a manageable network design, the instructor selected the tools so that they worked together as a comprehensive toolset for the course activities. It was important that the individual use of these tools did not seem disjointed and the structure and scheduling of each tool had a specific purpose for meeting the course objectives. Although a number of cloud technology tools were used, they intersected meaningfully for specific language learning tasks.

Cloud Technology Tools: For a brief description of how each cloud technology tool - Google + communities, Blogger, Google Hangouts, Instagram, Google Slides, and Tackk was used to meet the course objectives, please see Appendix 1.

In addition to these tools, students could choose any other social networking site to find examples for completing their assignments. Students stated that they used Facebook, Twitter, Pinterest, YouTube, Vine, Tumblr, and others. They shared their examples in the Google+ community. They had total flexibility to incorporate some of these tools into their final PLN project. Students mentioned (and showed) that they followed native Spanish speakers and Spanish news (or sports or entertainment) accounts in these social networks, which was not a requirement for the class. Two students even communicated with the instructor via twitter in Spanish. All of this is evidence for the emergence of social autonomy, so crucial to language learning.

Many specific features of the tools that were used lend themselves to networked learning. Students become co-creators by finding the relevant examples and creating a timeline of them for their classmates, contributors by sharing their findings and learning from each other, and negotiators by navigating diverse social media sites to find the relevant examples and clearly presenting them to their classmates.

Table 1 shows when the different tools were used during the semester. It provides a summarized structure for the 16-week course and the sequence in which the different tools were used.

Table 1. Use of tools during the semester

	LMS	Tackk	Google+ Community	Instagram	Google Hangouts	Blogger	Google Slides
8/25/2014	Required	Required	Required			Required	
9/1/2014	Required	Required	Required			Required	
9/8/2014	Required	Required	Required		Required	Required	
9/15/2014	Required	Required	Required		Required	Required	
9/22/2014	Required	Required	Required		Required	Required	
9/29/2014	Required	Required	Required		Required	Required	Required
10/6/2014	Required	Required	Required		Required	Required	
10/13/2014	Required	Required		Required			
10/20/2014	Required	Required		Required	Required		
10/27/2014	Required	Required		Required	Required		Required
11/3/2014	Required	Required	Required		Required	Required	
11/10/2014	Required	Required	Required		Required	Required	
11/17/2014	Required	Required	Required		Required	Required	
11/24/2014	Required	Required	Required			Optional	
12/1/2014	Required	Required	Required		Required	Optional	
12/8/2014	Required	Required	Required	Optional		Required	Optional

Micro Level: The Teaching of the Subjunctive

In order to see how these interactions worked on a daily basis, we decided to explore how one particular activity, namely the review of the subjunctive tense, took place and impacted the development of learner autonomy. This was part of Learning Objective #1 (The student will achieve a higher level of proficiency in Spanish by reviewing advanced grammar topics, which will be practiced via social media).

During the course of the semester, three weeks were allotted to studying the proper usage of the subjunctive. Beginning with the forms themselves, the review of the subjunctive then moved to normal use in three grammatical contexts: noun clauses, adjectival clauses, and adverbial clauses. Most of the students had already studied the subjunctive in previous courses, since the topic is usually introduced at the end of first-year Spanish, and then covered again at the intermediate level and in more advanced levels. The only students who were unaware of the subjunctive were the three native speakers. Thus the review was useful for them as well, since they could recognize correct or incorrect use of the subjunctive but did not know the underlying principles. The goal was for students to remember (or learn) what the subjunctive was and be able to recognize it when they saw it produced by native speakers in different social media outlets.

Because the subjunctive is used often in Spanish but only rarely in English, it can be difficult to grasp fully. Many advanced speakers of the language still make mistakes when trying to produce it. To achieve the aforementioned goal, the following steps had to be considered when designing the activity:

Step 1 - Comprehend the Concept: The online textbook used during the full course was a website, Spanish Grammar Online, created by Dr. Enrique Yepes from the University of Bowdoin. This book/website was chosen because it contains very clear explanations in English and also has many exercises that can be completed online. Some of the exercises had to be submitted for a grade, but most of them were not required. Instead, students could complete them, take a screenshot of their results, and send them to the instructor as extra credit. Approximately 30% of the students took advantage of this option. Reading the book entries about the subjunctive was a required first step for every student. The instructor did not provide any formal instruction. Thus this was designed as an autonomous exercise to comprehend the subjunctive.

Step 2 - Recognize the Subjunctive: Once the students completed the first step, they then had to apply their learning of the subjunctive by identifying correct examples from actual social media posts, and demonstrate their understanding by posting materials from global online resources. The students were required to perform the following tasks: (1) find an example of subjunctive use in social media, (2) post a link to the example and an image (if Google+ does not create the image), (3) add specific information about the example, e.g. number of the grammar section in the online textbook, explanation of what the example shows (e.g.: subjunctive in noun clause). In theory, students would also validate their learning through interactions with peers. Interactions between students did not occur naturally, however, so the instructor chose to make two comments mandatory. This intervention was intended to increase interactional discourse.

Step 3 - Apply the Subjunctive in the Students' Own Usage: The third step was to incorporate the subjunctive into their own writing when creating their blog posts on Blogger. To receive the highest grade for their posts, students had to send a draft to the instructor and mark clearly which sentences included the subjunctive, so that they could be reviewed before posting to the public. This was an optional step (to be done only if the student wanted an "A" for their blog post), only some 10% of the students chose to perform this task. More than half the students did not incorporate the studied grammatical items into their blogs.

Step 4 – Provide Learning Support through Effective Scaffolding: Support for learning the subjunctive was provided through the Google Hangout sessions. These served as virtual office hours for students who wanted to seek clarifications. Students were required to participate in at least two sessions during the course of the semester. Ninety percent of the students utilized this resource, many more often than the requirement, and reported it to be very useful.

RESULTS

Data Collection and Methodology

Data was primarily obtained from three sources: (1) an online survey, conducted after the mid-term point in the semester and completed by eighty percent of students; (2) focus groups interviews led by a research assistant, with forty percent participation; (3) student posts in the Google+ community over a period of three weeks, which were analyzed in detail to ascertain the level of student engagement. See Appendix 2 for the survey questions, Appendix 3 for a complete summary of the answers to the focus group questions, and Appendix 4 for information on how levels of engagement were established.

The online survey and the focus group interviews were centered on three main issues: (1) access - technical difficulties, hardware or software issues, lack of knowledge about a tool; (2) participation - students' willingness to interact with others, opinions about the Google+ community and other tools in terms of ease of use or usefulness; (3) deep learning – demonstration of Spanish language acquisition based on coursework, etc. Analyzing the students' posts also provided information on student engagement in one specific task within a limited period.

This triangulation of data from the survey, focus group, and evidence of participation in the cloud-based learning spaces permitted observation both at the macro level of the course and at the micro level of learning the subjunctive. It allowed the authors to examine the students' perceptions regarding access, participation and deep learning, as well as the level of student engagement in the course. The following section will present these two levels in more detail.

The first part of the results will focus on presenting which aspects of the pedagogical design worked in promoting autonomy for each of the three learning objectives. This will be followed by a summary of several challenges found in pedagogical design when integrating the cloud technology tools for Spanish language learning.

The summary of results provided below are divided into two sections: 1) results for the entire course are described under the Macro level results, with a focus on accomplishment of the three learning objectives, 2) results specific to the teaching activity of the subjunctive are covered under the Micro level results.

Macro Level Results: Learning Objectives

Learning Objective #1: The student will achieve a higher level of proficiency in Spanish by reviewing advanced grammar topics, which will be practiced via social media.

Several elements relating to access contributed to the emergence of autonomy in the activities for this learning objective. The level of comfort with the use of cloud technology tools and the ease of dialogic discourse in the grammar activities was high enough for two students to express preference for collaboration and communication within the class group through Google+ rather than Blackboard. One student described his ability to make meaning when he wrote that the grammar activities were "easier to understand when you can see it and manipulate on your own than just learning it from someone who lectures." Student survey results indicated that they valued the human element in the interactions, emphasizing their appreciation of "learning from real people" and "sharing the grammar learning with each other." They added that "learning from real Spanish language examples on the social media" validated their understanding of the Spanish language grammar concepts. Deep learning was conveyed by students in statements that affirmed their awareness of how they were learning. One student highlighted that the Instagram activity (in which students posted daily pictures accompanied by a sentence using the aspect of grammar being studied) helped her think about Spanish actively every day. Thus the Instagram-based task was an effective practice tool for strengthening her knowledge of Spanish grammar. The instructor had suggested Duolingo, an online program for practicing Spanish grammar, as an optional open educational resource for the students. Because Duolingo was not compulsory, only thirty percent of the students in the class used it as a resource for their learning. One student, however, showed autonomy by using Duolingo to consult with external users (i.e. who were not in his class) to check his translation homework before submitting it to the instructor. This proactive approach of reaching out to an open resource within the networked environment outside the classroom showed that students were negotiating their own paths of learning within the digitally networked classroom.

Figure 1 shows a student posting an example of the use of the subjunctive after the word "quizá" (maybe). A mini-conversation develops when the instructor mentions that the image comes from a famous Spanish online store. Another student responds that she has visited the site, using the phrase "acabo de visitar" (I just visited the website), which contains another one of the grammatical structures reviewed in the course. A second student also comments on the use of the subjunctive as well as the quote itself.

Learning Objective #2: The student will identify some key concepts related to digital citizenship, such as digital footprint, content curation, privacy and ethics and will develop their own personal learning network to be used to augment their knowledge of the culture and language of the Spanish speaking world.

With the exception of one student, who opted out of the course (at the beginning of the semester) because of challenges with technological access, students did not exhibit any resistance to the use of cloud technology tools. This is an important factor, given that the course was completely online and participation in Google+, Blogger and Instagram assignments formed a primary part of the course. At least three students stated that they occasionally felt overwhelmed having to participate across different cloud technology tools. By the end of the semester, however, they had become more comfortable with the technology. Two students who were in their sixties took the initiative to meet with the instructor on campus to gain the necessary proficiency with cloud technology tools. This was a powerful example of

Figure 1. Student showing an example of the subjunctive from an image in Pinterest

taking charge of one's own learning, especially since these were not regular students enrolled for the entire undergrad program. At the end of the semester, these students explicitly shared their enthusiasm at being able to continue using Google+ community and Instagram even after the end of the course.

Students learned to participate multi-modally in order to develop their sense of autonomy. For example, several features of Google+ provided a variety of participation opportunities: Google Hangouts allowed for face-to-face interactions with the instructor, while the Google+ community was used for specific collaboration tasks. Instagram was seen as beneficial by students for "forcing [them] to participate." The simple Instagram task requiring students to post appropriate pictures to demonstrate their knowledge of Spanish was quoted as "enjoyable." In using the Google+ community, students had to find effective ways to manage their discourse and provide quality feedback to peers. With almost no prompting, students chose to use the "+1" feature to validate the learning summarized in a peer's post. As one student wrote, "the course was overall enjoyable and helped me to learn not just as student but as a person."

This distinction of seeing oneself as a person who is a lifelong learner, as opposed to a student within a limited, semester-bound context, was an important factor in the development of learner autonomy. Students also indicated that on their own initiative, they "followed" some of these native speakers or Spanish language news accounts to augment their learning. Another characteristic of learner autonomy was brought out through students' awareness of a deep learning approach. Students seemed to be cognizant of "learning how to learn" by combining their participation in the different cloud technology tools to shape their language learning process. Many students commented that the search for examples in real-life feeds (from other social media sites such as Twitter or Pinterest, which were not part of their regular coursework) taught them about digital citizenship in Spanish-speaking countries and in their own lives.

More than half of the students in the class also said they were highly motivated to continue using these social media tools for their learning much beyond the scope of this course. In addition to tools such as Twitter or YouTube used in the class, one student added many more, including Skype, Viber, WhatsApp, and Snapchat. For this student, the purpose of using several tools was to communicate directly with her Spanish-speaking friends from other countries.

Learning Objective #3: The student will learn how to create a blog where he/she will be able to reflect on both the advanced grammar as well as the social and cultural aspects learned throughout the course.

All of the students were able to use the Google Blogger platform to create their own blog for posting their assignments. According to the student survey results, student stated that there were few issues with access. Students also stated in the online survey that the level of technology skills required was not too high. The opportunity to navigate through the different cloud technology tools helped each student to arrive at his/her own individual preferences. For example, one student thought that the use of Instagram was more effective in grasping the grammar concept than the way in which the learning activity was designed within Google+. The blog served the dual purpose of summarizing the students' learning experiences in the cloud environment and demonstrating their understanding of the grammar concepts, since they had to write entirely in Spanish. Students used their learning of Google Slides (which they were required to embed into their blogs for one assignment) in this course to work with students in another course who had not used Google Slides before. Their ability to transfer knowledge and technological skillset was clearly illustrated in the sociocultural context of learning Spanish. One representative student comment was that "I have learned about the uses of social media in many different countries from Google+ and our blogs." Because of her interactions in social media, one student could distinguish between Spanish in the classroom and Spanish used by native speakers from different Spanish speaking countries. According to the student she was able to make such a critical observation only because of the opportunity to engage in Spanish through Google+ with native speakers outside the U.S and online resources.

Figure 2 shows a sample student blog. Because these are public blogs, the instructor asked that students not use their real names, but instead create a pseudonym, in this case "Ava." On the right side of the screen, the student incorporated a blog roll of her classmates' blogs so that she could easily access them when she needed to make comments (a required task in the course). In this particular post, the student has embedded a Google Slide she had created to talk about social networking in Spain (each student had to research one specific Spanish-speaking country).

Micro Level Results: Teaching the Subjunctive

To understand this pedagogical design in greater depth, we will move from the results of student learning at the macro level (observations about the entire course) to the results observed at the micro level of a specific activity. This activity description for teaching the subjunctive has already been completed above. Following is a summary of results from the students' coursework for the activities related to the teaching of the subjunctive:

Students demonstrated their learning of the subjunctive in different ways Many students were able to find excellent examples of subjunctive use in quotes by native speakers, particularly in Pinterest. One student found a very funny video in Vine with another good example. A few interesting dialogues developed. One conversation in particular was not about the subjunctive, but about a topic in life in general, saying good-bye to loved ones (in Spanish) (see Figure 3). This reflected how the student's own interest guided her to another learning point outside the subject.

Figure 2. Example of a student's blog

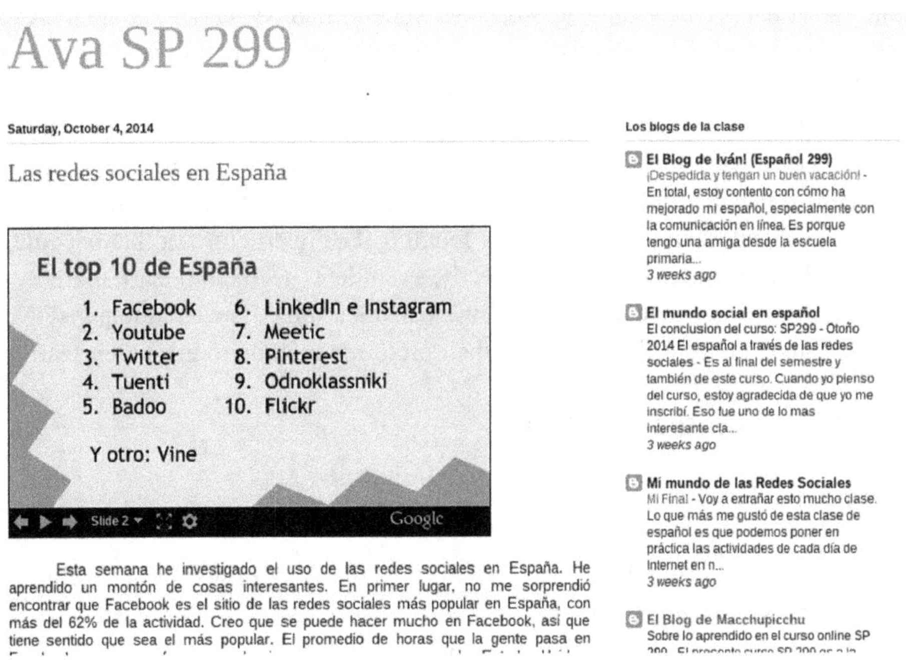

Figure 3. Reviewing the subjunctive in Google+ community

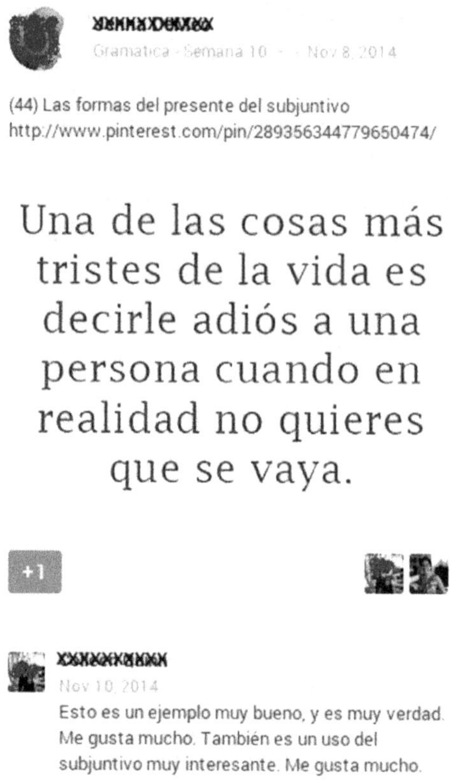

This student's example shows good understanding of the subjunctive in noun clauses after "querer que" (to want someone to do something).

To avoid using formal teacher-taught approaches, students had been asked not to use examples from open resource materials created by Spanish teachers. Instead, the instructor had recommended that that students show how the subjunctive is used by native speakers in informal interactions. Going against this advice, a few students kept choosing examples produced by teachers. In one instance, the student chose a YouTube video with specific rules on how to use the subjunctive in adjectival clauses. The instructor commented that she found it boring, but two of the students (in addition to the student who created the post) commented on how useful they found it. The instructor felt that her rule of not using teachers' materials had been then "broken" correctly, as students seemed to learn more from that video than from an example of native speaker use (unanticipated learning).The unanticipated learning for the instructor was that students were able to choose their preferred method to meet their learning objective.

Challenges for Pedagogical Design

Macro Level Issues

The purpose of creating a Personal Learning Network as the final project was to strengthen Spanish language competency and foster learner autonomy within a learning community. Students were required to use cloud technology tools such as Google+ communities, Google Hangouts, Tackk, and Instagram.

Each student had a unique process for developing a customized PLN, and was expected to autonomously enhance his/her Spanish language competency. In her reflection process at the end of the semester, the teacher practitioner identified several issues in the pedagogical design that she intends to resolve for the next run of this course:

- The way in which the learning design combined different cloud technology tools was quite complex. The need to handle multiple cloud technology tools within an online course was overwhelming for the students at the beginning of the course. There was a steep learning curve in the beginning, although an improved level of comfort led to ease of use before mid-semester.
- The week-by-week structure was rigid, requiring students to work in sequence with a particular cloud technology tool for a limited amount of time. For example, the self-study grammar activity from Week 2 to Week 4 required follow-up posts in Instagram only up to Week 5. This structured linear pedagogical design actually proved detrimental to the free flow of dialogue and participation across the different learning spaces.
- Discourse management and the feedback system across the learning spaces seemed constricted because interactional dialogues took place only within the learning space assigned for that activity. Creating overall connectivity between learning spaces was a huge challenge.
- The means for assessing results was not robust enough to measure deep learning: The setup of a digitally networked classroom did not easily accommodate unanticipated learning, particularly when strict time deadlines were necessary to maintain the flow of the course. There were also strict rules for grading, such as "post two examples and two comments," which may actually limit and curtail student participation and make connections more superficial (e.g.: "I comment because I have to").
- Although several points of interaction occurred between students and their peers, the instructor, and native speakers outside the boundaries of the course, it was difficult to know whether these were superficial connection points or whether in these cases participation through the connection led to deep learning.

Micro Level Issues

Although 80% of the students were able to understand the subjunctive and to apply their knowledge in their writing, the instructor faced many challenges in promoting autonomy. One student was unable to post due to technical difficulties during the three weeks and the instructor had to provide an individual task replacement. When problems in participation occurred, they were often related to learner motivation. None of the students added more than the two required posts or the two required comments to other students' post. Several students posted at the last minute, just before the deadline and thus not allowing time for other students to comment on their posts.

On some occasions, students posted incorrect examples. Although the instructor did provide feedback about incorrect posts, some students did not acknowledge these comments, leaving the instructor to infer there had been no follow-through. Thus, even though the classic process of the initiation from the instructor, response from the student, and feedback from the instructor did occur, this initiation-response-feedback loop becomes meaningful only when it goes through several iterations and learning is reinforced. In this case, the single iteration of the initiation-response-feedback loop did not progress further to build continuity and died prematurely, whereas it could have been extended further to strengthen Spanish learning.

In Figure 4, the student chose a good example (a video of a song with many instances of the subjunctive) and the instructor validated it. Another student asked a specific question, i.e. "what is the name of the song?" but the first student did not respond to either of the two comments.

Figure 5 shows how a student used an incorrect tense/mood ("tengo" = I have), and the instructor then modeled the correct usage of the subjunctive without explicitly correcting her sentence in the following exchange ("tuviera" = I had). Whether the student picked up on this correction is unknown, but there were several layers of interaction rather than just a single response. Even though the responses are short, they kept the conversation alive by acknowledging the instructor's comment.

Figure 4. Example of feedback loop dying after minimal interaction

Figure 5. Example of dialog on Instagram

After analyzing in detail the posts made by students in the Google Plus Community (see Appendix 4 for information on how we did this), the results about engagement by the students in these fora are shown in Tables 2 and 3.

Almost 30% of participants were highly engaged, about 30% were moderately engaged and around 40% were poorly engaged (see Table 3).

We observed a high degree of variability at the student level. For the two cases of complete zeros, one was a student who could not post for medical reason during the three weeks, and another was a sixty-year old student who was having problems with access and was therefore given an alternative task. Besides these two, only three students were consistent over the period of the three weeks, one at the highest level, the second at the moderate level, and lastly one at the poorly engaged level.

DISCUSSION

The results presented in the previous section from the pilot study can be broadly categorized under four main challenges.

Challenge #1: Given the high variability among learners, how can the instructor create a design that can benefit all learners?

Table 2. Engagement at the classroom level during the three weeks of the subjunctive activity- by total number of posts for that week

Week 10	Week 11	Week 12
13	15	14
13	11	12
11	10.5	10
10	7	8
7.5	7	7
7	7	7
5.5	6.5	7
5	5.5	6
4	4	4
4	1	3
3	0	2
2	0	0
0	0	0
0	0	0

Scale:
15 - 9: Highly engaged
8 - 5: Moderately engaged
4 - 0: Poorly engaged

Table 3. Engagement at the individual student level

	Week 10	Week 11	Week 12
Student 1	13	7	10
Student 2	13	11	12
Student 3	5.5	7	7
Student 4	4	4	3
Student 5	4	6.5	8
Student 6	0	0	0
Student 7	10	7	6
Student 8	0	0	0
Student 9	7.5	5.5	4
Student 10	11	0	14
Student 11	3	10.5	2
Student 12	5	1	0
Student 13	2	15	7
Student 14	7	0	7

Scale:
15 - 9: Highly engaged
8 - 5: Moderately engaged
4 - 0: Poorly engaged

An analysis of learner responses in the activity involving the subjunctive revealed high variability among learners, as seen from the data on the level of engagement. Such variability is not uncommon in a higher-ed classroom. The challenge for the teacher practitioner in handling this variability is further compounded by the context of applying cloud technology tools, where student response could vary based upon access and participation.

The final project, which required the creation of a PLN, is a case in point. In the task-based activities during the course, students were exposed to at least five cloud technology tools: Google+ community, Google Hangout, Instagram, Blogger, and Tackk. In addition, students also integrated other social media tools on their own initiative, such as Pinterest, Twitter, Tumblr, Vine, etc., to find grammar examples. They could show their learning of grammar and other topics covered during the course by choosing a subset from this master list of tools and combining tools in any order. To provide evidence of understanding the subjunctive, for example, students posted items from a variety of social media sites - Instagram, Tackk, and Google+. They could extend their learning to a tool that was not required, such as Twitter. In this way, each student learned step by step to create a unique PLN. Creating a PLN in this way gave each student the opportunity to pursue multiple paths of learning, thus acknowledging that each student was a unique learner in tailoring their process for the emergence of autonomy.

On paper, this seemed to suggest that each student could trace his or her own individualized path of learning, moving in different directions. Nevertheless, the rigid framework of the 16-week semester and the common goal to be achieved at the end of the course seem to totally ignore the variability among learners. Essentially, everyone was expected to get to the final point within the given parameters. Even though students start at different points, all students are expected to end at the common point of a learning network. In this case study, for example, one student sent an email to the instructor the week before the final project was due, expressing concern because she still did not know what a PLN was and how she could create one. On the other end of the spectrum, another student demonstrated the PLN she had already created using a web tool called Symbaloo, which had not even been mentioned in the course. Symbaloo allows the user to create all the tools of a PLN in a single screen, effectively displaying the learning from the PLN.

Challenge #2: How can learning spaces be designed within a networked learning environment in a way that fosters learner autonomy?

When the traditional classroom becomes a digitally networked classroom, the learning scenario takes on a greater complexity due to the web of possibilities now available to the learner. The emphasis may shift away from the centrality of classroom interactions to an open, learning-by-discovery mode.

It may be necessary to examine whether the move from the tradition LMS to Google+ communities was, in fact, an enhancement of the design. It could be said that the change was a move from a closed space (Blackboard) to another closed space, since the Google+ community for this class was set up as a private space. This nevertheless appears to be a step in the right direction, for the following reasons: limitations in the Blackboard application force interactions to remain rigidly structured, while Google+ communities allowed for richer interactions and easier flow. As also mentioned earlier (see Appendix 1), Google+ communities situate learning inside a true social network, and several students took this opportunity to practice Spanish by following native speakers or news sites on the larger Google+ network. In addition, although the community was private and can be erased by the instructor, in theory it is still available to students once the semester ends. All of the resources that were posted there are available to the community of learners. The same can be said of Blogger, which allowed students to create a portfolio or diary of their learning that can be accessed at any point in the future. In this case, student has 100% ownership. Finally, many students suggested in their comments that they took advantage of the mobile capabilities of Google+, such as push notifications that alerted them when other students posted, or the ability to post directly from the phone. Although Blackboard has a phone app, it does not function as well as the Google+ app.

If the digitally networked classroom is to be effective, the pedagogical design must be further enhanced. There is no certainty that use of the Google+ community or Blogger created an optimal environment for the emergence of autonomy, since there are only limited examples of students reaching out beyond the class community, and none of the students commented more than the required two times on either Google+ posts or other blogs. In addition, the sheer number of cloud technologies used in this case also proved to be a hindrance for the students in general, particularly at the beginning. Many mentioned that it was a complicated structure to navigate. Such a situation can lead to frustration rather than the intended goal of fostering learner autonomy.

The students' lack of comfort level with cloud technology tools could also be an obstacle to the pedagogical design. Some students expressed frustration when they were asked to embed their Google Slides presentation into their blogs, for example. For the students, issues of comfort level stemmed from privacy and visibility concerns. Although many of the activities were conducted in the private space provided by the Google+ community, some were completely open, such as the Instagram challenge, which was mandatory for three weeks. One student in particular expressed that he was not "comfortable" with Instagram, both the tool itself and the idea of posting public pictures and getting comments from strangers. He decided not to do it, and thus received a zero for the assignment. He did not communicate his feelings to the instructor. This was discovered later when reviewing the answers to the survey. Research has already shown that students are often more comfortable when they are able to post anonymously (Roberts, 2013).

All of the students who signed up for the course had willingly signed up for learning in the online environment, but the requirement to engage with cloud technology tools and build a PLN was unique to this instructor's teaching practice. Understandably, some students showed resistance to engaging in digital activities that demanded more than just minimal interactions via the Blackboard discussion board.

One practical strategy that could have been implemented is an informal periodic check-in with students throughout the course to ascertain their comfort level in handling the cloud technology tools. Responses concerning comfort level could be collected through anonymous posts. The virtual office hours provided by the Google Hangout sessions did help in dealing with affect-related issues such as anxiety concerning the technology skills needed for posting on Google+ or writing a comment on Tackk. Another possible strategy is to allow anonymous posts within the cloud-based activities, and then merely observe how community-building emerges. This would necessitate a high degree of trust and creativity on the part of the instructor when assessing learning.

Challenge #3: How can digital discourse be fostered in a manner that leads to community building?

The extent to which the benefits of digital connectedness led to deep learning and strengthening of Spanish language is difficult to measure. If networked learning is seen as "learning in which information and communications technology is used to promote connections: between one learner and other learners; between learners and tutors; between a learning community and its learning resources" (Goodyear et al., p. 1), then several points of connection did happen between peers, between the students and open resources, and the student and the instructor. A community of learners was definitely established. This is evident from the many incidental points of connection between the students and peers, and between students and external expert resources. These points of connection failed to form a meaningful learning community. Several points of connection within the Google+ community, Blogger and Instagram appeared to be at the surface level. Evidence of learning was visible, but reciprocity in interactions was lacking. The initiation-response-feedback loops went up only to one or two levels, and didn't complete loops of communication, or link forward to the next loop. Points of connectedness were often lost and community building seemed weak.

One pedagogical challenge that all teacher-practitioners are eager to solve is that of creating an optimal cloud-based learning space in which the students are eager to participate. This is a fundamental question of learner motivation. In the subjunctive activity on Google+, students had to choose pictures depicting the subjunctive. When the instructor observed poor participation in this specific activity, she intervened and required two responses to peer posts. The authors observed that although 60% of the students completed the required two posts, not a single student went beyond that. In an ideal environment, true engagement would happen because students would want to participate, as opposed to being required to participate.

One practical strategy might be to present a master database of possibilities and allow students to trace their own learning pathways for reaching the goal that they have chosen. Students could also be encouraged to define their goals for Spanish learning at the beginning of the course. This might motivate the group of students to work as a community, empowering each other to accomplish their goals. The teacher would be available as a facilitator, but the prompts would be triggered by the community of learners. This would address a fundamental issue of learner motivation. Knowles' andragogical principles of learning have clearly identified setting one's own goals and taking initiative as key to developing as self-directed learners (Knowles, 1975).

Challenge #4: How to bring about a paradigm shift in the role of the teacher that will more effectively facilitate learning in the digitally networked classroom? How to arrive at a balance between providing guided structure and allowing the freedom that promotes learner autonomy?

The academic domain of Language Acquisition has been at the forefront in the study of learner autonomy since the 1980s. According to Little (2003), "the process of 'autonomization' has been strongly influenced by neo-Vygotskian psychology, which sees learning as a matter of supported performance and emphasizes the interdependence of the cognitive and social-interactive dimensions of the learning process."

Within the context of a highly structured course, the instructor's role could be authoritarian in controlling the flow of dialog. Thus, in spite of the desire to promote autonomy, the instructor might be doing a disservice by acting in opposition to this very intention. One of the ways in which the course design might be disempowering students is by expecting them to demonstrate learning in a very specific way, while failing to account for unpredictable paths that students might take based upon their own motivations.

When facilitation within a networked environment continues to use traditional approaches to define, observe, and assess participation, it constitutes a serious obstacle to learner motivation. This case study raises the important question: given that here is a need for guiding learners and also providing freedom in networked interactions to create an optimal space for the development of autonomy, how can the pedagogical design strike the right balance in skillfully combining guidance and freedom? The next section attempts to answer this question by considering the rhizomatic approach as a possible model for digitally networked classrooms.

CONSIDERATIONS OF THE RHIZOMATIC MODEL AS AN IDEAL APPROACH FOR THE DEVELOPMENT OF LEARNER AUTONOMY

Why the Need to Consider the Rhizomatic Approach to Learning?

The results from our case study revealed several limitations for the teacher practitioner designing the learning spaces for an optimal networked learning experience. This points out the importance of learning from existing models of networked learning that could be more effective in promoting autonomy.

The Rhizomatic approach originally proposed by Deleuze and Guattari in 1987 is a preferred model since it is built on the basic premise that learning is naturally non-hierarchical, non-linear, unpredictable, and thrives in a networked system. The idea of the rhizome, a visual metaphor to explain a way of thinking, was constructed in their Capitalism and Schizophrenia project. Winn and Lockwood (2013, p. 221) summarize the rhizomatic pedagogy succinctly: "the rhizome - a flat, horizontal root system – suggests the immanent, transformative connectedness of the world and constitutes a corrective to an arborescent logic of stand-alone 'trees'. The rhizome privileges the connecting line rather than the isolated point. It is an endlessly proliferating assemblage of lines which connect from the middle. Connectivity without center, boundaries, beginning or end, is the first principle of the rhizome."

Cormier, who is currently experimenting with rhizomatic applications in online courses, interprets Deleuze and Guattari's idea of a rhizome as "a creeping rootstalk, … a stem of a plant that sends out roots and shoots as it spreads." Within a rhizomatic framework, "ideas are multiple, interconnected, and self-replicating." In applying this model to an online MOOC course, he sees it as akin to any learning process with no clear identifiable beginning or end. (Cormier, 2011). Cormier emphasizes that learning in such a space is essentially non-linear and grows in an unstructured, haphazard manner. "As a story for learning, it is messy, unstable and uncertain. … As with the rhizome, the rhizomatic learning experience is multiple, [and] has no set beginning or end, – "a rhizome creates through the act of experimentation" (Cormier, 2012). The Lincoln school of media in the U.K experimenting with the rhizomatic approach as a pedagogical model have built on Cormier's work on looking at the community as a curriculum (Coley et al., 2012).

This philosophical construct is significant as a knowledge model because it factors in ways of learning that the formal education system does not even begin to consider – that students pursue unexpected haphazard paths in a digital networked classroom to reach their learning goals, that unanticipated instances of learning by discovery is a valid form of learning. This Rhizomatic approach, in which the learner chooses to join a learning network at any point, participate in the learning based upon the learner's own intentions, and figure out when to leave or revisit the network, is strongly attuned to promoting autonomy. In recent years, it has taken on greater relevance for digital networked learning. With the advent of cloud technology tools, there is an urgent need to expand learning spaces beyond the standardized and closed environment of the institutional LMS. As Groom and Lamb (2014) recently mentioned "every hour spent online inside an LMS is one in which students are not engaging the wider web in a spirit of critical inquiry.

They are in a system; they are being managed." What sets the rhizomatic model apart from the rest of the well-established education principles is that it does not ignore these important aspects of learning.

Characteristics of the Rhizomatic Learning Model: Enabling an Intuitive Heuristic

This section links the basic tenets of a rhizomatic approach as outlined above to the case study of the Spanish language course described in section 2. When designing the networked learning space for the Spanish language course using the several cloud-based tools, there was no clear objective to apply the rhizomatic model. Post-hoc observations, however, show that several elements in the design of the cloud-based networking space in the case study reflect characteristics of the rhizomatic approach to learning.

Mackiness (2014) has culled six key characteristics from Deleuze and Guatari's work. These six characteristics serve as concrete learning traits to denote "connected learning". The characteristics are: connections, heterogeneity, multiplicity, asignifying rupture, cartography, and decalcomania. Mackiness presents these six characteristics against the background of a test case of an online course called Rhizo14 that applied these rhizomatic principles.

In Table 4, Mackiness' description of each characteristic is presented with a concrete example of how this characteristic was demonstrated within the present case study.

One student in the class created a PLN by curating many different resources in a single space using the tool called Symbaloo. It contained social networking links (Facebook, Twitter, Pinterest, etc.), language learning links (Duolingo, WordReference), and other multicultural links, like one for Barcelona Soccer, Univision TV channel, music in Spanish (Pandora) and also the course communications via the Blackboard LMS and her e-mail. This exemplified a rhizomatic approach by this student to build connections for strengthening Spanish across the different cloud technology tools.

Table 4. Rhizomatic characteristics in this case study

Rhizomatic characteristic	Description by Mackiness, based on the original work of Deleuze and Guatari	Example of learning observed in our case study
Connections	"a rhizome ceaselessly establishes connections"	Students had options to go to different social networking sites. They also could use Google Hangouts to clarify learning issues and connect with peers. They made connections in Instagram and Duolingo.
Heterogeneity	"any point of a rhizome can be connected to any other point"	The course provided the students with a master plan of cloud-based tools, of which each student could use a subset in combination to arrive at an individualized PLN.
Multiplicity	"a complex structure that does not reference a prior unity"	Students could strengthen their Spanish by tracing any of the multiple pathways available to them.
Asignifying rupture	"connections are constantly breaking (de-territorialization) and reforming(re-territorialization)."	Although not "constantly" students chose to participate in certain networks (like Instagram or Duolingo) of their own accord, deciding when to join the network and when to pull away.
Cartography and decalcomania	"like a map, not a tracing"	In their final projects, the creation of a PLN, students were asked to show a map of connections. We have mentioned how one student even found a platform, Symbaloo, to host all the elements of her learning map together.

Although this case study demonstrates an attempt to apply rhizomatic principles, it was very limited in its impact for fostering learner autonomy.

The primary focus of this case study is the teacher practitioner's role in creating an effective pedagogical design. So, the important question is: What is the role of the teacher-practitioner when implementing a Rhizomatic approach? One may argue that if the locus of control rests solely with the learner, is there a need for a teacher-facilitator in this networked rhizome? Irrespective of the myriad scenarios for learning available to the student, the locus of control always lies primarily with the student. Teachers still have a vital role to play as facilitators. According to Cormier (2011), the role of teacher-facilitators in this context is to maintain a suitable learning context "within which a conversation can grow." Just as important as teaching is the creation of a suitable learning space, where the learner can grow in multiple non-predetermined, connected pathways. Little (2003), who has been studying learner autonomy in foreign language acquisition since the 1990s, states - "the teacher's role is to create and maintain a learning environment in which learners can be autonomous in order to become more autonomous." Thus the instructor's role is not merely to instruct, but more to create a suitable learning space in which rhizomatic connections between different points can evolve, where discourse can thrive, and where all learning is essentially unpredictable.

CONCLUSION

For more than three decades, the domain of foreign language acquisition has focused on the challenge of promoting learner autonomy. Extending this research to the digitally networked classroom is the logical next step. The design and delivery of pedagogical models can be effective, however, only when the complexity of the learning scenario in a digitally networked classroom is more clearly understood. This case study has highlighted the challenges involved in integrating cloud technology tools by critically analyzing the structure of the activities and participation by students within a digital discourse, and also carefully examining the role of the teacher. Through this analysis, this study raises awareness of the dangers inherent in applying standard pedagogical approaches without adapting them to digitally networked learning environments. It is therefore highly relevant to the scholarly community of foreign language teachers who may be involved in similar innovations and facing comparable challenges. As an alternative theoretical framework, the rhizomatic approach opens up a new avenue for strengthening language learning in networked learning contexts. The rhizomatic pedagogical framework provides a foundation for developing concrete strategies and solutions. This case study presents a comprehensive overview of potentials and pitfalls that need to be considered when using cloud-based applications to foster learner autonomy.

REFERENCES

Beetham, H., & Sharpe, R. (2013). *Rethinking Pedagogy for a Digital Age: Designing for 21st Century Learning*. London: Routledge.

Coley, R., Lockwood, D., & Omeara, A. (2012). Deleuze and Guattari and photography education. *Rhizomes: Cultural Studies in Emerging Knowledge, 23*. Retrieved 30 December 2014, from http://www.rhizomes.net/issue23/coley/index.html

Cormier, D. (2008). Rhizomatic Education: Community as Curriculum. *Innovate: Journal of Online Education, 4*(5). Retrieved 30 December 2014, from http://davecormier.com/edblog/2008/06/03/rhizomatic-education-community-as-curriculum/

Cormier, D. (2011, November 5). *Rhizomatic Learning – Why we teach?* Retrieved January 14, 2015, from http://davecormier.com/edblog/2011/11/05/rhizomatic-learning-why-learn/

Cormier, D. (2012, December 13). *Trying to write Rhizomatic Learning in 300 words*. Retrieved January 14, 2015, from http://davecormier.com/edblog/2012/12/13/trying-to-write-rhizomatic-learning-in-300-words/

Dalsgaard, C. (2006). Social software: E-learning beyond learning management systems. *European Journal of Open, Distance and E-Learning, 2006*(2). Retrieved 30 December 2014, from http://www.eurodl.org/materials/contrib/2006/Christian_Dalsgaard.htm

Deleuze, G., & Guatarri, F. (1987). *A thousand plateaus: Capitalism and schizophrenia* (B. Massumi, Trans.). Minneapolis, MN: University of Minnesota Press.

Goodyear, P., Banks, S., Hogdson, V., & McConnell, D. (Eds.). (2004). *Advances in research on networked learning*. Boston: Kluwer Academic.

Groom, J., & Lamb, B. (2014). Reclaiming innovation. *EDUCAUSE Review, 49*(3). Retrieved from http://www.educause.edu/visuals/shared/er/extras/2014/ReclaimingInnovation/default.html

Halttunen, K. (2011). Pedagogical Design and Evaluation of Interactive Information Retrieval Learning Environment. In *Teaching and Learning in Information Retrieval* (pp. 61–73). Berlin: Springer. doi:10.1007/978-3-642-22511-6_5

Holec, H. (1981). Autonomy and Foreign Language Learning. Oxford, UK: Pergamon. (first published 1979)

Hurd, S., Beaven, T., & Ortega, A. (2001). Developing autonomy in a distance language learning context: Issues and dilemmas for course writers. *System, 29*(3), 341–355. doi:10.1016/S0346-251X(01)00024-0

Knowles, M. S. (1975). *Self-directed learning: A guide for learners and teachers*. New York: Association Press.

Lian, A. P. (2004). Technology-enhanced language-learning environments: A rhizomatic approach. In J. Son (Ed.), *Computer-assisted language learning: Concepts, contexts and practices* (pp. 1–20). New York: Universe.

Little, D. (2003). Learner autonomy and second/foreign language learning. *Subject Centre for Languages, Linguistics and Area Studies Good Practice Guide*. Retrieved 30 December 2014, from https://www.llas.ac.uk/resources/gpg/1409

Mackness, J. (2014, June 24). *Principles for Rhizomatic Thinking*. Retrieved January 14, 2015, from https://jennymackness.wordpress.com/2014/06/24/principles-for-rhizomatic-thinking/

Martin Bosque, A., & Munday, P. (2014). Conexión, colaboración y aprendizaje más allá del aula: #InstagramELE. In *Proceedings from the Second Annual Conference of Applied Linguistics for the Teaching of Foreign Languages*. Madrid: Nebrija Procedia. Retrieved 14 January 2015, from http://www.nebrija.com/la_universidad/servicios/pdf-publicaciones/ActasNebrija_SegundoCongreso.pdf

Roberts, L. D., & Rajah-Kanagasabai, C. J. (2013). "I'd be so much more comfortable posting anonymously": Identified versus anonymous participation in student discussion boards. *Australasian Journal of Educational Technology*, *29*(5). doi:10.14742/ajet.452

Rose, D. H., & Meyer, A. (2002). *Teaching every student in the digital age: Universal design for learning*. Alexandria, VA: Association for Supervision and Curriculum Development.

Sasser, T. (2012). Bring Your Own Disruption: Rhizomatic Learning in the Composition Class. *Hybrid Pedagogy*. Retrieved 30 December 2014, from http://www.hybridpedagogy.com/journal/bring-your-own- disruption-rhizomatic-learning-in-the-composition-class/

Veletsianos, G., Kimmons, R., & French, K. (2013). Instructor experiences with a social networking site in a higher education setting: Expectations, frustrations, appropriation, and compartmentalization. *Educational Technology Research and Development*, *61*(2), 255–278. doi:10.1007/s11423-012-9284-z

Warschauer, M., & Liaw, M. (2011). Emerging technologies for autonomous language learning. *Studies in Self-Access Learning Journal*, *2*(3), 107–118.

Winn, J., & Lockwood, D. (2013). Student as Producer is hacking the university. In H. Beetham & R. Sharpe (Eds.), *Rethinking Pedagogy for a Digital Age: Designing for 21st Century Learning* (pp. 218–229). New York, NY: Routledge.

Yepes, E. (n.d.). *Spanish Grammar Libro digital Herramientas de español: Online Advanced Spanish Book*. Retrieved January 13, 2015, from http://www.bowdoin.edu/~eyepes/newgr/ats/

KEY TERMS AND DEFINITIONS

Cloud Technology Tools: Set of tools, such as any type of software, which is based online via a shared infrastructure. Users access these tools from their devices without having to manage the hardware or software.

Digitally Networked Classroom: A digital environment in which the learner is connected to other learners, the instructor, and open educational resources. The learner uses these connections for the benefit of his/her learning.

Learner Autonomy: Learner takes charge of his/her learning. The demonstration of autonomy is always anchored to a context. The learner is able to show the initiative to problem solve to achieve a specific goal by being less dependent on a teacher.

Pedagogical Design: A set of theoretical constructs, patterns and/or procedures, employed by the teacher practitioner in the learning environment.

Personal Learning Network: A learning network formed by an individual with the objective of connecting with others and open resources for informal learning.

Rhizomatic Learning: Learning based on the idea of the rhizome, a root which grows according to its environment, in an unstructured and unpredictable manner, with no clear center.

Social Networking Sites: Web based sites which connect people with similar interests. Each user has a space and can connect with other users and see others' connections.

Subjunctive in Spanish: A verbal mood which is used to express states of unreality such as volition or emotion. It usually appears in three grammatical contexts: nominal, adjectival or adverbial subordinate clauses. It is much more widely used in Spanish than in English.

APPENDIX 1

List of Tools Used in this Course

Google+ communities is currently the second-largest social networking site, with more than 340 million users. It was chosen to meet the teaching objectives for various reasons. Because of its global reach, students could already establish connections with a population outside the class. Students could easily post different types of media, such as YouTube videos, Pinterest Pins, Tweets, Facebook post, etc. One important strength in providing feedback was the comment feature. The commenting system was very simple to use and very clear, unlike some of the threaded discussions on a more traditional LMS, where comments can easily get "lost." In addition, students who have turned on notifications on their phones can know when someone has commented on their posts. Lastly, it includes the +1 symbol, similar to the "like" in Facebook, which can be used by students and instructors to "reward" good postings and/or comments. Thus, students can also see which postings were better at responding to the questions asked.

Blogger is a blogging platform owned by Google. Each student had their own blog, created with the Google owned platform Blogger. This platform was used for the following reasons: It can serve as portfolio of what was learned in class. Students can use it after they finish the course. Students comment on each other's blogs and learn from each other. Blogs can be shared with the larger community by the instructor or the member themselves. Students could have a blog roll of their classmates' blogs right inside their blog, so they could easily know when someone posted or they could comment. In addition, because it is a very popular platform, there are already many how to guides and videos, both in English and in Spanish that can be incorporated as resources for students, without the instructor having to create them.

Google Hangouts is a video tool that allows you to have video conversations with up to ten people. There is one modality, Google Hangouts on Air, which can be recorded and shared later through YouTube. During the course of the semester there were eleven Google Hangouts on Air. They were spaced out, having almost one Hangout per week. Any member of Google+ can participate in the Hangouts, which are video sessions organized by one person, in this case the instructor. Each student was required to participate in at least two Hangouts. Only one student did not participate in any, and several students participated in more than two. The Video Hangouts were recorded and later posted in YouTube and shared in the course Google+ Community, as well as in Blackboard. On the Hangouts, the instructor went over the instructions on the Grammar units or the Modules or projects. Students had a chance to ask questions about the course or about assignments, as well as to get to know each other a bit better, as this was the only time they could actually see each other.

Instagram is a social networking site based on pictures. Users post images and other uses can like them or make comments. They also use hashtags to group pictures according to themes or location. In order for the students to initiate collaboration with people outside of the classroom learning community, they participated in a challenge using Instagram for three weeks during the semester. There was a prompt for each day of the month, and anybody who wanted to participate took a picture relating to that prompt, wrote a quote for it, and tagged it with the word #InstagramELE. The students in were asked to write sentences related to the grammar being studied during those weeks, add the common tag of #InstagramELE, add also a tag for the class, #SP299OL14, and try to interact with people in the larger community by posting comments on other peoples' pictures and responding to the comments they obtained. This challenge, #InstagramELE is something that exists outside of this course. For more information about, see Martin Bosque & Munday, 2014.

Google Slides is a presentation tool which can be used collaboratively as a shared learning space. It can be easily embedded into blogs. Students used it firstly on their own (shared with the instructor), then for their group project, collaborating with other students, and lastly for the final individual project. This built practice in an incremental fashion to move to the next collaborative group project with peers.

Tackk is a tool that facilitates the creation of webpages that can be customized with multimedia elements such as videos, pictures, polls, etc. It was used primarily to enhance the design and communication within Blackboard, since the pages are easily embeddable into Blackboard and improve the normal look of a Blackboard page. Beyond design, they were also very useful because they have a comment stream at the end of each page. This allowed students to write questions or comments which could be seen by everyone.

APPENDIX 2

Mid-Term Survey Questions

Link to the survey: https://docs.google.com/forms/d/1Tk-Ovh_4AXm07P9KXMtliZjiN226LsPN-Oea9oAoMYI/viewform

1. Access - Please, indicate your agreement with each of the statement below:
   [1] Strongly Disagree [2] Disagree [3] Undecided [4] Agree [5] Strongly Agree
   - I am able to complete all the tasks required with the technology I have
   - I am able to complete all the tasks required with the technology I know how to use
2. Do you experience frustration with any technical aspect of the course? Could you give a specific example?
3. Participation - Please, indicate your agreement with each of the statements below:
   [1] Strongly Disagree [2] Disagree [3] Undecided [4] Agree [5] Strongly Agree
   - I like to participate in collaborative learning experiences
   - Our Google+ Community is easy to use for collaboration
   - Our Google+ Community is useful for collaboration
4. The intention of using Goole+ community was to promote networked learning. Do you have an example of collaborative learning which has taken place during the course so far?
5. Do you think that the tools used in the course so far (Blackboard, Google+, Tackk Boards, Google Hangouts, Instagram, etc.) promote your participation?
6. Could you give two specific examples of your own learning (about Spanish language and culture or other topics) through any of the tools we use?
7. Attitude - Please, indicate your agreement with each of the statement below:
   [1] Strongly Disagree [2] Disagree [3] Undecided [4] Agree [5] Strongly Agree
   - Time constraints make it difficult for me to participate often
   - It is hard to maintain a smooth and continuous contact with all members of the group.
   - I prefer to post assignments close to the deadline
   - The tools we use enhance the content of the course
   - The tools we use enhance my own learning.

8. Have you used any other tool not mentioned here to work or communicate with your peers in this class? Could you let me know which ones and how you used it?
9. Do you have any suggestions to improve the communication in the course?
10. Do you have any other suggestions about the course

APPENDIX 3

Table 5. Summary of the answers to the focus group questions

	Access	Participation	Attitude	Deep Learning
Google Plus Communities	It was easy to access but felt very overwhelming in the beginning. I felt like it was difficult in the beginning, I don't use Google Plus but I liked it towards the end. I had trouble with the Google slides. Also, I didn't know how to do an embedded post. Google app was very useful. Google plus was 100% better than Blackboard. Easier to use, read and to look at they are more organized. Getting notifications helped me to stay in touch with work and between sessions.	I had a positive experience because everyone participated. The discussion boards were very interesting. Blackboard not as active as Google Plus. I felt there was a lot of participation and Google Plus was very convenient. Google plus has several options that allows many different opportunity to collaborate.	I felt very connected to the students in my group, in fact I felt connected to other students outside of my study group as well. This was my first online course and I felt that everyone was learning on the same level. The professor created a community (within Google Plus) it was easy to find and to look at. I don't know what Google Plus would be used for outside of an academic setting.	Before starting this class I used my computer in the usual way meaning email, doing homework…the basics. But now with all of the tools introduced and used in the course I feel more confident. I did my own research on how to embed a post. I did start using it outside of the class, it came in handy for my micro-economic class. It was a group project that we were all doing a presentation – slideshow kind of thing so we had one common link that we could all work on at the same time. I set up the file and sent everyone the link. I would have never known about it if I hadn't used Google in the course (SP299).
Google Hangouts	My computer wouldn't work but I could view the videos on the app on my phone. I had difficulty with understanding how to record the video.			Based on what I learnt about the google tools in this course, I used it to work on a collaborative project in another course.
Instagram	Loved everything about the class.	I am an outlier because I didn't really do one of the assignments because I'm not really familiar with Instagram. I was not emotionally comfortable with posting pictures on Instagram, I didn't do that particular assignment.	It is easier to send a picture via Instagram than it is to email it.	This has helped in other aspects of my life including my work and family life.

continued on following page

Table 5. Continued

	Access	Participation	Attitude	Deep Learning
		*Initially when the course started I had a BlackBerry and I couldn't access the social media tools easily. For the sake of this course, I bought a smartphone and really like using the smartphone.		
Twitter	I found people (kids in Spanish speaking countries) speaking in their natural language and how they go about everyday just tweeting.			
Duolingo	2 students mentioned the use of Duolingo in the class.			
Tackk	Not mentioned			
All tools combined for Networked Learning	At the start it was difficult but after getting into the rhythm of the class it became easier. Enjoyed the online format. Wished there were more online courses with same type of format. Enjoyed taking the online class. I had never used Google Plus, Blogger or some of the other social media tools used in the class. I felt like I was going all over the place online and not to mention this was my first online course. I liked that everyone had to use the same space to do their work and when other students posted words I didn't know I looked them up. The hardest part was knowing where to go.	The professor gave several tools for the non-native speakers to continue to practice their Spanish. Even as a native speaker the professor has given several tips on the use of technology as well as the ability to practice Spanish. The online format is very convenient and very necessary for students that do not live close to the University. I thought it was really cool that if I didn't have my computer I could go on my phone and use the apps.	Initially when the course started I had a BlackBerry and I couldn't access the social media tools easily. For the sake of this course, I bought a smartphone and really like using the smartphone. I felt I needed to get a smartphone to participate in the class although I was thinking of purchasing one before the start of the class. If it wasn't because we had such a lenient teacher I don't know if I would have done as well in the class. I think it was easier to participate in this class. When I am in (on ground) class there really isn't a lot of participation to begin with, I feel like I am raising my hand so there isn't dead silence because it's awkward.	I did not felt that the level of technology was too much. In fact I learned a lot that I feel will help me move forward in my other courses. Also, I would have thought that the younger students would have known more about the technology used in the course but we all learned together. We all learned a lot. The course was overall enjoyable and helped me to learn not just as student but as a person. *I had never used Google Plus, Blogger or some of the other social media tools used in the class. I felt like I was going all over the place online and not to mention this was my first online course. I liked that everyone had to use the same space to do their work and when other students posted words I didn't know I looked them up.

continued on following page

Table 5. Continued

	Access	Participation	Attitude	Deep Learning
	I learned how to do a screenshot on my computer. The class really introduced me to a lot more than I had ever used before. I think we pretty much covered everything (in our discussion). The technology portion of this class made it much easier to communicate than in other online courses. To see post was a lot more appealing to follow along with what others were doing was a simple click of the mouse. I learned more about the language because of the online class format. The grammar it's easier to understand when you can see it and manipulated on your own than just learning it from someone who lectures. Modern use of the language. Kids today in Spanish speaking countries are using social media.		But I think we are more motivated to do the online participation because we are constantly getting notifications that people are posting that that I am falling behind so I have to get on this.	*The class really introduced me to a lot more than I had ever used before. I think we pretty much covered everything (in our discussion). It helped more than we could have ever brought to it.

- Student felt that there should be more online courses in all department.
- Student stated that in their previous class the professor(s) would explain via power points but didn't take it further. Once the class was over there was no follow-up.
- The professor was a lot more involved than previous experience of online course. The professor was communicating with us a lot more than other professors do in online courses.
- Professor sent weekly updates of what the class had to do. Not sure if would have been the same if it had been another professor because I'd never taken another online class.

PLEASE NOTE if you see an * it means that the comment fell into more than one category.

APPENDIX 4

The level of engagement in the Google Plus Community Posts for Weeks 10, 11 and 12 of the semester (when we reviewed the subjunctive) was established following these guidelines.
We gave points for the following:

- 1 point per post
- 1 point for each comment to one of his/her posts
- 1 point for each comment made to another student's post
- 1 point if there was evidence of communicating (that is, if the comment was something more than "great post!")
- 1 point if there was evidence of learning by their comment

We took off points for the following:

- 1 point for every instance in which the student did not answer a question addressed to them in the post.

According to the points obtained by the students, we established this scale:

15 - 9 points: Highly engaged
8 - 5 points: Moderately engaged
4 - 0 points: Poorly engaged

Compilation of References

Ahmad, A. (1987). Jameson's rhetoric of otherness and the 'national allegory. *Social Text, 17*(17), 3–25. doi:10.2307/466475

Aitchison, C. (2009). Writing groups for doctoral education. *Studies in Higher Education, 34*(8), 905–916. doi:10.1080/03075070902785580

Aitchison, J., & Lewis, D. M. (Eds.). (2003). *Introduction. New media language*. New York, NY: Routledge.

Aleman, A. M., & Wartman, K. L. (2009). *Online social networking on campus: Understanding what matters in student culture*. New York, NY: Routledge.

Alexander, B. (2006). A threat to professional identity? The resistance to computer-mediated teaching. In M. Hanrahan & D. L. Madsen (Eds.), *Teaching, technology, textuality: Approaches to new media* (pp. 27–35). New York, NY: Palgrave Macmillan. doi:10.1057/9780230523302_3

Allen, I. E., & Seaman, J. (2015). G*rade level: Tracking online education in the United States.* Babson Survey Research Group and Quahog Research Group. Retrieved from http://onlinelearningconsortium.org/read/survey-reports-2014/

Allen, G. (2000). *Intertextuality*. London: Routledge.

Anderson, B. (1983). *Imagined Communities. Reflections on the Origin and Spread of Nationalism.* London: Verso.

Annan, K. (2000). *We the peoples: The role of the United Nations in the 21st century.* New York: United Nations.

Appadurai, A. (2008). Disjuncture and differences in the global cultural economy. In S. During (Ed.), *The Cultural Studies Reader* (pp. 216–226). New York: Routledge.

Araujo, B., Carmona, J. F., Parra, J., & Chávez, R. C. (2014). Digital Explorations Along the Borderlands: Transfronterizo Youth, Testimonio and Personal Learning Networks. *International Journal of Information Communication Technologies and Human Development, 6*(2), 16–31. doi:10.4018/ijicthd.2014040102

Arola, K. L. (2010). The design of Web 2.0: The rise of the template, the fall of design. *Computers and Composition, 27*(1), 4–14. doi:10.1016/j.compcom.2009.11.004

Arthur, W. B. (2009). *The nature of technology: What it is and how it evolves*. New York, NY: Free Press.

Ashcroft, B., Griffiths, G., & Tiffin, H. (2002). *The empire writes back: Theory and practice in post-colonial literatures* (2nd ed.). London: Routledge.

Asing-Cashman, J., Gurung, B., Limbu, Y., & Rutledge, D. (2014). Pre-service teachers' computer self-efficacy beliefs in using free and open source tools (FOSTs): An empirical investigation. *International Journal of Teaching and Learning in Higher Education, 26*(1), 66–77.

Atkinson, D. et al. (2015). Clarifying the relationship between L2 writing and translingual writing: An open letter to writing studies editors and organization leaders. *College English*, *77*, 383–386.

Austin, A. E. (2009). Cognitive apprenticeship theory and its implications for doctoral education: A case example from a doctoral program in higher and adult education. *The International Journal for Academic Development*, *14*(3), 173–183. doi:10.1080/13601440903106494

Ball, C. F. (2004). Show, not tell: The value of new media scholarship. *Computers and Composition*, *21*(4), 403–425. doi:10.1016/S8755-4615(04)00038-6

Baltzersen, R. K. (2013). The importance of metacommunication in supervision processes in higher education. *International Journal of Higher Education*, *2*(2), 128. doi:10.5430/ijhe.v2n2p128

Bannon, L. (2011). Reimagining HCI: Toward a more human-centered perspective. *Interaction*, *18*(4), 50–57. doi:10.1145/1978822.1978833

Barad, K. (2003). Posthumanist performativity: Toward an understanding of how matters comes to matter. *Signs (Chicago, Ill.)*, *28*(3), 801–831. doi:10.1086/345321

Barassi, V., & Treré, E. (2012). Does Web 3.0 come after Web 2.0? Deconstructing theoretical assumptions through practice. *New Media & Society*, *14*(8), 1269–1285. doi:10.1177/1461444812445878

Barker, C. (2008). *Cultural Studies: Theory and Practice*. Los Angeles, CA: Sage Publication.

Barnard, W. M. (2004). Parent involvement in elementary school and educational attainment. *Children and Youth Services Review*, *26*(1), 39–62. doi:10.1016/j.childyouth.2003.11.002

Barrett, H. C. (2006). Using electronic portfolios for formative/classroom-based assessment. *Classroom Connect Connected Newsletter*, *13*(2). Retrieved from https://electronicportfolios.org/portfolios/ConnectedNewsletter.pdf

Barron, B. (2004). Learning ecologies for technological fluency: Gender and experience differences. *Journal of Educational Computing Research*, *31*(1), 1–36. doi:10.2190/1N20-VV12-4RB5-33VA

Barton, D., & Hamilton, M. (2000). Literacy practices. In D. Barton, M. Hamilton, & R. Ivanič (Eds.), *Situated literacies: Reading and writing in context* (pp. 7–15). London: Routledge.

Bawashi, A. S., & Reiff, M. J. (2010). *Genre: An introduction to history, theory, research, and pedagogy* (C. Bazerman, Ed.). Anderson, SC: Parlor Press.

Bawden, D. (2008). Origins and concepts of digital literacy. In C. Lankshear & M. Knobel (Eds.), *Digital literacies: Concepts, policies, and practices* (pp. 17–32). New York: Peter Lang.

Baym, N. K. (2002). Interpersonal life online. In L. A, Lievrouw & S. Livingstone (Eds.). Handbook of new media: Social shaping and consequences of ICTs (pp. 62-76). London: Sage Publication.

Bazerman, C. (1994). Systems of genre and the enactment of social intentions. In A. Freedman & P. Medway (Eds.), *Genre and the new rhetoric* (pp. 79–104). London, UK: Taylor & Francis, Ltd.

Bazerman, C. (2004). Speech acts, genres, and activity systems: How texts organize activities and people. In C. Bazerman & P. Prior (Eds.), *What writing does and how it does it: An introduction to analyzing texts and textual practices* (pp. 309–340). New York, NY: Routledge.

Bazerman, C. (2008). Theories of the middle range in historical studies of writing practice. *Written Communication*, *25*(3), 298–313. doi:10.1177/0741088308318025

Bazerman, C. (2009). Genre and cognitive development: Beyond writing to learn. In C. Bazerman, A. Bonin, & D. Figueiredo (Eds.), *Genre in a Changing World*. West Lafayette, IN: The WAC Clearinghouse and Parlor Press. doi:10.4000/pratiques.1419

Bean, J. C. (2011). *Engaging ideas: The professor's guide to integrating writing, critical thinking, and active learning in the classroom*. John Wiley & Sons.

Beetham, H., & Sharpe, R. (2013). *Rethinking Pedagogy for a Digital Age: Designing for 21st Century Learning*. London: Routledge.

Beldarrain, Y. (2006). Distance Education Trends: Integrating new technologies to foster student interaction and collaboration. *Distance Education*, *27*(2), 139–153. doi:10.1080/01587910600789498

Berlak, A. (2008). Challenging the hegemony of whiteness by addressing the adaptive unconscious. In V. Lea & E. J. Sims (Eds.), *Undoing whiteness in the classroom: Critical educultural teaching approaches for social justice activism* (pp. 48–66). New York, NY: Peter Lang.

Berlin, J. (1988). Rhetoric and ideology in the writing class. *College English*, *50*(5), 477–494. doi:10.2307/377477

Berlin, J. (1992). Poststructuralism, cultural studies, and composition classroom: Postmodern theory in practice. *Rhetoric Review*, *11*(1), 16–33. doi:10.1080/07350199209388984

Berners-Lee, T., Cailliau, R., Luotonen, A., Nielsen, H. F., & Secret, A. (2003). The world-wide web. In N. Wardrip-Fruin & N. Montfort (Eds.), *The new media reader* (pp. 791–798). Cambridge, MA: The MIT Press.

Bezemer, J., & Kress, G. (2008). Writing in multimodal texts: A social semiotic account of designs for learning. *Written Communication*, *25*(2), 166–195. doi:10.1177/0741088307313177

Bhabha, H. K. (1994). *The location of culture*. London: Routledge.

Birkerts, S. (1994). *The Gutenberg elegies: The fate of reading in an electronic age*. Boston: Faber & Faber.

Bitzer, L. (1968). The rhetorical situation. *Philosophy & Rhetoric*, *1*, 1–14.

Bizzell, P. (2014a). Toward "transcultural" literacy. In B. Horner & K. Kopelson (Eds.), *Reworking English in rhetoric and composition: Global interrogations, local interventions* (pp. 131–149). Carbondale, IL: Southern Illinois University Press.

Bizzell, P. (2014b). We want to know who our students are. *PMLA*, *129*(3), 442–447. doi:10.1632/pmla.2014.129.3.442

Blau, I., & Caspi, A. (2009). What type of collaboration helps? Psychological ownership, perceived learning and outcome quality of collaboration using Google Docs. In *Proceedings of the Chais conference on instructional technologies research* (Vol. 12).

Bolter, J. D. (2001). *Writing space: Computers, hypertext, and the remediation of print* (2nd ed.). Mahwah, NJ: LEA.

Bowie, J. L. (2012). Rhetorical roots and media future: How podcasting fits into the computers and writing classroom [Audio podcast]. *Kairos, 16*(2). Retrieved from http://technorhetoric.net/16.2/topoi/bowie/index.html

boyd, d. (2007). Why youth (heart) social network sites: The role of networked publics in teenage social life. In D. Buckingham (Ed.), *Youth, Identity, and Digital Media*. Cambridge, MA: The MIT Press.

Braaksma, M. A. H., Rijlaarsdam, G., Couzijn, M., & van den Bergh, H. (2002). Learning to compose hypertext and linear text: Transfer or interference? In R. Bromme & E. Stahl (Eds.), *Writing hypertext and learning: Conceptual and empirical approaches* (pp. 15–37). Boston, MA: Pergamon.

Brandt, J. E. (2012). Google Apps for Education and accessibility: Review of research. *Maine CITE*.

Bransford, J. D., Brown, A. L., & Cocking, R. R. (Eds.). (2000). *How people learn: Brain, mind, experience, and school.* Washington, DC: National Academy Press.

Bransford, J. D., & Schwartz, D. L. (1999). Rethinking Transfer: A Simple Proposal with Multiple Implications. *Review of Research in Education, 24*, 61–100.

Brereton, J. (Ed.). (1995). *The origins of composition studies in the American college* (pp. 1875–1925). Pittsburgh, PA: University of Pittsburgh Press.

Breuch, L. K. (2005). Enhancing online collaboration: Virtual peer review in the writing classroom. In K. C. Cook & K. Grant-Davie (Eds.), *Online education: Global questions, local answers* (pp. 141–156). Farmingdale, NY: Baywood.

Brockmeier, J., & Olson, D. R. (2009). The literacy epesteme: From Innis to Derrida. In D. R. Olson & N. Torrance (Eds.), *The Cambridge handbook of literacy* (pp. 3–21). Cambridge, UK: Cambridge University Press. doi:10.1017/CBO9780511609664.002

Brooke, C. G. (2009). *Lingua Fracta: Toward a rhetoric of new media.* The University of Michigan: Hampton Press.

Brown, M. E., & Hocutt, D. L. (in press). All composition is local, even in the Googleverse: Glocalizing the composition classroom with Google Apps for Education. In R. Rice & K. St.Amant (Eds.), *Thinking globally, composing locally: Rethinking online writing in the age of the global internet.* Boulder, CO: University Press of Colorado.

Brown, J. D., & Rodgers, T. S. (2003). *Doing second language research.* London: Oxford University Press.

Bruffee, K. A. (1986). Social construction, language, and the authority of knowledge: A bibliographical essay. *College English, 48*(8), 773–790. doi:10.2307/376723

Brummett, B. (1979). *Three meanings of epistemic rhetoric.* Speech communication association annual convention, San Antonio, TX.

Bruner, J. (1986). *Actual minds, possible minds.* Cambridge, MA: Harvard University Press.

Bruner, J. (1996). *The Culture of Education.* Cambridge, MA: Harvard UP.

Bruner, J. (2002). *Making stories: Law, literature, life.* New York, NY: Farrar, Straus, and Giroux.

Burke, K. (1966). Language as symbolic action: Essays on life, literature, and method. Berkeley, CA: The University of California Press.

Burrill, D. A. (2005). Out of the box: Performance, drama, and interactive software. *Modern Drama, 48*(3), 492–512. doi:10.3138/md.48.3.492

Butler, J. (1993). *Bodies that matter: On the discursive limits of "sex".* New York: Routledge.

Caeton, D. A. (2009). Agency and Accountability: The Paradoxes of Wiki Discourse. In M. Barton & R. Cummings (Eds.), *Wiki Writing: Collaborative Learning in the College Classroom.* Ann Arbor, MI: University of Michigan Press; doi:10.3998/dcbooks.5871848.0001.001

Caffarella, R. S., & Barnett, B. G. (2000). Teaching doctoral students to become scholarly writers: The importance of giving and receiving critiques. *Studies in Higher Education, 25*(1), 39–52. doi:10.1080/030750700116000

Caine, R., & Caine, G. (2011). *Natural learning for a connected world: Education, technology and the human Brain.* Teachers College Press.

Çakıroğlu, Ü. (2014). Analyzing the effect of learning styles and study habits of distance learners on learning performances: A case of an introductory programming course. *The International Review of Research in Open and Distributed Learning, 15*(4). Retrieved from http://www.irrodl.org/index.php/irrodl/article/view/1840/3004

Callon, M. (1986). Some elements of sociology of translation: Documentation of the scallops and the fishermen of St. Brieuc Bay. In J. Law (Ed.), *Power, action, & belief: A new sociology of knowledge?* (pp. 196–229). London: Routledge.

Calvillo-Gámez, E. H., Cairns, P., & Cox, A. L. (2011). Assessing the core elements of the gaming experience. In R. Bernhaupt (Ed.), *Evaluating user experience in games: Concepts and methods* (pp. 41–71). London: Springer.

Campbell, R., & Green, D. (Eds.). (2000). *Literacies and learners: Current perspectives.* Prentice Hall.

Canagarajah, S. (2014b). *Clarifying the relationship between translingual practice and L2 writing.* Paper presented at The 2014 Maryland Conference on Academic and Professional Writing, University of Maryland, MD. Retrieved September 4, 2016, from https://www.academia.edu/16051926/Clarifying_the_Relationship_between_Translingual_Practice_and_L2_Writing

Canagarajah, S. (2002). *A geopolitics of academic writing.* Pittsburgh, PA: Pittsburgh UP.

Canagarajah, S. (2013a). English as translingual. In *Translingual practice: Global Englishes and cosmoplitan relations* (pp. 56–75). London: Routledge.

Canagarajah, S. (2013b). Negotiating translingual literacy: An enactment. *Research in the Teaching of English, 48*(1), 40–67.

Canagarajah, S. (2014a). In search of a new paradigm for teaching English as an international language. *TESOL Journal, 5*(4), 767–785. doi:10.1002/tesj.166

Canagarajah, S. (2016). Translingual writing and teacher development in composition. *College English, 78*(3), 264–272.

Carstensen, J., Golden B., & Morgenthal JP. (2012). Cloud Computing Explained. In *Cloud Computing* (pp. 23-56).

Carter, L. (2003). Argument in hypertext: Writing strategies and the problem of order in a nonsequential world. *Computers and Composition, 20*(1), 3–22. doi:10.1016/S8755-4615(02)00176-7

Castells, M. (2012). *Networks of Outrage and Hope: Social Movements in the Internet Age.* Cambridge, UK: Polity Press.

CCCC. (2013, March). *A position statement of principles and example effective practices for online writing instruction (OWI).* National Council of Teachers of English.

CCCC. (2013, March). A position statement of principles and example effective practices for online writing instruction (OWI). *National Council of Teachers of English.* Retrieved from http://www.ncte.org/cccc/resources/positions/owiprinciples

Changchit, C. (2014). Students' perceptions of cloud computing. *Issues in Information Systems, 15*(1), 312–322. Retrieved from http://iacis.org/iis/2014/60_iis_2014_312-322.pdf

Charmaz, K. (2006). *Constructing grounded theory: A practical guide through qualitative analysis.* London: SAGE Publications.

Charney, D. (1994). The effect of hypertext on processes of reading and writing. In C. L. Selfe & S. Hilligoss (Eds.), *Literacy and computers: The complications of teaching and learning with technology* (pp. 89–112). New York, NY: MLA.

Chavez Chavez, R. (2003). Our responsibility: A perspective on "Taking a stand". *Teacher Education and Practice, 16*(2), 156–170.

Cheng, B., Wang, M., Moormann, J., Olaniran, B. A., & Chen, N.-S. (2012, April). The effects of organizational learning environment factors on e-learning acceptance. *Computers & Education, 58*(3), 885–899. doi:10.1016/j.compedu.2011.10.014

Cheung, C. K., & Dubey, A. (2011). Enhancement and expansion of language education in the internet era role of web 2.0 technologies. *Journal of Current Issues in Media and Telecommunications*, *2*(4), 387–403.

Cho, K. L., & Jonassen, D. H. (2002). The effects of argumentation scaffolds on argumentation and problem solving. *Educational Technology Research and Development*, *50*(3), 5–22. doi:10.1007/BF02505022

Christensen, G., Steinmetz, A., Alcorn, B., Bennett, A., Woods, D., & Emanuel, E. J. (2013). The MOOC Phenomenon: Who Takes Massive Open Online Courses and Why? Working Paper. *Social Science Research Network*. doi:10.2139/ssrn.2350964

Clark, J. E. (2010). The digital imperative: Making the case for a 21st –century pedagogy. *Computers and Composition*, *27*(1), 27–35. doi:10.1016/j.compcom.2009.12.004

Coiro, J., Knobel, M., Lankshear, C., & Leu, D. (2008). Central issues in new literacies and new literacies research. In J. Coiro, M. Knobel, C. Lankshear, & D. Leu (Eds.), *The Handbook of Research on New Literacies* (pp. 1–21). New York: Lawrence Erlbaum.

Coiro, J., Knobel, M., Lankshear, C., & Leu, D. J. (2008). Central issues in new literacies and new literacies research. In J. Coiro, M. Knobel, C. Lankshear, & D. J. Leu (Eds.), *Handbook of research on new literacies* (pp. 1–21). New York: Taylor & Francis Group.

Coley, R., Lockwood, D., & Omeara, A. (2012). Deleuze and Guattari and photography education. *Rhizomes: Cultural Studies in Emerging Knowledge, 23*. Retrieved 30 December 2014, from http://www.rhizomes.net/issue23/coley/index.html

Collins, A., Brown, J. S., & Holum, A. (1991). Cognitive apprenticeship: Making things visible. *American Educator: The Professional Journal of the American Federation of Teachers, 15*(3), 6-11, 38-46. Retrieved from: http://elc.fhda.edu/transform/resources/collins_brown_holum_1991.pdf

Collins, A., Brown, J. S., & Newman, S. E. (1986). *Cognitive Apprenticeship: Teaching the Craft of Reading, Writing, and Mathematics* (No. BBN-6459). BBN Labs Inc. Retrieved from: http://eric.ed.gov/?id=ED284181 (ERIC Document Reproduction Service No. ED 284181)

Collins, A., Brown, J. S., & Newman, S. E. (1986). *Cognitive Apprenticeship: Teaching the Craft of Reading, Writing, and Mathematics* (No. BBN-6459). BBN Labs Inc. Retrieved from: http://eric.ed.gov/?id=ED284181(ERIC Document Reproduction Service No. ED 284181)

Collins, F. L. (2012). Researching mobility and emplacement: Examining transience and transnationality in international student lives. *Area*, *44*(3), 296–304. doi:10.1111/j.1475-4762.2012.01112.x

Collison, G., Elbaum, B., Haavind, S., & Tinker, R. (2000). Facilitating Online Learning: Effective Strategies for Moderators. Atwood Publishing.

Connelly, L. (2015, April). *Technology in the Classroom: Google Drive*. Poster presented at Undergraduate Research and Arts Forum at Michigan State University, East Lansing, MI.

Connor, U. (2008). Mapping multidimentional aspects of research. In U. Connor, E. Nagelhout, & W. V. Rozycki (Eds.), *Contrastive rhetoric: Reaching to intercultural rhetoric*. Philadelphia, PA: John Benjamins B.V. doi:10.1075/pbns.169.19con

Conrad, R. M., & Donaldson, J. A. (2004). *Engaging the online learner. Activities and resources for creative instruction.* San Francisco: Jossey-Bass.

Conrad, R. M., & Donaldson, J. A. (2011). *Engaging the online learner. Activities and resources for creative instruction (updated version).* San Francisco: Jossey-Bass.

Conrad, R. M., & Donaldson, J. A. (2012). *Continuing to engage the online learner: More activities and resources for creative instruction* (Vol. 35). John Wiley & Sons.

Cook, K. C. (2005). An argument for pedagogy-driven online education. In K. C. Cook & K. Grant-Davie (Eds.), *Online education: Global questions, local answers*. Farmingdale, NY: Baywood Publishers. Baywood's Technical Communications Series.

Cooper, M. (1986). The ecology of writing. *College English, 48*(4), 364–375. doi:10.2307/377264

Cooper, M. (2010). Being linked to the matrix: Biology, technology, and writing. In S. A. Selber (Ed.), *Rhetoric and technologies: New directions in writing and communication* (pp. 15–32). Columbia, SC: University of South Carolina Press.

Cooper, M. (2011). Rhetorical agency as emergent and enacted. *CCC, 62*(3), 420–449.

Cooper, M. (2011). Rhetorical agency as emergent and enacted. *College Composition and Communication, 62*(3), 420–449.

Cooper, M. M. (2007). Learning digital literacies. In G. E. Hawisher & S. Selfe (Eds.), *Multimodal composition: Resource for teachers, new dimensions in computer and composition* (pp. 181–186). Hampton Press, Inc.

Cope, B., & Kalantzis, M. (Eds.). (2000). *Multiliteracies: Literacy learning and the design of social futures*. London: Routledge.

Cormier, D. (2008). Rhizomatic Education: Community as Curriculum. *Innovate: Journal of Online Education, 4*(5). Retrieved 30 December 2014, from http://davecormier.com/edblog/2008/06/03/rhizomatic-education-community-as-curriculum/

Cormier, D. (2011, November 5). *Rhizomatic Learning – Why we teach?* Retrieved January 14, 2015, from http://davecormier.com/edblog/2011/11/05/rhizomatic-learning-why-learn/

Cormier, D. (2012, December 13). *Trying to write Rhizomatic Learning in 300 words.* Retrieved January14, 2015, from http://davecormier.com/edblog/2012/12/13/trying-to-write-rhizomatic-learning-in-300- words/

Costanzo, W. (1994). Reading, writing, and thinking in an age of electronic literacy. In C. L. Selfe & S. Hilligoss (Eds.), *Literacy and computers: The complications of teaching and learning with technology* (pp. 11–21). New York, NY: MLA.

Coursera.org. (2015). *About Coursera*. Retrieved 4 April 2015 from http://www.coursera.org

Creswell, J. W. (2008). *Educational research: Planning, conducting, and evaluating quantitative and qualitative research.* Pearson Education, Inc.

CUE Powerful Learning. (2015). *Sugata Mitra: The Future of Learning* [Video file]. Author.

CUE 2015 Annual Conference. (n.d.). Retrieved from https://www.youtube.com/watch?v=y-e9WRMWcdI

Cuestas, A., & Fazzi, V. (2012). The use of ICTs in the English class: An enriching experience. *Puertas Abiertas,* (8). Retrieved from http://www.memoria.fahce.unlp.edu.ar/art_revistas/pr.6019/pr.6019.pdf

Cummins, M., Johnson, L., & Adams, S. (2012). *The NMC horizon report: 2012 higher education edition*. The New Media Consortium.

Czerniewicz, L., Deacon, A., Fife, M., Small, J., & Walji, S. (2015). Introduction to MOOCs: definition and characteristics. *MOOCs: CILT position paper.* Retrieved from http://docplayer.net/13741959-Moocs-introduction-to-moocs-definition-and-characteristics-cilt-position-paper.html

Czerniewicz, L., Deacon, A., Small, J., & Walji, S. (2014). Developing world MOOCs: A curriculum view of the MOOC landscape. *Journal of Global Literacies, Technologies, and Emerging Pedagogies*, *2*(3), 122–139. Retrieved from http://joglep.com/files/7614/0622/4917/2._Developing_world_MOOCs.pdf

Dalsgaard, C. (2006). Social software: E-learning beyond learning management systems. *European Journal of Open, Distance and E-Learning, 2006*(2). Retrieved 30 December 2014, from http://www.eurodl.org/materials/contrib/2006/Christian_Dalsgaard.htm

Danowski, D. (2006). Anyone? Anyone? Anyone? Leading discussions in cyberspace: e-Journals and interactivity in asynchronous environments. In J. Alexander & M. Dickson (Eds.), *Role Play: Distance Learning and the Teaching of Writing* (pp. 97–108). Cresskill, NJ: Hampton Press.

Davis, M., & Yancey, K. B. (2014). Notes toward the role of materiality in composing, reviewing, and assessing multimodal texts. *Computers and Composition*, *31*, 13–28. doi:10.1016/j.compcom.2014.01.001

Deleuze, G., & Guatarri, F. (1987). *A thousand plateaus: Capitalism and schizophrenia* (B. Massumi, Trans.). Minneapolis, MN: University of Minnesota Press.

DeMeyer, A. (2013). The future of doctoral education in business administration. *Journal of Management Development*, *32*(5), 477–486. doi:10.1108/02621711311328264

Dennis, E. E. (1998). Foreword. In J. V. Pavlik (Ed.), *New media technology* (2nd ed.; pp. ix–x). Boston, MA: Allyn and Bacon.

Denton, D. W. (2012). Enhancing instruction through constructivism, cooperative learning, and cloud computing. *TechTrends*, *56*(4), 34–41. doi:10.1007/s11528-012-0585-1

DePew, K. E., Spangler, S., & Spiegel, C. L. (2014). Getting past our assumptions about Web 2.0 and community building: How to design research-based literacy pedagogy. In M. Limbu & B. Gurung (Eds.), *Emerging Pedagogies in the Networked Knowledge Society: Practices Integrating Social Media and Globalization* (pp. 120–143). Hershey, PA: IGI Global. Retrieved from.

DePew, K., & Lettner-Rust, H. (2009). Mediating power: Distance learning interfaces, classroom epistemology, and the gaze. *Computers and Composition*, *26*(3), 174–189. doi:10.1016/j.compcom.2009.05.002

Deterding, S., Dixon, D., Khaled, R., & Nacke, L. (2011b). *From game design elements to gamefulness: Defining "gamification"*. Paper presented at the MindTrek '11, Tampere, Finland. Retrieved November 27, 2014 from https://www.cs.auckland.ac.nz/courses/compsci747s2c/lectures/paul/definition-deterding.pdf

DeVellis, R. F. (2012). *Scale development: Theory and application* (3rd ed.). Los Angeles, CA: Sage Publications, Inc.

Devi, P., & Gaba, T. (2013). Cloud Computing. *International Journal of Advanced Research in Computer Science and Software Engineering*, *3*(5), 1246–1251. Retrieved from http://www.ijarcsse.com/docs/papers/Volume_3/5_May2013/V3I4-0494.pdf

Devitt, A. (1993). Generalizing about genre: New conceptions of an old concept. *College Composition and Communication*, *44*(4), 573–586. doi:10.2307/358391

DeVoss, D., McKee, H., & Selfe, R. (Eds.). (2009). *Technological ecologies and sustainability* [PDF e-book]. Retrieved September 4, 2016, from http://ccdigitalpress.org/tes/TES_COMBINED.pdf

Dizard, W. (2000). *Old media and new media: Mass communications in the information age* (3rd ed.). New York, NY: Longman.

Dobrin, D. N. (1994). Hype and hypertext. In C. L. Selfe & S. Hilligoss (Eds.), *Literacy and computers: The complications of teaching and learning with technology* (pp. 305–315). New York, NY: MLA.

Dobrin, S. I. (2011). *Postcomposition*. Southern Illinois University Press.

Dobrin, S. I., & Weisser, C. R. (2002). Breaking ground in ecocomposition: Exploring relationships between discourse and environment. *College English*, *64*(5), 566–589. doi:10.2307/3250754

Dobson, T. M., & Willinsky, J. (2009). Digital literacy. In D. R. Olson & N. Torrance (Eds.), *The Cambridge handbook of literacy* (pp. 286–312). Cambridge, UK: Cambridge University Press. doi:10.1017/CBO9780511609664.017

Domahue, C. (2016). The "trans" in transnational-translingual: Rhetorical and linguistic flexibility as new norms. *Composition Studies*, *44*(1), 147–150.

Donahue, C. (2009, December). 'Internationalization' and composition studies: Reorienting the discourse. *CCC*, *61*(2), 212–243.

Dryden, L. M. (1994). Literature, student-centered classrooms, and hypermedia environments. In C. L. Selfe & S. Hilligoss (Eds.), *Literacy and computers: The complications of teaching and learning with technology* (pp. 282–304). New York, NY: MLA.

Duffy, J. (2014, April 2). *The best cloud storage solutions*. Retrieved August 30, 2014, from http://www.pcmag.com/article2/0%2c2817%2c2413556%2c00.asp

Duffy, P. (2008). Engaging the YouTube Google-Eyed Generation: Strategies for Using Web 2.0 in Teaching and Learning. *The Electronic Journal of e-Learning*, *6*(2), 119 – 130. Retrieved from http://www.ejel.org/volume6/issue2

Duggan, M., Ellison, N., Lampe, C., Lenhart, A., & Madden, M. (2015). *Social Media Update 2014*. Pew Research Center. Retrieved from http://www.pewinternet.org/2015/01/09/demographics-of-key-social-networking-platforms-2/

Duin, H., & Hansen, C. (1994). Reading and writing on computer networks as social construction. In C. L. Selfe & S. Hilligoss (Eds.), *Literacy and computers: The complications of teaching and learning with technology* (pp. 89–112). New York, NY: MLA.

Echeng, R., Usoro, A., & Majewski, G. (2013). *Acceptance of Web 2.0 in learning in higher education: An empirical study of a Scottish university*. Paper presented at the IADIS International Conference Web-Based Communities and Social Media 2013, Prague, Czech Republic.

Ehlers, U. D. (2009). Web 2.0 - e-learning 2.0 - quality 2.0? Quality for new learning cultures. *Quality Assurance in Education*, *17*(3), 296–314. doi:10.1108/09684880910970687

Engels-Schwarzpaul, A. C., & Peters, M. A. (Eds.). (2013). *Of Other Thoughts: Non-Traditional Ways to the Doctorate: A Guidebook for Candidates and Supervisors*. Springer Science & Business Media. doi:10.1007/978-94-6209-317-1

Engeström, Y. (1990). *Learning, working and imagining: Twelve studies in activity theory*. Helsinki: Orienta-Konsultit Oy.

Eom, S. (2010). *Relationships between e-learning systems and learning outcomes: A path analysis model*. Paper presented at the 2010 IEEE 10th International Conference on Advanced Learning Technologies (ICALT), Sousse, Tunisia. doi:10.1109/ICALT.2010.147

Erichsen, E. A., & Bolliger, D. U. (2011). Towards understanding international graduate student isolation in traditional and online environments. *Educational Technology Research and Development*, *59*(3), 309–326. doi:10.1007/s11423-010-9161-6

Ertmer, P. A., Ottenbreit-Leftwich, A., Sadik, O., Sendurur, E., & Sendurur, P. (2012). Teacher beliefs and technology integration practices: A critical relationship. *Computers & Education*, *59*(2), 423–435. doi:10.1016/j.compedu.2012.02.001

Ertmer, P. A., Ottenbreit-Leftwich, A., & York, C. S. (2007). Exemplary Technology-using Teachers: Perceptions of Factors Influencing Success. *Journal of Computing in Teacher Education*, *23*(2), 55–60.

Esnault, L. (2008). Web-based education and pedagogical technologies: Solutions for learning applications. Hershey, PA: IGI Global. doi:10.4018/978-1-59904-525-2

Eyman, D., & Ball, C. E. (2014). Composing for digital publication: Rhetoric, design, code. *Composition Studies*, *42*(1), 114–117.

Fairclough, N. (2006). *Language and globalization*. New York, NY: Routledge.

Feenberg, A. (1991). *Critical theory of technology*. New York: Oxford University Press.

Fichten, C. S., Ferraro, V., Asuncion, J. V., Chwojka, C., Barile, M., & Nguyen, M. N. et al. (2009). Disabilities and e-learning problems and solutions: An exploratory study. *Journal of Educational Technology & Society*, *12*(4), 241–256.

Fichter, D. (2005). The many forms of e-collaboration: Blogs, wikis, portals, groupware, discussion boards, and instant messaging. *Online*, *29*(4), 48–50.

Fish, S. (2011, Dec 26). The order of things changeth. *The New York Times*. Retrieved 15 February 2015 from http://opinionator.blogs.nytimes.com/2011/12/26/the-old-order-changeth/

Ford, L., & Amaral, D. (2006). Research on parent involvement: Where we've been and where we need to go. *BC Educational Leadership Research*, *3*(March), 1–20.

Foucault, M. (1982). The Subject and Power. *Critical Inquiry*, *8*(4), 777–795. doi:10.1086/448181

Fraiberg, S. (2010). Composition 2.0: Toward a multilingual and multimodal framework. *College Composition and Communication*, *62*(1), 100–126.

Fraiberg, S. (2010, September). Composition 2.0: Toward a multilingual and multimodal framework. *CCC*, *62*(1), 100–126.

Freebody, P. (2007). *Literacy education in school: Research perspectives from the past, for the future.* Australian Council for Educational Research.

Freire, P. (2001). *Pedagogy of the oppressed*. New York, NY: Continuum.

Gaillet, L. L. (2009). A socially constructed view of reading and writing: Historical alternatives to "Bridging the Gap.". In L. Ostergaard, J. Ludwig, & J. Nugent (Eds.), *Transforming English studies: New voices in an emerging genre* (pp. 163–178). West Lafayette, IN: Parlor Press. Lauer Series in Rhetoric and Composition.

Gasser, U., Palfrey, J., & Becker, M. B. (2012). *Mapping Cloud Interoperability in the Globalized Economy: Theory and Observations from Practice.* NCCR Trade Regulation Swiss National Center of Competence in Research.

Gay, L. R., & Airasian, P. (2003). *Educational research: Competencies for analysis and applications*. Pearson Education Inc.

Gee, J. P. (2007a). What video games have to teach us about learning and literacy? (Rev. and updated ed.). New York: Palgrave Macmillan.

Gee, J. P. (2007b). *Good video games + good learning: Collected essays on video games, learning and literacy*. New York: Peter Lang.

Gee, J. P., & Hayes, E. (2011). *Language and learning in the digital age*. New York: Routledge.

Ghefaili, A. (2003). Cognitive apprenticeship, technology, and the contextualization of learning environments. *Journal of Educational Computing, Design & Online Learning, 4*(1), 1-27. Retrieved from: https://wss.apan.org/jko/mls/Learning%20Content/Aziz%20-%20Cognitive%20Apprenticeship.pdf

Gibson, J. (1979). *The ecological approach to visual perception*. New York: Houghton Mifflin.

Giddens, A. (1984). *The constitution of society: Outline of the theory of structuration*. Berkeley, CA: University of California Press.

Gillen, J., & Merchant, G. (2013). From virtual histories to virtual literacy. In G. Merchant, J. Gillen, J. Marsh, & J. Davies (Eds.), *Virtual literacies: Interactive spaces for children and young people* (pp. 9–26). New York, NY: Routledge.

Gilroy, P. (1993). *The black Atlantic: Modernity and double consciousness*. Cambridge, MA: Harvard UP.

Giltrow, J. (2002). Meta-genre. In R. Coe, L. Lingard, & T. Teslenko (Eds.), *The rhetoric and ideology of genre: Strategies for stability and change* (pp. 187–205). New York, NY: Hampton Press.

Giroux, H. (1985). Critical pedagogy, cultural politics and the discourse of experience. *Journal of Education, 167*(2), 22–41.

Giroux, H. (2011). *On Critical Pedagogy*. New York, NY: Continuum.

Goffman, E. (1973). *The presentation of self in everyday life*. Woodstock, NY: The Overlook Press.

Goggin, G. (2012). *New technologies and the media*. London: Palgrave Macmillan.

Gonzales, L. (2015). Multimodality, translingualism, and rhetorical genre studies. *Composition. Forum*, 31.

Goodyear, P., Banks, S., Hogdson, V., & McConnell, D. (Eds.). (2004). *Advances in research on networked learning*. Boston: Kluwer Academic.

Google Apps Help. (2014). Google Apps user guide to accessibility. *Google Apps Help Center*. Retrieved from https://support.google.com/a/answer/1631886?hl=en&ref_topic=3035040

Google. (n.d.). Productivity Tools. *Google for Education*. Retrieved from https://www.google.com/edu/products/productivity-tools/

Gosper, M., McNeili, M., Woo, K., Phillips, R., Preston, G., & Green, D. (2011, November). Web-based lecture technologies and learning and teaching: A study of change in four Australian universities. *Journal of Asynchronous Learning Networks, 15*(4), 84–95.

Graupner, M., Nickoson-Massey, L., & Blair, K. (2009). Remediating knowledge-making spaces in the graduate curriculum: Developing and sustaining multimodal teaching and research. *Computers and Composition, 26*(1), 13–23. doi:10.1016/j.compcom.2008.11.005

Grodal, T. (2003). Stories for eye, ear, and muscles: Video games, media, and embodied experiences. In M. J. P. Wolf & B. Perron (Eds.), *The video game theory reader* (pp. 129–155). New York, NY: Routledge.

Groom, J., & Lamb, B. (2014). Reclaiming innovation. *EDUCAUSE Review, 49*(3). Retrieved from http://www.educause.edu/visuals/shared/er/extras/2014/ReclaimingInnovation/default.html

Guattari, F. (1989). The three ecologies. *New Formations, 8*, 131–147.

Gurung, B. (2013). Emerging pedagogies in networked knowledge communities. In M. Limbu & B. Gurung (Eds.), *Emerging Pedagogies in the Networked Knowledge Society: Practices Integrating Social Media and Globalization* (pp. 1–24). Hershey, PA: IGI Global.

Gurung, B. (2014). Emerging pedagogies in the networked knowledge communities. In M. Limbu & B. Gurung (Eds.), *Emerging Pedagogies in the Networked Knowledge Society: Practices Integrating Social Media and Globalization*. Hershey, PA: IGI Global. doi:10.4018/978-1-4666-4757-2.ch001

Gurung, B., & Chávez, R. C. (2011). Transformative multicultural engagement on a web 2.0 interface. In G. Kurubacak & T. V. Yuzer (Eds.), *Transformative online education and liberation: Models for social equality* (pp. 15–46). Hershey, PA: IGI Global. doi:10.4018/978-1-60960-046-4.ch002

Gurung, B., & Rutledge, D. (2014). Overlapping of personal and educational digital engagement. *Computers & Education*, *77*, 91–100. doi:10.1016/j.compedu.2014.04.012

Gutari, F. (2013). Can Children Teach Themselves? *Scientific American*. Retrieved From http://blogs.scientificamerican.com/observations/can-children-teach- themselves/

Haas, C., & Neuwirth, C. M. (1994). Writing the technology that writes us: Research on literacy and the shape of technology. In C. L. Selfe & S. Hilligoss (Eds.), *Literacy and computers: The complications of teaching and learning with technology* (pp. 319–335). New York, NY: MLA.

Halasek, K., McCorkle, B., Selfe, C. L., DeWitt, S. L., Delagrange, S., Michaels, J., & Clinnin, K. (2014). A MOOC with a view: How MOOCs encourage us to reexamine pedagogical doxa. In Invasion of the MOOCs: The promises and perils of massive open online courses (pp. 156-166). Anderson, SC: Parlor Press.

Hall, K. (2004). *Literacy and schooling: Towards renewal in primary education policy*. Aldershot, UK: Ashgate Publishing Limited.

Halttunen, K. (2011). Pedagogical Design and Evaluation of Interactive Information Retrieval Learning Environment. In *Teaching and Learning in Information Retrieval* (pp. 61–73). Berlin: Springer. doi:10.1007/978-3-642-22511-6_5

Hampden-Turner, C., & Trompenaars, F. (2000). *Building cross-cultural competence: How to create wealth from conflicting values*. New Haven, CT: Yale University Press.

Handa, C. (2004). *Visual rhetoric in a digital world: A critical sourcebook*. Bedford, MA: St. Martin's.

Hardt, M., & Negri, A. (2000). *Empire*. Cambridge, MA: Harvard UP.

Haring-Smith, T. (1994). *Writing Together: Collaborative Learning in the Writing Classroom*. New York: Harper Collins College.

Harris, J. (1995). Negotiating the contact zone. In *Landmark Essays on Basic Writing* (pp. 27–42). Erlbaum.

Hartley, J. (2007). Teaching, learning and new technology: A review for teachers. *British Journal of Educational Technology*, *38*(1), 42–62. doi:10.1111/j.1467-8535.2006.00634.x

Hartnett, M., George, A. S., & Dron, J. (2011, October). Examining motivation in online distance learning environments: Complex, multifaceted, and situation-dependent. *Examining Motivation in Online Distance Learning Environments: Complex, Multifaceted, and Situation-Dependent, 12*(6). Retrieved October 5, 2015 from http://www.irrodl.org/index.php/irrodl/article/view/1030/1954

Hasrati, M. (2005). Legitimate peripheral participation and supervising Ph.D students. *Studies in Higher Education*, *30*(5), 557–570. doi:10.1080/03075070500249252

Heidegger, M. (1977). *The question concerning technology*. New York, NY: Harper and Row.

Heider, J. S. (2015, July). Using digital learning solutions to address higher education's greatest challenges. *Pub Res Q*, *31*(3), 183–189. doi:10.1007/s12109-015-9413-8

Helfand, D. (2013, July 8). Watering the Roots of Knowledge through Collaborative Learning. *The Chronicle of Higher Education.*

Herrick, D. R. (2009, October). Google this!: using Google apps for collaboration and productivity. In *Proceedings of the 37th annual ACM SIGUCCS fall conference: communication and collaboration* (pp. 55-64). ACM. doi:10.1145/1629501.1629513

Hilligoss, S., & Selfe, C. L. (1994). Studying literacy with computers. In C. L. Selfe & S. Hilligoss (Eds.), *Literacy and computers: The complications of teaching and learning with technology* (pp. 336–340). New York, NY: MLA.

Hocks, M. E. (2003). Understanding visual rhetoric in digital writing. *College Composition and Communication, 54*(4), 629–656. doi:10.2307/3594188

Hocks, M. E. (2008). Understanding visual rhetoric in digital writing environments. In T. R. Johnson (Ed.), *Teaching composition: Background readings* (pp. 337–362). New York, NY: Bedford/St. Martin's.

Ho, L. A. (2009, Autumn). The antecedents of e-learning outcome: An examination of system quality, technology readiness, and learning behavior. *Adolescence, 44*(175), 581–599. PMID:19950871

Holec, H. (1981). Autonomy and Foreign Language Learning. Oxford, UK: Pergamon. (first published 1979)

hooks, b. (1994). *Teaching to Transgress: Education as a Practice of Freedom.* New York: Routledge.

Horner, B., & Selfe, C. L. (2013). *Translinguality/trasmodality relations: Snapshots from a dialogue.* Unpublished working paper, University of Louisville. Retrieved September 4, 2016, from http://louisville.edu/workingpapers/doc/self-horner-working-papers-version

Horner, B., Lu, M., Royster, J. J., & Trimbur, J. (2011). OPINION: Language difference in writing: Toward a translingual approach. *College English, 73*(3), 303–321.

Horner, B., Lu, M., Royster, J., & Trimbur, J. (2011). Language difference in writing: Toward a translingual approach. *College English, 73*(3), 303–321.

Hornig, S. (2010). What do children write in science? A study of the genre set in a primary science classroom. *Written Communication, 27*(1), 87–119. doi:10.1177/0741088309350159

Howland, J. L., Jonassen, D. H., & Marra, R. M. (2012). *Meaningful learning with technology* (4th ed.). Boston, MA: Pearson Education.

Hsu, Y. C., Hung, J. L., & Ching, Y. H. (2013). Trends of educational technology research: More than a decade of international research in six SSCI-indexed refereed journals. *Educational Technology Research and Development, 61*(4), 685–705. doi:10.1007/s11423-013-9290-9

Huh, K. (2006). Korean mothers' perspectives of schooling in the United States. *Primary English Education, 12*(2), 337–361.

Hui, K.-c., Pan, Z., Chung, R. C.-k., Wang, C. C. L., Jin, X., Göbel, S., et al. (2007, June 11-13). *Technologies for e-learning and digital entertainment.* Paper presented at the Second International Conference, Edutainment 2007, Hong Kong, China. doi:10.1007/978-3-540-73011-8

Humphreys, S. (2003). Online multi-user games. *Australian Journal of Communication, 30*(1), 79–91.

Hurd, S., Beaven, T., & Ortega, A. (2001). Developing autonomy in a distance language learning context: Issues and dilemmas for course writers. *System, 29*(3), 341–355. doi:10.1016/S0346-251X(01)00024-0

ISTE Standards for Teachers. (2016). Retrieved April 1, 2016 from http://www.iste.org/standards/iste-standards/standards-for-teachers

Jacobs, H. H. (Ed.). (2010). *Curriculum 21: Essential education for a changing world.* Alexandria, VA: Association for Supervision and Curriculum Development.

Jaeger, P. T., Lin, J., & Grimes, J. M. (2008). Cloud computing and information policy: Computing in a policy cloud? *Journal of Information Technology and Politics, 5*(3). Retrieved from http://www.urniacs.umd.edu/~jimmylin/publications/Jaegeretal2008.pdf.

Jain, M. K., Singh, R., & Shrivastri, S. (2015). Privacy Preservation and Authentication Method in Cloud Computing. *International Journal of Advanced Research in Computer Science and Software Engineering*, *5*(12), 596–600. Retrieved from http://www.ijarcsse.com/docs/papers/Volume_5/12_December2015/V5I12-0251.pdf

James, R. (2014). ICT's participatory potential in higher education collaborations: Reality or just talk. *British Journal of Educational Technology*, *45*(4), 557–570. doi:10.1111/bjet.12060

Janta, H., Lugosi, P., & Brown, L. (2014). Coping with loneliness: A netnographic study of doctoral students. *Journal of Further and Higher Education*, *38*(4), 553–571. doi:10.1080/0309877X.2012.726972

Jenkins, H. (2012). *Convergence Culture: Where Old and New Media Collide*. New York: New York University Press.

Jenkins, S. (2003). Foreword. In J. Aitchison & D. M. Lewis (Eds.), *New media language*. New York, NY: Routledge.

Jibber Jobber. (2014). *The Ultimate Interview Question #JobSearch* [Blog post]. Retrieved fromhttp://www.jibberjobber.com/blog/2014/11/12/the-ultimate-interview-question-jobsearch/

John, N. A. (2013, March). Sharing and web 2.0: The emergence of a keyword. *New Media & Society*, *15*(2), 167–182. doi:10.1177/1461444812450684

Johnson, E. (2014). Toward the building of a cross-disciplinary doctoral research and writing culture. *Journal of University Teaching & Learning Practice*, *11*(1), 4. Retrieved from http://ro.uow.edu.au/jutlp/vol11/iss1/4

Johnson-Eilola, J. (1994). Reading and writing in hypertext. In C. L. Selfe & S. Hilligoss (Eds.), *Literacy and computers: The complications of teaching and learning with technology* (pp. 89–112). New York, NY: MLA.

Johnson-Eilola, J. (1997). *Nostalgic angels: Rearticulating hypertext writing*. Norwood, NJ: Ablex Publishing.

Johnson-Eilola, J. (1998). Living on the surface: Learning the age of global communication networks. In I. Snyder (Ed.), *Page to screen: Taking literacy into the electronic era* (pp. 185–210). New York, NY: Routledge. doi:10.4324/9780203201220_chapter_9

Johnson-Eilola, J., & Hea, A. C. K. (2003). After hypertext: Other ideas. *Computers and Composition*, *20*(4), 415–425. doi:10.1016/j.compcom.2003.08.014

Johnson, L., Becker, S., Estrada, V., & Freeman, A. (2014). *The NMC horizon report: 2014 higher education*. The New Media Consortium.

Johnson, R. R. (1998). *User-centered technology*. New York: State University of New York Press.

Jonassen, D. H. (2006). *Modeling with technology: Mindtools for conceptual change* (3rd ed.). Columbus, OH: Merrill/Prentice Hall.

Jones, N., & Vollmers, G. (2008). Using web-based technologies for transformative hybrid distance education. In L. Esnault (Ed.), Web-based education and pedagogical technologies: Solutions for learning applications (pp. 37-55). Hershey, PA: IGI Global. doi:10.4018/978-1-59904-525-2.ch003

Jordan, J. (2015). Material translingual ecologies. *College English*, *77*(4), 364–382.

Joyce, M. (1988, November). Siren shapes: Exploratory and constructive hypertexts. Academic Computing.

Juul, J. (2005). Games telling stories? In J. Raessens & J. Goldstein (Eds.), Handbook of computer game studies (pp. 219-226). Cambridge, MA: The MIT Press.

Kain, D., & Wardle, E. (2014). Activity theory: An introduction for the writing classroom. In Writing about writing (2nd ed.). Boston, MA: Bedford/St. Martin.

Kang, Y. W. (2011). *Hybrid interactive rhetoric engagements in Massively Multiplayer Online Role-Playing Games (MMORPGs): Examining the role of rhetors and audiences in generative rhetorical discourses.* (Dissertation). The University of Texas at El Paso. Ann Arbor, M.I. UMI.

Kaplan, R. (1966). Cultural thought patterns in intercultural education. *Language Learning*, *16*(1), 1–20. doi:10.1111/j.1467-1770.1966.tb00804.x

Karunasena, A., Deng, H., & Kam, B. (2013). *Investigating the enabling role of Web 2.0 technology for interactive e-learning in Australia.* Paper presented at the 24th Australasian Conference on Information Systems, ACIS2013, Melbourne, Australia.

Kember, S., & Zylinska, J. (2012). Introduction. In S. Kember & J. Zylinska (Eds.), *Life after new media: Mediation as a vital process* (pp. xiii–xx). Cambridge, MA: The MIT Press.

Keramati, A., Afshari-Mofrad, M., & Kamrani, A. (2011, May). The role of readiness factors in e-learning outcomes: An empirical study. *Computers & Education*, *57*(3), 1919–1929. doi:10.1016/j.compedu.2011.04.005

Kessler, S., & McKenna, W. (1985). *Gender: An Ethnomethodological Approach.* New York: Wiley.

Kiernan, J. E. (2015). Multimodal and translingual composing practices: A culturally based needs assessment of second language learners. *Journal of Global Literacies, Technologies, and Emerging Pedagogies*, *3*(1), 302–332.

Kim, K. J., Liu, S., & Bonk, C. J. (2005). Online MBA students' perceptions of online learning: Benefits, challenges, and suggestions. *The Internet and Higher Education*, *8*(4), 335–344. doi:10.1016/j.iheduc.2005.09.005

Kincheloe, J. L., & McLaren, P. (Eds.). (2007). *Critical pedagogy in the twenty-first century: Evolution for survival.* New York: Peter Lang.

Kittle, P., & Hicks, T. (2009). Transforming the Group Paper with Collaborative Online Writing. *Pedagogy*, *9*(3), 525–538. doi:10.1215/15314200-2009-012

Knobel, M., & Lankshear, C. (2008). Introducing TPCK. In American Association of Colleges for Teachers (Ed.), Handbook of Technological Pedagogical Content Knowledge (TPCK) of Educators (pp. 3-27). New York, NY: Routledge.

Knobel, M., & Lankshear, C. (1999). *Ways of knowing: Researching literacy.* Sydney: Primary English Teaching Association.

Knorr, E., & Gruman, G. (2008, April 7). What cloud computing really means. *Infoworld.* Retrieved from http://www.infoworld.com/d/cloud-computing/what-cloud-computing-reallymeans-031

Knowles, M. S. (1975). *Self-directed learning: A guide for learners and teachers.* New York: Association Press.

Knox, J. (2014). Digital culture clash: "massive" education in the E-learning and Digital Cultures MOOC. *Distance Education, 35*(2), 164–177. doi:10.1080/01587919.2014.917704

Koh, M. H., & Hill, J. R. (2009). Student perceptions of groupwork in an online course: Benefits and challenges. *International Journal of E-Learning & Distance Education, 23*(2), 69–92.

Kolb, D. (1994). Socrates in the labyrinth. In G. P. Landow (Ed.), *Hyper/text/theory* (pp. 323–342). Baltimore, MD: Johns Hopkins University Press.

Kolko, B., Nakamura, L., & Rodman, G. (2000). *Race in Cyberspace*. New York: Routledge.

Krause, S., & Lowe, C. (2014). *Invasion of the MOOCs*. Anderson, SC: Parlor Press.

Krelja Kurelovic, E., Tomljanovic, J., & Ruzie-Baf, M. (2012). *The use of Web 2.0 tools in education from the point of view of future teachers.* Paper presented at the MIPRO 2012 - 35th International Convention on Information and Communication Technology, Electronics and Microelectronics, Opatija, Croatia.

Kreps, D., & Pearson, E. (2009). Community as commodity: Social networking and transnational capitalism. In N. Panteli (Ed.), *Virtual Social Networks: Mediated, Massive, and Multilayers Sites* (pp. 155–174). Eastbourne, UK: Macmillan. doi:10.1057/9780230250888_9

Kress, G. (1999). "English" at the crossroads: Rethinking curricula of communication in the context of the turn to the visual. In G. Hawisher & C. Selfe (Eds.), *Passions, pedagogies, and 21st Century technologies* (pp. 66–88). Logan, UT: Utah State University Press.

Kress, G. (2003). *Literacy in the new media age*. New York, NY: Routledge. doi:10.4324/9780203164754

Kress, G. (2005). Gains and losses: New forms of texts, knowledge, and learning. *Computers and Composition, 22*(1), 5–22. doi:10.1016/j.compcom.2004.12.004

Kress, G. (2010). *Multimodality: A social semiotic approach to contemporary communication*. London: Routledge.

Kumar, S., Johnson, M., & Hardemon, T. (2013). Dissertations at a distance: Students' perceptions of online mentoring in a doctoral program. *International Journal of E-Learning & Distance Education, 27*(1). Retrieved from http://ijede.ca/index.php/jde/article/view/835/1481

Kuuti, K. (1996). Activity theory as a potential framework for human-computer research. In B. A. Nardi (Ed.), *Context and consciousness: activity theory and human-computer interaction* (pp. 17–44). Cambridge, MA: MIT Press.

Kwan, B. S. (2009). Reading in preparation for writing a PhD thesis: Case studies of experiences. *Journal of English for Academic Purposes, 8*(3), 180-191. DOI:10.1016/j.jeap.2009.02.001

Lam, E. (2006). Re-Envisioning language, literacy, and the immigrant subject in new mediascapes. *Pedagogies, 1*(3), 171–195. doi:10.1207/s15544818ped0103_2

Lam, P., & McNaught, C. (2006). Design and evaluation of online courses containing media-enhanced learning materials. *Educational Media International, 43*(3), 199–218. doi:10.1080/09523980600641403

Lamsal, T. (2013). *Fleeing Mai Fair: Bye bye Guddusingh.* Retrieved 15 June 2014 from http://tikalamsal.com/2013/10/

Landow, G. P. (1992). *Hypertext: The convergence of contemporary critical theory and technology.* Baltimore, MD: Johns Hopkins University Press.

Lankshear, C., & Knobel, M. (2006). *New literacies: Everyday practices and classroom learning*. Berkshire, UK: Open University Press.

Lankshear, C., & Knobel, M. (Eds.). (2008). *Digital literacies: Concepts, policies, and practices*. New York: Peter Lang.

Lantz-Andersson, A., Vkigmo, S., & Bowen, R. (2013). Crossing boundaries in Facebook: Students' framing of language learning activities as extended spaces. *International Journal of Computer-Supported Collaborative Learning*, *8*(3), 293–312. doi:10.1007/s11412-013-9177-0

Latour, B. (1987). *Science in action: How to follow scientists and engineers through society*. Cambridge, MA: Harvard UP.

Latour, B. (1990). Om aktor-netvaerksteroi. Nogle fa afklaringer og mere end nogle fa forviklinger. *Philosophia*, *25*, 47–64.

Latour, B. (1996). *Aramis. Or the love of technology* (C. Porter, Trans.). Cambridge, MA: Harvard UP.

Latour, B. (2005). *Reassembling the social: An introduction to actor-network-theory*. Oxford, UK: Oxford University Press. Clarendon Lectures in Management Studies.

Latour, B. (2005). *Reassembling the Social: An Introduction to Actor-Network-Theory*. Oxford: Oxford UP.

Lauer, C. (2009). Contending with terms: "Multimodal" and "Multimedia" in the academic and public spheres. *Computers and Composition*, *26*(4), 225–239. doi:10.1016/j.compcom.2009.09.001

Lauer, J. (1993). Rhetoric and composition studies: A multimodal discipline. In T. Enos & S. C. Brown (Eds.), *Defining the new rhetoric* (pp. 44–54). Newbury Park, CA: Sage.

Lave, J., & Wenger, E. (1991). *Situated learning: Legitimate peripheral participation*. Cambridge University Press. doi:10.1017/CBO9780511815355

Law, J. (1992). Notes on the theory of the actor-network: Ordering, strategy and heterogeneity. *Systems Practice*, *5*(4), 379–393. doi:10.1007/BF01059830

Lawson, C. (2008). An ontology of technology: Artifacts, relations and functions. *Techne*, *12*(1). Retrieved January 28, 2011 from http://scholars.lib.vt.edu/ ejournals/SPT/v12nl/pdf/lawson.pdf

Leckart, S. (2011). The Stanford education experiment could change higher learning forever. *Wired*. Retrieved 20 March 2015 from http://www.wired.com/2012/03/ff_aiclass/

Lee, A. (2008). How are doctoral students supervised? Concepts of doctoral research supervision. *Studies in Higher Education*, *33*(3), 267–281. doi:10.1080/03075070802049202

Lee, H., Parsons, D., Kwon, G., Kim, J., Petrova, K., Jeong, E., & Ryu, H. (2016). Cooperation begins: Encouraging critical thinking skills through cooperative reciprocity using a mobile learning game. *Computers & Education*, *97*, 97–155. doi:10.1016/j.compedu.2016.03.006

Leont'ev, A. N. (1978). *Activity, consciousness and personality*. Englewood Cliffs, NJ: Prentice-Hall.

Lévy, P. (1997). *Collective Intelligence: Mankind's Emerging World in Cyberspace*. New York: Plenum Trade.

Lewin, T. (2013). Universities abroad join partnership on the web. *New York Times*. Retrieved 5 April 2015 from http://www.nytimes.com/2013/02/21/education/universities-abroad-join-mooc-course-projects.html

Lewin, T. (2013, April 30). Colleges Adapt Online Courses to Ease Burden. *The New York Times*. Retrieved from http://query.nytimes.com/gst/fullpage.html?res=9E02E5D7163BF933A05757C0A9659D8B63&ref=tamarlewin

Lewis, G. (2010). *Basics About Cloud Computing*. Retrieved from http://resources.sei.cmu.edu/asset_files/WhitePaper/2010_019_001_28877.pdf

Lian, A. P. (2004). Technology-enhanced language-learning environments: A rhizomatic approach. In J. Son (Ed.), *Computer-assisted language learning: Concepts, contexts and practices* (pp. 1–20). New York: Universe.

Licona, M., & Gurung, B. (2011). Online multicultural education discussion: Praxis retained. *Multicultural Education*, *9*(1), 2–8.

Lievrouw, L. A., & Livingstone, S. (Eds.). (2002). *Handbook of new media: Social shaping and consequences of ICTs*. London: Sage Publication.

Liew, A. (2007). Understanding data, information, knowledge and their inter-relationships. *Journal of Knowledge Management Practice*, *8*(2). Retrieved from http://www.tlainc.com/articl134.htm

Li, G. (2006). What do parents think? Middle-class Chinese immigrant parents' perspectives on literacy learning, homework, and, school-home communication. *School Community Journal*, *16*(2), 27–46.

Li, G. (2007). Second language and literacy learning in school and at home: An ethnographic study of Chinese Canadian first grades' experiences. *Literacy Teaching and Learning*, *11*(2), 1–31.

Limbu, M. (2012). Mapping "Bottom up" pedagogy in the age of digitally globalized world. *Nelta Choutari: Nepalese ELT practioners meet the world.* Retrieved August 25, 2012 from http://neltachoutari.wordpress.com/2012/03/01/mapping-bottom-up-pedagogy-in-the-age-of-digitally-globalized-world/

Limbu, M. (2013). *Emerging pedagogies in the networked knowledge society: Practices integrating social media and globalization*. Academic Press.

Limbu, M. (2014). *Digital rhetoric and global literacies: Communication modes and digital practices in the networked world*. Academic Press.

Limbu, M. (2011a). *Cross-cultural-composition 2.0: Mapping/remapping spaces of Language minority students in the contact zones*. Berlin, Germany: LAMBERT Academic Publishing.

Limbu, M. (2011b). Processing first-year college writing via Facebook pedagogy in linguistically and culturally diverse first-year composition classes. *Journal of International Students.*, *1*(1), 59–62.

Limbu, M. (2012). Teaching Writing in the Cloud: Networked Writing Communities in the Culturally and Linguistically Diverse Classrooms. *Journal of Global Literacies, Technologies, and Emerging Pedagogies*, *1*(1), 1–20. Retrieved from http://joglep.com/files/7613/5174/0862/ML.pdf

Limbu, M. (2013). Digital and global literacies in networked communities: Epistemic shifts and communication practices in the cloud era. In G. Verhulsdonck & M. Limbu (Eds.), *Digital rhetoric and global literacies: Communication modes and digital practices in the networked world* (pp. 131–153). Hershey, PA: IGI Global.

Limbu, M. (2013). Digital and global literacies in networked communities: Epistemic shifts and communication practices in the cloud era. In G. Verhulsdonck & M. Limbu (Eds.), *Digital Rhetoric and Global Literacies: Communication Modes and Digital Practices in the Networked World.* Hershey, PA: IGI Global. Retrieved from.

Limbu, M. (2014). Emerging Pedagogies in the Networked Knowledge Communities: Interweaving and Intersecting Global Communities in the 21st Century Global Village. In M. Limbu & B. Gurung (Eds.), *Emerging Pedagogies in the Networked Knowledge Society: Practices Integrating Social Media and Globalization* (pp. 61–86). Hershey, PA: IGI Global Publishing. doi:10.4018/978-1-4666-4757-2.ch003

Limbu, M., McCool, M., & Zheng, X. (2013). Writing Across Cultures: Understanding and Teaching Writer Responsibility and Reader Responsibility Writing. *Journal of Global Literacies, Technologies, and Emerging Pedagogies*, *1*(2), 56–70.

Lin, Y. T., Wen, M. L., Jou, M., & Wu, D. W. (2014). A cloud-based learning environment for developing student reflection abilities. *Computers in Human Behavior*, *32*, 244–252. doi:10.1016/j.chb.2013.12.014

Lister, M., Dovey, J., Giddings, S., Grant, I., & Kelly, K. (2009). *New media: A critical introduction* (2nd ed.). New York, NY: Routledge.

Little, D. (2003). Learner autonomy and second/foreign language learning. *Subject Centre for Languages, Linguistics and Area Studies Good Practice Guide*. Retrieved 30 December 2014, from https://www.llas.ac.uk/resources/gpg/1409

Lotherington, H., & Jenson, J. (2011). Teaching multimodal and digital literacy in L2 settings: New literacies, new basics, new pedagogies. *Annual Review of Applied Linguistics*, *31*, 226–246. doi:10.1017/S0267190511000110

Lu, M., & Horner, B. (2012). *Translingual literacy and matters of agency*. Unpublished working paper, University of Louisville. Retrieved September 4, 2016, from http://writing.uncc.edu/sites/writing.uncc.edu/files/media/docs/Min-Zhan_Lu_and_Bruce_Horner_Translingual_Literacy_and_Matters_of_Agency(1).pdf

Luke, A., & Freebody, P. (1997). Shaping the social practices of reading. In S. Muspratt, A. Luke, & P. Freebody (Eds.), *Constructing critical literacies: Teaching and learning textual practice* (pp. 185–225). Cresskill, NJ: Hampton Press, Inc.

Lu, M.-Z. (1994, December). Professing multiculturalism: The politics of style in the contact zone. *CCC*, *45*(4), 442–458.

Lunsford, A. A., Fishman, J., & Liew, W. (2013). College Writing, Identification, and the Production of Intellectual Property: Voices from the Stanford Study of Writing. *College English*, *75*(5), 470–492.

Lyons, W., Scroggins, D., & Rule, P. B. (1990). The mentor in graduate education. *Studies in Higher Education*, *15*(3), 277–285. doi:10.1080/03075079012331377400

Mackness, J. (2014, June 24). *Principles for Rhizomatic Thinking*. Retrieved January 14, 2015, from https://jennymackness.wordpress.com/2014/06/24/principles-for-rhizomatic-thinking/

Madge, C., Meek, J., Wellens, J., & Hooley, T. (2009). Facebook, social integration and informal learning at university: It is more for socializing and talking to friends about work than for actually doing work. *Learning, Media and Technology*, *34*(2), 141–155. doi:10.1080/17439880902923606

Maher, M. A., Gilmore, J. A., Feldon, D. F., & Davis, T. E. (2013). Cognitive apprenticeship and the supervision of science and engineering research assistants. *Journal of Research Practice, 9*(2), Article M5. Retrieved from http://jrp.icaap.org/index.php/jrp/article/view/354/311

Manovich, L. (2001). *The language of new media*. Cambridge, MA: The MIT Press.

Manovich, L. (2003). New media from Borges to HTML. In N. Wardrip-Fruin & N. Montfort (Eds.), *The new media reader* (pp. 12–23). Cambridge, MA: The MIT Press.

Maranto, G., & Barton, M. (2010). Promise and Paradox. *Computers and Composition*, *27*, 36–47. doi:10.1016/j.compcom.2009.11.003

Marcelo, C., Yot, C., & Mayor, C. (2015). University teaching with digital technologies. *Media Education Research Journal*, *13*(45), 117–124.

Martin Bosque, A., & Munday, P. (2014). Conexión, colaboración y aprendizaje más allá del aula: #InstagramELE. In *Proceedings from the Second Annual Conference of Applied Linguistics for the Teaching of Foreign Languages*. Madrid: Nebrija Procedia. Retrieved 14 January 2015, from http://www.nebrija.com/la_universidad/servicios/pdf-publicaciones/ActasNebrija_SegundoCongreso.pdf

Marx, K. (1978). On the Jewish Question. In R. Tucker (Ed.), The Marx-Engels Reader (pp. 26-46). New York: Norton and Company.

Matrix Center for Digital Humanities and Social Sciences. (2015). Facilitating Learning in Digital Spaces. *Matrix.msu.edu.* Retrieved 4 April 2015 from http://www2.matrix.msu.edu/portfolio-item/facilitating-learning-in-digital-spaces/

Matsuda, P. K. (2014). The lure of translingual writing. *PMLA*, *129*(3), 478–483. doi:10.1632/pmla.2014.129.3.478

McAuley, A. (2010). The MOOC model for digital practice. *Elearnspace.org.* Retrieved 4 April 2015 from http://www.elearnspace.org/Articles/MOOC_Final.pdf

McCool, M. (2010). Rethinking the problem of linguistic categorization for global search engines. *Rhetoric. Professional Communication and Globalization*, *1*(1), 60–76.

McKee, H. A., & DeVoss, D. N. (Eds.). (2013). Digital writing assessment & evaluation. Logan, UT: Computers and Composition Digital Press/Utah State University Press. Retrieved from http://ccdigitalpress.org/dwae

McKorkle, B., Halasek, K., Clinnin, K., & Selfie, C. L. (2016). Negotiating world Englishes in a writing-based MOOC. *Composition Studies*, *44*(1), 53–71.

McMillan, S. J. (2002). Exploring models of interactivity from multiple research traditions: Users, documents, and systems. In L. Lievrouw & S. Livingston (Eds.), *The handbook of new media* (pp. 163–182). Thousand Oaks, CA: Sage.

Means, B., & Olson, K. (1997). *Technology and education reform: Studies of education reform.* Washington, DC: U.S. Government Printing Office.

Mejias, U. A. (2013). *Off the network: disrupting the digital world.* Minneapolis, MN: University of Minnesota Press. doi:10.5749/minnesota/9780816678990.001.0001

Mell, P., & Grance, T. (2011). *The NIST Definition of Cloud Computing (NIST Special Publication 800-145).* Gaithersburg, MD: National Institute of Standards and Technology.

Merrill, M. D., Barclay, M., & van Schaak, A. (2008). Prescriptive Principles for Instructional Design. In J. M. Spector, M. D. Merrill, J. van Merrienboer, & M. P. Driscoll (Eds.), *Handbook for research on educational communications and technology* (3rd ed.; pp. 173–184). New York: Lauren Erlbaum Associates.

Metcalfe, J. (2006). The changing nature of doctoral programmes. *Wenner Gren International Series, 83*, 79. Retrieved from: http://www.portlandpress.com/pp/books/online/fyos/083/0079/0830079.pdf

Micciche, L. R. (2014). Writing material. *College English*, *76*(6), 488–505.

Mignolo, W. D. (2007). Delinking: The Rhetoric of Modernity, the Logic of Coloniality and the Grammar of Decoloniality. *Cultural Studies*, *21*(2), 449–514. doi:10.1080/09502380601162647

Miller, C. R. (1984). Genre as social action. *The Quarterly Journal of Speech*, *70*(2), 151–167. doi:10.1080/00335638409383686

Miller, C. R. (1994). Rhetorical community: The cultural basis of genre. In A. Freedman & P. Medway (Eds.), *Genre and the new rhetoric* (pp. 67–78). London, UK: Taylor & Francis, Ltd.

Miller, C. R. (2010). Foreword. In S. A. Selber (Ed.), *Rhetoric and technologies: New directions in writing and communication* (pp. ix–xii). Columbia, SC: University of South Carolina Press.

Minović, M., Štavljanin, V., Milovanović, M., & Starčević, D. B. (2008). Usability issues of e-learning systems: Case-study for Moodle learning management system. In R. Meersman, Z. Tari, & P. Herrero (Eds.), *On the move to meaningful internet systems: OTM 2008 Workshops* (pp. 561–570). Berlin, Germany: Springer. doi:10.1007/978-3-540-88875-8_79

Minow, M. (1993). From "Justice Engendered". In P. Smith (Ed.), The Nature and Process of Law (pp. 201-218). New York: Oxford University Press.

Mircea, M., & Andreescu, A. I. (2011). Using cloud computing in higher education: A strategy to improve agility in the current financial crisis. *Communications of the IBIMA*, *2011*, 1–15. doi:10.5171/2011.875547

Mishra, P., & Koehler, M. J. (2006). Technological pedagogical content knowledge: A framework for integrating technology in teacher knowledge. *Teachers College Record*, *108*(6), 1017–1054. doi:10.1111/j.1467-9620.2006.00684.x

Mitchell, K. (2012). A social tool: Why and how ESOL students use Facebook. *CALICO Journal*, *29*(3), 471–493. doi:10.11139/cj.29.3.471-493

Mitra, S. (2007, February). Kids can teach themselves. *Ted Talk* [Video file]. Retrieved fromhttps://www.ted.com/talks/sugata_mitra_shows_how_kids_teach_themselves?language=en

Mitra, S. (2013, February 28). Build a School in the Cloud. *Ted Talk* [Video file]. Retrieved from http://www.ted.com/talks/sugata_mitra_build_a_school_in_the_cloud#t-27842

Mol, A. (2011). Actor-Network Theory: Sensitive terms and enduring tensions. *Kölner Zeitschrift für Soziologie und Sozialpsychologie*, *50*(1), 253–269.

Mol, A., & Law, J. (1994). Regions, networks and fluids: Anaema and social topology. *Social Studies of Science*, *24*(4), 641–671. doi:10.1177/030631279402400402 PMID:11639423

Montgomery, A. P., Hayward, D. V., Dunn, W., Carbonaro, M., & Amrhein, C. G. (2015). Blending for student engagement: Lessons learned for MOOCs and beyond. *Australasian Journal of Educational Technology*, *31*(6), 657–670. doi:10.14742/ajet.1869

MOOC Research. (2015). *Reports*. Retrieved 4 April 2015 from http://moocresearch.com

Moore, J. (2005). *The SLOAN Consortium Quality Framework and the Five Pillars*. SLOAN-C. Retrieved January 5, 2015 from http://sloanconsortium.org/publications/books/qualityframework.pdf

Moos, D. C., & Azevedo, R. (2009). Learning with computer-based learning environments: A literature review of computer self-efficacy. *Review of Educational Research*, *79*(2), 576–600. doi:10.3102/0034654308326083

Moreira. (2010). Actor-network theory. In *Encyclopedia of Science and Technology Communication*. SAGE Publications.

Morey, S. (2012). Digital ecologies. In S. L. Dobrin (Ed.), *Ecology, writing theory, and new media* (pp. 106–121). London: Routledge.

Morgan, D. L. (2004). Focus groups. In S. N. Hesser-Biber & P. Leavy (Eds.), *Approaches to qualitative research: A reader on theory and practice* (pp. 263–285). New York: Oxford University Press.

Morris, L. V. (2013). MOOCs, Emerging Technologies, and Quality. *Innovative Higher Education*, *38*(4), 251–252. doi:10.1007/s10755-013-9263-2

Motaghian, H., Hassanzadeh, A., & Moghadam, D. K. (2013, January). Factors affecting university instructors' adoption of web-based learning systems: Case study of Iran. *Computers & Education*, *61*(1), 158–167. doi:10.1016/j.compedu.2012.09.016

Murray, M., & Jackson, P. (2009). *Web 2.0 in the classroom: The possibilities*. Paper presented at the Proceedings of the 2009 International SIGED: IAIM Conference, Phoenix, AZ.

Murray, J. H. (2003). Inventing the medium. In N. Wardrip-Fruin & N. Montfort (Eds.), *The new media reader* (pp. 3–10). Cambridge, MA: The MIT Press.

Nace, F. (2015). *Messaging the mindset: An intelligent approach to systemic change in education*. Washington, DC: Rowman & Littlefield Publishers.

National Institute for Standards and Technology (NIST). (2011). *The NIST Definition of Cloud Computing*. Retrieved from http://nvlpubs.nist.gov/nistpubs/Legacy/SP/nistspecialpublication800-45.pdf

Neff, J. M., & Whithaus, C. (2008). *Writing across distances & disciplines: Research and pedagogy in distributed learning*. New York, NY: Lawrence Erlbaum Associates.

Nehme, M. (2010, October29). E-learning and students' motivation. *Legal Education Review*, *20*, 223–239.

Nelson, M. E. (2006). Mode, meaning, and synesthesia in multimedia L2 writing. *Language Learning & Technology*, *10*(2), 56–76.

Nelson, R. M., & DeBacker, T. K. (2008). Achievement Motivation in Adolescents: The Role of Peer Climate and Best Friends. *Journal of Experimental Education*, *76*(2), 170–189. doi:10.3200/JEXE.76.2.170-190

Nepal Wireless Networking Project (NWNP). (2014a). *Mission*. Retrieved from http://www.nepalwireless.net/content.php?id=27

Nerad, M. (2012). Conceptual approaches to doctoral education: A community of practice. *Alternation, 19*(2), 57-72. Retrieved from: http://alternation.ukzn.ac.za/Files/docs/19.2/04%20Ner.pdf

Neupane, D. (2011). *Memories*. Retrieve 12 August 2013 from https://dhrubazdiary.wordpress.com/2011/08/16/memories/

New London Group. (1996). A pedagogy of multiliteracies: Designing social futures. *Harvard Educational Review*, *66*(1), 60–92. doi:10.17763/haer.66.1.17370n67v22j160u

NWNP. (2014b). *Our Story*. Retrieved from http://www.nepalwireless.net/content.php?id=48

Nye, D. E. (2006). *Technology matters: Questions to live with*. Cambridge, MA: The MIT Press.

O'Brien, H. L., & Toms, E. G. (2007). What is user engagement? A conceptual framework for defining user engagement with technology. *Journal of the American Society for Information Science and Technology*, *59*(6), 938–955. doi:10.1002/asi.20801

Orchovacki, T., Granic, A., & Kermek, D. (2013, December). Evaluating the perceived and estimated quality in use of web 2.0 applications. *Journal of Systems and Software*, *86*(12), 3039–3059. doi:10.1016/j.jss.2013.05.071

Orlikowski, W. J. (2000). Using technology and constituting structures: A practice lens for studying technology in organizations. *Organization Science*, *11*(4), 404–428. doi:10.1287/orsc.11.4.404.14600

P21. (n.d.). *Framework for 21st century learning*. Retrieved April 11, 2016 from http://www.p21.org/about-us/p21-framework

Pahl, C., & Donnellan, D. (2002). *Data mining technology for the evaluation of web-based teaching and learning systems*. Paper presented at the E-Learning 2002 World Conference on E-Learning, Montreal, Canada.

Palfrey, J., & Gasser, U. (2008). *Born digital: Understanding the first generation of digital natives*. New York, NY: Perseus Books Group, Basic Books.

Palloff, R., & Pratt, K. (2005a). *Collaborating Online: Learning Together in Community*. San Francisco: Jossey-Bass.

Palloff, R., & Pratt, K. (2005b). Learning Together in Community: Collaboration Online.*Proceedings 20th Annual Conference on Distance and Teaching and Learning*. University of Wisconsin.

Palmeri, J. (2012). *Remixing composition: A history of multimodal writing pedagogy*. Carbondale, IL: Southern Illinois University Press.

Pan, Z., Zhang, X., Rhalibi, A. E., Woo, W., & Li, Y. (2008, June 25-27). *Technologies for e-learning and digital entertainment*. Paper presented at the Third International Conference, Edutainment 2008, Nanjing, China.

Pannapacker, W. (2012). Digital humanities triumphant? In *Debates in the digital humanities*. Minneapolis, MN: U of Minnesota P. Retrieved 16 March 2013 from http://dhdebates.gc.cuny.edu/debates

Panteli, N. (2009). *Virtual social networks: Mediated, massive, and multilayers sites*. Eastbourne, UK: Macmillan. doi:10.1057/9780230250888

Papert, S., & Cavallo, D. (2000). *Entry Point to Twenty First Century Learning: A Call for Action at the Local and Global level*. Retrieved from http://learning.media.mit.edu/learninghub.html

Pappas, C. (2013, December 1). *Top 10 e-Learning statistics for 2014 you need to know*. Retrieved from http://elearningindustry.com/top-10-e-learning-statistics-for-2014-you-need-to-know

Pappas, C. (2015, May 26). *Top LMS Statistics and Facts For 2015 You Need to Know*. Retrieved September 18, 2015 from http://elearningindustry.com/top-lms-statistics-and-facts-for-2015

Parra, J. L. (2013). Developing technology and collaborative group work skills: supporting student and group success in online and blended courses. *Cutting-Edge Technologies in Higher Education, 6*, 287-337.

Paterson Primary School Information Handbook. (2009). Melbourne, Australia: Paterson Primary School.

Patton, M. Q. (2002). *Qualitative research and evaluation methods*. Thousand Oaks, CA: SAGE Publications.

Pavlik, J. V. (1998). *New media technology* (2nd ed.). Boston, MA: Allyn and Bacon.

Pavlik, J. V. (1998). Preface. In *New media technology* (2nd ed.). Boston, MA: Allyn and Bacon.

Pempek, T., Yermolayeva, Y. A., & Calvert, S. (2009). College students' social networking experiences on Facebook. *Journal of Applied Developmental Psychology, 30*(3), 227–238. doi:10.1016/j.appdev.2008.12.010

Pennycook, A. (2007). Language, localization, and the real: Hip-hop and the global spread of authenticity. *Journal of Language, Identity, and Education, 6*(2), 101–115. doi:10.1080/15348450701341246

Pennycook, A. (2008). English as language always in translation. *European Journal of English Studies, 12*(1), 33–47. doi:10.1080/13825570801900521

Pennycook, A. (2010). *Language as a local practice*. London: Routledge.

Piaget, J. (1929). *The Child's Conception of the World*. New York: Harcourt Brace Jovanovich.

Pickering, A. (1995). The mangle of practice: Time, agency, & science. Chicago, IL: The University of Chicago Press.

Porter, J. E. (2014). Framing questions about MOOCs and writing courses. In Invasion of the MOOCs: The promises and perils of massive open online courses (pp. 14-28). Anderson, SC: Parlor Press.

Porter, J. E. (2007). Foreword. In H. A. McKee & D. N. DeVoss (Eds.), *Digital writing research: Technologies, methodologies, and ethical issues* (pp. ix–xix). Cresskill, NJ: Hampton Press.

Postman, N. (1995). Virtual students: Digital classroom. *Nation (New York, N.Y.)*, *26*, 377–382.

Potts, L. (2008). Diagramming with Actor Network Theory: A method for modeling holistic experience.*Proceedings of the 2008 IEEE International Professional Communication Conference*. doi:10.1109/IPCC.2008.4610231

Potts, L. (2009). Using Actor Network Theory to trace and improve multimodal communication design. *Technical Communication Quarterly*, *18*(3), 281–301. doi:10.1080/10572250902941812

Poynton, T. A. (2005). Computer literacy across the lifespan: A review with implications for educators. *Computers in Human Behavior*, *21*(6), 861–872. doi:10.1016/j.chb.2004.03.004

Pratt, M. L. (1991). Arts of the contact zone. *Profession*, *91*, 33–40.

Prensky, M. (2001). Digital natives, digital immigrants part 1. *On the horizon*, *9*(5), 1–6. doi:10.1108/10748120110424816

Pressley, M. (2002). Effective beginning reading instruction. *Journal of Literacy Research*, *34*(2), 165–188. doi:10.1207/s15548430jlr3402_3

Preston, J. C. (2014). Online Doctoral Programs: Can They Produce the Business Scientists and Leaders Needed for the 21st Century? *International Journal of Leadership and Change*, *2*(1), 5. Retrieved from http://digitalcommons.wku.edu/ijlc/vol2/iss1/5

Purdy, J. P. (2010). The changing space of research: Web 2.0 and the integration of research and writing environments. *Computers and Composition*, *27*(1), 48–58. doi:10.1016/j.compcom.2009.12.001

Purvis, M., & Savarimuthu, B. T. R. (2009). *Computer-mediated socialnetworking*. Springer. doi:10.1007/978-3-642-02276-0

Rabkin, E. S. (2006). Audience, purpose, and medium: How digital media extend humanities education. In M. Hanrahan & D. L. Madsen (Eds.), *Teaching, technology, textuality: Approaches to new media* (pp. 135–147). New York, NY: Palgrave Macmillan. doi:10.1057/9780230523302_11

Radda, H., Cross, T., & Holbeck, R. (2012). Learning together: Perceived cognitive and behavioral outcomes of learners in a nontraditional, professional doctoral program. *Journal of Instructional Research,* (1). Retrieved from https://cirt.gcu.edu/ jir/documents/2012-v1/raddapdf

Radius Stories at the Edge. (2015). *Leveraging Cloud to Transform Education in Remote Areas of the World*. Retrieved from http://www.vmware.com/radius/leveraging-cloud-transform-education-remote-areas-world/

Rahimi, E., Van Den Berg, J., & Veen, W. (2014). Facilitating student-driven constructing of learning environments using Web 2.0 personal learning environment. *Computers & Education*, *81*, 235–246. doi:10.1016/j.compedu.2014.10.012

Rani, B. K., Rani, B. P., & Babu, A. (2015). Cloud Computing and Inter-Clouds - Types, Topologies and Research Issues. *Procedia Computer Science, 50*, 24-29. Retrieved from http://www.sciencedirect.com/science/article/pii/S1877050915005074

Rao, R. (1938). *Kanthapura*. London: George Alen and Unwin Ltd.

Reich, R. (1992). *The work of nations: Preparing ourselves for 21st century capitalism*. New York: Alfred A. Knopf.

Reid, A. (2008). Portable composition: iTunes University and networked pedagogies. *Computers and Composition*, *25*(1), 62–78. doi:10.1016/j.compcom.2007.09.003

Reyna, J. (2010). Google Docs in higher education settings: A preliminary report. In *Proceedings of World Conference on Educational Multimedia, Hypermedia and Telecommunications 2010* (pp. 1566-1572). Chesapeake, VA: AACE. Retrieved January 13, 2015 from http://jorgereyna.weebly.com/publications.html

Reynolds, N. (2004). *Geographies of writing: Inhabiting places and encountering difference*. Carbondale, IL: Southern Illinois University Press.

Rhoden, N. S. (2014). *A study of factors affecting the adoption of e-learning systems enabled with cultural contextual features by instructions in Jamaican tertiary institutions*. Colorado Technical University.

Rice, J. (2006). Networks and new media. *College English*, *69*(2), 127–133. doi:10.2307/25472197

Rice, J. (2006). The rhetoric of new media: Teaching a rhetoric of hypertext. In M. Hanrahan & D. L. Madsen (Eds.), *Teaching, technology, textuality: Approaches to new media* (pp. 148–161). New York, NY: Palgrave Macmillan. doi:10.1057/9780230523302_12

Rice, R. E. (2013). Preface. In F. L. F. Lee, L. Leung, J. L. Qiu, & D. S. C. Chu (Eds.), *Frontiers in new media research* (pp. 1–5). New York, NY: Routledge.

Richardson, W. (2007). In my view: Teaching in a Web 2.0 world. *Kappa Delta Pi Record*, *43*(4), 150–151. doi:10.1080/00228958.2007.10516471

Ritter, K. (2005). The Economics of Authorship: Online Paper Mills, Student Writers, and First Year Composition. *College Composition and Communication*, *56*(4), 601–631.

Roberts, L. D., & Rajah-Kanagasabai, C. J. (2013). "I'd be so much more comfortable posting anonymously": Identified versus anonymous participation in student discussion boards. *Australasian Journal of Educational Technology*, *29*(5). doi:10.14742/ajet.452

Robins, S. (2007, October 24). *Second Life in education* [Video file]. Retrieved from http://youtu.be/ueAcz7ZyFpM

Rodriquez, C. O. (2013). *MOOCs and the AI-Stanford like courses: Two successful and distinct course formats for massive open online courses. European Journal of Open, Distance, and E-Learning.*

Rogers, E. M. (2001). The Digital Divide [Abstract]. *Convergence (London)*, *7*(4), 96–111. doi:10.1177/135485650100700406

Rogers, M. A., Theule, J., Ryan, B. A., Adama, G. R., & Keating, L. (2009). Parental involvement and children's school achievement: Evidence for mediating processes. *Canadian Journal of School Psychology*, *24*(1), 34–57. doi:10.1177/0829573508328445

Rose, D. H., & Meyer, A. (2002). *Teaching every student in the digital age: Universal design for learning*. Alexandria, VA: Association for Supervision and Curriculum Development.

Roulston, K. (2010). *Reflective interviewing: A guide to theory and practice*. Los Angeles, CA: SAGE Publications. doi:10.4135/9781446288009

Rowe, M., Bozalek, V., & Frantz, J. (2013). Using Google Drive to facilitate a blended approach to authentic learning: Authentic learning and Google Drive. *British Journal of Educational Technology*, *44*(4), 594–606. doi:10.1111/bjet.12063

Royster, J. (1996). When the first voice you hear is not your own. *College Composition and Communication*, *47*(1), 29–40. doi:10.2307/358272

Rushdie, S. (1981). *Midnight's children*. London: Penguin Group.

Rushdie, S. (1988). *The satanic verses*. London: Penguin Group.

Russell, D. (1997). Rethinking genre in school and society: An activity theory analysis. *Written Communication, 14*(4), 504–554. doi:10.1177/0741088397014004004

Ryan, M.-L. (1999). Immersion vs. interactivity: Virtual reality and literary theory. *SubStance, 28*(2), 110–137. doi:10.1353/sub.1999.0015

Salmon, G. (2004). *E-moderating: The key to teaching and learning online*. Psychology Press.

Salmon, G. (2013). *E-tivities: The key to active online learning*. Routledge.

Sasser, T. (2012). Bring Your Own Disruption: Rhizomatic Learning in the Composition Class. *Hybrid Pedagogy*. Retrieved 30 December 2014, from http://www.hybridpedagogy.com/journal/bring-your-own- disruption-rhizomatic-learning-in-the-composition-class/

Scale, M.-S. E. (2010). Assessing the impact of cloud computing and web collaboration on the work of distance library services. *Journal of Library Administration, 50*(7-8), 933–950. doi:10.1080/01930826.2010.488995

Schertler, M., & Bodendorf, F. (2002). *Supporting communication processes in e-learning networks*. Paper presented at the International Conference on Computers in Education (ICCE 2002), Auckland, New Zealand. doi:10.1109/CIE.2002.1185924

Schmidt, D. A., Baran, A., Thompson, A. D., Mishra, P., Koehler, J., & Shin, T. S. (2009). Technological Pedagogical Content Knowledge (TPACK): The Development and Validation of an Assessment Instrument for Preservice Teachers. *Journal of Research on Technology in Education, 42*(2), 123–149. doi:10.1080/15391523.2009.10782544

Schmieder, E. J. (2008, March). Communication: The tool to interact with and control your online classroom environment. *International Journal of Instructional Technology and Distance Learning, 5*(3). Retrieved from http://www.itdl.org/journal/mar_2008/article2003.htm

Schuetze, H. G., & Slowey, M. (2002). Participation and exclusion: A comparative analysis of non-traditional students and lifelong learners in higher education. *Higher Education, 44*(3/4), 309–327. doi:10.1023/A:1019898114335

Scott, R. L. (1967). On viewing rhetoric as epistemic. *Central States Speech Journal, 18*(1), 9–17. doi:10.1080/10510976709362856

Selber, S. A. (2004). *Multiliteracies for a digital age*. Carbondale, IL: Southern Illinois University Press.

Selber, S. A. (2010). Introduction. In S. A. Selber (Ed.), *Rhetoric and technologies: New directions in writing and communication* (pp. 1–11). Columbia, SC: University of South Carolina Press.

Selber, S. A. (Ed.). (2010). *Rhetoric and technologies: New directions in writing and communication*. Columbia, SC: University of South Carolina Press.

Selfe, C., & Selfe, R., Jr. (2008). The politics of the interface: Power and its exercise in electronic contact zone. In Computers in the composition classroom: A critical sourcebook. New York, NY: Bedford/St. Martin.

Selfe, C. (1999a). Lest we think the revolution is a revolution: Images of technology and the nature of change. In G. E. Hawisher & C. Selfe (Eds.), *Passions, pedagogies, and 21st century technologies* (pp. 292–322). Logan, UT: Utah State UP.

Selfe, C. (1999b, February). Technology and literacy: A story about the perils of not paying attention. *College Composition and Communication, 50*(3), 411–436. doi:10.2307/358859

Selfe, C. (2009). The movement of air, the breath of meaning: Aurality and multimodal composing. *CCC, 60*(4), 616–663.

Selfe, C. L. (1999). *Technology and literacy in the twenty-first century: The importance ofpaying attention.* Carbondale, IL: Southern Illinois University Press.

Selfe, C. L. (2004a). Students who teach us: A case study of a new media text designer. In *Writing new media: Theory and applications for expanding the teaching of composition* (pp. 43–66). Logan, UT: Utah State University Press.

Selfe, C. L. (2004b). Toward new media texts: Taking up the challenges of visual literacy. In *Writing new media: Theory and applications for expanding the teaching of composition* (pp. 66–110). Logan, UT: Utah State University Press.

Selfe, C. L. (2009). The movement of air, the breath of meaning: Aurality and multilingual composing. *College Composition and Communication*, *60*(4), 616–663.

Selfe, C. L. (2009). The movement of air, the breath of meaning: Aurality and multimodal composing. *College Composition and Communication*, *60*(4), 616–663.

Selfe, C. L., & Hilligoss, S. (1994). Introduction. In C. L. Selfe & S. Hilligoss (Eds.), *Literacy and computers: The complications of teaching and learning with technology*. New York, NY: MLA. doi:10.1300/J054v02n01_01

Selfe, C., & Hawisher, G. (2004). *Literate lives in the information age: Narrative of literacy from the United States.* Mahwah, NJ: Erlbaum.

Selfe, C., & Richard, S. (1994, December). The politics of the interface: Power and its exercise in electronic contact zones. *College Composition and Communication*, *45*(4), 480–504. doi:10.2307/358761

Selfe, C., & Selfe, R. J. (2004). The politics of the interference: Power and its exercise in electronic contact zones. In J. Johnson-Eilola & S. A. Selber (Eds.), *Central Works in Technical Communication* (pp. 428–445). New York, NY: Oxford University Press.

Selinger, M. (2013). *Learning Hubs Where Learning Takes Place in a Digital World.* Retrieved from http://www.cisco.com/c/dam/en_us/about/ac79/docs/ps/Learning-Hubs.pdf

Sendall, P., Ceccucci, W., & Peslak, A. (2008). *Web 2.0 matters: An analysis of implementing web 2.0 in the classroom.* Paper presented at the Information Systems Education Conference 2008, ISECON 2008, Phoenix, AZ.

Sewell, W. H. Jr. (1992). *A theory of structure: Duality, agency, and transformation*. *American Journal of Sociology*, *98*(1), 1–29. doi:10.1086/229967

Shannon, C. E., & Weaver, W. (1949). *The mathematical theory ofcommunication.* Urbana, IL: University ofIllinois Press.

Sheldon, S. B., & Voorhis, F. L. V. (2004). Partnership programs in U.S. schools: Their development and relationship to family involvement outcomes. *School Effectiveness and School Improvement*, *15*(2), 125–148. doi:10.1076/sesi.15.2.125.30434

Shih, P.-C., Munoz, D., & Sanchez, F. (2006, November). The effect of previous experience with information and communication technologies on performance in a web-based learning program. *Computers in Human Behavior*, *22*(6), 962–970. doi:10.1016/j.chb.2004.03.016

Shin, D., & Cimasko, T. (2008). Multimodal composition in a college ESL class: New tools, traditiaonl norms. *Computers and Composition*, *25*(4), 376–395. doi:10.1016/j.compcom.2008.07.001

Shipka, J. (2011). *Toward a composition make whole.* Pittsburgh, PA: University of Pittsburg Press.

Shipka, J. (2016). Transmodality in/and processes of making: Changing dispositions and practice. *College English*, *78*(3), 250–257.

Shulman, L. S. (1986). Those who understand: Knowledge growth in teaching. *Educational Researcher, 15*(2), 4–14. doi:10.3102/0013189X015002004

Silvertone, R. (1999). *Why study the media?* London, UK: SAGE.

Skype. (n.d.). *What is the cloud?* Retrieved January 13, 2015 from https://support.skype.com/en/faq/FA12381/what-is-the-cloud

Sleeter, C., & McLaren, P. (Eds.). (1995). *Multicultural education, critical pedagogy, and the politics of difference.* Albany, NY: SUNY.

Smith, C. F. (1994). Hypertextual thinking. In C. L. Selfe & S. Hilligoss (Eds.), *Literacy and computers: The complications of teaching and learning with technology* (pp. 264–281). New York, NY: MLA.

Smith, S., & Hendricks, J. A. (2010). New media: New technology, new ideas or new headaches. In J. A. Hendricks (Ed.), *The twenty-first century media industry: Economic and managerial implications in the age of new media* (pp. 3–22). Plymouth, UK: Lexington Books.

Snoddy, R. (2003). Modern media myths. In J. Aitchison & D. M. Lewis (Eds.), *New media language* (pp. 18–20). New York, NY: Routledge.

Snyder, I. (2001). A new communication order: Researching literacy practices in the network society. *Language and Education, 15*(2-3), 117-131.

Sorapure, M. (2006). Between modes: Assessing student new media composition. *Kairos, 10*(2), 1–15.

Sorensen, C. (2014). Classrooms Without Walls: A Comparison of Instructor Performance in online. *MERLOT Journal of Online Learning and Teaching, 10*(4), 569-576. Retrieved from http://jolt.merlot.org/vol10no4/Sorensen_1214.pdf

Sourya, B. (2011). *Can Cloud Computing Help In Education?* Retrieved from http://cloudtweaks.com/2011/02/how-can-cloud-computing-help-in-education/

Spivak, G. C. (1999). *A critique of postcolonial reason.* Cambridge, MA: Harvard UP.

Stoll, C. (1995). *Silicon snake oil.* New York: Doubleday.

Street, B. V. (1993). *Literacy in theory and practice.* Cambridge, UK: Cambridge University Press.

Street, B. V. (2009). Ethnography of writing and reading. In D. R. Olson & N. Torrance (Eds.), *The Cambridge handbook of literacy* (pp. 3–21). Cambridge, UK: Cambridge University Press. doi:10.1017/CBO9780511609664.019

Sultan, N. (2010). Cloud computing for education: A new dawn? *International Journal of Information Management, 30*(2), 109–116. doi:10.1016/j.ijinfomgt.2009.09.004

Sunita & Prachi. (2013). Introduction to Cloud Computing. *International Journal of Advanced Research in Computer Science and Software Engineering, 3*(5), 1399–1401. Retrieved from http://www.ijarcsse.com/docs/papers/Volume_3/5_May2013/V3I5-0346.pdf

Sutherland-Smith, W. (2002). Weaving the literacy web: Changes in reading from page to screen. *The Reading Teacher, 55*(7), 662–669.

Su, Y., & Klein, J. (2010). Using scaffolds in problem-based hypermedia. *Journal of Educational Multimedia and Hypermedia, 19*(3), 327–347.

Swanson, K. W., West, J., Carr, S., & Augustine, S. (2015). Supporting Dissertation Writing Using a Cognitive Apprenticeship Model. In V. C. X. Wang (Ed.), *Handbook of Research on Scholarly Publishing and Research Methods*, (pp. 84-104). Information Science Reference, IGI Global.

Swarts, J. (2008). Information technologies as discursive agents: Methodological implications for the empirical study of knowledge work. *Journal of Technical Writing and Communication*, *38*(4), 301–329. doi:10.2190/TW.38.4.b

Swarts, J. (2010). Recycled writing: Assembling actor networks from reusable content. *Journal of Business and Technical Communication*, *24*(2), 127–163. doi:10.1177/1050651909353307

Takayoshi, P., & Selfe, C. (2007). Thinking about multimodaligy. In G. E. Hawisher & S. Selfe (Eds.), *Multimodal Composition: Resource for Teachers, New Dimensions in Computer and Composition* (pp. 1–12). Hampton Press, Inc.

Takayoshi, P., & Selfe, C. L. (2007). Thinking about multimodality. In C. L. Selfe (Ed.), *Multimodal composition: Resources for teachers* (pp. 1–12). Cresskill, NJ: Hampton Press, Inc.

Tavinor, G. (2005, April). Videogames and interactive fiction. *Philosophy and Literature*, *29*(1), 24–40. doi:10.1353/phl.2005.0015

Teo, T., Lee, C. B., & Chai, C. S. (2008). Understanding pre-service teachers' computer attitudes: Applying and extending the technology acceptance model. *Journal of Computer Assisted Learning*, *24*(2), 128–143. doi:10.1111/j.1365-2729.2007.00247.x

Tham, J. (Forthcoming). Audience, user, producer: MOOCs as activity systems. In E. Monske & K. Blair (Eds.), *Writing and composing in the age of MOOCs*. Hershey, PA: IGI Global.

Thatcher, B. (2010). Editor's introduction to first edition: Eight needed developments and eight critical contexts for global inquiry. Rhetoric, Professional Communication and Globalization, 1(1), 1-34.

Thatcher, B. (2005). Situating L2 writing in global communication technologies. *Computers and Composition*, *22*(3), 279–295. doi:10.1016/j.compcom.2005.05.002

Thiong'o, N. W. (1986). *Decolonising the mind: The politics of language in African literature*. Portsmouth: Heinemann.

Thompson, J. B. (1995). *The Media and Modernity*. Stanford University Press.

Thowfeek, M. H., & Hussin, H. (2008). Instructors' perspective on e-learning adoption in Sri Lanka: A preliminary investigation. *Communications of the IBIMA*, *6*, 124–129.

Thowfeek, M. H., & Salam, M. N. A. (2014, August). Students' assessment on the usability of e-learning websites. *Procedia: Social and Behavioral Sciences*, *141*, 916–922. doi:10.1016/j.sbspro.2014.05.160

Tomlison, J. (1999). *Globalization and Culture*. Cambridge, UK: Polity Press.

Tout, S., Sverdlik, W., & Lawver, G. (2009). Cloud computing and its security in higher education.*Proceedings of ISECON, 26*.

Tribe, M. (2001). Foreword. In L. Manovich (Ed.), *The language of new media*. Cambridge, MA: The MIT Press.

Tulley, C. (2013). Migration patterns: A status report on the transition from paper to eportfolios and the effect on multimodal composition initiatives. *Computers and Composition*, *30*(2), 101–114. doi:10.1016/j.compcom.2013.03.002

Upper Grand District School Board. (n.d.). *Parent Involvement Committee*. Retrieved from http://www.ugdsb.on.ca/pic/parentresources.aspx?id=17113#top

Vaidhyanathan, S. (2004). *The anarchist in the library: How the clash Between freedom and control is hacking the real world and crashing the system*. New York: Basic Books.

Valcke, M., Bonte, S., Wever, B. D., & Rots, I. (2010). Internet parenting styles and the impact on Internet use of primary school children. *Computers & Education*, *55*(2), 454–464. doi:10.1016/j.compedu.2010.02.009

Van Leeuwen, T. (2005). *Introducing social semiotics*. London: Routledge.

Veletsianos, G., Kimmons, R., & French, K. (2013). Instructor experiences with a social networking site in a higher education setting: Expectations, frustrations, appropriation, and compartmentalization. *Educational Technology Research and Development*, *61*(2), 255–278. doi:10.1007/s11423-012-9284-z

Vie, S. (2008). Digital divide 2.0: Generation M and Online social networking sites in the composition classroom. *Computers and Composition*, *25*(9), 9–23. doi:10.1016/j.compcom.2007.09.004

Vincent, J. (2006). Classroom writing: Multimodality and assessment in the writing classroom. *Literacy*, *40*(1), 51–57. doi:10.1111/j.1467-9345.2006.00426.x

Virilio, P. (1997). *Understanding pragmatics*. London, UK: Verso.

Vorderer, P., & Bryant, J. (2006). *Playing video games: Motives, responses, and consequences*. Mahwah, NJ: Lawrence Erlbaum Associates.

Vouk, M. A. (2008). Cloud computing—issues, research and implementations. *Journal of Computing and Information Technology*, *4*(4), 235–246. doi:10.2498/cit.1001391

Vygotsky, L. S. (1978). *Mind in society: The development of higher psychological process*. Cambridge, MA: Harvard University Press.

Walker, G. E., Golde, C., Jones, L., Bueschel, A. C., & Hutchings, P. (2008). *The formation of scholars: Rethinking doctoral education for the twenty-first century*. San Francisco, CA: Jossey-Bass.

Wan, L. (2010). *Application of Web 2.0 technologies in e-learning context*. Paper presented at the 2010 International Conference on Networking and Digital Society, ICNDS 2010, Wenzhou, China.

Warnick, B., & Heineman, D. S. (2012). *Rhetoric online: The politics of new media* (2nd ed.). New York, NY: Peter Lang.

Warnock, S. (2009). *Teaching writing online: How & why*. Urbana, IL: National Council of Teachers of English.

Warschauer, M. (2011). *Learning in the cloud: How (and why) to transform schools with digital media*. New York, NY: Teachers College, Columbia University.

Warschauer, M., & Liaw, M. (2011). Emerging technologies for autonomous language learning. *Studies in Self-Access Learning Journal*, *2*(3), 107–118.

Wertsch, J. (1998). *Minds as action*. New York, NY: Oxford University Press.

WhatIsCloud.com. (n.d.). *Basic Concepts and Terminology*. Retrieved from http://whatiscloud.com/basic_concepts_and_terminology/index

Williams, B. (2007). Foreword. In C. L. Selfe (Ed.), *Multimodal composition: Resources for teachers*. Cresskill, NJ: Hampton Press, Inc. doi:10.1016/B978-0-7506-8368-5.50002-0

Winn, J., & Lockwood, D. (2013). Student as Producer is hacking the university. In H. Beetham & R. Sharpe (Eds.), *Rethinking Pedagogy for a Digital Age: Designing for 21st Century Learning* (pp. 218–229). New York, NY: Routledge.

Winogard, T., & Flores, F. (1986). Understanding computers and cognition: A new foundation for design. Reading, MA: Addison.

Withrow, F. B. (2004). *Literarcy in the digital age: Reading, writing, viewing, and computing*. Lanham, MD: Scarecrow Education.

Wolff, L. (2010). Learning through Writing: Reconceptualising the Research Supervision Process. *International Journal of Teaching and Learning in Higher Education, 22*(3), 229-237. Retrieved from: http://files.eric.ed.gov/fulltext/EJ938558.pdf (ERIC Document Reproduction Service No. EJ 938558)

Wysocki, A. F. (2004). Opening new media to writing: Openings and justifications. In *Writing new media: Theory and applications for expanding the teaching of composition*. Logan, UT: Utah State University Press.

Wysocki, A. F., Johnson-Eilola, J., Selfe, C., & Sirc, G. (2004). *Writing new media: Theory and applications for expanding the teaching of composition*. Logan, UT: Utah State University Press.

Yancey, K. B. (2004). Looking for sources of coherence in a fragmented world: Notes toward a new assessment design. *Computers and Composition, 21*(1), 89–102. doi:10.1016/j.compcom.2003.08.024

Yancey, K. B. (2004). Made not only in words: Composition in a new key. *College Composition and Communication, 56*(2), 297–328. doi:10.2307/4140651

Yepes, E. (n.d.). *Spanish Grammar Libro digital Herramientas de español: Online Advanced Spanish Book*. Retrieved January 13, 2015, from http://www.bowdoin.edu/~eyepes/newgr/ats/

Young, R. (2004). *White mythologies: writing history and the west* (2nd ed.). London: Routledge.

Young, V., & Martínez, A. Y. (Eds.). (2011). *Code-Meshing as world English: Pedagogy, policy, performance*. Urbana, IL: NCTE.

Yu, R. (2014, May 2). Cable companies expand public Wi-Fi for customer loyalty. *USA Today*. Retrieved August 29, 2014, from http://www.usatoday.com/story/money/business/2014/04/30/cable-wifi/8525347/

Zagal, J., Chan, S. S., & Zhang, J. (2011). *Measuring flow experience of computer game players*. Paper presented at the AMCIS 2010. Retrieved October 10, 2015 from http://aisel.aisnet.org/amcis2010/137

Zeni, J. (1994). Literacy, technology, and teacher education. In C. L. Selfe & S. Hilligoss (Eds.), *Literacy and computers: The complications of teaching and learning with technology* (pp. 11–21). New York, NY: MLA.

Zhao, Y., & Frank, K. A. (2003). Factors affecting technology uses in schools: An ecological perspective. *American Educational Research Journal, 40*(4), 807–840. doi:10.3102/00028312040004807

Zhenghao, C., Alcorn, B., Christensen, G., Ericksson, N., Koller, D., & Emanuel, E. J. (2015). Who's Benefiting from MOOCs, and Why. *Harvard Business Review*. Retrieved from https://hbr.org/2015/09/whos-benefiting-from-moocs-and-why

Zoetewey, M. W., & Staggers, J. (2003). Beyond current-traditional design: Assessing rhetoric in new media. *Issues in Writing, 13*, 133–157.

About the Contributors

Binod Gurung, PhD., has a doctorate degree in curriculum and instruction from New Mexico State University, USA. His research interests include emerging educational technologies, online multicultural education, and critical pedagogies. His articles have appeared in Computer & Education, International Journal of Teaching and Learning in Higher Education, Multicultural Education, and Journal of Global Literacies, Technologies, and Pedagogies. He has also published several book chapters and an edited volume pertaining to the educational technology field.

Marohang Limbu is an assistant professor in the Writing, Rhetoric, and American cultures at Michigan State University, USA. Limbu is a co-editor of *Emerging Pedagogies in the Networked Knowledge Society: Practices Integrating Social Media and Globalization (2013)* and *Digital Rhetoric and Global Literacies: Communication Modes and Digital Practices in the Networked World (2014)* with IGI Global. Limbu is a founder and editor-in-chief of the journal, *Journal of Global Literacies, Emerging Pedagogies, and Technologies* (peer-reviewed quarterly journal). Limbu's current research interests include cloud technologies, networked pedagogies, South Asian studies, global literacies, global indigenous knowledge and/or global indigenous rhetorical traditions, intercultural communication, cross-cultural communication, and inter-epistemic communication.

* * *

Anita August is an associate professor of visual culture, creative writing and rhetoric and writing studies at Sacred Heart University, USA. August received her PhD in rhetoric and writing studies at the University of Texas at El Paso and her MFA in creative writing and critical studies at California Institute of the Arts. Her interdisciplinary research focuses on the areas of rhetorical visual theory and pedagogy, collective intelligence communities, and creative writing pedagogy. August reaches across disciplines to facilitate a dialogue regarding the social construction of visual imagery as a meaning-making practice and examines and theorizes the rhetorical power of visual imagery as discourse.

Maury Elizabeth Brown is an assistant professor of English at Germanna Community College in Locust Grove, Virginia and a PhD student in English at Old Dominion University. She also has experience as a corporate communications executive and as a K-12 teacher and instructional designer. She researches multimodal composition, digital and video rhetorics, new media, business, professional and technical writing, and games in education and culture. Through a focus on critical literacy and the human side of learning and technology, she hopes to develop in students the capacity for empathy that brings self-actualization and community.

Dilli Bikram Edingo, a PhD student at York University in York/Ryerson joint program Communication and Culture, is the author of *An Angel in the Wilderness* (2006), *G. B. Yakthumba: A Champion of Democracy* (2010) and the translator of *Two Faces of A Coin* (2008) and *Gopali Folklore and Folklife* (2009). He is the recipient of Apprenticeship Research Grant-2007 from Social Inclusion Research Fund by SNV-Nepal and Mini-Research Grant-2008 from University Grants Commission, Nepal. The areas of his research interest include new media, power, politics, digital technologies, globalization, transcultural, and/or intercultural communication, and indigeneity.

Katherine Emmons, PhD, has chaired over 20 PhD dissertations to completion, and has served as a committee member for many more. She is a faculty member in Education, with experience in teacher preparation, language and cultural diversity in the classroom, children's literature, global and international education, and online learning. She is a part time faculty member in online PhD programs at Capella University and Walden University, in addition to her full time position in teacher education in the United Arab Emirates.

Kate Fedewa is an academic specialist in the Department of Writing, Rhetoric, and American Cultures at Michigan State University, where she is also a member of the Writing in Digital Environments Research Center and an instructor of both first year writing and professional writing. Her research interests include student-centered pedagogy, identity formation, user experience, participatory culture, and the history of English language pedagogy.

Daniel L. Hocutt serves as web manager and adjunct professor of liberal arts at the University of Richmond School of Professional and Continuing Studies, where he has worked for over 15 years. He teaches "non-traditional" students composition and research methods, focusing attention on ways to make academic writing relevant in workplace situations. He is also a PhD student in English at Old Dominion University, focusing on the intersection of technology and human communication. His research interests include cloud-based collaborative composing; rhetoric, communication, and composition studies; professional and technical writing; new media studies; networks; and trickster studies. He finds composition endlessly complex and fascinating.

Kathryn Houghton is an academic specialist in the Department of Writing, Rhetoric, and American Cultures at Michigan State University where she teaches first-year writing, professional writing, and interdisciplinary humanities. Her research is primarily focused in editing and publishing.

Jialei Jiang is a PhD candidate specializing in Composition and TESOL at Indiana University of Pennsylvania. Her research interests include digital literacies and multimodal composition, second language acquisition and cloud-based writing, as well as multilingual writers and writing center practices. She is also interested in designing pedagogical tools to address issues in digital composition and second language learning.

Yowei Kang, Ph.D., is an Assistant Professor at Degree Program of Creative Industries and Digital Film, Kainan University, Taiwan. Kang received his PhD from University of Texas at El Paso, Texas. His research interests focus on digital game research, technology and rhetoric, composition pedagogy using digital game technology, and teaching English as a second language (ESL).

Jaya Kannan is the Director of Digital Learning at Sacred Heart University. She has a PhD in Computer Assisted Language Learning and more than 15 years of international teaching and research experience in the higher education setting. Her recent research interests involve the study of self-directed learning and the role of affect in the digital learning environment.

Pilar Munday is an Associate Professor of Spanish at Sacred Heart University. She received a BA in English Philology from the Universidad de Granada (Spain) and a Ph.D. in Theoretical Linguistics from New York University. Her teaching covers all aspects and levels of the Spanish Language, including Spanish Phonetics, Linguistics and Culture. Her research includes uses of technology in modern foreign language instruction.

Dhruba Neupane is a PhD candidate at the University of Waterloo, Canada. His current project explores translingual-transliterate practices of a South Asian immigrant population in Ontario. Drawing primarily on immigrants' own literacy practices and on new literacy and composition studies, postcolonial theories, transnational and diaspora studies (with a special attention to non-western rhetorical traditions and communicative practices), his ongoing study aims to expose various strategies, often unnoticed or elided in academia, that immigrant writers adopt as they participate in and challenge standard literacies.

Julia Parra is an assistant professor at New Mexico State University, College of Education, Department of Curriculum and Instruction, Learning Design, and Technology Program. She earned her degree of Doctor in Education in Learning Technologies from Pepperdine University's School of Education and Psychology. Dr. Parra has an overarching research focus on learning design, technology, and innovation and has conducted and published research in the areas of faculty/teacher professional development with technology and in technology-based environments; online/blended/HyFlex teaching and learning; cloud-based student collaboration; digital democracy, culturally-responsive teaching and learning; the relationships between pedagogy, content and technology (TPACK); personal learning networks, and MOOCs.

Ramesh Pokharel, PhD, taught wide varieties of undergraduate and graduate courses on English Studies at Tribhuvan University, Nepal for fifteen years. He did a PhD in Rhetoric and Composition from the University of Texas at El Paso, and taught English Composition, Technical Writing, Professional Writing, and Literature at the University of Texas at El Paso, Texas A & M University, College Station, and University of Houston for six years. He is currently doing a PhD in Language and Literacies Education at University of Toronto. His current research interest includes language policy, bi/multilingual education, language issues based social justice, multilingualism, and multiculturalism.

Byanjana Sharma, PhD, is the director and editor-in-chief in the *Dorling Publications*, Nepal. She completed her PhD from *Monash University*, Australia. Apart from being a published writer internationally and nationally, she has devoted a substantial amount of time in the field of English Language Teaching as a teacher educator. Her research interests include language and literacy teaching, professional development and teacher training in EAL and EFL contexts.

Jason Tham is a PhD student in the Rhetoric and Scientific and Technical Communication program at the University of Minnesota – Twin Cities, where he teaches first-year composition and technical and professional writing. He studies how emerging technologies invite different ways of thinking and learning, and the increasingly intense flow of information occurring among people and machines. One of his long-term projects is investigating the scale and intensity of interconnected complex learning networks in the digital communication context. His work can be found in "Society for Technical Communication's Intercom," "Journal of Technical Writing and Communication," "Journal of Interactive Technology and Pedagogy," and "Computers and Composition Online."

Index

G

H

K

L

M

N

O

P

Q

R

S

T

U

V

W

www.ingramcontent.com/pod-product-compliance
Lightning Source LLC
LaVergne TN
LVHW060419300926
849162LV00006B/1473